From Maastricht to Brexit

ECPR Press

ECPR Press is an imprint of the European Consortium for Political Research. It publishes original research from leading political scientists and the best among early career researchers in the discipline. Its scope extends to all fields of political science, international relations and political thought, with-out restriction in either approach or regional focus. It is also open to interdisciplinary work with a predominant political dimension.

ECPR Press Editors

From Maastricht to Brexit

Democracy, Constitutionalism and Citizenship in the EU

Richard Bellamy and Dario Castiglione

ecpr
PRESS

Published by the European Consortium for Political Research, Harbour House, 6-8 Hythe Quay, Colchester, CO2 8JF, United Kingdom

British Library Cataloguing in Publication Data
A catalogue record for this book is available from the British Library

ISBN: HB 978-1-78660-992-2

Library of Congress Cataloging-in-Publication Data Available

ISBN 9781786609922 (cloth)
ISBN 9781538157008 (pbk)
ISBN 9781786609946 (electronic)

ecpr.eu/shop

*To the younger generation of Europeans across Europe.
May they do better than our's at creating a demoi-cratic
European Union of which the UK forms a part.*

Contents

Acknowledgements

This book is a kind of intellectual journey. Admittedly, it started by chance, but reflected our shared interests in a normative political theory with institutional roots and practical relevance. As all such journeys, it has been a learning experience, discovering and developing new ideas, occasionally changing our minds, but, overall, pursuing some common and persistent themes and approaches, which we still regard as relevant to the European debate.

During these years, we have learnt a lot from many other scholars with whom we have collaborated in various international projects. They are too many to mention here, though some of them are acknowledged in the chapters of this book. We owe a particular debt to those who co-authored some of the articles here reproduced, and who kindly agreed to their publication in this volume, namely Sandra Kröger, Justus Schönlau and Albert Weale.

We would also like to thank the editors and the editorial team of the Press for having supported the publication of the work and the help they have given us throughout. We would also like to extend our gratitude to Alexandra Segerberg and Peter Kennealy, who were on the editorial board of the Press when we first discussed its publication.

1 October 2018

Original Sources

We thankfully acknowledge the publishers of the original articles for their kind permission to reproduce the material in the present form.

Chapter 1: Richard Bellamy and Dario Castiglione, 'The Normative Challenge of a European Polity: Cosmopolitanism and Communitarianism Compared, Criticised and Combined' in A. Føllesdal and P. Koslowski (eds.) *Democracy and the EU* (Springer, 1998), pp. 254–80.

Chapter 2: Richard Bellamy and Dario Castiglione, 'Normative Theory and the European Union: Legitimising the Euro-"Polity" and Its "Regime"', *European Journal of Political Theory*, Vol. 2, No. 1 (2003), pp. 7–34.

Chapter 3: Richard Bellamy and Dario Castiglione, 'Democracy, Sovereignty and the Constitution of the European Union: The Republican Alternative to Liberalism', in Z. Bankowski and A. Scott (eds.), *The European Union and its Order* (Blackwell, 2000), pp. 170–90.

Chapter 4: Richard Bellamy and Dario Castiglione, 'Building the Union: The Nature of Sovereignty in Europe's Political Architecture', *Law and Philosophy*, 16.4 (1997), pp. 91–115.

Chapter 5: Richard Bellamy, 'Sovereignty, Post-sovereignty and Pre-sovereignty: Reconceptualising the State, Rights and Democracy in the EU', in N. Walker (ed.), *Sovereignty in Transition* (Oxford: Hart, 2003), pp. 167–90.

Chapter 6: Richard Bellamy and Justus Schönlau, 'Constitution Making as Normal Politics: Disagreement and Compromise in the Drafting of the EU Charter of Fundamental Rights and Constitution'. [This is an unpublished piece bringing together: Richard Bellamy and Justus Schönlau, 'The Normality of Constitutional Politics: An Analysis of the Drafting of the EU Charter of Fundamental Rights', *Constellations: An International Journal of Critical and Democratic Theory*, 11.3 (2004) pp. 412–33 and Richard Bellamy and Justus Schönlau, 'The Good, the Bad and the Ugly: The Need for Constitutional Compromise and the Drafting of the EU Constitution', Lynn Dobson and Andreas Føllesdal, eds, *Political Theory and the European Constitution*, Routledge, 2004, pp. 57–71.]

Chapter 7: Dario Castiglione, 'Constitutional Politics in the European Union' [a shortened and edited version of chapters 1 and 2 of *Constitutional Politics in the EU: The Convention Moment and its Aftermath* (Palgrave, 2007)].

Chapter 8: Dario Castiglione, 'Back to the Future? The Euro and the EU's Silent Constitution Building', in ed. G. Moro, *The Single Currency and European Citizenship*, Bloomsbury Academics, 2013, pp. 218–31.

Chapter 9: Richard Bellamy 'The Liberty of the Moderns: Civic and Market Freedom in the EU', *Global Constitutionalism: Human Rights, Democracy, Rule of Law* 1.1 (2012), pp. 141–72.

Chapter 10: Dario Castiglione, 'Political Identity in a "Community of Strangers"', in Jeffrey T. Checkel and Peter J. Katzenstein (eds.), *European Identity*, Cambridge University Press, 2009, pp. 29–54.

Chapter 11: Dario Castiglione, 'Negotiating Language Regimes', in D. Castiglione and C. Longman (eds.), *The Language Question in Europe and Diverse Societies,* Hart Publishers, 2007, pp. 1–14 [this is a slightly revised version of the original article].

Chapter 12: Richard Bellamy and Dario Castiglione, 'The Uses of Democracy: Reflections on the EU's Democratic Deficit', in E. Eriksen and J. Fossum (eds.), *Democracy in Europe: Integration and Deliberation*, Routledge, 2000, pp. 65–84.

Chapter 13: Richard Bellamy, 'Still in Deficit: Rights, Regulation and Democracy in the EU', *European Law Journal*, 12.6 (2006), 725–42.

Chapter 14: Richard Bellamy, 'Democracy without Democracy? Can the EU's Democratic "Outputs" Be Separated from the Democratic "Inputs" Provided by Competitive Parties and Majority Rule?' *Journal of European Public Policy*, 17.1 (2010), pp. 2–19.

Chapter 15: Richard Bellamy and Sandra Kröger (2016) 'Beyond a Constraining Dissensus: The Role of National Parliaments in Domesticating and Normalising the Politicization of European Integration', *Comparative European Politics*, 14.2 (2016), pp. 131–53.

Chapter 16: Richard Bellamy and Dario Castiglione, 'Democracy by Delegation? Who Represents Whom and How in European Governance', *Government and Opposition* 46.1 (2011), pp. 101–25.

Chapter 17: Richard Bellamy and Dario Castiglione, 'Three Models of Democracy, Political Community and Representation in the EU', *Journal of European Public Policy*, 20.2 (2013), pp. 206–23.

Chapter 18: Richard Bellamy, 'An Ever Closer Union of Peoples: Republican Intergovernmentalism, Demoi-cracy and Representation in the EU', *Journal of European Integration*, 35: 5 (2013), pp. 499–516.

Chapter 19: Richard Bellamy and Albert Weale, 'Political Legitimacy and European Monetary Union: Contracts, Constitutionalism and the Normative Logic of Two-level Games', *Journal of European Public Policy* 22.2 (2015), pp. 257–74.

Introduction

From Maastricht to Brexit

Richard Bellamy and Dario Castiglione

The European Union (EU) presents a particular challenge to those who study it, which stems from the ongoing political and academic debates as to its ultimate purpose and character. Even Jacques Delors, whose famous Luxembourg speech of 1985 outlining his vision as President of the Commission for a more politically and socially as well as economically unified Europe, with ever more common institutions, has been seen as epitomising the federal conception of the EU, remarked that this ideal of Europe remained, and would continue to remain for the next thirty to forty years, a kind of 'unidentified political object' (*objet politique non identifié*). Indeed, he deliberately avoided characterising his view of Europe in conventional terms as either some kind of supranational superstate or an intergovernmental organisation, describing it rather as 'an entity [*ensemble*] enabling each of our countries to benefit from the European dimension and to prosper internally as well as hold its own externally'. The scope and form of that 'unidentified object' continue to lie at the heart of political divisions over the EU and academic analysis of it.

The difficulty confronting both political actors and academics in defining what kind of *objet* the EU is or might be derives not only from its novelty and complexity but also from the fact that endogenous and exogenous pressures have produced dramatic changes to its borders, competences and rationale over the past thirty to forty years. Think of the major shocks that have transformed the EU since 1985: the collapse of the Soviet Union in 1989 and the subsequent process of Enlargement to Central and Eastern Europe from 2004; the acceleration towards an ever closer Union with the signing of the Maastricht Treaty in 1992; the introduction of the Euro in 1999; the failed ratification of the proposed Constitutional Treaty in 2005; the financial crisis of 2008–2009 and the ensuing Euro crisis; and most recently the combined effects of the refugee crisis, the Brexit vote and the growing influence of nationalist and populist parties and discourses across Europe and beyond. All these largely unforeseen and perhaps unforeseeable events and developments mean that the EU in 2020 cannot but be quite different to the EU that Delors or anyone else could have reasonably imagined thirty-five years ago. Of course, all political societies change in unexpected ways before the eyes of their participants and observers, albeit at different speeds and with different intensities. In the case of the EU, however, these changes have been transformative to an exceptional degree, redefining its nature and objectives as well as altering its functioning and competences, and in the process testing its internal and external credibility.

Such changes pose obvious problems for the empirical analysis of the EU. Any such account risks lagging behind the rapid movement of facts and history. A timely reminder of this danger is the fact that by the time you read these lines, you will probably know whether or not Britain has withdrawn from the EU, and if so on what terms it has either gone or stayed, while at the time of writing these very same lines (in early January 2019), we remain in the dark over both these issues. But how far, and in what ways, do such empirical uncertainties matter for those of us who study politics and political forms from a more theoretical and normative perspective? Are contingent and unexpected events and circumstances a concern for political theorists? We believe they are, though in different respects than for the purely empirical accounts and analyses of social scientists and historians. The relationship between normative theory and empirical reality is not a straightforward one. Theoretical interpretation need not engage in either faithful description or explanation. Not only does normative theory self-consciously adapt the object of analysis to the particular theoretical lenses through which it observes it, but also political norms do not take reality as it is, but try to shape and direct it. Normative political theory is typically formulated in a specialised (occasionally esoteric) language, with the ostensible purpose of offering a second-order intervention on reality by providing schemes for the interpretation of that reality in the same way as empirical and historical studies do. However, these normative interpretations can also provide the basis for a first-order political action geared towards changing that reality, in much the same way as the ideas that citizens deploy when participating in politics do, albeit at a higher level of abstraction.

As a result, even a normative political theory focused on delineating a purely ideal society cannot be completely indifferent to either real human conditions and motivations, or to historical circumstances and contingencies – at least, not if it wishes to be action guiding. As David Miller has remarked, seen as a branch of practical reasoning, political theory cannot avoid some 'presuppositional grounding' in facts about the world or the proximate possible worlds it seeks to address (Miller 2008). Accordingly, the normative debates concerning not just the feasibility but also the desirability of constitutionalising or democratising the EU have to a considerable degree rested on rival empirical as well as normative assessments of the conditions and circumstances that make particular modes of legitimate governance plausible and necessary in the kind of societies we live at present. Different normative accounts of the tasks the EU should undertake and the ways it ought to be organised rest on contrasting empirical evaluations of the degree and implications of interconnectedness, social and technological developments, capacities for production, travel and communication, and accumulated (though highly dispersed, contested and differentiated) knowledge and culturally and institutionally embedded practices of moral and social living, for the ways democracy, constitutionalism and citizenship should and could be configured at the European level.

All this may not be so controversial, leaving as it does ample space for the disagreements over the relationship between facts and norms, ideal and non-ideal theory, and morally and realistically inclined political theory, that inform recent methodological debates within the discipline (Valentini 2012). Nevertheless, even putting these debates to one side along with our own, somewhat ecumenical, stance on them, it remains pertinent to ask of a book such as this: How far does its theoretical and normative assessment of the EU as a political *objet* depend on the vagaries of actual politics? If the EU was to disintegrate over the next few years, and our book's *objet politique non identifié* were to disappear, would our normative reasonings become void, and acquire a merely historical or even antiquarian value? Such a dramatic historical event would undoubtedly affect the whole field of EU studies. In a similar manner to the way the collapse of the Soviet Union and the Soviet bloc meant the demise of the sub-discipline of Soviet studies within the social sciences, and its partial relocation to departments of history, so it might be thought that a dramatic transformation or collapse of the EU would likewise consign the entirety of EU studies to those disciplines that specialise in worlds we have lost.

As we argue in a new concluding chapter (chapter 20), notwithstanding the many recent crises of the Union and some reversal of the integration process, we very much doubt matters are so desperate as to lead to the end of the EU. However, even if they were, we contend that would not make this book as redundant, say, as a textbook on the political system of the EU would become. Nor have new developments necessarily made earlier chapters outdated as would likewise be the case if such a textbook was to be based on the EU of 1992 rather than that of 2019. The reason is that the object of study of this book is not so much the process of European political and legal, as well as economic, integration per se, as the use of the EU as a case study for the investigation of the normatively appropriate institutional mechanisms for governing a world where the modern nation state–based foundations of politics, characterised by a fairly neat distinction between the internal state sphere (the domain of constitutional law and politics) and the international state system (the domain of international law and politics), has come under strain for multiple and long-standing reasons. For this purpose, the analysis of the past successes and failures of the EU remains as pertinent as the assessment of its current crises and possible future.

European integration and the resulting Union have come to acquire a paradigmatic value as a way of meeting the challenges of more globalised economies and societies, organising supra- and transnational legal and regulatory arrangements, and institutionalising a more internationalised politics, between and to some degree beyond nation states. The paradigmatic value of the EU experience does not necessarily make it a generalisable model. But we do not think that the logic of exceptionalism applies either. Naturally, the institutional forms of the EU and of its predecessor organisations are the product of particular historical circumstances and of contingent events and chains of decisions. However, one can develop more general and abstract normative arguments for supporting or opposing them. Moreover, were the EU to disappear, the challenges that have partly come to define it would not go away, nor would the theories and reasoning used to assess the EU automatically lose their force or cogency.

As we suggested in an article originally published in 2003, and reproduced here as chapter 2, the acceleration of political integration sanctioned by the Maastricht Treaty and already signalled in Delors's Luxembourg speech had meant even then that 'European politicians and peoples cannot avoid strategic-oriented action or normative argument concerning the purpose, underlying values, future shape and desirable structures' of the EU. This political necessity motivated what we then called the 'normative turn' in EU studies, and our own work was intended as a contribution to both political and academic discussions over the legitimacy of the Union. If anything, the necessity for some kind of normative justification of the EU has become ever more urgent over the past fifteen years. Yet that urgency stems not from the need to save the EU at all costs but because the problems the EU confronts go beyond the particular European experience or the contingency of the EU's strengths and weaknesses, being concerned with a more general transformation of politics in our own times. As we note in chapter 20, the difficult negotiations surrounding Brexit have made all too clear how the retreat from the EU and a return to a largely national conception of politics involves considerable normative as well as practical costs. Exit from the EU does not wish away the challenges confronting a people who want to maintain meaningful and legitimate democratic forms of governance in the political conditions of contemporary societies.

To a large extent, the arguments we develop in this book can be seen as arising from the very concerns that ostensibly led to Brexit: namely, how can citizens credibly and legitimately 'take back control' in the context of an ever more interconnected world, and to what extent is the EU a plausible and justifiable response to this challenge? As a result, we attempt to develop a general normative framework for understanding the character of this challenge and assessing the responses to it, that offers an accurate and coherent account of the normative demands underlying both. With regard to the challenge, chapter 1 develops an account we dub 'cosmopolitan communitarianism', that seeks to reconcile the normative demands of a cosmopolitan kind stemming from the current processes of globalisation with those of a communitarian kind stemming from the historical processes of state formation and national self-determination, and argues that the first need to be embedded within the second to be meaningfully action guiding for individual citizens and politicians alike. With regard to the response, chapters 2 and 3 then aspire to elaborate normative criteria for the design of legitimate institutions at the European level that are capable of meeting the normative demands of the cosmopolitan communitarian challenge. These criteria draw on the republican notion of freedom as non-domination, and lead us to propose that a legitimate EU needs to evolve forms of governance that are compatible with promoting non-domination between the member states, on the one hand, and their individual citizens, on the other. Originally developed in the aftermath of Maastricht, this framework has evolved through the analysis of a number of key issues, such as sovereignty, constitutionalism, Union citizenship and the democratic deficit, as these have emerged over the subsequent twenty-five years. It is to tracing this trajectory, and noting its remarkable robustness as an analysis of the vicissitudes of the EU over this period, that we now turn.

THE ARGUMENT OF THE BOOK IN CONTEXT

As we have noted above, and the title of this collection implies, these chapters were written in the years between the drafting of the Maastricht Treaty in 1991 and the Brexit referendum of 2016. In retrospect, the difficulties surrounding the ratification of the first can be regarded as presaging the growth of Euroscepticism across Europe of which the second provides the most extreme expression so far. These difficulties signalled the end of the 'permissive consensus' and the start of an ever more prominent 'constraining dissensus' (Hooghe and Marks 2009) as the post-war Breton Woods settlement of balancing 'Smith abroad' with 'Keynes at home' (Gilpin 1987, 359) gradually gave way to an ever more neoliberal version of Smith abroad reinforcing Hayek at home – a process enhanced in the EU by the creation of the single market (Streeck 2014). As the returns on such a policy gradually decreased, at least for certain non-mobile and unskilled groups, the demand for the EU to attain greater 'input' legitimacy to compensate for its waning 'output' success increased commensurately (Scharpf 2009). Yet, such demands have not always been straightforwardly for greater democracy at the EU level, as the debate around the EU's so-called democratic deficit has largely assumed. As the winning slogan to 'take back control' in the Brexit referendum suggested, the demand for greater democratic accountability has been expressed even more vociferously in terms of a claim either to return certain competences to the national level, or to reinforce domestic oversight of EU policy making (Kriesi 2016; De Vries 2018). The chapters in this volume chart the largely failed attempts of the EU and much of the academic literature to adequately address the increasing challenge posed by this demand for greater domestic control post-Maastricht.

To recall, the Maastricht Treaty was initially rejected in a Danish referendum, attracted only a *petit oui* of 50.7 per cent in an unprecedented French referendum, and was narrowly passed by the British parliament in the face of an exceptional rebellion of Conservative MPs against their own Prime Minister, John Major, and with the reluctant support of Labour MPs discontented over an opt-out from the Treaty's social provisions. The Single European Act of 1986 had had as its objective the creation of a single market within the then European Community by 1992. The Maastricht Treaty in many ways represented the recognition of this new reality, which had gradually taken the integration process into core state powers. In particular, it led to the introduction of the Euro, with applicant countries joining the European Exchange Mechanism and committing to avoid devaluing their currency for two consecutive years, to adopt 'sound' fiscal policies, with a pledge to keep inflation no higher than 1.5 per cent above the top three best-performing countries and long-term interest rates within 2 per cent of these countries, and to limit debt to 60 per cent of GDP and annual deficits to no greater than 3 per cent of GDP. All these undertakings considerably weakened the scope of domestic fiscal and economic policy, which was moved in a more economically liberal direction. The Treaty also introduced the status of European citizenship, which brought together the main entitlements individuals obtained from their member state belonging to what was now called the European Union (EU). However, as many commentators noted at the time (Everson 1995), these rights were primarily linked to the four freedoms at the heart of the single market and so mainly focused on those who moved from one member state to another. Finally, the Treaty extended cooperation in areas such as foreign and security policy and justice and home affairs, although these were as yet predominantly intergovernmental in character, with supranational institutions having less influence than in the core economic areas.

These changes all raised the issue of how far the EU's political arrangements could credibly provide ongoing democratic influence and control over the exercise of its increased competences. They also appeared to lock the member states into the logic of the free market revolution brought about by Ronald Reagan and Margaret Thatcher in the early to mid-1980s. Though the British Maastricht rebels often claimed to be defending the legacy of the former Prime Minister, the Single European Act has with some justification been called 'Thatcher's Plot' to snare the member states into 'Hayek's Trap' (Van Parijis 2016), as outlined by the liberal philosopher in his 1939 essay 'The Economic Conditions of Interstate Federalism'. Hayek had argued that the free movement of labour, capital, goods and services would drastically constrain the capacity of national governments to intervene in the economy, curtailing their use of indirect or direct taxation to regulate prices, labour or investment. Moreover, he also predicted that cultural heterogeneity would mean political integration would be unable to compensate for this loss of state capacity at the national level by replacing it at the supranational level. Such a multistate federation would lack an overarching national identity that might foster solidarity of a similar kind to that which had allowed redistribution from one economic sector to another within states. He doubted the 'French peasant will be willing to pay more for his fertiliser to help the British chemical industry' (Hayek [1939] 1948, 262). While the Maastricht Treaty was signed by twelve member states, the collapse of the former Soviet bloc post-1989 had already made evident the likely expansion of the EU to encompass the new democracies of Central and Eastern Europe. Therefore, the democratic challenge confronting the EU over this period related not only to the deepening of the economic integration process but also, and just as urgently, to its even more dramatic widening to a highly socially and culturally heterogeneous group of new members. As a result, the EU has seemed caught on the twin horns of Hayek's dilemma, with its single most concerted attempt at a solution – the ill-fated Constitutional Treaty – an abject failure.

As ever, it tends to be easier to identify problems, and do so with greater clarity, in retrospect than one can manage at the time. Nonetheless, it had seemed obvious to us that the step change in the integration process heralded by Maastricht risked outstripping what many citizens of the member states would regard as legitimate. Legitimacy would only be obtained if these measures could be credibly subjected to democratic control aimed at preserving a degree of social as well as political equality. At the same time, we doubted the plausibility and justifiability of simply scaling up the democratic mechanisms of the nation state to the EU level. Political identification with the EU remained weak compared to national and subnational identities and was getting progressively weaker, with the partial exception of some elite groups. Likewise, an integrated public sphere only existed in a highly fragmented and dispersed sense, and was similarly most common among mobile and educated professionals. Meanwhile, the intermediary structures of civil society necessary to support political mobilisation of a pan-European kind, such as a transnational party system, were also patchy and feeble and often created and financed by EU institutions. In these circumstances, enhancing the democratic authority of the European Parliament or other EU institutions merely risked deepening what Peter Lindseth (2010) has called the democratic disconnect with citizens.

As the argument of chapter 2 indicates, we believed neither of the two main schools of integration theory – neo-functionalism and liberal intergovernmentalism – fully appreciated this normative dilemma, or indeed the normative commitments implicit in their own accounts, while – as chapter 1 shows – we thought neither of the two main schools of normative international political theory – cosmopolitanism and communitarianism (which has more recently morphed into statism) – offered satisfactory responses to the empirical reality of the EU. We contended the EU was best conceived as lying betwixt and between supranationalism and internationalism, cosmopolitanism and statist communitarianism, in the manner that political scientists have often attempted to capture descriptively with such terms as 'multilevel'. We argued in chapter 3 that this cosmopolitan-communitarian normative constellation favours a republican more than a liberal account of politics – that of a 'mixed polity' rather than of a constitutional legal state, in which freedom as 'non-domination' rather than from interference per se, as provided by the standard set of liberal rights, offers the key norm for guiding institutional design.

In our writing – together, singly and with others – we have tried to explore the normative credentials of this picture of the EU as a deep form of international cooperation between democratic states. In this respect, our work aligns itself with a growing body of normative work (Rawls 1993; Christiano 2006, 2010; Miller 2007; Pettit 2010a, 2010b) that casts doubt on the democratic credentials of schemes for global democracy, while nevertheless seeking to provide the new and developing forms of international governance with democratic legitimacy. We propose the resulting republican model of international cooperation between democratic states as an alternative to liberal cosmopolitan theories of global democracy, using the EU as a case study (Bellamy 2019). On our republican account, European governance should be viewed in terms of a system of checks and balances between different states and their demoi. This system prevents any state dominating another, while promoting the possibilities of cooperation in areas where this is necessary either to secure their citizens certain necessary public goods only possible through international agreements, or to prevent certain public bads resulting from negative externalities only controllable by interstate action. Such goods and bads were initially primarily economic but security has also always been significant and both areas have been progressively broadened to encompass social and environmental issues and increasingly the protection of certain fundamental rights. Our claim has been that this model offers the only viable response to Hayek's trap. For it provides states with the capacity to regulate global markets in mutually beneficial ways rather than succumbing to them, as – for the reasons outlined by Hayek – would be likely to be the case in a more fully politically integrated EU of the kind advocated by liberal cosmopolitans of a federalist disposition.

From a substantive and political perspective, therefore, we contend that the kind of democratic normative theory we have developed in analysing the EU experience is not only the most appropriate to understand its nature and development but also offers some important answers to the legitimacy crisis that has affected the European project in the last few years, following the international economic crisis and more recently the result of the Brexit referendum. Many elements of our preferred republican model are in fact in place. Though far from perfect in its current configuration, the advantages of this arrangement have been a gradual deepening of reciprocal recognition and cooperation as the member states have negotiated mutually acceptable compromises to tackle their shared problems. From this perspective, the chief dangers to the EU's democratic legitimacy lie in the twin failures of the national governments and demoi to internalise through their domestic democratic processes the recognition and importance of this system of cooperation, on the one hand, and the attempts to replace Europe's complex, multilevelled and mixed system of government with common, uniform governing structures based on an alleged liberal democratic consensus, on the other.

A BRIEF SYNOPSIS OF THE BOOK

We have divided the chapters collected in the book into seven parts. This division is partly chronological, with the earliest essays coming first and the most recent essays last. However, there is also a shift from more general essays outlining the issues involved and our overall approach to them, and that are focused more on identifying problems than offering solutions, to more specific and detailed responses to the current crisis of democratic legitimacy within the EU.

As we noted above, the chapters in part I address the need for what we called a 'normative turn' in EU scholarship, and marked the first attempts by political theorists to grapple with the EU. They explore how we should understand the EU at an ontological level, as either cosmopolitan or (statist) communitarian, and examine the sort of normative approach (liberal or republican) that is most suitable for framing a response to the EU's particular governance issues. We make three key points. The first is that the empirical

argument that globalisation has eroded the capacity of nation states to provide for the security and welfare of their citizens is overstated. The second
is that any form of supra- or postnational (proto global) democracy at the
EU level will prove (and to some degree has proven) deficient in a variety of
related aspects: in terms of social and political equality, respect for diversity,
effective and fair democratic communication, and efficient and equitable
decision-making. The third defends a republican approach. We argue that the
aim of the EU should be to ensure non-dominating relations between states
that reflect the interests of their citizens. According to this criterion, interstate
relations should be mutually advantageous while preserving each state's
capacity to operate as a democratic political community.

Drawing on the analytical framework laid out in chapters 2 and 3, parts
II, III and IV focus on the 'polity' features of the EU. Adapting Max Weber,
we can define a polity as 'a political and legal order that exercises legitimate
power over a given territory and people'. As such, there are three dimensions
to a polity – the possession of sovereignty over a given domain, the existence
of a constitutional order that legitimates the exercise of power, and a citizenry
who identify with the polity as the appropriate locus for organising their collective affairs. The EU is generally regarded as both reflecting and promoting
the reconfiguration of all three elements from the national to the supranational
level. Yet, the character of this reconfiguration is open to debate. The chapters
collected in parts II to IV explore each of the three elements in turn, arguing
that states remain the fundamental component of the international order even
if the character of their relations has changed.

Cosmopolitan theorists have tended to characterise the EU as undermining
the sovereignty of states. On the one hand, they typically argue that sovereignty is being transferred upwards to the EU as it takes on certain competences. On the other hand, many also maintain that sovereignty itself is being
replaced by human rights and constitutional norms as the source of normative
legitimacy. Meanwhile, they contend that citizens are developing new forms
of postnational identity that reflect these two changes. As a result, they will
increasingly view EU-level politics as the main overarching focus of political
engagement. The chapters in part II dispute the views that sovereignty either
simply goes upwards or that it vanishes altogether. The true innovation of
the EU is instead that it creates more complex forms of shared and interconnected sovereignty. Therefore, we argue against more traditional unitary and
simplified conceptions of sovereignty, exploring a more pluralist and divided
conception as a way of conceiving the interactions between the various actors
within the European Union. Such a system, which in part reflects early modern and more republican ideas of the balance of power, shares and distributes
sovereignty in ways that remove the arbitrary power of any single agent or
agency. Through the resulting democratic negotiation between peoples, laws
have to be publicly justified in ways that give due recognition to difference.

The multiplicity of sites of governance and decision-making also enables them to be implemented more efficiently and with greater sensitivity to local variations. Thus, unity is constructed via a dialogue among a plurality, with the one being continually challenged, renegotiated and reconstructed as the other evolves and becomes more diverse. The doctrine of sovereignty was developed alongside the development of the modern state. As that political formation begins to fragment, it seems highly appropriate to return to the ideas and institutional structures it sought to supplant.

The chapters in part III engage with various phases and aspects of the EU constitutionalisation process, and with the question that dominated the first decade of this century and has tended to re-emerge during each of the EU's political crises: namely, does Europe need a constitution? At the end of the last decade, the European constitutional moment proved to be inconclusive. One of the reasons for this failure was that the question was wrongly put in more than one sense. Analytically, it is arguable that the EU already has a constitution of sorts; politically, the process was mismanaged by the European political elites; and normatively, the case for a written European constitution was not overwhelming. As was the case for sovereignty, our discussion of the EU's constitutional moment challenges current views of constitutionalism and their application to the EU. The chapters in part III examine three different aspects of the constitutional question. The first aspect is the nature of the European constitutional order, looking at both the making and the content of the EU 'constitution'. This order has emerged through different processes of constitutionalisation, comprising the fixing of the institutional structures of governance and the separation of powers at the European level, the definition through successive treaties of common areas of competence and collective decision-making procedures, and an interlocking legal system between the European and national levels based on the acquis communautaire. The existence of a constitutional order in this material sense was obscured during the constitutional debate, which focused almost exclusively on whether the EU should have a constitutional document, and on the symbolic value of such a document, rather than the content of the constitution and its role in the life of the EU polity. The second aspect we explore is the nature of constitutional politics in general and in the EU in particular. Here we argue that the process of constitution making reflected a typical republican compromise rather than a federal-liberal democratic consensus, and that the outcome of the EU constitutionalisation process should be read in that light. Constitution making is the combined result of intensely political constitutional moments and normal politics, with the law and the judiciary playing their part in organising and reflecting public views, but without any claim to representing a universal position capable of reconciling the disagreements of politics on purely substantive grounds. The third aspect is the very nature of the constitution and constitutionalism in a more globalised world, where the borders between states are more porous, and there are increased forms of cooperation and shared sovereignty. The EU is a paradigmatic case for such new forms of transnational and multilevel governance, for which traditional ideas of the constitution and constitutionalism have seemed inadequate. The conception of the constitution as an overarching document at the apex of a unified legal and political system no longer appears tenable even at the national level because it fails to capture in a few general principles the normative pluralism of modern societies, their sociopolitical differentiation and the more particularistic nature of social legislation. Constitutionalism itself needs to be rethought. In the European context, it needs to accommodate the national forms and practices of constitutional law, something requiring a more plural and flexible character, conceiving EU constitutionalism as an open-textured and continuously negotiated method of constitution building. Such an idea of constitutionalism reflects the basic intuition that the European constitutional order is a plural one, operating both at the supranational and national levels, and encompassing both the national and EU constitutions. The challenge for constitutional politics in the EU is how to conceive and operationalise conflict resolution in the context of such radical pluralism.

Part IV engages with the issue of EU citizenship, which many consider as perhaps the best way of legitimating the EU by creating a European demos willing to take part in a pan-European democracy. This argument has been developed in two directions, reflecting two distinct normative understandings of the political community. One type of argument for European citizenship rests on the construction (or emergence) of some form of European identity. This view is based on a more communitarian view of citizenship as resting on a sense of belonging, expressing itself in either ethnocultural or civic forms of identification with the community. The other type of argument for European citizenship is based on a more liberal and universalistic view of citizenship (and of the demos), grounded on fundamental human rights and the rule of law as the cement of the democratic community. Supporters of a European constitutional patriotism tend to combine these two understandings, but in a way which seems to oscillate between thin and thick views of the democratic community. Meanwhile, a third – transnational – form of citizenship has been advocated that sits between these two, seeking, in Benhabib's (2002, 2004) words, to 'disaggregate' and 'de-territorialise' political, civil and social rights – a view that has been developed in a republican direction by Bohman (2004, 2005, 2007). We reject the above arguments on various grounds. We criticise both communitarian and liberal conceptions of citizenship because they are partial and miss the important integrative function that political citizenship plays in modern societies. Such an integrative function requires not only a certain sense of belonging, and a catalogue of rights of membership, but also the participation of the citizens in making collective decisions in the

face of disagreements over values and conflicting interests. The three components – belonging, rights and participation – go together. Because belonging
and participation are weak at the EU level, so are rights. Contrary to the hopes
of most of those advocating supra-, post- or transnational views of EU citizenship, the development of Union citizenship rights by the ECJ has tended to
be of a market-reinforcing character that has weakened social solidarity and
political participation at the member state level without strengthening them
at the EU level. Yet, the fact of preexisting national allegiances, together
with the size and diversity of the EU, makes meaningful participation at the
EU level hard to justify or realise. So, with regard to belonging, rights and
participation, EU citizenship needs to be thought of as an adjunct to national
citizenship – a means for reinforcing national rights and gaining some of the
benefits of cooperation with other states.

The chapters in parts V and VI turn from the EU's 'polity' dimension to
its distinctive 'regime' or form of governance. In particular, they explore the
possibility of a form of EU democracy that allows EU citizens to combine
their new transnational and old national statuses, without creating a supranational status. This requires the careful construction of a complex institutional
system, through which citizens can express their democratic voice and exercise responsible control over political and administrative decision-making
at the European level, without, however, falling foul of the two related risks
of undermining established democratic channels to which people may more
readily relate, and eroding those thicker forms of social solidarity across
space and time that ensure durable cooperation and responsible behaviour
from citizens. None of these problems can be easily solved, and European
citizenship is far from being a panacea. Nonetheless, this is the challenge that
needs addressing in constructing an EU regime capable of both promoting
and sustaining the European polity in its present form.

Cosmopolitan views of the EU tend to favour a federal view of the EU polity
(Habermas 2001b, 2012, 2015), while proposing a solution to its democratic
deficit by suggesting the transferral of popular sovereignty upwards to the
European level. Conversely, technocratic views of the EU consider the European regime as something to which the principles and common mechanisms
of majoritarian democratic politics do not, or should not, apply (Majone 1996,
1998). Meanwhile, others have contended that the limitations of both these
proposals can be overcome by novel forms of consultation with civil society
groups that offer alternatives to standard forms of party-based, representative
democracy (Sabel and Zeitlin 2008). The chapters on forms of democracy
and representation in the EU offer a sustained criticism of all three positions
that either promote a vision of supranational democracy or consider European
policies as the exclusive province of regulatory and judicial decision-making,
or believe there can be forms of post-parliamentary democracy that do not

rest on the accountability of representatives to those they claim to stand for. These chapters criticise both postnational majoritarian and supranational non-majoritarian democracy at the EU level, while presenting a more sceptical view of the role that new forms of transnational democracy based on consultation with civil society groups can offer to address the democratic deficit. We suggest instead that new forms of international demoicracy, in which national parliaments play a much larger role than hitherto in overseeing the decisions of governments on EU affairs, should be explored and implemented in order to address the democratic and representative deficit at the EU level.

Such a kind of institutional development is in line with our normative assessment of the EU regime, which proposes a more positive model for EU democracy based on a republican view of politics grounded on the existence of multiple demoi. Part of the solution to the legitimacy crisis of the EU and to its democratic deficit is to think of the EU regime as a way of organising cooperation between democratic states and their peoples rather than as a mechanism for fully transcending them. Each of these states has its own internal systems of social justice for which its citizens are co-responsible thorough their equal participation within majoritarian systems of democracy. However, to the extent that the wealth and survival of these states depend on cooperation with other states, it seems appropriate that the costs and benefits of these arrangements be shared equitably. As is the case within each member state, non-majoritarian and counter-majoritarian mechanisms, and 'new forms' of governance, can be legitimised so long as their scope and operation are controlled by the majoritarian systems of the member states. At the European level, this implies that national democratic institutions, and not only national governments, should have a larger role in the decision-making process. When removed from such control, the European institutions cannot offer pan-European decision-making with anything but spurious and ineffective democratic credentials. It is only by empowering the European *demoi*, by giving them proper control over EU decision-making, and facilitating dialogue and cooperation between them and between their various democratic institutions, that it is possible to legitimate European governance across European societies.

The chapters in part VII conclude the volume by relating our arguments to the two main challenges currently confronting the EU: the Eurocrisis and Euroscepticism, of which Brexit is the most extreme instance. Both challenges stem from EU economic and legal integration outpacing the capacity and desire for political integration, leading to the undermining of democratic politics at both the EU and especially the member state level. By contrast, we suggest that our model of republican intergovernmentalism offers a credible response to both challenges that avoids creating a democratic deficit in either EU or member state politics. Rather, it revitalises and empowers both by revealing how the EU provides a framework within which the *demoi* of Europe can take back collective democratic control of their mutual relations.

CONCLUSION

Critics of our position – especially those holding more straightforwardly cosmopolitan and supra- or transnational views – might object that our account is too historically contingent. They contend that the only way to overcome the EU's present impasse is through an idealistic act of will that exploits the current crisis to take a great leap forward towards a more complete political union (Van Parijis 2016; Wolkenstein 2018). In the final chapter, written especially for this volume, we cast doubt on such proposals. Developing Claus Offe's diagnosis of a Europe entrapped (Offe 2015), we argue that this entrapment is as much normative as empirical. The empirical entrapment of the EU by the Euro crisis has resulted as much from the normative shortcomings of what Joseph Weiler (2012) has appositely termed the political messianism of Europe's political class as the policy failures that accompanied its introduction. Indeed the one led to the other. By failing to address the normative demands stemming from what in chapters 1 and 15 we refer to as the communitarian ghost in the cosmopolitan machine, Europe's political leaders now find themselves entrapped by a heightened level of Euroscepticism within all the member states that has reduced the prospects for pan-EU solidarity and forced the EU to adopt emergency measures of dubious efficacy and legitimacy. In sum, the EU finds itself ensnared by Hayek's trap. Accelerating political integration towards a federal union repeats the messianic mistakes of the past and will only deepen this entrapment. If the likely lesson of Brexit for the UK will be the realisation that domestic democratic control stands to be reduced yet further outside the EU than it was within it, the lesson for the EU should be that its role lies in promoting the capacity for democratic control of its member states – both alone and together, not least through the mutual control of their interactions and interrelations. In this respect, as Claus Offe and Ulrich Preuß (2016, 33) remarked before the referendum, both the impending Brexit crisis and the Greek crisis that preceded it should have been taken as opportunities to find ways of re-energising the democratic capacity of its members. In 2019, no less than in 1985, the normative task of the as-yet fully identified European political ensemble lies in fostering rather than subverting that capacity through promoting a demoi- rather than a demos-cratic Europe.

Part I

THE NORMATIVE TURN
IN EU STUDIES

A REPUBLICAN EUROPE?

Chapter 1

The Normative Challenge of a European Polity

Cosmopolitan and Communitarian Models Compared, Criticised and Combined[1]

Richard Bellamy and Dario Castiglione

I. A COPERNICAN REVOLUTION?

Consider for a moment how odd the European Union's political structure is.[2] It lacks the chief characteristics of a sovereign constitutional nation state – namely, a congruence of territory, functional authority and identity; a monopoly of legitimate violence within its borders; an exclusive control over the movement of goods and persons within its domain; a clear locus and hierarchy of authority and offices; offers little if any democratic accountability to those affected by its decisions; and has no preset limits to its area of competence. These features are largely loaned to it indirectly via the member states, which also offer it the main source of its legitimacy. Yet this transferral of powers does not occur in the institutionalised and consistent manner of a federal system. It is achieved in a piecemeal fashion, either through the internal dynamics of Community decision-making or as a result of periodic pacts and treaties between the various governments concerned. *Eppur si muove!* It has a life of its own. The treaties are not simple international agreements; they offer the basis for an independent legal system. The European agencies and bureaucracies amount to more than an intergovernmental organisation. They can generate and allocate revenue, regulate both public and private behaviour through legal and administrative directives, respond to pressure groups and organise elections, possess diplomatic status, and have the ability to conduct and conclude binding international negotiations on certain trade and security matters.

That an organisation that is not a state can nonetheless possess so many of its salient characteristics offers a challenge to much conventional thinking about politics. Indeed, we want to suggest that we need something like a Copernican revolution in our traditional political concepts if we are to comprehend the true nature of the European Union. In particular, the civic concepts of rights and democracy have to be related to those concepts associated with nationhood, notably state and popular sovereignty, in ways that do not assume a complete overlap or fit between the two groups. At stake is the normative underpinning of the respective claims of national and European legal and political institutions to be constitutionally superior within their distinct domains, and the issue of how far these spheres can be compartmentalised. Who has the authority to make decisions, about what, for whom and how have become questions that can no longer be easily avoided.[3]

The two dominant views of the EU within current British political debate, namely that of the pro-European neo-federalists on the one hand, and of the Eurosceptical neo-nationalists on the other, do not adequately capture this normative dimension of the European Union and the questions of political legitimacy it raises. In section 1, we shall attempt to offer a more theoretically nuanced approach by aligning different models of Europe with arguments stemming from the cosmopolitan and communitarian political moralities proposed by contemporary political theorists.[4] Each of these broad schools of thought represents ideal-types that can be associated with different versions of federalism and nationalism, respectively. Each also offers a distinctive account of democracy and rights that we employ, in section 2, to illuminate current debates over citizenship and judicial competences within the European Union. We conclude that when due weight is given to communitarian and cosmopolitan considerations, a less harmonious and more pluralistic view of the Union becomes both attractive and plausible.

II. THE COMMUNITARIAN GHOST IN THE COSMOPOLITAN MACHINE

Two complementary strands run through both the cosmopolitan and the communitarian accounts of rights and democracy: the normative and the sociopolitical. We shall examine each in turn for both theories. Although the two positions need not be as opposed as they are sometimes presented, important differences of emphasis are nonetheless present that have considerable practical implications for how we think about political institutions.

i) Cosmopolitan Globalists and Federalists

The normative basis of the cosmopolitan ethical thesis rests on a theory of human rights that combines individualism, universality and generality.[5] The moral implications of these rights can be cashed out in either interactional or institutional terms – in other words, either as pertaining to the actions of individual persons and agencies or as applying to the rules and procedures of certain institutional schemes. In a number of respects, the interactional case is practically weaker than the institutional. The perfect obligations necessary to uphold negative rights of non-interference can be conceptualised in global terms reasonably easily, since in principle at least they are costless and simply require individual forbearance. It is much harder to assign a global responsibility for positive rights to care and welfare which appear to rely on special obligations. Indeed, in the absence of any causal relation for the potential or actual harms involved, it is difficult even to justify positive action to secure negative rights worldwide, through the supply of peacekeeping forces and the like. The institutional view appears to fill this lacuna, since it potentially links us to a whole range of unknown others and provides a duty even to safeguard those negative rights we have not personally violated. The focus here is no longer on the direct relations between individuals, but on the justice of the practices and arrangements within which people are involved and jointly and severally responsible.

This institutional argument is contingent on the possible or actual existence of a global institutional scheme within which we all, to some significant degree, participate.[6] The sociopolitical strand of the cosmopolitan argument comes in here. Global socio-economic forces are held to have created a greater degree of interconnectedness within the world than ever before. Technological advances have internationalised production, distribution and exchange and transformed financial markets. Multinational corporations (MNCs), even when they possess a regional or national base, are said to organise their affairs on an international scale and respond to global market pressures. This internationalisation of markets is even more apparent in the financial sector, where new information technology has radically increased the mobility of economic units and to a large degree tied the world's major banking and trading centres into a single integrated network. New communications systems have also rendered ordinary people more aware of these global developments than ever before. The media, according to proponents of this thesis, have altered the 'situational geography' of social and political life by giving people direct access to distant events and creating new experiences, commonalties and frames of meaning that do not require direct physical contact – popular reactions to Tiananmen Square and the plight of the Kurds in the aftermath of the Gulf War being good examples of this phenomenon. A series of common cultural references – from the banality of soap operas through to greater popular awareness and knowledge of world events – have allegedly generated new solidarities as evidenced in transnational social movements such as Greenpeace and Amnesty International.

The above-mentioned processes are claimed to have weakened in turn the capacity of nation states to provide for the security and welfare of their citizens, and led to the creation of a number of international power blocks, regimes and organisations to facilitate their continued ability to do so by managing various areas of transnational activity. These institutions range from collective security arrangements such as NATO, through a variety of other intergovernmental organisations of different degrees of formality aimed at controlling various aspects of economic and social policy, such as the G7, to a number of international non-governmental organisations, some purely technical, like the Universal Postal Union, others more politically contentious, such as the IMF. All these organisations modify to one degree or another the freedom of action of states and undercut their capacity to operate as sovereign units. Consequently, their title to act as the agents of the sovereign will of their people has been likewise eroded. Effective decision-making and the sources of identification have in many cases passed elsewhere, or so at least it is alleged.

Finally, this move beyond the sovereign nation state is reflected in the body of international law that has grown up in the wake of these developments. Here individuals are gradually replacing states as the main subjects of the law. On the one hand, it has been recognised that individuals have rights and obligations that are independent of and go beyond those duties and entitlements they have as citizens of particular states – a point made most strikingly in war crime trials. On the other hand, the legitimacy of states has come to rest as much on the justice of their rule as on their de facto hold on power. The post-war international declarations of rights have reinforced this shift from state to individual, as have challenges to the notions of 'immunity from jurisdiction' and 'immunity from state agencies' which have hitherto operated as central principles of international law.

This global positivisation of individual moral rights brings the normative and empirical strands of the cosmopolitan thesis together. At least two broad possible views of the European Union can follow from this perspective. One version holds that the forces described above have undermined the nation state, but that a centralised federal Europe, that is itself not unlike a nation state writ large, can fill the gap. Another more truly cosmopolitan version is not so much supranational as postnational in orientation (Ferry 1992, 179–89), viewing moves towards federalism as an alternative to, rather than a new form of, the unitary sovereign state (Beaud 1995). By and large, political scientists – especially those of a functionalist disposition – have been drawn towards the first position. They have advocated the strengthening of the Union's supranational features – particularly the European Parliament and the Commission – and the phasing out of intergovernmentalism, and have welcomed the move towards common policies in the spheres of domestic justice and foreign affairs in addition to economic and social matters (e.g. George 1985, 1991; Keohane and Hoffman 1991). Lawyers, by contrast, have been the principal advocates of the second position. They have drawn inspiration from the gradual development of a single legal framework by the European Court of Justice, noting with approval its increasing tendency to appeal to human rights and its claims of Supremacy over the domestic law of member states and Direct Effect with regard to their citizens (Mancini 1989).[7] Needless to say, the reality falls far short of either version of the cosmopolitan ideal – a fact that communitarians are not slow in pointing out.

ii) Communitarians, Nationalists and the Sovereignty of States

Communitarians question both the normative and empirical aspects of the cosmopolitan thesis. With regard to the first element, they dispute the universalist and individualist rights-based starting point of the cosmopolitan case. Rather than viewing rights as foundational principles presupposed by all legitimate societies, communitarians contend they are best conceived as components of particular forms of life and their related patterns of human flourishing (Sandel 1987). Moreover, different communities are likely to prioritise different kinds and sets of rights. Indeed, even within a given conception of rights, conflicts between different sorts of rights involving incompatible and incommensurable values and interests tend to arise (Waldron 1989; Bellamy 1995). Such clashes can generally only be resolved by reference to the broader social picture of which they form a part. This wider social context is also important to motivate people to identify with rights and take on the burdens that upholding them usually entails. Finally, given their belief that the nature of our rights depends on the character of the society and the culture in which we live, communitarians tend to stress the priority of democracy over rights in the preservation of our liberty (Walzer 1981). A link is thereby established with national sovereignty. Nationality defines a common political culture and identity, that to be subjected to political control has to be tied to a democratic state (Walzer 1983, 28/9; Miller 1995, chap. 4).

Communitarians also contest the second, empirical, element of cosmopolitanism, questioning both the degree and consequences of the processes of globalisation and interconnectedness. It is possible to dispute, for example, the extent to which MNCs truly operate at a transnational level. As Hirst and Thompson have recently shown (1995), core capital, basic Research and Development, and management personnel and structures are mostly located within a main national base. The various political bodies and non-governmental agencies that have developed to cope with global problems of security and welfare tend to be international and intergovernmental rather than supranational. The UN, for example, far from representing a nascent form of cosmopolitan governance, as is sometimes argued (Held 1995, part IV), remains very much an instrument of the sovereign states which compose it – not least the superpowers, whose hold on the security council effectively blocks any move that might damage their interests (Zolo 1995, 27/8). Indeed, the major powers' effective control over the purse strings enables them to manipulate most important, and hence costly, initiatives requiring interstate cooperation, and to stop those that do not meet with their approval – witness the sabotaging of UNESCO by Britain and the United States (Jones 1995b).

Cosmopolitans also overlook the differential impact of global forces on different countries and the imbalances in the degree and nature of the inter-dependence that they create. By and large the wealthier and more powerful nations are net beneficiaries from global market forces, for example, while poorer states are either locked out of many of the networks or are subordi-nate partners and often damaged by global trade, becoming sources of cheap labour and resources, rather than developing strong economies of their own. Global environmental, health, security and other dangers that are no respect-ers of state borders are said to bind the peoples of the world together as shar-ing a common fate. However, they rarely affect all of them to an equal extent. When joint actions have shared consequences, such as the depletion of fish stocks, the cooperative action may be possible, although here too the standard free rider problems that arise with all public goods and bads mean that many countries will attempt to evade their responsibilities. Because the advantages and disadvantages are not usually mutual even with shared activities or prob-lems, the incentives for cooperative behaviour are usually lopsided (Jones 1995a, 75–7). Even within the EU, the substantial differences in economic performance, social standards and political interests between the member states have rendered the formulation of common policies far from easy. Brit-ain's acrimonious attempts to reduce the massive financial transfers to other EC states via the CAP reflect a genuine problem that potentially weakens the commitment to the Union of all the main contributors (Hirst and Thompson 1996, chap. 7; Jones 1993).

Although nations do form blocs for certain limited purposes, it is also impor-tant to note that these often have the goal of preserving state autonomy rather than diminishing it. Alan Milward's (1992) account of the European Commu-nity as a 'rescue' of the nation state is highly pertinent in this respect. The EU emerges from this analysis as being, in part at least, a reaction against the forces of globalisation. Indeed, many of its more 'social' corporatist and welfare ele-ments are in a number of respects anti-cosmopolitan – reflecting a desire to preserve the standards of member state workers against the effects of foreign competition. This feature has been highlighted by the exclusionary character of recent moves to create a European Citizenship, discussed below (Lyons 1996).

For related reasons, more homogeneous consumption patterns and a greater awareness of world affairs have not necessarily produced as much convergence in political identity among the general population as cosmopolitans assert. People distinguish a humanitarian concern with famine or other disasters in countries other than their own from the sort of formalised responsibilities they have for co-nationals. They may support initiatives such as Band Aid or give to Oxfam, but that is a long way from condoning increased taxation to expand the development aid budget, for example. Television, faster communication systems, greater job mobility and the like may have broadened people's horizons in certain respects and encouraged them to identify with a wider community, but the identification may not be so deep as the solidarities of old, based as they were on continuous, direct contact and personal involvement. Later in the chapter we shall produce some evidence from the EU to support this argument.

Just as we distinguished two different versions of the cosmopolitan ideal with regard to the EU, so two broad positions can be associated with communitarian thinking. On the one hand, there are conservative Eurosceptics of the British variety who think in terms of narrow national interests and conceive the nation in quasi-ethnic terms, resulting in a particularly hard-line position on immigration for example. On the other hand, there are civic nationalists. These tend to be more left wing and influenced by republican notions linking patriotism with democratic participation, as in the French tradition (Thibaud 1992; although see Miller 1995 for a British version, especially chap. 6). For different reasons, both groups will be reluctant to see a dilution of the inter-governmental character of the EU. However, while the first would dispute any shift in a federalist direction, the second would merely argue that until such time as a global identity and public culture develop, moral weight has to be given to the self-determination of different peoples. Attempts to force the pace will be seen as unjustified, but certain moves of a cosmopolitan kind are possible – even if the total transcendence of the nation state remains highly unlikely.

iii) Two Views of Rights and Democracy

Cosmopolitans and communitarians hold two different views of the nature of rights and democracy and the way they relate to each other. Cosmopolitans see rights as essentially self-standing. Their justification is independent of their recognition by any given society or culture and does not rely on democratic endorsement for its validity. Their scope and application are uniform and universal with individuals as their subjects. Citizenship and sovereignty are regarded as largely antithetical to rights, since they link them to membership of a state rather than regarding them as attributes of human beings as such. Even if democracy to some extent embodies the notion of equal rights, its procedures cannot always be counted on to uphold them. At best, it operates as a mechanism of imperfect procedural justice. Within the governmental and constitutional system, therefore, democracy has essentially instrumental uses as a means of allowing individuals to voice and protect their vital interests by controlling the decisions, usually indirectly via influence over their makers, which affect their lives. To the extent that those decisions have passed beyond, or in certain cases below, the nation state, then so must democratic institutions. What defines the demos is largely functional, making the parcelling out of popular sovereignty theoretically unproblematic even though there are numerous practical difficulties. In cases where democracy fails to offer the best protection for rights, or even endangers them, non-democratic mechanisms, such as judicial review or regulative agencies, are to be preferred (Pogge 1994; Ferrajoli 1996).

Communitarians regard rights as socially grounded and as oriented towards securing the participation of individuals within certain worthwhile collective practices. Democracy plays an important role in legitimising and justifying a particular understanding and interpretation of rights within a given society. Consequently, its instrumental qualities are valued far less than its intrinsic ones. Communitarians conceive democratic decision-making more in terms of deliberation on the common good than as a mechanism for the aggregation of individual interests. Moreover, they contend that compromise and the avoidance of a purely self-regarding stance are far more likely among a people who identify reasonably strongly with each other. It is no accident in this respect that the two paradigmatic examples of constitution making, namely France and the United States in the eighteenth century, were simultaneously instances of nation-building. For democracy implies the existence of a people who feel bound together. It is this sense of a shared fate and mutual responsibility that leads minorities to accept majority decisions, for example, and, perhaps more importantly, motivates majorities to take into account the opinions and concerns of minorities rather than excluding them altogether (Miller 1995, 96–9).

Judicial review tends to play a more subordinate role in this version of democracy to that accorded it in less communitarian accounts.[8] Majority tyranny, which offers a prime motive behind this legal protection of rights, is deemed less likely, and such judicial interference with the popular will be regarded as in any case illegitimate since the deliberations of the people provide both the rationale and the source of rights. Within this conception, democracy is itself a forum of principle that allows conflicting accounts and exercises of rights to be weighed and balanced against each other in ways that show equal concern and respect for the individual autonomy of others. There is no need, as some have argued, for judges to take on this role.

Indeed, there are numerous disadvantages associated with their doing so. Politics mobilises public support and commitment for taking on the burdens that are often entailed by granting particular rights. Moreover, the broader interests and values of diverse groups can be heard, and the defence of a particular right placed in the context of the whole range of policies being undertaken by the government and the wider needs and wishes of citizens. Judicial decisions tend to foreclose democratic involvement in policy making and thereby impair the identification of citizens with the rights they imply. Focus on the litigated case can also lead judges to ignore the knock-on effects of legal intervention for other equally important programmes, overlooking the way spending in one area might withdraw resources from others. In these ways, reliance on the courts may have the grave drawback of impairing democratic channels of communication, and risks producing the very unprincipled politics that supporters of judicial review believe render it necessary. In any case, it is doubtful that the judiciary is capable of withstanding the influence of the wider community, no matter how independent it may seek to be. Like other parts of the political system, it needs a degree of popular legitimacy to be authoritative. The danger is that only highly selective pressure groups will be able to exercise such influence, so that the courts will become a prey to those very 'sinister' interests they are supposed to overcome.[9]

When rights and obligations are nested within particular political communities, their cosmopolitan reach will clearly be affected. To the extent that our understanding of basic rights is coloured by the culture of our community, there are likely to be conflicts between the priorities and publicly recognised needs of different societies. State support for certain religions or languages may be important in some communities and regarded as illegitimate in others, for example. Even when the same rights are acknowledged, variations in local context may lead them to being interpreted and balanced in contrasting and not always compatible ways. In addition, there will be a feeling that 'charity begins at home' that will set limits on how much people will commit themselves to helping outsiders when that clashes with programmes, also motivated by rights considerations, of a domestic character. Thus, communitarians regard it as legitimate that a more generous national social security system, say, might be established at the cost of less spending on foreign aid overseas (Miller 1995, chap. 3 and 100–3).

Support for national sovereignty need not entail a view of international relations as an anarchic and amoral Hobbesean state of nature. Claims to self-determination for one group imply recognition of similar rights by others – including non-aggression and limited aid. To the extent that global interdependence does link states within institutional networks, they will have the sorts of obligations cosmopolitans advocate. Nonetheless, the absence of agreed metrics as to the value of resources or the relative worth of various rights and liberties will make arguments for a global redistribution of goods and services hard to cash out in practice – especially as such schemes can conflict with as well as support the autonomy of national communities. Still, it is reasonable to suppose that globalisation will produce forms of interstate cooperation in those areas such as defence, the environment and the economy where the capacity of states to act in autonomous ways has been seriously impaired. However, in most cases these cooperative schemes will be regarded as mechanisms for preserving rather than undermining national interests and self-determination, with transfers of decision-making power being largely conditional on the extent to which involvement in the relevant international body makes that possible (Miller 1995, 104–8).

iv) A Cosmopolitan Communitarianism?

In what follows, we shall argue that these two models shed light on a number of the debates and difficulties currently besetting the European Union. We have already identified four possible approaches to Europe – two stemming from the cosmopolitan and communitarian camps, respectively. We wish to propose a fifth approach that combines one from each of the schools of thought: namely the cosmopolitan globalist and the civic nationalist. It would be mistaken to regard the cosmopolitan and the communitarian arguments as totally at odds with each other, with the latter anti-liberal, anti-rights and anti-individualist, as certain commentators have claimed (e.g. Holmes 1993). Rather, they offer contrasting but to some degree compatible accounts of how we should think about individuality, rights and their relationship to the societies that embody them. Our claim will be that cosmopolitan morality only makes sense to the extent that it is embedded within a communitarian framework: a position we dub cosmopolitan communitarianism.

   Michael Walzer has recently explored the difference between the two schools in terms of a distinction between 'thick' and 'thin' moralities (Walzer 1994b, especially chap. 1). In his terms, universal human rights represent a 'thin', 'minimal' morality that all societies ought to uphold. But they do so in numerous 'thick', 'maximal' ways. Moreover, the individual rights bearers are similarly contextually defined. That is not to deny value-individualism, as is sometimes implied, but it is to reject those versions of methodological individualism that ignore the social dimension of personal identity and the development of autonomy (see Tamir 1993, chap. 1 for criticism of such views). According to this thicker, more communitarian view of rights and the individual, a pure cosmopolitanism offers an inadequate account of moral agency. For the cosmopolitan universalist agents are supposed to act on the basis of rational considerations of pure principle that abstract from their sense of identity as persons holding certain convictions and possessing particular attachments. By contrast, the cosmopolitan communitarian believes that both the principles and the moral motivations and character of those who follow them need to be fleshed out with natural sentiments and 'thick' concepts such as courage, honesty, gratitude and benevolence that arise out of specific ways of life. A pure cosmopolitanism cannot generate the full range of obligations its advocates generally wish to ascribe to it. For the proper acknowledgement of 'thin' basic rights rests on their being specified and overlaid by a 'thicker' web of special obligations. Welfare states, for example, have typically arisen in societies where there are strong feelings of social solidarity. These reinforce the formal obligations that arise from being members of an institutionalised scheme of political cooperation as citizens of the same state. Essentially, they create a sense of identification among a given group of people between whom it comes to be felt both legitimate and plausible that collectively binding decisions about the distribution of burdens and benefits should take place. That sense of commonness does not determine what its precise implications or content should be, but it does provide the basis on which such determination takes place. It defines the demos, as it were, for whom a form of democratic rule appears appropriate and plausible.

Nationalism has traditionally provided the ideological glue necessary to define a relatively circumscribed group of people and unify them around a set of shared institutions and practices that were sovereign over a well-defined territory. Political loyalty, accountability and legitimacy were tied in this way to state power and authority. Indeed, nationality was typically the creation of states and political elites seeking to consolidate their hold over their populations. Cosmopolitans deny the necessity and desirability of such attachments. They may, as Thomas Pogge (1994) does, grant them a certain empirical weight but not any moral significance. A mixture of voluntarist and utilitarian considerations of a broadly functional kind provides the only normatively relevant considerations so far as people's obligations to any particular polity are concerned (e.g. Simmons 1979). By contrast, our sketch of the communitarian argument has tried to suggest that largely unchosen commonalties of history, belief, geography and civic culture *do* have an ethical relevance. They supply the feelings of reciprocity, trust and commitment needed to supplement the ties of mere mutual advantage that result from individuals acting on the basis of rational self-interest alone. Such moral qualities have an important influence on the character of political life, since they increase people's willingness to engage in cooperative behaviour by raising their expectations and confidence in others. As David Miller (1995, chap. 2) has recently argued, far from encouraging self-interested and partial behaviour, the lessening of the tension between personal and collective goals within a group is likely to make an impartial stance more acceptable.

On this account, the normative aspect of the cosmopolitan argument will only go beyond a 'thin' humanitarian concern for others to the extent we live in a relatively 'thick' cosmopolitan civil society with a corresponding public culture. So far as the EU is concerned, this result might be obtained in one of two ways. Either Europe itself will coalesce into a civic nation, or it must operate as a Union of nations involving a degree of variable geometry combined with a fair amount of consensus on central issues and even certain elements of a common identity. We shall defend the second option below. It represents an example of the cosmopolitan communitarian position outlined earlier, whereby nations demonstrate civic attitudes not only internally but also to a greater or lesser extent externally, with basic 'thin' cosmopolitan sentiments thickening in various ways depending on the nature and degree of their interaction and involvement with other nations and even international allegiances possibly developing in some instances. The civic nation variant of the communitarian argument is extended in this way to accommodate aspects of both the globalisation thesis and a universal cosmopolitan morality, while denying the normative or empirical possibility of a European, let alone a global, civic nation. This position involves a rejection not only of an unqualified cosmopolitan globalism and universalism but also of the centralised Federalist version of the cosmopolitan argument and the Eurosceptical version of the communitarian case. The neo-functionalist Federalist line greatly overestimates the integrative potential of global forces and the capacity of people to transfer their allegiances. The Eurosceptical argument underestimates the new realities of global economic competition and has xenophobic overtones of a decidedly uncivic nature. In sum, they too are neither plausible nor desirable.

III. WHOSE EUROPE, WHICH COMMUNITY?

i) The Challenge of Maastricht

It is commonly claimed that the European Union currently finds itself at the crossroads. On the one hand, it operates as an intergovernmental organisation and its mode of governance is likened to a form of consociational confederalism. All four of Lijphart's consociational principles of grand coalition, segmental autonomy, proportionality and minority veto have typified deliberations in the Council of Ministers and negotiations surrounding the various treaties, for example. Moreover, these consociational mechanisms have had the aim and effect of rendering the integrative process consistent with the protection and, to some degree, the enhancement of national identities and interests (Chryssochoou 1994). These characteristics are basically compatible with a communitarian perspective. On the other hand, the EU embodies an extraordinary number of apparently supranational features – most particularly the European Court of Justice, and, to a much lesser extent, the European Parliament. The claim stemming from these bodies is that a new European constitutional order has gradually come into being possessing Supremacy over national law and Direct Effect upon individuals and agencies within the national jurisdictions of member states. Increasingly, the Court has justified its claims to judicial competence-competence as the authoritative interpreter of a 'higher' European law by reference to the protection of basic human rights. This development has been accompanied by calls for the European Parliament to have a greater role in the legislative process and the view that intergovernmentalism fails adequately to represent the interests of individual citizens – the so-called democratic deficit thesis (Mancini 1989). These arguments draw on cosmopolitan notions to underpin them.

Up until the Maastricht Treaty the tensions between these two dimensions of European integration rarely manifested themselves in practice. The jurisdictional and legislative expansion of the Court of Justice was largely controlled, and to a high degree abetted, by the member states – not least through a generous interpretation of Article 235 EC to allow a significant extension of the scope and powers of the Community. The shift to majority voting, combined with certain renewed worries on the part of national courts as to the integrity of their own position as guardians of their distinctive constitutional orders, has changed this situation and made governments far more sensitive to the Court's jurisdictional boundaries (Weiler 1994). These tensions are manifested in the Maastricht Treaty itself (Wincott 1994). Thus, while the Common Provisions in Title I, for example, emphasise the goal of an 'ever closer union of the peoples of Europe' (Article A), the Final Provisions in Title VII largely undercut them, not least by removing Title I from the jurisdiction of the Court (Article L). Another instance of this Janus-faced character of the TEU is the way subsidiarity is defined in both a devolutionary manner, to suggest that decisions should be taken 'as closely as possible' to the citizens (Article A and B), and in a potentially neo-federalist direction as a means for allocating different areas of competence that allows the Community to act even outside its 'exclusive' sphere when 'by reason of the scale or effects of the proposed action' it can achieve certain objectives more effectively than the member states (Article 3B EC). Most significant of all are the various Protocols attached to the Treaty incorporating various derogations from common policies, such as the British opt-out from the Social Charter and the possibility of opting out from EMU, the provisions for Danes to have privileged access to second homes in rural Denmark, and the protection of Irish anti-abortion law. These appear to threaten the central legal tenet of the Union, the acquis communautaire, and to open up the possibility of an à la carte Europe involving considerable variable geometry. Not surprisingly legal analysts have tended to be hostile to the Treaty, seeing it as reducing the capacity of the Court to produce a coherent legal order and denigrating the resulting constitutional structure as a patchwork of 'bits and pieces'. As one prominent legal commentator has put it, the Union displays 'more of a *bricoleur's* amateurism than a master bricklayer's strive for perfection and attention to detail'. The result, she continues, has jeopardised 'the cohesiveness and the unity and the concomitant power of a legal system painstakingly constructed over the course of some 30 odd years', threatening in the process 'the whole future and credibility of the Communities as a cohesive legal unit which confers rights on individuals and which enters into their national legal systems as an integral part of those systems' (Curtin 1993, 23/4, 67).

Two issues bring out the conflicts between cosmopolitan and communitarian concerns in the post-Maastricht climate particularly well – namely, the notion of European citizenship and the debate over the jurisdictional limits of the Union highlighted by the Maastricht decision of the German Constitutional Court. Both raise matters related to the contrast between the two models of rights and democracy discussed earlier, and indicate the problems of advocating democratic procedures in the absence of a demos and of assigning rights protection to judicial review. We shall examine each in turn, suggesting in the conclusion that resolving the tensions they reveal may be a matter of yet more *bricolage* rather than architectural design.

ii) European Citizens in Search of a Nation

The establishment of Union Citizenship in Articles 8 to 8e of the amended EC Treaty has been taken by certain commentators as representing a first, albeit highly inadequate, step towards the creation of a European demos. The chief criticisms from this cosmopolitan perspective have related to its limited nature and the huge anomalies that arise from its being tied to nationality as that is variously defined by the different member states – especially with respect to immigrants resident within the EU (Lyons 1996). Conspicuously little thought, however, has been given to the more communitarian-minded issue of how many people actually desire this status (although see Weiler 1996). In fact, most of the empirical evidence, such as the findings of the Eurobarometer poll, indicates a very low level of identification with Europe. Even though a majority of Europeans are broadly favourable to integration, it is largely on the grounds that it is a 'good thing' for their own country (an opinion expressed by 69 per cent of those polled in 1990). Only 14 per cent in a 1989 poll said they 'frequently' felt a 'citizen of Europe', while 48 per cent responded that they 'never' did so. Indeed, the only group that appears to feel a higher level of European compared to national consciousness are those working in the various

European institutions, who have a vested interest in fostering the European ideal (Wilterdink 1990, 77–85, 1993, 119, 128/9).

These findings reinforce some of the earlier criticisms of the globalisation thesis and suggest problems with the Federalist version of the cosmopolitan argument, which seems to depend on the development of a strong European civic nation. In spite of a considerable degree of economic integration and a significant number of common political institutions, there has been comparatively little convergence in civic attitudes and allegiances. Although the intensification of trade, transport, and communication links, greater labour mobility, and an equalisation of social conditions were important elements in the development of national identities in nineteenth-century Western Europe (Gellner 1983), they were never sufficient in themselves. In the case of the European Union, the crucial role played by centralised political institutions in unifying the economy is also missing, since the common market has been more the product of deregulation than regulation. Moreover, the growth of economic and social interdependence is not by any means centred solely on Europe, even if trade among the member states has increased more than commerce between them and the rest of the world. The European Union is also a remarkably open-ended project in terms of geographical scope, and potentially might include the most varied cultural and political traditions. Earlier nation state building projects usually had reasonably well-defined territorial ambitions that were linked to certain preexisting historical, linguistic and cultural boundaries. Although these sentiments were generally only shared by a dominant social group and had to be diffused among the rest of the population, there nevertheless was a sense of who was being united and where. No core cultural or geographical reference point seems to exist for the EU, however, beyond a vague commitment to certain unspecified 'principles of liberty, democracy and respect for human rights and fundamental freedoms and of the rule of law' (Preamble, TEU). Even the growing linguistic dominance of English, ironic given the general indifference of the British to the continent and the importance of French among the Eurocracy in Brussels, arises from its global significance rather than from its being a European language.

Postnationalist cosmopolitans, of course, will regard the absence of a sense of European consciousness as highly desirable. A constitutional patriotism centred upon universal liberal democratic values ought to be enough to unite all peoples around common political institutions, and avoids the exclusionary connotations of a form of citizenship based on a territorially and culturally specific national identity (Habermas 1992). Communitarians, however, contend that a high degree of identification forms a precondition for democracy. Without a sense of Europeaness, increasing the powers of the European Parliament risks making the democratic deficit more profound rather than less. Unless voters feel an institution is socially as well as formally legitimate, they will be disinclined either to take part in its decisions or to accept them (Weiler 1993). As rational choice theorists have been forced to concede, self-interest alone cannot explain participation in elections since the rational voter will always stay at home. Voting is a practice involving a number of specific obligations that go with the role of citizen. I need a civic identity, in other words, to be inclined to vote, and that only comes through membership of a specific polis with appropriate traditions. Likewise, unless there is a single right answer, I will only accept a decision as valid if I identify in some respect with those who make it. Given the plurality of ultimate values and the complex ways in which they interact, it is unlikely that clear-cut correct solutions can be discovered to many if any of the dilemmas that standardly confront governments over such matters as welfare, defence, health and education and the resources to be allocated to each of them. Rather, collectively binding solutions have to be constructed within specific contexts (Bellamy 1995). That entails involving those likely to be benefited or burdened by the outcome, and crucially getting those in the minority to accept the majority view. Once again, a feeling of belonging to a given community plays a vital part in legitimising the democratic process among those involved. It binds together a people and generates reciprocal ties that foster a disposition to consider the general welfare and to compromise where necessary.

Admission to citizenship for these reasons usually involves more than signing up to a set of abstract set of principles. Naturalised citizens, in particular, normally have to be inducted into a certain form of social and political life and declare a willingness to undertake certain duties. Education and the normal processes of socialisation provide a less formalised procedure for nationals. No such induction process exists at the European level, nor is it clear what it would entail. In this regard, it is noteworthy that in a 1989 Eurobarometer poll 59 per cent preferred the idea that the European Parliament should be organised around national criteria rather than the current political ones, even though as yet no European-wide parties, as opposed to groupings of national parties, exist. As Weiler (1996, 111) has pertinently remarked, at present there is as much reason for us to expect the Danes, say, to accept the legitimate authority of a German Bundestag to which they were given voting rights as that of the European Parliament.

iii) *Deutschland Über Alles? Das Maastricht-Urteil*

Similar points emerge from the second issue to be considered, that of the respective judicial competences of the ECJ and national constitutional courts.[10] Recent attention on this question has focused on the 1993 judgement of the German Constitutional Court in response to the challenge by Mr Manfred Brunner and others to the validity of Germany's accession to the

Maastricht Treaty. Brunner had argued that Maastricht violated Article 79 section 3 of the Basic Law, which forbids amendments affecting the role of the Lander in legislation and, via reference to Articles 1 and 20, that curtail either basic rights or the 'democratic and social' character of the republic and the sovereign authority of the German people as exercised 'through elections and voting and by specific organs of the legislature, the executive power, and the judiciary'. This sort of challenge had already been partly anticipated by the insertion in 1992 of a new Article 23 on participation in the development of the European Union. However, this Article had been careful to assert how the EU was governed by the same principles as those guaranteed by the Basic Law and had insisted that the Bundestag and, where appropriate, the Bundesrat had to be fully involved in the legislative evolution of the EU. In this way, it was hoped not to fall foul of Article 79. Brunner's point was that the making of Community law through majority voting within the Council of Ministers, combined with the European Court's assertions of Direct Effect and the Supremacy of Community over national law, effectively undercut the right of Germans to control their own affairs. The Lander were particularly affected in this respect, since in spite of all the fine talk about subsidiarity there is no real involvement of the regions in Community decision-making. Although the Constitutional Court rejected this particular challenge, it chose both to reassert the continuing sovereignty of the German people and to deny that either the European Court of Justice or any other European organ could claim competence over its own competence. In other words, it remained for the German Court alone to decide whether or not a European measure or development infringed the German constitutional order.

German popular sovereignty, it asserted, remained intact so long as national parliaments not only limited the extension of European functions but states also retained 'sufficiently important spheres of activity of their own in which the peoples of each can develop and articulate in a process of political will formation which it legitimates and controls, in order to give legal expression to what – relatively homogeneously – binds the people spiritually, socially, and politically together' (German Federal Court 1993, C I 2 b(2)). Their reasoning on this point was essentially communitarian – to be more than 'merely a formal principle of accountability', democracy had to be between a people who could influence each other's opinions and have an impact on those who governed them (German Federal Court 1993, C I 2 b(1)). This condition, they noted, is not met by the European Union, which possesses neither a demos nor mechanisms for effective democratic control over its decision-makers by any of its constitutive peoples, either severally or collectively. Consequently, the sovereignty of the German people required that 'functions and powers of substantial importance must remain for the German Bundestag' (German Federal Court 1993, C I 2 b(2)). To ensure that this situation persisted, the

Court had to retain its prerogative to review legal instruments emanating from European institutions 'to see whether they remain within the limits of the sovereign rights conferred on them or whether they transgress those limits'. The 'Law of Accession' was provisional, therefore, on subsequent European developments continuing to be compatible with the German constitutional order as interpreted by the Court (German Federal Court 1993, C I 3).

A cosmopolitan perspective that sees national and popular sovereignty as matters of instrumental rather than intrinsic importance will tend to regard the German Court's arguments for defending a specifically German form of democracy as somewhat beside the point. The key question is whether liberal democratic values are defended, not their national location or colour. This issue might have been supposed to be resolved in the late 1960s and early 1970s, when the German and Italian constitutional courts obliged the ECJ to declare that the protection of fundamental rights formed 'an integral part of the general principles of law' it had a duty to uphold.[11] This declaration had been motivated by the European Court's desire to uphold the Supremacy of European law against scrutiny by national courts for its protection of human rights – a matter they were often pledged to uphold but the ECJ apparently was not. Since no European Bill of Rights has been formally adopted by the Community to which the ECJ might refer, the Court said it would be guided by the rights protected in the constitutions of member states and international conventions – most particularly the European Convention on Human Rights.[12] Some commentators regarded this development as 'the most striking contribution the Court made to the development of a constitution for Europe' (Mancini 1989, 611). They have argued that 'there is hardly anything that has greater potential to foster integration than a common bill of rights, as the constitutional history of the United States has proved' (Cappelletti 1989, 395). They contend that it ought to be possible to draw from the various national constitutions and international conventions a 'common bill of rights' for the Community that 'by encapsulating the nature of the legal order that it underpins ... would create an integrationist *culture* of rights'. Indeed, Article F (2) of the TEU, which refers to the European Convention and common constitutional traditions as offering 'general principles of Community law', might be regarded as a step in this direction, although characteristically it sits alongside F (1) with its insistence that 'The Union shall respect the national identities of its Member States, whose systems of government are founded on principles of democracy'.

The use of the language of rights by the ECJ since 1970, however, provides ample evidence of the difficulties with this thesis, and goes some way to explaining the German Court's reassertion of its prerogatives. The key problem relates to the distinction between cosmopolitan and communitarian views of rights and democracy that we made earlier: namely, that even if all the member states endorse broadly the same set of rights and democratic principles, they have legitimately different views about their scope and their relative weighting with regard to both each other and other important values and interests that reflect valid cultural differences. The right to freedom of expression is accepted by all member states, for example, but in certain countries it is interpreted as warranting the special protection of linguistic minorities or a national language on the grounds that a people's culture provides the necessary context within which they express themselves as possessors of a specific identity. However, these protections can place restrictions on the free movement of goods, services, capital and labour which the Community is pledged to uphold. This conflict has been at the heart of a whole series of key cases: notably, Cinéthèque, Groener, Bond and ERT. The reach of Community law has come to appear increasingly open-ended so that there has been a disturbing tendency for the ECJ both to extend the range of its jurisdiction and to interpret rights in a largely market manner that shows scant respect for national constitutional values (De Witte 1991; Coppel and O'Neill 1992).

iv) A Right to Choose? *Grogan*

This process came to head in *Grogan*. In this case, the Society for the Protection of the Unborn Child brought an injunction against various office holders of student unions in the Republic of Ireland to prevent them disseminating information about British abortion clinics on the grounds that it infringed Article 40 (3) (iii) of the Irish Constitution. The matter was referred to the ECJ under Article 177.[13] Notwithstanding the Irish constitution's proclamation of a 'right to life of the unborn', abortion was treated by the Court as simply 'a medical activity which is normally provided for remuneration [and] may be carried out as part of a professional activity'. Consequently, it constituted 'a service within the meaning of Article 60 of the Treaty', rendering the case justiciable under Community law. The only reason the injunction did not contravene Article 59, prohibiting any restriction by member states on the freedom to supply services throughout the Community, was because the connection between the student unions and the British clinics was 'too tenuous'.[14] Had a formal relationship existed between the two, the ECJ might have decided very differently – a fact that led to a Protocol being added to the TEU expressly protecting the Irish clause. Whatever one's position on abortion, it is clear that the ECJ failed to consider the moral concerns underlying the Irish view (Coppell and O'Neill 1992, 685–9; although for a contrary opinion see Prosser 1996, 73–4). In many respects, however, the Court had no alternative but to decide as it did. All it can legitimately refer to are the economic freedoms that provide the EU with its main raison d'être. Drawing on certain putative common European democratic principles would provide no help here, since the measure is unique to Ireland. Indeed, almost all the hard

cases referred to above involve some national peculiarity. Moreover, they are
morally grey areas in which the weighing up of the competing considerations
involved proves hard in terms of pure principle alone, since at some point
these become indeterminate. Popular legitimacy comes in here, either directly
(as in a referendum such as the Irish held on abortion) or indirectly via political representatives or, even more loosely, yet just as effectively and important, through the general prestige a national court has within the political
system. Yet it is precisely this communitarian source of political legitimacy
that the Court lacks and is unlikely to be able to obtain.

Set against this background, we submit that the German Maastricht decision is unsurprising and defensible. Not everyone thinks so. Weiler (1996,
530–2), for example, has suggested that it represents a declaration of Cold
War – a standoff between the ECJ and national courts that, if either were to
call the other's bluff, risks undermining the whole legal integrity of the Union.
For the decision flies in the face of the ECJ's insistence that it alone has the
authority to decide whether a community measure is ultra vires (Article 173
EC), and that within its sphere 'the validity of a Community measure or its
effect within a Member State cannot be affected by allegations that it runs
counter to either fundamental rights as formulated by the Constitution of that
state or the principles of a national constitutional structure',[15] a point emphati-
cally reaffirmed by *Grogan*. However, the absolute supremacy of Community
law over domestic constitutional provisions has never been accepted by all
national supreme courts. In general, they have acknowledged the authority of Community law for reasons internal to the national legal order rather
than, as the ECJ would have it, because of its intrinsic Supremacy, and have
distinguished between alterations to basic principles of the national constitution and the transfer of certain powers. This picture suggests a pluralistic and
interactive, as opposed to a monistic and hierarchical, picture of legal systems
might be the most appropriate frame of analysis for understanding the relationship of EC to national law (MacCormick 1995, 1996, 143–50). It remains
to examine the plausibility of this account.

CONCLUSION: A MIDDLE WAY?

i) Mad Cows and Englishmen

What might be called hard-line cosmopolitans and communitarians find the
European Union something of a standing contradiction. The former argue that
the EU requires a framework of legally binding legitimising constitutional
principles and a system of supranational federal European political institutions that, within clearly demarcated spheres, are superior to either national

or regional bodies. The latter argue that there can be no ceding of national sovereignty and that the EU has already gone too far. The British BSE affair offers a characteristic confrontation between these two positions. Federalist-minded Europhiles saw the EU's action as a legitimate protection of individual interests in the context of a transnational market. It confirmed their image of the EU as a rational response to global economic and social forces that go beyond what national states can control, and that finds its justification in a growing liberal democratic consensus centred on the protection of human rights rather than state sovereignty. Sceptical Europhobes, in contrast, saw the EU's position as motivated by little more than the interests of rival producers in other member states. For them, the event fuelled their conception of the Union as a centralised and unaccountable Leviathan, that served the cultural and economic imperialism of the Euro-elite and undermined the national self-determination of particular peoples.

Both perspectives possess an element of truth, as well as a goodly dose of hyperbole and misunderstanding. If few people are likely to man the barricades to defend some supposed British birthright to eat diseased cow brains, cattle farmers had legitimate interests at stake that needed to be addressed. If the health risks were real and could not be ignored, it would be naive to portray the EU as a totally benevolent institution representing nothing but the putatively higher interests of the states that compose it. Not just the British but all governments were faced with the difficult task of balancing the demands of producers and consumers within their respective national constituencies against both genuine concerns about health and the need to cooperate with their economic and political partners. There is no obviously right way of reconciling all the various elements in play. Moreover, the division of responsibility in the evaluation of risk between individuals, governments and expert regulatory bodies is a notoriously grey area for those of a liberal temper. Here we come to what is perhaps the central problem when thinking about democracy and the EU – namely, the difficulty of deciding at what level such decisions should be taken and by whom. This fact suggests an alternative account of the EU as a somewhat messy composite arrangement that combines an uneasy mixture of national, intergovernmental and supranational elements that combine in ad hoc ways depending on the matter in play. While Eurofederalists and Eurosceptics have a tendency to regard this middle way as inherently unstable and unsatisfactory, we want to argue that it might offer the most illuminating picture of the EU's largely sui generis nature.

ii) Bricolage versus Architecture

On this middle view, which draws on moderate versions of the cosmopolitan and communitarian arguments, it proves perfectly possible to acknowledge both the validity of certain general norms and obligations and the need for supranational collective action in those areas where global processes have rendered it prudent to do so, without insisting that such acknowledgement need be of the same kind for all parties or require the adoption of a totally unified political system. Rather, it emerges from within the distinctive perspectives of the various participants and the dialogue that ensues between them.

It may be that increasingly common points of view, and hence a willingness to pool sovereignty, will eventually emerge. In an earlier article, we suggested that at such a time a 'democratic baptism' would still be necessary to provide the new institutions or constitutional framework with a thicker, more communitarian legitimacy than can be provided by principles of justice alone (Bellamy and Castiglione 1996b; see too Weale 1995, which inspired this suggestion, and Walker 1996, especially 280–3, who develops it). A somewhat similar and more detailed proposal is made by Thomas Pogge in his contribution to this volume, although we note that his more cosmopolitan orientation takes the existence of a demos somewhat for granted and he adopts a more instrumental view of the democratic process to ours. Nonetheless, we agree on the ultimate necessity of popular involvement in the constitutional process. The forms that it has so far taken have involved the systematic breaking of one of the principles of the separation of power, which assumes a distinction between the constituent power and the constituted powers. National governments are at present arrogating to themselves the powers to constitute a Union in which (it would seem) they themselves will have a fundamental role as institutional players. However, a word of caution is in order. Mass consultation on major constitutional issues can only take place in rather exceptional circumstances; otherwise the principles at stake risk being clouded by the relatively minor and transient concerns of 'normal' politics (Ackerman 1991), as the French Maastricht referendum illustrated. Such 'constitutional moments' are rare, and usually only appear when some disaster like a war has created a sufficient bond of solidarity among people to lead them to forget old differences and contemplate new allegiances. Such a moment gave rise to the European ideal in the first place, of course, but peace and prosperity have increasingly been taken for granted by subsequent generations, and their enthusiasm for the project has waned accordingly. Moreover, the integration process is in such a fluid state that there is a danger that any explicit attempt to legitimise the Union would ultimately backfire through being premature. New measures that people could claim not to have agreed to would be necessary – a complaint frequently made by British Eurosceptics, for example, to dispute the continued sway of the 1975 referendum on joining the then EEC.

Much more likely is a continuation of the current piecemeal process whereby the Union develops through a mixture of ad hoc agreements, periodic major intergovernmental reviews, and certain internal dynamics of the Community itself. In keeping with the German Maastricht decision, democratic legitimacy within this setup comes largely from national parliaments and courts. The chief objection, fuelled by Maastricht, is that this mechanism leads to a fragmented à la carte Union of opt-outs and variable tracks. At some level, it will undoubtedly be necessary for member states to agree what is and what is not optional. However, this cannot be decided a priori – as we have seen, conventional notions of what is or is not required for a political organisation to work are constantly challenged by the very existence of the EU. Rather, they have to be progressively negotiated. The normative foundations of this conception of the EU can perhaps be best characterised as a hybrid cosmopolitan communitarianism, in which different communities converge on a range of compatible perspectives on common goals and endeavours, rather than a communitarian cosmopolitanism, which assumes a universal consensus on principles and procedures. It suggests a civic Europe made up of different nations, rather than a homogeneous European civic nation. This approach may be more bricolage than architecture, but it has the great advantage of suggesting that the status quo may not be as unjustifiable and unstable as many have wished us to believe.

NOTES

1. Research for this chapter was supported by an ESRC award for a project 'Languages and Principles for a Constitution of Europe' (R000221170). We are grateful for the comments on earlier versions of audiences in Oslo, Bologna and Edinburgh and for the written observations of Andreas Føllesdal, Barry Jones and Barry Holden. We are also indebted to stimulating discussions of these themes with co-participants in the ESRC-sponsored research seminar series on Legal Theory and the European Union.

2. These opening reflections are inspired by Schmitter (1996), especially 219.

3. See Walker (1996) for a review of the growing impact of such issues in the recent legal and, to a lesser extent, political science literature on the EU.

4. For an overview of the debate, see Mullhall and Swift (1996). For the application of these two models to IR theory, see Brown (1992). We have offered a preliminary sketch of their relevance to European constitutional debates in Bellamy and Castiglione (1996b).

5. This paragraph essentially summarises the argument of Pogge (1994).

6. The exposition of this thesis in the next three paragraphs derives from Held (1995, chaps. 5 and 6).

7. For the contrast between the legal and political science paradigms, see Weiler, Haltern and Mayer (1995, 24–33) and Wincott (1995).

8. The role of judicial review in relation to rights and democracy has been debated most fully with regard to the part played by the Supreme Court in the United

States. The case for this has been made most forcefully by Ronald Dworkin (1985), especially 70/1, and that against by Cass Sunstein (1993). See Bellamy and Castiglione (1998), and Bellamy (1997) for a fuller examination of this debate, on which this paragraph draws.

9. For evidence to this effect with regard to the American Supreme Court, see Mackeever (1995).

10. The analysis here draws on MacCormick (1995) and Gustavsson (1996).

11. In case 11/70, *Internationale Handelsgesellschaft*, [1970] ECR 1125, 1134. See too case 29/69, *Stauder v. Ulm*, [1969] ECR 419, at 425 where the Court first stated that fundamental rights were 'enshrined in the general principles of Community law and protected by the Court'.

12. In case 4/73, *Nold (II)*, [1974] ECR 491, 507.

13. *The Society for the Protection of Unborn Children (Ireland) Ltd v. Stephen Grogan and others*, Case 159/90, 4 October 1991, reported in [1991] 3 CMLR 689. This analysis follows Coppell and O'Neill (1992, 685–9).

14. Opinion of the Advocate General of 11 June 1991, paras. 18, 21, 24.

15. Case 11/70, *Internationale Handelsgesellschaft*, [1970] ECR 1125 at 1134, [1972] CMLR 255 at 283, cited in De Witte (1991, 88).

Chapter 2

Legitimising the Euro-'Polity' and Its 'Regime'

The 'Normative Turn' in European Studies[1]

Richard Bellamy and Dario Castiglione

By raising fundamental questions about the ultimate goals and methods of European integration, Maastricht forced Europhiles and Eurosceptics alike to confront the legitimacy of both the Union itself and – as became apparent with the crisis of the Santer Commission – the institutional mechanisms employed to govern it. The need to publicly legitimise the EU has prevented the main political actors adopting a purely pragmatic approach, in which the EU's development is simply the incremental result of ad hoc calculations of national advantage. To a lesser or greater degree, European politicians and peoples cannot avoid strategic-oriented action or normative argument concerning the purpose, underlying values, future shape and desirable structures of what Jacques Delors once called *un objet politique non identifié*. Academics, too, have begun to discover that the integration process depends not only on functional efficiency or its furtherance of national economic or defence interests but also on people's ideals and perceptions. Consequently, explanation and justification have proved less easily distinguishable than earlier positivistic and behaviouralist models assumed.

This chapter seeks to clarify certain implications of the resulting normative turn in European studies.[2] Jean Monnet thought the Community would operate as a 'public utility state' and this broadly economic and utilitarian focus has been shared by many analysts of Europe.[3] More recently, however, there have been attempts by both academics and politicians to supplement and even modify the EU's market orientation through reference to the ideals of liberal democracy and proposals for a written constitution, a Charter of Rights and the strengthening of the European Parliament (Pinder 1994, 284; Habermas 1999). However, once we take seriously the normative content of

43

people's demands and beliefs, treating them as judgements and not merely as preferences, then legitimacy cannot be either reduced to performance per se or conceived in purely ideal terms (Beetham and Lord 1998; Bellamy and Warleigh 1998). People disagree not only over what goods ought to be produced but also about which institutions should produce them, when, how and for whom. Concepts of rights and justice are also disputed, likewise leading to debates over which institutions have the authority to decide certain issues, in what ways, for which people and so on. Because the EU results from and stimulates a dispersal of sovereign power and multiplication of political identities, disputes within the Union over both the good and the right are highly complex. Our claim shall be that this complexity is reflected in the EU's character as a polycentric 'polity' possessing a multilevel governance 'regime'. Though the efficiency and equity of this system could undoubtedly be improved, departures from such admittedly complicated and messy structures towards either a purely interest-based liberal intergovernmentalism or an idealistic federalism will weaken rather than strengthen legitimacy. The EU's evolution as both a 'polity' and a 'regime' has been an ongoing process of multiple negotiations over the normative issues raised by integration (Wallace 1985, 1996; Elgström and Jönsson 2000). Legitimacy will be enhanced only by constitutional and democratic mechanisms that foster rather than restrict such dialogues.

We begin in section 1 with an analysis of legitimacy. We argue it possesses an internal and an external dimension, the one linked to the values of the political actors, not least the European peoples, the other to the principles we employ to evaluate a political system and assess its effects for outsiders as well as insiders. Both dimensions apply to two distinct aspects of any political setup – its justification as a 'polity', where collective decisions can be made about particular issues, and the acceptability of the prevailing 'regime', or form of governance, whereby those decisions get taken. We claim these four elements of legitimacy are related and interact with each other. The internal and external legitimacy of a 'polity' is shaped by and shapes the internal and external legitimacy of the 'regime' that governs it. By contrast to many accounts (see the overview of this approach in Beetham and Lord 1998, chap. 4), performance figures as an aspect of both 'polity' and 'regime' legitimacy rather than being treated as an independent factor.

The next two sections deepen this analysis by examining, respectively, the normative weaknesses of many accounts of the 'polity'-building process and of proposals for improving the EU's 'regime'. We shall contend that the EU (and increasingly the member states too) suffers from a fourfold legitimacy deficit that involves, on the one hand, defining and legitimising what the EU qua 'polity' is and is for and, on the other, devising a legitimate 'regime' that corresponds to the Union's structure and does not overstep the degree of allegiance people are prepared to give it. Yet, many theories of European integration exclude normative and 'regime' considerations from their accounts of the 'polity'-building process, while certain theoretical (but also empirical) analysts of EU institutions and policy-making propose normative 'regimes' that fail to address the sui generis characteristics of the Euro-'polity'. Moreover, in both cases the roles played by what we refer to as the internal dimensions of legitimacy are ignored. Section 2 explores the weaknesses of theories of the EU 'polity' that bracket the issues of its 'regime' and internal acceptance by European citizens. Section 3 reverses this perspective. It criticises attempts to devise 'regimes' for the EU that ignore the character of its 'polity' and the complex ways its citizens identify with both the Union and each other. We shall argue that the process of unification has reconfigured both sovereignty and identity within Europe, altering in the process the internal and external legitimacy of the 'polity' aspect of the member states and the EU. Internally, the interests of the member states and their peoples cannot be taken as givens, because ideals and allegiances are being partly shaped by the EU. Externally, major modifications are also being introduced to the governance structures within which they operate. Function, territory and civic identity have begun to pull apart, so that the nineteenth-century construct of the homogenous, sovereign nation state no longer provides an adequate model 'polity' for the member states, let alone the EU. As a result, the standard normative vocabulary of rights, citizenship and representation has to be rethought in ways suited to the multiple civic identities and levels of governance that characterise the EU. In sum, a novel type of 'polity' requires a new form of 'regime' to govern it.

1. THE DIMENSIONS OF LEGITIMACY

The growing appreciation of normative considerations in European Union studies follows from the discovery that the strategic and evaluative aspects of politics matter: political actors are not simply motivated by short-term calculations of interests, while the political arrangements within which they operate have to be more than a convenient modus vivendi (Jachtenfuchs, Diez, and Jung 1998). As we noted, both aspects were raised by the questioning of the EU's legitimacy following Maastricht and its difficult passage through national legislatures and referenda. For very different reasons, both federalist orientated Europhiles and nationalistic Eurosceptics have questioned the 'polity' and 'regime' aspects of the EU. For the one, the EU 'polity' is too narrowly defined and its 'regime' too complex and dominated by élite bargaining. They wish the EU to encompass ever more tasks, to strengthen a pan-European democracy by such measures as giving more power to a

European Parliament, and to put in place a constitutional structure committed to common values (e.g. Duff 1994). For the other, the EU has become too much like a 'polity', encompassing too many issues that are more appropriately dealt with domestically. To the extent that they seek a constitutionalisation of the EU 'regime', it is to limit its political powers and reassert those of the people within their member states (e.g. Barry 1994).

The legitimacy issue has become increasingly prominent as the implications of monetary union, enlargement and cooperation in defence have been thought through (De Búrca 1996). Legitimacy can be defined as 'the normatively conditioned and voluntary acceptance by the ruled of the government of their rulers'. It involves both an internal and an external dimension, both of which apply not only to the type of 'regime' but also to the 'polity' itself. The *internal* dimension reflects the ways people within any organisation, including a state, relate to each other and to the institutions governing their lives. Such internal legitimacy arises from a fit with socially accepted norms, customs and beliefs, and formalised processes of authorisation through relatively direct or, more usually, various indirect forms of consent. The *external* dimension reflects a supposedly objective as opposed to subjective point of view, such as might be adopted from the outside (though not necessarily so). It stems from the justification of these institutions' rationale and their congruence with certain formal and substantive norms, such as legality and human rights, respectively.

The legitimacy of a 'polity' concerns the *subjects* and *sphere* of politics. The first term refers to how citizens are defined, the second to the ways the policy areas and geographical boundaries where political power is exercised are demarcated. Internally, the *subjects* who make and have to obey collective decisions must recognise each other as equal citizens and acknowledge the designated decision-making body as rightfully holding sway over a given *sphere* of their lives, be that *sphere* territorially or functionally defined. Such recognition is both contingently conditioned by such factors as language, culture, historical accident and geography and more deliberately agreed to by various forms of tacit, express or hypothetical consent, from referenda and oaths of allegiance to military service or mere residence. Externally, a 'polity' must meet certain formal and substantive criteria, such as are found in international law, both to obtain the recognition of other states or those who are excluded from citizenship, and to achieve the minimal standards of economic viability and justice for those on its territory, regardless of citizenship, to be morally obliged to support it.

The legitimacy of a 'regime' concerns the *styles* and *scope* of politics. The *styles* of politics refer to the manner in which institutions work – the electoral system, the relationship of the judiciary to the legislature and so forth. Internally, such legitimacy involves a mixture of conformity with traditional practices and expectations, such as surrounds the attachment of many British people to the monarchy, and a more active willingness to participate in some degree in making the institutions work, even if that is only by voting in an election or paying taxes. Externally, the *styles* of politics must possess the rational-legal characteristics associated with the rule of law if they are not to be so chaotic as to be unworkable and offer protection against various kinds of oppression and injustice, and uphold those rights implied by democracy, though these are more contentious. Only then will citizens feel securer supporting rather than opposing their rulers. Finally, the *scope* of politics refers to how far power can be exercised within its given *sphere* – for example, whether there can be economic intervention or merely regulation. Internally, legitimising a given *scope* for politics will once again be a matter of political culture and deliberative debate. Externally, legitimacy involves some division of the public and the private. In this respect, a constitution often tends to offer a distinctive *internal* conception of what are assumed to be the *external* characteristics of any legitimate regime.

Table 2.1 offers a diagrammatic representation of the above schema of the dimensions of legitimacy.

Three important observations are necessary at this juncture. First, though analytically distinguishable, the resulting four aspects of legitimacy identified

Table 2.1 The Dimensions of Legitimacy

Legitimacy	*Polity* sphere *and* subjects	*Regime* scope *and* styles
Internal **a) socially accepted norms**	Political identification among 'subjects' and between them and a particular power centre as having authority within a given 'sphere' (be it territorial, functional or both)	Institutions recognise ideals, interests and identities of governed
Internal **b) authorisation by (usually indirect) consent**	As in plebiscites and referenda over such issues as secession	Collective decisions seen as authoritative because involve mutual recognition
External **a) formal – established rules**	De jure compatible with international law	Legality – a regular system of governance/not arbitrary
External **b) substantive – freedom, justice, efficiency/ benefits**	Viable, existence does not entail oppression of insiders or outsiders	Not oppressive, unjust or incompetent

in the matrix are all interrelated. None on its own is more basic than the others or sufficient to make a political system or organisation legitimate. Each has knock-on effects for the others, with the character of one having implications for the configuration of the rest. For example, recent studies have noted how high levels of support for certain external 'regime' criteria, such as the principles of democracy, can lead citizens to an internal dissatisfaction with the character of the actual 'regime'. Thus, in Britain the politically dissatisfied are more likely to favour constitutional changes such as reform of the House of Lords (Dalton 1999, 75/76). However, these *external* criteria are in themselves too abstract to determine precisely what kind of 'regime' should be in place. There is a certain variation between different constitutional traditions on matters such as how 'freedom of speech' might be balanced against 'the right to privacy'. These differences reflect the *internal* legitimacy embodied in the political culture of the country concerned. Meanwhile, a 'regime' may satisfy standard external criteria of democratic acceptability but lack internal 'polity' legitimacy among the populace. Yet, if the *sphere* and *subjects* of politics appear inappropriate, then the *styles* and *scope* may ultimately come to be questioned both externally and internally without significant adjustment. For example, those Scottish Nationalists who dispute the legitimacy of the United Kingdom do not deny so much that the British political system meets standard democratic criteria as that it is not their democracy. However, this questioning of the UK's 'polity' legitimacy has nonetheless generated demands to adapt its 'regime' by incorporating devolution and possibly electoral reform. In Northern Ireland, Canada and Belgium, a similar dynamic has led to calls for minority group rights and various forms of power sharing at the executive and other levels of government. At the same time, the internal probing of the external dimensions of legitimacy is itself to some degree externally constrained. Proposals for secession, for instance, standardly must ensure not only that the resulting new 'polity' would be economically viable and secure but also the former parent state. Additionally, they should take account of the preferences of substantial minorities who favour staying with the parent state or a degree of autonomy of their own and so on. Such considerations may in their turn constrain the type of 'regime' the new 'polity' could legitimately adopt. Indeed, in many cases 'polity' legitimacy will depend on 'regime' legitimacy. Arguably, this has been the case in Northern Ireland, where greater regional autonomy has been made possible by a degree of executive power sharing.

Second, these four aspects of legitimacy are constantly evolving as people's interests and ideals change and social and economic life is transformed by technological and other innovations. For example, a greater awareness of environmental issues, itself linked to enhanced international interconnectedness in economic production and consumption, has resulted in changed perceptions of the shape of the 'polity' and of types of 'regime'. Thus, the *sphere* and *subjects* of politics in policy areas such as climate change have come to be seen as global. That has involved envisaging a new *scope* and *style* for politics, requiring novel forms of regulation by international agreements and agencies. Such changed perceptions have operated both at the élite level, albeit for the most part cautiously and conservatively, and more radically at the popular level, with the growth of transnational environmental movements.

Finally, performance as such does not appear within this scheme, except as a minimal external requirement of viability. Two reasons motivate this omission. One reason is that the impact of policy outputs generally, and economic performance in particular, may affect the allegiance of citizens to incumbent politicians but plays a minor role in shaping their confidence in a given 'polity' and 'regime' (McAllister 1999, 201–3). The legitimacy of these depends on more deep-rooted cultural values. Consequently, established democracies can retain support during quite extended periods of economic failure if both 'polity' and 'regime' have internal and external legitimacy, though citizens may severely criticise the government or even politicians in general. The other reason is that the four dimensions shape what counts as *legitimate* performance. Nobody values productivity per se. Rather, they want more of some things and less of others. Moreover, certain ways of producing a good may result in various bads, such as unemployment or pollution, while different goods can sometimes be in competition. So any increase in good A will have costs as well as benefits, including harmful or beneficial effects for goods B, C and so on. Thus, performance is an evaluative concept. Many of the norms shaping people's notion of *good* or *legitimate* performance stem from the cultural values underpinning both the 'polity' and 'regime'. These, either implicitly or explicitly – often via some constitutional norm – constrain what gets produced and how. Debate over performance usually remains within these norms. However, occasionally it challenges them, requiring that both 'polity' and 'regime' be rethought in certain respects. For example, during the Thatcher period in Britain, government policy gradually moved from suggesting that, within the existing rules, Conservatives could run the economy better than Labour, to seeking to change the social democratic character of the British state. The result was that of taking some *spheres* and *subjects* out of politics, while altering both its *scope* and *styles* through far-reaching privatisation programmes.

These observations have important implications for how we think about the legitimacy of the EU. Most politicians and citizens within the EU agree that the external dimensions of 'polity' and 'regime' legitimacy fall within a liberal democratic spectrum ranging from the social democratic to the moderate libertarian. However, this broad consensus does not in itself generate any particular allegiance to the EU.[4] For it is compatible with considerable disagreement over the internal dimensions of the EU. A liberal democrat could just as plausibly argue either that these values would be best defended at the

level of the nation state, with some minimal interstate cooperation for humanitarian purposes, or that they pointed to a cosmopolitan form of governance,
as that they required extensive European integration. These disagreements
over which *spheres* should be covered by the EU, and hence the degree to
which the citizens of member states should be its *subjects*, have important
implications for the *styles* and *scope* of the EU's political and legal system.
For example, the sort of 'regime' required to legitimately govern an essentially
intergovernmental free trade zone will not be as extensive as that needed for
a federal state, demanding considerably less in the way of democratic control.
At the same time, though, the creation of a European 'regime' of any type has
implications for the development of the EU 'polity' – constraining it in some
respects while sustaining and fostering it in others, many of which are hard to
predict. A limited 'regime' will restrict the policy areas into which the EU can
extend. Thus, Fritz Scharpf has suggested that because the EU's inadequate
democratic arrangements prevent it from offering the 'in-put legitimacy' of
'government by the people', it can only engage in those public policies where
the 'out-put legitimacy' needed to ensure 'government for the people' is sufficient (Scharpf 1999, 2, 6, 23, 203). Yet it should be noted that this thesis cannot be viewed simply as a purely 'external' form of performance legitimacy, as
some – notably Giandomenico Majone – come close to arguing (e.g. Majone
1996, especially 284, 287, 1998). For without the elements of 'internal' legitimation needed to define even those performance standards required for the EU
to be deemed an 'efficient' facilitator and regulator of transnational trade, it is
doubtful whether purely 'external' output legitimacy could justify more than
the threshold levels involved for humanitarian aid.

Even a restricted 'regime', however, will allow and encourage debates
about the nature of the 'polity' to occur, with demands for greater democratic
accountability, for example, fuelling the evolution of the EU into new policy
areas. Therefore, there is an element of truth in both the Eurosceptic argument
that 'regime' change in the EU must remain in step with the low levels of
'polity' allegiance it receives compared to member states, and the Europhile
counterargument that if the EU's 'regime' was strengthened, people would
look more favourably on the construction of a more extensive European 'polity'. What both sides of the debate miss are the mutual interactions of 'polity'
and 'regime', explored in the remainder of this chapter.

2. THE NORMATIVE AND 'REGIME'
DIMENSIONS OF THE EUROPEAN 'POLITY'

Despite their important differences, the hitherto dominant theories of European integration, namely neo-functionalism and liberal intergovernmentalism,

share a common aspiration to provide scientific explanations that minimise the independent role of the EU's 'regime' and normative ideals. Both focus on the EU's 'polity' legitimacy, regarding its 'regime' legitimacy as a secondary matter that is achieved largely indirectly. Both also adopt a predominantly instrumental and purely performance-based view of the development of the EU 'polity'. This perspective equates the internal aspect of the EU's 'polity' legitimacy with its success in securing the goods of peace and prosperity. Because these goods are basic to the ideals of a majority of the European peoples, no additional internal normative justification is assumed to be necessary. Since most people have an interest in maximising them, how far integration should proceed becomes largely a matter of cost-benefit analysis. External legitimacy is either transferred to the EU, or indirectly guaranteed, as a result of integration being promoted in accordance with international law by states that are themselves recognised as externally legitimate. Moreover, the terms of this external legitimacy are believed to be the same for all states and for the EU.

Thus, for neo-functionalists such as Haas, 'the public is ... concerned with income, price stability, better working conditions, cleaner air, more recreational facilities ... [and] does not greatly care whether these are provided by national government or by Brussels' (Haas 1958, 79/80). That such policies were increasingly coordinated at a European rather than a domestic level was the product not of idealism so much as the interconnected nature of modern economies. Such economic integration was predicted to prove self-sustaining. Because the different parts of the economy are linked, an economic spillover effect was expected whereby increasing integration in one area would lead to it proceeding elsewhere. The removal of constraints on the free movement of capital, services and labour would generate in turn an increasing number of common regulations, the need for a single currency and so on. In its turn, economic spillover would encourage and be accompanied by political spillover. Supranational organisations would arise to oversee the ever more integrated economy and themselves produce a self-reinforcing range of institutions. Because the cost-benefit calculations of integration are complex within a modern interconnected economy, the lead had inevitably to come from élites and technocrats. Indeed, they often operated by stealth to avoid the possible irrational prejudices and faulty instrumental reasoning of their electorates. However, it was expected that the 'loyalties and expectations' of all economic and political actors would gradually shift to where the action was – at the centre (Haas 1958).

On the neo-functionalist account, 'polity' construction creates its own 'regime' and internally legitimating norms. Moreover, these norms are treated as mere properties of the economic system that facilitate its healthy functioning. Satisfying standard 'external' aspects of legitimacy are assumed to bring the 'internal' aspects in their wake, with little interaction between the two. People will identify with the EU 'polity' and accept its institutions so long as integration provides certain desired goods and the means for controlling their supply without damaging productive efficiency, infringing international law, or inflicting injustice. As we saw, this position presupposes a consensus on what goods people want and an indifference to who delivers them, how and among whom they are distributed. However, such agreement has not obtained in practice. Indeed, it is precisely because people disagree about the *sphere* and *subjects* of a 'polity', that it needs a 'regime' where such issues can be raised and internal legitimacy generated. Moreover, as we also noted in the previous section, these debates can have knock-on effects for the type of external legitimation that are applied. If the EU begins either to act externally as a 'polity' when people internally regard it as an international organisation or vice versa, that will produce both an internal and an external legitimation crisis.

To some degree, it was the first scenario that undermined the neo-functionalist account when De Gaulle refused to contemplate an expansion of the Parliament's powers in agricultural policy (the Empty Chair crisis of 1965). Liberal intergovernmental approaches see themselves as filling the explanatory gap left by the failure of the economic and especially the political spillover mechanisms to work as smoothly as neo-functionalists had supposed. In his influential account of this thesis, Andrew Moravcsik proposes a tripartite argument whereby national governments first define an ordering of preferences in response to the domestic pressures of societal groups, second bargain among themselves to realise these interests, and third choose appropriate institutions to realise them (1993, 481, 1999, 20, 473). In this approach, the 'regime' and internal normative aspects of legitimacy are exogenous to the process of EU 'polity' building. They belong to the domestic realm, with national political institutions aggregating the interests of the population and so setting the agenda for their representatives. Though the theory does not specify the content of national government preferences, economic interests and the need to coordinate given economic interdependence are once again identified as the crucial factors (Moravcsik 1999, 473–5). Moreover, all interests are assumed to be pursued economically. The EU's chief purpose is to resolve collective action problems within a globalising economic environment. European agreements bind states to uphold common policies that reduce negative externalities while allowing them to recoup some of the benefits generated by positive externalities (Moravcsik 1993, 509–10, 1999, 35). Since all groups within a state will not benefit from such action, the profile of domestic preferences provides the 'bargaining space' within which interstate negotiations take place (Moravcsik 1993, 497, 1999, 36–8, 475–77). States have to weigh up the costs of negotiating and losing some freedom of action in the future against the benefits of integration. The chief gains of creating a settled European organisation rather than proceeding by ad hoc agreements are efficiency and stability, not least the removal of prisoner dilemmas and free riding (Moravcsik 1993, 512–14, 1999, 73–7, 485–9). However, the EU's 'polity' structures and its governing 'regime' remain firmly intergovernmental, albeit of a highly developed kind.

As with neo-functionalism, liberal intergovernmentalism sees normative legitimation as resting on largely invariable external standards. If the member states are recognised as legitimate and their agreements are compatible with international law and norms, then the EU must be legitimate. Provided its quasi-'regime' satisfies external criteria of legality and justice, it too is legitimate. However, the more the EU does resemble a 'polity' with a 'regime' of its own, the more problematic this scenario becomes. Rightly or wrongly, most of the electorates of all member states believe significant powers have been ceded to EU institutions and either wish them returned to domestic control or desire a strengthening of European controls. In other words, there is a mismatch between what they perceive as the changed external standing of the EU and its member states, on the one hand, and the forms of internal legitimacy they now receive, on the other. They believe the *sphere* and *subjects* of the EU are changing without either adequate authorisation or sufficient popular identification to allow the establishment of a 'regime' with sufficient *scope* and the requisite *styles* to offer accountable and effective governance.[5]

Although liberal intergovernmentalism appears to fill gaps left by neo-functionalism, the neo-functionalist spillover mechanism offers a theoretical source of internal legitimation that, at least in principle, would overcome problems in its position (Waever 1995; Diez 1999, 360). For even if we accept the EU is primarily intergovernmental in both 'polity' and 'regime' terms, it is doubtful liberal intergovernmentalism can avoid assuming the emergence of certain internal European norms and a related 'regime' to structure the bargaining of state actors (Wallace 1990, 215). Moravcsik himself concedes that geopolitical factors, that were generally more ideational than objective, mattered 'where the costs and benefits of cooperation were uncertain, balanced, or weak', predominating in issues – such as foreign policy coordination or purely institutional matters, such as the role of the European Parliament – with no immediate economic impact (Moravcsik 1999, 477). He also acknowledges that such factors were often connected to prestigious national leaders and could influence core national preferences (Moravcsik 1999, 478). However, he contends these were secondary to the commercial motivations to cooperate in various areas within an increasingly global and interconnected economy (Moravcsik 1999, 6/7, 473–7). Where such motivations were not present, integration rarely advanced. By and large, Moravcsik sees states as being pushed by key economic interest groups eager

to cooperate for mutual interest. He makes light of the likelihood of different state actors adopting different bargaining strategies and claims that the
payoffs and the rules of the game were clear to and agreed by all, that all saw
themselves as involved in a supergame rather than a series of one-shot games,
and that all concurred on the economic focus of the arrangements (Moravcsik
1999, 60–2). If true – and it is beyond the scope of this chapter to test these
empirical claims – then the decisions surrounding the choice for Europe were
fortuitously free of the dilemmas of collective action to which one might
otherwise have suspected them to be prone. After all, international politics is
replete with examples, from the failure to tackle global warming to the arms
race, where states have been tempted by free riding or caught in games of
chicken in ways that prevent them cooperating in mutually beneficial ways
(Hollis and Smith 1990, 137–41).

Even if European ideals and institutions were not necessary to bring about
European integration, however, many would contend have been products of
it. The focus on making choices and decisions misses the way the behaviour
of the main political actors is shaped by the ongoing processes of implementing them. As a number of commentators have noted (e.g. Wincott 1995b,
597–609), the liberal intergovernmentalist position has difficulty accounting
for the way the European Parliament and the European Court of Justice have
developed an authority of their own which is to some degree independent of,
constrains and moulds the decision-making of the member states (e.g. see
Vink 2001). In many respects, these developments provide a stable context
for bargaining to take place, which, for well-known reasons, rational actors
may be unable to provide for themselves (Wallace 1990, 225; Diez 1999,
361–3). They offer not only rules for the game, as historical institutionalist
accounts argue (e.g. Pierson 1996), but also, as constructivists have indicated
(Christiansen, Jorgensen, and Wiener 1999), roles for the actors involved,
even if they do not determine their actions anywhere near as strongly as
certain accounts suggest. Put another way, European law and institutions
help create normative expectations that fill the gaps in the various actors'
rational expectations of each other. Indeed, institutional arrangements may
even lock them into policies they come to find undesirable, such as continuing surpluses arising from the Common Agricultural Policy (CAP) (Scharpf
1988). Moravcsik partly grants some of these claims, but argues that most of
these institutional restraints and their consequences – including the apparently undesirable ones – were intended in order to commit all future governments to particular policies (Moravcsik 1999, 491–4). This thesis may hold
for the medium term but there are limits to how far-sighted one can be in the
long term. Consider the creative and ultimately incoherent ways in which
some American legal scholars refer back to the 'intentions' of the founders
to justify their interpretations of the American constitution (e.g. Bork 1990;

for a critique, see Sunstein 1993, chap. 4). Any attempts by future European lawyers or politicians to take this tack would similarly be doomed to fail. For good or ill, EU law and institutions such as the Parliament and commission have a dynamic of their own, albeit one still strongly constrained by intergovernmental decision-making.

In contrasting ways, neo-functionalists and liberal intergovernmentalists seek to bracket the question of the EU's 'polity' legitimacy from that of its 'regime'. Respectively, they see the latter either as a product of 'polity' formation or as its precondition (i.e. as a mechanism for national preference formation within the member states). Likewise, they separate internal legitimation from external legitimacy and assume the former to be non-normative in nature because people simply wish to maximise peace and prosperity. However, these attempts to partition normative issues ultimately fail. Debates over how far the extension of the EU's powers is either necessary or desirable have accompanied the whole course of European integration. These divisions occur within most member state populations and even many governments. They involve not only technicalities but also different ideological and ethical stances concerning the proper *sphere, subjects* and *scope* of EU politics, the *style* of accountability available and so on (Diez 1999). Contrary to the neo-functionalist position, these differences have meant that the 'spillover' from economic gains into enhanced internal legitimacy has been partial and patchy. Moreover, the fragility of the economic benefits and their contested nature has also produced some questioning of the EU's external legitimacy. Contrary to the liberal intergovernmentalist position, the normative as well as economic character of these disagreements renders them hard to aggregate, making a stable 'national' position that a government might represent hard to achieve. These kinds of disputes will only be resolved when purely instrumental reasoning gives way to moral argument and the belief that a certain course of action is right. Here norms are not mere rationalisations of material interests, they structure them. Mass normative opinions are not only operative in shaping the policies of élites towards Europe within the member states,[6] both formal and informal channels have also developed at the EU level whereby citizens can express such divergent opinions in ways that bypass national executives – most notably the European Parliament but also via subnational or transnational lobbying organisations of various kinds (Imig and Tarrow 2000). In addition, such bodies as the ECJ allow citizens to invoke European norms against national ones (e.g. *Cowan v. Le Trésor public* Case 186/87 [1989] ECR 195; *Konstantinidis v. Stadt Altensteig* Case C-168/91 [1993] ECR I-1191). Meanwhile, and for the present most influentially, deliberation between élites within European settings establishes patterns of socialisation whereby agreements result not from bargains but persuasive argumentation as to the merits of a given policy (Checkel 1999).

In other words, a European 'regime' has begun to emerge which offers a rival source of EU 'polity' development and external and internal legitimation to the member states.

At a mainly descriptive level, multilevel governance analysts of the EU have traced this intertwining of the various dimensions of 'polity' and 'regime' within the EU, noting that authority is now shared (and contested) between national executives and actors operating above and below the state, such as the EP and the regions, respectively (Marks, Hooghe and Blank 1996, 341/2). Moreover, these multiple levels coalesce in different ways according to policy area. No one set of institutions is ultimately responsible for all competences, while the membership and character of these institutions varies. For example, foreign, monetary and social policies require different types of agreement between different sets and sorts of actors concerning different *spheres* and *subjects*. To cite a notorious case, Britain is a full member of the EU, yet secured an opt-out from stage three of EMU and the Amsterdam Protocol (Article 73Q) on 'freedom, justice and security' and, until 1998, was exempt from the commitment to a common social policy. Different kinds of institutional arrangement govern these areas and the relationships between them are obscure to say the least. Thus, the Commission can promote binding accords between management and labour in areas such as health and safety that give these private non-state bodies a quasi-legislative power that can preempt both Community and Member State action (Arts. 117 and 118). The Western European Union is the EU's putative defence arm and as such 'an integral part of the development of the European Union' (Article J4), but only ten of the fifteen belong to it. As a result, the EU is polycentred as well as multilevelled (Schmitter 2000, 15–9). Put another way, there are multiple polities involving multiple 'regimes'. There are considerable overlaps between them but also certain tensions.

Multilevel governance rejects the liberal intergovernmentalist separation of domestic and international politics.[7] Though 'states are an integral and powerful part of the EU', these analysts note 'they no longer provide the sole interface between the supranational and the subnational arenas, and they share, rather than monopolise, control over many activities that take place in their respective territories' (Marks, Hooghe, and Blank 1996, 346/7). Thus, the Commission cannot be seen simply as an agent of the states (Marks, Hooghe, and Blank 1996, 358, 361). Not only is it able to exploit tensions among the states, but it also has various informational and agenda-setting advantages that give it a certain autonomy of action over often divided and temporary government officials and politicians. Likewise, the EP's growing power of co-decision has further limited the competence of both states and Commission, rendering the making of EU legislation a 'complex balancing act' among the main EU institutions (Marks, Hooghe, and Blank 1996, 364).

The existence of these distinctive sites of power to the state also means that non-state actors at subnational and transnational level can appeal to them when governments fail to respond to their needs. Capital and labour have long employed such tactics. However, other groups have also availed themselves of Union political structures. Indeed, it is now estimated that some 20 per cent of European groups are 'public interest' organisations covering the whole issue and ideological spectrum (Greenwood 1997).

Pressure by trans- and subnational groups, on the one hand, and the development of multiple levels of governance that cut across states either above or below, on the other, tend to reinforce each other. The latter facilitates the emergence of the former, who demand in their turn enhanced powers for the latter, even if this process has so far occurred unevenly and in fits and starts (Jeffrey 2000). Moreover, these institutions not only provide rules and norms that constrain purely calculative and self-interested economic behaviour but also offer a forum within which values and ideals as well as interests can be deliberated (Stone Sweet and Sandholtz 1997, 305; Christiansen, Jorgensen, and Wiener 1999, 541/2; Checkel 2001). However, the complexity of a multi-level system can increase the possibilities for inefficient and inequitable decision-making. Some commentators propose the best way of overcoming this situation is to provide the EU with a written constitution and more transparent and democratic decision-making (most influentially Habermas 2001). At this point, therefore, we need to reverse our perspective and ask how far the sui generis nature of the EU's 'polity' structure places normative constraints on the type of 'regime' it might adopt.

3. THE NORMATIVE AND 'POLITY' DIMENSIONS OF THE EUROPEAN 'REGIME'

The last section argued that the EU's 'regime' played an important role in shaping the EU 'polity', especially by offering various channels for its internal legitimation through discussion of which *spheres* and *subjects* should fall within its domain. This section argues that the character of the EU 'polity' shapes in its turn the character of the EU's 'regime'. Our argument starts from the, admittedly contentious, assumption that the multilevel account of the Euro-'polity' described above is roughly correct. Thus, we assume sovereignty to be partially dispersed between different policy *spheres* involving different *subjects*, for which different sorts of 'regime' might be appropriate. We also believe this situation to be fluid, and the dispersal of sovereign power to be partly horizontal as well as vertical (see Ruggie 1993, 172). The EU is very different, therefore, to a standard, albeit somewhat idealised, conception of a federal nation state. Within this arrangement, there is a strong political allegiance to the boundaries of the 'polity' and the competences of the subunits are relatively clear. Broad agreement exists over the complexion of the *subjects* and *spheres*, and hence who can decide what and where. The 'regime' distributes power vertically and hierarchically from the top down. Meanwhile, a shared political culture provides a rough consensus on the appropriate *styles* and *scope* of politics. In other words, the particular complexion of the 'polity' and 'regime' possess widespread 'internal' legitimation as an appropriate embodiment of the abstract liberal democratic values that offer the main sources of 'external' legitimacy. As a result, the 'regimes' of such states can combine a formal or informal constitution and tradition of judicial review that sets out the basic principles of the public culture, and a majoritarian system of democracy that operates within this constitutional framework. By contrast, the EU's 'internal' legitimacy is decidedly thin. Most people believe it to be useful without feeling deeply attached to it. There are profound disagreements about its respective competences vis-à-vis the member states and how the two relate to each other. Consequently its *spheres* and *subjects* are uncertain, and there is no shared 'political culture' as to the *styles* and *scope* of EU politics. As a result, we argue that it would be premature to either create a formal EU constitution, other than perhaps a simplification of the treaties, or to transform the European Parliament into a federal legislature (for a contrary view see Lord and Beetham 2001). Indeed, some contend that globalisation without and social and cultural differentiation within are undermining this model at the level of the nation state (Tully 2002). Instead, we need to see constitutional norms as the ongoing product of a dialogue between different demoi and different legal systems within the EU, through which both its 'polity' and 'regime' are being constantly recreated (Bellamy 2001b).

Constitutions are often assumed to normatively constitute both a 'polity' and its 'regime' by providing them with the external legitimacy offered by universal principles such as human rights (Dworkin 1995). However, as we have noted, such lists of rights are too abstract to offer in themselves much guidance as to how a regime should be organised. People reasonably differ over the justification of rights, their interpretation in particular contexts and the balance to be achieved between them (Waldron 1999, chap. 7). Not only philosophers and judges but also ordinary people disagree about such matters as whether pornography or racist opinions are entitled to protection under a right to freedom of speech, and the extent to which different forms of speech can or do infringe other rights, such as privacy and non-discrimination. The view one takes on these sorts of issues implies a certain conception of the good society: of the ways we should recognise and show concern and respect for others. Consequently, rights also require internal legitimation of both their 'polity' and 'regime' aspects (Bellamy 2001b). In fact, constitutions differ in the ways they balance rights because they offer internal interpretations of external legitimacy requirements that reflect national political and legal traditions. They reflect the *styles* and *scope* of politics adopted by certain *subjects* within a given *sphere*. When no congruence between sovereignty and identity obtains, then constitutions will lack internal 'polity' legitimacy because they cannot express the normative consensus of an already-existing 'people'. As a result, debates about the content and interpretation of constitutions, and the different *styles* and *scopes* these give to politics, will have a far greater tendency than within settled polities to shade into debates over the appropriate *sphere* and *subjects* within which a particular constitutional system can operate. For example, differences over the *scope* of monetary policy have produced in the EU context differences over its *sphere* and *subjects* too, with those outside EMU aspiring to a different configuration of the EU 'polity' to those within it.

In this situation, constitutions can no longer operate as the apex of a normative hierarchy in which they frame and offer the basis for democracy, as is the case in the standard federal model referred to above. Instead, they become coequal as part of a horizontal as opposed to a vertical division of powers. Legitimation of either a 'polity'-based demand, such as for greater regional autonomy, or of a 'regime'-based demand, like affirmative action, cannot be grounded in appeals to constitutional rights or popular sovereignty alone. Rather, the arguments invoke both: namely, that the character of a particular group of people warrants a certain understanding of their rights – including where and how they are implemented. These debates about constitutional rights are in practice, if not necessarily in principle, open-ended and ongoing. The judgements involved in applying abstract rights to concrete circumstances are inconclusive, and the ideals, interests and identities of those involved are constantly evolving as their situation and relations to each other change. Instead of a consensus that sets the terms of debate, therefore, constitutions have to be seen as part of a continuous series of dialogues and compromises as different groups seek to accommodate the views of others.

Jim Tully has noted how, even within established polities, multiculturalism and a renascent multinationalism have produced just such a dialogical turn in understanding constitutionalism (Tully 2001a). However, the situation within the EU is much more radical. Usually, multinationalism and to a lesser extent multiculturalism challenge 'polity' legitimacy indirectly and incrementally through ever more extensive changes to the 'regime'. By contrast, the EU's 'polity' legitimacy is both fragile and fragmented and has to contend with the much more robust existing 'polity' structures of the member states. Moreover, it involves a number of cross-cutting 'regimes' operating between different aggregations of 'polities'. Thus, the legitimacy of any EU constitution requires constitutional dialogues at both the 'polity' and 'regime' levels, with the two to some extent cutting across each other (Shaw 1999, 2000b, 2000c). The tensions currently present within the EU largely stem from attempts to block and circumnavigate such dialogues.

These fault lines are perhaps best illustrated by the series of confrontations between the ECJ and the German Federal Constitutional Court (BverfG). The ECJ has wished to make itself the guarantor of the external 'polity' and 'regime' legitimacy of community law, taking for granted that it possesses internal legitimacy as a distinct *sphere* with a determinate *scope*: most particularly the securing of the free movement of goods, services, labour and capital between the member states. Moreover, it argues European law has not only 'direct effect' but also 'supremacy' over even national constitutional law in these areas. However, the BverfG has carefully circumscribed these claims within an internal constitutional point of view of its own. Thus, the EU possesses internal 'polity' legitimacy because the BverfG accepts that Art 24 of the German constitution allows the transfer of certain legislative powers to international bodies (*'Solange I'* Internationale Handelsgesellschaft [1974] 2 CMLR 549). 'But', the Court went on (540), 'Art 24 ... limits this possibility in that it nullifies any amendment of the Treaty which would destroy the identity of the valid constitutional structure of the Federal Republic of Germany'. Importantly, it noted in particular the lack of a democratically elected and accountable EU legislature and the absence of constitutionally entrenched fundamental rights. 'So long as' a conflict between European law and the rights recognised by the German constitution was possible, the latter would prevail. Having obliged the ECJ to affirm its acknowledgement of human rights considerations as general principles of law, the BverfG has also accepted that it need not review secondary community legislation for compatibility with the basic law (*'Solange II'* Wunsche Handelsgesellschaft [1987] 3 CMLR 225). Yet it has not accepted that it is for the ECJ to decide what are community and what national matters, nor that it could not adjudicate on the constitutionality (within the German legal order) of either further extensions of the community or even changes in the practices of the ECJ (*Solange II, Brunner* [1994] 1 CMLR 57).

Though less fully expressed, most other national constitutional courts arguably hold a similar position (MacCormick 1995). The differences between the ECJ and the constitutional courts of the member states need not necessarily be a source of conflict if community law formed a 'discrete' order (Weiler 1999, chap. 3 suggests this sort of solution). After all, unlike the US Supreme Court, the ECJ does not presume national law to be 'nested' within community law and so does not assess the bearing of rights in what it regards as non-community areas, including those where a member state has obtained a derogation from community obligations (e.g. *Cinéthèque v. Fédèrations nationales des cinémas français* Cases 60-1/84 [1985] ECR 2605 and *ERT v. Dimotiki Etairia Piliroforissis* Case C-260/89 [1991] ECR I-2925å). However, difficulties still arise because, as we observed earlier, community and national affairs remain almost impossible to disentangle from each other. Decisions in one *sphere* invariably have knock-on effects for the other. Thus, there are clashes not only over economic priorities but also between the predominately market-orientated community values and various of the non-market social and cultural values of the states (e.g. *Grogan*). It is on these occasions that dialogue becomes inescapable.

So far, the ECJ and national courts have neatly skirted around such problem areas through tacit mutual accommodations. However, courts are imperfect vehicles for expressing either a national or a European community view that reveals how citizens identify with each other at either level.[8] The representative and accountable character of legislatures gives them an authority and legitimacy when seeking to accommodate different concerns and interests that courts do not possess (Waldron 1999). It is sometimes suggested that courts could acquire such qualities if their selection were more embedded in the political process. But that would be to subvert the separation of powers and the distinctive and valuable role courts play in upholding consistency, prospectivity and impartiality in the making and implementation of the law. It is these formal features of the rule of law that ensure that agreed policies are equitably and efficiently pursued. In this respect, EU law has provided the burgeoning body of European regulations with an all-important external legal-rational legitimacy (Majone 1996). However, as we noted earlier, to ensure that the law itself is 'for' the people in any substantive sense requires that it also possesses the internal legitimacy of having been made 'by' the people in ways that reflect the collective will. The relatively small number of judges cannot replicate the representative functions of a legislature and the diversity of opinions they normally contain. Moreover, their independence would be subverted if they were to be as accountable as we expect politicians to be. Yet in politics that accountability is crucial – for it is what obliges our representatives to take heed of the perspectives of ordinary citizens. None of this denies the vital role courts play in protecting the interests of individual citizens from the careless, inconsiderate and occasionally malicious actions of public and private agents and agencies. However, while litigation against an overpowerful state or corporation is an important feature of a democratic society, it is not a substitute for the democratic process. Courts properly focus on abuses of the law in individual cases. By contrast, democratic decision-making seeks to win the active assent of all citizens to a programme of collective policies. In circumstances where no consensus exists on what is the right or most just course of action, courts are in no position to take on this task. For it requires more than ensuring the law is equitably applied. It also involves securing compromises among a whole range of concerns, balancing the knock-on costs and benefits of pursuing policies in one area for those in others, and in consequence prioritising health and employment, say, over education and defence, and obtaining a willingness among citizens to pay for the requisite measures in one form or another.

It might be argued that the EU's unfolding constitutional order *is* the product of a political process – namely the intergovernmental conferences that decide changes to the treaties through political dialogue and compromise. The role of the courts, notably the ECJ, is then to simply interpret what 'we the people' have decided (Shaw 2000b, 24, 25–9). There are two difficulties with this view. First, it limits constitutional politics to specific transformative 'moments' rather than seeing it as ongoing aspect of 'normal' politics. However, truly constitutional moments tend to occur in exceptional times, such as following a war, when there is a widespread desire for a new beginning and a sense of common purpose. The IGCs cannot be represented as genuine constitutional moments in this sense. Rather, they are continuations of the daily debates within Europe concerning the EU's purpose and membership as well as its form of governance. As we have noted, with the 'polity' issue still unsettled it is impossible to make settled decisions about its 'regime'. Moreover, this situation is exacerbated by virtue of there being different European peoples who view the 'polity' as well as the 'regime' questions very differently from each other. Second, IGCs are not especially open or democratic fora. Only occasional referenda force politicians to account, and these are usually quite crude and not universally held. Nevertheless, as those following Maastricht and most recently in Ireland after Nice have revealed, they often indicate a failure of politicians in even the most Europhile states to carry their populations with them. What is required is an improvement in the 'normal' European democratic process, not constitutional settlements that further reduce the daily involvement of European citizens in political debate about the shape and character of the EU.

The recent declaratory European Charter of Fundamental Rights illustrates both these points. Despite emerging from a convention that was unusually open both in the range of interests represented and the transparency of its proceedings, neither its members nor the document that emerged have been subjected to democratic scrutiny (Shaw 2000b, 34–6; De Búrca 2001). As a result, it cannot claim the popular legitimacy some of the more enthusiastic convention members have wished to claim for it. It aimed at producing a mutually acceptable view of the rights community law should recognise. Yet, there is a danger that it risks freezing a particular view of rights rather than allowing their evolution as the EU itself evolves. In many respects, it codifies the status quo. Moreover, it does not get around the problem of the interaction between community and national law, notwithstanding its declared restriction to the former. Instead, it risks making the tensions worse by appearing to justify the pretensions of the ECJ to constitute a hierarchical 'regime' in the absence of adequate internal 'polity' legitimacy (Bellamy and Castiglione 2001). The European convention already provides a declaratory statement to which all member states subscribe: the community should do likewise. The crucial issue is how their various justifications, interpretations and balancing of rights can be related to each other in ways that satisfy the internal legitimacy of their respective polities (Bellamy and Castiglione 1997a, 2000b). Our analysis suggests this problem requires explicit procedures be set up for continuous dialogues not only between member state constitutional courts but also between their legislatures – the latter facilitated by the empowerment of new transnational democratic fora.

Meanwhile, the enhancement of European democracy in such ways is subject to similar constraints to those we have highlighted with regard to a European constitution (Banchoff and Smith 1999). Within a relatively homogenous people, who accept the legitimacy of both 'polity' and 'regime', then government by simple majority rule is warranted, with minorities protected by the constitutional consensus. But when the contours of the 'polity' are in dispute, such hierarchical decision-making risks being coercive. Actors must achieve the higher threshold of a mutually acceptable compromise characteristic of systems of governance. By contrast to governmental arrangements, governance involves horizontal relations between actors who are sufficiently interdependent to desire a collective agreement, yet practically independent or normatively distinct enough to make imposed solutions impractical or unjustifiable (Hirst and Thompson 1996, 183/4; Schmitter 2001). Governance operates as a form of partnership in which each partner benefits from cooperation with the others and would be damaged by their non-involvement, even if not to the same degree. It involves regular interaction over a whole range of policies rather than being an ad hoc and sporadic arrangement, so that those involved share certain norms and have a commitment to the process itself, albeit not of the absolutely binding kind associated with obligations to a state.

The balance between Commission, Council and European Parliament and the various levels largely reflect such horizontal governance relationships. Their inadequacies result from the poor democratic control exerted by the relevant 'polity' constituency over each one of them. The democratic deficit tends to be analysed in terms of strengthening the European Parliament as the only directly elected institution. Once again, the difficulty with this solution lies in its introducing a hierarchical 'regime' without the requisite internal 'polity' legitimacy. As Weiler has pertinently remarked, in the absence of a unified European demos, asking the European peoples to accept legislation by majoritarian voting in the European Parliament would be like expecting the Danes to acknowledge the legitimate authority of a German Bundestag to which they had been granted voting rights (Weiler 1996, 111). Indeed, the legitimacy crisis posed by strengthening European parliamentary government is even more acute than Weiler's analogy suggests. For social differentiation has produced an ever more complex and diverse society and economy. It has become difficult for one body either to adequately represent the range of values and interests or to produce regulations that are sufficiently attuned to the peculiarities of particular case, let alone to implement and enforce them. As a result, there has been a dispersal of political authority among a whole range of private and semiprivate actors, from privatised service providers, that increasingly run the once-nationalised utilities within most of the member states, through specialised agencies and regulators, such as private standardisation bodies like CEN or CENELEC, to voluntary and special interest organisations (as employed in the fifth environmental programme). This shift from parliamentary democracy to a 'democracy of organisation' has gone further in the EU than in any state (Anderson and Burns 1996). The promotion of social dialogue via Article 139EC has even produced an officially recognised partial privatisation of the legislative process (Bernard 2000, 279/80).

A situation of multiple European demoi operating across multiple polities requires a 'regime' that explicitly recognises and seeks to promote dialogue between them and the various ways in which they debate the changing dimensions of the proto-European 'polity'. As we have noted, the actual structure of the EU does in part reflect this concern. Thus, there are multiple channels of political representation for different sorts of political *subjects*: member states in the Intergovernmental Conferences and Council of Ministers, national political parties in the EP, selected functional interests in the Economic and Social Committee (ESC) and subnational territorial units in the Committee of the Regions. The avenue for reform lies in strengthening the democratic accountability of each and facilitating a more equitable dialogue between them. Elsewhere (Bellamy 1999, chap. 5, 2001b; Bellamy and Castiglione 2000b), we have argued that the most suitable norms for devising such a scheme derive from the neo-Roman republican tradition with its injunction that decision-making evade domination through 'hearing the other side'. The key to this approach lies in prioritising freedom rather than rights and justice. Given the latter are sources of disagreement, they cannot offer a framework for our political deliberations. By contrast, the emphasis on freedom stresses the importance of being able to continually renegotiate and dispute any given settlement (Tully 2001b). The focus is not on realising any particular end state so much as the capacity of the members of a political society to determine their way of life in a manner that reflects their diverse and evolving ideals, identities and interests. As a result, political arrangements have to be so structured to ensure each side engages with the concerns of others. The goal is to avoid domination by ensuring each affected group is a party to the decision and finds it mutually acceptable. The aim is not consensus but compromise through reciprocal accommodation.

Contestatory mechanisms are central to this scheme, providing the means for avoiding both false negatives and positives (Pettit 1999; Bellamy 2000b, 215/6). In parliamentary systems the ability to remove the government from office offers the best mechanism of this kind. In a system of governance, though, matters are not so straightforward because power is less centralised and the demos more fragmented (Anderson and Burns 1996). To some degree the dispersal of power is itself an aid. Multiple but interacting 'polities' and 'regimes' can offer checks and balances that can help secure mutual recognition. Such balancing largely justifies the weighted voting in the Council and distribution of seats within the EP, which biases representation against large states to ensure the smaller get a voice. However, EU institutions still leave grossly under-represented key concerns, from regions through to a whole series of non-business interests – from the unemployed, through ordinary consumers to public interest movements, including transnational coalitions of these groups. Giving a legislative as opposed to purely consultative function to bodies such as the Committee of the Regions and the Economic and Social Committee, while employing electoral mechanisms to make them more accountable and representative, would further recognise the multiplicity of 'regimes' and 'polities' in the EU and strengthen the balance of powers within its decision-making. Though the Commission consults a large number of NGOs, both informally and within the context of the comitology process, the process of selection remains haphazard and obscure, while the representativeness and accountability of these organisations are deficient, to say the least (Warleigh 2001). In this respect, the White Paper on Governance promises a major step forward, not least in providing a catalogue of which organisations are consulted and in proposals for ensuring they are answerable to their members. Granting citizens opportunity structures for a direct input in the legislative process via the right to initiate referenda and the passing of an American-style Administrative Procedure Act, to ensure the participation of all interested parties in the framing of regulations, would further enhance the contestatory powers of citizens.[9] These suggestions are obviously indicative rather than exhaustive of what might be done. To the extent the EU continues to be characterised by several Europes rather than one, we claim merely that these sorts of mechanisms are vital to ensure the internal democratic legitimacy of the EU's ongoing constitutional process.

CONCLUSION

Attention to the normative dimension of the EU has been stimulated by concern over its lack of legitimacy. We have argued that addressing this issue proves more complex than is sometimes supposed. Legitimacy operates across four dimensions, none of which are congruent within the EU or likely to become so. For different reasons, analysts of the EU have tended to ignore the interaction between 'polity' and 'regime', and to emphasise *external* at the expense of *internal* legitimacy. Putting all four dimensions together reveals the EU to be a polycentric 'polity' possessing a multilevel 'regime'. The result is that the EU conforms neither to the materialist realism of many theorists of intregration nor the high idealism of certain European federalists. Both descriptively and prescriptively it lies somewhere in between. As we have argued more fully elsewhere, this in-between character of the EU is best captured by the 'republican' notion of a 'mixed constitution', within which sovereignty is horizontally dispersed between different parts of the body politic so as to force all parties to deliberate with each other (see Bellamy and Castiglione 2000b; Bellamy 2003).[10] In the terminology of the present chapter, this setup allows internal legitimacy to emerge via a series of dialogues among the multiple European constituencies, which serve to construct both the EU 'polity' and its 'regime'. From this perspective, the main avenues for reform should be to improve the ability of the EU's institutions to check and balance each other and to enhance the contestatory power of ordinary citizens. Both these proposals would be hindered rather than helped by a written constitution and federal legislature.

NOTES

1. Research for this chapter was supported by an ESRC Grant L213 25 2022 on 'Strategies of Civic Inclusion in Pan-European Civil Society'. Earlier versions have been presented at seminars in Oñati, Florence, Edinburgh, Belfast and Montreal. We are grateful for the comments of Lars Tragardh, Peter Wagner, Neil Walker, Philippe Schmitter, Lynn Dobson, Alex Warleigh, Antje Weiner, Daniel Weinstock and Wayne Norman, among others, on these occasions, and for the detailed suggestions of the journal's three referees.

2. This chapter develops the argument of Bellamy and Castiglione (2000a). We are grateful for comments on those earlier papers, especially Shaw (1999, 2000a, 22–5) and Chryssochoou (2000, 2001, chap 6). The literature involving the normative analysis of the EU is now growing apace. By and large the lawyers promoted this turn, perhaps because law – especially constitutional law – is explicitly a normative order. Any list will necessarily exclude important work, so the following is meant to be illustrative rather than exhaustive: De Witte (1991); Habermas (1992); MacCormick (1995); Wincott (1995a); Walker (1996); De Búrca (1996); Curtin (1997); Craig (1997); MacCormick (1997); Shaw (1998, 1999, 2000b, 2000c); Weiler (1999); and Bankowski and Scott (2000). More recently, however, there has been a growing body of work that has built on collaboration between political theory and political science. See especially the following edited collections: Lehning and Weale (1997); Føllesdal and Koslowski (1997); Nentwich and Weale (1998); and Eriksen and Fossum (2000). See too Beetham and Lord (1998); Wiener (1998); Chryssochoou (1998);

and Schmitter (2000). In contributions to some of these volumes and in collaborative volumes of our own, we have attempted a similar mix that also draws on the legal literature – notably, Bellamy, Bufacchi, and Castiglione (1995); Bellamy and Castiglione (1996a); Bellamy (1996a); and Bellamy and Warleigh (2001). See too Bellamy and Castiglione (1997b, 2000b); and Bellamy and Warleigh (1998). For a recent overview, see Friese and Wagner (2002).

3. This has been particularly true of the functionalist and (in a different way) the liberal intergovernmentalist approaches discussed in section 2.

4. Habermas (1998, 118, 225/6) has argued that rights per se can provide the focus of a 'constitutional patriotism' for the EU. But an abstract agreement on the appropriate external criteria any 'polity' or 'regime' should meet will not tell you which 'polity' they ought to be realised in, or even the best form of 'regime' to do so. Both of these involve internal forms of legitimation that Habermas either ignores or simply assumes match his argument. For an explicit critique of Habermas's position, see Bellamy (2000a).

5. As noted, countries differ widely in their views of the EU. But although 51 per cent of European citizens in the most recent poll expressed support for the Union, only four member states (Spain, Portugal, Luxembourg and Ireland) recorded a majority satisfied with the way democracy works in the EU. By contrast, over 50 per cent in all but one member state (Italy) were satisfied with national democracy (Figures from Eurobarometer Report 52, April 2000 (based on research October–November 1999).

6. For a study of how such issues structured German policy towards EMU, see Merlingen (2001).

7. It should be noted that similar considerations also work against attempts to distinguish different levels of analysis within EU decision-making, from historic decisions about the nature of the EU system to sub-systemic policy-shaping (Peterson 1995). Because the four dimensions of *subjects, sphere, scope* and *style* are related, with a continuous interaction between European and member state considerations among the relevant actors, super-systemic issues will be raised in ordinary policy making and policy issues arise in historic decisions on the nature of the system. Differences of emphasis may of course exist, but they will not be clear-cut (a point, to be fair, that Peterson partly concedes at p. 85).

8. In his study of the spread of constitutionally based judicial review in Europe, Alec Stone Sweet (2000) notes how courts attempt to avoid legitimation problems by making pragmatic compromises that anticipate and so defer to what they presume will be the majority view. As we have noted elsewhere, and indicated above, this tactic is at best imperfect (see Bellamy 1999, chap. 7, 2001b).

9. These and other proposals are made in Curtin (1996, part V); and Schmitter (2000). See too Craig (1997, 119–24), who draws out their republican potential.

10. Although Friese and Wagner (2002, p. 355 note 45) may be correct to describe our thesis as a 'weak' form of republicanism when compared to Habermas's 'strong' version, we trust it is evident from the above that they are mistaken to suggest that we 'take it for granted that there is agreement about the Europeanness of many questions'. Indeed, our scheme is motivated in large part by our disputing that such agreement exists, with us looking to deliberation within this multilayered setting to create it.

Chapter 3

Democracy, Sovereignty and the Constitution of the European Union

The Republican Alternative to Liberalism[1]

Richard Bellamy and Dario Castiglione

The European Union (EU) has appeared to many analysts as an incoherent mix of the supranational and federal, on the one hand, and the international and intergovernmental, on the other. This hybridity makes democratic accountability problematic. The lines of responsibility are often unclear and many decisions get made betwixt and between the established mechanisms of democratic control as matters of executive or administrative discretion. Both criticism of and remedies for this situation standardly appeal to the norms and practices of liberal democracy. Those favouring a move towards greater integration advocate removing the democratic deficit within the EU by extending liberal democratic institutions to the European level through such measures as enhancing the powers of the European Parliament, formalising the evolving European constitution and instituting a quasi-federal distribution of sovereign power (e.g. Burgess 1989; Williams 1990; Bogdanor and Woodcock 1991). Those who adopt a more intergovernmental perspective, by contrast, maintain political authority must largely remain with the constituent nation states, since their linking of people, territory and community provides liberal democracy's only viable context (e.g. Barry 1994; Miller 1995; Moravcsik 1993).

In what follows, we shall contest this common starting point. We argue that the very global economic and social forces that have promoted European integration have undermined liberal democracy at the nation-state level without creating appropriate conditions for its establishment within a supranational European polity. As Schmitter and others have argued (cf. Schmitter's contribution in Marks, Scharpf, et al. 1996; Marks, Hooghe, and Blank 1996), a more complex, multilayered and hence multinational form of governance is coming into being. As critics rightly fear, these circumstances provide ample possibilities for the self-interested bargaining and blocking that have so frequently characterised European decision-making and produced measures such as the Common Agricultural Policy that are both suboptimal and inequitable. To avoid these dangers, however, requires a quite different approach to the standard liberal democratic solution – one we dub 'democratic liberalism', which draws on the neo-republican tradition in politics (Pettit 1997; Skinner 1998).

This analysis rests on a fuller account of the EU's democratic deficit than is usual. There are three dimensions to this phenomenon (Castiglione 1995, 61–3), two of which are rarely addressed. First, there is the democratic deficit in the narrow sense of the relative absence of any influence by ordinary citizens over European decision-makers and the policies they enact in their name (Williams 1990). Second, there is the federal deficit. This arises from the ambiguous relationship between the central EU institutions, such as the European Court of Justice, the European Parliament and the Commission, on the one hand, which claim a federal status within their respective domains, and national governments, parliaments, courts and bureaucracies, on the other, which frequently dispute or seek to qualify such claims (Neunreither 1994). Finally, there is the constitutional deficit (e.g. Pogge 1997, 160–2; Rubio Llorente 1998, para. 6.1). This refers to the lack of any systematic normative and popular legitimisation of European political institutions due to the paucity of sustained debate about their overall shape and reach – even by the political and bureaucratic élites.[2] If the first deficit focuses on democratic accountability and representation, the second raises the issue of the distribution of sovereignty and the third the problem of the EU's legitimacy. The three are interrelated. How one tackles the first of these deficits will largely be framed by one's thinking on the broader issues raised by the second and third. For the type and degree of democracy suitable for everyday political decisions rests to a great extent on the ways sovereignty is parcelled out and the degree to which it is regarded as legitimate for a given body to make them.[3] These dimensions define the content, scope and sphere of democracy – who makes decisions about whom and what, how, why, when and where.

This chapter elucidates the advantages of a neo-republican approach to the three deficits over more traditional liberal interpretations of democracy. Two clarifications are necessary. First, these two traditions are of course historically entwined and elements of both can be found in the political systems of most Western democracies (cf. Isaac 1988; Holmes 1995, 5). However, coexistence should not be taken for complementarity or overlap. As we shall argue below, republican justifications and conceptions of liberty, rights and the rule of law differ from the liberal's in important respects – most especially in relation to the nature and role of democracy.[4] Second, these models reflect contrasting views of the democratic ideal and hence of the norms that should inform democratic institutions.[5] Whereas liberal democratic norms provide a rationale for both majoritarian and consensual political systems, and federal and intergovernmental conceptions of the EU, we claim the emergent forms of multilevel governance call for rather different regulative norms deriving from a democratic liberal republicanism (see Scott 1998, for a parallel argument).

Section 1 argues that the complexity and pluralism of modern societies have undermined the constitutional consensus, hierarchical organisation of power and majoritarian decision-making characterising liberal democracy. Section 2 demonstrates that the threefold deficit within the EU arises out of these generic deficiencies of the liberal democratic model in global conditions. Strengthening liberal democracy will exacerbate rather than attenuate these problems, therefore. Section 3 introduces the concept of democratic liberalism. Of republican inspiration, this model of governance identifies the constitution with a political system that disperses power within civil society and encourages dialogue between the component parts of the body politic. Section 4 illustrates its normative and practical attractions for the EU.

I. LIBERAL DEMOCRACY

Liberal democracy rests on a distinction between the state and civil society. Liberals see constitutionalism as a normative framework that sets limits on and goals for the exercise of state power. Traditionally, its principles are grounded in a social contract designed to legitimate the state's monopoly of violence. According to this argument, free and equal citizens would only consensually submit to a polity that removed the uncertainties of the state of nature while preserving the most extensive set of equal natural liberties. Interference by the state or law is only justified to reduce the mutual interference attendant upon social life so as to produce a greater liberty over all. The separation of powers supposedly fosters this aim by preventing anyone from being judge in his or her own cause, thereby constraining the arbitrary and partial framing and interpretation of legislation. The rule of men is replaced by the rule of universal and equally applicable general laws.[6]

Two features of these arrangements are worth highlighting. First, as James Tully has observed, the normative consensus assumed by the 'modern' liberal conception of constitutionalism hypothesises a degree of uniformity among the constitutive people (Tully 1995, chap. 3). It assumes that behind different beliefs and customs lies a common human nature, a natural equality of status and shared forms of reasoning sufficient to generate agreement on constitutional essentials. What divergences remain are supposedly eroded as historical progress leads to more homogeneous and less stratified societies that conform to a similar pattern of social and political organisation, and stand in contrast to the ranked societies and cultural particularisms of the past. Nation-building further strengthens this process. As co-nationals, the people share a corporate identity as equal citizens of the polity.

Second, the rights-based approach goes together with a conception of freedom as non-interference and of the state as a neutral ringmaster, unconcerned with upholding any particular set of values.[7] This understanding of the constitution encourages in its turn a purely preference-based picture of the economy and an interest-based account of democracy. In each case, what matters is the degree outcomes correspond to the uncoerced choices and express desires of those concerned. The conditions of production and the protection of public goods enter with difficulty into this view of the economy. The first are assumed to be the result of voluntary contracts, the latter left up to the invisible hand. Likewise, politics becomes a competitive market within which rival interest groups bargain with each other, and involves no attempt to evaluate the interests concerned. Its purpose is purely instrumental: to protect against incompetent or tyrannous rulers by allowing their removal, and to aggregate preferences either through majoritarian voting or corporatist-style consensual politics, and encourage politicians to pursue policies that conform to such aggregate preferences.[8]

Liberals accept that economy and democracy need regulating when they threaten the constitutional structure. However, identifying when such threats occur and who possesses the authority to remedy them proves problematic. Because the economy forms part of the private sphere, there are difficulties about whether the requisite interference is either legitimate or perpetrates an even greater intrusion in people's lives than those it prevents. Such decisions cannot necessarily be left up to democratic governments, since interest groups may use the state's coercive power to further their personal goals. This dilemma raises a further source of tension between the hypothetical consent underlying the constitution and the express will of the people. Liberals try to avoid this crux by treating the constitution as a 'higher' law that provides the preconditions for the 'normal' legislation arising out of democratic politics. They see judicial review by a court buttressed by a bill of rights as the best bulwark against the democratic subversion of the constitution (Dworkin 1995, 2).

Cosmopolitans extend liberal accounts of the progress of society in a postnational direction. They contend that globalisation produces overlapping communities of common fate that require and render possible global regulatory bodies, such as the EU, underpinned by uniform, equal norms.[9] However, the very forces supposed to underlie this extension of liberalism have in reality given rise to new kinds of postmodern diversity that render a liberal consensus hard to sustain. For the same processes that drive globalisation have augmented functional differentiation in the economy and society and fostered multiculturalism. The consequent pluralism of interests and values, and the growing complexity of the social and economic systems, create difficulties for the liberal model of constitutional democracy. They render majoritarian decision-making more problematic, increase the difficulty of regulating the unaccountable power located in civil society and subvert the rights consensus upon which liberalism rests.

Within this new global context, liberal democracy promises more than it can deliver.[10] As a political regime it succumbs to a democratic, federal and constitutional deficit. Growing complexity and functional differentiation hinder democratic control by rendering problems more technical and less amenable to general regulations. The range and scale of decisions handled by unaccountable specialised bureaucracies, and involving considerable technocratic discretion, expand. The autonomy of many sectors of economy and society is increased. Globalisation may heighten interconnectedness but it has a highly variable impact on different classes, countries and social and economic sectors. As financial markets illustrate, this feature can weaken the ability of political institutions to impose collective decisions while improving the capacity for elite groups to evade and defect from them by shifting their capital around.

Having more supranational or global decision-making bodies will not help. They will be too distant to regulate in a suitably differentiated manner, and are likely to lack the capacity to implement any but the most general of norms. Nor is it clear that they will be able to count on much democratic legitimacy to act in any case. Voters already feel alienated by a political system that they can influence in only the most indirect and marginal ways. It is far from clear that they will identify to any significant degree with such remote institutions or that appropriately transnational political organisations will be capable of developing – witness the low turnouts and notable absence of European political parties in elections to the European Parliament.

The difficulty of making and enforcing collective decisions is further complicated by the spread of multiculturalism. Not only are geographically separated cultures brought into greater contact with each other, but improved social mobility renders states more pluriethnic as well. Different beliefs and identities prove less amenable than divergent economic interests to the democratic horse-trading liberals standardly employ to build stable and fair majorities. As a result, the likelihood of conflict or the oppression of minorities rises. This possibility can fuel demands for self-government and the creation of multiple demoi as opposed to an enlargement of the demos.

The net effect of these processes is to suggest a fragmentation rather than an extension of the democratic public sphere, which undercuts the hierarchical

organisation of sovereign power. The social complexity of highly differentiated advanced industrial societies results in a proliferation of autonomous
centres of power. These centres are capable of making decisions according to
a variety of functionally specific criteria within their respective domains, with
unpredictable knock-on effects for other parts of the social and economic
system. Citizens find themselves locked into a variety of these spheres, and
get pulled in opposite directions by the inner logic of each. Reconciling such
clashes proves highly problematic. The various areas of social life operate
with increasingly distinct and largely self-validating criteria. They become
ever more taken up with their own concerns and tend to interpret the world
from their own perspective, generating incommensurable and incompatible
claims (Luhmann 1981).

Similar difficulties bedevil the constitutional entrenchment and judicial
protection of the basic liberties (Bellamy 1999, chaps. 2 and 7). Liberals
claim the constitution can provide a neutral framework for politics that rests
on a separation of the right from the good. But this distinction proves practically elusive. How and when rights to privacy and to freedom of speech
clash, for example, involve invoking contentious notions of the presence and
absence of constraints which may be normatively and empirically evaluated
from a range of reasonably different perspectives, giving divergent answers
in each case. Moreover, the legitimacy and implementation gap is likely to
be even greater than with the political system. Use of precedent means that
legal judgement has an inbuilt tendency to self-referentiality. Legitimation
comes either indirectly, via the legislature or through a widely held normative
consensus. If the influence of the former is weak, and the latter has ceased to
exist, then law is forced to operate in a vacuum and be largely self-validating
and practically impotent.

The deficiencies of the liberal democratic model are linked. Poor democratic accountability is fuelled by the inadequacy of a territorial and hierarchical distribution of power, and the inappropriateness of applying general,
uniform constitutional norms to complex circumstances. As we shall see, the
deficits of the EU are to a large extent symptomatic of this general liberal
democratic malaise, and so unlikely to be cured by further doses of liberal
democracy.

II. THE LIBERAL DEMOCRATIC DEFICIT OF THE EU

Analysis of the EU from a liberal democratic perspective has been especially
prevalent among legal scholars.[11] They focus on the establishment of a common market through a process of 'negative' integration: the removal of trade
barriers and restrictive practices, and the institution of the four freedoms

guaranteeing the free movement of capital, goods, services and persons. As lawyers noted early on (Stein 1981), the jurisprudence of the European Court of Justice quietly, and with a remarkable degree of tacit political support, effected the constitutionalisation of the emerging body of European economic law. Through a series of landmark decisions, the Court asserted European law operated with direct effect on individuals and was an independent source of obligations and rights,[12] had supremacy over the national legal systems of member states within its domain.[13] It also described the founding Treaties as the European Community's 'constitutional charter' rather than a mere international agreement,[14] and maintained the Court's position as the competent authority to decide when European law applied and how.[15]

The Court's justification of its role in establishing and upholding the European constitution rests on impeccable liberal democratic grounds. It alleges a normative consensus exists to ensure maximal equal liberty and facilitate social interaction on terms that are the same for all. Thus, 'the preservation of the Community character of the law' requires 'ensuring that in all circumstances the law is the same in all states of the Community'[16] and has 'identical effects over the whole territory of the Community'.[17] Likewise, the Court assumes a federal organisation of power, with certain aspects of state sovereignty definitively ceded to the Community.[18] Hence, EU measures derive their validity solely from European law and cannot be challenged on the basis of a conflict with national laws – even those of a constitutional status – 'without the legal basis of the Community itself being called into question'.[19] National courts must apply the rulings of the ECJ, ensure due process for the exercise of the four freedoms and uphold a general principle of non-discrimination on the basis of nationality, while national legislatures may become liable for failures to adequately implement EU laws.[20] Finally, the Court has regarded the European Parliament as 'an essential factor in the institutional balance intended by the treaty', reflecting 'at Community level the fundamental democratic principle that the peoples should take part in the exercise of power through the intermediary of a representative assembly'.[21]

As already suggested, this legal picture of the EU partly conflicts with the state-centric perspective commonly adopted by political scientists.[22] Moreover, tensions both between member states and between them and various European institutions have heightened recently. These strains reflect the way the liberal democratic version of constitutionalism espoused by the Court exacerbates the threefold democratic deficit described above. At the constitutional level, stress has manifested itself most clearly in conflicts over the interpretation of rights. We noted earlier how pluralism enhances incommensurable and incompatible understandings of rights and their appropriate balance. The potential clashes that result are apparent in conflicting opinions over rights protection offered by the ECJ and national constitutional courts.

The ECJ has read fundamental rights into European law to stem challenges to its competence and the supremacy of EC legislation by the German Federal and Italian constitutional courts. They argued that since their national constitutions contain bills of rights, whereas the European constitution does not, they had an obligation to scrutinise EC law for conformity to German and Italian fundamental rights and to invalidate or dispense with measures that failed to meet the requisite standard.[23] The ECJ felt constrained to reassure national courts that the general principles of EC law implied rights protection. The Court contended it drew inspiration from common institutional traditions and international treaties acknowledged by the member states – most particularly the European Convention on Human Rights. Regardless of origin, however, these rights become EU rights and as such subject to interpretation 'within the framework of the structure and objectives of the community'.[24] Although Germany initially accepted the ECJ's reassurance, the Italian court has not. Outright confrontation has so far been avoided, but many doubt it can be evaded in the long run (De Witte 1991; Shaw 1996, 188–95).

The ECJ has espoused a narrowly economic liberal view of rights analogous to that of the US Supreme Court during the Lochner era. It has played a significant part in the privatising of hitherto nationalised enterprises, and the weakening of welfare systems within the member states. This libertarian account of rights has produced tensions in a number of areas. The ECJ has been relatively intolerant of minority language rights, regarding them not just as restrictions on the four freedoms that can increase transaction costs by, for example, requiring multilingual labelling but also of freedom of expression, although they could be equally interpreted as defending the latter.[25] In *Grogan* the dilemma posed by the Irish constitution's protection of the right to life of the unborn child was largely sidestepped, though the Court's definition of abortion as a 'service' clearly poses problems for the Irish state's attempts to deny its citizen's access to it.[26] These debates reveal how legitimacy cannot be based on an alleged overlapping consensus on shared liberal democratic principles and the rule of law. In spite of considerable agreement on these matters, and the amended Article F TEU notwithstanding, substantial divergences remain. Nor does an appeal to maximising liberty help.[27] As we saw, the Court has consistently appealed to a narrowly negative and economic view of freedom in its judgements in these cases, yet this notion is often what is in dispute. The rights of national constitutions are often intended to prevent the removal of valued opportunities by the market. The boot-strapping operation of the ECJ in creating a European Constitution is a remarkable example of the self-validating nature of law. Yet this validity comes called into question when confronted by the fact of normative disagreement.[28] Significantly, the Court has suggested that accession by the Community to the European

Convention would compromise the autonomy of EC law – exactly the problem faced by national legal orders.[29]

The Court's assertion of the supremacy of EC law suggests a federal structure based on the hierarchical ordering of sovereign power, in which the particular interpretation and implementation of general formulations can be devolved down to subordinate bodies. The same is true of the much-vaunted doctrine of subsidiarity, albeit from the other end of the telescope. Recent developments within the EU suggest a very messy picture, however, with no clear division of powers between federal and lower levels. The principle of subsidiarity in the Amsterdam Protocol (and Articles A TEU, 3b EC) is masterfully vague, allowing both wide and narrow interpretations that can make almost anything or nothing the province of the Community. No criteria are offered for determining either what proximity to citizens entails, or when a matter can or cannot 'be sufficiently achieved by the Member States' on their own. Although Maastricht and Amsterdam extend qualified majority voting by the Council of Ministers into new areas and raise the prospect of a dramatic expansion of common policies in the monetary, defence and justice spheres, these developments are hedged around with arrangements 'for derogations where warranted by problems specific to a member state' (Arts. K 15–17, 12 [formerly K7 TEU] and 5A [formerly K2 TEU] of the Treaty of Amsterdam, and Article 8b EC). Thus many of the new policies allow for multiple speeds, variable geometry and a Europe à la carte. The first type of variation that accepts different rates and methods of implementation of policies such as VAT harmonisation poses no great difficulty to the ideal of a homogeneous, federal Europe. The second and third are far more problematic. The former suggests a distinction between core issues that all should adhere to and peripheral ones that may be optional, the Schengen system being a plausible example of such an optional policy. The latter suggests a far more smorgasbord approach, with Britain's opt-out from stage three of EMU and the Amsterdam Protocol (Article 73Q) on 'freedom, justice and security' being notorious instances. Perhaps most important of all, Maastricht introduced the notion of the three pillars of the European Union. The first comprises an enlarged European Community, the second and third deal with foreign and security policy and justice and home affairs, respectively. The important feature of this arrangement from our perspective is that in the last two areas the mode of operation is essentially intergovernmental and the ECJ has no inbuilt jurisdiction. Pressure to adopt uniform policies is consequently much less. As such, this system invites variation, derogations and multi-tracks.[30]

Such variability is made even more likely by the way the levels and complexity of decision-making have increased, with a greater range of non-state actors being involved in the process. Thus there are not only new powers for

the European Parliament (Article 137 EC), including a highly complicated
co-decision procedure (Article 189b EC),[31] but also a new advisory Committee of the Regions involving unspecified subnational units (Article 198a EC)
and the possibility of semi-corporatist arrangements involving the Commission in dialogue with labour and management when drafting social policy
(Annex I, Protocol 14, Articles 3 and 4 EC). Such groups play an increasingly
important role within the comitology process in any case. Indeed, there are
now over 3,000 interest groups and a 100 regional offices based in Brussels. As analysts of the EU who take a multilevel governance approach have
stressed, these developments are eroding state sovereignty without creating
a European superstate with its own internal hierarchy (cf. Schmitter's contribution in Marks, Scharpf, et al. 1996). Rather, function and territory have
begun to pull apart, with a variety of authorities operating at different levels –
from sub- to supranational – in each domain. These are not hierarchically
ordered with exclusive control over specific areas of policy. They overlap and
are involved in continuous negotiation with each other, often in somewhat
informal fora.[32]

This increasingly complex configuration of sovereign power has profound implications for the EU's democratic deficit in the strict sense of the
term. The European Parliament and Court have a shared federal vocation,
and tend to buttress each other's claims. Thus the ECJ has seen enhanced
legislative powers for the Parliament as augmenting its own democratic
legitimacy and has staunchly defended its prerogatives.[33] Likewise, the
Parliament has tried to take a lead in bypassing the intergovernmental
process and suggesting the enactment of a European Constitution jointly
with the national parliaments.[34] These attempts have not gone unchallenged, however. The amended TEC did strengthen the European Parliament in certain respects. In addition to increased powers, most notably
the co-decision procedure (Article 189b EC), member state nationals were
bestowed the right to vote and stand in European elections on the basis of
residence alone as part of the new status of citizen of the Union (Article
8b EC), and 'political parties at European level' were solemnly declared
to be 'important as a factor for integration within the Union' that 'contribute to forming a European awareness and to expressing the political will
of the citizens of the Union' (Article 138a EC). Yet there has been little
popular enthusiasm for these developments and some active antagonism.
Far from being steps towards a pan-European political system,[35] uptake
of European political rights remains significantly lower than in national
elections. When asked in a recent poll how they describe themselves: by
nationality only, nationality and European, European and nationality, or
European, respondents divided 45 per cent, 40 per cent, 6 per cent and
5 per cent, respectively (Eurobarometer Report No. 48, March 1998). Thus
there is little evidence of a European demos or a shared political culture.

The difficulties referenda ratifying Maastricht experienced in France and Denmark have been interpreted by some as indicating a popular reaction against further European integration, although the influence of purely domestic political factors on voters makes this hard to assess. More unequivocal was the challenge thrown up by the German Federal Constitutional Court in its judgement in the *Brunner* case. This decision not only disputed the ECJ's competence-competence in adjudicating on the applicability of European law but also argued that popular sovereignty within Europe was exercised primarily through national parliaments rather than the European Parliament because there was no European people.[36] The 'no demos' thesis has haunted discussion of the EU's democratic deficit ever since. A number of commentators have criticised a perceived volkish reasoning behind the German Court's argument.[37] While this interpretation is open to dispute, it is certainly true that national elections give member state citizens only limited control over European developments. The consociational decision-making of the Council of Ministers and IGCs manifest all the democratic shortcomings critics have levelled at that system in domestic arenas: namely, elitism, conservatism and the stifling of dissent and new voices. However, most commentators accept one cannot take a unified European demos for granted, and that European political institutions lack legitimacy as a result (Chryssochoou 1996). There is now growing agreement on the need to talk of dual or even multiple citizenship, reflecting our various political allegiances and membership of a variety of demoi – territorial, cultural and functional – with little congruence between them (Weiler 1996).

The above suggests that the liberal democratic model of the EU has succumbed to all three aspects of the democratic deficit.[38] Instead of a constitutional consensus, we have a number of competing and overlapping constitutional traditions. Instead of a federal organisation of sovereignty, we have an emerging multilevel mode of governance involving a mix and dispersal of sovereign powers over a number of areas. Instead of a unified democratic system based on a uniform citizenship of the union, we have multiple demoi operating at different levels and kinds of political aggregation. So far, commentators have been inclined to regard this picture as a mess, castigating the post-Maastricht settlement for producing 'a Europe of bits and pieces' (Curtin 1993), that Amsterdam confirmed instead of remedying. And from a liberal democratic perspective, it is messy. By contrast, democratic liberalism finds this picture more congenial.

III. DEMOCRATIC LIBERALISM

Democratic liberalism harks back to a pre-liberal conception of constitutionalism that identified the constitution with the social composition and form of government of the polity (Bellamy 1996b). Much as we associate a person's physical health with his or her bodily constitution and regard a fit individual as someone with a balanced diet and regimen, so a healthy body politic was attributed to a political system capable of bringing its various constituent social groups into equilibrium with each other. The aim was to disperse power so as to encourage a process of controlled political conflict and deliberation that ensured the various social classes both checked and ultimately cooperated with each other, moving them thereby to construct and pursue the public good rather than narrow sectional interests.

As Quentin Skinner (1998) and Philip Pettit (1997) have shown, the heart of the republican approach lies in a different conception of freedom to the liberal's. Liberty is seen as a civic achievement rather than a natural attribute. It results from preventing arbitrary domination rather than an absence of interference tout court. Domination denotes a capacity to intentionally control and diminish an agent's realm of choice, either overtly through various explicit forms of restraint or obstruction, or covertly by more subtle forms of manipulation and influence. Arbitrariness rests in the power to exert domination at whim, and without reference to the interests or ideas of those over whom it is exercised. Pettit notes that an absence of interference can be consistent with the presence of domination. Those with such power may simply choose not to wield it. Social relations will be adversely affected nonetheless. Likewise, seeking to reduce interference may in given contexts be compatible with leaving certain agents or agencies with considerable power over others. For example, attempts to reduce the arbitrary hold men have traditionally exerted over women in marriage have been challenged on the grounds that they are too intrusive and themselves involve a greater degree of interference. Similar arguments have been used against laws to protect employees from unscrupulous employers. Even social liberals, such as L. T. Hobhouse (1964 [1911], 71), accept that the onus of proof rests on the proponents of state intervention to show that less interference is thereby created overall. Republicans, by contrast, see debate about the legitimacy of interference per se as misconceived. They concentrate on providing a non-dominating environment where citizens can lead secure lives, plan ahead, and live on a basis of mutual respect – conditions which may require intervention (Sunstein 1993).

This view of liberty shapes the republicans' distinctive linkage of the rule of law with the distribution of power and democracy. Instead of the constitution being a precondition for politics, political debate becomes the medium through which a polity constitutes itself. This occurs not just in exceptional, founding constitutional moments, but continuously as part of an evolving process of mutual recognition. Domination and arbitrary power involve more than an infringement of the formal rule of law espoused by liberals. It is entirely possible to promote general rules based on whim or self-interest and that entails a gross curtailment of people's freedom of action. The generality and universality requirements can also seem themselves arbitrary if employed to disqualify special rules that refer to properties that apply to only some groups – as when maternity leave for women or affirmative action policies are accused of being discriminatory, or when such considerations are used to block any form of regulation which might seek to focus on particular contexts or outcomes (Hayek 1960). Such formal criteria appear particularly inadequate at tackling structural forms of domination, where discrimination and selective blindness have been built into the institutions, norms, social and economic relations, and procedures within which the rules are framed.

Contemporary liberal jurists try and get around these difficulties by adopting a more substantive view of the rule of law, identifying it with the upholding of rights by an independent judiciary. As we noted, this approach proves problematic. A political constitutionalism takes a different tack. Justice becomes identified with the process of politics. Political mechanisms not only ensure all are subject to the laws and that no one can be judge in their own case – the traditional tasks of the separation of powers – but also that the laws connect with the understandings and activities of those to whom they are to apply – the side benefit of dispersing power so that more people have a say in its enactment. *Audi alteram partem* forms the watchword of legal fairness, not the formal or substantive properties liberals associate with the law (Pettit 1997, 189; see also Hampshire 1991, 20/1).

'Hearing the other side' within a pluralist polity implies respecting that people can be reasonably led to incommensurable and incompatible understandings of values and interests, and seeing the need to engage with them in terms they can accept. This criterion places constraints on both the procedures and the outcomes of the political process (Gutmann and Thompson 1996, 57; Cohen 1996, 100–1; Benhabib 1996b). It obliges people to drop purely self-referential or self-interested reasoning and to look for considerations others can find compelling, thereby ruling out arguments that fail to treat all as of equal moral worth. Political actors must strive for common ground through mutually acceptable modifications leading to a fair compromise.

Political compromise takes the place of a pre-political consensus, for the clashes of principle and preferences associated with pluralism preclude substantive consensual agreement.[39] How such compromises are to be achieved, and what counts as a fair hearing, depends on the issue and the character of the groups debating it. Where the clash concerns divergent preferences, then a fair compromise is likely to be achieved through splitting the difference or some form of barter. Here fairness makes the proportionate weighting of preferences appropriate. For the political equality espoused by democrats would be violated in cases where a majority vote meant that the preferences of a group that constituted two-thirds of the population always held sway, and those of the remaining third never got a look in. But the character of the compromise is different in matters of principle. Here the object will be to ensure equal consideration of the content and intrinsic importance of different values for particular groups of people, so that they seek solutions that are acceptable to a variety of different points of view. Instead of bargaining, participants in this sort of dispute negotiate and argue. In the case of bargained compromises, preferences can be taken as exogenous to the system and democracy seen in largely instrumental terms. A negotiated compromise involves a more deliberative model of democracy, that leads to preferences being shaped and ranked endogenously through the democratic process itself as otherwise inaccessible information regarding the range and intensity of the moral and material claims involved comes to light. Achieving this result requires that groups reach a sufficient threshold to have a voice that people take seriously. With very small groups, that may involve more than proportionate voting power, with others somewhat less will suffice.

The emphasis placed by the neo-republican approach on compromise should not be confused with the consensus model of democracy as identified by Arend Lijphart (1984). There are two important differences that distinguish it from both consociationalism and other forms of corporatist politics. First, as noted above, it does not take preferences as exogenous to the system, but considers democratic deliberation as a way of filtering and changing preferences (cf. on a similar line of argument, Mansbridge 1992). Second, whereas elites are central to consociational and standard corporatist politics (Lijphart 1977, 1984), they play a subordinate role in the deliberative model discussed here. As Jane Mansbridge argues, 'traditional corporatist models focus on external negotiation' (1992, 42). They assume elites act as mediators and brokers of compromises that can be translated into legislative measures. By contrast, 'more recent democratic corporatist models' stress 'internal negotiation, in which leaders also negotiate with members of their interest groups to reach agreements that members can accept as binding' (42). These models share the neo-republican desire to mobilise the 'moral resources' of deliberative democracy (cf. Offe and Preuß 1991) and make the 'quest for understanding' (Mansbridge 1992, 42) a central feature of the process of changing one's own and others' preferences in order to achieve fair compromises.[40]

Political system builders often overlook that different sorts of policies call for different kinds of compromise, and hence for a different quality of decision-making. Yet these considerations prove more crucial than functional efficiency when deciding the level at which decisions are to be made, how groups should be represented and the degree of autonomy particular bodies or sections of the community may claim. They are integral to a political constitutionalism, with its intimate linking of justice, the rule of law and the democratic dispersal and division of power. In the ancient ideal of mixed government, the favoured mechanism was to assign particular governmental functions to different social classes. In contemporary societies, the answer lies in multiplying the sites of decision-making power and the forms of representation employed for different purposes.

Within a more complex and differentiated social context, centralised and hierarchical ways of distributing power will be inadequate. Territorially based representation has to be supplemented by functional and cultural forms within particular sectors. Social and cultural interests are often territorially dispersed, or located below any specific territorial unit. Empowering certain groups may require their representation within a specific location, or across a given sector, or in the case of vertical cleavages, according to segment. Workplace democracy and parent governors at schools are examples of the first; corporatist representation of unions, employer organisations and professional associations of the second; consociational representation for given ethnic, linguistic, religious and cultural groups of the third. Such mechanisms allow minority opinions to have both a degree of autonomy within their own sphere combined with a say in collective decision-making. On the one hand, all groups (those asking for special consideration included) are obliged to consult the broader interests and concerns of society as a whole. On the other, these same mechanisms operate as checks and balances on the purely self-interested or partial exercise of power.

Democracy plays a central role in this system, protecting against arbitrary rule and enabling the educative engagement with others.[41] Interests are not simply advanced and aggregated, as in liberal accounts of the democratic process. They get related and subjected to the criticism of reasons, transforming politics into a forum of principle. In consequence, the need diminishes for a judicially monitored principled constitution to frame democracy. Judicial review can track whether reasoned debate occurs, but need not substitute for an absence of such deliberation. Democracy also operates within civil society as well as the state. Power is not simply devolved down in a hierarchical manner to lesser levels of the state, as in a standard federal system. It is dispersed among semiautonomous yet publicised private bodies. In this way, politics shapes rather than being simply shaped by social demands.

Republicanism has often been attacked for being impractical and undesirable. Critics contend the liberties of the ancients had to give way to those of the moderns as societies grew in scale and diversity, and the protection of individual rights came to override vain attempts to secure an elusive collective welfare. This picture proves historically and substantively flawed. Far from assuming homogeneity, the republican model was a response to social division and class conflict. As the American federalists appreciated, territorial size and social differentiation are positive aids rather than blocks to republican government, since a plurality of voices and power centres is conducive to deliberation and a process of mutual checking. Although groups were excluded in the past – notably women and slaves – the same holds for liberal democracy, and the difficulties of updating republicanism are less than those confronting liberalism. For the focus on domination and the relation of social to political power makes the active inclusion of all groups far more essential to the republican model than the liberal, with its traditional distrust of state interference in civil society. Nor is republicanism inimical to the acknowledgement of the standard liberal set of individual rights to freedom of expression, association, bodily integrity and the like. On the contrary, it compels recognition of them since they are integral to the whole process of political deliberation. It also allows the democratic balancing of their relative weight in relation both to each other and to additional values and interests depending on the issue and the people involved.

Far from aiming at or assuming the achievement of a monolithic general will or common good, the purpose of such deliberation is to construct a compromise that specifically acknowledges diversity in the ethical reasoning of agents. Dispersing power helps both the appropriate mix of voices to be heard and the peculiar circumstances of particular contexts to be taken into account. Not only can general rules can be tailored to a wide variety of objects and concerns, and their implementation and monitoring enacted to meet the special requirements of a given situation and constituency but also – and often more importantly – specific norms can be established to meet special circumstances and relevant differences, and collective decisions brokered among conflicting points of view.

This same quality facilitates the handling of complex problems. Complexity proves problematic for hierarchical forms of decision-making whenever a gap exists between public standards and their specification and monitoring. It arises where the actors involved are highly miscellaneous and there is a large degree of cognitive indeterminacy as to the causal relationships between them, and contestability as to how the various factors might be evaluated. These features prevent the decomposition of complex issues into their component parts because there will be no clearly demarcated ends or interests to be served. Environmental regulations typically display these characteristics, with people disputing both the costs and benefits and the cause and effects of pollution. In such cases, devolved deliberation can lead to a problem-solving approach that seeks a suitably integrated solution to the issue that tries to accommodate the multifarious perspectives of those concerned.

Thus a democratic liberalism simultaneously addresses all three of the deficits we identified above. For the democratic making of decisions (democratic deficit) is linked to the dispersion and devolution of power to provide an appropriate mix of social forces and levels of governance (federal deficit), with both being part and parcel of a political constitution that unites law, efficacy and legitimacy (constitutional deficit). It remains to see how suited it is to the EU.

IV. THE DEMOCRATIC CONSTITUTION OF EUROPE

The republican model offers a normatively appealing and empirically plausible response to all three dimensions of the EU's democratic deficit.[42] At the constitutional level, an institutional space needs to be created where those bodies delegated with the task of upholding national constitutional values may enter into dialogue with each other to resolve disputes over competences and clashes of values. Joseph Weiler has suggested that a European Constitutional Council comprising members of the national constitutional courts or their equivalents might serve this purpose (Weiler 1996, 120–1). While welcoming this idea, we would modify it in two respects. First, Weiler fears challenges by constitutional courts to the supremacy of European law and the competence-competence of the ECJ threaten the legal integrity of the Union. He likens the potential standoff between the two to one of Mutual Assured Destruction. We believe he goes too far. The absolute supremacy of Community law over domestic constitutional provisions has never been accepted by all national supreme courts. They have acknowledged the authority of Community law for reasons internal to the national legal order rather than, as the ECJ argues, because of its intrinsic Supremacy, and have distinguished between alterations to basic principles of the national constitution and the transfer of certain powers. As Neil MacCormick has observed, this analysis suggests a pluralistic and interactive picture of legal systems might be a more appropriate frame of analysis for the relationship of EC to national law than a monistic and hierarchical one (MacCormick 1995). From this perspective, the ECJ need not assert the Supremacy of any given set of laws over others but merely seek mutual accommodations in areas of friction.

Examples of this approach already exist in some areas. In his examination of the effect of European integration on private law, Christian Joerges notes how European regulations give recognition to the interests and concerns of non-nationals within an interdependent economic order, but that decentralised fine-tuning by national courts enables the accommodation of the different standards and safeguards provided by the legal systems of the member states (Joerges 1997). For example, the ECJ's 1990 decision in *GB-Inno-BM*,[43] when it ruled that Luxembourg's prohibition of leaflets advertising price reductions by a Belgian supermarket restricted the rights of consumers and traders, was a response to a situation in which Luxembourg citizens habitually cross-border shop rather than an assertion of the supremacy of European economic law. By contrast, the 1995 decision in *Alpine*

Investments,[44] upholding Dutch prohibitions against firms in Holland market-
ing commodities futures by cold-calling even in member states that had no
such prohibition, acknowledged that Dutch authorities had good reasons for
their regulations without suggesting that states such as Belgian should adopt
them too. Indeed, one might argue that the ECJ's desire to sidestep outright
confrontations with national constitutional courts in cases such as *Grogan*
indicates less a failure of nerve and more the acceptance of the pluralistic and
compromising approach we advocate.

This observation brings us to our second divergence from Weiler. Our
model does not insist on high levels of uniformity or normative consensus
as a test of the rule of law. It demands the more substantive assurance that
laws track the multifarious interests and values of those concerned. This
aim is met by a dispersal of power designed to achieve an appropriate mix
of voices instead of a formal separation of powers. It also suggests that
democratic fora may be better than judicial ones for debating such issues,
since they are likely to be more representative and possess greater popular
legitimacy. Democratic procedures should nonetheless be such as to ensure
that the debate is appropriate to the constitutional principles at stake. Thus,
only considerations that affirm and relate to the standing of the parties as free
and equal citizens should be admissible, and a supermajoritarian decision rule
might be necessary to foster such argumentation. A European Constitutional
Council need not be an exclusively judicial body, therefore. It could be more
like the French *Conseil d'État*.

Similar reasoning leads us to reject a standard federal organisation of sovereignty, whereby the residue of central power is devolved on a territorial basis
from the top down to smaller units. As we noted above, certain functions are
too dispersed, are carried out in highly divergent and changing circumstances,
and have such complex causes and effects, as to make either the centralised
monitoring or devising of general regulations inappropriate. Problems have to
be solved in a more contextual and ongoing manner that brings the relevant
parties together. The fora required will be as diverse as the issues under
consideration: from schools and hospitals to the workplace. Membership will
be similarly diverse and overlapping, including in these cases providers, cus-
tomers, those with specialized knowledge and other affected parties. As we
have indicated, the guiding principle of representation should be to ensure an
equitable and informed dialogue rather than equality per se. The result is that
purely self-interested bargaining becomes more difficult.

This picture fits well with multilevel governance approaches.[45] These
have stressed how public policy making within both the EU and the member
states is more fragmented and decentralised than is often supposed, involving a wide range of actors. In consequence, both state-centred perspectives
and supranational accounts prove inadequate. Neither the member states nor

Brussels can control the policy agenda. EU organisations lack the capacity to push a European view, with the Commission having to vie with the other EU bodies while being split into numerous competing Directorates and surrounded by a variety of specialist committees. Within this setup, purely national interests also prove hard to push, partly because the complexity of the issues often makes it unclear where these lie, and partly because they have to compete for a voice with policy experts and transnational interest groups.

There are encouraging signs of the emergence of a republican politics of compromise within this system. At the intergovernmental level, the EU has been characterised as a confederal consociation, for example. All four of Lijphart's criteria for a consociational system – grand coalition, segmental autonomy, proportionality and minority veto – have typified the deliberations of the Council of Ministers and negotiations surrounding the various treaties (Lijphart 1977; Chryssochoou 1998). These consociational mechanisms have had the aim and effect of rendering the integrative process consistent with the protection and, to some degree, the enhancement of national identities and interests. Moreover, the Council and Intergovernmental Conferences (IGCs) have divided legislative authority with the European Parliament and Commission. Paul Craig (1997) and Neil MacCormick (1997) have also given a republican rationale to this arrangement. They see it as embodying the notion of institutional balance typical of a mixed commonwealth that represents the various interests and constituencies involved within the EU far better than making the EP the principal legislative body could.

At the other end of the policy process, Joanne Scott (1998) has argued that the 'partnership' principle employed within Community structural funding can also be interpreted in republican terms. Partnership demands that Community development operations

> be established through close consultations between the Commission, the member state concerned and the competent authorities and bodies – including within the framework of each member state's national rules and current practices, the economic and social partners, designated by the member state at national, regional, local or other level with all parties acting as partners in pursuit of a common goal.[46]

She argues that partnership shares power across different levels of government, with the Community recognising that member states are not single units and that actors outside the official public sphere also merit a political voice. Thus, it 'does not involve the parcelling out of limited pockets of sovereignty, but a genuine pooling of sovereignty'. In other words, it ensures the mixing of voices that is distinctive to the democratic liberal approach, promoting dialogue by dividing power. At the same time, the example shows how international solutions to global problems can build on local initiatives.

Of course, the compromises of the present system are frequently based on bargaining rather than negotiation and reflect a modus vivendi that entrenches rather than challenges current inequalities of power and wealth. They are also brokered mainly by elites with an interest in maintaining the status quo. A genuine republican scheme for Europe must look at ways of enhancing popular influence and involvement in the policy process. Proposals for the associative democratic governance of Europe by Paul Hirst (1994, 139–41), Philippe Schmitter (1996), and Joshua Cohen and Charles Sabel attempt just this (1997). To realise the republican device of dispersed sovereignty and the participatory ethic that goes with it, they advocate a scheme of vouchers, redeemable against public funds that citizens can distribute to associations of their choice. These associations can constitute themselves on a variety of different bases, such as religion, ethnicity, profession or locality, and serve a range of purposes, from the provision of a particular service in a given place through to a more comprehensive range of services equivalent to a welfare system. The only limits on them are that they permit exit, are democratic in organisation and meet certain conditions of viability. Associationalism is a reformist strategy that does not supplant but supplements, and offers an alternative to, existing bureaucratic and market mechanisms. Though often seen as mutually exclusive, these last two actually go together. For the regulative failures of the market produce the need for ever more stringent control by a central bureaucracy, be it the member states or the EU, which in turn generates allocative inefficiencies that only the market seems able to remedy, thereby leading full circle. More dispersed decision-making that draws together local groups on issues such as regional development or schooling offers an alternative. The associational system publicises areas that liberalism treats as private without becoming part of a state bureaucracy or subject to centralised legislatures. Rather, knowledge is pooled within a number of confederal institutions that group associations and determine revenue-raising powers.

In this model, a deliberative account of democracy focused on the removal of domination is intrinsic to the way politics resolves both the constitutional and federal deficits. At the constitutional level, this conception of democracy welcomes a heterogeneity of viewpoints rather than shunning them as impossible to sum. It offers the best means for ensuring decisions are informed by relevant concerns and so avoid dominating those they affect. As a result, conflicts of values and interests can be confronted as problems to be resolved rather than as threats to the very nature of legal and political authority that one should try and avoid by deferring to a higher authority. At the federal level, it provides a rationale for creating multiple sites for decision-making that reflect the plurality of our political identities and the complexity and diversity of the problems requiring regulation.

This scheme aids a process of positive as well as negative integration. The removal of constraints requires positive changes too, of course, but these have often proved inimical to initiatives requiring greater collective action. For example, the developing social agenda of the EU, with its focus on the problems of exclusion, uneven economic development and employment opportunities, and the rights of workers and immigrants, seems far better characterised in terms of the removal of domination rather than of interference. So too does a more collaborative policy in the realm of security and home affairs. In other words, a more devolved and flexible political structure for the EU need not inhibit greater European integration. On the contrary, while the process may be more differentiated, greater legitimacy and efficacy may well render it deeper too.

CONCLUSION

The European Union's democratic deficit has often been attributed to the absence of a fully fledged liberal democratic and federal constitutional structure. We have challenged that analysis and argued that many of the legitimation problems within the EU stem from this very model of politics. Instead, we have advocated an alternative constitutional regime that draws inspiration from the republican tradition. We have argued that this approach fits the differentiated and non-statist character of European integration better than the liberal model can, while being more legitimate from a normative point of view. We do not say European constitutional development will take this path, merely that a future multinational European polity could be 'a Republic, if you can keep it'.[47]

NOTES

1. Research for this chapter was supported by an ESRC Research Grant on 'Sovereignty and Citizenship in a Mixed Polity' (R000222446). For helpful comments, we thank Tony Downes, Neil MacCormick, Jo Shaw, Jim Tully, Alex Warleigh, participants at the conference on 'Liberal Justice and Political Stability in Multinational Societies' organised by the Groupe de Recherche sur les Sociétés Plurinationales, McGill University, the TSER EURCIT Network Workshop in Reading, and seminars at the Universities of Essex, Brussels, Lisbon, Leeds and Paris.

2. Even Liberal Intergovernmentalists acknowledge that 'Europe stands ... before a series of ongoing constitutional debates', and that 'the focus in the future ... will be on the construction of a legitimate constitutional order for policy-making responsive

to the desires of national governments and their citizens' (Moravcsik and Nocolaïdis 1998, 34).

3. Our main interest is the 'normative' as opposed to the 'popular' or 'social' sense of legitimacy. For these distinctions see De Búrca (1996), Weale (1994, 1995), and Beetham and Lord (1998).

4. See for example the work of Cass Sunstein (1993) and Bruce Ackerman (1993) on how a republican perspective alters traditional liberal interpretations of the United States Constitution. The republican theory advocated here is more neo-Roman than 'civic humanist' (for this distinction, see Skinner 1998 and Pettit 1997). The neo-Roman version looks to Machiavelli and has a realist edge that is more welcoming to pluralism than the rather soggy communitarianism of the neo-Aristotelian civic humanist tradition (cf. Sandel 1996, and Pettit's review 1998). While the Aristotelian view involves a politics of virtue, the neo-Roman tradition focuses on the institutional side of republicanism.

5. Whereas Lijphart's famous classification, for example, looks at different ways the democratic ideal might be realised in different circumstances (e.g. 1977, 4; 1984, 21–3), our argument adds a further dimension and suggests that different institutional arrangements may require different normative foundations linked to different conceptions of democracy (Bellamy and Castiglione 2000).

6. See for example the French Declaration of the Rights of Man and the Citizen of 1789, especially Articles 1, 2, 4, 6, 14 and 16, and compare with Rawls (1971, 60).

7. The French Declaration of the Rights of Man and the Citizen of 1789 and Rawls (1971) once again provide exemplary instances of this mode of thinking.

8. We consider majoritarian and consensual forms of democracy to reflect the same liberal ideal, although, as we note below, certain institutional arrangements of consensual democracy may also be congruent with the neo-republican approach.

9. For a defence of this cosmopolitan approach, see Held (1995), and from a more strictly normative perspective, Pogge (1994), Beitz (1994) and Ferrajoli (1996). See also several of the contributions to Archibugi et al. (1998). In our own contribution to that volume and in other related essays (Bellamy and Castiglione 1997a, 1997b), we have explored the pros and contras of the cosmopolitan view. For a sceptical discussion of the effects of globalisation, see Hirst and Thompson (1996).

10. What follows draws on Zolo (1992).

11. Recently, Kenneth Armstrong and Jo Shaw (1998) have remarked on the tendency to simplify the integrative role of law by considering the 'legal order as a constitutional order' and by 'overstating ... the coherence of purpose achieved by the Court of Justice' (148). We use this now familiar story not to suggest that it is true (or that it fully reflects the complexities of the legal order as an 'autonomous institution'), but as a significant example of the liberal democratic interpretation of the EU. The reservations raised by Armstrong and Shaw to such an interpretation can only add to the doubts we have on the ability of the liberal democratic model to address the three deficits. Likewise, we do not wish to underplay the tensions between federal and intergovernmental visions of integration, nor the centripetal contribution made by the latter to this process (Weiler 1991). The ECJ's position is merely the most fully developed example of the liberal democratic vision of Europe. The resilience of such

a view is illustrated by Judge Mancini's recent plea for European statehood, while its 'strategic' (more than simply descriptive) import is evident from Weiler's reply: 'The most interesting issue in my eyes is not the what of this case for statehood, but the who and the how' (both in Mancini and Weiler 1998).

12. Case 26/62 *Van Gend en Loos v. Nederlandse Administratie der Belastingen* [1963] ECR 1.

13. Case 6/64 *Costa v. ENEL* [1964] ECR 585.

14. *Van Gend en Loos* and Case 294/83 *Parti Ecologiste 'Les Verts' v. European Parliament* [1986] ECR 1339.

15. The above-mentioned cases and successive interpretations of Article 177 EC.

16. Case 166/73 *Rheinmühlen-Düsseldorf v. Einfuhr- und Vorratstelle für Getreide und Futtermittel* [1974] ECR 33.

17. Case 48/71 *Commission v. Italy (Art Treasures II)* [1972] ECR 527.

18. *Commission v. Italy (Art Treasures II)*.

19. Case 11/70 *Internationale Handelsgesellschaft* ([1970]) ECR 1125 p. 1134.

20. Cases 6, 9/90 *Francovich v. Italian State (Francovich I)* [1991] ECR I-5357.

21. Case 138/79 *Roquette Frères v. Council* [1980] ECR 3333.

22. For classic statements, see Hoffmann (1982) and Moravcsik (1993, 1995). For more recent discussions of the interplay between legal and political integration processes, cf. Weiler (1991) and Wincott (1995).

23. For example German Federal Constitutional Court, *Internationale Handelsgesellschaft* [1974] 2 CMLR 549.

24. *Internationale Handelsgesellschaft* , Case 4/73 *Nold v. Commission* [1974] ECR 503; Case 374/87 *Orkem v. Commission* ECR [1989] ECR 3283.

25. See Case C-260/89 *ERT v. Dimotiki Etairia Piliroforissis* [1991] ECR I-2925 for this judgement.

26. Case C-159/90 *SPUC (Ireland) Ltd v. Grogan,* [1991] ECR I-4685.

27. On the limits of such attempts to extend rights from their original strict economic dimension to a broader constitutional meaning, see Armstrong (1998, 167–68).

28. Indeed, as Eleftheriadis (1998) notes, the Court's and its academic supporters' tendency to address the constitutional issue from a 'doctrinal' perspective simply begs the question of the 'normative justification of the new legal order' (269).

29. Opinion 2/94 Accession by the Community to the ECHR (28.3.1996). In this Opinion the Court put forward two separate reasons for rejecting accession. The first suggested that Article 235 EC was not an adequate ground, since it was 'part of an institutional system based on the principle of conferred powers' (i.e. from the member states). Jo Shaw (1996, 197) argues that the court was backtracking from the high ground taken in Opinion 1/91 Re the Draft Agreement on a European Economic Area [1991] ECR I-6079, where it seemed instead to assert unequivocally the autonomy of EC law. This may be true, but such political caution on the Court's part is tempered by the second reason adduced against accession. This reinforces Opinion 1/91 and considers the Community system as an established one, whose 'entry into a distinct international institutional system' would 'entail a substantial change'. Indeed, national courts could appeal to the same argument with equal force. On the complex interaction between European and national legal orders, within a worldwide network

of legal communications, see Maher (1998), who not only argues for a pluralistic analysis of their relationship, but also notes that when national systems assimilate European laws and directives, they must evaluate the latter's impact on 'the links between existing law and the social process being regulated' (246/7), if their own fundamental equilibrium as legal systems is not to be upset.

30. Amsterdam modified the system, removing immigration and asylum policy from the renamed third pillar to the first, suggesting the Union structure remains fluid. Britain, Ireland and Denmark in any case obtained opt-outs (Article 73Q).

31. Extended at Amsterdam, but often to areas where unanimity rather than QMV operates in the Council.

32. For a discussion of the interplay between formal and informal aspects of the decision-making process, with particular reference to the role of subnational authorities, cf. Bomberg and Peterson, who, on a more general note conclude that 'it is striking how little the EU acts to iron out national differences' (1998, 235).

33. Case C-70/88 *Parliament v. Council* (Chernobyl) [1990] ECR I-2041, Article 173 EC).

34. OJ 1994 C61/155.

35. Simon Hix (1995), for instance, suggests that the development of a transnational party system at the European level is hindered by the present institutional structure of the Union, and by the poor understanding that political and other institutional actors have of the role that modern parties can play in the legitimation of the EU. His suggestions, though rather minimalist, can perhaps be better accommodated by the kind of neo-republican approach outlined below.

36. *Brunner* [1994] 1 CMLR 57 at 87.

37. See the debate between Grimm (1995) and Weiler (1995).

38. Symptomatic aspects of the inability of the present model of politics to go beyond a superficial treatment of the various features of the 'democratic deficit' have been illustrated by Hix (1995) in relation to the public sphere, Norris (1997) in relation to representation, Laffan (1996) in relation to the affective dimension of integration, Lodge (1994) in relation to problems of transparency and Geddes (1995) in relation to immigration and third-country nationals. Not all these authors may agree with the thrust of our critique, but their analyses aptly illustrate our reservations.

39. What follows draws on Bellamy and Hollis (1999).

40. Consociational democracies have traditionally been seen as non-homogenous societies in which the principle of unified sovereignty nonetheless applies. Our model, instead, aims to address the issue of a polity where sovereignty is dispersed both vertically and horizontally. For a brief discussion of this point, see Bellamy and Castiglione (1997b, 441–45).

41. Pettit (1997, 30) and Skinner (1998, 74 n. 38) stress the first benefit but regard the second as a civic humanist rather than a neo-Roman concern, which smacks dangerously of 'positive' liberty. Putting history to one side, substantively we do not believe a 'weak' positive appreciation of the virtues of participation can be totally excised from republicanism.

42. J. Habermas (1996a, esp. chap. 7 and Appendix II; and 1996b) claims there is a middle way between republicanism and liberalism, which he applies to the EU.

However, he conflates republicanism with the contemporary communitarianism of Michael Sandel and Charles Taylor. These theories lack the emphasis on social conflict and liberty as non-domination that characterise the neo-republicanism of our account. See Pettit's review of Sandel (Pettit 1998). As a consequence of Habermas's failure to see this difference, the deliberative aspect of his thesis is highly idealised; while the increasingly prominent neo-Kantian features of his position, with their emphasis on rights-based constitutionalism, place him firmly, or so we maintain, in the liberal democratic camp.

43. Case 362/88 *GB-INNO – BM v. Conféderation du commerce luxembourgeois* [1990] ECR I-667.

44. Case C-384-93 *Alpine Investments BV v. Minister van Financièn* [1995] ECR I-1141.

45. For an overview, see Marks, Hooghe, and Blank (1996). We have also drawn inspiration from Philippe Schmitter's contributions to Marks, Scharpf, et al. (1996).

46. Council Regulation 2081/93 OJ 1993 L193/5, Article 4(1), cited Scott (1998, 181).

47. This phrase is attributed to Benjamin Franklin, who is said to have uttered it in response to an inquiry when leaving the Philadelphia Convention as to what type of regime had been agreed upon.

Part II

RETHINKING SOVEREIGNTY

Chapter 4

Building the Union

The Nature of Sovereignty in the Political Architecture of Europe

Richard Bellamy and Dario Castiglione

The alleged crisis of the nation state is a commonplace among many writers on Europe. The arguments for this thesis are all too familiar. The related processes of globalisation and social differentiation have undermined the state's claims to sovereignty. It neither controls the most important decisions in the economy or defence, nor expresses a common identity capable of sustaining a shared sense of justice and a commitment to the collective good. The future lies with new forms of political and social order that take us below and beyond the sovereign nation state, to regional and global blocs regulated by a cosmopolitan legal system based on individual human rights. So far as Europe is concerned, imperatives of both a functional and a normative nature impel the creation of an ever closer Union.

We believe these reports of the nation state's demise to be exaggerated. The impact of global forces and the associated pressures towards greater social individuation have been far from uniform, and the normative claims of national cultures and group identities show few signs of diminishing. The capacity of the nation state to act as the primary locus of administrative, legal and political power and authority may have been weakened but not in ways that necessarily point in a cosmopolitan direction. Rather, both the allegiances of citizens and their forms of economic, social and political interaction, cooperation and organisation have become a complex mixture of the subnational, national and supranational. Instead of convergence on a common normative framework and a single set of institutions, such a highly differentiated social system is characterised by numerous subsystems each governed by its own rules and practices.

Sovereignty does not lose its relevance in such a situation. If anything, the need for authoritative mechanisms capable of mediating between diverse values and interests increases rather than diminishes. However, sovereignty does need to be reconfigurated to reflect the competing attachments and norms emanating from the various spheres of people's lives, and the complexities of the relationships that exist between them. If politics is defined by the questions of who gets what, when, where and how, then the answers increasingly must be in the plural – different people, in different ways and employing different criteria according to the context and the good concerned. That suggests that sovereignty will also be plural, because more dispersed, with different persons or bodies having the power to decide in different circumstances, without there necessarily being any single, hierarchical system of decision-making.

In what follows, we shall pursue this notion of a pluralist conception of sovereignty as a way of conceiving the interaction between the various actors within the European Union. On this understanding, the member states, citizens, regions, the various Community institutions and so on each represents a semiautonomous component of a far-from-homogenous political system. They interact in different ways, respond to different sorts of problem and represent different constituencies. Drawing on our earlier work in this field (1996b, 1997a, 1997b), we shall characterise the resulting mixed polity in terms of a combination of the normative and empirical elements to be found in cosmopolitan and communitarian political moralities. Each of these broad schools of thought offers a particular model of the political architecture for Europe, involving different understandings of sovereignty and legitimacy. Whereas the first favours federal arrangements of various kinds, the second emphasises the centrality of the component nation states. Sections 1 and 2 examine each of these schools respectively, noting that both contain a range of positions some of which are more compatible with those from the alternative camp than others. Section 3 presents a view of Europe as a mixed commonwealth which draws on those more complementary elements in a manner we dub cosmopolitan communitarianism. The resulting amalgam may be more bricolage than grand architectonic design, but none the worse for that.

1. FEDERAL ARCHITECTURE

Supporters of various federal arrangements share the fundamental intuition that material and ideal developments since World War II have severed the historical connection between political legitimacy and collective self-determination on the one hand, and identification with a unitary state, defined by its territorial borders and a high degree of cultural and linguistic homogeneity, on the other. To differing degrees, they accept that national and state units will, and should, retain some capacity for autonomous self-organisation. But they believe that the political and legal structure of the new European polity must rest on a number of key centralised institutions and be based on principles of rights, justice and the rule of law of a fairly universalistic nature. It is this two-level structure of the polity that makes it a federation, even though the fundamental legitimacy of this arrangement lies in the values and efficacy of the centralised level.

There are two versions of federalism: a more conventional view centred on a federal state, and a more philosophical position that sees federalism in terms of a set of legal principles that take us beyond notions of the state. The more traditional understanding takes federalism to be both a form and a principle of state organisation. The nation state (even in the idiosyncratic form of the United Kingdom) traditionally developed as a unitary and highly centralised polity, where powers remained under the strict control of the central authorities and were only devolved for administrative and functional reasons. Federal states, by contrast, offered a more divided model of sovereignty and the representation of interests, expressed in the idea of dual citizenship. The federal model seemed better adapted to conditions of cultural and linguistic diversity, or situations where for either historical or geographical reasons there was no great homogeneity within the state. Historically, federalism was also conceived as a vertical form of checks and balances, which by dividing the legislature against itself would ensure the balanced and diffuse representation of views and interests as well as the reciprocal control and limitation of local and centralised powers. Because of its essentially dual nature, the political significance of federalism has varied according to historical circumstances. Demands for state federalism have played an important part in processes of state consolidation, as in the formation of the United States and in present-day Europe, but have also been instrumental to the disaggregation of more unitarian polities, as with the introduction of federal structures in Germany and Spain, and demands for devolution in Britain and Italy.

This view of federalism does not imply a denial of the centrality of state formations in contemporary politics (i.e. a congruence of territory and competences, supported by a monopoly of force in the hands of legally established authorities). Nor does it doubt that sovereignty is an important attribute of political states. It questions instead whether – given the increasingly interconnected nature of economies and, in the present nuclear age, of defence – single European nation states retain sufficient power and authority to act effectively as sovereign states. As Herman Heller suggested in the 1920s (Heller 1927, chap. 10), a federal Europe does not mean the abolition of state sovereignty itself, but its partial or total transference to a different level, deemed more capable of exercising it with efficacy.

In contemporary Europe, state federalism of this kind need not be justified on the purely negative ground of the nation state's loss of effective sovereignty. Less immediately instrumental reasons have also been advanced. After all, the ideals of peace and prosperity motivated the originators of the European movement, and continue to inspire many of the current proponents of a federal Europe.[1] There is no denying that during the last 200 years nationalist ideologies have greatly contributed to support and justify discrimination, oppression and power politics, within and outside Europe, with appalling human consequences. Supranationalism, on this view, promotes peace by breaking down the barriers between peoples and strengthening communication and reciprocal understanding between them. It builds on the more idealistic and universally oriented features of a common European culture (rationality, tolerance, diversity, civility, etc.), and treats national ties as atavistic throwbacks of less civilised times.

Parallel considerations link federalism to prosperity. Jean Monnet's functionalist method and strategy may be construed as an administrative and institutional response to the spontaneous development of a European civil society, characterised by the rapid increase in transnational exchanges and economic and cultural cooperation that have been instrumental in sustaining high levels of productivity and welfare distribution. According to this view, the piecemeal construction of the administrative and legal machinery (even more than the political structure) of a still-in-the-making European federal state has put into place the institutional framework needed to support the autonomous development of a European economy and society (Schmitter 1996, 228–29). This position involves a conception of the European Union as an inherently dynamic system, whose constitution, unlike those of fully established states, must both mirror and promote a process of continuous change and integration (Schuppert 1995, 331).

This model of Europe involves a new kind of cooperative federalism (Heun 1995, 185–87). This does not rest on a constitutionally fixed division of competences between the various levels of the federal structure but encourages the setting up of new formal and informal structures of cooperation both between the component states and between them and the federal state. This functionalist conception of federalism and its evolution envisages a more technocratic model of the state as a kind of enterprise association. It rests on an a-political vision of civil society as consisting primarily of economic and social activities that can be regulated and harmonised using legal and administrative procedures alone.[2]

There remains a fundamental ambiguity in the project of a European federal state. Its underlying ideals of peace and prosperity are presented as having universal value, making the European Union a model for others to imitate; but the very means by which peace and prosperity can be ensured – from economic competitiveness to border control – may in some cases imply the exclusion of others (poor nations and economic migrants) from their benefits. Indeed, state federalism in Europe may need the construction of a European identity with both its encompassing and exclusionary features. These particularist implications are rejected by the second, more cosmopolitan, interpretation of a federal Europe.

This version equates federalism with a radical criticism of state sovereignty. The principles underlying this position are the recognition of the dignity and basic liberties of the individual, and the fact that these fundamental rights apply generally and universally. According to the individualist understanding of these principles adopted by most cosmopolitans, obligations are either self-chosen or dependent on one's (interactional and/or institutional) relationships with other individuals.[3] No nation, or any other ascriptive community, has moral worth apart from that attaching to its individual members. All particular political allegiances are dissolved in a world community of human beings, with legitimate sovereignty meaning no more than the power to enact the principles of cosmopolitan justice. Most cosmopolitans contend, however, that it does not follow that the only legitimate political unit is a world state. Such a polity is as impracticable as it is inadvisable because of the threat that such a concentration of power might pose to individual liberty and rights (Pogge 1994; Archibugi 1995). The world 'society' advocated by cosmopolitans does not necessarily imply a concentration of sovereignty. On the contrary, it may best be served by the dispersion of sovereignty (hence their advocacy of federalism) beyond the traditional unit of the (nation) state, and by its dissolution as a form of ultimately personalised collective agency. Cosmopolitan federalism represents a challenge both to the nation state and to the idea of sovereignty itself.

The cosmopolitan view understands federalism not as a form of state, but mainly in juridical terms as 'law without a state' (Koopmans 1992, 1051). This position harks back to medieval constitutional theories, which distinguished jurisdiction (*jurisdictio*) from governance (*gubernaculum*) (MacIlwain 1958, chap. 4). Fundamental laws, rights and privileges, and the whole juridical apparatus were considered as the main brakes on the power of the political ruler. In international law, this line of argument was carried into the modern world by the jurisprudential tradition that understands the law of the nations (jus gentium) to be not the product of agreements between sovereign states, but the legal framework of an ideal *civitas maxima* within which sovereign states operate (Kelsen 1920, chap. 9; Ferrajoli 1995). Such a conception implies that the juridical order of the state is not a closed unit, and that its sovereignty is therefore subject to important limitations both in its internal and external dealings. From a cosmopolitan perspective, the problem has often been that the validity of the superior law lacked practical

application. This lacuna has now been partly addressed by the positivisation of human rights via various international conventions and declarations
and the establishment of international organisations, such as the UN and the
International Court of Justice, with the function of implementing them, even
if their capacity to do so remains highly limited in practice (Held 1995, chaps.
5 and 6; Ferrajoli 1996). These mechanisms go some way towards fulfilling
the cosmopolitan ideal, as expressed by Kant, of law-governed relationships both within the state, when this gives itself a 'civil constitution', and
between states, when they accept to be united in a 'lawful *federation* under
a commonly accepted international right' (Kant 1991, 90). As a result, in a
cosmopolitan federation, sovereignty – in its absolute sense, as the authority
to make the ultimate decision – is dissolved in the impersonality of the law.

Our reference to the medieval lineage of the modern cosmopolitan view
of the dissolution of state sovereignty has perhaps more than historical significance. Some of the institutional models favoured by cosmopolitans have
something in common with medieval pluralist structures of power, such as
the Holy Roman Empire. This entity was a 'political body constituted around
a juridical organization' (Winckler 1992, 19), where the issue of *plenitudo
potestatis* was a deeply contested one. The European Union may be considered the primary example of the 'return' of this model of federal Empire. Its
constitutionalisation mainly through the jurisprudence of the European Court
of Justice, the apparent dispersion of sovereignty because of the overlapping
competences at national and European level and the ambiguous nature (international or federal?) of the treaties that have given rise to the Union and the
Community – all these factors taken together have produced a complex polity
with an elaborate structure of administrative and legal powers, with no single
hierarchy and no overarching authority to which all other powers are clearly
accountable. Similarities with the premodern structure of the federal Empire
may end here, however, for cosmopolitans argue for the dissolution of state
sovereignty on normative grounds that reflect postnational, rather than supranational, developments (Ferry 1992). It is not just globalisation and social
differentiation that make the difference. Cosmopolitans see these processes
as providing the opportunities rather than the reasons for rejecting the moral
value of communitarian attachments. The crisis of the nation state has opened
up a whole number of other issues on which cosmopolitans contest traditional
conceptions of legal and political sovereignty.

The main cosmopolitan challenges concern ideas of democracy and political identity in the nation state. The postnational challenge to democracy has
two aspects to it. First, it rejects the idea that democracy is, in essence,
'people rule', pointing out that democratic sovereignty cannot be absolute,
since this would risk allowing democracy to abolish itself. Democracy must
rest on self-standing rights, which need constitutional entrenchment in order

to be protected against even democratic majorities. On the face of it, this seems a criticism of the majority principle as the main rule of democracy. In fact, it strikes at the core of democratic theory by questioning the legitimating role of the demos as both the constituent power and the basic unit on which the boundedness of the democratic community ultimately rests. By displacing the demos from its central position, cosmopolitans also undermine the idea of popular sovereignty. They substitute the former with the 'civil multitude',[4] and the latter with the more impersonal sovereignty of the law, which becomes the proper object of a cosmopolitan patriotism. From this point of view, the integration of Europe and the redistribution of popular sovereignty are theoretically unproblematic. Since cultural, national and similar ties are deemed morally insignificant, setting the boundaries and scope of political and administrative units are matters of practical convenience alone. Territorial contiguity and economic viability rather than a sense of belonging are the decisive factors (Pogge 1994).

The second aspect of the cosmopolitan challenge to traditional ideas of democracy is based on the recognition that in complex societies there is a disjunction between the political-administrative sphere, where decisions are taken, and the public sphere – in the Habermasian sense of those private and semiprivate associations that act in the public realm – where opinions are formed and debated (Ferry 1992, 148–66). In modern national democracies, representative institutions are meant to link the two spheres by rendering the executive power publicly accountable through the formal mechanisms of a parliamentary regime. This procedure has now become both technically difficult, due to the complexity of the issues and the number of decision-making levels involved, and politically problematic, because of the apparent inability of the political machinery to give expression to a common will in highly differentiated societies. Cosmopolitans maintain that this enervation of political representation can be offset by the diversification of the technical and the critical functions of the state. The latter is increasingly located in the informal institutions comprising the public sphere, such as the media, professional associations, charities and similar bodies. These are located in civil society and are said to exercise constant control over the political and administrative process. Together with the judicial power, they assume the dual function of legitimating political and administrative decisions, by exposing them to the test of public reason more than that of popular consent, and of limiting the power of the political and technocratic apparatuses by giving publicity to their actions. As a consequence, the main democratic deficit in the European Union, as presently structured, does not lie in the limited powers vested in the institutions of direct representation, but in the lack of a fully developed and integrated European society and public sphere.

The other main cosmopolitan challenge to nation-state sovereignty concerns the idea of political identity. Its questioning follows directly from the deconstruction of the demos into a 'civil multitude', with important consequences for citizenship and territoriality. In modern societies, the law already recognises that there are rights of the person, to which all are entitled irrespective of their affiliation to a particular political community. Citizenship rights, however, still have an exclusionary character. In increasingly globalised societies, so it is argued, such a distinction is not warranted (Turner 1997, esp. 15–17; Ferrajoli 1994). Obligations towards others' negative and positive rights should not be restricted by community or national boundaries. The globalisation of responsibility implies that state sovereignty be both broadened, by requiring the state to intervene beyond the confines of the immediate interests of its citizenry (as in, for example, the Bosnian crisis), and narrowed, by sanctioning a general and universal right to free movement and to take up residence. In a very limited sense, European citizenship, as imperfectly introduced by the Maastricht Treaty, goes some way towards bridging the gap between human and citizenship rights, which seems integral to the idea of communal identity, and which the emergence of nation states widened further.

On the basis of this criticism of the privileged status normally associated with membership of a political community, the very idea of political unity and the right of self-determination that goes with it may only be justified on instrumental grounds (Margalit and Raz 1990; Beitz 1994, 131–35), and be strictly within the legal framework of a cosmopolitan federation. This makes an entitlement to political self-determination for both ascriptive and voluntary groups conditional on a number of factors concerning, on the one hand, their relevance and encompassing nature, and on the other, the effects that self-determination may have on both groups' members and non-members. The territorial boundaries of these units cannot be assumed on simply historical or allegedly 'natural' grounds, they may need to be continuously negotiated and renegotiated. Cosmopolitan federalism, therefore, has no privileged place for national sovereignty in the political architecture of the European Union. Nor does it regard issues of national sovereignty as carrying special weight in the process of constitutionalisation of the European Union, thus denying that the nation states are (or should be) the *Herren der Verträge*.

This radical criticism of national sovereignty does not exclude that there may still be a place for nation states. According to at least one version of cosmopolitan federalism, a certain sociopolitical homogeneity between the political units comprising the federation is needed to prevent its transformation into a federal state.[5] In other words, states may remain relatively independent so long as they are sufficiently similar for centralised schemes of redistribution or mechanisms for mediating conflicts of legal norms to be unnecessary. In the European Union, however, that requirement could be met by autonomous regions, which may be better equipped to address local needs and demands, as much as by existing national states.

Cosmopolitan federalism may also support more radical solutions to the political architecture of the European Union by advocating either a vertical or a horizontal dispersion of sovereignty. The former solution (Held 1995; Pogge 1994) insists that what matters is the best level at which a decision-making unit can satisfy the conditions of maximum decentralisation (units that are as small as possible) and optimal centralisation (units that include as equals all persons significantly and legitimately affected by the relevant decisions). This vertical dispersion of sovereignty would have the added benefits of creating a multilayered structure, strengthening the vertical system of checks and balances and of the division of powers, and encouraging a cosmopolitan culture that favours multiple identifications. The horizontal dispersion of sovereignty[6] addresses a different aspect of the crisis of the nation state, by suggesting a model of social federalism that shifts the focus of decision-making processes from a territorially based to a socially based representation of interests. This is not as far-fetched a proposal as it may perhaps seem, for some features of European integration have de facto anticipated such a move. There is an obvious danger of corporatism, which could perhaps be offset by guaranteeing both a diffuse system of representation and a centralised dialogue based on strong normative criteria. This may have costs in terms of both political democracy and formal legitimacy, but would be aimed mainly at increasing social legitimacy in the European Union. The proposals for either a vertical or a horizontal dispersion of sovereignty, however, seem to be particularly vulnerable to the kind of criticisms more generally directed against the cosmopolitan position. Namely, that they are too abstract and disregard the open-textured nature of discussions about the substantive legitimacy of decision-making units.[7] To imagine the political architecture of the European Union without taking questions of political identity seriously may court serious danger. This, by contrast, is the starting point for models of political architecture based on a communitarian mode of argument.

2. NATION-BASED ARCHITECTURE

Current defences of nation states and of their sovereignty within the political architecture of the European Union rest on a belief in the importance and justifiability of collective forms of self-determination that are not simply seen as instrumental to individualist values and interests. Defenders of these positions place great weight on the communitarian argument that there are no disembedded selfs. Individuals need communities with which to identify, in

order both to make sense of their lives and to give substance to their autonomy of judgement and action. Communal self-determination is an important
part of this autonomy, but the kind of community needed and the form that
self-rule should take are still open questions to which many different answers
can be given. National sovereignty in Europe requires some arguing, therefore, even from a communitarian perspective.

The first set of arguments contests the claim that national sovereignty
has been eroded by globalisation.[8] Three main ripostes are offered. The first
suggests that globalists fail to recognise the important conceptual distinction
between the limitation and the transferral of sovereignty. The nation state's
incapacity to control economic and environmental dynamics, for instance,
results in a de facto limitation of the state's external sovereignty, without this
having any major legal or political implications that signify the transferral
of sovereignty to some other body. The second suggestion is that globalists
overrate the impact that globalisation has on the capacity of the nation state
to control socio-economic processes. The development of international and
intergovernmental – more than supranational – institutions should be seen as
attempts by nation states to keep their power, rather than as revealing a loss
of sovereignty. Nation statists, for example, can defend monetary unification
for much the same reasons that state federalists do, by suggesting that this is
the only way in which political communities can keep financial markets under
control. The all-important difference, which has significant implications for
institutional design, is that while federalists consider a central European bank
as part of a broadly federal structure, supporters of nation-state sovereignty
look on it as an interstate institution. The third criticism questions the globalists' view that the state has lost control over its territory. It suggests that,
although this may be the case in a number of areas involving economic regulation, capital circulation, information and technological developments, it is
not so in the crucial area of human mobility. Indeed, if anything, states in the
late twentieth century have a firmer grip over the great majority of their own
population; while there are no longer opportunities for mass migrations on the
scale of those that took place in the past up until World War I.

The second set of arguments in support of the nation state suggests that at
present the nation state is still the main collective entity capable of offering
a stable, encompassing and relevant identity to its members; of guaranteeing
recognition by other such collective bodies; and of providing the basic unity
necessary for the exercise of political self-determination.[9] The privileging of
the national dimension can be argued on strongly organic grounds, emphasising ethnic and racial identity, a narrow conception of past history, and a
commonality of language and culture. This clearly can give rise to extremely
unpleasant forms of nationalism. But some of the same elements can also be
integrated into a civic understanding of national identity that constructs it in

broadly voluntary terms and is respectful of the person as separate from the community.[10]

Civic communitarians, however, may find it difficult to demonstrate that nations should be privileged over other communities. In principle, there seems to be no particular reason why identity, recognition and self-determination should be better served by nations than by any other group or corporate body. This difficulty is not greatly different from that encountered by cosmopolitans in establishing the optimal level for the vertical distribution of sovereignty. Cosmopolitans argue for it in purely instrumental terms, so that there is always the possibility that a group within the political community may argue for sovereignty on certain matters to be moved either upwards or downwards. Similarly, civic communitarianism allows all kinds of groups to claim recognition, without there being any substantive principle on the basis of which to match processes of contextual identification with the allocation of sovereignty.[11] It would seem to follow that 'tribalism', as the universal attribute of human beings to join in groups, requires that self-determination be attached to any group claiming to have a common identity and demanding to be recognised by others. But the primacy of identity, though maintained in principle, is denied by civic communitarians in practice. Indeed most of them accept that political self-determination is an important precondition for sustaining identity itself and for guaranteeing its recognition. They conclude, therefore, that political personality should be granted only to those 'tribes' that are politically viable. In the modern world, this implies a number of conditions: territorial contiguity, to facilitate decision-making and its application; mutual trust, to guarantee social dealings with the minimum of force; the sense of being an active and lasting community, where everyone feels some direct or indirect involvement in its affairs; some shared belief and common identification, but neither too fixed nor based on ascriptive characteristics, so that they are congruent with social differentiation and do not undermine the territoriality condition; and a capacity to mix particular attachments with consideration for the community as a whole, both of which may be needed to sustain a sense of justice and solidarity. Of the many communities we inhabit, nations seem to approach such conditions best, and so are commonly regarded as the natural focus of political sovereignty.[12]

A number of other arguments are often given in support of maintaining national sovereignty as a central feature of the European Union. First, it is suggested that political and administrative uniformity bring with them social and cultural homogenisation. This would undermine the pluralism of traditions, institutional settings and styles of life for which Europe is often praised, and which is considered to be a vital ingredient in sustaining an autonomous civil society. Historically, this pluralism has been fostered by the multiplicity of nations that comprise Europe, and by a fundamental balance of power between them. This circumstance has prevented the establishment of a single empire on the European continent, maintaining instead a 'concert of nations'. Federal structures at the European level and a diminution of national self-rule would have a negative impact on social and cultural pluralism, posing a threat to individual and collective liberties (Thibaud 1992, 101–7).

Secondly, communitarians insist that democracy – which everyone agrees is one of the fundamental values on which the European Union ought to rest – needs to foster a sense of unity and a minimum of common identity in the people, so that everyone is prepared to accept the democratic game of majorities and minorities. Without this background assumption, there is no fundamental bond on which to rely, and no trust between the citizens that the rules of the game will be kept. Deep and irreconcilable divisions may set in, driving the democratic community apart and making democratic rules and institutions irrelevant.[13] As with arguments on nationality, so conceptions of the 'people' can be based on either organic (ethnic-historical-cultural) or artificial (civic-voluntary) constructions. However, the kinds of criticism of federal projects that these conceptions imply amount to the same thing. These projects are considered either unrealistic (state federalism), because there is no European demos, or anti-democratic (cosmopolitan federalism), because it would undermine democratic forms of legitimacy. It is also added that projects to construct a European demos contradict the original, and often repeated, aim of an 'ever closer Union of the *peoples* of Europe'.[14] Federalists seem to advocate a melting-pot strategy, something which was never intended, and which may turn out to be either impracticable or counterproductive for democracy both at the European and, indirectly, at the national level.

Thirdly, communitarians regard the idea of European citizenship with a certain suspicion. At one level, they consider the introduction of European citizenship alongside national citizenship as deeply problematic because of the conflict of allegiances that this may give rise to. In a fully integrated federal system, dual citizenship expresses the participation of the citizen in two different sets of institutions – one at the national and the other at the local level. Those conflicts that emerge from this vertical dispersion of sovereignty are conflicts between institutions. They do not concern the citizen directly, and do not test his or her allegiance to the political community, except in the extreme case of secession. But in a less integrated system, a plurality of citizenships would seem unworkable (Aron 1991–1992). This reason for the communitarians' rejection of multiple citizenship is compounded by a more fundamental objection they raise against cosmopolitanism. Communitarians emphasize that citizenship implies both rights and obligations and that the disjunction of the idea of citizenship from a community-based sense of solidarity and reciprocity would render citizenship highly problematic. A sense of commonalty and a minimum degree of homogeneity seem to be required for citizenship, therefore, as they were for the definition of the demos.

What all these arguments amount to is that political self-determination requires a community of fate. The European Union in its present form is at most an individualist based form of state. There do not seem to be the conditions for Europe itself to become a community of fate capable of sustaining democratic forms of government and principles of social citizenship. Such a development is both highly problematic and detrimental to social and cultural pluralism. Recent attempts at forging a European identity to sustain and justify greater integration have resulted in the shallow symbolism of self-celebration. The celebration of Europe per se, rather than its various national cultures and values, tends to be strikingly contentless (Thibaud 1992, 50). The famous fantasy bridges of the ill-fated new European banknotes are a good illustration of this phenomenon.

Communitarian models of the European Union agree that nation states are the *Herren der Verträge* and that the Union can at most be regarded as an 'association of states' (*Staatenverbund*), retaining full external sovereignty, but willing to pool it together in order either to coordinate their actions in matters of common interest or to increase their influence and bargaining power in international affairs. The transference of sovereignty from the states to the Union is limited and conditional and has no implications for internal sovereignty therefore; nor does it envisage a vertical dispersion of sovereignty. These sorts of considerations, for instance, motivated the German Constitutional Court's Maastricht judgement reaffirming its competence-competence at the national level.[15]

But there are other aspects of the political architecture of the Union on which communitarians diverge. On the whole, three main positions can be identified, arising out of different conceptions of the nature of the national community and of politics. The first is based on strongly organic conceptions of the nation and the people harking back to nationalist values and aspirations and demanding the scaling down of all federal-like institutions of the Union. At the core of this position is a deep suspicion of external influence and the conviction that any form of organic cooperation risks jeopardising the sovereignty of the nation. The second model, usually associated with British Eurosceptics and their 'hostility' to things European, mixes a traditional defence of national sovereignty on broadly nationalist grounds with the neoliberal conviction that economic matters escape politics and so should not be subject to state intervention but left to market mechanisms. In this scheme, the European Union is a form of technical-administrative association (*Zweckverband*),[16] whose power is narrowly limited to guaranteeing the existence and the functioning of a European-wide free market. There may be spillovers into other areas, but these should remain strictly subordinate to the primary technical and economic objective of the formation of a common market. The individualist 'universalism' of this position clashes with the rhetoric on the strengthening of the national economy, so that, echoing nineteenth-century traditions, economic individualism is harnessed to a would-be politics of national supremacy. In European terms, this means the acceptance of those supranational institutions and established cooperative procedures which ensure open and competitive markets, but the preservation of national sovereignty by limiting the functional expansion of supranational institutions and by keeping the veto power of the nation states.

While the previous two models appeal to a more nationalistic oriented communitarianism, the third is based on a civic-democratic (as opposed to a national) idea of sovereignty, which needs preserving both because it is crucial for self-determination and because of its formative and civilising role. As was suggested earlier, from such a perspective post- and supranational developments are seen as jeopardising the way in which democracy itself works – either because the new polity would lack the social preconditions for democratic decision-making or because it would not need democratic processes of will formation. Supporters of this position, however, accept that a 'natural' move towards a larger European polity is possible, and indeed to a certain degree auspicable, insofar as this is functional to propping up the 'civic' aspects of the nations of Europe. Ideas of civicness and civility are bridges to more universalist considerations, suggesting an alternative model to the 'individualist' European Union as it has so far been constructed. It substitutes 'voice' for 'exit' mechanisms, for example, and tries to preserve difference where homogeneity seems to set in (Thibaud 1992, 41). Civic nationalists are critical of those moves that expropriate nations of their external sovereignty, which in their view also undermine internal sovereignty and self-determination. But, in principle, it is not averse to a pulling together of external sovereignty in forms that preserve the democratic configuration of internal sovereignty itself.[17] They also depart from the nationalist version of communitarianism by accepting that the construction of the European Union is a two-way process not only of preserving national identities in Europe but also of making the nations of Europe more European. In their view, both processes need to be seen as contributing to keeping alive civic and democratic values and practices.

3. A MIXED COMMONWEALTH

Models of the European Union inspired by a mixture of communitarian and cosmopolitan arguments give a more positive gloss to the two-way transformation of national politics acknowledged by civic communitarians. They tend to combine a communitarian appreciation of the importance of identity politics within a civic and democratic setting, with the recognition that globalisation and supra- and postnational processes have already altered the structure of state sovereignty beyond what communitarians are prepared both to admit and to allow. In many respects, the gradual constitutionalisation of Europe that has so far occurred confirms the intuition at the root of this third group of models, that there is something fundamentally new, or, as is often said, sui generis, in the constitutional structure of the European Union, and that such novelty is captured by neither federal nor nation-based forms of political architecture. What distinguishes this third position is a certain support both for the open, piecemeal nature of the constitutionalisation process and for a constitutional structure that mixes national and federal elements. But, given the post-Maastricht crisis of confidence, supporters of this position have felt compelled to distance themselves from a purely functionalist justification of the piecemeal process and from the vacuity of the sui generis formula, both of which tend to ignore questions of legitimacy (Schmitter 1996, 21–22). Thus, there have recently been a number of attempts to give theoretical and institutional substance to the reconfiguration of sovereignty that comes with the construction of the European Union as a new form of polity.

A first consideration, captured by Duverger's suggestion that a neo-federalist structure is in the making in Europe (Duverger 1995), follows from the simple observation that the basic units of the new polity are fully formed nation states, commanding strong allegiances from their citizenries and with long-established histories, well-developed identities and rooted institutional traditions. The development of a federation-like structure at the European level cannot avoid confronting and accommodating the demands that come from these national dimensions of politics. In recognition of all this, Joseph Weiler has proposed a dual form of citizenship, as in traditional federal structures, but based on different sources of allegiance and identification (Weiler 1996, 113–16). This, he believes, can be achieved by decoupling the idea of citizenship at the European level from its elements of nationhood. The European demos, formed on the basis of universalistic values and principles, as implicit, for instance, in Habermas's idea of constitutional patriotism, should not supplant the national Demoi, but only act as a civilising force keeping under control the emotional drive and particularist focus of national citizenship. Such a dual form of citizenship and legitimacy would not simply require a vertical dispersion of sovereignty, but its more nuanced articulation, by giving to representation at national and European levels different functions, as perhaps suggested by a postnational vision of the European polity. It may also imply, as Neil MacCormick has argued, a vision of internal sovereignty in the European Union as dependent on distinct legal and political systems, the validity of whose actions is a function of coordination and cross-referencing, both between centre and periphery and between individual states (MacCormick 1993, 1996, 143–50). This takes us beyond the sovereign state, into a pluralist, and implicitly contested vision of sovereignty.

The polycentric polity that is therefore emerging is a definite departure from the nation state, mainly because it implies a dissociation of the traditional elements that come with state sovereignty: a unified system of authority and representation controlling all functions of governance over a given territory. The personalised character of traditional sovereignty, associated with the idea of a *government*, is substituted by a more diffuse, and hence impersonal, idea of multilayered *governance* (on this, see Hirst and Thompson 1996). The underlying logic of such a system of governance is nonetheless unclear. Domenico Majone has argued that while national institutions still maintain a semblance of unified control over the territory, they are complemented by European institutions, whose character is mainly regulatory, and which concern areas with increasing problems of externalities in decision-making (e.g. the economy and the environment).[18] Philippe Schmitter has noticed, however, that although the European level of governance is increasingly affecting all areas of policy making, a multiplicity of institutional and semi-institutional arrangements between different partners are encouraged (Schmitter 1996). This institutional flexibility tends to blur the lines of identity and jurisdiction and, according to Schmitter, may develop either towards a form of *consortium*, with nation states still in control of the areas and forms of cooperation, or towards a *condominium*, which implies a 'variation in both territorial and functional constituencies' (Schmitter 1996, 136).

In spite of the many differences of analysis, we wish to suggest that all these attempts agree on the basic intuition that the polity that is gradually emerging is a 'mixed commonwealth':[19] that is, a polity where the subjects of the constitution are not homogeneous, but a mixture of political agents sharing in the sovereignty of the polity under different titles. In practical terms, this implies that neither the nation states nor the citizens of the European Union are the sole, exclusive subjects of the constitution; but that they both, together with other new sociopolitical agents, may contribute to the democratic construction of a democratic Europe. It also implies that political means of mediation and reconciliation have a primary role, to which legal means and institutions need to be subordinated. For democratic deliberation has a capacity that legal mechanisms lack to build new allegiances and identities, and to negotiate workable compromises when a consensus on new forms of common life cannot be achieved (Bellamy 1995, 153–75).

Proponents of the 'mixed commonwealth' hypothesis also demonstrate a certain scepticism towards traditional views of political architecture. Both federal and nation-state versions presuppose a unified and systematic vision of the principles that should guide the construction of the European polity.[20]

But the political architecture of a mixed commonwealth clearly implies a mixture of principles, which must in part reflect the willingness of the political agents to redefine their identities and practices. Such a mixture is more likely to emerge and be accepted as legitimate as the result of time and as part of a process of selection of procedures and institutions by trial and error. What distinguishes this position from traditional functionalist justifications is the appreciation of the element of design, which is central to constitution-making processes that take on board the need for both formal and social legitimacy. It is this conception of the open-ended nature of the constituent process, which may look more like bricolage than political architecture, that for the time being unifies those who favour the construction of a mixed commonwealth.

The result may not have the symmetry and proportionality that come with the principles of classical architecture. It may perhaps lack the dynamism and sense of material, surfaces and space typical of modernism. But it is not necessarily going to be a hotchpotch of half-digested architectural idioms, like many postmodern buildings. Perhaps, more than structural architecture – whose image is conjured up by the 'pillars' of the Maastricht Treaty – urban development is a better metaphor for the construction of a mixed commonwealth. This may not involve as much careful planning, precise engineering and unity of conception than is thought necessary in creating a single building or a group of buildings. It may rather require that mixture of design and spontaneous development that is so much part of successful urban environments, where a plurality of groups and individuals dwell, and in which they satisfy their different needs and desires.

NOTES

1. On the role of ideals in the construction of the European Union, see Weiler (1995).

2. On the anti-political conception of civil society, see Taylor (1995, 215–20).

3. On various understandings of cosmopolitanism, see Pogge (1994, 89–98).

4. In Kantian terms, a 'civil multitude' is composed of cosmopolitan citizens – those, that is, that are bound by both the civil constitution and the idea of cosmopolitan right; see Kant (1991).

5. On the condition of 'political homogeneity', see Beaud (1995, 299–302).

6. On social federalism in Europe, see Telò (1994).

7. On the relationship between substantive legitimacy and the boundedness of the democratic community, see Weale (1995, 86–9).

8. This paragraph essentially summarises arguments found in Hirst and Thompson (1996).

9. A discussion of the distinction between identity, recognition and self-determination is found in Taylor (1994).

10. On a possible distinction between ethnic and liberal nationalism, see MacCormick (1996).

11. The indeterminacy of the communitarian argument on the natural unit for self-determination is evident in Walzer (1994a).

12. The arguments suggested at the end of this paragraph are based on Miller (1994); see also Miller (1995).

13. On the relationship between democracy and Demos, see Grimm (1995, 36–47); and Rusconi (1996).

14. On this contradiction, see Weiler (1996, 110–13).

15. For discussions of the judgement of the Federal Constitutional Court of Germany on Maastricht, MacCormick (1995); and Herdegen (1994).

16. On this form of association in Europe, see Winter (1995, 7–9).

17. In a state, or a political unit, *external* sovereignty is the power to act autonomously, while *internal* sovereignty means 'who' has the authority to make decision. On this distinction, see MacCormick (1995, 98–100); and Ferrajoli (1995, chap. 2).

18. For a discussion of the European polity as a 'regulatory state', see Majone (1994, 77–101, 1995). For a discussion of regulation and economic models in Europe, see Wilks (1996).

19. We owe this concept to Neil MacCormick.

20. For a defence of a fully coherent and cohesive system, see Curtin (1993).

Chapter 5

Sovereignty, Post-sovereignty and Pre-sovereignty

Three Models of the State, Democracy and Rights within the EU[1]

Richard Bellamy

Few would deny the established pattern of sovereign states faces practical and normative challenges. The capacity and right of existing states to exercise supreme authority within their territory, control access to it and speak for their citizens outside it have all become harder to sustain and justify. The related processes of globalisation and social differentiation have enhanced interconnectedness at an international level while producing greater heterogeneity at regional and local levels. These forces have reduced the ability of states either to frame independent socio-economic, foreign and defence policies, or to draw on or forge a national identity capable of sustaining an allegiance to the public good and the political institutions and decisions that define and uphold it. Increasingly, if to varying degrees and with many qualifications, citizens question not only the functional competence of states to provide for their economic and personal security but also the legitimacy of even democratic states to define and uphold, let alone override, their rights.

Though most people concede these problems exist, both academics and the general public debate their severity and implications. There are two main views. The first view contends that states either have retained their sovereignty but developed new strategies to defend it, or are in the process of transferring it to other bodies (e.g. Jackson 1999, 423; James 1999, 457; Sørensen 1999, 590). Either way, sovereignty remains central to the nature of politics. The second view argues that we both are and should be going beyond the sovereign nation state towards a postnational politics based on human rights (e.g. Held 1995, 135; Linklater 1998, 29, 32, 34, 50/51; Ferrajoli 1996; Habermas 1999, 118–20). Sovereign authority is being curtailed, both formally and in fact, without it passing to other bodies. A government that is bound by domestic and international human rights charters can no longer claim to be entitled to do whatever it wishes with its population, even if its policies are democratically sanctioned. If sovereignty is by definition inconsistent with such limitations, then these arrangements must entail its transcendence. For sovereignty has not been embodied in the law or the courts. Their authority is normative rather than political, grounded in justice rather than the command or force of those in power.

These two views involve contrasting perspectives on the relationship between the state, democracy and rights. The first, pro-sovereignty, view treats state and popular sovereignty as mutually dependent. People can only rule themselves if they, usually through their representatives, possess supreme authority within a given domain, albeit indirectly through controlling those who govern in their name. Consequently, any weakening of state sovereignty either undermines democracy, or involves a transfer of sovereign power elsewhere and so requires a parallel shift of democratic control. Meanwhile, rights only have standing through being enshrined in law by the sovereign body – which in a democracy is the legislature. Thus, state sovereignty defines the demos and their ability to rule, and popular sovereignty defines rights. By contrast, the second, post-sovereignty, view sees both forms of sovereignty as a potential threat to rights. State sovereignty can hinder humanitarian intervention against oppressive regimes, and popular sovereignty can produce tyrannous majorities. As a result, they have to be limited (and, in consequence, their claims undermined) by rights mechanisms, such as constitutional and international charters. On this account, state and popular sovereignty possess no intrinsic worth or legitimacy. They are only instrumentally valuable as a means for the protection and promotion of rights. Indeed, pre-political rights, which attach to individuals by virtue of their humanity, provide the very basis for politics. So, rights define both the polity, as a convenient functional unit for fostering rights, and democracy, through providing the rationale for the right to vote (e.g. Pogge 1994).

There is a certain symmetry about these two views. Both are premised on sovereignty being fundamentally political, supreme and agent or agency-based. Hence, if political sovereignty has not been defended or transferred it must have evaporated. This chapter disputes this common premise. Sovereignty and allegedly post-sovereignty views turn out to be two sides of the same coin. Neither the rule of persons nor the rule of law can be sustained without the other. Therefore, attempts to make one or other supreme will become locked in a vicious circle. Consequently, the contrast between sovereignty and post-sovereignty turns out to be overdrawn. Sovereign power never has been, nor indeed could be, purely political, in the sense of ruler-based. Sovereignty has always required normative recognition of some kind which both constrains and facilitates its exercise (Hart 1961, chaps. IV and VI). Law and rights standardly provide such a normative basis for political power. Yet, contrary to the claims of post-sovereigntists, sovereignty does not thereby dissolve but becomes vested in these fundamental norms and those charged with their interpretation and implementation. For rights can clash and may be subject to conflicting interpretations over their application to particular cases, so a 'supreme' court may have to exercise finality of decision of a direct or more indirect kind and rely on political authorities to back its decisions. These arrangements may tame sovereignty and reduce the opportunities for certain kinds of oppression, but they can also create new problems associated with weak governance and a lack of democratic accountability. Meanwhile, the normative basis of the law's sovereign authority remains contested, apparently resting more on might – the power to enforce a particular view – than consensus on the right. So, the transfer thesis errs through not recognising that political sovereignty is not self-sufficient and that legal norms alter its basis, manner of application and areas of competence, while the evaporation thesis is mistaken in its turn in denying that key elements of sovereign political power still persist, being both necessary to and unsettling the normative sovereignty of the law.

However, it would be mistaken to believe that some form of sovereignty is unavoidable. We are apt to forget how recent the doctrine of sovereignty is, originating only in the sixteenth and seventeenth centuries to buttress the novel claims of absolute monarchs. As such, it involved a conscious and, at the time, contentious and contested, critique of an alternative view that was concerned with the maintenance of a pre-sovereignty condition and a corresponding form of politics (for a useful historical account, see Franklin 1991). According to this republican theory, power was best distributed and shared rather than concentrated. So republicans advocated a mixed constitution, involving a balance of powers between different political institutions and sections of the community. The aim of these arrangements was to ensure no person or body had the capacity to act in an arbitrary manner. To the extent finality of decision existed in this setup, it was a systemic feature, requiring the cooperation of all relevant agents and agencies, rather than residing in any one of them. As a result, all collective decisions had to be negotiated by citizens or their representatives to show they were publicly justifiable and treated the values and interests of those they affect with equal concern and respect. So, the rule of law results from the rule of persons, but without invoking either the sovereign will of a *demos* or assuming consensus on a sovereign *Grundnorm*. Rather, its basis and safeguard lie in negotiated agreements between heterogeneous persons located within different levels and branches of government. Because no group or person is sovereign over any other, the tyranny of any minority or majority must give way to deliberation and the construction of laws that deal fairly with others. Within this scenario, therefore, democracy and rights finally come together.

In what follows, I shall defend both the theoretical coherence and the practical plausibility of the pre-sovereignty approach. Updated as a theory of 'mixed sovereignty', its division of sovereign power proves curiously suited to a world where conflicting claims to sovereignty abound. As debates about the character and future of the EU illustrate, this issue is of more than academic interest. The EU is seen by many as a test case for whether, and if so in what ways, state and popular sovereignty are being transformed. Proponents of the sovereignty view interpret the EU as either an intergovernmental organisation that allows its constituent states to maintain their prerogatives in new circumstances (e.g. Moravcsik 1993, 473) or a federal state in the making that shall ultimately take on the powers hitherto held by its members (e.g. Pinder 1994). By contrast, others see the EU as potentially a new kind of post-sovereign entity, which might regulate solely on the basis of rights (e.g. Linklater 1998, chap. 6), although left and right disagree over how far these rights are positive as well as negative. However, I shall argue that it also has many of the characteristics of the 'pre-' or 'mixed' sovereignty conception of a polity and that republican constitutional arrangements offer the most normatively attractive way to ensure its complex structures meet the twin demands stemming from democratic politics and legal rights (see too Bellamy and Castiglione 2000b).

I begin, in section 1, with an analysis of the relations between political and legal sovereignty that provides the framework for an assessment of the transformation from sovereignty to post-sovereignty in section 2. Both have drawbacks and advantages, while sharing a fundamental incoherence. Section 3 then outlines and defends the pre-sovereignty conception of the mixed constitution as the true alternative to a sovereignty-based political system. Throughout I will refer to developments within the EU to illustrate aspects of my argument.

1. THE DIALECTIC OF POLITICAL AND LEGAL SOVEREIGNTY

The rationale for sovereignty lies in the supposed need for some ultimate adjudicator of all conflict in a world where consensual agreement on the right and the good cannot be counted on. The sovereign is the agent or agency where the buck stops and a final decision gets made. The only alternative is said to be an anarchic state of war.[2] Therefore, the core element of sovereignty is the possession of 'supreme authority'. However, theorists from Bodin and Hobbes onwards have argued that to secure this supremacy sovereignty must be unlimited and hence in certain crucial respects 'absolute' and 'unitary' or 'indivisible' as well (Bodin 1992, 1–4, book 1 chap. 8). For a start, it is claimed the status cannot be partial. As Georg Sørensen has put it, sovereignty is like being married, you either possess this status or you do not, one can no more be a 75 per cent sovereign than 75 per cent married (1999, 593). Similarly, sovereignty cannot be shared or distributed, because then no one agent or agency will have finality of decision. Still, it need not involve total power in the sense of directly coordinating everything, an impossible task in a society of any size and complexity. Many tasks can be delegated and some left to semiautonomous authorities. All that sovereignty requires is that in the event of a clash of authorities the sovereign's decision prevails. In this respect, it can operate as a 'threshold concept' (Lee 1997, 241, 245).[3] Nevertheless, in a sovereign system power can only be devolved vertically and in a hierarchical manner. Delegated authorities, be they officials or agencies, remain under the control of the sovereign, who sets and can change their terms of reference, remove them from office and even abolish the position altogether. Likewise, the sovereign decides which areas can be governed by the autonomous decisions of individuals or private agencies. Even federal arrangements must leave finality of decision with a superior body at the centre. From this sovereignty perspective, a system based on a horizontal distribution of power is tantamount to anarchy, lacking coherence and consistency. Yet, as we will see, this is the very arrangement proposed by pre-sovereignty theorists.

Such supreme authority was traditionally associated with the political sovereignty of a ruler. However, a problem arises at this point, which brings us to the central dilemma surrounding the practice of sovereignty noted in the introduction. For it is doubtful that political sovereignty could be sustained or consistently exercised without the support of law, or law, contrary to Hobbes's and Austin's view (Hobbes 1991, 80), be reduced to the commands of the sovereign. Sovereignty must be de jure as well as de facto. The sheer political capacity of a government to exert power over a community, or of the populace – in the case of popular sovereignty – to assert their interests, will not ensure they are regularly obeyed or listened to. If only might decides who has the right to command, then unless an agent is so powerful as to be truly unassailable, their supremacy will always be subject to fluctuations in the prevailing balance of power. Moreover, an omnipotent authority would raise even more serious concerns. Any sovereign powerful enough to rule by might alone would have no incentive not to be so tyrannous as to make the uncertainty of a sovereignless world more preferable to the certainty of oppression.[4] So political sovereignty is legitimated and exercised through domestic and international law. Legal institutions establish the right of sovereigns to rule and systematise their ruling by embodying it within legal rules. However, if political sovereignty is constituted and regulated by law, its absoluteness, indivisibility and supremacy seem called into question. Political sovereignty appears to be limited, shared or even supplanted by legal sovereignty. Yet legal sovereignty in its turn seems compromised. For law, while a semiautonomous system, also needs political power in its turn to render it effective and legitimate, most typically within a democracy through the direct or indirect tacit and active consent of those to whom it applies. Thus, law and politics appear deeply intertwined. Each supports the other but in so doing seem caught in a vicious circle that challenges the very logic of sovereignty (for this intertwining of law and politics, see MacCormick 1995, 95–100; Loughlin 2000).

One attempt to unravel this dilemma is to distinguish the 'polity' and the 'regime' dimensions of sovereignty, treating the former as the primary, politically 'constitutive' element, and the latter as the secondary, legally 'regulative' aspect.[5] That way politics provides the basis and raw material for law. In this account, the polity dimension of sovereignty concerns where, over whom and by who power is exercised. In other words, it defines the functional and territorial 'spheres' where politics can operate, and the 'subjects' who rule or are ruled through the established political procedures within these spheres. As such, it involves both the internal exercise of power over and by subjects within certain domestic spheres, and the foreign employment of power to defend or extend the polity externally. The regime dimension of sovereignty concerns how and when power is exercised. It refers to the extent or 'scope' of politics, for example, whether it entails intervention and redistribution or simply regulation, and the 'styles' of politics, such as the type of electoral system, the form of democratic decision-making and so on. Regimes too are not only domestic, within a polity but also increasingly well-developed in foreign affairs between polities.

Following Georg Sørensen, we can align this distinction between 'polity' and 'regime' with a division between the 'constitutive' and 'regulative' rules of sovereignty (Sørensen 1999, 591–97). Constitutive rules define the aims, actors and possible moves within any activity, while regulative rules govern how such a constituted activity might be carried out. Thus, the constitutive rules of soccer differentiate it from rugby, and various regulative rules structure how soccer should be played. It is possible to change a regulative rule, like the off-side rule or the number of yellow cards needed to be sent off or suspended, without altering the constitutive rules either at all or so much that one effectively invents a new game. Yet, as the games analogy reveals, the distinction between the two is not hard and fast. Changes in the one have knock-on effects for the other, with modifications in the regulative rules often having the incremental effect of changing the game. Sørensen argues the constitutive elements of sovereignty consist of 'states with a delimited territory, a stable population, and a government', possessing 'constitutional independence' and operating in the context of the 'international society of states' (1999, 592/3). He claims this basic model has remained essentially unchanged since the seventeenth century. What has altered are the regulative rules, most particularly via the development of more extensive international regimes to regulate trade, security and human rights, most of which have internal implications for the domestic sovereignty of states as well as their external relations with each other (Sørensen 1999, 596–98). Even as closely integrated a regime as the European Union can still plausibly (if not uncontentiously) be seen as having sovereign states as its constitutive units, though he grants that this may turn out to be a case where alterations of the regulative rules ultimately undermine the sovereignty game (Sørensen 1999, 602–4).

This historical analysis provides an interesting interpretation of the supposed transition from sovereignty to post-sovereignty, examined in the next section, that apparently reconciles the primacy of political sovereignty with the growing role of a putative post-sovereign legal challenge to its constitutive supremacy. However, I believe it ultimately fails. Sørensen likens sovereign states to elements of an antecedent activity, such as driving cars, and regulative legal rules to the Highway Code (1999, 595). Thus, the political sovereignty of a territorially located *demos*, who make up the 'polity', is 'constitutive' of its own legal regulatory 'regime'. For the former is presupposed by, establishes and ultimately legitimates the latter. In this way, it appears one could have a sovereign political 'polity' which nonetheless provides its own limited legal 'regime'. Yet by what right does the *demos* possess such constitutive power? As Sørensen also notes, the external status of sovereign states rests on their mutual recognition and collective agreements as mediated by international law (1999, 593). Internally, too, constitutional norms identify and can reconfigure the right of any *demos* to rule. Think of the way excluded groups, women, workers, religious and ethnic minorities, came to be recognised as part of the *demos* (see Bellamy and Castiglione, 2004a). So regimes, both external and internal, are also constitutive – they provide the Hartian 'rules of recognition' or Kelsenian *Grundnorm* that authorise and facilitate the exercise of sovereign power (Hart 1961, chap. VI; MacCormick 1995, 98). Thus, the distinction between 'constitutive' and 'regulative' rules refers to elements of both the 'polity' and the 'regime', returning us once more to the vexed relations between de facto and de jure sovereignty, politics and law, democracy and rights, and the original dilemma of the competing claims of political and legal sovereign power.

2. FROM SOVEREIGNTY TO POST-SOVEREIGNTY

Taking the above analysis into account, the alleged shift from sovereignty to post-sovereignty can now be more fully described and assessed, and compared with an account of pre-sovereignty in the following section. A sovereignty-based system assumes an autonomous polity possessing an independent regime with a single supreme authority exercising finality of decision over all issues at the apex of a vertical and hierarchical distribution of power. Sovereignty so conceived is standardly thought to be fundamentally political, being exercised either by a single unelected ruler, or the people – usually through their elected representatives. Law is required to stabilise any regime, giving it the coherence and consistency needed for the efficient exercise of power, but its source must ultimately lie in the commands of the de facto ruler – be that a person or the people. Such power is said to possess three defining characteristics – it must be 'absolute', because independence cannot be qualified or limited, 'unitary', because it must apply to all matters and cannot be shared or divided, and 'supreme', because it must be final. As a result, sovereignty is linked to a territorial nation state as the only viable context for such power to be exercised. Only here can rulers claim a monopoly of decisional power over a given sphere and its subjects that admits of no higher or superior authority or limitation. The sovereignty of states and their rulers is even said to be self-constituting – deriving from their mutual recognition within the society of states.

Post-sovereignty theorists believe this account presents a relatively easy target, with both the absolute and unitary conditions having been so weakened as to have fatally weakened claims by any political agent or agency to supremacy of the requisite kind (for a good overview, see Held 1995, chaps. 5 and 6). With regard to absoluteness, I have already remarked how they can point out the ways law is semiautonomous from the state – constituting its very existence and establishing the norms and rules that define the rights and duties of states and their office holders towards their citizens and those of other states or none. The *Rechtsstaat* is not only domestic but international, with international law an explicitly non-state system of law. As a result, the constitutional independence of states has come to be regarded as 'absolute' only to the extent it meets certain formal and substantive conditions of legitimacy – otherwise there would be grounds for humanitarian intervention. International agreements and organisations have also reduced the autonomy of states to act in certain important spheres in ways that affect the 'unitary' condition. Though states and their representatives are the prime actors within organisations such as NATO, the WEU or the EU, their interactions and collaborations are so numerous and intense as to have profoundly modified their independence of action. Sovereignty has been to a degree 'pooled' or shared with other states and partly divided, with finality of decision over clashes with regard to certain economic, strategic and even social and civil policies passing to bodies such as the WTO, the UN or the European Court of Human Rights. Such pooling and dispersing of power is of course particularly intense in the European Union (see Wallace 1999, 503), but exists to a degree for almost all states. Finally, enhanced regional autonomy has increasingly challenged the hierarchical pattern of standard federal systems, pushing them closer to confederalism or consociationalism where shared decision-making is the norm in crucial or sensitive areas, with vetoes or opt-outs challenging 'finality' at the centre.

The pro-sovereignty theorist's fallback position in the face of these developments is to assert that ultimately states can always withdraw from such arrangements or choose not to comply. For example, though the Treaty on European Union has no formal provision for secession, it is generally granted that this possibility exists. It is this option that leads Sørensen to assert that though the regulative rules governing the normal exercise of sovereignty may have changed, the constitutive rules of sovereignty remain the existence of states with the de facto political capacity to act as supreme authorities (Sørensen 1999, 603). Yet, practically neither the one hegemonic economic and strategic superpower, the United States, nor pariah states, such as Libya or Iraq, can totally disengage and still act effectively or even, in the case of the latter, have their statehood respected. If sovereignty has not been totally eroded, therefore, even at the constitutive level it has been profoundly weakened and changed in character. In particular, states have to recognise the legal sovereignty exercised by various domestic and international courts, the supreme authority in certain areas of various international organs that they have created through their agreements, and a more general need to negotiate with other states, bodies, regions and even ordinary citizens in order to act.

Nonetheless, it remains true that, contrary to the claims of post-sovereignty theorists, sovereignty has not thereby passed away. For domestic and international courts, regulatory agencies, intergovernmental organisations and the like can all operate as supreme authorities in discreet areas without being either absolute or unitary. For example, the European Court of Human Rights is the ultimate forum for deciding whether the law of signatory states infringes the European Convention, but its manner of operation and competences are strictly circumscribed. In other words, though there has been a parcelling out of sovereign powers and changes in their mode of operation, this process has involved the piecemeal transfer and weakening of sovereignty, not its demise. The result has been a fragmentation of the comprehensive polity and associated regime typical of the nation state into a number of different policy or functional 'polities', each working at different levels of aggregation and with its own distinctive 'regime'.[6] This development reduces certain sorts of abuses associated with the concentration of sovereign power, with regulators and the courts promoting procedures and policies that can lead governments to take rights more seriously. It also means that law can be tailored to local preferences and circumstances. However, there are also drawbacks to this development. When there is a single and powerful locus of sovereignty the lines of responsibility are clearer; it is easier to prioritise policies and consider how they fit together, noting the ways tackling one issue in a certain way may facilitate or hinder efforts elsewhere; and delivery can be more effective through being more direct. The task of ensuring democratic accountability is also simplified, as is the process of collective deliberation among a people in order to negotiate an agreement on which public goods should be supported, by whom and why. In a dispersed system, there are more opportunities for free riding and compliance may be harder to monitor, while officials and politicians can find it easier to escape scrutiny and control.

In a recent essay, Jim Tully has noted three trends whereby many of the global economic and legal processes that are undermining or weakening state sovereignty have also damaged democratic government and the rule of law (Tully 2002, 204). The first trend arises from the manner international legal and regulatory regimes foster certain of the worst as well as the better features of global capitalism. They protect the rights underlying free trade but often in ways that disadvantage poorer countries and persons, especially as powerful states are usually in a position, as the prime enforcers of these regimes, to defect or fail to comply with measures that go against their interests. Even within advanced capitalist states, there has been an erosion of socio-economic and cultural rights. For these processes of global juridification rarely bring in their wake parallel mechanisms for maintaining democratic account-ability. Yet, democracy has been the prime mechanism whereby people have attempted to ensure that lawmakers and enforcers treat their views and interests on these issues with equal concern and respect. It has been through democratic contestation, for example, that women and workers won the vote and obtained important rights protecting them at home and in the workplace. Instead, power increasingly passes to democratically unaccountable bodies, such as international corporations and tribunals, technical regulatory authori-ties and so on.

The second trend refers to the ways the devolution of power within estab-lished states not only increases the opportunities for democratic self-gover-nance for regions and minority nations but also produces weaker political units that are unable to challenge the global pressures for economic deregula-tion, low taxation and flexible labour markets. As a result, there is a further reduction in the resources available for these political units to provide the public goods and services required to secure the well-being of their citizens. Education, health, the environment, and the infrastructure all suffer. All too often, what coercive power these small states do possess is dedicated largely to suppressing the social unrest and criminal behaviour associated with the growing inequality and poverty produced by indiscriminate policies of economic liberalisation.

Finally, the third trend concerns the growth of executive power and the decline of democratic deliberation and decision-making within traditional representative institutions. The growth of global regulatory regimes and intergovernmental organisations, on the one hand, and the privatisation of many public services or their contracting out to semiautonomous agencies and QUANGOs, on the other, has removed many areas of decision-making from adequate scrutiny by domestic legislatures. In any case, representatives remain too dependent on parties that, with the decline of mass membership, are ever more tools of the leadership, to wield much influence. By contrast, well-organised interest groups, media corporations and unelected experts are increasingly influential. Not surprisingly, citizens have become less attached to parties and more motivated by sectoral concerns and single causes, issues and campaigns. Some of these developments have been both beneficial and successful, contributing to the creation of transnational movements in areas such as the environment. But they also reflect a general privatising of political life and a move away from a concern with the public good and integral collective agreements.

The EU reflects both the positive and the negative aspects of this passage from sovereignty to post-sovereignty. Positively, European integration has promoted peace and prosperity between the member states, with increased interaction modifying national self-interest and fostering cooperation to tackle transnational problems such as cross-border pollution. The commitment to certain standards of liberal democracy has also bolstered the new democracies of Spain, Greece and Portugal, while often prompting progressive reforms within the more established democracies in areas such as the equal treatment of men and women. Negatively, however, the removal of barriers to the free movement of goods, services, capital and persons, and the enshrining of these 'four freedoms' within European law, has had certain of the deleterious effects associated above with the trend towards global juridification: threatening local self-determination, linguistic and cultural diversity, and risking a 'race to the bottom' in certain welfare provisions and employment and social security rights. Clashes between the European Court of Justice and national constitutional courts over the interpretation and ranking of rights in these areas have been common, with no settled procedure for their satisfactory resolution. Intergovernmental agreements have enhanced executive power, removing certain crucial economic and security decisions from effective parliamentary or popular control at the national level without, as the EU's notorious 'democratic deficit' attests, establishing effective forms of accountability at the supranational level. Meanwhile, the EU remains a 'weak' polity – lacking the legitimacy to engage in redistributive and interventionist as opposed to regulatory policies, and often not possessing the capacity to implement and secure compliance for even these measures. Yet little support exists for remedying these defects by turning the EU in its turn into a sovereign political unit. For example, though national identities have to some degree fragmented, with people showing increasing regional and transnational allegiances, very few people claim to have a European identity or would welcome EU-wide collective decision-making.[7]

The move towards a condition beyond or post-sovereignty poses in a new form the paradox surrounding the purpose and practice of sovereignty examined in the last section. For the very processes that have tamed sovereignty have also rendered it both necessary and no longer possible. Though the heightened complexity and social differentiation of contemporary societies constrain the ability of sovereign states to dominate their citizens, they also enhance both value pluralism and the oppressive power of private institutions, thereby raising the problems of deep disagreement, freeriding and the powerlessness of the weak before the strong which sovereignty claims to resolve by authoritatively defining right and wrong, acting as the supreme arbiter, and compelling all to obey. Post-sovereignty theorists seek to overcome this difficulty by arguing there can be agreement on rights – the framework within which we resolve our disagreements about the nature of the good life – and indeed that without such an agreement no use of sovereign power can ever be legitimate. So conceived, post-sovereignty takes us not beyond sovereignty, so much as towards a basis for the legitimation and limitation of sovereign power. Yet in the process it empowers the judiciary, creating a legal sovereignty that is often as arbitrary as, if generally weaker but also less accountable, than the political sovereignty it displaces. For rights to property, privacy, freedom of speech, bodily integrity and so on are deeply contentious, yielding disputes every bit as heated as (and usually linked to) those occasioned by people's more comprehensive beliefs – as debates over such matters as welfare, freedom of the press, pornography and abortion amply show. Therefore, the challenge has to be to retain certain key elements of, and offer a coherent basis for, a sovereign system, notably effective and democratic government, within the new conditions of a post-sovereign world of multiple polities, regimes and identities and without losing some of the welcome curbs on arbitrary power these developments have produced. Put another way, a legitimate unity has to be constructed out of plurality without creating 'a common Power to keep them all in awe' (Hobbes 1991, 88). The next section proposes the arrangements of a pre-sovereign system as being best suited to this task.

3. FROM PRE-SOVEREIGNTY TO MIXED SOVEREIGNTY

The arguments for sovereignty developed by Bodin and Hobbes, which so many commentators on this issue take as their starting point, involved the conscious criticism of what had hitherto been the standard view – namely, that even within monarchical systems power should be mixed in ways that blocked any one agent or agency acting in an arbitrary manner (Franklin 1991, 301–5; Bodin 1992, book 2 chap 1. especially 103–5; Hobbes 1991, 225). A view associated with the Roman constitution and republicanism, its central tenet was that a well-ordered political system rests on the 'the Empire of laws and not of men' (see Harrington 1992, 8, 20). However, this condition does not replace political with legal sovereignty. Not only is the idea of a putatively non-political judicial branch a largely post-sovereignty notion but also it was clear to these theorists that even natural law has to be interpreted and applied, thereby giving discretionary power to those charged with doing so. If laws were not to reflect the mere whim or will of the ruler, thereby dominating and potentially oppressing the ruled, but apply equally and consistently to all, so none could be above the law, while being so formulated as to show all citizens equal concern and respect, then rule by an agent or agency over others had to be replaced by a system of popular self-rule (Skinner 1998, 74/5). Yet, this proposal should not be equated with popular sovereignty. Republican theorists did not conceive of 'the people' as a homogeneous group. Quite the contrary, they were well aware of their class and religious divisions. So the system they advocated was one where each person was to count equally with others. As the seventeenth-century neo-Roman republican theorist James Harrington put it, in an explicit critique of Hobbes, it is only when all are equal in the making of the laws that they will be 'framed by every private man unto no other end (or they may thank themselves) than to protect the liberty of every man' (Harrington 1992, 19/20).

Thus, a pre-sovereignty system involves bringing together democracy and the rule of law in such a way that there is neither legal nor political – including popular – sovereignty. Instead, citizens have to engage with each other as political equals and negotiate collective agreements that embody reciprocity and a willingness to 'hear the other side', neither ignoring nor overriding other people's concerns so long as these too embody mutual respect. The key to promoting such dialogue lay in the idea of a 'mixed' constitution that both distributed and shared power: the very two devices that the sovereignty theorists were to criticise, though they acknowledged both could be found in the Roman and other constitutions. Two central mechanisms within this peculiarly republican regime facilitate the distribution and sharing of power: the 'separation of powers' and the 'balance of power' (Bellamy 1996b, 436).

The first, distributive, mechanism reduces the discretionary aspect of the law, preventing it degenerating into a mere command. The second, sharing, mechanism encourages the law to track the interests of those to whom it applies and gives them a sense of ownership over it. Taken together, they serve to remove the sovereignty of any agent or agency, thereby blocking the abuse of power while facilitating and legitimating its constructive and more differentiated use. As a result, the law becomes more sensitive to the diversity of ideals, interests and situations within the polity.

Though the institutional forms taken by the mechanisms for distributing and sharing power may require adjustment to reflect new social and political problems, cleavages and structures, the logic behind them remains much the same. The 'separation of powers' distributes sovereignty by dividing the legislative from the executive and judicial functions to prevent any person or group becoming a judge in their own cause. Separating those who formulate the laws from those entrusted with their interpretation, application and enforcement brings all within the law. The legislators are constrained in their ability to decree ad hoc or self-serving laws by the judiciary's role in applying the law to all in an impartial and consistent manner. Meanwhile, the discretionary and interpretative powers held by the executive and judicial branches are checked because exercised under laws they do not make. However, there are two well-known problems with this thesis. The first concerns the conceptual and practical difficulty of separating functions. For example, when judges adjudicate on which rules apply in given cases, they often end up setting precedents that come to constitute new rules. Similarly, officials frequently create rules in the course of implementing a law, while legislators are inevitably concerned with how the laws they frame will be interpreted and applied to specific cases. Thus, the three functions are interrelated, with each branch of government engaged to some degree in the activities of the other. The second problem arises at this point. For the constraints imposed by what functional separation is possible will be undermined if all branches of government represent similar groups and interests. Having each function run by different people will not necessarily prevent their working for a partial interest if all belong to the same party or class. This problem has been particularly acute in systems, such as the British, where the executive controls the legislature and can exert direct and indirect influence over the judiciary through appointments or other ways.

The notion of the 'balance of power' comes in here. This device seeks to share the various functions between different groups and classes of people. Historically, the various branches of government were assigned to different classes. For example, in Montesquieu's famous depiction of the British constitution, executive power belongs to the Crown, while the legislative lies largely with the Commons and partly with the Lords, who also control the judicial branch through the law Lords. The sharing of power is more usual today through systems of representation that ensure a variety of different constituencies can obtain an equal voice, and by multiplying the sites of decision-making. Thus, bi-cameral systems typically employ different methods of election for the two houses, while corporatist and consociational systems share powers among different functional, cultural or religious groups. Likewise, federalism, workplace democracy and associationalism provide ways of multiplying the sites and levels of decision-making, be they factories, schools, neighbourhoods or regions. Through sharing and distributing power, a balance is produced between the various interests and values of individuals and groups within the polity, obliging them to interact in ways that oblige them to treat each other fairly and with reciprocity. Harrington famously expressed this point in terms of the fable of the girls and the cake, who ensure a fair division by having the one who cuts the cake take the last slice (Harrington 1992, 22–5, 64–7). A mixed constitution similarly divides sovereign powers so as to avoid the possibility of any person or group being able to pass public measures for personal or sectional advantages.

Because nobody can get their way without the support of others, the mixed constitution obliges citizens and governments to engage in a process of public justification to show why the policies they advocate truly promote public interests. Republicanism is committed to a conception of dialogical reason. The watchword of such reasoning is to 'listen to the other side' (*audi alterem partem*), which carries with it 'a willingness to negotiate over rival intuitions concerning the applicability of evaluative terms' (Skinner 1996, 15/16; Pettit 1999). Such public justification involves more than a lowest-common denominator test, whereby the only legitimate collective rules relate to goods that de facto are in everyone's rational interest to have publicly provided. In this case, those able to provide for themselves could object to supporting collective arrangements and even standard public goods might be deemed unacceptable. Instead, public justification entails the giving of reasons that are shareable by others and so carries with it a commitment to dialogue and mutual understanding.[8] Common rules should not only treat all individuals as moral equals capable of autonomous action but also be attentive to the variety of circumstances in which they find themselves and the diverse forms of practical reasoning they adopt. Consequently, legislators must drop purely self-interested and self-referential reasoning and look for forms of argument that could be accepted by other individuals who are similarly constrained. In other words, there will be an assumption that in evaluating laws we start by taking into account the effects of their general performance for securing the various generic goods that one could expect individuals to value in the different situations they might find themselves. This assumption implies neither that all are similarly situated nor that they value the same goods. On the one hand, it would exclude any arguments that failed to heed the plight or concerns of others and could not be plausibly shared. So, self-serving arguments by the prosperous that there could never be grounds for mutual aid would be unlikely to pass this test. On the other hand, it merely requires that arguments be made in terms all could relate to. This requirement is consistent with groups or individuals either pointing out how their peculiar circumstances create special demands which would be felt by others in their place, or requesting their currently ignored claims be recognised on grounds of fairness by drawing parallels with certain existing entitlements of others. When incommensurable goods and values are in play, it also allows for collective agreements to take the form of a compromise involving reciprocal concessions of various kinds (Bellamy 1999, chap. 4).

A critic might argue that this system smuggles in both a sovereign *Grundnorm* of 'hearing the other side', along with the values of reciprocity and equality of concern and respect that derive from it, and a sovereign 'people', who ultimately decide. Being essentially an argument from democracy, it must surely rest on both a set of constitutional democratic rights and a *demos*. But the norms do not in any sense precede or frame the practice of dialogue, they are intrinsic to it and only emerge within it. Thus, there is no preexisting consensus on rights. Rather, rights – including those on which the democratic process itself rests – are identified through contestation, negotiation and compromise, often between highly divergent views. Likewise, there is no unitary *demos* but rather multiple *demoi* who must make their claim to be recognised and listened to through dialogue with others. Is the process as a whole to be regarded as sovereign then? Only in a sense that renders the term meaningless. No agent or agency holds the power of supreme authority. Unity here depends not on an authoritative *command* but on normative *agreement* between the various parties. Indeed, it is the inability of any agent or agency to force a decision that partly motivates the search for such an agreement. It might still be objected that even if the internal regime lacks a sovereign, the polity must operate as a sovereign unit. Even if true, in foreign as in domestic affairs the executive must be accountable to the system as a whole, so external sovereignty is also not the prerogative of any agent. However, the external sovereignty of a polity is standardly balanced and increasingly shared with other polities. Mixed international regimes can complement their domestic counterparts, as we shall see the EU illustrates. After all, early modern mixed constitution theorists had the German Empire as their model.

Because the mixed constitution privileges neither rights nor democracy, it undermines both legal and political sovereignty. Demands for new rights highlight this mutual dependence of rights and democracy and its essentially pre- and anti-sovereignty logic.[9] It is sometimes argued that progressive change depends on either a political sovereign able to compel powerful social groups to give up their privileges, or a legal sovereign able to curb majority or minority tyranny by upholding individual rights. But arguably quite the opposite is the case. Calls for new rights generally challenge the prevailing ways politics and law are constituted. Standardly, they involve political recognition for new categories of people and legal recognition of new types of claim, both of which are linked to altering the way power is shared and distributed by reconstituting the 'polity' and 'regime'. From this perspective, sovereignty merely entrenches the domination of hegemonic groups. Therefore, widening the practice of dialogue involves further fragmenting rather than strengthening sovereignty. For example, the demand for workers' social and economic rights went hand in hand with the demand for the vote. They claimed these rights on the basis of an entitlement to citizenship, as being capable of taking part in a process of public justification concerning the ways they should be treated equally or unequally to others. As a result, they criticised the prevailing definitions of both people and rights for being inconsistent with the practice of dialogue. They questioned property as a qualification for voting and a largely negative conception of rights that blocked interfering with the ways property owners conducted their business. The constitutive and regulative rules of the dialogical game were dramatically changed as a result. Thus, the nature of the 'polity' altered as the economy became a legitimate sphere for political regulation and workers were recognised as active rather than passive subjects. The character of the 'regime' similarly altered as new 'styles' of politics, such as mass parties and union activism, became accepted, and the 'scope' of politics came to embrace more interventionist and redistributive policies. These alterations to the 'polity' and 'regime' produced new forms of sharing and distributing power through schemes such as industrial democracy and corporatism. For it is only through dispersing power in this way that rights gains can ultimately be secured and maintained. Later movements for women's and multicultural rights have followed a very similar trajectory.

Law and politics play complementary roles in these campaigns. The judiciary and legal system operate as an important counter to democracy, ensuring that legislation is consistently applied and forms part of a coherent body of law. The legal system stabilises the status quo, so that citizens know where they stand and can plan ahead, and can even be the starting point for an internal critique of the existing system when it fails to live up to its own legal/constitutional standards. Though distinct, however, law does not have an authority that is entirely separated from or superior to politics, based on some putative fundamental values that are immune to political criticism. For it is through politics that law, including constitutional law, is promulgated and legitimised. So rights campaigns are first and foremost political in nature, seeking to change the political and hence the legal constitution of the system, opening both to fuller forms of public justification. As we saw, these changes generally involve introducing greater diversity in both the loci and forms of civic participation. These innovations include multiplying the sites of legal decision-making and rendering legal procedures more consultative and accessible. In some circumstances, limited entrenchment of certain rights may be advisable to guard against myopia or carelessness on the part of the legislature, but this too must be subject to some form of democratic entrenchment. Meanwhile, appeal to democracy does not rest on the sovereignty of any given *demos* because the construction of the people is also contested within these democratic dialogues, and new forms of civic identity asserted that multiply the range of *demoi* participating within the system. Think of the way transnational social movements have challenged the sovereigntist's view of the *demos* as territorially located.

A mixed constitution is well suited to pluralist and complex societies, allowing policies to be responsive to local difference without the weakening of governance or concern with the common good that sovereignty theorists fear. Dispersing power obtains a hearing for the diverse preferences and reasons of different individuals, ensuring the peculiar circumstances of particular contexts get taken into account. General rules can be tailored to a wide variety of objects and concerns, and their implementation and monitoring enacted to meet the special requirements of a given situation and constituency. In certain cases, specific norms can even be established to meet special circumstances and relevant differences. However, respect for plurality is always balanced against the need to engage with the collectivity. Sharing and distributing sovereignty not only gives minorities a degree of autonomy but also curbs their ability to act arbitrarily or independently, thereby promoting collaboration that recognises difference. Consequently, strong government action is fostered rather hindered. Because positive measures must be devised in ways that take into account the variations typical of highly differentiated societies, they are both fairer and more efficient. As a result, they have greater legitimacy and are more likely to be undertaken and implemented.

It might be argued that talk of pre-sovereignty seems at best misleading and at worst impractical and incoherent after three centuries when politics has been dominated by claims to sovereignty. But in circumstances in which these claims have proliferated and entered into conflict with each other, the republican approach is effectively to mix these different quasi-sovereign agents and agencies so they cancel each other out, thereby de-sovereigntising sovereignty. The potential for a shift to a mixed sovereignty system is well illustrated by the EU. I remarked earlier how the EU has been portrayed as betwixt and between a sovereign and a post-sovereign system, being both intergovernmental and federal, on the one hand, and a regulative rights-based legal regime, on the other. Yet some of these apparently paradoxical features, along with many of its achievements, arguably arise from the EU's having evolved into a mixed sovereignty system. Recent analyses of the EU have stressed its 'multilevel' nature, involving a mixture of sub-state, state and supra-state actors and decision-making fora. As a result, authority is now shared (and contested) between national executives and actors operating above and below the state, such as the European Parliament and the regions, respectively (Marks, Hoogue, and Blank 1996, 341/2). Moreover, these multiple levels coalesce in different ways according to policy area. No one set of institutions is ultimately responsible for all competences, while the membership and character of these institutions varies. For example, foreign, monetary and social policy require different types of agreement between different sorts of actors concerning different policy spheres and affecting different sets of people. This multilevelled structure is also reflected in the interaction between EU law and that of the member states. At least since 1964, the European Court of Justice has considered the Community (now Union) as constituting a distinct legal order, with its own internal norms of validity (see *Costa v. ENEL*, case 6/64). However, there is no European *Grundnorm* or *demos* underlying this European constitutional order, qualifying it as a 'higher' order to those of the member states. Rather, it exists alongside, and occasionally in tension with, the legal orders of the member states, each of which also possesses distinct norms of validity, including distinct criteria concerning the relevant situations where EU law applies and is valid. The application and enforcement of rights and obligations under EU law remain matters for the authorities of the member states. Each must individually obtain democratic approval either directly, through referenda, or indirectly, through the national parliament, for any major legislative changes arising from further European integration, and national courts justify their acceptance of Community law by reference to these domestic processes (see MacCormick 1995, 255; Weiler 2001).

From the perspectives of the sovereignty and post-sovereignty positions, the EU structures can appear messy and incoherent. On the one hand, political supremacy appears to lie with neither the member states nor the supra-state organs of the EU, but between them all in differing ways and combinations according to the policy area. On the other hand, the juridification of this regime is similarly partial and unclear. European legal norms exist, but they do not have a clear-cut constitutional supremacy as a 'higher law' above the legal norms or even the political decisions of the member states. By contrast, from a mixed sovereignty point of view, this situation represents a highly desirable state of affairs. It represents a distribution and sharing of sovereign power between the different peoples of Europe that obliges them to negotiate collective policies in ways that reflect the various interests and values of those concerned. Thus, Neil MacCormick has seen the sharing of legislative authority between the European Parliament, the Council and the Commission as conforming to the rationale of a mixed constitution – producing a healthy balance between transnational, national and supranational interests (Mac-Cormick 1997; see too Craig 1997; Bellamy and Castiglione 2000b). It could be added that their deliberations are increasingly supplemented by other channels of representation for other sorts of political subjects, with selected functional interests being represented in the Economic and Social Committee (ESC) and the obscure comitology process, subnation interests in the Committee of the Regions (CR) and so on (Curtin 1997).

Of course, there is no denying the many shortcomings of these arrangements – the purely consultative role of the ESC and the CR, the imperfect balance between large, medium and small states, the difficulties of getting transnational interests represented, and the relatively weak democratic accountability of government representatives on European matters, among other failings (Schmitter 2000). But these problems should not obscure the central achievement of this mixed sovereignty system – namely, the reciprocal modification of national interests, both vis-à-vis each other and increasingly with regard to their subnational communities, and their collaboration in promoting collective interests. This process of negotiation and compromise has been as true of the development of EU law, where human rights policy evolved through successive challenges by various national constitutional courts to the ECJ, as it has been of the politics (e.g. Internationale Handelsgesellschaft Case 11/70 [1970] ECR 1125, p. 1134, Internationale Handelsgesellschaft [1974] 2 CMLR 549, *Nold v. Commission* [1974] ECR 503, *Frontini v. Ministero delle Finanze* [1974] 2 CMLR 372, *Rutili v. Minister for the Interior* Case 36/75 [1975] ECR 1219, *Nicolo* [1990] 1 CMLR 173). A reassertion of sovereignty at either the national or the European level would not only remove this delicate balance but also be deeply delegitimising. For if integration has not created a European identity, it has produced a profound modification and partial Europeanisation of national identities. At the same time, the weak governance and poor accountability typical of a largely regulatory and juridical regime remain the EU's chief shortcoming, and would only be intensified by it moving further towards a post-sovereign system. Instead, attention should be focused on improving the EU's mixed constitution in ways that further enhance the reciprocal interaction and dialogues between its multiple *demoi* and levels of governance.

CONCLUSION

This chapter has challenged the contrast between sovereignty and post-sovereignty. If the one prioritises politics, the other makes law supreme. Each has its drawbacks, and neither ultimately proves possible. The first risks equating might with right, while the second overlooks how right needs the might resulting from the assent of those to whom it applies to be effective and legitimate. Both wrongly assume that sovereign power cannot be divided – in the first case thereby justifying a concentration of power, in the second ignoring the power wielded by organs other than the state – including the courts. Finally, though each presents itself as a solution to the problem of an absence of unity, each ends up proposing a unity as the source of political or legal sovereign authority – be it a homogenous *demos* or a consensus on rights. A pre-sovereign system escapes these difficulties. It shares and distributes sovereignty in ways that remove the arbitrary power of any single agent or agency. Through the resulting democratic negotiation between peoples, laws have to be publicly justified in ways that give due recognition to difference. The multiplicity of sites of governance and decision-making also enables them to be implemented more efficiently and with greater sensitivity to local variations. Thus, unity is constructed via a dialogue among a plurality, with the one being continually challenged, renegotiated and reconstructed as the other evolves and becomes more diverse. The doctrine of sovereignty was developed alongside the development of the modern state. As that political formation begins to fragment, it seems highly appropriate to return to the ideas and institutional structures it sought to supplant.

NOTES

1. Research for this chapter was supported by an ESRC Grant L213 25 2022 on 'Strategies of Civic Inclusion in Pan-European Civil Society'. I am grateful to Dario Castiglione, Ian Hunter, Philip Pettit, Jim Tully and Neil Walker for their comments on an earlier version.

2. For example, Hobbes (1991, 90) who links plurality in judgements with the 'war of every man against every man' and argues only a 'common power' can establish both 'right and wrong' and legal order in such circumstances.

3. Cited in Walker (1998, 33–4).

4. The classic statement of this objection is of course Locke (1960, II 93, 328).

5. As I understand it, Bodin attempted to make this move by distinguishing what is standardly translated as 'state' ('polity') from 'government' ('regime'), and arguing the Prince could be sovereign over the one while limited in the other. Though Bodin ultimately abandoned this argument, rightly noting its incoherence, it was taken up by others, such as Pufendorf, later (see Franklin 1991, 307, 317).

6. Again, this development has gone further within the EU than elsewhere (see Marks, Hooghe and Blak 1996, 341).

7. For example, a recent Eurobarometer Report (52 April 2000 – based on research October–November 1999) records that while an average of 46 per cent of European citizens believe their country has benefited from the EU, only 4 per cent see

themselves as exclusively European and 6 per cent as European and nationality (e.g. European-Irish or European-British). Most, 42 per cent, regard themselves at best as nationality and European (e.g. as French-European or Danish-European). Earlier polls produced very similar results.

8. This is a deliberate weakening of the formulation of Scanlon (1999), whose account of public reasoning I otherwise follow. It arises from thinking that pluralism requires greater flexibility and compromise than he believes necessary. See Bellamy (1999), introduction and chap. 3.

9. What follows draws on and develops themes in Tully (1999, 161); Bellamy (2001b); and Tully (2002).

Part III

CONSTITUTING THE EU

Chapter 6

Constitution Making as Normal Politics

Disagreement and Compromise in the Drafting of the EU Charter of Fundamental Rights and Constitution[1]

Richard Bellamy and Justus Schönlau

The draft Constitution for the European Union has been criticised in some quarters for being the product of low politics, not high principle. Rather than aspiring to the elevated standards of deliberative argument supposedly set at Philadelphia,[2] the Convention on the Future of Europe is charged with being characterised by shabby bargains to accommodate various sectional interests, especially those of member state governments. As a consequence, critics contend the resulting document lacks the clarity and precision that could have been achieved had it issued from a rational consensus on common values and procedures. Instead, they view it as lengthy and overly complex, mixing empty verbosity with detailed and potentially unworkably complicated formulae that reflect a series of compromises designed to keep all the parties happy.[3]

This chapter questions a key assumption underlying such criticisms concerning the need to distinguish 'constitutional' from 'normal' politics. These two forms of politics are often treated as distinct species of the same genus (e.g. Ackerman 1991, 3–33). Whereas the latter supposedly involves a focus on policy considerations and the promotion, balancing and aggregation of sectional interests, the former is portrayed as a more high-minded affair. It consists of deliberation on the common good to arrive at a consensus on those principles required to show each person equal concern and respect (e.g. Elster 1996; Cohen 1996, 95–119). As such, it comes as close as possible to the ideal politics of an original contract between free and equal citizens.

Proponents of this interpretation maintain that if everyone is constrained to reason in an open and equitable manner, uninfluenced by purely private advantage, prejudice or other kinds of unjustifiable partiality, the contractors will converge on a conception of justice that is both fair and in the public interest. By contrast, normal politics is said to be the realm of shabby compromises, in which self-interested parties bargain for personal or sectional gain, only accepting what they have to in order to get as much of their way as they can (e.g. Habermas 1996a, 127, 165–67, 181–83). Consequently, the outcomes of constitutional politics – most notably constitutional rights – provide the preconditions for normal politics and may legitimately constrain it (e.g. Dworkin 1996, introduction).

We dispute this contrast and the relationship it proposes between these two political settings. We do not wish to deny that just as certain concerns of contemporary eighteenth-century politics, most notably slavery, marred the proceedings at Philadelphia of two centuries ago, so the Brussels Conventions were sometimes unduly preoccupied by passing issues or the need to conciliate particular interests. One does not have to be a cynical realist to expect any real political process to fall short in some measure from the ideal. However, there are also many occasions when conflicting views and interests cannot but be taken into account. As we shall show, disagreements over matters of constitutional principle are often reasonable and involve policy differences that cannot be ignored. As a result, political deals have to be struck to achieve a compromise. In these respects, there are often good reasons for constitution making to resemble the ordinary process of legislation.

Constitutional politics are typically linked to dramatic 'moments' such as a civil war, revolution, military defeat or some other national disaster or major turning point (Ackerman 1991, 266–94). In these cases, it is necessary to rebuild the structures of normal politics and normalise the antagonisms of opposed groups. Less dramatic instances, such as the three rounds of constitutional politics in Canada since the mid-1960s, have had similar aspirations – namely, to bring antipathy to the prevailing regime within the fold of normal politics. We contend this process of normalisation arises not because constitutional politics stands outside and differs from normal politics, but on the contrary because it reveals that conflicts on matters of principle are amenable to the normal political processes. Disagreements about constitutional principles are frequently well founded, both reflecting and lying at the heart of normal political divisions. Consequently, a consensus beyond these political disputes is not available. Rather, mechanisms have to be found whereby people can live with their disagreements. As a result, constitutional politics reaches an accord not through some or all disputants being converted to a common point of view, but via a normal political process of give and take that allows the parties to reach mutually acceptable compromises in which each recognises the views of others without necessarily agreeing with them. As with ordinary legislation, there need be nothing shabby about such deals.[4] They involve a complex mix of bargaining and principled argument that belies attempts to distinguish normal from constitutional politics by associating the former exclusively with the first and the latter with the second. Politics tout court necessarily employs elements of both, combining them in different ways according to the nature of the issue being discussed, so as to find solutions all can live with.

Our analysis focuses on the two Conventions that drafted the EU Charter of Rights and the doomed Constitutional Treaty. The earlier Convention was broadly welcomed and its perceived success to some degree encouraged the use of the 'convention method', as it came to be known, to tackle the broader issue of institutional reform through the writing of a Constitution. We start, in the first section, by outlining why normal political compromise over constitutional essentials can be necessary. We argue that because fundamental constitutional principles, such as rights, are subject to reasonable disagreements, the conditions of public reason held to typify 'constitutional' politics will be insufficient to produce a consensus. The second section explores the various types of normal political compromise available, and their suitability for resolving different sorts of dispute. The third section illustrates these points through an analysis of the two Conventions. We conclude by suggesting the success of these, as with other, conventions lay not in their extraordinary character so much as their normality. As a consequence, we ought perhaps to treat their conclusions as part of, and reformable by, normal politics too, rather than according them the superior status standardly attributed to the Charters and Constitutions resulting from such meetings.

WHY COMPROMISE? THE NATURE OF POLITICAL DISAGREEMENT

Compromise is sometimes portrayed as a shoddy capitulation, whereby principle gets sacrificed to self-interest and short-term advantages. For example, in the case of a Constitution it might be supposed that it should be based on principles that ought to be embraced by all who endorse liberal and democratic values rather than simply balancing the particular interests of those currently affected. Such calculations, critics of compromise standardly argue, can only lead to incoherence and injustice. Yet, compromise can also indicate a laudable willingness to see another's point of view, thereby showing a decent respect for difference. If there are divergent and competing views and interests, each of which is well founded, then, if a collective agreement is necessary, it seems both prudent and justified to seek an accommodation between them.

142   *Chapter 6*

There are various circumstances that might render such compromises necessary (Bellamy 1999, chap. 1). These range from contingent or logical conflicts in satisfying particular human goods, of not being able to fund, say, both libraries and swimming pools, differences between divergent conceptions of the good, such as the clash noted by Machiavelli between the Christian and the Pagan life, to the pull of different sorts of moral claim, such as the tension between consequential and deontological considerations. Not all goods and values can be accommodated in a given social space and, to the degree they are incommensurable as well as incompatible, ranking them will prove a difficult task. Though certain philosophers believe that they can, at least in principle, resolve such dilemmas, no such proposed resolution commands universal assent. As John Rawls has pointed out, what he calls the 'burdens of judgement', defined as 'the many hazards involved in the correct (and conscientious) exercise of our powers of reason and judgement in the ordinary course of political life' (Rawls 1993, 53–6), place limits on what we can justify to others. Even the best-argued case can meet with reasonable dissent due to such factors as the complex nature of much factual information and uncertainty over its bearing on any case, disagreement about the weighting of values, the vagueness of concepts, the diverse backgrounds and experiences of different people, and the variety of normative considerations involved in any issue and the difficulty of making an overall assessment of their relative weight (Rawls 1993, 56–7). As a result, 'many of our most important judgements are made under conditions where it is not to be expected that conscientious persons with full powers of reason, even after free discussion, will all arrive at the same conclusion' (Rawls 1993, 58).

Even the most basic of constitutional principles, namely fundamental rights, can be subject to disagreements resulting from these sources. For example, think of the debates over breaches of privacy. It is often difficult to identify these not just because the empirical details may be unclear but also (and most importantly) because people differ over the boundaries of the concept, hold different accounts of the public interest, where it overrides the right to privacy, view personal responsibility differently and so on. They have different views of when a right exists to be breached in the first place. Indeed, the laws in many states differ on this point. For example, France and Germany protect the privacy of public figures more than Britain or the United States. Thus, although all EU member states share a commitment to human rights, when it came to drawing up the Charter of Fundamental Rights they frequently divided over the *substance* of rights, or which rights we have and why, the *subjects* of rights, or who may possess them, the *sphere* of rights, or where they apply, the *scope* of rights, or how they relate to other rights and values, and the *securing* and *specification* of rights, or the type of political or judicial intervention and the precise set of entitlements that are needed to protect them, both in general and in particular cases (for a full analysis of debates over these dimensions of rights, see Bellamy 2001a, especially 17–21). Members of that Convention disputed whether rights covered social and economic matters as well as civil and political issues, if they applied simply to EU institutions or the domestic arrangements of the member states as well, their impact on certain collective national interests, how far, if at all, they covered all persons residing within the EU territories as opposed to EU nationals alone, the ways they were to be framed – abstractly or very specifically, as policy goals or clear entitlements, and the extent to which the Charter was simply a declaratory statement or legally binding. As we shall see, parallel divisions also characterised the second Convention on the Future of Europe.

THE POLITICS OF COMPROMISE

In circumstances of reasonable disagreement, deliberation will not necessarily act as a funnel that leads the disputants to converge on a single position. There is no better argument none can reasonably reject and no compelling reason for anyone to transform their position to adopt another's. We submit that people overcome this impasse by dropping the search for a strong consensus (in the sense of all being converted to a particular view) and looking instead for mutually acceptable compromises (this section summarises Bellamy 1999, chap. 4; see too Benjamin 1990). In this case, all the parties remain convinced that their own position would be the best, at least given their own concerns, but come to appreciate that reasonable alternative perspectives exist that ought to be acknowledged in some way as well. In other words, compromise need not be simply a matter of prudence but also of principle, reflecting a willingness to 'hear the other sides'. Here deliberation works more like a filter, weeding out purely self-interested moves in order to reveal those positions that ought to be accommodated and those that should not (Bohman 1998, chap. 2). This process achieved, then different sorts of compromise may well be available, depending on the issue in dispute.

Roughly speaking, there are three broad kinds of compromise, each of which has a number of variations, with the version adopted depending on the character of the parties and the differences dividing them. The first kind seeks a direct compromise between the different viewpoints. One of the commonest methods consists of *bargaining* and arises in what Albert Hirschman has called 'more-or-less' conflicts (Hirschman 1994, 203–18). In these cases, the disputants are either arguing over a single good whose meaning they share, or are able to conceive their various demands as being translatable into some common measure – usually money. Thus, when employees haggle over wages or house buyers over the price of their prospective home, they may have issues other than money in mind – such as the need to work late or the proximity of a railway line in these two examples – but they can nevertheless put a price on their concern that enables the parties to agree a mutually satisfactory deal. However, many conflicts cannot be resolved so easily because the positions are incommensurable or incompatible with each other. In these instances, more complex compromises are required. A more sophisticated style of bargaining involves *trading* to mutual advantage, whereby each gets some if not all of what they want. For example, most political parties have to engage in a degree of log-rolling to get elected. This procedure brings into a single party various groups that may disagree over many issues but who prioritise them differently. If three groups are split over the possession of nuclear weapons, development aid and a graduate tax, but each values a different one of these more than the others, it may be possible for them to agree to a package giving each the policy they value most while putting up with another with which they disagree in an area that matters less to them. Of course, sometimes the result can be a programme that is too inconsistent to be tenable or attractive. Here, it might be better for the groups to shift to an agreed *second best*. Some conflicts appear intractable at the level of abstract principle but can be resolved through the *negotiation* of the details. What appear to be standoffs between incompatible views sometimes arise through the various positions being under articulated. Thick description may help clarify the distinctive weight of different demands. Each party may agree that reasons of different weight or involving different sorts of consideration are involved. Or it may be possible to reason casuistically and by analogy from those cases where there is agreement to others where abstractly there appears to be a standoff. Judges often use precedents in this way (Sunstein 1996).

The second kind of compromise consists of various attempts to skirt around the disagreement. For example, people often employ *trimming* to avoid talking about the issues that divide them and seek either to find agreement on other grounds or to take them off the agenda altogether. This technique resembles the way neighbours of opposed religious beliefs steer clear of discussing religion so as to remain sufficiently friendly to cooperate on school runs. It is partly employed by Rawls when advocating the avoidance of 'comprehensive' moral theories in politics (1993, xvii, 141–44), and is familiar in constitutions in the form of 'gag-rules' (Holmes 1998, 19–58; Rawls 1993, 151, note 16). From this perspective, the very decision to have a Bill of Rights can be regarded as a compromise agreement to remove certain divisive issues from the political agenda. A variation of this technique is *segregation*. Here the attempt is to contain potentially conflicting issues or differing groups of people by placing them within distinct spheres. Granting ethnic or national minorities limited forms of self-government and consociational forms of democracy provide examples of this approach.

The third kind of compromise employs a procedural device to overcome deadlock. Third-party arbitration is one common mechanism of this kind, where trust is placed in the arbitrator to do the balancing in an impartial manner according to a fixed set of rules. Majority voting is another example of this approach. In this case, the disputants compromise on a procedure they all accept as fair even if they will continue to disagree on the merits of the actual decision itself. Such methods appear justified wherever agreement on substance seems unlikely because of time constraints or the character of the differences dividing the parties.

All three kinds of compromise, along with their variants, are standard political techniques and frequently combined. Each has its respective merits and demerits, according to the issue and the perspectives of the people concerned. Take religious education in a multicultural society. Trading might yield ecumenical solutions or concessions in other areas that certain religious groups regard as more important, such as special rights like Britain's exemption of Sikhs from wearing crash helmets on motorcycles. Or it might be better to trim or establish as a shared second best that schools are strictly secular. Societies that are deeply segmented along religious lines have often adopted various forms of segregation, such as consociationalism (Lijphart 1968). Sometimes a minority group engages in negotiation to get accepted. For example, British Muslims have pointed to analogies with established liberal or Christian practices to get certain of their claims recognised as legitimate and to promote understanding of them (Modood 1993, 87–91).

It will be objected that compromise will only be equitable if the relative power of the parties concerned is so divided that all get a hearing but none has the ability to force concessions to meet perverse or unjust claims. In fact, compromise shares the concern with political equality that animates democracy. Namely, it 'requires the view that we must recognise everybody with whom we communicate as a potential source of argument and reasonable information' (Weale 2007, 57). It is vital, therefore, that different viewpoints are fairly represented in the decision-making process. One advantage of constitutional over normal politics may be that this is more likely to be the case. As we shall see was the case in the Convention, different viewpoints tend to be so represented that even minority positions get a hearing, while the public character of their deliberations and the need for near unanimity encourage participants to appeal to shareable reasons rather than prejudice or self-interest when making their arguments. However, here too the difference between constitutional and normal politics is largely a matter of degree rather than of kind. Most political systems seek to ensure fair and reasonable decision-making through adopting a suitably proportional electoral system, drawing constituency boundaries in certain ways, dividing legislative power and so on.[5]

The critique of majoritarianism, the most common objection to normal politics, needs qualifying in this regard. An insistence on unanimity may give small groups an effective veto over decisions that amount to minority tyranny – a fear some voiced in both Conventions on certain issues. By contrast, majority voting can be the fairest decision procedure, as May famously showed (1952, 680–84), and, as Condorcet revealed (1976), may be more likely to be right than individual judgement. Of course, both these results assume ideal conditions that rarely obtain in practice (Dahl 1989, 144–50, 160–62). However, for this reason, strict majoritarianism is unusual in real political systems. Most legislatures are elected via systems that produce multiple parties and a degree of representativeness that makes coalition building necessary.[6] As pluralists have long noted, even within dominant parties majorities get constructed from minorities. Legislative majorities are often in reality supermajorities of the population as a whole, reflecting a wide spectrum of public opinion. As a result, bargaining is also less common than critics of majoritarian politics often contend. As we saw, bargaining can be appropriate, but on many issues it fails to do justice to the values and concerns in play. Yet, the need for coalition building and more complex compromises render it relatively rare. Instead, voting normally follows on from protracted discussion and diplomacy in which trading, second best and negotiation tend to be more important than straightforward bargaining. Thus, the structures of constitutional politics are also closer to those of normal politics than is sometimes granted.

In fact, the most unsatisfactory compromises arise not from majority rule so much as the mechanisms used to avoid it – notably, trimming, segregation and non-aggregative, pure procedures. In skirting around a problem and taking it off the agenda, trimming and segregation can ignore or even create an injustice. The use of both these mechanisms to deal with slavery in the antebellum south is a clear case in point. That is not to say that they are always inappropriate. For example, segregation can promote the self-government and autonomy of certain minorities, even if there always have to be safeguards against the oppression of those other minorities that inevitably arise within the new political unit. Likewise, removing a contentious issue, such as religion, from the agenda can overcome conflict on this issue. However, such measures can also build up resentment and turn opposition to those policies were religious views are relevant into a critique of the entire regime. As a result, opponents can be tempted to evade or subvert the normal political process, rather than engaging and finding an accommodation with those of different views. Some have argued that by settling the abortion through a judicial ruling on the Constitution rather than a normal political compromise, opponents of abortion in the United States have been tempted to adopt just such tactics, putting their energy into capturing the court rather than engaging with their adversaries (Glendon 1991, 58–60; Tushnet 1999, 138–40). As a result, the issue has become a zero-sum game, in which the complexities of the situation that render disagreement reasonable and compromise both possible and appropriate are all too often ignored by both sides.

Pure procedures prove poor for slightly different reasons. They can produce what Dworkin has called a 'checker-board' compromise, such as the view that people with birthdays in odd years can have abortions and those in even ones not (1986). Such solutions might seem a way of splitting the difference between opposed groups. After all, half the female population having access to abortion is better for pro-choicers than none, just as anti-abortionists would prefer to stop half the possible abortions rather than allowing them all. Nonetheless, they seem arbitrary in their effects. More generally, pure procedures have no filtering mechanisms, and let irrational and intolerant positions stand unchallenged. In some circumstances, though, a formal procedure, and even a check-board solution, can be justified. Different jurisdictions can have different policies without any injustice or absurdity, while a rotating presidency, say, is rather different to a rotating policy. The one is likely to result from segregation, the other from certain power-sharing arrangements. It would also be wrong, as Dworkin does, to characterise majority voting as naturally tending to checker-board compromise. In general, as we have seen, it promotes an integrative rather than a distributive solution, which seeks to bring together different positions in a single, collective decision by means of a procedure all can recognise as fair. Indeed, compromise works best when it combines a respect for diversity with the maintenance of unity and solidarity.

So conceived, compromise shares the aspiration of consensus to reach an agreement that treats all with equal concern and respect. To this degree, it possesses many of the normative attractions the proponents of consensus associate with their ideal. However, it differs by achieving this result through reflecting rather attempting to transcend normal political divisions. While a constitutional consensus, if it were possible, could claim to offer a framework for politics for all time, a constitutional compromise will mirror the context in which it is elaborated. As a consequence, a constitutional politics based on compromise will resemble normal politics not just in its processes but also in its decisions. For they will mirror the prevailing differences.

It follows that the resulting Constitution ought to be allowed to evolve as people's circumstances and views change. Most scholars concede the need for some updating,[7] but many regard it as best done by the judiciary drawing out the contemporary implications of abstract principles that themselves derive from a consensus on justice sub specie aeternitatis. However, if the legitimacy of any constitutional settlement rests on its being a fair compromise for given circumstances, in which the way principles are framed and balanced simply mirror what seemed fair to those parties that existed at a certain time, then arguably the Constitution needs itself to be part of an ongoing process of normal politics rather than removed from it. We shall return to this point in the conclusion. First, though, we need to explore how far the Conventions can be characterised as exercises in the normal politics of compromise.

EUROPE'S CONSTITUTIONAL COMPROMISE: AN ANALYSIS OF THE CONVENTIONS

Neither of the two Conventions needed to take on a grand constitutional role.[8] Indeed, many of those who set up these bodies, and some participants in them, saw their task as being merely to reorganise in a clearer manner what was already provided for in existing case law and treaties. However, the 'convention method' was regarded as being more suitable than an IGC for even these more limited tasks because it was believed that their composition and procedures were likely to favour a more constitutional politics of deliberation and consensus as opposed to the bargaining and deal making typical of normal politics. We believe normal politics, including on occasion that of IGCs, can be more deliberative and principled than this contrast suggests.[9] Here, though, we wish to show that despite both Conventions meeting the standard criteria people set out for constitutional politics, they nevertheless had to resort to the normal political arts of compromise to achieve a settlement. The types of compromise tended to vary with the nature of the disagreements they confronted, and as with ordinary legislation some proved more felicitous than others.

Both Conventions conformed to the ideal conditions for a democratic deliberative setting as nearly as is realistically possible.[10] First, their size was reasonably optimal. The Charter Convention had 62 members, that on the Future of Europe 102 full members (shadowed by an equal number of substitutes) plus a President and two Vice Presidents. As such, neither was so large that they favoured oratory over argument, with those speakers most versed in rhetoric coming to the fore. Rather, all members could participate in discussion.

Second, even if there was minimal direct consultation with the electorate over their deliberations or conclusions, the Conventions were also more than usually representative of European public opinion in terms of the range of ideologies and interests they included and consulted. Bargaining typically takes place among a small group of like-minded actors, who do not need to consult either experts or stakeholders, and for whom making a decision proves more important than getting it right. A larger group, involving a number of stakeholders and experts, is more likely to raise problems and divergent perspectives, all of which need to be explicitly addressed. Though imperfect in their involvement of interested groups, both Conventions were more than usually representative of EU opinion. Like EU decision-making more generally, they involved national, transnational and supranational representatives, along with formal and informal consultations with subnational groups.[11] However, unusually the weighting was towards parliamentarians in the national and European parliaments. In the Charter Convention (what follows draws on De Búrca 2001), national parliamentarians accounted for thirty (or two from each of the fifteen member states, usually from the main government and opposition parties) and European parliamentarians for sixteen of the sixty-two representatives. By contrast, member state governments and the Commission only had one representative each, making sixteen in all. Nevertheless, only 16 per cent were female and all were white. Two representatives each from the Council of Europe and the ECJ had observer status, and the European Council had indicated that other European bodies, such as the Ombudsman, the Committee of the Regions and the Economic and Social Committee, be invited to give their views and an 'appropriate exchange' be entered into with the candidate countries for Union membership (Conclusions of the Cologne European Council, 3.4.06.1999, Annex IV). In addition, the Convention was encouraged but not required to invite 'other bodies, social groups, or experts' to give their views (ibid., spelt out further in Conclusions of Tampere European Council, 15–16.10.1999, Annex). The Convention on the Future of Europe had a very similar composition but encompassed the parliamentarians and government representatives of the ten candidate and three applicant countries as well and had two Commission members (what follows draws on Shaw 2003, 57–66). Thus, it contained fifty-six national parliamentarians and twenty-eight representatives of the heads of national governments, while the delegation of the members of the European Parliament remained at sixteen. There were also thirteen observers from the Committee of the Regions (six), the Economic and Social Committee (three), the social partners (three) and the European Ombudsman. As before, female participation fell well below the 40 per cent recommended by the Commission in its policy on gender balance. Only seventeen women were among the full conventionnels, although there were twenty-one female substitute members, and only two of the twelve-member presidium were women and none of the three-member Presidency.[12] Even more disturbingly, acknowledgement of the EU's multicultural character was yet again conspicuous by its virtual absence. There was only one nonwhite member, the UK government's alternate delegate Patricia Scotland. However, the second Convention was also required to consult widely and civil society was given the opportunity to engage with the Convention via a variety of means – such as an organised

Forum with its own website, via a Compact between particular groups designed to make their submissions more effective, through regular meetings with Jean-Luc Dehaene, the vice president charged with coordinating civil society inputs, and a 'jamboree' organised to coincide with the plenary meeting of late June 2002. Though criticised for still being unrepresentative, these events did allow women and minority groups, among others, some access to the proceedings.

Third, though most Charter Convention members belonged to institutions potentially affected by the Charter, most lacked a strong interest in preventing it undermining these bodies. They were either senior figures nearing retirement, middle-ranking politicians unlikely to achieve major office or, in the case of certain governmental representatives, relatively independent academics or lawyers. This was not so true of the Convention on the Future of Europe, though, which governments came to take an all too active interest in. Several key players, like the British government's representative Peter Hain or Belgium's Louis Michel, held ministerial rank, and several member states decided to upgrade their representation in the Convention to their foreign ministers as the debates intensified. For example, the Spanish representative, Ana Palacio, became foreign minister in the summer of 2002 and the German foreign minister Joschka Fischer took over from Glotz after the 2002 German elections and was highly influential in the later stages (see also Schönlau 2004).

Fourth, the deliberations of both Conventions were largely public without being in the glare of publicity. The debates, hearings and the documents submitted to them were public, and a dedicated website made their proceedings reasonably easy to follow from outside and allowed submissions from any interested individual or group. Most debates were held in open, plenary sessions. As a result, their processes were public enough to ensure transparency and oblige participants, however hypocritically, to employ the language of impartial reason rather than of mere self-interest. But its meetings were not so publicised as to encourage grandstanding and rhetorical overbidding aimed at courting or palliating groups outside the Convention. Moreover, if total secrecy encourages bargaining, partial secrecy can allow free and frank discussion. In the second Convention a number of smaller working groups frequently proved crucial for brokering agreements in sensitive areas. More importantly, a key role in both cases was played by the presidium, which met in secret and placed drafts before the Conventions to amend or accept. The Charter presidium consisted of a chair elected by the Convention, Roman Herzog, a former president of both the federal republic of Germany and its Federal Constitutional Court, and three vice-chairs chosen respectively by the national parliamentarians, the European parliamentarians, and the representatives of the member state governments (who were represented by the delegate of whichever state held the rotating EU presidency at the time). That of the second Convention involved its President, Valery Giscard d' Estaing, and the two Vice Presidents chosen by the European Council before the Convention started its work, as well as two Commissioners, two Members of the European Parliament, three government representatives, two national Parliamentarians and a representative from the candidate countries. Herzog's authority ultimately proved greater than Giscard d' Estaing's: his Convention was less politicised, he was an acknowledged expert on constitutional law and he had been 'elected' by the Convention itself. As a result, Herzog's presidium was better able to act as a third-party arbitrator than d' Estaing's, which was often accused of being autocratic and failing adequately to respond to, or consult with, the Convention.[13]

Finally, both Conventions had a strong incentive to reach a mutually acceptable outcome. The European Council had ordained that a draft Charter was to be presented for approval 'when the chairperson ... deems that the text of the draft Charter elaborated by the body can eventually be subscribed to by all the parties' (Conclusions of Tampere European Council, 15–16.10.1999). The Charter Convention's chair, Roman Herzog, took this instruction to mean that votes on individual proposals were to be avoided and that decision-making should be as consensual as possible, involving the support of all four components of the Convention (national governments, national parliamentarians, the European members of Parliament and the Commission representative). This interpretation was not uncontentious, and was felt by some to hide real divisions and by others to give too much power to minority opinions.[14] Still, the final draft was approved by a 'consensus minus two' at the plenary.[15] The Laeken mandate formalised Herzog's consensus approach, with Valery Giscard d' Estaing treating 'consensus' as something between unanimity and majority vote. However, many found his interpretation of this rule obscure.

Nevertheless, notwithstanding these near optimal discursive conditions, the resulting constitutional consensus within both Conventions actually consisted of a series of normal compromises aimed less at normative agreement than mutual acceptability. We shall take each Convention in turn. As we noted above, the Charter Convention debates reveal cleavages over six dimensions of rights – their substance, subjects, sphere, scope, the ways to secure them and their specification. A major divide concerned the legitimate sphere of the Union's activity. Some, like the British government's representative Lord Peter Goldsmith, maintained 'the task of this Convention is to make existing rights at European Union level more visible' (Goldsmith 2000a, 2000b). They wished to restrict the Charter to those rights derived from the sources to which the Council had referred them for guidance. Others, like the Italian government's delegate, Stefano Rodotà, thought the Charter should go beyond the ECHR and give 'substance to European citizenship' (personal communication). They wanted to draft a new and substantially wider document that extended into areas not covered by earlier instruments, such as biotechnology, and that might even provide the foundation of a future federal European polity. As a result, the debate over the EU's sphere partially overlapped with familiar philosophical and ideological differences over the substance of rights. Some wanted social rights included, others viewed them as policy choices that lie within (and must be compatible with) a domain established by civil and political rights. This debate was also related to discussions over whether all rights, some or none, should extend to subjects other than citizens of the Union (a status currently restricted to nationals of the member states). Some considered fundamental rights as logically including all humans, others considered them as attributes of citizenship. Different accounts of the nature of rights also tend to produce divergent understandings of the scope of various categories. Not surprisingly, conservative parties tended to emphasise market-based and process rights protecting formal equality, while social democrats favoured placing social rights on a par with traditional civil and political rights as necessary to ensure these were of equal worth to all. These differences also informed the major divisions over the status of the Charter and how, if at all, it should be secured. Some insisted the Charter should be legally binding, others contended the Cologne conclusions had made clear it would only be declaratory. Naturally, all these issues had an impact on the way the various rights came to be specified.

Significantly, the Convention did not divide into two distinct groups of minimalists and maximalists, with debates so polarised between them that compromise became difficult. Because a maximalist on matters of substance might be a minimalist over which subjects or spheres should be included, there were cross-cutting divisions. The groups who agreed or disagreed about one dimension differed from those who agreed or disagreed over another. Nor was a maximalist position necessarily always the most just, with all detractions from it being motivated by national or group self-interest rather than principle. To a large extent, disagreements took place in the context of general agreement on the importance of rights. All member states are signatories of the European Convention on Human Rights (ECHR), along with other international instruments, and possess some form of domestic bill of rights. Though special interests may have motivated some arguments, this applied as much to maximalist as to minimalist positions. However, most divisions mirrored, albeit at a lower level of sophistication, debates in the academic literature between cosmopolitans and liberal nationalist communitarians, Kantians and utilitarians, choice and benefit theorists and so on. In other words, they are rights-based differences between and over the nature of rights rather than between proponents and opponents of rights.

The solution to these disagreements lays in the types of compromise outlined above. Forms of bargaining that simply split the difference proved possible to a remarkable degree. For example, the substantive debate between proponents and opponents of workers' rights reached a compromise whereby the proposal for a 'right to work', in the sense of an entitlement to a job, became modified to the more free market sounding 'freedom to choose an occupation and a right to engage in work' (Article 15).[16] Other compromises in this area involved trading, whereby a package was agreed giving each side some of what it wanted. Thus, a deal was done whereby Article 29 establishing a right of access to a free placement service was included in return for a relatively open-ended 'right to own, use, dispose or bequeath his or her lawfully acquired possessions' and the recognition of the 'freedom to conduct a business' (Articles 17 and 16, respectively).[17]

Part of the controversy surrounding social rights arose from many aspects of social policy not falling within the EU's current competence.[18] Consequently, even those who substantively favoured social rights did not necessarily support them in the Charter because they did not wish to expand the Union's sphere. Here too trading offered the solution, with Articles 51 and 52 representing a compromise of this kind that gave something to both minimalist and maximalist stances on this issue. The former gain by the first article, which limits the Charter's application to EU institutions and the implementation of EU law by the member states (51: 1) while explicitly ruling out the creation of any new competence (51: 2). However, the latter gain by the second article, which indicates that limitations on these rights are not justified by the subsidiarity principle (52: 1) and that when they coincide with rights in the ECHR, acceded to by all member states, have the same scope as there (52: 3), though allowing the Charter and Union law to exceed them. This concession to the sphere minimalist in the event allowed a fairly maximalist view of the scope of social rights to enter into the Charter, even when it was doubtful if they did fall within the EU's competence, as was the case with social security (Article 34) and health care (Article 35) (though these were only granted 'in accordance with the rules laid down by Community law and national laws and practices').

When it came to the tricky issue of the subjects of Charter rights, segregation provided the solution. The Cologne mandate had been ambiguous on this question, listing not only the supposedly universal rights contained in the ECHR but also 'the fundamental rights that pertain only to the Union's citizens' (Conclusions of the Cologne European Council Meeting), thereby implying not all the rights included in the Charter would automatically be rights of 'every person'. Many Convention members expressed their concern about limiting rights to EU citizens, which some saw as incompatible with the substance of human rights as universal entitlements.[19] However, it was also possible that extending EU rights to all persons would result in a minimalist position as regards both their sphere and scope. The resolution of this complex dispute was a multilayered compromise involving distinguishing five categories of rights according to their subject. So the 'classical' fundamental rights and freedoms (i.e. those taken mainly from the ECHR) are formulated as 'rights of every person', those rights based on the EC/EU Treaty provisions on citizenship are rights of 'every EU citizen', then there are rights, such as for example 'social security and social assistance' (Article 34) which are addressed to 'everyone residing and moving legally within the European Union', while some other rights (e.g. Articles 27, 28, 30 and 31) provide rights for 'every worker' or for 'every child' (Article 24.3). Finally, the Charter introduces a new category of rights addressed to 'any Union citizen and any natural or legal person residing or having its registered office in a member state' (Articles 42, 43 and 44). So, by segregating between different categories of rights and stipulating carefully who could hold them, the classes of people counting as subjects of EU rights could be expanded.

Nevertheless, not all issues relating to the identity of the subjects of rights could be dealt with in this way. A particularly pertinent example was the right to join and found political parties at the European level. Compromise on this right was only achieved by a form of trimming that involved moving from the particular policy to a higher level of abstraction. Originally the presidium had proposed a separate article specifying that 'every citizen' had the right to join and found parties (Convention 17 of 20.03.2000). This proposal sparked a controversial debate over whether such an important political right could and should be restricted to EU citizens, and what provisions ought to be made for immigrants. In response, the presidium proposed a second draft of this article which drew a distinction between the right to join a political party, which it gave to 'everyone', and the right to found political parties, which was to be restricted to 'every citizen' (Convention 28 of 05.05.2000). After another debate and a number of written alternative proposals, the presidium withdrew this idea and decided to drop the whole article from the Charter's chapter on citizens' rights. Instead, parties are now referred to only in the abstract in the second paragraph of Article 12, which covers the much less controversially universal right of 'freedom of assembly'.

As the above examples show, compromises over one dimension of rights tended to interact with, and often ease, compromises in other dimensions. As a result of this process, agreement on the Charter as a whole gradually developed. However, there was always a danger of the various compromises coming apart whenever the ways they fitted together as part of a composite package came under close scrutiny. For reasonable disagreements remained, particularly over the substance of many rights and the status of the Charter. These differences were largely overcome by concentrating on particular issues and treating the decisions as the product of a pragmatic attitude of give and take rather than a consensus on rights. Indeed, sometimes the language of rights was dropped altogether.[20] For example, in the areas of consumer and environmental protection, it proved impossible to settle on a formula based on individual rights. Instead, an agreement was reached on a general policy aim or 'principle' as it was termed. Thus, Article 37 does not give a right to a clean environment but merely declares 'A high level of environmental protection and the improvement of the quality of the environment must be integrated into the policies of the Union and ensured in accordance with the principle of sustainable development'. Likewise, Article 38 states 'Union policies shall ensure a high level of consumer protection'.[21]

Thus, as table 6.1 indicates, the Charter involved multiple compromises over each dimension of rights. A 'constitutional' consensus could not be found through convergence on a uniquely reasonable position. Instead, mutually acceptable concessions between reasonable and occasionally incompatible views were sought and found. These compromises involved bargaining as much as deliberative argument, although the latter more often than not informed the former, which were founded as much in conflicts of principle as in competing interests. In many cases, it was not the right itself that was in dispute so much as the policy implications that might be drawn from a given interpretation of it. Sometimes, as in the debate over the right to join and found parties, the issue was resolved by trimming to a level of abstraction that left the right sufficiently fuzzy as to allow a variety of interpretations. However, in most cases, the desire was to reduce the scope for judicial discretion by either segregating the right to protect national jurisdictions or specifying a given interpretation, in which case a trade-off usually was necessary over some other right in another policy area. As a result, the Charter came to resemble a piece of ordinary legislation not just in the way it was framed but also in its substance.

By and large, both the Charter and the process that gave rise to it have been regarded as successful, and it was incorporated into the draft Constitution more or less unchanged as part 2 of the draft Constitution.[22] By contrast, the draft Constitution has been less well received.[23] Undoubtedly, it was taken much more seriously by the public and politicians and is rather more contentious. Yet, this did not lead to the dominance of pure bargaining. True, it was not entirely absent. Certain national governments attempted to force through concessions by using the threat of a veto – especially in the very last phase of the Convention when time pressures meant that such tactics could be used without having to be justified before the Convention as a whole. For example, Germany and France were each able to overturn a previously agreed extension of qualified majority voting to an area of particular sensitivity to them: namely, immigration and access to the labour market, and trade in cultural

Table 6.1 Compromises in the Rights Convention

Dimension of Rights	Type of Compromise				
	Bargaining	Trading	Segregation	Trimming	Third-Party Arbitration
Substance	Right to work (Article 15)	Article 29 in return for Articles 16/17	Linguistic segregation on the religious issue in preamble (German text is different)	Question of legal status of the Charter – Herzog's 'as if' approach	Overall agreement on the Charter as a package (final decision about Charter was left to IGC)
Subjects			Five categories of rights holders in the Charter	Question of political parties (now only mentioned indirectly)	Question of application to member states 'only when they are implementing Union law' left to the ECJ
Sphere	'Solidarity' as principle in preamble in return for less substantive social rights	Article 51/52 setting limits to Charter applicability	Principles rather than rights on environment and consumer protection	Agreement that Charter would only be applicable to EU institutions, not directly to member states	
Scope		Article 51/52 setting limits to Charter applicability but making Charter 'minimum standard'		Linguistic trimming; earlier drafts spoke of EU 'guaranteeing rights' – replaced by 'recognises rights'	
Securing and specification	Introducing the reference 'under the conditions provided by Community law and national laws' in contested articles	Article 51/52	Later addition of 'explanatory statements' by presidium (now part of the Charter text in draft Constitution)		

goods, respectively. However, the commonest kind of compromise was based on negotiation, with procedural devices, trimming and segregation also playing a part.

Examples of negotiated compromise include the involvement of national parliaments in monitoring subsidiarity (see the protocols on the role of national Parliaments and on the application of the principles of subsidiarity and proportionality). The debate about how to uphold the principle of subsidiarity without overly curtailing the EU's capacity to act or jeopardising the efficiency of its law-making power, was initially polarised between those seeking the creation of a third chamber representing national parliaments and others advocating very little, if any, change to the current (weak) system of enforcement. The compromise solution integrated both points of view. Though national parliaments were not formerly involved in EU decision-making, their role is strengthened. They must now be kept informed of EU developments and have the possibility of issuing 'early warnings' when they believed the principle of subsidiarity to be under threat, supplemented with the ultimate sanction of bringing cases before the European Court of Justice via the national governments.

Another successful integrative compromise resulted from the negotiations about the division of competencies between the European Union and its member states. A core question of the Laeken mandate, this issue provoked heated debate during the early stages. Some, notably the German Länder, wanted a fixed catalogue of competencies, others were wary of prematurely fixing EU structures in their current state. As with the agreement on national parliaments, a compromise was forged within a working group. The proposed solution was to introduce three basic categories of competencies (exclusive and shared competencies and a category of 'supporting, coordinating or complementary action', Articles I-13, I-14 and I-17), as well as special provisions for specific policy areas (economic and employment policy, foreign and security policy, Articles I-15–16) and a flexibility clause which allows the Union to adopt measures for which it does not have specific competencies, but which are necessary to obtain the objectives of the Union (Article I-18).[24] The safeguard against excessive use of this latter provision is the unanimity requirement and the necessary consent of the European Parliament (Article I-18.1) and the specific reference to the subsidiarity monitoring mechanism (Article I-18.2) and the exclusion of harmonisation (Article I-18.3). This complex compromise seems to have satisfied most if not all Convention members that the right balance had been struck.

Procedural compromises were naturally crucial to the Union's institutional arrangements. The principle of equality of member states was frequently invoked in the debates about them, with equal rotation promoted as its clearest expression. This was introduced at Treaty level in its basic form in the article on the rotation of the Presidency of the Council of Ministers (Article I-24), even though various proposals had been made for elected Chairs of these bodies. Nevertheless, the specifics of the 'equal rotation' are left for the European Council to decide, 'in accordance with the conditions established by a European decision of the European Council' (Article I-24.7).

On the whole, however, the need to develop coherent policy-making structures meant that more complex procedural solutions were adopted. The system for the election of the President of the European Commission as introduced by Article I-27 represents a good compromise in this respect. It combines the two logics (the intergovernmental and the supranational) of European integration: the European Council proposes a candidate by a qualified majority, for the EP to elect by a majority. The somewhat vague formula that in choosing the candidate the European Council should take 'into account the elections to the European Parliament' is a compromise solution which allows room for some flexibility until a more stable European party system has emerged.

As far as trimming is concerned, it is difficult to establish in many cases which issues could have been debated by the Convention, but were not included as a matter of choice or reasoned decision. On the whole, the Convention sought to avoid the vagueness and deliberate ambiguities that were often employed to reach agreements at IGCs. From this point of view, trimming was seen as a failure. However, as we noted earlier, one issue which was consciously (and largely successfully) removed from debate was the contents of the EU Charter of Fundamental Rights. While the Laeken mandate had clearly indicated that a solution had to be found on the questions of if and how the Charter should become part of the constitutional treaty, it did not mention the contents of the Charter. Yet there were voices in the second Convention's early debates that criticised certain aspects of the Charter and seemed to imply the need to reopen the issues decided by the first Convention. Nevertheless, the working group on the Charter very clearly stated that 'the content of the Charter represented a consensus reached by the previous Convention. ... The whole Charter – including its statements of rights and principles, its preamble, and, as a crucial element, its "general provisions" – should be respected by this Convention and not be re-opened by it' (Conv 354/02:4). Given that it is unclear that the decisions of the second Convention could have been any different to the first in this regard, trimming on this issue was probably the best solution.

Segregation was also a tool employed by the Convention in the search for agreement. Clearly, reserving certain decisions within the EU context for member states or even subnational actors is a form of segregation. To some degree, a clearer demarcation of state competences in certain areas was employed to allow greater integration in others. In this regard, the new arrangements for protecting subsidiarity represented a compromise between the groups in the Convention who clearly pushed for further centralisation of competencies, and those who wanted to roll back integration and give powers to the national level. This sort of compromise was not possible in all issue areas, however, with foreign affairs and common defence and security policy proving particularly tricky. Various forms of flexible integration have been offered as one way of getting round this problem. The idea of enhanced cooperation (Article I-44), for example, allows those countries wishing to embark on further integration in certain areas to do so without waiting for the agreement of those member states that are unwilling or unable to participate. The challenge is to balance such a clause against the danger of an overall dissolution of the European Union or the creation of a two-tier system if the mechanism is used too often. The procedure for enhanced cooperation in Article I-44 of the Constitution therefore introduces a large number of safeguards (such as non-exclusivity of the groups forging ahead, the rule that enhanced cooperation be used as a 'last resort', only upon authorisation by the Council and with a minimum of one-third of member states as participants, etc.) to ensure it does not lead to the development of permanent parallel groups of member states. Once again, it represents a fair balancing between the demand for unity and consistency, on the one hand, and for diversity and autonomy, on the other.

Similar reasoning lies behind the institutionalisation of the Euro-group, where different speeds of integration are already established. By adopting specific provisions for those countries which have adopted the Euro (Article I-15 and Articles III-194–202), decisions about monetary issues are to a certain extent segregated. While it seems obvious that EU members belonging to the Euro naturally have to take certain decisions together without those who do not belong to the single currency, the inclusion of such specific provisions at the constitutional level raises the question of whether a permanent closure might be established of the Euro-group vis-à-vis a minority of non-Euro member states. This impression is exacerbated by the fact that the Constitution also contains a section on 'transitional provisions' (Articles III-197–202) on member states that do not (yet) fulfil the criteria for Euro-membership, but it does not seem to provide for member states to decide not to join the single currency at all. How these provisions will interact with political reality is a matter for future analysis, but there is at least the danger of segregation being imposed by the majority on the minority.

So, as table 6.2 shows, the Convention on the Future of Europe also presents an array of different sorts of compromises. Of course, some compromises will be regarded as more felicitous than others. Some believe the Charter and Constitution trim too much. For example, many believe the first excludes non-EU nationals on too many issues and skirts around social rights, while others fear

Table 6.2 Compromises in the Constitutional Convention

Bargaining	Negotiating (trading, log-rolling, second best, etc.)	Procedural Pure (e.g. lottery or rotation)	Procedural Imperfect (e.g. majority – or qualified majority – decision-making)	Trimming	Segregation
Last-minute exceptions to qualified majority voting introduced by individual powerful players – cultural trade (France), immigration (Germany)	Early warning system on subsidiarity for national parliaments – protocol division of competencies: no rigid catalogue, but categories (Articles 11–17)	General principle of equal rotation for presidency of sectoral council formations (Article 23.4)	Election of Commission president by majority of European Parliament on proposal by qualified majority of the Council (Article 26.1)	No re-discussion of the Charter compromises	Strengthening of subsidiarity control via national parliaments; principle of enhanced cooperation of member states which want to go further (Article 43)

the second is silent on too many issues in the area of economic governance, where no agreement could be reached beyond the status quo (working group final report: Conv 357/02). The system for the definition of the qualified majority (Convention draft Article 24) likewise attracted considerable criticism and ultimately proved too contentious for the IGC. In a further round of compromise negotiation, the IGC agreed on a more refined system giving extra protection to smaller states – albeit, arguably at the expense of clarity and efficiency (Article I-25 Constitution). To a large degree, we can regard these less satisfactory compromises as representing distributive rather than integrative solutions, where those with most power were able to ignore or partially block the demands of others. As we acknowledged, this is always a danger with normal politics. Ironically, though it is precisely this possibility that Constitutions and Charters are supposed to guard against. At least within a normal political process, an oppressed group can rally, build new alliances and seek to get its opponents to think again. That becomes much harder when a poor compromise gets entrenched as part of the very constitution of normal politics. One has only to think of the ways the electoral college system has distorted recent Presidential elections within the United States, enhancing the likelihood of a minority winner by grossly over weighting the votes of the electors in small states and reducing the campaign to a battle over a few swing states (for details and criticism, see Dahl 2002, chap. 4), to become aware of how provisions that seemed the best available (if less than satisfactory) solution to an impasse at one time can live on to become even more unfortunate later. As a Constitutional Treaty, the Constitution has to be ratified by an IGC and by every member state according to its own constitutional requirements. Moreover, the Constitutional Treaty requires the same cumbersome procedure for future changes to the Constitution.[25] Given the normality of its drafting, however, it seems obvious that a more normal way to adapt the new document to changes has to be found.

CONCLUSION

The Convention has been greeted in many quarters as offering a new method for legitimating European integration – one that differed from the politics of compromise held to characterise intergovernmental conferences where principle was allegedly subordinated to national interests (e.g. Deloche-Gaudez 2001). We have argued this contrast is overdrawn. The Convention setting can help filter out overtly self-serving arguments but it cannot funnel reasoning towards a consensus that abstracts from and rises above normal politics. To a great extent, this is because matters of principle, such as rights, or of the foundations of politics, such as voting systems, are subject to the reasonable disagreements that animate normal political debate. Moreover, given these disagreements result from the complexity of people's circumstances and experiences, compromises not only are achieved using the stratagems of normal politics but also reflect the prevailing normal political divisions on the issues of the day. The main achievement of constitutional politics is not to resolve or go beyond these divisions so much as to render people aware of them and to normalise them within mutually acceptable agreements that take them into account. In this respect, the comparative representativeness of both Conventions has been crucial, as has been their relative openness to civil society.[26] Yet this inclusiveness makes the need for compromise more rather than less likely, since it almost certainly increases the diversity of views and interests that need to be accommodated.

Are the results of such processes compromised as a result? Those disappointed by what they regard as the unfortunate political manoeuvring of both the Charter Convention and more especially that on the Future of Europe might be tempted to argue that academics, bureaucrats or members of the judiciary rather than politicians should draft constitutional documents. Such a proposal would be misguided. First, there is no reason to believe that any group containing the standard range of views on these questions would be any less likely to diverge on the points that have divided these (and other) conventions. After all, constitutional courts frequently split and have to make decisions by majority vote, while their agreements are often 'incompletely theorised' and either trim from their principled disagreements or involve negotiation on the basis of analogies with other cases (Sunstein 1996, chap. 3). Second, a frequent complaint about the EU is that too many important decisions get taken by experts and technocrats. As the elected representatives of citizens, politicians arguably have greater standing legitimately to make what are necessarily political choices on their behalf. Interestingly, António Vitorino, the Commission representative at the Charter Convention, was of this view, arguing that the 'wise combination of the Community and national sides and, above all, the parliamentary predominance will help bolster the draft Charter's legitimacy in the eyes of a public that is often critical of the complex decision-making machinery at European level' (quoted in De Búrca 2001, 131). A supposedly ideal normative consensus would simply have indicated the exclusion of a number of widely held positions from the drafting body and so delegitimise its conclusions.[27] Finally, this argument misconceives the role of a Constitution. The necessary employment of normal politics within Constitution making reflects the purpose of constitutions themselves as much as the process of drafting them. Rather than treating constitutions as somehow superior to and literally constituting normal politics, they should be seen as a form of mutual recognition that normalises political divisions (Shaw 2003, 47–52; Tully 1995, 30). Their success lies not in remaining outside normal politics but in informing it – and not merely via blind obedience to constitutional norms but also through citizens critically challenging and defending them. In other words, perhaps the prime virtue of the normality of constitutional politics resides in turning the resulting Constitution into part of the basic vocabulary of normal political debate. It achieves this effect not through bypassing everyday political divisions but by engaging with and reflecting them using the resources of normal politics.

This last point raises a more general issue about the status of constitutions and charters with regard to normal legislative processes. If they are akin to normal legislation in both their drafting and their content, ought we to give them special production and make them a source for the judicial review of the laws passed by the legislature? Doing so might itself be seen as a necessary compromise if certain issues are so divisive, or people deemed so careless or myopic, that they are likely only to be handled reasonably through trimming them from the normal political agenda and handing their protection to a third party.[28] Yet there is also the danger that a charter could freeze a given position or prove so vague in its guidance as to give undue scope to judicial discretion. For example, both criticisms have been raised against the EU Charter and Constitution. While some see them as a turning point in the EU's evolution (e.g. Eriksen 2001; Habermas 2001a), others believe the EU is evolving so fast that they are premature (Weiler 2000, 95–7, 2003, 7–23). The difficulty is that those rights and procedures that are clearly spelt out may merely reflect current concerns and become outdated, while those in more contentious areas are so loosely formulated they could be interpreted in quite contradictory ways. For example, two of the main issues for the future of the EU concern its competences vis-à-vis the member states, especially with regard to social policy, and the status of third-country nationals. As we noted, these were areas where the Charter employed extensive trimming and segregation. It could be the very mention of these topics within the Charter will ensure that future policy takes the rights involved extremely seriously.[29] Yet, the experience of domestic charters suggests this may involve legislatures either leaving principled issues up to courts or seeking to anticipate their judgements. Either way, politicians (and to some degree ordinary voters too) will have ceased to think about rights and discuss them for themselves (see Stone Sweet 2000, for the European experience; and Tushnet 1999, for the United States). Moreover, in circumstances of deep disagreement, a court's interpretation may be as divisive as any other,[30] so that its and the Charter's authority themselves become an issue within the political debate, putting the legitimacy of EU institutions into question and reducing the capacity of the system to broker necessary compromises. Arguably, something like this scenario has arisen in Canada over precisely these sorts of concerns (Fudge 2002, chap. 18). In such circumstances, it may be better to improve the competency of normal politics to decide such constitutional questions – especially if they are likely to be raised on an almost continuous basis. This proposal would involve designing normal political institutions in such a way that compromises had the openness and fairness we found in the Conventions. For instance, instead of seeking to discover a definitive list of EU competences or agree on the principles that might decide this issue, both impossible tasks – as the numerous attempts to give substance to the term subsidiarity has revealed all too well, the draft Constitution for the EU suggests allowing national parliaments to contest extensions of the EU beyond what they regard as its legitimate sphere (Protocol on the Application of the Principles of Subsidiarity and Proportionality, CONV 850/03, para. 5, 230). Such democratic mechanisms reflect the contemporary need for constitutional settlements to be open to a continuous process of democratic legitimation in order to respond to the evolving and differing ideals and interests of their citizens and the rapid changes of modern economies and societies.

In sum, the difference between constitutional politics and normal politics is not as deep as it is often claimed. Many 'constitutional' questions can and have to be solved by normal politics, and the institutions of a political system should be designed to allow a normalised constitutional dialogue. Constitutional conventions, such as the Convention on the Future of Europe, may help kick start a global process of reform. But if constitutional politics is simply a version of normal politics, reifying the compromises achievable at a particular time within a constitutional settlement may prove a considerable hindrance to any future, incremental reforms made necessary by changing circumstances and views. Given the rapid expansion and growing diversity of the EU and the dramatic transformations of modern economies and societies, such limitations are likely to be encountered sooner rather than later. Therefore, in the medium to long term, the redesign of normal politics to allow constitutional issues to be regularly debated, deployed and developed with due consideration may be preferable to taking them off the political agenda altogether or reserving them exclusively to extraordinary fora. In other words, constitutionalists should focus attention on the political constitution of the polity or organisation, that is, its system of ongoing decision-making for the settling of differences, rather than on vain attempts to establish legal, rights-based constitutional foundations that seek to go beyond political divisions.[31] So far as the EU is concerned, an appropriate place to start might be to consider how the experience of the two Conventions could be used to replace the IGC with a flexible, efficient and normal way of resolving constitutional conflicts in the future and adapting the Constitutional Treaty, should it be ratified, to changing concerns and circumstances.

NOTES

1. This chapter draws on two earlier essays by the authors (Bellamy and Castiglione 2004b, 2004c). We are grateful to Daniel Halberstam for encouraging us to draw out further some of the implications of these two pieces.

2. Although see Dahl (2002, chap. 2), who notes how the Philadelphia delegates had 'to engage in fundamental compromises to agree on any constitution at all' (12).

3. The response of *The Economist* (2003, 9), which had earlier produced its own draft EU Constitution, was typical in this respect. As their commentator wrote, 'There was always a risk that the Convention would not design a particularly good constitution. What was harder to imagine was that the Convention would produce a text which would worsen the very problems it had been instructed to address ... [yet this] is what it has somehow contrived to do'.

4. While we can only examine the normality of constitutional politics here, we would equally wish to insist on normal legislative politics having many of the qualities reserved by some to abnormal constitutional deliberations (see Waldron 1999). However, we would also want to stress that even on matters of principle, politics cannot be too high flown. To resolve principled disagreements that defy any consensus, we often need to use a range of bargaining and procedural techniques to achieve a compromise.

5. For a survey of how different forms of representation ensure minorities reach a sufficient threshold to have a voice, see Phillips (1995).

6. Lijphart's analysis of twenty-one stable democracies revealed only six as conforming to this pattern (Lijphart 1984; Dahl 1989, 15660).

7. Even 'originalists' in the United States, such as Bork (1990), who stress the importance of remaining faithful to the words and intentions of the framers, end up engaging in selective updating whenever the 'original' meaning proves too ambiguous or inconvenient for them to abide by it. On the inevitability of interpretation and updating, see Sunstein (1996, chap. 8).

8. Both the Conclusions of Cologne European Council Meeting 3-4.06.1999, Annex IV, establishing the Charter Convention and the Laeken Mandate, European Council 15.12.2001, Document SN 273/01 setting up the Convention on the Future of Europe played down the constitutional aspects of these bodies' tasks. Such attempts by upstream authorities to constrain constitution-making bodies are not untypical, since they worry their power might be subverted. Like similar bodies in the past, though, both Conventions tended to strain their remit to the limit and the decision to draft a Charter and a Constitution, respectively, was taking early on.

9. Some analysts even claim international negotiations can produce the sort of rational consensus expected of constitutional politics (e.g. Risse 2000). Though we see such accounts as skirting around the difficulties in the way of real consensus – which is strange for academics who must rarely leave a seminar not disagreeing with someone – and hence of confusing all well-motivated agreements with a convergence on 'the truth', they do at least show that diplomacy is more than mere self-interested bargaining.

10. The discussion that follows employs the criteria Elster (1996, 107, 117) derives from his analysis of the Philadelphia, Paris and Frankfurt conventions.

11. Given that regions often have some constitutional independence, their involvement was weak. In the Charter Convention, the only formal requirement was to consult the Committee of the Regions (Conclusions of the Tampere Council 15/16.10.1999, Annex, A iv). However, where, as in Germany, the second house is a federal chamber, the national parliamentary delegations included a regional representative. The Convention on the Future of Europe had observers from the Committee of the Regions, but again no formal regional representatives – although Neil MacCormick, a Scottish Nationalist, was an alternate member of the European Parliament's delegation in the Convention and raised regional issues on matters such as minority language policy. See MacCormick (2004).

12. N.B. Membership of the Convention and its sub-bodies changed over the seventeen months of the Convention's existence.

13. A number of critical first-hand accounts have already been published; see, for example, Einem (2004); Kiljunen (2004); and Stuart (2003).

14. For a critical view, see Voggenhuber (2001). On one occasion in the Charter Convention, the attempt by the acting chairman Mendez de Vigo to put a presidium proposal to a vote nearly led to a walkout of a large number of Convention members who insisted that votes were not allowed under the Cologne/Tampere mandates (debates on document Conv 36/00 on 06.06.2000, as summarized in Deutscher Bundestag, *Die Charta der Grundrechte der Europäischen Union* (Berlin, 2001, 285)). The stalemate over the new voting rules, initially opposed by Spain and Poland, provoked a similar discussion in the second Convention.

15. The last plenary meeting of the Convention took place on 02.10.2000 during which the 'consensus of the Convention on the draft Charter of Fundamental rights was declared by the Convention's president to the applause of all but two delegates.

16. The following Articles of the Charter of Fundamental Rights are quoted with the Article numbers given in the version of Charter endorsed by the EU member states at the Nice summit in December 2000.

17. This 'trade-off', explored below, was struck by Iñigo Mendez de Vigo in the European Parliament delegation between the Socialists and Social Democrats, on the one hand, and the Conservatives and Christian Democrats, on the other.

18. See Convention debate on 03.04.2000 as summarised in Deutscher Bundestag (2001, 253/54). The Cologne mandate had stated that social rights from documents like the European Social Charter should only be included 'insofar as they do not merely establish objectives for action by the Union', a view supported by the head of the Convention secretariat, J. P. Jacqué, who argued that the Community could not promote human rights but only uphold a minimum set of judicially enforceable standards (De Burca 2001, 134/5). As we shall see, the Convention partly dissented from this restricted view.

19. Johannes Voggenhuber was most clearly against any restriction (interview 10.10.2000). Most other Convention members accepted that for practical reasons, and with reference to the Cologne mandate, the Charter would include different categories of rights holders.

20. See the debate of 5.6.2000 over whether the Charter could distinguish between 'genuine rights' and 'mere principles' (Deutscher Bundestag 2001, 279–84).

21. In the 5 June debate Herzog used the protection of the environment as an example of a 'principle' which was not an individual right, but should still bind the member states. Summarised in Deutscher Bundestag (2001, 279–80).

22. The main change is that the British pushed through the incorporation of the Praesidium's explanatory notes into the body of the Charter (Part II, Title VII, Articles II-51–54, CONV 850/03, pp. 59–60) largely because these were taken as limiting its 'scope' more clearly to EU institutions and policies (see the White Paper 2003, 39 para 102). There is also now a commitment to attempt to accede to the European Convention on Human Rights (Part 1, Title II, Article 7, para 2, CONV 850/03, p. 8).

23. See the minority report attached to the final document by eight full and substitute members of the Convention (Conv. 851/03 Annex) and the editorial 'On the Future of the Convention Method' by Arnull (2003, 573/4).

24. References to the Articles in the Constitution refer, unless specified otherwise, to the 'Consolidated Version of the Treaty establishing a Constitution for Europe', published as document CIG 87/04 on 06.08.2004. This has a different numbering with regard to earlier drafts.

25. Articles IV-444 and -445 do envisage the possibility of a 'lighter' revision procedure for moving issues from the unanimity role to qualified majority voting (Article IV-444) and on specific internal policy issues (Article IV-445). Yet in both cases the thresholds to take these decisions are high (Article IV-444 requires unanimity in the Council and assent of the European Parliament, Article IV-445 requires ratification by the member states).

26. For an assessment of how far these virtues are to be found in the Convention on the Future of the Union, see Shaw (2003, 53–67).

27. It is noteworthy how often the term 'compromise' has been used approvingly in regard to the draft EU Constitution, just released at the time of writing. For example, the pro-EU *Le Monde* 15–16 June 2003 even headlined its report 'Un texte de compromis pour un Union á 25'.

28. This is a standard argument for rights-based judicial review (e.g. Freeman 1990, 353/4).

29. Rights-foundationalists, who advocate far-reaching judicial review, often make this sort of claim for Bills of Rights (e.g. Dworkin 1986, 32).

30. Indeed, it may well suffer from falling short of people's expectations as to substance and scope while overreaching them as regards the sphere of the EU. For a critique of past performance in this regard, see Coppel and O'Neill (1992, 669–92).

31. Significantly, the articles on the workings of the Institutions proved among the most contentious of the proposed draft Constitution (CONV 724/03 p. 1). However, from the perspective argued for here, the proposals for revision are too complex and make reform too difficult. Even changes to part III (the EU policies) technically require a full treaty revision procedure, with unanimity in the Council, national ratification including referenda where necessary and so on (see note 23).

Chapter 7

Constitutional Politics in the European Union

Dario Castiglione

One of the problems, perhaps the main problem, that the 'Convention on the Future of Europe' had to face when it set out to draft a constitution was not so much whether it would succeed in writing a constitution that might satisfy the majorities of European citizens and all member states, but whether it *could* write a constitution at all. The original sin of European constitutionalism is that it tries to apply categories (those of the constitutional discourse) that have been developed for polities which have a fundamental element of political 'unity', even though they can take the form of either centralised or federal states. The European Union and its preceding institutional expressions started life, instead, as a form of international cooperation. As such, there is an underlying resistance to the very idea of a fundamental political 'unity' between the different members of such an organisation. In this sense, the challenges that the Convention faced were both practical and theoretical, and empirical and normative.

Indeed, for some time, legal philosophers, political theorists, theoretically inclined lawyers and political scientists have contributed to shaping a normative vocabulary and sharpening the analytical tools for coming to terms with the fundamental ambivalence of political integration. The central question, as already indicated, is that the European integration process has come to symbolise the crisis of one of the central categories on which modern political theorising has rested since Hobbes's time, namely the distinction between the kinds of relationships that apply *within* a state and those that apply *between* states. The partial breaking down of such a distinction has important consequences for how we think of politics itself and of its interlocking domains.

It is for these reasons that an understanding of the Convention consists not only in questioning whether writing the EU constitution was a way of making the European Union more legitimate, efficient and democratic but also whether the very writing of an EU constitution was either possible or legitimate in the first place. I start, accordingly, by trying to clarify some of the central categories that apply to constitutional politics in the EU.

THE MEANING OF CONSTITUTIONAL POLITICS

In examining the literature, one finds that 'constitutional politics' has no settled meaning. One of the available meanings takes constitutional politics to be an aspect of 'judicial power' (Stone Sweet 2000). This derives from the defining role that the written constitution and the process of judicial review of legislation have acquired in many modern democracies, following in particular the American model, but with reference also to a number of European *Rechtsstaat* traditions. The role that constitutional courts and the process of constitutional interpretation and adjudication play in limiting and redirecting legislation and policy making can be considered intrinsically *political*, and studied as a form of *politics*. This understanding of constitutional politics therefore focuses on the way in which political issues and policy making are influenced by the judicial process and by judicial actors, through means and modes of arguing that are typical of the judicial process and system, but that, insofar as they operate on substantive policies, can be considered political in the narrow sense, as determining the substance of the decisions and not just offering a 'frame' or the 'rules of the game' for arriving at the decisions themselves. A second meaning of constitutional politics takes a reverse view of the relationship between constitutional reality and politics by looking at ways in which political action contributes to the creation of a stable structure of rules, norms and expectations within which ordinary politics operates. The focus here is on the capacity that political decisions and circumstances have to determine a higher order of rules and to produce a constitutional structure, even when this is not formalised as such. A third meaning, finally, identifies constitutional politics with the more specific processes of constitution making and constitutional transformation, and it looks at the particular qualities and normative purchase that political action has, or need to have, in order to produce a higher set of rules and laws. These three meanings of constitutional politics are not in complete opposition to each other. Indeed, they occasionally tend to coincide, so that, for instance, the exercise of judicial power can be seen as a form of constitution making; or constitution making can be considered as being successful only if and when political action generates the background conditions within which a more formalised document or set of norms acquires true constitutional status. As we shall see in the course of our discussion, all three meanings are at play in the way in which the EU has consolidated in some kind of polity.

The ambiguous meaning of 'constitutional politics' partly reflects ambiguities in the use of ideas of 'constitutionalism' and the 'constitution'. In one
sense, constitutionalism is a modern political doctrine. It refers to a series of
principled arguments for the limitation of political power in general and of
government's sway over the life and rights of citizens in particular. Although
one may conceive the means for the limitation of political power in many different ways, in the course of the last two centuries, these limitations and their
underlying principles have been embodied in the institutions and practices of
the modern constitutional state, with at their centre a written constitutional
text (Castiglione 1996). By constitutionalism, in a second sense, one can thus
refer to the complex of institutions that characterises a constitutional regime;
a form of state, and an organisation of government, that is, that embodies the
principles of constitutionalism. This double meaning is very similar to that
which applies in the case of the term 'socialism', which is used to indicate
either the ideology or the political regime – and occasionally both at the
same time. There remains, however, some important difference between the
analytical use of constitutionalism as a regime, and its normative meaning,
so that discussions of European constitutionalism and its transformations
(Weiler 1999) may be taken to refer to either the introduction of some kind of
constitutional charter and constitutional law in the EU system of governance,
or to a discussion of what kind of public philosophy should guide such a form
of governance.

Although it would at first appear less evident, the ambivalence in the uses
of constitutionalism also applies to the understanding of the constitution
itself. In a more obvious sense a constitution is, as Paine said, 'a thing ...
in fact': something that has 'a visible form', and can be quoted 'article by
article' (1989, 81). But of course, Paine was here making a point against the
Ancient and unwritten tradition of English constitutionalism. Even though,
in its modern sense, the constitution is usually intended as a document setting out the higher law (or 'constitutive' rules) of a state; by the constitution
a number of other 'things' are also intended, such as the act through which
something is constituted, the basic norm according to which other laws and
legislation can be judged, and the structure or inner characteristics defining
a political order. Such a variety of meanings suggests that different roles are
attributed to the constitution within organised legal and political systems,
and that such roles can be looked at either analytically, as having a *function*
within the system, or normatively, as determining how the system *ought to*
work. Thus, to agree on what a constitution is or does may not be that easy,
even when one takes it to be the linchpin on which the modern constitutional
state rests. This distinction between the functional and normative role of the
constitution is partly at the basis of the two narratives of constitutional politics we identify in this chapter, one more concerned with the way in the which

the EU has acquired a constitutional order, while the other more attentive to the legitimacy of such a constitutional order.

There is, of course, as mentioned at the beginning, the added complication that the EU, and the other institutional forms in which European integration has temporarily crystallised over the past fifty years, cannot readily be conceived as having state properties; or at least not in the same way in which one traditionally thinks of the state, as consisting (in broadly Weberian terms) in a unified territorial entity, where the central authority exercises a legal monopoly of power, and the citizenry accepts such an exercise as having some form of legitimacy (i.e. where power does not rest on force alone). In modern constitutional democracies, the constitution (in its various meanings) is said to be playing various important roles, such as legitimating power, insofar as it seems to authorise it; or conferring unity to the legal and political system, by acting as the crucial link between these two systems of social organisation (Luhman 1992); or ensuring the loyalty of the citizens, by offering itself as a cultural and normative point of reference for the citizens' allegiance to the political system and their identification with the political community. In all these three roles, however, the capacity of the constitution to perform those functions is seen as dependent on the fact that there is some form of unified structure of power that the constitution helps to put together and organise in some hierarchical form. This is precisely what is meant to be lacking at the European level, where certainly at the beginning of the integration process, and arguably still nowadays, authorisation, legitimacy, integration, allegiance and enforcement are fundamentally mediated by the member states, and therefore reflect the fragmented structure of power typical of the international system, and not (or not yet) the more unified and homogeneous one of the constitutional state. In order to talk meaningfully of constitutional politics in the EU (in either its functional or normative version), it is therefore necessary to make some sense of the divided image of the EU, as both an international organisation and a polity in the making. *Hic Rhodus, hic salta!*[1]

THE EMERGENCE OF THE EUROPEAN CONSTITUTIONAL ORDER

One way, the most obvious one, of telling the story of constitutional politics in the EC/EU is to look at how the European constitutional order has come to life; or, as Alec Stone Sweet has put it, how has it happened that the EC/EU has metamorsophised 'from an international regime, founded on the precepts of international law, into a multi-tiered, quasi federal polity' (2000, 160). This is hardly an uncontested fact, but even those that hang on to the view that EU politics still operates as an international law regime (Grimm 1995), or that

EU decision-making is in essence intergovernmental (Moravcsik 1999), must offer some account of the consolidated nature of the Community legal and institutional order, and of what J. H. H. Weiler has described as the virtual foreclosure to member states of the *exit* option from Community obligations (1999, 31). Weiler himself has illustrated the emergence of European constitutionalism, meant as a constitutional regime, by looking at its 'geology', at how it was first conceptualised from a number of practical and theoretical perspectives (1999, 221–37). Following, in a slightly modified form, Weiler's own characterisation of what he considers the three main approaches during the foundational phase, we here distinguish between a historical (an adaptation of what Weiler calls 'doctrine' approach), a legal and a political reading of the emergence of the European constitutional order. These three readings offer a complex view of the 'constitutionalisation narrative'. We shall look at them in the reverse order.

Neo-functionalism and Supranational Politics

The political science approach is probably the least self-consciously constitutional of these three readings, but it offered the first sustained attempt to identify a new kind of order, as this was emerging from the European integration process. This version of the constitutionalisation narrative developed through a series of, often competing, 'grand theories' of European integration, starting with the intellectual breakthrough represented by neo-functionalism (Haas 1958). This is not the place where to reassess that theory and its intellectual history, but from a more specific constitutional perspective, its contribution can be summarised under several headings. For one, neo-functionalism entrenched the idea that there was a new, supranational dimension to politics. Interest formation and mediation were no longer taking shape exclusively within the two distinct, but mutually supportive sights of national statehood and the international arena. Moreover, the supranational dimension was not characterised by domination (as in the cases of imperial and colonial relationships), but it was emerging from the interactions of separate social and institutional actors, who operated (already at the national level) with a certain degree of autonomy, and who found it convenient to think of their interests and of the scope of their actions as something that reached beyond the nation state, connecting in this with other groups and institutions similarly operating with a regional framework in mind. Neo-functional theories and analyses propped up the idea of the new supranational dimension by suggesting that it had a dynamics of its own based on the concept of 'spillovers', and that its emergence was further reinforced by the very fact that it produced (and empowered) new institutional actors operating at the supranational level. Finally, both the mechanisms of functional development and adaptation, and the relative autonomy attributed to the supranational institutions overseeing integration, became part of a minoritarian, but self-conscious federal strategy for the promotion of the supranational level as an important, if not the dominant, political arena.

The partial demise of neo-functionalism, following a number of sustained attacks on some of its central tenets (Moravcsik 1999; Milward 1992) and the realisation that its teleology of integration was not consistently and unequivocally sustained by either empirical analysis or general political developments, should not detract from the fact that neo-functionalism contributed to the conceptualisation of the integration process, making this and the European institutions specific objects of analysis. Such analysis has since been carried forward through other methodological perspectives which, though rejecting some of the fundamental premises and guiding concepts of neo-functionalism, have nonetheless taken seriously the emergence of a supranational space and the autonomous role played by some of the European institutions. Neo-institutionalism, multilevel governance and, in a way, constructivism have offered a more nuanced way of conceiving the interactions between the national and the supranational levels, and how it is this mixture of levels, of institutional and normative constraints, and of competing constructions of political meaning that determines the constitutional underpinning of politics in the EU and the countries comprising it.

Judicial Constitutionalisation

In spite of the increasing attention showed by political scientists to the structural elements in European integration and politics, a constitutional discourse was relatively slow to emerge in this literature. This may have something to do with the general inattention towards constitutional matters in much of political science and political theory for several decades after the middle of the twentieth century (Bellamy and Castiglione 1996). Not so among the lawyers. The second, and arguably the most influential reading of the constitutional narrative, is the one focused on the emergence of a new legal order at the European level, and how particularly the European Court of Justice was instrumental in fixing both its character and the way in which such a supranational legal order related to that of the member states. The story of the so-called judicial constitutionalisation has been told many times, and in a variety of forms, but its basic outline is undisputed (though its significance remains contested). At the centre of this version of the constitutionalisation narrative there is the action of the European Court of Justice (ECJ) and how this, in the often-quoted words of Eric Stein, 'fashioned a constitutional framework for a federal-type structure', while working in 'benign neglect' from its basis in 'the fairyland Duchy of Luxembourg' (1981, 1). The constitutional order, in this case, is not (at least on the face of it) the product of a slow evolutionary process, as intended from a neo-functionalist perspective; nor is it the sedimentation of institutional logics and the way in which these both constrain and produce path-dependency. The constitutional order emerges instead as the by-product of a piecemeal, but purposive process of rationalisation of the legal system through case law, in which the Court plays a pivotal role in its dealings with private litigants and national courts. The assumption here is that the de facto legal system emerging from the integration process, the acquis communautaire, was given constitutional shape by the establishment of a series of ordering principles of European jurisprudence. These principles are usually identified as the Supremacy, and the Direct Effect doctrines (De Witte 1999); though one may also add *preemption* and the protection of human rights (Mancini 2000, 7–14; Weiler 1999, 22–5), and in a second period *indirect effect*, and *governmental liability* (Stone Sweet 2000, 163). Most of these doctrines are associated with particular legal cases and how the ECJ's rulings over them have become the cornerstones of the new constitutional order. To deal only briefly with Supremacy and Direct Effect: the doctrine of Supremacy, first established in *Costa v. ENEL* (ECJ 1964), maintains that community law has primacy over national law in view of the obligations that member states have incurred through agreements signed with other member states at the European level; and that national legislators cannot therefore legislate in a manner that is inconsistent with such agreements, while national judges have a 'duty to disapply' (De Witte 2000, 190) laws that may undermine such binding agreements. The doctrine of *direct effect*, first formulated in the *Van Gend en Loos* case (ECJ 1963) just before the *Costa* case, established instead the applicability at the national level of various legislative and regulative acts ('regulations', 'treaty provisions' and 'directives'). This would hold true even in those cases where national authorities either failed to make provisions for such application in a reasonable time, or the national law clashed with the spirit of the directives and regulations. Although the two rulings of the EJC (and others that have followed along the same path) remain controversial in their justification, their combined effect has been to suggest that there is a common legal order at the European level and that this has a kind of hierarchical structure that makes it similar to what applies at the national level.

There is an interesting ambivalence in this understanding of the judicial constitutionalisation of the EU. On the one hand, it is clear that the constitutional order so conceived, as a coherent system organised around a number of key principles and doctrines, is the product of 'judicial creativeness'; on the other hand, the action of the ECJ is presented as nothing more than the rational interpretation and coherent systematisation of principles already included in the acts and intentions of the national governments and the political actors who promoted and signed the EC/EU founding Treaties, thus giving form

and direction to the process of integration. The fact, of course, is that the difference between judicial 'creativeness' and judicial 'rationalisation' depends
on how one interprets what Stein called 'benign neglect', and on whether
one assumes that such neglect has persisted over time, from the foundational
phase of the 1960s and 1970s until nowadays (cf. also Weiler 1999, 191/2;
De Witte 1999, 194–98). The relationship between the kind of constitutional
jurisprudence defined by the ECJ, and the way in which this has been viewed
by member states' governments and Parliaments, as well as by ordinary and
constitutional courts at the national level, is an exceedingly complex story,
but posing the problem in this terms makes it clear that the view of judicial
constitutionalisation as the single-handed product of the ECJ is an oversim-
plification in which both supporters and critics occasionally tend to fall. In
any case, the view of the Court as the actor unpacking the logical implications of the intentions of the Treaties' signatories, and of the 'fact' that the
Treaties themselves have created 'a Community of unlimited duration', with
'real powers stemming from a limitation of sovereignty or transfer of powers
from the States to the Community' (ECJ 1964, 593), is something that must
necessarily rest on a particular reading of the history of treaty making in the
EC/EU. This is indeed the third version of the constitutionalisation narrative
to which we referred at the beginning of this section, the one dealing with the
chronicle of the formal and political acts through which member states have
locked themselves in the integration process.

From the Treaties to the Constitution

At the centre of this version there is the conceptual distinction between *treaty*
and *constitution*, an issue to which we shall return later from a more theoretical perspective. For the time being, we may to look at the issue from a more
historical perspective.[2] Here, we shall only attempt a summary overview to
assess its broad significance. The historical view seems to suggest that constitutional development in the EU/EC should be conceived as a linear evolution
from 'treaty' to 'constitution', as the effect of cumulative developments from
economic to political integration. In fact, a closer examination of the various
phases seems to undermine such an image, offering a much more complex
picture of changes and continuities.

The nature of the organisational structure within which to frame the process of European peaceful cooperation after World War II was a matter of
contention and experiment from the very beginning. The rhetorical appeal
to the idea of a 'constitution' was there from the outset. This emerged in
between the lines of numerous official documents and declarations, and motivated a number of failed attempts to establish a more solid ground for political cooperation. In spite of the difficulty that the more radical federal project

encountered in the Europe of the 1950s, the Treaty of Rome made explicit reference to the aim of an 'ever closer union', thus making the point that its underlying aspiration went beyond that of a common international treaty. Such a reading of the early beginnings paints a picture of competing projects rather than slow piecemeal evolution, as indicated by the neo-functionalist narrative. On the one hand, there was the consolidation of federal aspirations, which had already emerged in interwar Europe; and on the other, the political realism of member states' governments and political elites at large, who by the end of the 1950s saw with increasing scepticism some of the federal ambitions underlying cooperation, which they also perceived as a threat to their own positions of power.

The evident impracticability of a federal project contributed to the shifting of the focus of economic cooperation towards more functional instruments and piecemeal agreements. This, however, did not stop the formation of a basic institutional structure mixing intergovernmental and supranational institutions, a structure that has remained in place to the present day. Increasingly, the process of treaty-creation saw the involvement of other political actors besides national governments. This process acquired a somewhat self-reflexive nature, and gave voice to supranational interests as these became progressively embodied by the European institutions. So, both the institutional structure and the way in which the integration process progressed became a site for the redefinition of the public interest from an exclusively national basis to one where supranational elements started intruding.

Although for a long period throughout the 1970s and part of the 1980s no new major 'constitutional' initiative seemed to emerge, the period was one of development and consolidation of the supranational dimension. Issues like the extension of qualified majority voting, the role played by the more distinctively elected institutions such as the Parliament, the more explicit recognition of a solidaristic component in the enlargement of the communitarian institutions to other European countries, or the increasing perception that the integration project needed to get closer to the citizens – all such issues testify to the fact that there was more to the EC than a series of intergovernmental treaties. The very logic of market integration seemed to require the (partial) abandonment of the unanimity principle, and the construction of a European-wide collective interest in a number of policy areas. As a consequence of such attempts at redefining the boundaries within which to consider common interests and hence common policies, the question of the democratic nature of representation in the European institutions started to emerge as a widely discussed issue. Moreover, the introduction of direct elections to the European Parliament in 1979 rather paradoxically made more, rather than less evident that there were unresolved questions of both political representation and political competence within the institutional structure of the Community.

Paradoxically, the more a constitutional dimension was put in place, the more it seemed that there was a constitutional gap (hence a gap of legitimacy) at the centre of the EU/EC.

By the end of the 1980s, the introduction of the Single European Act, and the rapidly changing geopolitical configuration of Europe, with the collapse of the Soviet regimes, significantly accelerated the series of intergovern-mental conferences and Treaty reforms, which in the past two decades have profoundly changed the relationship between the EU, the member states and European citizens. From the perspective of the more historical narrative that we are here considering, the intergovernmental conferences became, or at least started to be perceived as, the true markers of constitutional devel-opment in the EU. Over time, the IGCs have become events where some form of genuine negotiation and confrontation over different visions of the future of Europe have started taking place amid the more traditional – yet inevitable – low-level bargaining and log-rolling. By the time the upheavals of 1989 and the foundation of a new 'European Union' in the early 1990s had forced a more open 'constitutional' phase onto the European agenda, European integration had finally (and perhaps irrevocably) become an issue of genuine political contestation in almost all member states. In this context, the Maastricht ratification crisis marked the end of the permissive consensus, and output legitimacy as the quasi-exclusive basis for an elite-driven integra-tion process, even though, as had happened in previous occasions, this did not produce a clear move towards a more defined constitutional project. At Maastricht, and at the following IGCs, the contours of the project for politi-cal integration remained undefined, even though monetary unification, the formation of a definite common framework for macroeconomic policy and enlargement to the post-communist countries, provided a historical opportu-nity for doing so.

In spite of all this, and in spite of the more cautious attitudes triggered by the popular reactions to Maastricht, the age of constitutional politics seemed to have finally dawned on Europe. Thus, a *political* debate on the 'future of Europe' became inevitable, something that was reflected in the not always successful attempts to broaden participation in the process of institutional reform of the Union. Such an attempt could be considered as a way of finding new forms of ex ante legitimacy for constitutional politics in the EU. This move led to the Cologne summit, in 1999, to set up a new body (later called a 'Convention') to draft the EU Charter of Fundamental Rights; and eventu-ally to the Laeken Declaration setting up the 'Convention on the Future of Europe', with the task of defining the EU's constitutional agenda. One of the key moments of this more 'historical' narrative of European constitutionali-sation remains, of course, Joschka Fischer's speech at Humboldt University in May 2000, when the then German foreign minister forcefully proposed an overtly 'constitutional' path for the future of Europe. This was followed by a series of other political speeches along the same lines, making sure that the Constitution had become a political, and not simply an academic, issue.

Fifty years after the early discussions about some form of political integration, the European political debate had come full circle and acknowledged the need for an explicit 'constitution' within which to inscribe the integration process. The main difference, this time, was the recognition, at least in the public rhetoric, that such a development would need some form of direct democratic legitimacy. This could partly be achieved ex ante, through the Convention process; and ex-post through popular or parliamentary ratification. With the Laeken Declaration, the EU entered into the most explicitly constitutional phase of its development yet. It is at this juncture – meant here in a conceptual rather than merely historical terms – that the issue becomes no longer that of the nature and effects of the constitutionalisation process, but that of its legitimacy. It is to this that we now turn.

THE SUPRANATIONAL CONSTITUTION AND ITS LEGITIMACY

As the 'historical' reading of the constitutionalisation narrative suggests, the ideas of constitutionalism and of the constitution were present in the political debate from the very beginning of the integration process. Nevertheless, it took some time for the notion that the EC/EU had acquired some kind of, at least functional, constitution to be accepted. Weiler (1999, 3–9), for one, has remarked on this inversion of the traditional way of conceiving modern constitutionalism (but not, of course, of 'ancient' ideas of the constitution), by figuratively making use of the biblical passage in *Exod* 24:7, where the people of Israel are said to have declared their acceptance of the book of Covenant with the words: 'we will do, and hearken'. There would seem to be some incongruence in ante-posing the deeds ('we will do') to the act of listening and declaring one's willingness to obey ('and hearken'). In Weiler's metaphor, the 'doing' stands for the process of material constitutionalisation, while the 'hearkening' represents the legitimate way in which a constitutional order is established: 'the deliberative process of listening, debating, and understanding' (1999, 5). This debate over the sources of legitimacy is at the core of what we here describe as the 'supranational constitution narrative'.

Such a narrative overlaps with the debate on the 'democratic deficit' (for a recent statement on this, cf. Føllesdal and Hix 2005) and with what has become the standard account of the way in which the democratic deficit in the EU has emerged as a consequence of the partial exhaustion, or inadequateness, of its output form of legitimacy (Scharpf 1999; Beetham and Lord

1998). Indeed, the idea of legitimacy has played an increasingly important role as a way of linking the theoretical-normative debates with the reality of ongoing integration. At least since the early 1970s the question has been asked of how the current system or even further integration could be justi-fied, in particular in the face of decreasing public support as measured by opinion polls. The realisation grew that apart from successful policy deliv-ery (output legitimacy), democratic input and probably some kind of social recognition (identification) were needed to maintain the legitimacy of the emerging European polity. Informal constitutionalisation (through the ECJ or the gradual institutionalisation of certain practices) was increasingly seen as playing an ambiguous role in the EU's 'quest for legitimacy' (De Burca 1996). On the one hand, it was seen as necessary to develop and consolidate the system, thus ensuring its continuous functioning. On the other hand, it was criticised for excluding and further alienating the citizens from the pro-cess of integration, also provoking the occasional backlash from the member states as the guardians of the democratic interests of their citizens. As more questions were raised on how to ensure that a European-wide polity could be normatively legitimate, the very idea of democratic legitimacy in suprana-tional conditions came under scrutiny. The same question obviously applied to democratic constitutionalism and the constitution. Indeed, the debate over the nature of democratic legitimacy in the EU has inevitably got entangled with the question of whether Europe needed a written constitution (Habermas 2001a).

Does Europe Need a Constitution?

In a strange way, the discussion about writing the European constitution took over from where the narrative of the neo-functionalists floundered, offering a moment of closure to the integration process as it had been described by the neo-functionalists. The constitution was an obvious, and theoretically unproblematic, aim for those who conceived the future of Europe in federal terms. Indeed, the constitution seemed to provide some 'meaning and pur-pose' (Nuotio 2004) to the integration process, determining once and for all what it has been called its *finalitè* (Walker 2003). Since many identified the *finalitè* of the European integration process with the establishment of a new form of statehood at a supranational level, the constitution was conceived as the sanctioning that political integration was, on the whole, complete. By fix-ing the structure of internal power, assigning precise competences at national and supranational level, and between the various European institutions, the constitution would establish a new architecture of sovereignty within the EU and its member states. From such a perspective, the constitution would contribute to making the EU more legitimate, efficient and democratic. But if the constitution is meant to confer legitimacy to the EU as a state-like entity, where does the legitimacy of the constitution itself come from? The normative narrative of constitutional politics becomes therefore embroiled with the discussion of what is the nature and legitimacy of the 'constitution' in supranational conditions.[3]

This discussion has developed along two parallel lines of dispute, two faces, so to speak, of the same medal, involving, on the one hand, the identification of the 'constituent power' in the EU constitutional order; and, on the other, the characterisation of the nature of the foundational document of such an order: whether this should be regarded as a 'treaty' between states, or as a 'constitution' of the European people. The German jurist Dieter Grimm has perhaps been the most authoritative and consistent voice arguing against the view that the European Union can, at this stage of its development, meaningfully give itself a constitution (Grimm 1995). Grimm remarks that the emergence of modern constitutions is intrinsically linked to the way in which positive law operates at two levels over the public domain. The first level establishes the legitimate source of state power and regulates the operations of government. The second level follows from the exercise of state power itself, but it acquires force insofar as state power has been bound by the rules set down at the first level. Grimm argues that this is not the way in which Community law has operated over the years, and that any attempt to constitutionalise it comes against the intractable question of who are the 'masters' of the Treaty, the ultimate repositories of sovereignty in the EU legal and political system: that is, the true constituent power. According to Grimm, the 'constituent power' remains with the member states, who, as actors within an international system, are not subject to the constitutional discipline typical of first- and second-order positive law, as it applies in constitutional states, where instead the constituent power dissolves itself into the 'constituted powers' as a result of the creation of a constitutional order. Grimm's argument here is that, due to the dominance of the separate state actors, the EU legal space lacks the distinctive structural properties of constitutional law. Attempts to introduce some form of constitutionalisation remain partial and superficial until the EU can claim some form of self-sufficient statehood *independently from the member states*. According to this view, the European constitution cannot legitimate European statehood and democracy, since it presupposes some form of established statehood.

Even if we assume that Grimm is right in his analysis of the structural limits to be overcome in order for the EU to have a constitution, it could be argued that the post-Laeken process and the 'Treaty establishing a Constitution for Europe' were meant to create the background political conditions for constitutional politics and constitutional law. This raises the other point of controversy, intriguingly captured by the decision made in the Convention to mix the languages of international and constitutional law by referring to the agreed document as both a 'treaty' and a 'constitution', or as they put it: a treaty establishing a constitution, where it remains unclear where the 'text' of the treaty ends and that of the constitution starts. This linguistic solution, however, only highlights the problem. As suggested by Bruno De Witte (2004), a close exegetical analysis of the language of the approved text, and of the formal status of the document itself, seems to support the case that the way in which the document was both conceived and formulated is entirely within the tradition and language of international treaty making, showing the clear intention of the drafters to confirm, rather than weaken, the position of the member states as the 'High Contracting Parties', who have the power to bound themselves to the agreements set up in the Treaty, within the limits set by their own *separate* constitutional orders. Such evidence, however, does not in itself seem conclusive, for there is nothing to prevent the possibility that a treaty may become the basis for a self-contained constitutional order, as it happened in the German case towards the end of the nineteenth century. In this respect, the intentions of the framers are of limited guidance. In fact, it is part of the 'constitutionalisation' thesis to suggest that the passage from an international regime to a constitutional order has been on the whole unintended.

But there is another way of putting the sceptical argument against a federal Europe and against the idea that the EU is already in the position to give itself a constitution. This is generally known as the 'No-demos' thesis (Weiler 1999). Simply put, this argument suggests that without some kind of unified people there cannot be democracy – and therefore that any European state without a European people would necessarily be undemocratic. The issues commonly raised in relation to the 'No-demos' thesis are of three kinds. One concerns the deliberative presuppositions for democracy to operate. Such presuppositions comprise a diffuse and fairly integrated European public sphere, a working representative system at the European level, and even more obviously the ability to communicate and understand each other through a shared language. Although in some limited and/or rudimentary forms, these elements are already present in the EU, it is difficult to see how such conditions can operate beyond the narrow circle of European elites, something that would make it difficult for a European-wide political system to have a genuine popular character. The second issue raised by the 'No-demos' thesis concerns the way in which, in a democracy, people are prepared to accept collective decisions that have redistributive implications out of a sense of solidarity with the other members of the community. The nature and boundary of such solidarity are strongly contested, but historically in Europe democratic citizenship has developed in parallel to a solidaristic conception of the national community. A working democracy at the European level would therefore need some form of connective solidarity to ensure that people were willing to accept as legitimate the application of the majoritarian principle across a series of important policy decisions. The third issue, finally, is that of cultural diversity. Whereas the experience of democracy within the nation state has tended to coincide with a certain homogeneity of the people – or, more often, with a nation-building project, which relied on processes of democracy- and citizenship-formation in order to get firmly established – in the EU, cultural and national diversity is both pervasive and tends to be considered a value worthy to be preserved rather than overcome.

In each of its forms, the 'No-demos' thesis once again proposes the question of sovereignty and the unresolved (perhaps unsolvable) question of the nature and role of the constituent power.[4] In the experience of national constitutionalism, the ultimate appeal to the demos, as both a unitary and self-constituting subject ('We, the people'), has played an important role as the alleged source of, and the legitimating influence over the exercise of power by the political and legal institutions – the 'constituted powers'. The question is whether this self-constituting model can be reproduced at a European level, in a situation in which the national demoi still cling both to the separateness of their interests and to demands for the recognition of their sociocultural differences. It is here that the narrative of the 'supranational constitution' comes into its own. In other terms, if one does not start from the assumption that a quasi-federal structure is the natural *telos* of the integration process, how is it possible for constitutional politics to operate at a supranational level?[5] The answer to this question has taken two main forms, which represents the two divergent readings of the 'supranational constitution' narrative. One reading concentrates on the idea that the making of the constitution is the result of a *constitutional moment*; the other reading emphasises the idea of the constitution as the result of a *process* of continuous negotiation and interpretation of constitutional law and of the underlying constitutional order – a process that requires time and that operates at different levels.

Constitutional Moments

The 'constitutional moment' version of the normative narrative has found inspiration in the work of the American constitutionalist Bruce Ackerman (1991), and it has more recently been popularised in the idea that the European Constitutional Convention should be considered a New Philadelphia. In both Ackerman's and the popular version, the writing of the constitution has an important 'generative' quality, which depends on the effect in time that the constitution has over the working of the political and legal systems. In other words, on how successful and long-lasting a constitution is. This implies a series of 'descriptive' statements, which can only be judged ex-post.

But from a more normative perspective, the evaluation of a constitutional moment involves an assessment of the specific *generative* qualities of the constitutional moment, and of the way in which such generative qualities take *form*. Identifying the generative quality and the specific forms of constitutional moments is another way of posing the question of the sources of legitimacy. In other words, a constitutional moment is such, if it is capable of bringing into being the fundamental elements that give legitimacy to a polity and to its political regime. Here views may diverge on whether what matters is more an outcome-based assessment of legitimacy – a constitutional moment is therefore assessed on the kind of constitutional order it produces and on the substance of the constitutional document; or whether legitimacy is seen in more procedural terms – if, for instance, the constitutional moment succeeds in either mobilising the citizenry or producing public deliberation and a higher form of consensus.

The Constitutional Convention has offered an interesting terrain for developing and debating the validity of the more procedural approach, and particularly the normative and socio-psychological basis for a deliberative approach to democracy and constitutionalism. A number of authors have engaged with the issue of the nature of discourse and agreement in politics, and what normative force principled deliberation and agreement (as opposed to contractual bargaining) may carry with them (see the contributions in Eriksen, Fossum, and Menéndez 2004; Eriksen 2005). By applying certain aspects of Habermas's communicative theory, they see the prolonged phase of institutional discussion and transformation in Europe since Maastricht as a way of constructing the unity of the European polity on the basis of a reflexive form of problem solving that makes appeal to shared norms and progressively entrenched commitments. From such a perspective, the introduction of the 'convention method' can be seen as a decisive improvement on the IGC, for it would seem to introduce a more dispassionate way of arguing about the organisation of the European institutions, appealing to general reasons, instead of taking narrow national interests as the basis for log-rolling and the bargaining-type of intergovernmental politics dominating the signing of previous Treaties in the history of European integration.

But this position presents some problems, for it offers an idealised view both of what happens in discussions on constitutional issues, and of the 'convention' experience itself, besides suggesting a somewhat artificial separation between constitutional questions and fundamental policy issues, thus assuming that the former are a better ground on which to build consensus at the European level. The normative quality of constitutional deliberation can be questioned from two distinct perspectives. The first does not necessarily imply a rejection of the analytic and normative contentions made by advocates of the superiority of constitutional deliberation. According to this view, although it is difficult to prove empirically that particular agreements are the result of rational deliberation, or that they reflect a rationally motivated consensus, it may still be true that the contextually induced restrains of constitutional deliberation create incentives through which agents are motivated to reach agreements based on more dispassionate principles and reasoning, and that such agreements have a strong 'integrative' function, establishing something stronger than a simple modus vivendi. From such a perspective, the work of the Constitutional Convention looks like a genuine attempt at substituting a more deliberative and supranational style of constitutional politics to the bargaining model based on strong national interests as instantiated in the practice of the IGCs. However, even though the process may look distinctive, it remains to be seen whether the outcome of the Constitutional Convention – that is, the kind of constitutional document that it managed to produce – went beyond the kind of substantive compromises that have characterised much of treaty making in the EU (Magnette 2004). Indeed, the very fact that the constitutional draft prepared by the Convention needed approval by the IGC may cast some doubt on the idea that the writing of the Constitutional Treaty represents a real break with past experience. Moreover, the stalling of the ratification process can be cited as further proof that the deliberative character of the process does not guarantee a consensual outcome.

Constitutional deliberation can also be questioned from a second, and normatively more radical, perspective. For it can be argued that the negotiations in the Constitutional Convention showed that a number of key constitutional questions can only be settled by 'normal' political means, and by trade-offs between policy issues within a wider context, and that indeed such a bargaining style of politics is both unavoidable and justifiable, since political compromises are intrinsic to all forms of democratic politics. Compromises are not to be rejected because they may fall short of some idealised form of consensus, but judged contextually and according to their capacity to favour social and political integration, besides producing some distributive outcomes accepted by those involved. Compromise, and not consensus, is the form of agreement that better reflects political pluralism in modern times, and this is no different in either normal or constitutional politics (Bellamy and Schönlau 2004).

This second challenge undermines the *categorical* distinction between constitutional and normal politics, denying that they can be easily distinguished on the basis of their normative value. In the European case, some commentators go even further and question whether the recent phase of constitutional politics, which has focused discussion on the EU institutional framework, and on what the EU is, or should become, may be the best ground on which to build consensus at a European level. Andrew Moravcsik, for instance, maintains that talks on the constitution, far from consolidating the integration process, have opened up a Pandora box, risking destabilising the 'constitutional settlement' reached throughout the 1990s (Moravcsik 2002, 2005). This position, however, denies that there is a crisis of legitimacy in the EU, while assuming that its de facto supranational constitutional order needs no explicit normative basis, for it ultimately rests on the democratic legitimacy of the member states. Even allowing for Moravcsik's point on political prudence, it would seem difficult to maintain that the emergence of an explicit constitutional discourse in Europe is a largely manufactured event, particularly when one considers that it has developed within the context of an unprecedented process of enlargement, and that it follows from a phase of profound changes in the nature and extent of the economic integration process. If anything, the constitutional debate testifies of the need to find a new balance between the EU institutional structure and its policy-making ambitions. Arguably, Europe's constitutional moment should not be identified with the Laeken process of writing a documentary constitution, but with the new phase of political integration that started at Maastricht (Weiler 1999, 3/4). From such a perspective, the Convention and the Constitutional Treaty look more like the concluding acts of a protracted constitutional moment, whose fundamental features are not those enshrined in the articles of the constitutional text, but momentous political decisions such as the Enlargement, the introduction of a common currency, of an independent European Central Bank, and of the Stability Pact. It is partly ironic that such decisions are not regarded as 'constitutional', and that they have been taken with very little popular involvement, without a European-wide discussion (Weiler 2002). But as the ratification crisis of 2005 shows, in the eyes of the European public there is very little difference between what the EU *is* and what it *does*, so that at the moment of considering the ratification of the Constitutional Treaty many voters found it problematic to distinguish between what the Constitution *says* (i.e. what is in the actual text of the constitution) and what, in their view, it *stands for* (i.e. how they consider the European Union and its impact upon their everyday life). It is little surprising, therefore, that present and future enlargement, immigration, and social and economic policies – all issues that are not affected by the introduction of the Constitutional Treaty – have played such an important part in the way in which people voted in the French and Dutch referendums. It is a sign that constitutional politics cannot be limited to institutional matters, but it is inevitably entangled with some of the substantive issues associated with normal politics.

There is, however, another side to the idea that the normative character of constitutional politics needs a constitutional moment, something that breaks the routine of normal politics. This is connected with the importance of symbolism as part of constitutional politics. The point has been made forcefully by Jürgen Habermas, when he intimates that 'as a political collectivity,

Europe cannot take hold in the consciousness of its citizens simply in the shape of a common currency. The intergovernmental arrangement at Maastricht lacks that power of symbolic crystallization which only a political act of foundation can give' (2001, 6). According to Habermas, the constitution can act as a catalytic point in the 'circular creation' of Europe as a political community, coming as the constitution does at the end of an already advanced process of social, economic and political integration, and, in turn, helping to put in motion the construction of a European-wide civil society, a common public sphere, and a shared political culture (2001, 16–21). Underpinning this operation there is what Habermas calls 'constitutional patriotism', a form of allegiance to the political community, which rests on abstract and universal principles of a civic kind. A lively debate has developed around this idea and whether it may rightfully become part of a European identity (Friese and Wagner 2002; Lacroix 2002; Kumm 2005) but from Habermas's perspective, the main question is whether the focus on the constitution could help foster such an allegiance. In other words, the writing of the constitution would be part of a constitutional project aimed at enlarging our circle of solidarity at a European level and to create the conditions for a 'federation of nation-states' (Habermas 2001a, 15).

In Habermas's and other supporters' view of the need for a constitution, as a strong normative and symbolic statement, the constitution is part of a constructivist gambit intended as the beginning of the process of construction of a political demos in Europe. But as Neil Walker has argued (2004a, 2004b, 2005a), the way in which the Constitutional Treaty has taken shape did not reflect one single project or conception of the EU constitution and European constitutionalism. For Walker, a number of very different influences have shaped both the text and the form taken by the drafting process of the Constitutional Treaty, comprising positions expressing various shades of scepticism against constructive and documentary constitutionalism, and even extending to those who were in principle hostile to it. From such a perspective, the Constitutional Treaty reflects a compromise between different views, and is the basis for future political and intellectual battles. Thus, the current debate on whether its text may be rescued after the defeats in the French and Dutch referendums is beside the point. The real issue is whether the halting of the constitutional moment simply signals a temporary retreat of constructivists and federalists constitutional projects, or it is the sign of a process of reversion of the broader constitutional agenda set at Maastricht.

The Processual Constitution

The fuzzy definition of a European constitutional moment highlights the difficulties besetting any attempt to reproduce the traditional concepts of national constitutionalism at a European level. One of the key ideas of those who tend to emphasise the postnational character of the constitutional path in the EU is that constitution making in it cannot be characterised as an *event*, but as a *process* (Shaw 2003a). This is no trivial disagreement. It takes us back to some of the themes discussed apropos finality and constitutional moments. In point of substance, there may be no difference between a constitutional order achieved through a gradual process and one agreed at a particular moment. Indeed, many who throughout the years have applauded the role of the European Court of Justice in upholding the existence of a new European constitutional order now welcome the fixing of the Constitution by the Convention. According to them, after a period of de facto constitutionalisation, we have entered a phase when a more definite constitutional settlement needs to be formalised in view of the profound changes introduced by the single market, monetary unification and enlargement. Moreover, both legitimacy and democratic deficits need urgent attention, something that may only be achieved by fixing Europe's institutional architecture and the rights of the European citizens.

This kind of argument, however, presents two problems. By accepting that a constitution of sorts was already in place, it makes the present moment less foundational, thus posing the problem of what the relationship is between the past and the future constitutional order. By emphasising the legitimacy deficit of the European institutions, it becomes vulnerable to the counterargument that fixing the European Constitution at this particular moment risks freezing the status quo, making it less acceptable to the European citizens. A more gradual process, instead, may be better at tracking and directing the political sentiments of the European peoples as they are asked to widen their sense of solidarity. It may also be more flexible and therefore better equipped at developing institutional arrangements so to make them seem relevant to policy projects and policy objectives in which citizens can more immediately recognise their interests and for which they may more readily mobilise.

This argument about a more 'processual' understanding of constitution making has many facets, involving different elements of constitutional politics. One is concerned with the relationship between formal and informal moments in the making of the constitutional order, emphasising, for instance, how treaty reform in Europe cannot be seen as a simple succession of different treaties each amending the other, and characterised by intergovernmental bargaining (Greve and Jorgensen 2002; Farrell and Héritier 2003). A second element consists in a more systemic understanding of how both law and politics operate but also of how they interact by producing a 'structural coupling' between them, so that constitutional politics is the result of various institutional dialogues and the way in which they come to interact (Greve and Jorgensen 2002). A third element concerns the way in which the development of European community law has changed the structural context in which different branches of law operate at the national level, forcefully impacting on the relationship between private and public law in the member states' legal systems, contributing to redrawing some of the boundaries between them, while in particular problematising the relationship between private and public autonomy. This process is part and parcel of the open constitutionalisation of the EU legal system (Joerges 1997; Joerges and Everson 2004).

EUROPEAN CONSTITUTIONALISM
AS WORK IN PROGRESS

One manifestation of the disagreement over whether the Constitution should be conceptualised as either an event or a process is on how to consider the present Constitutional Treaty. Giuliano Amato has put this question in a humorous way, by talking of the Constitutional Treaty in terms of the 'gender' of this document. He wished, or so he says, that the newly born text were a 'girl' (*una femmina*) but has to acknowledge that, in fact, it was a 'boy' (*un maschio*). In his view, the Convention did not produce a 'constitution' (*costituzione*, a feminine noun in Italian) but a 'treaty' (*trattato*, masculine).[6] Amato is convinced that the real point of difference lies in the power of revision that the Draft attributes to the national governments and not to the European institutions, thus favouring an interpretation of the nature of the EU as still an international organisation operating according to intergovernmental principles. And yet the Draft does not present itself as a simple 'treaty' but as a 'constitutional treaty', or, in other contexts, as a 'treaty establishing a constitution'. This would seem to signal that the process of constitutional definition of the European Union is still very much open and in the making.

Moreover, and perhaps more importantly, the nature of the European Constitution is in doubt. Indeed, many believe that the idea of the constitution as traditionally applied to the national context is no longer adequate in the transnational and multilevel context characterising European governance. Such inadequacy has two sources. One is in the very conception of the constitution as an overarching document at the apex of a unified legal and political system. Such a conception has been said to be no longer tenable even at the national level, because it would be unable to capture in a few general principles the normative pluralism of modern societies, their sociopolitical differentiation, and the more particularistic nature of social legislation (Fioravanti 1992).

The other source of inadequacy is the changing nature of constitutionalism, which in the European context needs to accommodate the national forms and practices of constitutional law. According to many, this gives to European constitutionalism a plural character, which needs to make a virtue of the necessity to enter in dialogue with diverse traditions and also find forms of accommodation between parallel legal and constitutional orders. One of the formative principles of European constitutionalism is therefore that of being tolerant, as Weiler maintains,[7] or as Maduro (2000) says: 'we have to start reasoning in the realm of what could be called couterpunctual law. ... The discovery that different melodies could be heard at the same time' (De Witte 2002; Shaw 2003a). From such a perspective, writing the constitution now as a more traditional text may risk jeopardising what may be construed as perhaps the greatest achievement to date of the European constitutional order, that of allowing for an ongoing political and constitutional conversation to go on across Europe.

This idea of constitutional toleration and of a constitutional conversation is closely connected to the recognition of the fact that there are different demoi at the heart of the construction of the EU as a polity (Maduro 2003). For Weiler (2001) the *Sonderweg* of European constititutionalism consists of renouncing the desire to look for a 'positive' common constitutional culture, but accepting that there are different national constitutional cultures. Similar echoes can be found in other authors (Nuotio 2004; Shaw 2003a), applying to EU constitutionalism an open-textured and continuously negotiated (both internally and externally) method of constitution building. The principles that guide it, however, are still very much a matter of experiment and contention and may apply beyond the EU experience (Slaughter 2004). The basic intuition, however, is that the European constitutional order is a plural one, operating both at the supranational and at the national level, and encompassing both the national and the EU constitutions (Pernice and Kanits 2004). As Neil MacCormick says, 'a pluralistic analysis ... shows the systems of law operative on the European level to be distinct and partially independent of each other, though also partially overlapping and interacting' (1999, 119). In itself, this is not a difficult state of affairs to perceive and analyse. The problem is how to conceive and operationalise conflict resolution in the context of such radical pluralism. This is indeed the challenge for constitutional politics in the EU. In this sense, European constitutionalism is still work in progress.

NOTES

1. In the somewhat garbled and transformed sense of 'this is the crux of the matter' that Hegel and Marx conferred to Aesop's original: 'Hic Rhodus, hic saltus', which was meant instead as a challenge to the boasting of braggarts.

2. For this reconstruction, I am indebted to Justus Schönlau.

3. From a federalist perspective, the legitimacy of the constitution is not a real problem, or at least its legitimacy is no different from that one may attribute to the

constitution of a state. There is here a difference between those who think that European statehood can be easily disjointed from nationhood, and that European democracy and constitutionalism therefore require a federal-like structure (Mancini 2000, XXVI), and those who take more seriously the conundrum of constitutionalising a supranational entity.

4. The circularity that the issue of 'constituent power' poses to constitutionalism is similar to that raised by the possibility of establishing a democracy according to democratic means (Dahl 1989, 207). In either case, something prior and *discontinuous* seems to be presupposed in order to establish a constitutional or a democratic regime.

5. This does not exclude that Europe's supranational constitution may not resemble traditional federal constitutions. In fact, this is very likely. The issue here is not one of substance but of legitimacy. Discussions about the supranational constitution, even when they are in favour of a European constitution, start from the assumption that this cannot be justified on the basis of an already established statehood at the European level.

6. Cf. G. Amato, 'Prefazione', in Ziller (2003, 9). Ziller discusses Amato's distinction in the main text at 47/8.

7. Weiler (2003a). Weiler's argument about the plural nature of the European constitutional order is clear, but his use of the idea of 'toleration' as applied to the interrelation between different constitutional orders is rather confusing, unless it is meant as a generic attitude to intercultural dialogue. On the difficulties raised by recent debates on toleration, see McKinnon and Castiglione (2003).

Chapter 8

Back to the Future?

The Euro and the EU Silent Constitution

Dario Castiglione

For the first time in more than twenty years it has perhaps become possible to imagine a breakup of the European Union (EU) and the collapse of its experiment in supranational governance. The crisis of the Euro and the difficulties in finding a generally agreed solution to the sovereign debts issue have posed once again the question about fundamentals: What is the EU, and what is it for?

The issue of definition has troubled European Union politics for some time. The 'what is?' question seems a necessary presupposition for both political understanding and political organisation. In order to understand the way in which the EU works and is organised, there must be 'something' that we take the EU to be. For a while, the obvious answer to this question was that the EU (or the various communities that have led to it) was an international organisation, which emerged piecemeal from a series of treaties and various agreements between an expanding number of countries in Europe. Its main object was the solution of problems of economic coordination and cooperation, while its underlying purpose was to prevent economic competition from becoming the ground for power politics between European nation states, whose destructive results were evident from the experience of the first half of the twentieth century. The growing importance of the phenomena and inner dynamics of economic integration challenged that perception and made the 'what is' question more problematic. Famously, Jacques Delors once called the European Community *un objet politique non identifié*. This formulation signals a division between those who wish to treat the European Union as a distinctive, almost unique, object of political research, situated in the middle between a 'state' and an 'international organisation', and those that dismiss with impatience such vague formulas, for they regard talk of exceptionalism as a way of obfuscating rather than illuminating political reality. As it often happens with the emergence of new phenomena, we are witnessing a battle between different approaches, different theories and different political projects, with the likely result that both our knowledge and practice of politics will be affected by such disputes over what the EU 'is', or is 'becoming'.

The dispute over the nature of the EU has been complicated by two dynamic aspects of European integration, which have made the EU an even more elusive target. Both the geographical reach of the Union and its shared competences have progressively increased, without a clear sense of where the limits to such expansive processes lie. These dynamics, and their surrounding uncertainties, have generated a number of theoretical questions, which are not only concerned with what the EU *is*, but with what it *ought to be*. In particular, legal and political theorists have started asking questions regarding the legitimacy upon which the body of EU laws rests, and on the EU's own specific identity. These questions came to the political boil, so to speak, at the start of last decade, and materialised around the debate on whether the EU needed a Constitution, for this was taken to define the empirical character of the Union as well as its values and aspirations. In the eyes of its supporters, the EU Constitution would have defined the *finalité* of the Union itself, while sanctioning once and for all its aspirations to be a fully political, even a state-like, entity.

As everyone knows, that debate concluded with the political defeat of the constitutional gambit. And yet, it may be worth starting our discussion of the present financial and monetary crisis of the EU by reflecting on what happened, and what did not happen during the constitutional phase that opened more than ten years ago. The reason for doing this is that, as I shall try to suggest in the remainder of this chapter, the European constitutional debate was a missed opportunity, not so much because it did not produce a Constitution, but because it failed to clarify the terms of the constitutional issue. The focus of that debate was too much on institutional and symbolic issues, whose relevance is undisputed, but which ended up diverting the general attention from other, and more informal, aspects of the EU Constitution, which, if anything, have even more relevance to how the Union works and to its significance in the life of its citizens. Accordingly, in this chapter, I wish first to go over what the European constitutional debate of last decade missed, and then look at how the EU silent Constitution, which mainly escaped public debate a decade ago, is now firmly at the centre of the present crisis. Unless the EU and its citizens deal with these silent, but ever more visible, aspects of the EU constitutional fabric, the exit from the present crisis risks leading either to a political impasse or to increasing, and possibly dramatic, tensions within the Union itself.

A MISTAKEN CONSTITUTIONAL MOMENT?

When, at the beginning of the new millennium, the European institutions and the member states put in place the process to draft a European Constitution, the debate that ensued was as much about the substance of the constitutional document as the significance of the constitutional moment itself. Nonetheless, some important aspects of European Constitution making were missed in that debate, or at least not enough attention was paid to those who raised them. One such aspect concerns the relationship between constitutional and normal politics, and how this also relates to the interplay between institution building and framework policies. It is worthwhile to return to such a discussion to better understand the nature of the present financial crisis as part of an ongoing Constitution-making process in Europe.

One of the reasons given in support of a European Constitution, eventually named a 'Constitutional Treaty', and which, after the failure of the ratification process, resulted in the Lisbon Treaty, was that the very making of the Constitution would contribute to the legitimacy of the European integration process. Such a position was based on the idea that there exists a *categorical* distinction between constitutional and normal politics, and that the former has particular normative and legitimating properties. This, however, was an issue of contention in the debate of the time. Some commentators questioned whether constitutional politics, focusing discussion on the EU institutional framework, and on what the EU is, was the best ground on which to build consensus at a European level. Andrew Moravcsik, for instance, maintained that talks on the Constitution, far from consolidating the integration process, had opened up a Pandora's box, risking destabilising the 'constitutional settlement' reached throughout the 1990s (Moravcsik 2002, 2005). Moravcsik's position, however, denied that there the EU suffered from a crisis of legitimacy, assuming instead that its de facto supranational constitutional order needed no explicit normative basis, for this ultimately rested on the democratic legitimacy of the member states.

But even allowing for Moravcsik's point on political prudence, it would seem difficult to maintain that the emergence of an explicit constitutional discourse in Europe was a manufactured event, particularly when one considers that it developed within the context of an unprecedented process of enlargement, and following from a phase of profound changes in the nature and extent of the economic integration process. If anything, the constitutional debate testified to the need for finding a new balance between the EU institutional structure and its policy-making ambitions. From such a perspective, Europe's constitutional moment should not be identified with the specific process, which started with the Laeken declaration, and took shape through the Constitutional Convention, of writing a documentary Constitution, but with the overall phase of political integration that started years earlier at Maastricht (Weiler 1999, 3/4). From such a perspective, the Convention and the proposed (but not ratified) Constitutional Treaty look more like the concluding acts of a protracted constitutional moment, whose fundamental features are not those enshrined in the articles of the constitutional text, but more momentous political decisions taken such as enlargement and the introduction of a common currency taken across a period of years. The ironic fact, as it will be discussed later, is that such decisions were not regarded as 'constitutional', and that they were taken with very little popular involvement, without a European-wide discussion (Weiler 2002). In spite of this, as the ratification crisis of 2005 eventually showed, in the eyes of the European public there was very little difference between what the EU *is* and what it *does*, so that when the moment of ratification came, many voters found it problematic to distinguish between what the Constitution *said* (i.e. what was in the actual text of the Constitution) and what, in their view, it *stood for* (i.e. how they considered the European Union and its impact upon their everyday lives). It is not surprising, therefore, that issues such as enlargement, immigration, and social and economic policies – all issues that were not affected by the introduction of the Constitutional Treaty – played such an important part in the way in which people voted in the French and Dutch referendums, which eventually determined the fate of the Constitutional Treaty. This is a clear sign that constitutional politics cannot be limited to institutional matters, but that inevitably involves some important policy issues, which are usually associated with normal politics.

This entanglement of institutions and policies and of constitutional and normal politics raises two general questions. One is the question of the relevance of the issues that at the time were at the centre of the constitutional process, and the other is the precise impact that constitutional politics makes when compared to ordinary politics. On the issue of relevance, as Joseph Weiler (2002) said at the time, constitutional mobilisation had the perverse effect of diverting attention from the really momentous changes that, as already noted, had occurred in the European Union, and which had instead been managed either pragmatically or by taking decisions by default, thus excluding the citizens from debating and deciding on such issues. On the really hard choices confronting Europe the formal constitutional process made little or no impact.

This argument on the 'irrelevance' of the European constitutional debate can lead to two different conclusions. One, of more local consequence, is that there was a failure in the European political class to decide which issues to place at the centre of the public debate. The other, of more general relevance, suggests that there is no real difference between constitutional and ordinary politics, or at most it is *strategic* rather than *categorical*. In a broader sense, constitutional politics is the kind of action that a series of favourable circumstances converge to create by offering a 'window of opportunity' within which it is possible to operate so as to determine the character of a polity and of its regime for a relatively long period of time. From this perspective, constitutional politics can only be judged consequentially, by looking at the effects it produces.

But there are a number of other important elements following from this 'strategic' sense of constitutional politics that should also be noticed. First, constitutional politics is not tantamount to producing a formal Constitution, a document, that is, that has the formal qualities of constitutional law, distinct from ordinary legislation. The object of constitutional politics is more often the interconnection between the political (the more substantive organisation of power) and the formal Constitution. At times, it may concern changes in the 'material' Constitution, by which one should understand important pieces of legislation or of organisation of the state, which do not need to be part of the formal Constitution itself. In view of this, it is impossible to define the province of constitutional politics in a way that excludes ordinary politics.

Secondly, because of its partly consequentialist character, constitutional politics finds its validation in the way in which ordinary politics makes it its own point of reference. In relation to the more 'intrinsic' properties of constitutional politics, these can be seen as a possible effect of the 'window of opportunity' contingency and of the capacity of both leaders and citizens to operate in such a way to exploit the moment by organising political attention and activating mechanisms of broader acceptance and allegiance within the community (Olsen 1997, 217–20; Castiglione 1995). In the modern conditions of democratic societies, sustained public debate and the mediation of 'strong publics' make an important contribution to the emergence of broad forms of principled and strategic agreement, and practical convergence, at least in the long term (Eriksen and Fossum 2002).

But all this does not necessarily require a higher level of consensus, which is almost impossible to achieve even between reasonable citizens, in view of their diversity of values, interests and empirical assessments, besides considerations on the complexities of social choice and its subject matter. Agreements in constitutional politics, as in ordinary politics, are points of equilibrium often reached through a variety of considerations and strategies, involving arguments, bargaining and negotiating processes, compromises, incomplete theorisation, and strategic arguments. What is sometimes considered as the binding character of constitutional consensus is at its origins – even when it emerges from truly exceptional moments of collective crisis and mobilisation, which are indeed rare – the product of a number of more or less principled compromises. At first, these compromises result in a modus vivendi. Over time and by the effect of common and continuous engagement both in the business of ordinary politics and in ongoing deliberative and decision-making experiences, such a modus vivendi may consolidate in a shared framework, always open, however, to different interpretations or to sudden collapse – as the experience of constitutional democracies amply testifies. To conclude on this point, if constitutional and ordinary politics cannot be clearly and categorically distinguished from each other on either their substance or because of their properties, and if nonetheless there is a more strategic sense in which such a distinction can occasionally become operative, there is no simple way of saying whether constitutions, and their normative appeal, are either the product of extended processes or decisive events. Indeed, it is probably safer to assume that both aspects tend to contribute to the making of a Constitution.

There is, however, another side to the idea that the normative character of constitutional politics needs a constitutional moment, something that breaks the routine of normal politics. This is connected with the importance of symbolism as part of constitutional politics. During the constitutional debate, this point was made forcefully by Jürgen Habermas, when he maintained that 'as a political collectivity, Europe cannot take hold in the consciousness of its citizens simply in the shape of a common currency. The intergovernmental arrangement at Maastricht lacks that power of symbolic crystallization which only a political act of foundation can give' (2001, 6). According to Habermas, the Constitution should have acted as a catalytic point in the 'circular creation' of Europe as a political community, coming as the Constitution normally does at the end of an already advanced process of social, economic and political integration, and, in turn, helping to put in motion the construction of a European-wide civil society, a common public sphere and a shared political culture (2001a, 16–21). Underpinning this operation there is what Habermas has called 'constitutional patriotism', a form of allegiance to the political community, which rests on abstract and universal principles of a civic kind. Indeed, at the time and since, a lively debate has developed around this idea and whether it may rightfully become part of a European identity, but from Habermas's perspective the main question was whether the focus on the Constitution could help fostering such an allegiance. In other words, whether the writing of the Constitution would be part of a constitutional project aimed at enlarging our circle of solidarity at a European level and at creating the conditions for a 'federation of nation-states' (Habermas 2001a, 15).

In Habermas's and other supporters' view of the need for a Constitution, as a strong normative and symbolic statement, the Constitution was part of a constructivist gambit intended as the beginning of the process of construction of a political demos in Europe. But, as Neil Walker argued at the time (2004 and 2005), the way in which the Constitutional Treaty took shape did not reflect a single project or conception of the EU Constitution and European constitutionalism, but different one. Indeed, as Walker argued, a number of very different influences shaped both the text and the form taken by the drafting process of the Constitutional Treaty, comprising positions expressing various shades of scepticism against constructive and documentary constitutionalism, and even extending to those who were in principle hostile to it. From such a perspective, the Constitutional Treaty was a compromise between different views, thus being open to future political and intellectual battles. Indeed, the fact that the text of the Constitutional Treaty was eventually rescued by more or less ratifying it in the form of the Lisbon Treaty, even if it was politically defeated in the French and Dutch referendums, shows that the documentary text itself, and the kind of consensus that it reflected, was not of decisive importance. Of greater importance was whether the halting of the constitutional moment determined by the ratification crisis, should be interpreted as a temporary retreat of the broadly federalist project, or whether it was the beginning of a reversion process of the kind of constitutional agenda that was put in motion at Maastricht. In a way, this dilemma is exactly the same as the one posed by the current monetary and financial crisis – though perhaps in reverse: whereas the ratification crisis could be seen as a temporary retreat, the current crisis may demand a leap forward, if one wishes to avoid the unravelling of the integration project as a whole.

But there are other aspects of the constitutional phase that may be useful to consider before coming to the current crisis. One thing that emerged from the ratification crisis is that throughout the constitutional phase public debate was never fully engaged. Whatever popular participation and public debate eventually emerged, they were rather the effect of growing opposition to the Constitutional Treaty than a positive campaign on the merits of the Constitution. Low levels of popular mobilisation and lack of debate are often explained as the consequence of a lack of salience of institutional and constitutional issues in the lives of European citizens. This argument often complements the one already mentioned, according to which the French and Dutch electorates rightly voted on issues of policy rather than on the text of the Constitutional Treaty. Enlargement and monetary union were substantive policy decisions with considerable constitutional implications, though they were treated as part of 'normal' politics with no real public discussion encouraged. In those instances where public debate surfaced at the national level, as in the British case about the Euro, it was more for the presence of a strong opposition rather than for a genuine desire to engage in a well-informed public debate. It is therefore hardly surprising, and certainly not unexpected, that once a popular debate emerged over the Constitutional Treaty as part of the ratification process, this was focused as much on the main policy changes that have shaped the EU since Maastricht as on the Constitution itself.

For this reason, one should look at the constitutional moment in a broader historical-political context. The more immediate and most obvious aspect of such a context is given by the process of enlargement, which, in spite of being protracted through time, and conceived as the preserve of the European political elites, has become a dominating political issue, posing numerous political and institutional challenges to the European Union and its current member states (from agriculture to redistribution policies across countries, from minority rights to internal migrations and border control).

A second context within which to see the emergence of the constitutional agenda is the social question. This had become more evident since the late 1990s, during the period when there was a return of social democratic parties to government in many European countries after a long phase of neoliberal governments and policies. Although the season of third-way-governments (most of them in ideological and electoral retreat as soon as they were elected) was short, and although there was no concerted attempt to move towards a more 'social Europe', it nonetheless contributed to the shift of popular perception from a market-based to a more welfare- and rights-based vision of Europe. So far, this shift of emphasis has produced no real shift in policies, but the relevance of such a theme during the ratification debate cannot be easily dismissed. If anything, the current crisis has made the social issue even more relevant; indeed, how Europe will deal with the social dimension as economic integration progresses and internal mobility increases is a question with profound constitutional ramifications.

Thirdly, and as I shall discuss more in detail in the next section, part of the political context for the constitutional debate was clearly determined by monetary unification. Although this was at the time presented as the natural completion of the single market, it can be construed as the beginning of a more ambitious integration process, involving fiscal and other macroeconomic decision-making processes that may need more careful coordination, greater flexibility and responsiveness in order to be managed in relation to the economic cycle. The need for a different institutional setting for economic management at the European level has since become more apparent due also to the slowing down of economic development in the EU area.

In conclusion, the constitutional phase should not be seen as completely separate from normal politics. On the contrary, it was the expression of the EU coming to terms with the changes and challenges posed by the transformed political context produced by increasing integration. From such a perspective, one can more easily make sense of the 'ratification crisis' as the expression of a wider malaise and dissatisfaction, reflecting a crisis of legitimacy: a sign that the increasing powers and functions of the EU needed more definite support from European citizens. The constitutional phase tried to bring to conclusion what had been started at Maastricht. In a way, it was the moment when European citizens and European peoples were asked whether Europe had a 'common future'. The problem was that the question was put too generally and in the wrong way, without explaining what such a common future entailed in terms of both benefits and sacrifices. This is what the present monetary and financial crisis has finally disclosed, by showing the centrality that the 'economic' Constitution has for the future of Europe, even though this was a question that was firmly out of the agenda of the constitutional debate during the last decade.

THE CONSTITUTIONAL IMPORTANCE
OF MONETARY UNIFICATION

I have argued so far that the present financial crisis should be seen in broad constitutional terms, and that indeed the monetary system introduced by the Euro, and the implicit restructuring of the European financial architecture that followed from it, are part of the (silent) EU Constitution, even though they were hardly discussed during the constitutional phase that never was. I have also implicitly argued that the present crisis should be considered as a continuation of the protracted 'constitutional moment' that started at Maastricht. I now want to make clear the particular sense in which the establishment of the Euro has constitutional relevance, but, at the same time, that such a constitutional status does not exclude the principles of monetary policy to be discussed politically and democratically. This partly follows from the way in which I have set up the relationship between constitutional and normal politics in the previous section but also from the way in which we should understand the principle of democratic legitimacy as operating at the European level. In the present context, the latter argument will only be developed in a compressed form.

In order to discuss the impact that the introduction of the Euro has had on the EU constitutional fabric, it is probably best to start from a number of basic statements, which are obvious, but nonetheless often forgotten, and that therefore risk confusing the argument. First, when we assess the importance of the introduction of the Euro from both a political, social but also symbolic perspective, it is vital to remember that the Euro does not stand in isolation, but is part of an international monetary and financial system. This, as we shall readily see, has important consequences, also because it makes more difficult to compare the role and place of the Euro in comparison with other currencies at different historical periods, thus making the usual rhetorical move of a comparison between the Euro and previous national currencies (in particular the German Mark) rather untenable.

From a more practical and symbolic perspective, the introduction of the Euro in the strict sense of this being a currency for exchange is far less important than, say, the introduction of credit cards and new electronic forms of payment. The latter have truly revolutionised our social and imaginary relationship with money and with the credit system as whole. Looked at from this more broadly social and anthropological perspective, the impact of the Euro, and of the way in which it may affect our daily dealings as either consumers or citizens, is slight, and should not be overstated.

Indeed, when we consider the way in which the Euro may affect our citizenship status and our citizenship practices, or may have a constitutional impact, it is important to distinguish between the various meanings in which we may refer to the Euro. Roughly speaking, there are three general senses: as a monetary entity (as part of a credit system); as a particular currency (within a practical system of exchange); and as coinage, including banknotes (as a material token). The relationship between citizens and the Euro is distinctively different, depending on which one of these senses it is meant. This is something that gets confused when, for instance, evidence gathered through opinion surveys is brought to bear on discussions about the impact or public acceptance of the Euro. These tend to overstate the way in which the 'currency' sense is more directly perceived by people in terms of their attachment, or identification, with a particular material representation of a monetary and credit system whose work is more difficult to perceive physically, if not through very indirect economic processes, which may ultimately affect one individual or family in terms of income or purchasing powers.

Even though the symbolic and practical issues in connection to coinage (or the printing of paper money) have some social relevance, and in spite of the practical policy issues that may arise from the sense connected to the currency function of the Euro, the most important constitutional dimension of the introduction of the Euro is linked to its broad monetary function as part of an international monetary system, and as a means of exchange within an economic area cutting across countries that still maintain separate political and legal system. Notice that the introduction of the Euro, in this more specific sense, has an effect not just on the member states that have adopted the new currency but also on those who belong to the EU but have decided to stay outside the Eurozone. Indeed, as the interconnection of the financial crisis has showed recently, the presence of the Euro is of relevance for the whole international monetary system, and its role within such system is of far greater significance than the one the individual national currencies had in the past, for no other reason than the magnitude of the economic area that the Euro covers in comparison to each individual national currencies in the past.

In its broader monetary sense, the introduction of the Euro has meant the establishment not just of a new currency but also of a new network of institutions, and of the altering of the previous financial and monetary relations between large areas of the EU. The systemic nature of this change, with effects, as I have already remarked, both within individual countries and on the international monetary and financial system as a whole, makes its management extremely difficult, particularly in a situation where political power is still dispersed. One of the arguments often made in relation to the establishment of a common European currency within a more globalised economy is that this is more resilient to the pressures that come from external powers and from the markets in general. However, this is true only insofar as it is possible to have some unified management of some of the financial, credit and monetary levers that affect the performance and stability of a monetary system. Although some of these have been unified under the control of the Central European Bank, most of them are still in the hands of national governments, and therefore the overall effect on the management of the currency is not necessarily of greater empowerment vis-à-vis external and market forces.

Moreover, and from a constitutional perspective this is of even greater significance, the introduction of the Euro has by and large meant the abandonment of previous practices and institutions through which the monetary system was both regulated by and linked to the political system. It is often forgotten that, whatever form they took, monetary institutions were embedded in both political and economic national contexts, which, whether fairly or unfairly, efficiently or inefficiently, provided a set of rules and practices through which economic and broadly social interests were represented in the process of decision-making that resulted in various aspect of monetary policy. The introduction of the Euro does not simply pose the question of whether new institutions of a supranational character have taken the place of national institutions and actors, but whether and how the new institutions perform not simply the technical functions of monetary decision but also those of social intermediation. This issue is of particular relevance because the introduction of the Euro has created an institutional network for monetary policy that is very different from the structure that operated at national levels, giving greater autonomy to the European Central Bank, when compared to its national counterparts (Crouch 2000).

From a democratic perspective, the changes in the institutional network that determines monetary policy, and therefore important aspects of macroeconomic management, have significant consequences and pose two main questions. The first one, as already mentioned, concerns the embeddedness of this institutional network within democratic practices and institutions, guaranteeing broad representativeness, public scrutiny, and operational transparency, so that the policy outcome has sufficient legitimacy to gain acceptance. The second one is whether the main policy objectives that have been fixed as regulating principles of the activity of increasingly independent monetary authority at the EU level can be regarded as socially neutral, and the policy process as responsive enough to other paramount considerations that need to regulate the living within a democratic community.

Given the constitutional and democratic relevance of introducing the Euro and the particular institutional architecture that was established for its system of governance, it is paradoxical, as mentioned in the previous section, that no serious debate took place about these issues during the constitutional phase. The broad terms of the already established EU economic Constitution were never discussed because regarded as being outside the political agenda. But the reverse is true. From a political economy perspective, the introduction of the Euro was part of a political project, which we can characterise through the two central mechanisms for monetary governance. The first is the high degree of autonomy given to the European Central Bank in deciding monetary policy. The second is the introduction of the 'stability pact', aimed to control prices (keeping inflation low), and to control the public deficit, while excluding its structural use. In a way, both these issues represent the answers to the two democratic questions I referred above. The greater autonomy given to the European Central Bank is directly related to the question of democratic representativeness and social embeddedness; while the 'structural' policies that the Bank is meant to pursue pose the problem of the social scope of such policies.

With respect to the question of the autonomy of the Central European Bank, this is normally justified in terms of credibility, and argued in the language of the principal-agent theory. From the perspective of principal-agent theory, democratic representation and regulatory delegation look rather similar, since they can both be nested in an overall chain of 'delegation of powers' from citizens to non-majoritarian institutions, passing through legislative and executive bodies, and occasionally public bureaucracies (Braun and Gilardi 2006, 4–11). However, as the literature on regulatory delegation shows, at a more substantive level some of the operations, as well as the mechanisms of role-formation and agent's motivation, are distinctive, following dynamics of their own, which are not entirely reducible to political, or even bureaucratic forms of representation. Majone (2005, 64–7) characterises the reasons for delegation as being primarily of two kinds: the reduction of decision-making costs, and the enhancement of commitment and long-term credibility. These two reasons align the principal's and agent's preferences in different ways to produce two divergent accounts of delegation. Delegating to reduce decision-making costs assumes that principal and agent share similar preferences. Indeed, the main problem for this kind of delegation is to ensure there are no 'agency losses'. As a result, principals need to design selection procedures and post-delegation mechanisms that avoid dangers such as 'shirking' (when agents follow their own preferences irrespective of their principals'), 'slippage' (perverse institutional mechanisms that make agents' preferences diverge from their principals'), and 'capture' (when agents collude with the actors whose behaviour they are meant to regulate) (Cohen and Thatcher 2005). This form of delegatory representation parallels that of mandated political representatives, for whom electoral mechanisms serve to guard against these risks. However, it is unclear that appointed, non-majoritarian bodies have anything as effective as electoral accountability to keep them on their toes. Indeed, their main representative claim rests on the second reason, which by contrast requires that delegates be insulated against the need for undue responsiveness to their principals' preferences. This is indeed what is normally advocated in the case of Central Banks.

The rationale for delegation to guarantee market credibility and maintain commitments assumes principals suffer from akrasia and act for short-term personal advantages at the expense of long-term collective benefits, even if they ultimately stand to gain from them. Principals can avoid this dilemma by adopting a pre-commitment strategy, and selecting agents whose incentive structure coincides with the long-term commitments required by markets rather than the short-term popularity politicians (or governments in the European case) typically need to court. One consequence of this de-alignment of preferences between principal and agent is to increase agents' discretion and relax considerably, if not completely, the accountability and control conditions to which they are subjected. Agents no longer 'represent' their principals own short-term understanding of their interests and preferences, but rather respond to their principals' supposed second-order preference. This involves their agents acting according to their own 'independent' judgement as to where their principals' first-order interests and preferences lie *in the long term* so as to produce the commitment and credibility required by the market. Thus, when the European Central Bank acts as a non-majoritarian regulatory agent in monetary matters, it does not directly represent the governments of the member states, or the EU legislative bodies, but rather 'represents' the long-term interests of the European Union and of its member states, even if its reading of these interests and preferences diverges from how the other institutional actors perceive them.

Whether one agrees or not with this representation of regulatory delegation is besides the point in our context. Indeed, a number of democratic objections could be raised against such a justification for the Bank's independence. However, in the case of the Central European Bank, the way in which this has been set up has created a situation in which its credibility seems to depend entirely from it only pursuing inflexible and overcautious policies, precisely because it lacks the kind of flexibility that other Central Banks (The Federal Reserve in the United States, for instance) have by the fact that they are not entirely impermeable to political pressure (Fitoussi 2002). The Bank's inflexibility in trying to be seen as 'credible' is further aggravated by the fact that monetary policy at the EU level is isolated from fiscal policy, and can only be conducted in a pro-cyclical fashion, thus drastically reducing the mix and variety of policy tools that it is at its disposal. The comparison often made between the European Central Bank and the Deutsche Bundesbank in terms of prestige and policies is extremely deceiving from many points of view. First, the policies of the Bundesbank were conducted in a very different economic, monetary and financial context, and in relation to particular political, cultural and economic conditions of West Germany. Secondly, the institutional context in which the Bundesbank operated was very different, and so the mix of interests that it was trying to serve, which were far more homogenous than those that the European Central bank needs to attend. Thirdly, the size of the economy of West Germany, even if relatively large in international terms, was far smaller than the one of the EU economic zone nowadays, so that this also offered greater latitude of action. In short, to use the Bundesbank as a model for the European Central Bank is both wrong and deceptive.

From a more policy perspective, the pro-cycle, anti-inflationary policies linked to the European Central Bank, besides reflecting a certain neoliberal ideological perspective, it has also meant a rigidity in policies, which has resulted either in the inability to adopt efficient policies quickly or in a less transparent modus operandi, since the monetary and fiscal authorities cannot readily justify policies that they may regard appropriate, but which seem to contradict the guiding principles of European monetary policy. This has also resulted in a certain slowness to adapt to the economic and financial contingencies, and also a high degree of inflexibility in adapting to either territorial or social diversity within the Eurozone, thus making policies less, and not more legitimate, in the eyes of the European citizens.

In conclusion, the introduction of the Euro and the (silent) constitutionalisation of both monetary policy institutional architecture and objectives suffer from important democratic deficits, and can hardly be regarded as socially neutral. Although this was evident from the start, the debate on the Constitution that dominated EU politics during the past decade failed to engage with the problems that the Euro posed for the democratic governance and legitimacy of the EU. The recent financial and economic crisis has, however, exposed these very problems. If Europe is our common future, and if a single monetary system is part of it, we need to have a more democratic, representative and legitimate way to run it and to establish its principles and objectives. We are back to one of the central constitutional issue for the EU, but this time with a vengeance. *Hic Rhodus, hic salta.*

Part IV

CITIZENSHIP, IDENTITY AND LANGUAGE

Chapter 9

The Liberty of the Moderns?

Market Freedom and Democracy within the EU[1]

Richard Bellamy

With the Euro crisis creating pressures for a fiscal union within the Euro-zone, the compatibility of a free market with political freedom in the EU has become an especially pressing issue. The four market freedoms establishing the free movement of capital, labour, services and goods define the EU's core purposes. In many respects, these four freedoms are the archetypal 'modern freedoms' praised by the French political theorist Benjamin Constant in his lecture of 1819 on 'The Liberty of the Ancients Compared to those of the Moderns'. In this chapter, I shall argue that Constant's analysis of the passage from ancient to modern liberty proves instructive for understanding the contemporary dilemma of how to combine market with political freedom in the EU.[2] Constant argued that commerce had undermined the ancient form of political liberty, that of direct participation. Certain interpreters have seen this argument as suggesting an inherent tension between 'liberalism' and 'repub-licanism', markets and democracy, which is exemplified by the EU (Scharpf 2009, 174–78). They contend that – unchecked – the EU's four market free-doms might undermine democratic citizenship within the member states, with-out being able to create anything as substantial at the European level. In their view, the result will be the erosion of the democratically constituted social rights and policies typical of these states by EU-led pressures for an unre-stricted free market (Scharpf 2009, 192–98). Yet, Constant maintained that modern liberty was compatible with a new kind of political liberty, representa-tive democracy (Constant 1819, 325/6). Likewise, some analysts have argued that the EU can adopt similar political arrangements to those found in the member states (Hix 2008), and even that the freedoms associated with modern liberty offer a basis for establishing the political rights typical of representative democracy on postnational grounds (Habermas 1998, 116–18). Indeed, Article 8A of the Lisbon Treaty declares, 'The functioning of the Union shall be founded on representative democracy'. However, others believe the EU presages new forms of transnational (Benhabib 2008; Kostakopoulou 2008), or supranational, citizenship (Majone 2001) that can detach social from political rights, and the democratic 'outputs' of economic equity and efficiency from any democratic 'input'. This chapter explores all these possibilities.

The first section outlines Constant's classic diagnosis of the shift from 'ancient' to 'modern' liberty. It examines why he thought political liberty remained 'indispensable' in a commercial age, and regarded representative democracy as compatible with modern liberty. As we shall see, though, Constant believed representative democratic institutions could only function in cultural and social conditions that are not themselves the products of the civil liberties he associated with modern liberty – indeed; they assisted practices that potentially undermined these conditions. The second section describes how these conditions facilitated the development of representative democracy within European nation states. These states combined modern civil and commercial liberties with the representative form of political liberty in the manner imagined by Constant. However, this combination involved three factors – national identity, a social contract among citizens and political parties – that all modify the individualistic and private character of modern liberty. These factors are shown to be largely absent from the EU, raising the question of whether the social and cultural conditions exist for the institutions of representative democracy at the EU level to be effective. Some commentators have contended that a new, postnational basis can be found for them; others argue that new forms of transnational and supranational citizenship are emerging that go beyond representative democracy. The third section investigates these possibilities. I examine three accounts, each of which seeks to do away with one of the three factors highlighted above as necessary for representative democracy at the national level. I start with Habermas's (1996a, appendix 2) 'postnational' argument that public autonomy can be seen as logically entailed by the modern liberty of private autonomy, with a constitutional patriotism flowing from individual rights replacing nationalism as a civic bond. I then turn to Benhabib's (2004, chap. 4, 2008) 'transnational' view that 'freedom of movement' has deterritorialised certain social rights, and decoupled them from the reciprocal bonds of economic and political participation that ground them in the member states. Finally, I explore Majone's (1996, 2001) technocratic defence of 'supranational' forms of non-majoritarian governance for certain key EU functions, with party competition replaced by selective consultation with experts and civil society groups. I argue all these schemes overlook certain key features of modern liberty that Constant identified as making political liberty difficult to achieve, yet as necessary as ever.

FROM ANCIENT TO MODERN LIBERTY

Constant's account distinguishes between different conceptions of liberty, the formal entitlements and practices that are associated with them, and the social, cultural and economic conditions needed to render these entitlements and practices plausible and effective. He equated the ancient conception of liberty with collective autonomy and the modern conception with individual autonomy (Constant 1819, 310–12). Ancient liberty consisted of the political freedom provided by the collective participation of all citizens in ruling the polity. Although citizens enjoyed a superior civil status to non-citizens, such as slaves or women, their public duties largely extinguished their opportunities for freedom in the private sphere. Indeed, private interests were regarded as inherently partial and detracting from an attachment to the public good. The political freedom of being ruled by oneself rather than by others could only be obtained collectively and through the sacrifice of all personal freedom. Only such total involvement could ensure politics was not captured by particular interests and all citizens devoted themselves to the public good.

By contrast, modern liberty was predominantly civil rather than political, and mainly exercised in the private and social sphere. Instead of civic duty, modern liberty encouraged individuals 'to occupy their days or hours in a way which is most compatible with their inclinations or whims' (Constant 1819, 311). It was fostered by individual rights to freedom, such as the civil freedoms of conscience, association, speech and movement, and above all by the freedoms of contract and property ownership. The latter went hand in hand with commerce, which had undermined the small-scale, slave economies supporting ancient liberty and provided the socio-economic conditions favourable to modern liberty.

Constant welcomed this development as having expanded both the types of freedom open to people and the range of social classes who could enjoy them. He also thought the spread of modern liberty through commerce had made political oppression less likely. People had become more jealous of their private liberty and suspicious of all government rules and regulations that might inhibit it. They also looked to trade rather than war to enrich themselves, thereby reducing the capacity of rulers to embark on military adventures that increased their own wealth and power. Instead, rulers became dependent on private banks and taxpayers for their revenues, with their income likewise relying on trade and industry. Nonetheless, if 'individual liberty' was 'the true modern liberty', 'political liberty is its guarantee' and remained 'indispensable' (Constant 1819, 323). Constant worried that in their enjoyment of their private liberties, citizens might neglect and even subvert these political guarantees (Constant 1819, 323/4). The difficulty was that the very factors that made these guarantees necessary also encouraged their neglect and subversion.

Though Constant thought all individuals had an interest in the rights associated with modern liberty, he appreciated that not everyone necessarily had an equal interest in every one of them or in upholding them on an equal basis for all. Nor did he think a free market would inevitably harmonise each person's pursuit of their own interest with a similar pursuit by everyone else in ways that promoted the best interests of all. The particular interests of different individuals could and did clash. Following Adam Smith (Viner 1958; Winch 1978, 97/98), Constant saw commerce as potentially corrupting from a civic point of view, reducing sympathy for others and encouraging cupidity – dangers all too evident in the 'monopolizing spirit' of the mercantile system (Constant 1815, 217/18). Certain political structures, not least an impartial legal system, were needed to secure the civil rights related to individual liberty and ensure all respected them. Political mechanisms were also necessary to resolve conflicts and solve coordination problems – such as the supply of public goods. One solution might be to charge independent administrators with the task of providing these guarantees, leaving individuals free to engage in their private pursuits. As he caustically observed, it was an offer those in authority were all too happy to make, being 'so ready to spare us all sort of troubles, except those of obeying and paying!' However, the Napoleonic regime had revealed the error of trusting to self-declared 'enlightened' despots. Tempting though this solution might appear to individuals who felt they had better things to do than engage in politics, it would be 'folly' to hand over political power to any group of people without being able to ensure they served the interests of the ruled rather than their own (Constant 1819, 326).

Therefore, a modern form of political liberty had to address the same two key political tasks of ancient liberty: namely, to guard against the uncertain virtuousness of the guardians of liberty, and to gain the support of the citizenry for certain common rules and regulations. Moreover, it had to do so for the self-same reasons as those that had motivated the ancients – the concern that politics might be captured by 'factions' and employed for personal gain. Even modern liberty required a degree of civic virtue to induce citizens to guard the guardians who provided the political guarantee of their freedom, and to see the necessity for such political guarantees in the first place (Constant 1819, 327/8). Yet, this civic virtue could not be of the kind associated with ancient liberty. That version had involved the dropping of private interests for the public interest. By contrast, to be compatible with modern liberty, civic virtue and politics more generally had to be consistent with citizens regarding the furthering of their private interests as the main purpose of their freedom.

Constant contended that representative democracy provided a form of political liberty of the requisite kind. It embodied the 'eternal rights to assent to the laws, to deliberate on our interests, to be an integral part of the social body of which we are members' (Constant 1819, 324) in a way attuned to the liberties of the moderns. To assent to the laws, citizens did not have to be directly involved in decision-making themselves. They elected 'hired stewards' to do it for them, leaving them plenty of time for their private affairs. Constant saw these representatives very much as delegates and stressed the importance of their being directly elected to ensure their accountability and responsiveness to the electorate (Constant 1815, 202, 206). It was as delegates rather than trustees that they were authorised 'to deliberate on our interests' on our behalf. Representative democracy involved a very different conception of the public interest to that associated with ancient liberty. Instead of being distinct from all private interests, it was the product of their aggregation and negotiation. The role of representatives was to represent the diverse private interests of their electors, and produce legislation that responded to their concerns. The general interest could only arise from 'the negotiation that takes place between particular interests'. This required 'the representation of all partial interests which must reach a compromise on the objects they have in common' (Constant 1815, 205). A representative must remain 'partial towards his own electors', therefore, because the 'impartiality of all' only resulted when 'the partiality of each of them' was 'united and reconciled' (Constant 1815, 206). The upshot of this system was to make all citizens feel 'an integral part of the social body'. For each citizen could claim an equal responsibility for and stake in the laws given they had been made by their elected representatives so as to reflect their interests. In this way, 'political liberty, by submitting to all the citizens, without exception, the care and assessment of their most sacred interests, enlarges their spirit, ennobles their thoughts, and establishes among them a kind of intellectual equality which forms the glory and power of a people' (Constant 1819, 327).

On Constant's account, therefore, representative democracy retains the links found in ancient liberty between self-government, the public interest, and civic virtue, on the one side, and liberty, on the other. However, it reworks their rationale and functioning to coincide with the modern liberty of individual autonomy, with its focus on social and personal life, rather than the essentially political collective autonomy characteristic of ancient liberty. It makes politics less onerous and reconceives the public interest in terms of private interests. Yet, neither of these features will of themselves overcome the key problem of factionalism, which is likely to be an even greater danger under modern as opposed to ancient liberty. Other aspects of Constant's institutional design address this issue to a degree. For example, he recommended a clear separation of powers, with an independent judiciary to police infringements of basic rights and a constitutional monarch with the power to dissolve parliament. But the 'bastion' of individual freedom remained 'the existence of a large and independent representation' (Constant 1815, 289).

It alone enables citizens to guard the guardians and legitimise the reciprocal modifications to their private interests needed to construct the public interest.

Constant hoped political participation itself might generate some of the civic virtue needed for these tasks. However, it is doubtful it can do so if citizens lack any disposition towards public spiritedness in the first place. If individuals are simply concerned to promote their own interests as much as possible, then they will remain tempted to free ride on the civic virtue of others, and to devote their own political energies to rent seeking. Fostering mutual dependence through federal arrangements that allowed each local faction to block the self-interested behaviour of other factions, as he also recommended, will be insufficient to promote their common interests efficiently and equitably. It simply invites the universalising of factionalism. It will produce either deadlock or generalised rent seeking by representatives attempting to buy the support of their followers, neither of which is likely to be optimal or just unless the parties are equal to start with. Even then prisoner's dilemmas and other quandaries of rational choice will arise. To avoid these difficulties, individuals need to be disposed to view the exercise of their own private rights in ways that take into account and accommodate their similar exercise by others.

The dilemma had been appreciated as endemic to commercial republics by Montesquieu and Smith, on whom Constant drew (Winch 1978, 97–99), as well as the authors of *The Federalist* (Elkin 2006). They too had sought to devise political institutions that economised on virtue, while recognising that in politics as opposed to markets private vice rarely generates public benefits. However, like other French liberals, Constant was more attentive to the role cultural and social conditions play in fostering appropriate political attitudes than the Anglo-American tradition has tended to be (Siedentop 1979). He had witnessed the failure not just of the French Revolution's attempt to reinvigorate ancient liberty but also of the Napoleonic attempt to establish an Empire of modern liberty through the Code Napoléon against the rise of nationalism.

Two such conditions underpin Constant's analysis of representative democracy. First, he noted how a shared political culture fosters allegiance both to political institutions and one's fellow citizens. As he remarked, 'the natural source of patriotism' was found in 'a vivid attachment to the interests, the ways of life, the customs of some locality' (Constant 1813, 74). As Mill later argued (Mill 1861, chap. 16), drawing on Constant and other French liberals (Siedentop 1979, 172–74), such national sentiments make representative democracy possible by facilitating public debate in ways that reduce factionalism (Miller 2009, 208–13). For a start, it will be easier to have a discussion among the public as a whole if there are shared cultural instruments, such as a common media – newspapers and, nowadays, television and radio programmes – that address and are accessible by all, not least because they are in a common language all can understand. Such instruments help different sections of society to inform and respond to each other. It becomes harder for governments to play them off against one another and to pander to sectional rather than public opinions commanding broad support. A political culture also supplies shared values that provide citizens with a basis for debating matters of collective concern. For citizens and their representatives to feel obliged to respond to and accommodate the views and interests of others, they must consider the arguments their interlocutors raise are more than private opinions and concerns. A common stock of values, that all recognise as important for the political community, aids discussion and compromise. It provides agreement on the sorts of points that can be raised and need to be addressed and responded to, even if there is disagreement about their relative importance and the most appropriate response. In their absence, people will just talk past each other. The sharing of values and language can also help build trust among the electorate by highlighting common sympathies and priorities. Politics can be less about gaining advantages for one's own group or oppressing rival groups, and more about what set of policies best balances the different concerns of individuals so as to achieve the most satisfactory outcome for all.

Second, similar issues arise if there is a lack of interdependence of interests and individuals do not possess a roughly equal stake in the collective decisions affecting them (Christiano 2006). These conditions supply both an equal right, as a matter of fairness, for all members of the political community to have an equal say in how it is run, and stimulate the sort of cross-cutting cleavages whereby people who find themselves opposed on one issue are on the same side on others. Both conditions reduce the prospect of majority tyranny. Though people will have a greater interest in some issues than others, everyone involved in politics will have a more or less equal interest in the totality of collective decisions. They will be able to compromise by trading votes between the issues that matter to them and those that they regard to be less important, and will be less likely to be consistent winners or losers as a result. This reasoning underpinned the traditional limitation of the vote to property owners, a view Constant fully endorsed. He distinguished landed from 'industrial' property in this respect. Only the former 'binds man to the country where he lives, surrounds his departure from it with obstacles, creates patriotism through interest' (Constant 1815, 218). Land alone gave each member of the association 'a common interest with the other members of the association' (Constant 1815, 214). It signified involvement in common cultural, social and economic structures, and a commitment to their future efficient and equitable functioning. The moveable 'industrial' property of labour and trade was less affected by such structures, and its possessors had less of a common interest in supporting them and ensuring they operated in a fair way.

Given the topic of this chapter, it is significant that Constant regarded the absence of these two conditions as a chief failing of the Napoleonic Empire (Fontana 2002, 126/7). This project had endeavoured to unite Europe around the benefits of a uniform model of good governance encapsulated in the Code Napoléon. 'The same code of law, the same measures, the same regulations, and if they could contrive it gradually, the same language, this is what is proclaimed to be the perfect form of social organisation' (Constant 1813, 73). However, 'a fictitious passion for an abstract being, a general idea stripped of all that can engage the imagination and speak to the memory' could not replace the 'genuine patriotism' that springs from 'local customs' (Constant 1813, 73/4). Uniform laws also overlooked local diversity. In this respect 'large states have great disadvantages. Laws proceed from a place so remote from those places where they must be applied, that frequent and serious errors are the inevitable result' (Constant 1813, 77). Good governance needed more than a uniform imposition of the rules and rights of private interest. If laws were to be sensitively and impartially applied and adhered to, in ways that reinforced public goods while being sensitive to local differences, then institutions of political liberty that could draw on shared cultural norms and common interests were necessary.

Though Constant never mentions *The Federalist*, one can assume that he would have regarded its proposals as incompatible with these two preconditions for representative politics as the Napoleonic Empire. A large size might aid the checks and balances needed for the negative task of blocking factions, as *Federalist* 10 famously maintained, but – at least within Europe – he would have regarded such a solution unavailable. Europe was too diverse for the common culture and interests he believed were needed for the positive task of constructing and generating allegiance to a shared public interest. In these respects, his conception of modern political liberty is more 'republican', more concerned to preserve those qualities of ancient liberty that 'achieve the moral education of citizens' (Constant 1819, 328), than *The Federalist* – hence his preference for an association of European nation states.[3] Yet, he feared this possibility was endangered not just by Napoleon but also by the corrosive effects of commerce, which was turning the European peoples into 'a great mass of human beings, that ... despite the different names under which they live and their different forms of social organization, are essentially homogeneous in their nature' (Constant 1813, 52/3). If the 'natural' source of civic pride was local, the danger was such a mass would be little more than an agglomeration of self-seeking private individuals.

The various dilemmas Constant diagnosed as bedevilling the combination of modern liberty and democracy are all too evident in the current Euro crisis. On the one hand, the financial crisis and the high levels of sovereign debt that have resulted from it reveal both the need for market regulation and the tendency not to do so when a merchant class with highly moveable property and little stake in the polity capture governments (Mair 2011). If economies are not socially and politically embedded, they are prone to various forms of market failure (Polanyi 1944). On the other hand, the difficulties of getting agreement on a suitable rescue package among the Eurozone members follow from the type of democratic politics that Constant associated with modern liberty, in which agreement requires Pareto improvements for all the parties involved. This reasoning will only provide a rationale for Germany and the other solvent states to guarantee the sovereign debt of those states likely to default so long as it is compatible with enlightened national self-interest as the solution to an assurance game. However, if the appeal begins to shift so that it is less to enlightened national self-interest and instead to the collective self-interest of the Union as a whole – that is, if the sacrifices called for from either the debtor or the creditor states rise beyond a certain threshold and look to be uncompensated in the medium or even the long term – then cooperation will weaken (Scharpf 1997, chap. 6). In the view of many national politicians and their electorates, it would appear that we are perilously close to this situation – hence the tentativeness of the proposals being made to resolve the situation. The EU has traditionally sought to overcome such problems by imposing a non-political solution via the Commission or the European Court of Justice, or in this case the European Central Bank. However, such solutions are also only likely to prove stable and acceptable in the case of a symmetrical prisoner's dilemma, in which uniform rules and cooperation will benefit all and the problem is to avoid free riding (Scharpf 2009, 183–85, 189/90). A key difficulty with the Euro, though, has been that the underlying constellation of interests, in this case, does not conform to this pattern. It is not just that certain countries failed to abide by the conditions of the Stability and Growth Pact and keep public spending under control but also that the economies of the participating states have proven too diverse. In other words, Constant's critique of the Napoleonic Empire's technocratic imposition of uniform norms and regulations applies with particular force here. The problems currently confronting the EU are increasingly characterised by asymmetric conflicts of interest. In these cases, an appeal to mutual national self-interest ceases to be credible and must be to the collective self-interest of the Union as a whole – as has occurred in current calls to 'save the Euro' and with it 'Europe'.[4] Yet, to construct a European public interest in these circumstances requires a pan-European democratic politics capable of overcoming national self-interest. At this point, the issues raised by Constant's analysis of modern liberty become highly relevant. As I noted, the EU upholds the civil liberties necessary for a free market. What remains to be seen is if sufficient cultural and social conditions exist at the European level to imbue those who enjoy this pan-European modern liberty with sufficient elements of the civic spirit of the ancients for a political union based on the principle of representative democracy to be possible.

THE MODERN UNION OF POLITICAL
AND COMMERCIAL LIBERTY

Contrary to Constant's expectations, commerce did not end the military conflict (Wenar, and Milanovic 2009). Representative democracy was only firmly established in Europe after two world wars and a third, cold, war. Nevertheless, the liberal democratic states that gradually emerged from the nineteenth century onwards could be said to involve precisely the marriage he anticipated between political and market freedom. Moreover, he has been proved justified in believing that there could be no liberal (civil and commercial liberty) regimes that were not also in some meaningful sense democratic (political liberty) regimes too, and vice versa. Yet, this modern form of political liberty depended on the two factors Constant had identified as necessary, a common culture and common interests, being preserved in a form he had thought potentially incompatible with commercial liberty: namely, nationalism and a social contract between unpropertied labourers and those possessing industrial property, plus a third factor, political parties, that he had not anticipated. These respectively generated the common values and idiom, the alleviation of conflicts of interest, and the creation of ideological rather than factional political associations that were needed to engender enough elements of the public spiritedness and social solidarity typical of the citizenry of the ancient polity for the less demanding, yet more inclusive, representative democracies to work in ways that promoted rather than subverted the public goods appropriate to a modern system of liberty.

As we saw, Constant feared modern liberty was dissolving cultural differences and creating common tastes as well as economic bonds that were transnational in character (Constant 1813, 52/3). Yet, a desire for similar consumer products does not seem to have eroded national sentiments. Indeed, to some degree, the development of unified markets for production and exchange promoted nationalism as local practices were replaced by a common economic and cultural system tied to a single state (Gellner 1983). These economically driven processes of nation-building fed into the development of a national political demos (Rokkan 1974). The resulting national cultures possess many of the hallmarks of ancient liberty in being created by the state, often through compulsory education programmes, and stressing a common public bond of a civic kind that is superior to, and partly shapes, an individual's private preferences. They also ensure a shared language or languages necessary for a common public sphere. Meanwhile, as he noted, size remains important. The representative system can only be stretched so far. Citizens not only rightly feel their vote counts for less if a political community gets too big (Dahl and Tufte 1973, 13ff) but also larger communities tend to be more diverse – culturally, socially and economically – making it less likely all have an equal stake in the issues on which they have an equal say, and increasing the chances of persistent minorities and hence of majority tyranny (Christiano 2006).

Second, in addition to cultural bonds, a community of interest among citizens has been buttressed by a social contract promoting a degree of reciprocity in economic relations (Offe 2000, 67/8). Market rights have been supplemented and constrained by social rights in exchange for a willingness to work and pay taxes. Though Constant followed Smith in regarding commerce as socially beneficial, like Smith he appreciated its operations might be attended by conflicts generated by the large inequalities it promotes in patterns of ownership and income (Winch 1978, 98/99; Marshall 1950; Barbalet 1988). By basing the franchise on 'landed' property alone, he had attempted to exclude the conflict between capital and labour from politics, and prevent commercial interests capturing the political process (Constant 1815, 217). In a commercial world, however, insistence on a landed property qualification became increasingly untenable. Meanwhile, mass mobilisation in two world wars undermined his contention that the 'patriotism' required 'to die for one's country' involved a lesser commitment to, and understanding of, its interests than possession of land (Constant 1815, 214). Instead, they prompted the enfranchisement of the unpropertied, with public systems of social assurance and education offering an alternative to propertied wealth for ensuring a citizen could act and think independently without being dependent on particular private interests (Mann 1987). In the process, class conflict was attenuated sufficiently to be containable within the democratic system. However, in return, participation in the economy, at the very least through being available for work if able to do so, became both a legal requirement and an expectation of one's fellow citizens for those seeking the full social and political benefits of citizenship. This expectation that a universal entitlement to social welfare will be reciprocated by everyone's doing their bit to contribute to the welfare of others when they can, obtains support in its turn from citizens feeling they belong to a national political community (Miller 1995, 83, 93). Again a degree of commonality has helped both to create a social bond and increase confidence that one's fellows will act justly by you if you act justly towards them (Galston 1991, 215–24).

Finally, Constant shared his contemporaries' distrust of parties (e.g. Hume 1741, Essay 8). However, for a mass electorate, the process of combining the disparate views of millions of citizens and bringing them to bear on representatives, while avoiding both factionalism and clientelism, has depended on the development of political parties defined by ideology or programmes rather than patronage networks or the narrow interests of their members, and obliged regularly to compete for power in free and open elections (Lipset and Rokkan 1967). As early analysts of modern democracies noted (Bryce 1921, 119; Schattschneider 1942, 1), parties play an ineliminable role in the 'modern' form of political liberty by channelling the pursuit of private interests in a more public direction, and making political participation cost effective in terms of time and effort. Electoral competition forces parties to construct coalitions of different interests and unite them behind a programme of government to obtain a majority. As a result, different private interests are brought to accommodate each other and seek common ground, and so come, in part at least, to shape their demands in terms of a broader and more public interest. Parties also economise on the time citizens have to give to informing themselves about the merits and failings of their potential and actual rulers and the views of their representatives and fellow citizens. Mutual criticism by rival parties highlights electorally salient information, while party discipline controls and vets representatives.

However, party competition only tends to work well when those involved are not additionally divided by ethnic, religious, linguistic and cultural divisions or overly polarised by class conflicts: conditions provided by a common nationality and social rights. For these factors prevent politics becoming zero-sum and allow ideologically or programme based parties to unite very diverse groups around a number of mutually intersecting concerns that cut across cultural and class cleavages. At the same time, as Constant noted, political participation helps give citizens a sense of responsibility for and control over these policies, with electoral pressures serving to shape national political culture and the social system. Our confidence that the laws treat those subject to them in an equitable manner is strengthened through their being open to contestation through fair political processes in which each citizen's vote is treated with a reasonable degree of equal concern and respect.

Therefore, though contemporary representative democracies are liberal-democratic, with the ancient liberty of direct collective political participation transformed by the modern liberties of freedom of choice, the exercise of autonomous judgement about how to lead one's life, and the separation of public and private, their practices are shaped by cultural bonds Constant feared might be destined to disappear, social bonds he had not imagined as possible, and political mechanisms of a kind he had thought pernicious. All three factors serve to constrain the operation of modern liberty in various ways so as to render it compatible with a commitment to collective decision-making. Part of the difficulties with establishing any degree of political liberty within the EU arises from the fact that the continued unfolding of modern liberty appears to have done little to abate the importance of the first factor, while potentially making the second and third factors increasingly problematic.

Far from national and cultural differences decreasing, they have become ever more significant. Thus, multinational states, such as Britain, Belgium and Spain, have begun to fragment along linguistic, religious and ethnic lines and been subject to increasing calls for self-government on the part of territorially concentrated minority groups and, in certain cases, even secession (Kymlicka 2001, 212/13). Cultural criteria have, if anything, increased in importance for those seeking access to citizenship from outside, with many states enfranchising non-resident co-nationals while remaining reluctant to grant full citizen rights to resident aliens (Joppke 2001). By contrast, welfare settlements have been under pressure since the 1980s from governments influenced by New Right thinking, with global markets often invoked as having helped promote such neoliberal policies. Despite some modest retrenchments, though, social rights have remained remarkably robust in the face of such onslaughts and there is little evidence that globalisation has forced a reduction in welfare spending in order to maintain international competitiveness, though some restructuring has taken place (Swank 2002, 276). However, what remains strong is the view that welfare forms part of a contract between citizens which involves duties as well as rights. Whether justified or not, citizens have demanded governments pursue policies that guard against putative welfare 'scroungers' and have been sensitive to 'economic' immigration if that is felt to detract from the employment opportunities available to existing citizens or to place additional burdens on social services such as housing, hospitals and schools, without any compensating gain in tax revenue towards their maintenance and improvement (White 2003, chap. 1). Meanwhile, all advanced democracies are witnessing a slow but steady decline in electoral turnout, along with a shift towards more focused – and, in certain respects, more privatised and factional – forms of political participation, as party membership has declined even more rapidly than voting (Hay 2007, 12–6). Citizens appear to see politics increasingly through the lens of commercial and civil liberty. It is the mechanism through which private interests are pursued and individual rights upheld. There has been a commensurate rise in consumer groups and single-issue movements, particularly in areas such as consumer rights, and the increased resort to the law by those with the resources to do so (Pattie, Seyd, and Whiteley 2004, 275–80). Contemporaneously, there has been a move towards the sort of depoliticisation Constant feared as citizens have come to distrust politicians and the political process. Ever more areas of public life have been handed over to 'expert' regulatory bodies of one kind or another that claim to govern on the basis of the 'public interest', yet with few, if any, mechanisms for ensuring accountability to the public (Hay 2007, 91–5).

All three of these developments pose a challenge for the development of a system of representative democracy at the level of the EU. If national sentiments remain strong for defining political membership and the boundaries of the political community, then how can the EU compete with such allegiances? Likewise, if social rights are rooted within national systems of welfare and solidarity, how can they be disembedded without potentially further weakening the bonds of reciprocity among citizens that sustain them? Finally, without the support of pan-European cultural or social bonds, how can a European party system develop and politics avoid becoming the preserve of myriad pressure groups and depoliticised administrative bodies?

Unsurprisingly, the EU performs poorly on all three of the factors that have made a modern form of political liberty possible in the member states (Bellamy 2008). With regard to the first factor of cultural identification, Eurobarometer surveys consistently indicate that less than 10 per cent of EU citizens have a strong sense of EU identity, with only 50 per cent feeling even a weak attachment – and that strongly secondary to their local and national ties.[5] Likewise, so far as the second factor of social rights goes, opinion polls also show little support for the EU taking responsibility for welfare. Issues relating to socio-economic rights, insofar as they involve health, welfare and education, all have a low level of legitimacy as EU competences, with 65 per cent or more of European citizens regarding these as exclusively national responsibilities. Finally, on the third factor of political parties, these exist at the European level purely as groupings of national parties within the European Parliament, with the take up of EU-level political rights at a lower level and declining faster than within the member states. Average turn out in elections to the European Parliament runs at below 50 per cent and in many countries are as low as 25 per cent, with each increase in parliamentary power being accompanied by a decline in turnout in European elections, which continue to be fought largely on domestic issues (Hix and Marsh 2011). Among the 12 million EU citizens resident in another member state turn out is even lower, with the proportion of non-national EU citizens even registering to vote ranging from a mere 9 per cent in Greece and Portugal to 54.2 per cent in Austria.

It might be argued that just because these factors do not exist now does not mean they could never exist in the future. However, their emergence within the EU is preempted by their presence in the member states, while the processes that promoted them there, not least war, are unlikely to be repeated (Offe 2003, 73/4; Miller 2008, 145/6). For example, there is considerably more diversity on Constant's two elements of a shared political culture and common interests in Europe than in the United States (Baldwin 2009). Views on abortion policy are often taken as a proxy for religious and moral values more generally, with the United States notoriously divided on the issue.

However, if one compares Swedish policy, where on average there are over 17 abortions a year per 1,000 women, with the far more restricted Irish policy, which allows for only 6 abortions a year per 1,000 women, then the division is as great, if not greater. Moreover, despite the spread of English as the lingua franca of the educated European classes, a European media has failed to develop even among this class. Possibly the only newspapers that enjoy a pan-European readership are the mildly Eurosceptic *Financial Times* and the US *Herald Tribune*. Meanwhile, social differences are similarly wide, with the gap between the per capita income of the poorest West European country (Portugal) and the richest (Norway) being three times that between the poorest US state (Mississippi) and the richest (Connecticut). Thus, in the short to medium term at least, it appears doubtful that within the EU modern liberty can be linked to political liberty on the same basis as in the member states, as has often been assumed would be necessary for the EU itself to become a 'representative democracy' as Lisbon directs (Hoffman 1966, 868). The differences in the crucial dimensions are simply too great and have deepened rather than diminished over the past fifteen years (Shore 2004), despite the dramatic increase in EU competencies over this same period. However, others have argued that the novelty of the EU lies in promoting new types of citizenship that do not rely on these three factors but are based on the civil liberties of the moderns alone. It is to the plausibility of such schemes that I now turn.

EU CITIZENSHIP AS THE LIBERTY OF THE MODERNS

EU citizenship can be seen as the archetype of a purely modern conception of political liberty. Though only citizenship of a member state gives access to EU citizenship, it does not itself relate directly to any of the three factors that led to the establishment of liberal democracy within nation states. Instead, citizenship of the Union stems from the four quintessentially modern commercial liberties that lie at the heart of the EU – namely, the free movement of labour, capital, goods and services. At an early stage, these four commercial freedoms became associated with a broader set of civil rights linked to a right to equal treatment and the absence of discrimination on grounds of nationality (Article 12 EC) or 'sex, racial or ethnic origin, religion or belief, disability, age, or sexual orientation' (Article 13 EC). Although initially tied to economic issues such as employment and pay, successive judgements of the European Court of Justice (ECJ) came to interpret the commitment to equality as an implicit component of any legal system that seeks to take individual rights seriously. Following the establishment of the status of Union citizenship in 1992 with the Maastricht Treaty, the Court has gradually come to read the four freedoms through the lens of Article 18 EC, giving every Union citizen the right to move and reside freely in the territory of other member states. By 2001, the Court felt bold enough in one such case – *Grzelcyk*, involving students studying in a different member state to their own – to adopt a rhetorical formula it has regularly employed ever since: namely, that 'Union citizenship is destined to be the fundamental status of nationals of the member states, enabling those who find themselves in the same situation to enjoy the same treatment in law irrespective of their nationality, subject to the exceptions as are expressly provided for'.[6] A number of commentators have argued in similar terms, welcoming this new status as signalling the move towards a new form of citizenship beyond the nation state (e.g. Kostakopoulou 2008).

In what follows, I shall explore the plausibility of this attempt to build the political and social liberties associated with citizenship on modern commercial and civil liberty alone. I shall examine three contrasting accounts, each of which seeks to minimise the need for one of the three factors that made the modern form of political liberty possible within the member states. Each will be shown to suffer from one or more of the pathologies of modern liberty feared by Constant. The first account, provided by Habermas, attempts to create a postnational identification with the EU through a constitutional patriotism to EU-wide rights. Yet, his argument ignores both the local roots of civic patriotism noted by Constant and the tensions between private and public autonomy that Constant showed lay behind the undermining of ancient by modern liberty. The second, transnational account, offered by Seyla Benhabib, reflects on how EU citizenship has come to 'disaggregate' citizenship rights and to 'deterritorialise' certain social rights (Benhabib 2004, 153–5, 2008, 46/47). However, her enthusiasm for this development overlooks how it generates a commercialisation of citizenship that undermines the social contract at the national level that gives rise to these rights in the first place. The third, supranational technocratic account of Majone (2001) suggests the benefits of political liberty can be provided by proxy and without parties – through expert regulators and selective consultation with civil society. Yet, this solution offers an updated version of the Napoleonic version of good governance that Constant recognised as more likely to subvert than strengthen liberty.

Habermas contends EU legitimacy requires the development of a postnational form of Union citizenship that derives from identification with European-level rights (1996, appendix 2) and supported the proposed Constitutional Treaty as a necessary means to achieve this result (Habermas 2001a). To be valid, he believes international law must conform to the 'democratic principle' by incorporating the preconditions for political accountability within it. He sees this incorporation arising through the civil and commercial liberties of the moderns providing the new foundations for the liberties of the ancients. Indeed, his general theory can be seen as an attempt to unite ancient and modern liberty, republicanism and liberalism (see Habermas 1998, 68/9, and 2001b, 116–18, where he uses these terms, and 1996, 99–104). On the one hand, he argues that private autonomy requires social as well as the standard civil rights for its exercise. On the other hand, he contends that these self-same rights are the basis for, and can only be legitimised through, democratic processes. In this way, civil and civic liberties go hand in hand as mutually entailing each other. At the same time, rights can thereby offer an alternative basis for democratic citizenship to membership of a national political community, making possible its extension to the European and potentially the global level (Habermas 2001b, 98–103).

There are a number of problems with this thesis, some prefigured in Constant's analysis of modern liberty. Both logically and empirically his linking of private and public autonomy is too neat (Christiano 1996, chap. 1; Weale 2007, 106–15; Bellamy 2007, 210–12). As Constant noted, there is at the very least a tension between the time and effort that has to be devoted to politics and the pursuit of one's private activities (Constant 1819, 316/7; Weale 2007, 108). True, it might with some justification be argued that in the circumstances of social life private autonomy depends on public regulation. However, this raises the problem that the private autonomy of different citizens may often clash, as may their views as to the appropriate public rules and goods needed to uphold and foster it. Such conflicts reflect their differing preferences and moral values, and the general difficulties that attend identifying and agreeing on what count as good outcomes and the best ways to secure them given the complexities and openness of most social processes. R. P. Wolff (1970) showed many years ago how to portray public policies and laws as expressions of the autonomous will of the people as a whole requires either an implausible account of collective agency or an ethical naturalist account of 'real freedom' of the kind objected to by liberal critics of 'positive' freedom. Indeed, many theorists who adopt this approach have a tendency to compile such extensive lists of the rights and policies needed to secure the preconditions of democratic autonomy that one wonders what would remain for citizens actually to decide democratically (e.g. Held 1995, 153–56, 190–201). Such accounts seem entirely circular – they obtain a spurious democratic legitimacy for their preferred list of rights by so defining democracy that it inherently involves them, so that any democratic consideration of their normative importance and practical implications becomes at best unnecessary at worst self-contradictory.

These conceptual problems become all the more manifest when one considers how the functional and cultural diversity of modern societies multiplies the various spheres of life, each with their different guiding values and priorities, and the plurality of moral codes and valuations of different individuals and groups of people operating within and between them. These processes are themselves the result of modern liberty, yet they increase the potential for tensions and conflicts between the diverse activities of citizens and make convergence on the preconditions for private and public autonomy even less likely. To these difficulties need to be added those linked with the very territorial extent of the proposed postnational political communities. As we saw, Constant noted how size matters (Constant 1813, 76/77), diminishing both the impact any citizen feels he or she may make on collective decision-making and the identification they may have with their fellow citizens (see too Miller 2009, 212/13).

What leads a given group of people to coalesce around a particular con-stitutional settlement would appear to be less its intrinsic merits and more a preexisting belonging to the polity and people to which it applies. To quote Constant again (1813, 73/4), patriotism does not issue from 'a fictitious passion for an abstract being' but 'a vivid attachment to the interests, way of life, the customs of some locality' (see too Shore 2004). After all, every member state already has its own constitutional settlement which embodies liberal democratic values. However, that has not diminished the demand for enhanced self-government or even secession by national minorities within these states. Why, then, should one expect the existence of an EU-level constitution to enhance support for the EU? In fact, only 27 per cent of citi-zens say an EU constitution per se would strengthen European citizenship. Indeed, only 32 per cent of Europeans know their rights as citizens and only 43 per cent claim to understand what the term 'citizen of the EU' means.[7] All the peoples of Europe might value rights, but they have different valuations of them. Within the member states their disagreements in these respects are settled through democratic and judicial decisions that reflect a national politi-cal culture. However, we saw that take up of EU political rights are limited, as is identification with EU-level institutions – a circumstance that has led the German Federal Constitutional Court for one to question the democratic legitimacy of the ECJ and EU law to claim constitutional competence over domestic understandings of constitutional rights.[8]

Nevertheless, Habermas is right to fear the disembedding of rights from a functioning democratic system that can mesh their private exercise with the public goods that provides their rationale (see Raz 1994, chap. 3 for this collective dimension of rights). The dangers attending such a development emerge clearly from a consideration of the 'disaggregation' and 'deterritori-alisation' of rights Benhabib celebrates. As initially designed, Union citizen-ship was supposed to be proof against this arising. Not only is it restricted to citizens of a member state but also, the ECJ's rhetoric notwithstanding, the Treaty insists it must 'complement and not replace national citizenship' (Arti-cle 17 (1) EC). Meanwhile, with the exception of the right to vote in elections to the European Parliament, the EU itself does not provide citizens with goods or services through EU funds or agencies. Rather, what EU citizenship offers is access on a par with national citizens to engage in economic activity with, and enjoy the services and benefits provided by, another member state. It is only activated through a citizen moving to, or trading with, another member state through the exercise of the four freedoms. So, Union citizenship does not offer a form of dual citizenship with the EU per se. Rather, it allows EU citizens to pursue their commercial liberties on a par with nationals of another member state to their own. Moreover, certain 'limitations and conditions' were instituted to protect various non-market liberties associated with national citizenship. Thus, the 1990 Residence Directives, later repealed and incorporated into Article 7 (1) b and c of Directive 2004/38, together with certain provisos of what are now Articles 39, 43 and 49 EC, restrict the right of residence to those engaging in economic activity or possessing adequate funds not to become a burden on the national system of social assurance and covered by sickness insurance. The four freedoms also do not apply in areas that are 'wholly internal' or involve restrictions based on public policy, security and health (*Uecker*[9]). Recently, though, these limitations have been implicitly and explicitly challenged by ECJ rulings to the effect that Union citizenship offers a Treaty based, directly effective right of its own. It is these decisions that have fleshed out a form of market citizenship at the EU level that potentially conflicts with political and social citizenship at the member state level (Everson 1995).

In a series of cases, the Court has increasingly argued that the restrictions protecting national citizenship have to be applied in a 'proportional' manner (*Baumbast*[10]) that do not deprive Union citizens of a right to move and reside that exists independently of their pursuit of any economic activity (*Chen*[11]), thereby creating new rights for non-workers (*Sala*,[12] *Trojani*[13]), students (*Grzelczk*) and jobseekers (*Collins*[14]), weakening public interest derogations that excluded non-nationals from certain public service jobs (*Marina Mercante Espanola*[15]), and altering what could be considered a 'wholly internal' matter (*Avello*,[16] *Chen*, *Rottmann*,[17] *Zambrano*,[18] although see *McCarthy*,[19] which arguably reasserts the internal rule). In a parallel move, the Court has also questioned the previous understanding that the state provision of healthcare and education are not 'services' in the commercial sense of Articles 49, 50 EC, but legitimately correspond to the democratically decided collective preferences of the citizens of each of the member states, reflecting national financial priorities and other public interest considerations (e.g. *Commission v. Austria*,[20] *Humbel*[21]). As such, these services had not been subject to the prohibition on restrictions of the freedom to provide services. However, decisions such as *Swartz*,[22] *Kohll*,[23] *Geraets-Smits*,[24] *Mueller-Faure*[25] and *Watts*[26] have undermined this reasoning by allowing individuals to escape national processes of rationing these goods by shopping for alternatives elsewhere in the Union. *Grzelczyk* held that 'a certain degree of financial solidarity' now existed between the member states. Yet, though the Euro crisis suggests that such solidarity is decidedly limited, the Court has consistently refused to treat national fiscal concerns as posing restrictions on the exercise of European liberties – even treating national rules against tax avoidance as violations of free capital movement. Finally, there have been a series of judgements that have prioritised EU-level economic freedoms over member state–level social rights (*Viking*,[27] *Laval*,[28] *Rueffert*[29] and *Luxembourg*[30]). In these cases, the Court has attempted to impose a uniform, minimum standard of wage legislation that overrides local collective bargaining agreements, thereby hindering the exercise of union rights.

In various ways, these decisions uncouple the rights of individuals freely to pursue their personal goals and interests on an equal basis to others either from economic participation within and a contribution to, or membership of and identification with, the polity in which one resides (Scharpf 2009, 191–98). Consequently, many citizenship rights, including access to important social and economic benefits, have been disassociated not just from political citizenship but also from what we have seen have become the standard prerequisites for obtaining the same: namely, an economic stake in the fortunes of the state, membership and a degree of identification with it, and political participation in shaping and sustaining the goods that it provides its citizens. It is this process that has produced what Benhabib calls the disaggregation of citizenship (Benhabib 2008, 46/47), whereby the synthesis of civic with commercial and civil liberties achieved within the nation state has been pulled apart as the latter have become detached from the three factors we identified as linking them to the former. Instead, modern commercial liberties have become the trigger of themselves for access to certain civic liberties: notably, the ability to vote and stand in local and European elections when residing in another member state, and admission to social benefits that hitherto have been both privileges of political citizenship and part of their foundation.

Although an advocate of 'another cosmopolitanism', Benhabib's transnational position shares the general cosmopolitan endorsement of such moves as following their critique of the moral arbitrariness of borders, and the exclusionary nature of state-centred citizenship (Carens 1987; Nussbaum 1996). Even though many, if not all, of these rights apply only to EU nationals rather than all non-citizens resident within a member state, and to that extent are unsatisfactory, cosmopolitans are apt to regard any deterritorialising and denationalising of citizenship as a step in the right direction. However, there is a split within the cosmopolitan camp over what universal obligations we owe to all humans, and the mechanisms that might be necessary to uphold them. Libertarians see the liberties of the moderns in largely negative terms, as merely necessitating the removal of barriers that interfere with free exchanges between individuals (Kukathas 2003, 572). On this view, there was little need for Union citizenship as a social or political status – it was sufficient to uphold the four freedoms as inherent aspects of a 'common market', avoiding welfare and political rights as creating potential distortions with its free operation while supporting the possibility of economic migration from poor to rich countries as consistent with a genuinely free market in labour. By contrast, more socially minded cosmopolitans have argued that rich countries also have more positive obligations towards the poor (e.g. Pogge 2008). Theorists differ as to how far these extend, but most contend some redistribution is warranted given that the wealth of the rich depends in part on their having exploited the resources of the poor and deployed their superior bargaining position to gain favourable terms of trade.

The quandary confronting social liberals, though, is that the institutional capacity for securing the libertarian, market-reinforcing view of the liberties of the moderns is far greater than that for implementing the market-correcting view they favour. As Fritz Scharpf has noted (1999, 54–8), ever since *Cassis de Dijon*[31] the ECJ has effectively constitutionalised free competition within the EU, overriding the political judgement of national legislatures on the reasonableness of their environmental, health and safety, and other regulations whenever it felt they lacked an adequate public interest defence. The opening up of the full range of public services to competition, so that Union citizens may choose from a range of providers, is simply an extension of this logic. Yet, this possibility potentially undermines the social contract within each of the member states without establishing any at the EU level (Scharpf 2009, 198). For example, the decision in *Watts* simply enables those citizens who are sufficiently mobile and proactive to seek a given health treatment in another member state to jump the waiting lists and other restrictions that national services employ to prioritise the spending of limited resources among different kinds of health care (Newdick 2006). As such, it certainly enhances the 'modern liberty' of those citizens able to take advantage of this option. But, given that national budgets are not infinitely elastic, their doing so may be at the expense of the health or other social needs of many of their fellow citizens. Moreover, these other individuals are not in a position to contest such Court decisions through the political system. Instead, their collective civic liberty has been undercut by this extension of an essentially commercial liberty.

Benhabib appears to acknowledge this dilemma in seeking to distinguish the 'human rights' claims made by refugees, asylum seekers and migrant workers from the deregulatory legal framework promoted by global capitalism – what she calls the *lex mercatoria* (Benhabib 2007, 22, 33). Yet, this theoretical argument overlooks how in practice the language of the first has often been deployed to legitimise the second. Like others (Caporoso and Tarrow 2008; Kostakopoulou 2008; Kochenov 2011) she has seen the Court's extension of rights to free movement and to non-discrimination on the basis of nationality to those outside the labour market as marking a move from its market bias to one based in rights. She argues they reflect a cosmopolitan duty of 'hospitality' that, in time, ought to enable migrants from poor countries to gain access to the social rights of wealthier states (Benhabib 2008, 22/23, 36). However, in many respects, the Court has simply deployed the language of human rights to further extend its market logic. By portraying the negative rights associated with market-reinforcing liberties as extensions of humanitarian duties not to unduly interfere or exploit others and to uphold basic rights, it has been able to overcome all democratic objections on the part of the member states. These have not been examples of 'democratic iterations' as Benhabib claims (2007, 33), but rather a means to trump national exercises of self-determination (Scharpf 2009, 193).

The difficulties of extending positive rights on the basis of free movement are both normative and practical. Normatively we incur such obligations to our fellow citizens through being associated with them within a given political system that possesses the capacity to determine and compel obedience to the rules governing our social and economic interactions with each other. Through the exercise of our civic liberty we are co-responsible for these rules, and so have a mutual obligation to ensure they operate in as equitable and impartial manner as possible. We also help sustain them through our economic activity and taxes. However, if we can claim these rights without incurring the related obligations, say by forcing my fellow citizens to pay for a service in another country that as a result of collective decisions in which I could and probably did participate is unavailable or less available to me in my country of full citizenship, then this social and political compact is undone. Meanwhile, citizens do not exist in such relations with non-citizens. International organisations – even highly developed ones such as the EU – have limited powers and are authorised not by citizens directly but by their states. They are voluntary agreements to pursue certain circumscribed common purposes for the mutual benefit of the parties concerned. Cosmopolitans are sometimes inclined to suggest that we should create global institutions capable of treating all individuals equally, given that membership of any given state is a mere accident of birth – and even, somewhat contentiously given its continued intergovernmental character and manifest democratic failings, to view the EU as demonstrating the possibility of such schemes (e.g. Held 1995, 111–13, 254/55; Cohen and Sabel 2006). However, this proposal confronts the normative problem of already-existing states. As a matter of consistency, our enjoyment of the rights of citizenship may imply a duty to ensure that everyone can also enjoy this right. Yet, the right of everyone to be a citizen of some state does not entail that we all must be citizens of a global state or federation of states. Indeed, the continued role played by national political cultures in defining the boundaries of citizenship, and the problems of establishing effective political mechanisms within large-scale, multinational political systems, suggests the attempt to do so would be ill fated (Sangiovanni 2007).

Certain analysts have suggested that these concerns with EU democracy and its impact on welfare policies are misplaced. The legal regulation required to uphold the market rights that form the EU's core business is both uncontroversial, given that it is Pareto-efficient and reflects common interests, and best administered by expert, technocratic bodies that are immunised from potentially distorting political interferences (e.g. Majone 2001; Moravcsik 2002). Such matters are of low electoral salience and often depoliticised even within the member states. However, this argument raises Constant's main worry regarding the 'liberty of the moderns': namely, that individuals will be tempted to delegate their safe-keeping to 'Enlightened' rulers promising to act on behalf of public utility (Bellamy 2010).

As he noted, such schemes have three main weaknesses: they offer no safeguard against factionalism; they fail to encourage a patriotic identification with public policies; and offer no means for 'guarding the guardians'. All three apply here. First, regulators have no incentive to respond to the concerns of the public, and no effective mechanism for gathering information on what those concerns may be. Constraining the access of the general public raises the risk of regulators being 'captured', or unduly influenced, by certain sectoral groups, and producing policies that are inequitably and possibly inefficiently partial to those interests (Coen and Thatcher 2005).

Second, there is a danger that citizens will lack a sense of ownership of these regulations, disputing their point even when they are in their own interests, and become alienated from those who uphold them. The fact that less than 50 per cent of citizens think 'EU membership is a good thing' – not just in Eurosceptic Britain (where only 33 per cent think it good and 25 per cent regard it as 'bad') or Finland (36 per cent 'good', 25 per cent bad) but also in traditionally Europhile nations such as France (44 per cent good) – sits ill with the view that civic engagement is unnecessary for the EU's legitimacy so long as the 'outputs' provided by the independent technocracy are themselves legitimate.[32] Moreover, it is disputable precisely how uncontentiously win-win market-making regulatory policies are – even taking into account the compensation offered by the Social Fund and other mechanisms to overcome short-term costs for particular groups. As Majone acknowledges, redistributive policies do require more democratic legitimacy than purely regulative ones (Majone 1996, 294–96). For in these cases it is likely to prove even harder to get citizens to buy into the provision of public goods that may appear prima facie to conflict with their personal exercise of their civil and commercial liberties.

Finally, this argument overplays the domestic analogy, underestimating the ways elected politicians control non-majoritarian regulatory bodies in the member states. The autonomy of domestic regulatory bodies is generally limited by various screening and sanctioning mechanisms that allow the political principals to control their technocratic agents. Though many formal instruments appear too costly and arduous to employ with any regularity, potentially impugning the neutrality of the agency and thereby undermining its chief asset, or risking associating the political principals with any failure, a range of less overt and informal measures prove as effective. By selecting friendly yet independent experts, with no direct party or other link to government, and managing the effectiveness of the body through their hold on information or role in implementing its recommendations, politicians can shape the institutional incentives in such ways that regulators propose congenial policies (Thatcher 2005, 347). At the EU level, the plurality of principals and the ability of the Commission to develop a complex network of overlapping agencies, all reduce this influence while introducing the dangers of conflicting forms of accountability. Moreover, the possibilities for regulatory capture are increased by the closeness of EU regulation to various 'stakeholders' – notably business and unions (Coen and Thatcher 2005, 341/2). Domestic regulators also come under diffuse public pressure from the media and other organs of the national public sphere – a pressure that is far harder to exert at the EU level given the virtual absence of a pan-EU public sphere. One can hardly regard monetary policy as of low electoral salience, yet the European Central Bank is far more independent from public and political opinion than any of its member state equivalents.

Some analysts argue that these difficulties can be overcome by selective consultation with an emerging European public formed of transnational civil society groups (Sabel and Zeitlin 2007). Yet, in the absence of shared identities, reciprocal social relations and proper parties, the political liberties pursued by Union citizens are of a markedly individualistic rather than a collective kind (Scharpf 2009, 176–78). They consist of special interest and single-issue groups and court actions that typically seek benefits for the individuals themselves and their supporters, while transferring the costs onto others (Warleigh 2006; Kroger 2008; Harding 1992). These channels invariably promote rather than counterbalance factionalism and rent seeking (Olson 1974).

CONCLUSION

This chapter has employed Constant to explore the problems and necessity of combining the commercial liberty of the moderns with a viable form of political liberty that possesses certain key qualities of the liberty of the ancients, albeit in a new guise. Section 1 discussed Constant's argument that representative democracy provided the solution. He believed it economised on civic virtue sufficiently to be compatible with the liberty of the moderns, while offering a mechanism for securing that liberty on an equal basis for all citizens that could guard against free riding and rent seeking by rulers and ruled alike. However, he also thought representative democracies would only operate in this way provided citizens shared a political culture and had an equal stake in political decisions. Section 2 described how these conditions came to be met within nation states thanks to nation-building, a social contract among citizens and the development of political parties. It also showed these three factors to be absent from the EU – a possibility Constant had himself foreseen in his critique of Napoleonic Empire. Section 3 then looked at Union citizenship as an example of basing civic rights on the civil and commercial liberties of the moderns alone, without any of the conditions that have rendered them compatible with political liberty within the member states. I argued that Constant's fears have turned out to be well founded. Of themselves, these liberties cannot generate the civic bonds needed for representative democracy. However, shorn of the reciprocal bonds and constraints that such collective decision-making generates, Union citizenship confers rights without responsibilities. It risks unpicking welfare arrangements within the member states without having the capacity to generate them at the EU level, while encouraging a form of politics that benefits organised special interests rather than the public interest – be it that of each member state or of Europe as a whole. The Euro crisis has been seen by many as an opportunity to push forward with both fiscal and political union (Duff 2011). Whether circumstances require such dramatic changes lies outside the scope of this chapter. What has been suggested, however, is that there are both considerable sociocultural obstacles to subjecting the market-driven economic imperatives behind this policy to democratic controls at the EU level, and that such control is essential if the economic liberties of the moderns are not to result in the self-defeating pursuit of private benefits at the expense of various public benefits – including the collapse of the market itself. If, as Constant's thesis suggests, there are democratic limits to European unification, then further economic and political integration may risk compounding market failure with political failure. It might be preferable to limit both political and economic cooperation to those tasks achievable by his preferred option of a union of democratic European nation states.

NOTES

1. I am grateful to stimulating discussions at the Universities of Aberystwyth, Bremen, Cornell, Luiss, Manchester, Princeton and Syracuse, and CEPC in Madrid, the Royal Netherlands Cultural Institute in Rome, ARENA in Oslo and the Diplomatic

Academy in Vienna, with Daniele Archibugi, Charles Beitz, Carlos Closa, Erik Eriksen, Michelle Everson, John Fossum, Christian Joerges, Chris Lord, Sebastiano Maffettone, Andrew Moravcsik, Glyn Morgan, Philip Pettit, Johannes Pollak, Sidney Tarrow and Michael Zürn offering useful observations. Welcome written comments came from Oliver Gerstenberg, Sandra Kröger, David Owen, Christine Reh, Fritz Scharpf, Albert Weale and this journal's referees and editors, especially Jim Tully.

2. The following is not intended as intellectual history – I employ Constant for my own purposes. As Foucault responded to critiques of his account of Nietzsche, 'The only valid tribute to thought such as Nietzsche's is precisely to use it, to deform it, to make it groan and protest. And if commentators then say that I am being faithful or unfaithful to Nietzsche, that is of absolutely no interest' (Foucault 1980). That said, the view presented does appear to accord with much recent historical commentary – see Jeremy Jennings (2009). Jeremy also kindly read section 1.

3. I'm here attributing to him reasoning similar to that of Miller (2008).

4. For example, German finance minister Wolfgang Schäuble as reported in *The New York Times*, 18 November 2011, http://www.nytimes.com/2011/11/19/world/europe/for-wolfgang-schauble-seeing-opportunity-in-europes-crisis.html.

5. Figures come from Eurobarometer 60, 62 and 67.

6. Case C-184/99, *Grzelczyk v Centre Public d'Aide Sociale d'Ottignies-Louvain-la-Neuve* [2001] ECR I-6193, para 31.

7. The Gallup Organisation, 'Flash Eurobarometer No 294. European Union Citizenship – Analytical Report' (October 2010).

8. Lisbon judgement of 30 June 2009, 2 BvE 2/08, 2 BvE 5/08, 2 BvR 1010/08, 2 BvR 1022/08, 2 BvR 1259/08, 2 BvR182/09. See too the Maastricht judgement of 12 October 1993, 2 BvR 2134, 2159/92.

9. Case C-64-65/96, *Uecker and Jacquet* [1997] ECR I-03171.

10. Case C-413/99, *Baumbast* [2002] ECR I-07091.

11. Case C-200/02, *Zhu and Chen* [2004] ECR I-9925.

12. Case C-85/96, *Martinez Sala* [1998] ECR I-02691.

13. Case C-456/02, *Trojan*i [2004] ECR I-07573.

14. Case C-138/02, *Collins* [2004] ECR I-02703.

15. Case C-405/01, *Colegio de Oficiales de* Marina Mercante Espanola [2003] ECR- I-10391.

16. Case C-148/02, *Garcia Avello* [2003] ECR I-11613.

17. Case C-135/08, *Rottmann* [2010] ECR I-1449.

18. Case C-34/09, *Ruiz Zambrano* [2011] ECR I-0000.

19. Case C-434/09, *McCarthy* [2011] ECR I-0000.

20. Case C-147/03, *Commission v. Austria* [2005] ECR I-05969.

21. Case C-263/86, *Humbel* [1988] ECR 5365.

22. Case C-76/05, *Schwarz and Gootjes-Schwarz v. Finanzamt Bergisch Gladbach* [2007] ECR I-6849.

23. Case C-158/96, *Kohll* [1998] ECR I-1935.

24. Case C-157/99, *Geraets-Smits v. Stichting Ziekenfonds VGZ* [2001] ECR I-5473.

25. Case C-385/99, *V.G. Muller-Faure v. Onderlinge Waarborgmaatschappij O.Z. Zorgverzekeringen U.A* [2003] ECR 1-4509.

26. Case C–372/04, *Watts v. Bedford Primary Care Trust* [2006] ECR I–4325.

27. Case C-438/05, *International Transport Workers' Federation and Finnish Seamen's Union v. Viking Line* [2008] IRLR 143.

28. Case C-341/05, *Laval v. Svenska Byggnadsarbetareförbundet* [2008] IRLR 160.

29. C-446/06, *Dirk Rüffert v. Land Niedersachsen* [2008] IRLR 467.

30. Case C-319/06, *Commission v. Luxembourg* [2008] ECR I-4323.

31. Case C-120/78, *Rewe-Zentral AG v. Bundesmonopolverwaltung für Branntwein* [1979] ECR 649.

32. Eurobarometer, 'The Future of Europe', May 2006, 27.

Chapter 10

Political Identity in a Community of Strangers

Dario Castiglione

In this chapter I argue that the construction of European *political* identity does not need to rest on a definite conception of what it is to be Europeans. This is so for two reasons: one has to do with the transformation of the very conception of political identification with one's own community in modern societies; the other with the mixed nature of the European Union as a multi-level polity, comprising both intergovernmental and supranational levels of governance. Any normative discourse about political identity in Europe will have to accommodate these two facts.

Political identity is both a social and a historical construct. As a social construct, it reflects the institutional nature of the political community. As a historical construct, its emergence and consolidation are bound up with historical contingencies and with the way in which competing narratives and ideologies shape the self-perception of the members of the community. As suggested in the introductory chapter to this volume, 'Europe's identities exist in the plural', and so it is for the more specific sense of political identities.

But there is an important functional element to political identity, insofar as this plays an important role in sustaining the allegiance and loyalty that citizens have to their political community. In this respect, the different kinds of motivations and cultural and psychological constructions that make different people identify with a political community may be a matter of indifference, as long as political identity helps to bring the members of a community together. On the other hand, the content of political identity may matter a great deal insofar as it helps to determine the character and self-understanding of a political community.

The purpose of this chapter is to examine the state of the debate about European political identity, concentrating on its more normative aspects. In the first section, I show how this debate is intrinsically connected to that of the nature of the European political community and therefore it suffers from the same ambiguities and uncertainties. Sections 2 and 3 present two different conceptions of European political identity, reflecting a nation-based and a postnational understanding of politics in the European Union, respectively. As I argue throughout, the nation-based conception fails to appreciate the changing nature of political identity in a more globalised and internationalised world – which is the first 'fact' I mentioned at the beginning. In this respect, the kind of 'constitutional patriotism' propounded by Jürgen Habermas offers a more sensitive understanding of how we identify with our political community and what is the basis for political allegiance in the contemporary world. However, as I discuss in section 4, Habermas's postnational position fails to come to terms with the second 'fact': the mixed nature of the European Union, and with the profound differences that exist within the European polity. In such conditions, European political identity cannot be constructed on the basis of putative European values, but needs to be supported by the more conflictual mechanisms of democratic politics and inter-institutional balance. The concluding part of the chapter builds upon the critical analysis of constitutional patriotism by suggesting a different way of conceptualising European political identity, one more attuned to live with persisting conflicts. This is partly due to the diminished role that force (both internal and external) plays in the self-understanding of modern political communities, so that it becomes easier to reconcile the demands of different nested political identities, even when these tend occasionally to enter into conflict with one another.

I. POLITICAL IDENTITY AND POLITICAL COMMUNITY

The idea of political identity is a complex one. It contains two distinct senses, which for good reasons are often collapsed together, but whose analytical distinction is nonetheless important. One refers to the way in which political action and institutions contribute to processes of individual and collective *identification* and differentiation; the other to the way in which this process of identification provides the ground for political *allegiance* in a political community.

Different forms of political identification do not need to clash. As an individual, one can simultaneously play different political roles, in the same way in which one has different social and personal roles in life. There is no contradiction in feeling a sense of belonging to functionally different organisations. In some respect, certain political roles – for instance, being a political activist, a member of a trade union or of a pressure group, a partisan voter and a citizen of a political community – can even support each other insofar as they all contribute to determine the way in which one makes sense of one's political identity. The case is not dissimilar when we consider identification with territorially, rather than functionally, different entities: with the city, the region and the nation; or even, though sometimes more problematically, with the different levels of either a federal or composite political system (Katzenstein 2005, 81). In fact, in the latter cases, dissonance may be due to cultural rather than strictly political aspects of personal or group identification.

When we take political identity in the specific sense of allegiance, it is, however, a different story. This is because political communities – communities that claim the legitimate use of force over their members – require some form of allegiance and loyalty, which has a somewhat exclusive nature both in the way in which it makes claims over our solidarity with our fellow citizens (i.e. internally), and in the way in which it demands us to support our own community against external threats (Taylor 1998).

Differentiating between these two senses of political identity has some relevance when we come to the European case. European political identification is in itself unproblematic. It has been rightly argued that it does not need to be in direct opposition to either national or regional identities, since they can all easily cohabit in a nested structure causing neither psychological nor cognitive dissonance (Risse 2004, 248–49). This represents what in the introduction to this volume is called the 'positive-sum nature' of European identity; and although the development of a particular attachment to Europe, or more specifically to the EU as a political entity, may impact on the way in which we perceive other forms of institutional and territorial identification, the latter need to be neither abandoned nor subordinated to the European level. It is, after all, possible to be and feel both British and English (or Spanish and Catalan; or Italian and Sicilian) at the same time, though these are complex historical constructions that conjure up different kinds of meanings and associations, and which rest on different political and cultural experiences that have on occasion taken divergent or even opposite directions (on the relationship between Britishness and Englishness, cf. Colley 1992; Pocock 1995; Aughey 2007, among many).

As one would expect, things are somewhat more complex with regard to European identity in the sense of political allegiance to the EU. In modern democratic societies, this sense of political identity is bound up with the practices of citizenship and has a recognisably 'projectual' nature, which results from the way in which elites try to ensure that the political system, or a political project, have enough popular support. Moreover, the projects and narratives of political identity have been adapted and made functional to the requirements of sovereignty and territoriality, and therefore conceived as exclusive to either a particular state or a particular nation. The emergence of a distinctive European political identity necessarily enters in some kind of collision with the more historically and politically sedimented allegiances towards the nation state. Such a conflict and its overcoming can be conceptualised in two different ways. The first, and most obvious one, is a conflict of content, so to speak. From this perspective, European citizens are asked to change the priority of their political allegiances by identifying with a different territory and expressing loyalty towards different sovereign institutions. Hence, the EU and the European institutions come to take the place that was of the nation and the national state. The second is a more radical conceptualisation, insofar as the EU, as a transnational entity, does not simply take the place of the nation states, but effectively undermines the very principles of territoriality and sovereignty. This changes both the form and function of political identity, as the latter would seem to play a different role within the political system.

From a more theoretical and normative perspective, the current debate about European political identity oscillates between these two positions: a more traditional statist and nation-like conception of identity, which sees the European Union as a nation writ large; and a postnational conception which sees the EU as a new form of state. Indeed, since Maastricht (though not just because of Maastricht) the question of the *political form* of the European Union has become part of a European-wide debate. Even though it remains true that the 'quasi-constitutional' structure, and the institutional organisation of the European Union, has stabilised for some time, its political form – in between an international organisation and a full-grown political community – remains both controversial and largely unresolved (Castiglione and Schönlau 2006). As it became even more evident in the course of the ratification debate about the now abandoned Constitutional Treaty, there are many reasons why such stabilisation appears either unsatisfactory, or threatening, or illusory, depending on the different points of view. For many, the Constitutional Treaty was meant to bring some kind of closure to the protracted phase of economic and political integration, and to establish the limits of geopolitical enlargement, processes which had proceeded piecemeal and 'functionally' since the 1950s, but had dramatically accelerated with the German unification and the collapse of the Soviet sphere of influence at the end of the 1980s. It could be argued that, with the failure of the Constitutional Treaty, and the retreat into the more traditional territory of intergovernmentalism during the preparation of the Treaty of Lisbon, the supremacy of the member states as the 'masters of the Treaty' has been re-established. But this is more likely to be a temporary swing of the pendulum. Intergovernmentalism and supranationalism remain poised in an uneasy equilibrium within the institutional structure of the European Union, and, from this perspective, the Treaty of Lisbon does not change the status quo.

The debate about European identity is part and parcel of this conundrum of the political nature of the European Union. Indeed, it is one aspect both of the debate on how to interpret the nature of the EU, and of the political attempt to influence what the EU will become. For, if the European Union is or is becoming a political community of sort, its stability and sustainability require that its members share some sense of being part of it. But if the nature of such a community is unclear, the sense of belonging that people may have towards it may be equally confused. Hence the present sense of 'anxiety' and 'uncertainty', and fundamental 'ambiguity' of which the introduction of this book speaks. The image which is evoked in the introduction of a ship losing direction is not unfamiliar in the European debate, conjuring up similar images of journeys, crossroads and destinations, which have been part of the discourse of European *finalité*. Nonetheless, when these images, or the very discourse of *finalité*, are applied to political identity, they tend to become somewhat paradoxical, or at least circular (Walker 2002; Castiglione 2004).

In the European case, this circularity takes two forms. On the one hand, it is unclear what comes first, either a European political identity or the consolidation of the European Union as a political community – the well-known discussion about the European Demos (Weiler 1999). On the other hand, as remarked in the introduction to this volume, there appears to be a double movement of politicisation and depoliticisation involving political identity. European identity is increasingly becoming an issue of deep political controversy both across Europe and within individual member states. At the same time, the search for a European identity is intended as a way of establishing a common ground for overcoming political differences. Thus, European identity becomes politicised at the very time when it is invoked as the depoliticised ground on which Europeans should recognise each other. This paradox of politicisation and depoliticisation is not peculiar to European political integration. It was already present in the process of nation-state formation, but there it was often solved (or perhaps obscured) by appeals to the more cultural aspects of national identities as the substratum of political identities, something that, as we shall see, is more problematic in the European case.

II. NATION-LIKE CONCEPTIONS OF EUROPEAN POLITICAL IDENTITY

The difficulty of matching cultural and political identity in Europe is particularly evident when we examine those positions that look at European political integration as a process of scaling up the dimension of the political community. The implication here is that the European integration process poses the question of the scale of politics but does not change the fundamental categories of sovereignty and nationhood, which remain dominant in Europe politics, inscribed as this is within the more general context of the international system of states and of international law (Grimm 1995).

These positions are important because they remain extremely influential at a political and popular level. Indeed, when looked at from a strictly political perspective, the debate about political identity has been dominated by the simple alternative between national and European identity, the former favoured by the Eurosceptics, the latter by the Eurofederalists. In spite of their political division, both Eurosceptic and strongly federal conceptions of the EU tend to agree on the nature of the issue at stake, whether or not the centre of political gravity, and therefore of primary allegiance, should be moved from the national to the European level. They disagree, of course, on the opportunity of such a move. This way of looking at the EU as a direct challenge to national identity is a zero-sum game between European and more local political identities. It reproduces an older discussion about dual citizenship (see Aaron 1974), which applies to federal as well as to multinational systems of state governance, where the component parts are strong or distinctive enough, in terms of language or other historical and cultural features, that their existence poses the problem of political allegiance in more acute terms.

In terms of the conception of political identity, Eurosceptics and enthusiastic Eurofederalists share a similar belief in the dominance of traditional conceptions of (national) statehood and sovereignty, according to which politics (and democratic politics at that) needs a 'thick' conception of political identity, since this is necessary to guarantee both political allegiance and social solidarity. This belief can either take a more culturalist (even ethnic and narrowly nationalistic) turn or be articulated in a more liberal or civic-democratic language (Thibaud 1992; Tamir 1993; Miller 1995, 2000). Of course, for the Eurosceptics and for those who put great store on a historical conception of nationality as the cement of the political community, a European political identity is out of the question. If anything, the kind of deep-seated Euroscepticism, based on an 'integralist' agenda (see Holmes's contribution to this volume) has developed a kind of European anti-identity, based on a vision of Europe as a centralising bureaucratic empire. But the possibility of a European political identity in its traditional sense is at the core of a federal vision of the European Union, what is sometimes referred to by its opponents as Europe as a superstate. This position predicates a fully sovereign EU, with an independent foreign policy, on the ground that this, and not a loose European confederation, would be capable of delivering security and welfare to all European citizens in a way in which the member states are no longer capable of doing (Morgan 2005). This position is sometimes identified with a vision of 'fortress-Europe', which replicates some of the nation- and state-based categories, such as sovereignty and the congruence between territory and culture, at the

EU level, in order to preserve Europe as an area of political influence and prosperity within the context of twenty-first-century international politics. 'Fortress Europe' or Europe as a 'superstate' would seem to require a positive sense of political identity not dissimilar from the one that traditionally operated at the nation-state level. The debate about the cultural and religious origins of Europe that was sparked by the drafting of the Preamble of the Constitutional Treatise (Castiglione et al. 2007, chap. 10), and that on whether Turkey should be allowed to join in the European Union, highlight a conception of political identity that sees this as fundamentally rooted in a shared and largely homogeneous cultural background, offering positive motives for identification as a strong basis for political allegiance. What is important in this context is to emphasise that this conception of political identity makes no distinction between the process of identification and that of securing political allegiance, so that loyalty towards a community is possible only if there is some strong element of identification that holds people together beyond the mere fact that they may be part of the same political community. In this sense, political identification is always, to a certain degree, based on cultural aspects of mutual recognition, and therefore European political identity is hardly distinguishable from a more general idea of European identity.

Naturally, the idea of a common European identity can be presented as either the result of the historical uncovering of a common past (Christian Europe, Enlightened Europe, etc.), or as a more constructivist operation identifying the European roots in a narrative whose starting point is Europe's present. Indeed, the latter operation is often presented in the guise of the former. Whether rooted in its historical and cultural past or 'imagined' (Anderson 1999), the political identity of a European superstate seems nonetheless to require not only strong positive identification but also a certain sense that such an identity is distinct from that of others. Recent events have provided interesting opportunities for the formation of an oppositional political identity, where anti-Americanism and anti-Islamism can easily form the content for a political identity mainly conceived in opposition to an 'other'. Yet, it is evident that there are deep divisions in Europe, which may undermine both projects. From this perspective, Enlargement provides a telling paradox for Europe as a superstate (see Case's contribution to this volume). On the one hand, it offered a vision of Europe as a definite geopolitical entity, finally reunited within its 'cultural' and 'historical' confines; on the other, it introduced in the EU very different self-understandings of Europe, of its history and of its mission. In this respect, the relationship with the United States is a crucial one, and one that divides European countries (against each other) and European society (within each country) more than it may unite them. The same is true of religion, something that has become even more complex since Enlargement.

But, from the point of view of the construction of a European political identity, one should not dismiss the role that negative elements play alongside more positive ones. Although, as we said, articulated in entirely negative and oppositional terms, the influence of Euroscepticism as part of a discourse of European identity should not be underestimated. It is only plausible to imagine Euroscepticism as a permanent feature of EU politics, one articulating in a populist language, or in the form of anti-politics, a strong resistance against some of the centralising and bureaucratic tendencies of the European integration process. Issues such as migration and how to deal with a multicultural society provide the integralist position with ammunition for their defence of traditional conceptions of national sovereignty, territorial integrity and cultural nativism, thus making discourses of a dominant European identity rather vulnerable for the foreseeable future.

In this perspective, it is interesting to notice two particular phenomena linked to the recent process of enlargement. From the point of view of many of the 'old' member states, those comprising the area traditionally described as 'Western Europe', the issue of internal mobility – which was so central to the ideological construction of a 'common market' – has recently become much more controversial in view of the fact that large numbers of skilled and unskilled workers from new East European member states have started making use of the freedom of movement allowed them by the integration process (see Favell, in this volume). The integration process has paradoxically contributed to re-activate a number of 'national' reflexes in the attempt to provide social protection for local populations. Enlargement has also produced paradoxical results in Central and Eastern Europe. The rather protracted process of integration and the emergence of deep divisions in international affairs between what has come to be known as 'New' and 'Old' Europe have contributed to the emergence of Euroscepticism in some of the new member states. This has partly undermined the prevalent conviction in those countries soon after 1989 that there were no tensions between the rediscovery of their national sovereignty and their joining the European 'family', in the form of becoming members of the EU. In fact, for many of these countries joining the EU was meant as an assertion of national sovereignty, something that they may not be prepared to relinquish too readily by diluting it within the larger confines of the European Union.

This discussion of the contradictory ways in which Enlargement and integration seem to have affected the construction of a European political identity and of a sense of belonging to the European Union shows how difficult it is for a European identity conceived in a nation-like fashion to displace more traditional national identities and allegiances. This is probably a reflection of the fact that, whether conceived as an intergovernmental or a supranational organisation, Europe is not a nation writ large. From a normative perspective, a postnational conception of European political identity looks more promising.

III. CONSTITUTIONAL PATRIOTISM AS EUROPEAN POLITICAL IDENTITY

The main exponent of a postnational conception of European political identity is probably Jürgen Habermas, who has deployed the idea of constitutional patriotism – an idea originally developed in the context of German constitutional culture (Müller 2007, chap. 1) – as the centrepiece for a normative conception of political identity adapted to postnational conditions. This section will explore the analytical and normative elements of Habermas's position. However, Habermas's position does not stand in isolation; it is part of a longer history of positions that, contrary to what we have seen in the previous section, maintained that the European process of integration undermined a purely national and state-based view of politics (Haas 1958). The neo-functionalist literature in particular offered a reading of the integration process that tried to capture the piecemeal way in which post-war (Western) Europe was being created as a single economic and political space. As part of this process, it was suggested that the emergence of the European Communities, and later of the Union, weakened territoriality and sovereignty as the unifying principles of both internal and external political action.

As noted in this volume's introduction, the gradual construction of a European identity, not in opposition to national and local identities, but as the natural reflection of the emergence of new supranational political structures and practices to which people grew increasingly accustomed, and which they supported more on the basis of rational calculations than emotive attachments, was part of this vision of functional integration (Haas 2000, 322–52; Marks 1999, 69–71). Such a vision of political identity does not deny that national borders matter in the reality of politics and in people's own self-understanding as political agents; but, in the words of Robert Schuman, it suggested that the importance of borders and of nation states was 'de-emphasised' in the new architecture of political space and political action (Haas 2000, 322). The kind of conception of political identity that follows from this vision is the reverse of the one we saw in the previous section. Whereas a nation-based conception collapses identification and allegiance together, the postnational conception separates the two, conceiving allegiance and loyalty in a more rationalistic and abstract rather than in an emotive way, somewhat detached from cultural and psychological processes of identification.

This position gives very little importance to political identity as an 'exclusionary' identity. The allegiance we may have to the system of laws and rights developed by the EU (even against our own government/country) comes from the universality of the principles upheld by that system, or by the efficiency-driven imperatives of the market and of bureaucratic administration. According to such a perspective, all we need to do to in order to sustain social and political obligations at the European level is to cultivate a kind of universal citizenship attuned to the rights of others, or to disregard altogether discourses of democratic citizenship and political identity, while relying entirely on other mechanisms of formal and substantive legitimacy.

But there is a different and more 'republican' conception of postnational politics, which does not devalue the importance of identification as part of the political integration process, and does not completely separate identification from allegiance. It insists instead on the importance of a politics of identity as part of a new normative framing for democratic politics at a supra- and postnational level. Jürgen Habermas has developed such a version by proposing 'constitutional patriotism' as the basis for political identity at a European level. This is a kind of patriotism (hence a particular attachment to the European polity), but one that in Habermas's view should be based on a 'civic' (and cosmopolitan) understanding of the principles underlying the European polity. It should therefore be open to the inclusion of the 'other' but remain rooted in a self-understanding of the European perspective, thus combining both universalist and particularist instances. This is what it makes it both attractive and distinctive as a normative reading of European identity.

In a recent treatment of the issue, Habermas (2006, chap. 6) distinguishes two moments of his argument. He first addresses the question of whether European identity is 'necessary', and secondly whether it is 'possible'. The first part of the argument is implicitly directed against the kind of liberal and functional conceptions of postnational citizenship that, as already argued, put little emphasis on the emotional attachments that ground citizens' loyalty towards the community and the political system. The second part is an answer to those who believe that national attachments are still the only viable basis for political identity.

Habermas's demonstration of the need for a European political identity is partly based on the negative argument that both the explanatory and the political force of the traditional functional narrative of the integration process as self-propelling are now exhausted. He identifies the three main challenges facing the European Union in governing Enlargement, managing the political consequences of increasing economic unification, and redefining the role of Europe within the new geopolitical situation created by 9/11 and the Bush administration's foreign policy, particularly in the Middle East. While the spillover character of economic and social integration as envisaged by the neo-functionalist model did not require a 'common European consciousness' (2006, 68), each of these challenges ask for a definite awareness on the part of the citizens, since they are increasingly asked to recognise the discipline of majorities and minorities within a much enlarged community, and accept the redistributive effects of more 'positive' forms of integration. Moreover, a common foreign and security policy needs more overt forms of opinion and will formation, and therefore the development of a European public sphere.

For Habermas, the decision taken at Laeken in 2001 to start a more overt discussion about writing a European constitution was therefore a timely way of addressing the shortcomings of the neo-functionalist narrative of, and approach to, European integration. A Constitution (or a Constitutional Treaty, as it emerged from the Convention on the Future of Europe) offered a moment of closure to the debate about *finalitè*, providing the basis for a new form of statehood at a supranational level, and for fixing the structure of internal power in the EU. But there is another aspect to the overt process of constitution making that Habermas has been stressing and that has relevance for our discussion of why Europe needs a political identity. According to him, a normative conception of constitutional politics needs a constitutional moment, something that breaks the routine of normal politics and introduces an important moment of symbolism in constitutional politics (Castiglione et al. 2007, chap. 2). 'As a political collectivity', Habermas writes, 'Europe cannot take hold in the consciousness of its citizens simply in the shape of a common currency. The intergovernmental arrangement at Maastricht lacks that power of symbolic crystallization which only a political act of foundation can give' (2001a, 6). In this sense, the Constitution represented a catalytic point in the creation of Europe as a political community, coming at the end of an already advanced process of social, economic and political integration, and helping to put in motion the construction of a European-wide civil society, a common public sphere, and a shared political culture (2001a, 16–21).

As we know, that opportunity was not seized, but this does not necessarily contradict Habermas's first part of the argument about political identity, that Europe *needs* to activate citizens' consciousness in the process of political integration, and that therefore an explicit form of political identity is necessary. It poses, however, a problem for the second part of his argument, that such a political identity is *possible*.

Habermas's argument on the feasibility of European political identity moves in three stages. The first concerns the postnational nature of the political identity itself. The second engages with the substance of a European political identity. And the final with the political forces most likely to generate it. I shall try to summarise briefly these three parts of Habermas's argument in the remainder of this section, while I shall address what I take to be its shortcomings and a possible alternative conception in the next two sections. As for the nature of European political identity, there is a sense in which this is not very different from national forms of political identity. Against those who stress the more culturalist and communitarian aspects of national political identity, Habermas remarks that, historically, national consciousness emerged as a form of 'solidarity amongst strangers', of a fairly abstract nature with strong legal mediations (2006, 76/77). From such a perspective, the real issue about the feasibility of a European political identity is not whether it exists already, but what are the conditions for it to exist.

There are, however, as Habermas admits, important ways in which the nature of a European political identity may depart from its national counter-parts. Such a political identity may need to be more overtly 'constructed' and more 'cosmopolitan' in nature. The former aspect is largely due to changed historical and political conditions. Whereas national political identity has often emerged in situations of revolutionary struggle and through processes of democratisation which conferred to it an important element of pathos; this is not so in the case of the construction of European political identity, which needs to emerge more mundanely from the everyday dealings of the European citizens, in conditions that are already governed by democratic principles and practices.

The second departure of European political identity from its national coun-terpart follows, according to Habermas, from a series of developments that can already be observed in the nation states, particularly since the second half of the twentieth century. This is its more universalistic character, due mainly to the 'internal dynamic' of the democratic process, which contributes to shaping the references for public discourse in terms of issues of justice, rather than simply of national interests (Habermas 2006, 77). Habermas also detects a 'peculiar switch in emotional fixation from the state to the constitu-tion' (78), which corresponds to the way in which civic solidarity grows not so much out of identification with a national community, but of membership in a democratic polity – in other words, there is a shift from processes of identification that sees the state and the community in relation to the outside, with processes that emphasise the preservation of a particular liberal and democratic order within the community. In sum, with respect to its nature, Habermas believes that European political identity is feasible insofar as it is an extension of national forms of consciousnesses.

The second stage in Habermas's argument about the feasibility of a Euro-pean political identity is concerned with the kind of more substantive values that make Europe distinctive in the present historical and geopolitical condi-tions. This is an important point, since it engages directly with the question of how the kind of more cosmopolitan political identity that Habermas believes Europe is developing relates to its historical roots, and how these are to be identified. The nearest that Habermas has come to define such roots is in his 'manifesto' on 'what binds Europeans together', which he co-signed with Jacques Deridda at the height of the European debate on the war in Iraq

(Habermas 2006, chap. 3). The context is important, since at the time Habermas maintained that the diffuse popular opposition in Europe against the invasion of Iraq was perhaps the first real manifestation of a European public opinion, and of the possibility of the formation of a pan-European public sphere. Moreover, in spite of the divisions between the European governments, the expression of the European voice in the form of popular protest seemed to be a moment of both self-assertion and self-confidence. But, to come to the substance, Habermas suggests the following list of achievements and values as being part of Europe's historical heritage (2006, 46–8):

- first, the kind of secular politics that has emerged from the separation between state and church throughout the modern period;
- second, the importance placed on politics and the state as instruments to correct the operations of the market;
- third, the diffuse awareness of the paradoxes of progress, something that Habermas links to the way in which the party system has developed in Europe promoting internal ideological competition;
- fourth, the way in which class differences and class struggles in Europe have fostered social solidarity and generally an ethos towards achieving social justice;
- fifth, a strong sensitivity towards the violation of personal and bodily integrity, which partly derives from Europe's own confrontation with its unsavoury past, and which is at the heart of European rejection of capital punishment;
- sixth, the recognition of the need to domesticate state power through international organisations, which is also the product of a reflection on Europe's internal wars;
- seventh, the way in which the experience of decline (in terms of colonial power and global influence) has determined a certain capacity for self-reflexivity.

The third and final stage in Habermas's argumentation for the feasibility of a European's political identity is of a more immediate political nature, and seems to be based on the conviction that the political core of European integration remains firmly in the Franco-German axis. As he says in answer to a question about the role that different countries (particularly the Eastern European ones) may play in the EU:

> The changing tempo of European unification has always been determined by the agreement between France and Germany to keep the process moving forward. … as the Eurozone demonstrates, there is already a Europe of different speeds. (Habermas 2006, 52)

This is both an observation on the internal politics dynamics of the European Union and a fairly realistic assessment of where the power engine of the Union still lies.

IV. THE PLACE OF CONFLICT AND CONSENSUS
IN EUROPEAN POLITICAL IDENTITY

There is much that is attractive in the Habermasian position about European political identity. As we have seen, he rightly outlines the limits of those positions that underestimate the role that a shared sense of belonging may need to play at this stage of the integration process. Although not original, his argument for the necessity of a certain political identity in a community whose functions are increasingly political is compelling.[1] Such political identity cannot simply reflect unmediated and unreflective processes of identification. This is not so in the context of the nation state, and, as Habermas suggests, it is even less likely to be so in a supranational context, where political identity will have to be more artificially constructed and more mediated by legal and political experiences and institutions. But Habermas recognises that political allegiance needs some kind of socio-psychological basis and cannot be just an abstract kind of attachment. In this respect, Habermas's position is much closer to the one defended by those who believe in Europe as a superstate, with the difference that Habermas is convinced that the kind of constitutional patriotism he advocates for Europe is a particularlist reading of more universal principles, and that, as we have seen, the 'identification with the state mutates into a orientation to the constitution' (2006, 78). This, for Habermas, is the postnational core of modern political identity.

But there are limits and tensions in the way in which Habermas tries to reconcile particularism and universalism in his construction of European constitutional patriotism. These can be addressed by raising two main objections against it.[2] First, there is the issue of the role and identification of the substantive values on which Europeans converge. Secondly, there is the issue of the way in which the construction of political identity is related to the nature and conditions of the European polity. I shall discuss these two issues in this section, and take up again the more general question of what lies at the core of a postnational conception of political identity in the concluding section of this chapter.

Political Identity and European Values

With respect to the issue of the values underlying European constitutional patriotism, this is not an easy position to maintain with coherence. It requires a difficult balance between a justification of cosmopolitan values (which are therefore universal in nature) and a more communitarian explanation (hence one that is linked to particular features of the community) of how they have emerged, how they have become our own, and how ultimately they contribute to distinguish us from others. There is no doubt that moral justification of attachments to particular communities, or of the ethics of citizenship in general, may need to do precisely such a reconciliation between these two tendencies (Apia 2005; Bellamy and Castiglione 1998). But the Habermasian position seems still uneasily poised between a defence of universal values that is too 'thin' to mobilise people's allegiance and loyalty and a reconstruction of European values that may become too 'thick' in the way in which Europeans use it as a form of identification.[3]

Habermas's position can sometimes be interpreted as purely cosmopolitan, so that adherence to liberal democratic principles on its own is sufficient to generate a patriotic allegiance to any just society. In other instances, however, Habermas's attempt to present his argument as a distinctively 'European' account, risks transforming his argument into a form of supranationalism. In his reconstruction of the historical roots of European values, Habermas greatly exaggerates both the degree of system and value convergence within the EU, and the extent to which political and national values can be separated.

In fact, Europe is far more diverse, and the sense of Europeaness among its peoples far shallower than Habermas allows. He also underestimates both the elements of negative identification we discussed in section 2, and the eclectic (and sometime contradictory) way in which collective identities emerge. As a consequence, his vision of European values and value convergence is both over-optimistic and overconfident, in spite of the fact that he himself makes reference to the reflexive and self-critical way in which Europeans deal with their unmastered past. Moreover, his political insistence on the need for a 'core' Europe to force the pace of political unification and identity construction underestimates the tendencies towards administrative centralisation implicit in the European project as it has developed so far, while it underplays the dangers that come from either the exercise of hegemonic power by a small elites, or the possibility of domination of certain territorial coalitions over others.

Habermas seems strangely uninterested in the multiplicity of cleavages that traverse the European Union. His construction of constitutional patriotism fails to confront the more contingent aspects from which political identity emerges. In this respect, his is too an idealised picture of Europe's geopolitical role, one that fails to perceive the importance that both the post-Maastricht developments and Enlargement have played in forming the still confused self-understanding of the European polity (see chapters by Case and Kaeble in the original volume in which this chapter was published).

Habermas seems also oblivious to the difficulties that the project of constructing a value-based identity that is not exclusionary may present. Insofar as the European values are presented as 'our' values, there is always a tendency to construct them in opposition to those of others and therefore to exclude the others. In the reality of a growingly multicultural and diverse Europe, where mobility and immigration play a much larger role than in the near past, such an insistence on values, even on universal values, risks being socially and culturally divisive rather than being a unifying force. Moreover, in some cases, it is difficult to see what makes certain values specifically our own, if not a selective reconstruction of the historical evidence. Take, for instance, the explicit reference that Habermas makes to the 'social privatisation of faith' as something that divides Europe from the United States, when he says that 'a president who begins his official functions every day with a public prayer and connects his momentous political decisions with a divine mission is difficult to imagine' (2006, 46). Although the public show of religious zeal may be alien to most political cultures in Europe, the way in which religion plays a public role in Europe is probably as much a matter of contention in the United States than across Europe and, crucially, within each of the European countries. Arguably, the role of religion within European public cultures has recently become, if anything, more prominent, not least as the effect of Enlargement (cf. Byrnes and Katzenstein 2006).

The tendency in Habermas's analysis of value convergence to show a common European political culture tends to constrain the diversity of Europe. Unwittingly, his proposal promotes the very talk of an ethnic Europe he seeks to avoid, offering the idea of Europe as a superstate, or Fortress Europe a spurious legitimacy in order to retain an allegiance to putatively common constitutional values. In other words, Habermas fails to see both the inevitable dangers (i.e. the exclusionary side) of any construction of political identity, and the deeply ingrained divisions of European political culture, which cannot be easily reconciled by a broad Enlightenment view of European identity.

The Constructive Role of Democratic Conflict

The failure, in my view, of Habermas's attempt to construct European political identity mainly on abstract values is that his conception of democratic politics is over-reliant on the idea of consensus, downplaying the important role that political conflict has in it. Although he views value converge and the rights that follow from this, as the result of communicative processes within the public sphere, the difficulty with his theory is that beyond the most abstract level, and sometimes even here, there is considerable disagreement about the way in which values translate into particular policies and institutional arrangements, and on the foundations and character of rights, and the way in which they can be applied to particular issues. Debates and conflicts over values and rights not only provide the substance of many political debates, they also produce different accounts of the nature of the political (Bellamy and Castiglione 2008). The same goes for political identity and how this affects the practice of citizenship. Neither is simply constructed on a set of political values and political rights. Rather, political identity is partly expressed in the way in which, as citizens, we go about claiming rights or participating in politics at different institutional levels.

A different way in which to see the formation of political identity in Europe, one more attuned to the issue of democratic disagreement and conflict rather than consensus, is to emphasise the structural as opposed to the value and legal mechanisms as the key factor of European constitutionalism – most particularly the balance and separation of powers produced by the EU's unique mix of intergovernmental, supranational and transnational decision-making mechanisms. Hence, European political identity needs to be adapted to the plurality of demoi and legal systems that have both legitimated and fostered European integration. The involvement of different peoples and different nations is also an important factor in ensuring a flexibility of approach that takes into account the very different economic and social circumstances of the member states – a factor that has become all the more important with Enlargement. From this perspective, the appeal to constitutional patriotism risks being a purely rhetorical exercise, and may occasionally stifle the ongoing constitutional dialogue that has so far led to an increasing sense of mutual respect and recognition, combining both diversity and an ever closer Union of peoples rather than a nationalistic creation of a European people.

Although multilevel governance undermines the sense of unity and purpose that characterises traditional forms of democratic power, it does not necessarily exclude the introduction of other forms of more diffuse democratic participation and deliberation, thereby giving the citizens the opportunity to have a say on what matters in their life. It is in the practice of common deliberation on common problems that the European citizens can develop a sense of sharing a common identity and of solidarity. In terms of democratic participation, Europe offers opportunities as well as apparent losses. European politics is undeniably often characterised by log-rolling and horse-trading between national governments in defence of sectoral interests of various degrees of legitimacy. However, it also offers fora for a more deliberative style of politics – one that is partly detached from the constraints imposed by modern-day party politics, and sometimes better able to combine individual and democratic perspectives with those advanced by expert bodies. But, the reverse also holds true. For intergovernmentalism has also allowed some particular interests to be successfully defended against the force of simple majoritarianism within a given national community. It is arguably the very diversity and mutually balancing character of the various policy-making polities and regimes comprising the European Union that places it in a better situation to represent the variety of rights, interests and identities that characterise citizenship in modern societies. In this respect, European political identity needs to reflect the institutional plurality that characterizes political Europe.

CONCLUSION: THE TIES THAT BIND
A COMMUNITY OF STRANGERS

The more conflictual and divided image of political identity that I have here suggested takes us back to the question from which this chapter started. Has the relationship between political identification and political allegiance changed as the effect of the growing internationalisation of politics of which the European integration process is part? Part of answer, as Habermas correctly identifies, is already inscribed in the experience of the nation state.

The ties that bind a political community together can be seen not only as a form of 'social cement' but also as a form of 'political allegiance', a distinction that runs along similar lines to that made by Ulrich Preuss between 'Transaktions-Wir' (we-transactions) and 'Solidaritäts-Wir' (we-solidarity) (Preuss 2005). The reason why these separate elements are often confused is due to the fact that the historical experience of the nation state has linked the two in an inextricable knot. But the two aspects are separate and somewhat captured by the paradox expressed by the idea of a 'community of strangers'. Such an idea is somewhat counterintuitive, if we adhere to the distinction famously made by Tönnies between 'community' (*Gemeinschaft*) and 'society' (*Gesellschaft*). According to Tönnies, 'all kinds of social co-existence that are familiar, comfortable and exclusive are to be understood as belonging to *Gemeinschaft*.... In *Gemeinschaft* we are united from the moment of our birth with our own folk for better or for worse. We go into *Gesellschaft* as if into a foreign land' (Tönnies 2001, 18).

When we speak of a 'political community' we do not mean the cosy and intimate relationships that attain in small groups. Our life in a political community is mostly conducted as a series of relationships in a *Gesellschaft*, in the sense meant by Tönnies. But we do not treat our political community as a 'foreign land', nor do we treat the other members as 'strangers'. Modern political and sociological discourse has therefore been careful to suggest that, although our life in large modern societies is a life among strangers – a life, that is, characterised by anonymous relationships in the public sphere, mediated by the market, the law, the institutions of public and private administration, and by various forms of associations – our destiny as members of a political community is instead linked to that of others, with whom we live in an *inclusive* relationship of relative familiarity and identity, and on whose solidarity we trust. The question then becomes in what sense can the European Union be a society of strangers (even more so than a nation state) and at the same time be a 'political community'? And how is it possible for this to happen without entering into direct conflict with the fact that nation states also claim a very similar status and our loyalty?

One way of answering this question is perhaps to take a step back and look at the way in which the modern conception of political allegiance is linked to the conception of the modern state. In discussing the nature of the 'modern' form of political community, Weber (1968) emphasises three elements characterising the organisation of a collectivity of people: (1) a territorial space; (2) the availability (and virtual monopoly) of physical force; and (3) the wide scope of the community's social action (beyond that of the satisfaction of common economic needs, or of other specialised functions). The crucial point for our discussion is the second one. The availability of the use of force can be used externally but also, more routinely, internally. The use of force is crucial in defining the relationship between the community and the individual, since it defines the extent of the obligations of the member towards the community itself. With regard to the internal use, physical force is functional to backing up the member's obligations, while excluding the private use of physical force, if not in narrowly defined circumstances. With regard to the external use, the community requires that the individual participates in the defence of the interests of the community. Weber talks of this 'common political struggle of life and death' as the political community's 'particular pathos', and as needing 'enduring emotional foundations'. According to Weber, such emotional foundations come from the ties of memory, even more than those of cultural, linguistic and ethnic identities (Weber 1968).

If Weber is right about the modern form of political community, it is easy to conclude that the European Union is neither a political community nor is it likely to become one soon. However, as we have already seen, our conception of the political community has changed somewhat. Indeed, Weber himself notices that the kind of 'discipline' required of members of a political community finds its roots in more military kinds of organisation in which citizens were directly involved for the defence of the community. This raises the interesting point of whether, in our modern political societies, where more and more nation states have abandoned the practice of national conscription and use instead professional armies, the ordinary citizen is indeed required to commit what Weber calls the 'ultimate' sacrifice in defence of the community. Of course, one may envisage exceptional circumstances in which the entire population may need mobilising, but this could indeed be true of natural cataclysms or other situations where people may need no particular

motivation to participate in the operations of rescue at the risk of their own
life. There may still be some important sense in which the political community needs the allegiance of its members, and we may also not like the way
in which the arrangements for war and security have been privatised, but the
close connection between the idea of a political community and the expectation that its members may 'ultimately face death in the group interest' is not
as obvious nowadays as it was in Weber's time. From this point of view, the
recognised inability of the European Union to inspire such extreme forms of
sacrifice does not exclude it from performing other functions of a political
community, as long as it can mobilise people's solidarity in other respects.

But there is more. As Hegel, for one, had already perceptively noticed, it is
mistaken to think of patriotism mainly as a 'readiness for exceptional sacrifices and actions' (1952, 164). Hegel describes patriotism as a more ordinary
and banal sentiment, which makes us see how our own life depends on the
operations of the political community. It is a form of trust, or, as he put it, 'the
consciousness that my interest, both substantive and particular, is contained
and preserved in another's (i.e. in the state) interest and end'. It is from the
daily exertion (and self-conscious realisation) of this form of trust that 'arises
the readiness for extraordinary exertions'. The point here is not about the
nature of patriotism (as a virtue or as a vice, and what its proper content may
be) but the way in which the individual may relate to the community, for
if the sense of obligation can be cultivated through more ordinary acts and
exertions, we may have no need to find deep 'emotional' roots to it, but a
mixture of rational self-interest, habituation, and cultivation of a sense of the
collective interest. This point is closely linked with another made by Hegel
in his comment to the same passage on patriotism, in which he remarks that
'commonplace thinking often has the impression that force holds the state
together, but in fact its only bond is the fundamental sense of order which
everybody possesses' (1952, 282). If Hegel's interpretation of patriotism is
convincing, the European Union needs to cultivate its political identity neither in the heroic form of the 'ultimate sacrifice' nor in high-principled form
of constitutional patriotism, but rather in the more banal sense of the growing perception that European citizens may have that the Union contributes to
maintain a fundamental (though multilayered) institutional and legal order
within which they can exercise their liberty.

Finally, there is the fact that the internalisation of politics, and the form
of 'open statehood' that increasingly characterises the relationship between
states, particularly within the European Union, is changing the state of affairs
that Weber seems to presuppose to his analysis of the role of force as a constitutive element of the modern state. Nowadays, it is indeed less clear whether
the emotional and imaginary rootedness of national patriotism is what is
required to sustain political communities in the twenty-first century. It is

possible to imagine a more variegated pattern, something that is not unknown in history. In his dialogue *On the Laws*, Cicero, for instance, talks about the affection that one has to one's 'fatherland' (based on one's memories and the idea of custom and tradition) as different from that one has towards the 'commonwealth' (based more on the importance of laws and the republican institutions), and how ultimately the latter should prevail over the former. His was a more 'republican' (in the classical, historical sense) interpretation of the demands of the political community, and it may be as inadequate today, if applied to the EU, as the invention (or rediscovery) of common European memories. But what it may tell us is that open statehood may mean more fragmented identities and allegiances, and the possibility of these entering into conflict with each other. However, there is no reason to believe that such conflict should be unmanageable. Of course, there will always be a danger that conflicts and disagreement may degenerate into a standstill or even violence. But the solution to this may lie more in imagining how an interlocking political space may need interlocking systems of trust, solidarity and allegiances, none of which may need to be absolute, rather than thinking that we can reproduce the absolute demands of national citizenship at a European level.

NOTES

1. Habermas's argument is here part of a more general turn towards a normative discussion of the extent and rational of the European integration; for a list of other works arguing along similar lines, see Bellamy and Castiglione (2005, fn. 2).

2. For a criticism of the Habermasian position along similar lines, see Laborde (2002).

3. The following paragraph is indebted to Bellamy and Castiglione (2004).

Chapter 11

Negotiating Language Regimes

Dario Castiglione

Is there a language question in 'diverse societies'? In the volume on *The Language Question in Europe and Diverse Societies* (Castiglione and Longman 2007)[1] we suggest that there may be more than one, and that the nature of the questions raised by language use in such societies is both complex and multifaceted. The particular angle from which we look at these questions is one that tends to emphasise the role of language in a political community. This is a perspective that has become more salient as modern societies have become both more porous in their relations with each other and more internally differentiated. In the recent past, the political role of language appeared to be less problematic; for language was meant to be, on the one hand, an important element of distinction between different political communities, and, on the other, one of the main instruments for binding the members of the community together. Both these functions have been weakened as the combined effects of globalisation and multiculturalism have impacted on the internal and external dynamics of the political community. This is particularly evident in the European Union, where questions about the political role of language are mostly avoided, due to what is generally considered to be the intractable nature of its multilingual regime. But avoiding the problem does not solve it. Moreover, the avoidance strategy tends to obscure the nature of the questions posed by multilingualism in modern societies, and consequently the variety of measures and solutions that these may require. This collective volume on language in politics is meant to raise precisely such questions, thus contributing, if not to their solution, at least to identifying the problems and engaging in a discussion of the possible solutions.

Although the more theoretical and normative contributions to the volume apply to diverse societies at large, the majority of its chapters take the European experience, and the EU in particular, as their main focus of analysis.

This, of course, narrows the range of problems and experiences encompassing the language question, but, at the same time, offers a sustained analysis
of how this question applies to the European case, at least in its transnational
(rather than subnational) dimension. The other common feature of the contributions to this volume, their already-mentioned focus on the political
dimension of language, is enriched by the diversity of approaches characterising the various chapters, thus providing some basis for a dialogue between
disciplines: from politics to sociolinguistics, from law to anthropology, from
political sociology to normative theory. Part of the aim of this volume is to
suggest that only by entering into such a dialogue and by developing a sustained exchange of insights may it be possible to give a satisfactory account
of the language question in diverse societies. Indeed, such an interdisciplinary
approach has played an important role in the emergence of sociolinguistics
during the last fifty years, a discipline whose main scope is to study from
both a micro- and a macro-perspective the interactions between language and
society (Coulmas 1997, 1–3). Nonetheless, the more specific question of how
to deal with multilingualism in diverse societies has tended to be framed in
mainly political and legal terms. Bringing in the knowledge of sociologists,
linguists, anthropologists, educationalists and indeed sociolinguists is meant
to broaden the framework, offering a richer account of what language and
communication both entail and mean for individuals, groups and societies at
large.

THE NATURE OF DIVERSITY

Having outlined the general scope and intent of the volume, the rest of this
contribution aims to offer a more general context within which to place the
other contributions. It does so first by providing a few considerations on the
nature of diversity, secondly by offering a summary account of the questions
raised by multilingualism, followed by a discussion of how to deal with it
politically, and finally by giving a brief overview of the topics covered by the
individual contributors to this volume and of some of the lines of research
that may follow from their analysis. The idea of diverse societies is one where
'diversity' is given a prominent role, not just as a descriptor but also – albeit
often implicitly – as a norm: as the recognition that 'diversity' has a particular meaning and/or value for the society in question. This is evident in the
way in which the EU, for instance, describes itself as a community 'united
in diversity', which is, after all, the way in which its linguistic regime is also
characterised. But the idea of 'unity in diversity' poses a series of complex
challenges. As Europe, for instance, becomes a more integrated area of
economic production and exchange, there are greater opportunities for both

development and coordination between sectors, activities and institutions that have similar problems and interests. This provides a definite push towards unity, while narrowing the range of diversities. And yet, it may also increase the degree of inter- and intra-territorial difference (at European, national and subnational levels), making social cohesion more problematic. Moreover, the integration process needs to come to terms with the sheer variety of national and subnational situations, as they are determined by social and demographic factors, by particular cultural and institutional histories, and by the political composition and the kind of lifestyles and aspirations diffused in each country or region of Europe. This variety has recently increased, both quantitatively and so to speak qualitatively, as the result of enlargement, making this aspect of diversity more problematic, as attested by the number of languages that are now officially recognised in the institutions of the EU. The sociocultural diversity of the EU is further complicated by the presence of large minorities that are the product of recent and not so recent immigration waves. In Europe, in contrast to the American experience, such minorities have been assimilated to only a limited degree, and insofar as their values and lifestyles are not supported by a separate territorial authority, their 'diversity' poses yet another challenge.

But diversity is not just a *condition* of the European society. As I have already hinted at, due to several ideal and material processes, it has become a *value* of the European experience of integration (the purpose of the integration *process* being 'an ever closer union of the *peoples* of Europe'). This is a point worth considering, since the dominant perspective has been to treat diversity as a *problem* that needs to be either accommodated or overcome. By contrast, in both the EU's official communications and the self-consciousness of many of its citizens, diversity has a *constitutive* role (the EU as a 'Union of *peoples*'), which has important implications for both its identity and its evolving structure of governance. Furthermore, there may be different forms and ideas of diversity, some more backward-looking, emphasising belonging, others forward-looking, emphasising hybridity. The role of language, for instance, can be characterised in either way, as the accretion of past experiences, or as the malleable instrument for engaging with people in a fast-changing world. But, in general, there are at least five kinds of interrelated diversity that one may want to consider in describing the range of differences present in modern diverse societies.

1. There are differences that have a national and cultural dimension (including minority nations), most of which may also manifest themselves as linguistic differences.
2. There are differences produced by the existence of legal and political regimes at state, regional, supranational and international levels.

Although, on the face of it, these are organisational differences that can be altered at will and with a certain facility, they tend to assume a more cultural and entrenched nature as time passes, so that they are often hardly distinguishable from the more specific national and cultural differences.

3. There are ethnic and religious differences, which in themselves are distinct, but which can also be overlapping. Although in theory, the ethnic differences are ascriptive, while the latter are voluntary, religion itself is rarely a matter of choice in the lives of individuals.

4. There are social and economic differences that are associated with the modern economy and the processes of globalisation. These are differences of income, class and status that overlap and often tend to reinforce each other. They may also result in cultural differences, or, increasingly, in a process of individuation.

5. Finally, there is a complex group of differences based on gender, lifestyles and needs, often made more relevant and entrenched by the kind of socio economic processes mentioned under (4) above.

These types of diversity are not exclusively European, but common to all advanced economies in which the division of labour has led to differentiated spheres of economic and social life. What is distinctive of modern diverse societies is their appreciation that the social pluralism that comes from such diversities is considered a 'fact' with an important normative component, determining the way in which we ought to interact with each other. This appreciation and consequent attitude is also the product of a postcolonial view of race and a post-feminist view of gender. All together, they have produced a new positive attitude towards diversity and the propagation of discourses of recognition. The discourse of multiculturalism in Europe, as in other parts of the world, has tried to capture such a new attitude of respect for and recognition of diversity. But multicultural policies, as many critics are only too ready to point out, present modern democratic societies with problems of formulation, instrumentation and implementation if the recognition of deep diversity is to be combined with the equal treatment of citizens. Language is one prominent area of debate about the opportunities and shortcomings of multicultural policies.

In the EU, however, contemporary diversity and its discourses have been grafted onto the particular historical experience of a plurality of nations and peoples with their respective institutions, social arrangements, cultures, habits, traditions and, of course, languages. At the same time, the process of Europeanisation has created supranational and postnational structures and arrangements with the overlapping of cultural, political, legal and social spaces – all of which require more intense forms of exchange and communication. These developments have produced a complex pattern of diversity, with demands for recognition and difference sometimes competing with demands for efficiency, justice, equality and social cohesion.

From these considerations, it follows that one of the fundamental criteria for the development of a European form of governance is that of *governing diversity by valuing diversity*. In truth, this is not always possible, nor is it right in all circumstances, since there are also elements of diversity that are negative and that may be the source of intractable conflicts. Moreover, conflict management through bargaining, compromise and consensus-building is a difficult art, which can be achieved only through various institutional devices cutting across law, politics and education. In the case of linguistic differences, particularly when they are both widespread and entrenched as in the European case, finding both the instruments and the guiding principles for a policy that governs diversity by *valuing* it, would seem an impossible task. To face such a task requires, first of all, identifying the particular questions posed by multilingualism in diverse societies.

THE CHALLENGES OF MULTILINGUALISM

In a most obvious sense (natural) languages function as an instrument of communication between people but also as a social bond. Whichever side one takes on the origins of languages, as nature or convention, it is apparent that a language is not simply an abstract means of communication between different people, but – like all other such social 'institutions' – it binds them together, while offering them a ground for identification and belonging. Besides, as a means of social exchange, it offers opportunities for power politics and social domination. Thus, communication, identity and power are all processes in which language matters.

On the face of it, the first challenge posed by multilingualism is that there is more than one currency in which communication, identity and power relationships can take place in society. This poses obvious problems of efficiency, complicating all three sets of social relationship, thus endangering the unity of the society in question. Economically, transaction costs are greater, particularly if exchanges take place between people who speak different languages. Politically, people may find it more difficult to come to an agreement, since besides all other barriers, they also need to overcome the one posed by the difficulty in communicating and finding a way of understanding each other. Moreover, linguistic differences are, more often than not, part of a broader pattern of cultural differences due to different historical traditions and experiences developing in different parts of the world across time. But it is perhaps less remarked, at least in a political context, that multilingualism poses not simply the problem of 'conflict' between different systems of communication but also that of 'communication' between these very systems (Laponce 2002, 587). In other words, two languages that come to share part or the whole of the social space in which they operate enter into some relationship with each other, either as systems of communication, which are subject to transformation by the very fact of coming into contact with each other, or as alternative systems of communication for individuals who happen to operate in a social environment where two or more systems of communication apply equally. The crucial point is that both 'conflict' and 'communication' affect languages and the relationship of the community of speakers (as a whole or as individuals) with a language (their own or any other that is available to them within the same social space).

In other words, in a bilingual or multilingual environment, there are two sets of linguistic effects, which derive from the particular way in which two or more languages either enter into conflict or communicate. These effects impact on the languages themselves as systems of communication but also on the community of speakers who predominantly identify with one language or another, and on the individuals whose interests and identity are variously related to language use and intra-group communication. This complex set of relationships is already evident in the context of social and personal bilingualism that may arise from inter-linguistic marriages, or from the close proximity of different linguistic communities. It acquires a more pregnant meaning, however, when bilingualism takes the form of diglossia, that is, in those contexts where the languages available are not used interchangeably across all roles and levels of social discourse, but contextually, according to specific rules and conventions differentiating the use of one language from the other. There are cases in which diglossia may be regarded as merely functional, as when there may be a more or less tacit agreement between members of a community (or family) to speak one language privately (or at home) and another in public (which is often the case with dialects). There are other cases in which diglossia serves to separate the sacred from the profane, thus establishing a linguistic hierarchy and reinforcing a separation of roles, as when, for instance, it was the practice in the Catholic Church to use Latin in religious services (indeed, remnants of this system are still in place). But when diglossia applies to the political sphere, the functional reasons take on a more direct and divisive meaning, establishing a hierarchy of status and power. In such a case, the variety of relationships that diglossia establishes between languages, groups and individuals become more contested and the direct object, not only of personal psychology, but of political struggle. One of the issues raised by multilingualism in politics is whether there is any alternative to political diglossia (i.e. where one language is selected as the language of the political sphere), and whether any other arrangement is stable enough to guarantee effectiveness of communication while ostensibly offering equality of treatment and dignity to all linguistic groups comprising the political community.

LANGUAGE AS A POLITICAL PROBLEM

Until recently, the subject of multilingualism in political societies was only perfunctorily addressed, for it was often assumed that the legal and political systems of modern nation states required a common language in order to function. The question of the diversity of languages was seen as operating at the margin of the nation state: either as part of the assimilation process of migrant communities, or as part of the accommodation of relatively small, but concentrated, linguistic minorities. On the rare occasions that language emerged as a *political* issue, it was either as part of a discourse about national character or as a challenge to the supposed unity of the political 'nation', rather than to its monolingualism. The other political contexts in which multilingualism mattered were, of course, those of direct domination through either imperial or colonial power.

Lately the issue has acquired a new salience, due mainly to the new sensitivity towards diversity and recognition discussed above. Issues of language diffusion and language use have become part of a moral and political discourse meant to address questions of rightful entitlements and policy programmes, beside the more traditional issues of political domination. In their comprehensive introduction to a volume on *Political Theory and Language Rights* (2003), Will Kymlicka and Alan Patten have identified two series of issues, one concerned with practical and the other with theoretical questions, which have contributed to raising the awareness that language matters politically. Their list of practical problems comprises ethno-linguistic conflicts (in Eastern and Central Europe), subnational linguistic demands (in Western Europe), immigrants' linguistic enclaves (e.g. Hispanics in the United States), transnational political contexts (the European Union) and the protection of 'biodiversity' (protection of small minority languages). In different ways these developments have contributed to put linguistic diversity onto the political and legal maps. Kymlicka and Patten also list two broad theoretical developments, namely the debate on multiculturalism and that on the deliberative features of democracy, as factors contributing to the new awareness of the importance of language issues, insofar as these are considered to be relevant to the definition of visions of politics and society that engage with the broader questions of social and political cooperation in diverse societies.

In fact, and looking at these developments from a broader perspective, it may be argued that the new literature on language has grown around the cluster of practical and theoretical issues, such as those identified by Kymlicka and Patten, which have to do with the perceived crisis of the modern nation state as the main locus of legitimate political action both internally and at the international level. Interest in linguistic issues has therefore emerged at the intersection of three main debates, which are of both practical and theoretical relevance, and which have characterised recent work in the social sciences, and in particular in politics, law and sociology. Multiculturalism, globalisation and postcolonial discourses of cultural diversity are such debates, providing the background against which the issue of multilingualism has acquired both new meaning and political urgency.

Most of the practical developments listed by Kymlicka and Patten are determined and/or characterised by the interaction between these three main processes. In the case of the ethno-linguistic and the subnational conflicts that have emerged across Europe, these are only superficially the expression of a return to past nationalist feelings. For multiculturalism, globalisation and postcolonialism are radically changing the model of statehood in which nationalism thrived in the nineteenth and twentieth centuries. As we have already seen, the questions of identity and diversity, which are posed by new forms of migration, by the emergence of transnational political action and communication, and by the diffusion of new ecological sensibilities, are shaped in intricate ways by the combined effects of multiculturalism and globalisation, and given a different value in our postcolonial cultures.

When we move to the context provided by theoretical developments, the multicultural and deliberative debates singled out by Kymlicka and Patten can similarly be deconstructed along the three lines here suggested. The recent debate about multiculturalism obviously involves a redefinition of the relationship between particularity and universality, and between the individual and the community (or communities) that is determined as much by the internal differentiation of the political body as by the increasing porousness of national legal and political systems to global forces and influences. The emergence of a more global dimension, however, has its problems, for it has become increasingly difficult and contested to advance universal claims from within any single belief system.

The issue of deliberation would seem to be distinct from those of multiculturalism, globalisation and postcolonialism. And indeed, there are internal developments of democratic theory that make this debate independent from those other issues. However, it is true that one of the reasons for the growing attention given to deliberative processes in relation to the legitimation of legal and political decision-making is due to the fact that these have been partly depersonalised, while becoming less dependent on a hierarchy of norms and institutions within which the modern constitutional state tends to frame both law and politics. The crisis of sovereignty affecting the nation state encourages the rediscovery of the intrinsic discursive elements of law and politics, making the legitimacy of the institutions depend not on superior norms and authority, but on how people reason, negotiate and communicate with each other.

Now, in different ways, multiculturalism, globalisation and postcolonialism have reintroduced *culture*, and the attitude one has towards other people's culture, as a political issue. Linguistic diversity is part of this general problem. But the politics of language, as an aspect of the politics of culture, is both simpler and more complex. It is simpler, insofar as it offers a relatively easy test for the identification of issues of cultural identity and for the elaboration of cultural (i.e. linguistic) policies. In this respect, language is a good example of why and in what sense culture matters in politics and law. It is also simpler because language is a paradigmatic example of the relationship between universalism and particularism and of that between the individual and the community. Indeed, language is something that only comes in a particular form and can only exist as the product of social and interpersonal interaction. And yet, language – in the abstract – is one of the fundamental and universal human capacities. Moreover, individuals can grow up as bilingual or can learn another language with relative ease. In certain conditions, they can make a second language their own, using it to their own advantage, and without this causing them any problem in terms of their personality or detracting from their sense of identity.

But the politics of language present some difficulties, for the way in which language conjugates universalism and particularism, individual and collective expression, often complicates issues of identity, while rendering political choices starker, since the more traditional strategies of toleration, indifference, side-to-side cohabitation, and separate flourishing cannot easily apply in the case of language as they might more readily to other aspects of culture or to religion.

For all the reasons mentioned above, language has become a new political issue. Multilingualism, in particular, poses a political problem in two different contexts. One consists of those situations in which there are minorities whose main language of social communication is different from that of the majority (this poses more of a problem of social bilingualism). The other context is when there are many languages of social communication, and the question is whether or not to give privileged status to one of them within the legal-political system (this poses the problem of political diglossia as defined above). Some recent political and sociolegal literature on language has mainly addressed issues linked to minority languages, but with the solidification of the political and legal structure of the European Union, the question of a truly plurilingual polity has also become a specific theme for reflection – even though other cases such as India already existed.

Although at a more abstract level the two contexts may pose similar questions, it is apparent that there are important differences between them, both in relation to the kind of arguments that one may wish to use in support of multilingualism, and in relation to the policies to be adopted for such recognition and/or maintenance of languages. It is also debatable whether the two contexts – one characterised by the presence of one or more linguistic minorities, and the other by plurilingual political communication – can each be treated consistently, abstracting from the assessment of the precise form that multilingualism takes in particular circumstances. For example, with respect to minority languages, does the size of the population of speakers and its territorial concentration make a difference to the kinds of demands that the speakers of that minority language can make on the majority speakers? And with respect to multilingual communication, should arrangements for public communication be sensitive to historical circumstances and take on board general issues of economic and ideological domination?

Without entering into the details of these two contexts, it is here possible to assume that they pose relatively different problems and theoretical questions. Indeed, the suggestion advanced earlier on, that multilingualism poses both conflict and communication issues, and that these apply to languages, groups and individuals, suggests that there are some distinctive differences between tackling the issue of language in one context or the other, since the dynamics of conflict and communication between languages may apply differently in situations characterised by the presence of minority languages from those of plurilingualism. Moreover, different aspects of language planning would seem to be relevant to either of these contexts. Traditionally, language planning has been concerned with policies aimed at different features of a language: its 'corpus', its 'status' or its 'use'. Social bilingualism and political diglossia may affect differently the body and standards of a language, and may have different effects on the 'corpus' of either the 'dominant' or the 'weak' language in a social community. The level of protection (or promotion) that a language needs from (or towards) its own speakers is something that is difficult to determine, and for which there may not be a general abstract solution that applies indifferently to both deterritorialised linguistic minorities and linguistic groups within more or less defined borders and with institutions of their own. The issue of 'status' has immediate and diffuse relevance for political diglossia, particularly if the language of the public sphere has strong historical and/or cultural connotations, which make it difficult for other linguistic groups to accept without reservations. But it is also relevant in situations of social bilingualism, where there are large enough communities which for some reason tend to preserve and transmit their language of origin. Finally, the issue of 'use' is directly linked to that of 'status', and it may indeed be even more relevant to devising different policies for language planning.

However, most of the recent literature on the protection of language status and on the political and legal implications of language use has tended to gloss over such distinctions, while dividing on three broad theoretical and ideological approaches. In different fashions, they insist on different ways of looking at the relationship between speakers and their own language, or between speakers of different languages who may need to communicate with each other in a sociopolitical context. A first approach concentrates on the kinds of entitlement that a speaker (or a community of speakers) acquires in relation to their own language, producing a series of perfect and imperfect obligations in other speakers. A second approach focuses on the way in which language is inextricably linked to the speaker's identity – or to the collective identity of a community of speakers. This approach may result in an entitlement-based theory, but it can also be used to support a more republican view of how the political community shapes and assimilates individuals through language acquisition. Finally, a third approach makes use of the broadly liberal vocabulary of justice and fairness in order to evaluate issues of equality and the relative costs and benefits that speakers of different languages may accrue in their exchanges through some common medium. These three approaches tend to produce different political theories of language and different policy proposals. But it remains to be seen whether they are flexible enough to apply to different multilingual contexts, and whether their principles are mutually exclusive, or instead can be combined in some coherent fashion.

SOME CONTRIBUTIONS ON THE LANGUAGE QUESTION

The chapters comprising our volume on *The Language Question* reflect some of the issues raised in the previous discussion of language as a political question. Some of the chapters illustrate the theoretical approaches just outlined, but none of them takes a straightforward entitlement-based position. Although language rights are an easy way in which to formulate the issue of language protection, besides establishing minimum standards for citizens' access to public provisions, none of the contributions to the volume in question sets out a complete theory of language rights. Alan Patten, for instance, is interested in the more general formulation of a political theory of language based on justice and fairness. In doing so, he considers what he calls the 'triangle' of language policies (recognition, harmonisation and maintenance) in terms of the different ideas of equality supporting them. Omid Shabani, on his part, emphasises the importance of identity, but he does so from the perspective of constitutional patriotism, which, in his view, considers language in its 'communicative' function, so that this should not be regarded as a natural aspect of the identity of a people, but a factor actively contributing to the formation and transformation of their political identity. In his contribution, Peter

Kraus underscores the importance of a policy of recognition of linguistic and cultural diversity as part of a dynamic process involving at the same time the formation of a common identity and formation of a common space for communication. The latter, however, will need to rely on the reflexive capacity to acknowledge that such a commonality rests on a diversity of identities and languages.

The following three chapters in the book focus on the status of minority languages from a variety of disciplinary perspectives: historico-linguistic, anthropological and legal. Sue Wright and Reetta Toivanen raise a number of questions on the way in which language relates to group identity. This complicates issues of language rights, for it makes it more difficult to assimilate a particular language to a particular group identity. Niahm Shuibhne turns to the legal dimension of language use, analysing both the direct and indirect influence of EC directives and case-law jurisprudence on language issues. She suggests that the EC's piecemeal legal intervention is filling the gap left open by the lack of a general and coherent EU policy. Moreover, she suggests that although there is no specific European competence on language, the integration process is changing the European linguistic map, so that some form of intervention may, in fact, be required.

The remaining four chapters carry on the discussion of language in the European Union by partly returning to some of the theoretical problems raised in the opening chapters but also dealing with multilingualism intended as the context for plurilingual political communication. Miquell Strubell analyses the official documents and the official rhetoric of language diversity at the European level, which is generally considered to be the cornerstone of the EU language policy. As he and Longman demonstrate, however, this policy operates at a very superficial level, hiding a series of linguistic practices and language regimes at the institutional and semi-institutional levels that go against the high-minded but often impractical pronouncements behind the official support for linguistic diversity. Moreover, as Chris Longman illustrates and Philippe Van Parijs further discusses, the European language regime operates within a more general context in which English is progressively becoming a lingua franca. Neither of them considers this to be necessarily in antagonism with language pluralism and with policies supporting some form of it. Indeed, Van Parijs suggests that there are powerful reasons that militate in favour of promoting the generalised use of English as a lingua franca in Europe, but at the same time that a number of corrective strategies need to be pursued in order to reduce the linguistic unfairness and disadvantages that come with the dominance of one natural language over others. Finally, Philip Schlesinger raises the issue of language diversity and the formation of a European public sphere. He returns to some of the issues of identity and communication raised by Shabani, emphasising that, for a European space of communication to emerge, a common language is not sufficient. Linguistic dynamics within Europe should therefore be seen as part of a more general process of communication dynamics and identity construction.

CONCLUSION

When taken together, the chapters of this collection seem to widen the scope of the more recent political literature on language rights. Indeed, as noticed in the previous section, most of the contributors seem to pursue a line of enquiry that bypasses or goes beyond the strictly entitlement-based approach of much of the literature on language protection and linguistic minorities. Language rights may be necessary as an instrument of defence against political and cultural oppression. They may have a role in those cases where the viability of minority cultures and the self-determination of certain communities are under threat (Patten and Kymlicka 2003, 32–7; Skutnabb-Kangas and Phillipson 1995). But language rights cannot be the beginning and the end of a politics of language in democratic societies. This should be obvious from the discussion above of the complex way in which multilingualism is based on both conflictual and communicative relationships involving different agents. But there are also other reasons. An obvious one is that the internal development of both language and language communities cannot be fixed, since they depend on the complex relationships between innovation and tradition, and between individual choices and collective constraints. Another reason is that a situation of multilingual communication requires an intricate web of negotiations through which different people and groups may come to recognise each other and understand each other's needs, and these are unlikely to be regulated simply by legal rights. Moreover, as I have hinted at by distinguishing the context of social bilingualism from that of political diglossia, the issue of multilingualism in diverse societies has many aspects which touch on different levels of interaction, from the social to the political, from the legal to the cultural.

For instance, if we take the case of the European polity, the language issue has relevance in five interrelated areas:

1. As the instrument of public debate within the political institutions (its use in Parliament and the other main institutions, such as the European Court of Justice, the Commission, the Council).
2. As the instrument of intra-institutional communication within the administrative machinery of the EU and between civil servants and experts in the conduct of normal administrative business.
3. As the instrument of communication between the citizen and the administration (rights of enquiry, petition, political pressure and lobbying, etc.).

4. As the main vehicle for the formation and diffusion of public debate and opinions (the general public sphere, and the way in which different specialised publics interact within the public sphere, and how this feeds in, controls and influences institutional deliberation and decision-making).
5. Finally, as a general instrument of social communication.

In each of these areas different considerations about rights and power need to be made in order to find a system that reflects the demands of both cultural diversity and political and economic cooperation and solidarity.

In this respect, the problem of multilingualism in a democratic society may turn out to be a 'constellation' of problems, which may need addressing from a variety of theoretical and normative perspectives and with a variety of policies, leading to overlapping linguistic regimes, rather than depending on the application of a single principle or by the listing of general linguistic rights. The strategy of 'negotiation', therefore, may apply particularly well to an issue that, as it was suggested towards the beginning of this introduction, may need policies for the governance of diversity, not by suppressing it, but by highlighting its relative value in different situations and circumstances. This strategy is particularly appropriate to the governance of linguistic diversity in society, given that this is what we often do in intra-linguistic communication when translating from one linguistic code to another. As Umberto Eco remarks: 'translation is based on negotiation, this being a process according to which, in order to obtain something, we need to renounce something else – and by the end the players should come out with a sense of reasonable and reciprocal satisfaction, in accordance with the golden principle that one cannot have everything' (2003, 18, my translation).

In conclusion, one particular line of enquiry that I think may follow from the variety of contributions comprising this volume is that the governance of linguistic diversity may require, in the first instance, the negotiation of different linguistic regimes across society and politics. The particular normative principles and institutional arrangements that may apply to each regime, and how they can be made to work together, is, however, an open question to which the contributions here discussed make a contribution, but which will need further reflection and practical experimentation.

NOTE

1. This is a slightly revised version of the original article, which introduced the collective volume edited by Dario Castiglione and Chris Longman on *The Language Question in Europe and Diverse Societies: Political, Legal and Social Perspectives.* Hart Publishers, 2007. The volume comprises the following contributions: Alan

Patten, 'Theoretical Foundations of European Language Debates'; Omid A. Payrow Shabani, 'Language Policy of a Civic Nation-State: Constitutional Patriotism and Minority Language Rights'; Peter A. Kraus, 'Intercultural Recognition and Linguistic Diversity in Europe'; Sue Wright, What is a Language? The Difficulties Inherent in Language Rights'; Reetta Toivanen, 'Linguistic Diversity and the Paradox of Rights Discourse'; Niamh Nic Shuibhne, 'Minority Languages, Law and Politics: Tracing EC Action'; Miquel Strubell, 'The Political Discourse on Multilingualism in the European Union'; Chris Longman, 'English as Lingua Franca: A Challenge to the Doctrine of Multilingualism'; Philippe Van Parijs, 'Europe's Linguistic Challenge'; Philip Schlesinger, 'The Babel of Europe? Networks and Communicative Spaces'. These texts are here occasionally referred as 'the chapters of this volume', by which is meant the original volume on *The Language Question and Diverse Societies*.

Part V

THE DEMOCRATIC DEFICIT

Chapter 12

The Uses of Democracy

Reflections on Europe's Democratic Deficit[1]

Richard Bellamy and Dario Castiglione

Like the child in the fairy tale, many European Union scholars protest the 'Emperor has no clothes'.[2] Though the EU dresses itself up in the rhetoric of democracy – a fundamental requisite for member states – it is covered at best by only the scantiest democratic fig leaf. So far, however, the Union's failure to acquire the trappings of democratic decency has been of little political consequence. This fact should give commentators pause for thought. It suggests either the European ruling élites are cynically testing how far they can get away with their deception, or that current denunciations of a democratic deficit are oversimplified.

A number of European analysts now take the latter view and have become more circumspect about just calling for more democracy. We agree with them. Talk of a democratic deficit begs various questions that are rarely asked: namely, why is democracy valuable, will Europe gain from using it as opposed to other forms of decision-making, what form must it take to achieve these results – deliberative, majoritarian, consociational, a mix of all three, or something quite different from these – and how, if at all, can it be implemented in the European context? This chapter represents a modest attempt to address them.

We begin, in section 1, by distinguishing two dimensions of the EU's legitimation crisis, to which talk of a democratic deficit is intimately related. The first concerns the genesis and character of the European polity, the second the type of democratic regime most suited to it. Discussion of the latter dimension often overlooks its connection to the former by regarding democracy per se as intrinsically good. However, as we argue in section 2, the value of democracy is best measured by its benefits. These will only be present if the forms and procedures of a democratic regime fit the complexion of the polity and population to which they are applied. Section 3 follows through this analysis by examining the weaknesses of what for many defines contemporary democracy – namely, majority rule. Section 4 concludes that if, by virtue of containing multiple demoi, the EU is a mixed polity, it requires a mixed democratic regime involving a variety of decision rules and the dispersal of sovereign power between different bodies and diverse locations.

1. LEGITIMATION CRISIS?

Maastricht focused the minds of supporters and opponents of the European project alike by raising fundamental questions about its methods and ultimate goal (cf. Weiler 1999, chap. 1). Up to then, question begging had been an intrinsic part of the principal integration strategy. According to the so-called Monnet or Community method, Europe was to be made 'in the details' through administrative means and elite bargaining. Legal rules and democratic decision-making merely offered ex-post endorsements of an already-existing reality. This method had the advantage of allowing a federal structure to be formed by stealth, while keeping nation states in control of the overall direction of the process. As a result, it pleased both federalists and intergovernmentalists, and has proved compatible with analyses from each of these perspectives. Political debate and directly consensual forms of legitimation were eschewed as either irrelevant to technical matters or inappropriate for interstate bargaining. Moreover, discussion of the ultimate shape and scope of the EU was carefully avoided.[3] The project possessed the social legitimacy offered by good economic performance and responsiveness to demands from infra-national groups and organisations (or European civil society at large), and the formal legitimacy provided by the international law framework (pacta servanda sunt) within which the various Treaties were agreed. But its political legitimacy was the indirect and weak result of the negotiations having been carried out by elected national politicians and their civil servants.

Recently, however, social and legal legitimacy has become more problematic, and the need for direct political legitimacy correspondingly greater (Beetham and Lord 1998; Schmitter 1996, 1998). In the immediate post-war period, peace and prosperity were seen as obvious public goods that required coordinated European action to be achieved (Weiler 1999, chap. 7). The end of the cold war and a slowing up of fifty years of steady growth have changed that perception. What is required to secure these basic goods is now more disputed. Many analysts contend peace depends on states simply being liberal democracies rather than on their joining together into a single unit. Likewise, global markets certainly necessitate interstate cooperation to establish free trade and regulate them, but how much beyond that is less clear. The old social democratic consensus on such matters has come increasingly under attack from the new right and the experiments with privatisation adopted in almost all the member states since the 1980s. The Common Agricultural Policy, for example, is likely to prove ever more contentious, as are the degree and character of regulations in areas such as health and safety and the environment which impose direct costs and produce only diffuse and indirect benefits. As friction over issues such as fishing rights reveal, nation states are not averse to defecting from collective arrangements whenever it seems in their short-term interest to do so and free riding on the efforts of others. The proliferation of opt-outs over matters such as the Euro testifies to increasing disagreement over what economic and social policies are in the common interest. Meanwhile, expansion to the East and attempts to extend the public goods supplied by the EU are liable to heighten these tensions by raising the costs and decreasing the benefits available to existing members.

The formal legitimacy offered by law has been unable to make up for the lessening of the EU's social legitimacy. Indeed, in some respects, the dramatic growth in legal integration may have exacerbated the situation. Even those scholars who believe the member states still control the overall process accept that the gradual constitutionalisation of the Treaties through successive judgements of the ECJ and Intergovernmental Conferences means some form of supranational constitution is in the making, requiring a reconsideration of the methods, aims and principal agents of integration (Moravcsik and Nicolaïdis 1998). However, this extension of legal integration has often appeared to overstep not only what seems socially and economically warranted but also the substantive values and express wishes of the populations of the member states. This conflict has been particularly evident in the clashes between the ECJ and national constitutional courts in cases such as *Grogan*, where the ECJ's defence of the EC's core principles, the four market freedoms, has been opposed to an even higher law emanating from the national demos of the member state involved (Coppel and O'Neill 1992; De Witte 1991). A similar concern lay behind the German Federal Constitutional Court's Brunner ruling (Grimm 1995) and the uneasy ratification of the Maastricht Treaty by the British parliament and in referenda in Denmark and France. In these situations, the formal legality of the ECJ's judgements proves no substitute for its lack of substantial legitimacy (McCormick 1995, 1996; Eleftheriadis 1998). The Court's increasing willingness to refer to notions of rights that strictly speaking lie outside the domain of European law indicate the dilemma it now finds itself in (Shaw 1996). However, since these rights can be subject to incommensurable interpretations by different national jurisdictions, this manoeuvre does not circumvent the possibility of conflict but merely moves it to a more fundamental level (Bellamy 1995). One prominent legal commentator has even likened the potential standoff between the ECJ and national constitutional courts to the Cold War policy of Mutual Armed Destruction (Weiler 1996).

The retreat of the Community method and its associated political strategies and forms of legitimation has produced a shift to an 'intentionalist' paradigm that relies on more direct forms of consensual legitimacy (Streeck 1996; Offe 1998). For the exhaustion of the EU's social and formal legitimacy can be remedied only through an explicit political commitment to a particular form of Union. As a result, academic attention has focused on the EU's democratic deficit with a renewed urgency and European studies have taken a corresponding 'normative turn'.[4]

A full diagnosis of the EU's current political legitimation crisis requires two interrelated tasks that EU scholars have too often kept distinct. The first involves analysing the nature of the emerging European polity, the second exploring what type of regime or system of governance best suits it so as to deliver the democratic goods on which political legitimacy rests. Integration theorists have tended to concentrate on the polity formation aspect of the question and democratic theorists on the regime aspect. However, theories of political integration that do not address its democratic character are normatively blind and lack a sense of where they ought to be headed, while democratic theories that are formulated in ignorance of the political shape of the EU prove empirically empty and so unable to make the democratic ideal a reality. Rendering the EU politically legitimate entails seeing how the two might mutually influence each other, with the character of the EU polity shaping the form the democratic regime takes and being in its turn shaped by democratic decision-making.

The distinction between polity and regime (Schmitter 1996) reveals two dimensions to political legitimacy. The polity dimension concerns the legitimacy of the political community as a bounded entity wishing to determine its affairs. Democratic theory per se cannot resolve this problem, since democracy presupposes a relatively autonomous group among whom its decisions are binding (Dahl 1989; Weale 1995, 1997, 1998). In the modern world, nation states have come to represent the 'natural' locus of political decision-making, sanctioned internally by their monopoly over the legitimate use of force and externally by a system of international law based on state sovereignty. Throughout the past two hundred years, claims to political autonomy and self-determination have been couched in terms of either nationhood or statehood, therefore, with the one very often meant to imply the other. Recent developments towards global governance, of which the European Union is considered one of the most developed instances, have been taken to prise open the internal connection between nation and state, as well as to undermine the logical structure of state governance. On the one hand, it is argued that nationhood no longer supplies the sociocultural glue political integration requires to operate with the unconditional assent of the people living in a given territory (Curtin 1997; Habermas 1992a, 1996; Ferry 1992). On the other hand, the congruence between territoriality and functional competence underlying (hierarchically ordered) state power is said to have broken down (Schmitter 1996a, 1996b). These developments supposedly point to the new European polity being postnational in character and post-state in form. At present, however, these are mere tendencies, defined in largely negative and ideal terms as 'non-state' and 'non-national'. They operate in a global environment of overlapping, and often depersonalised networks of governance, and have yet to emerge in their positive and concrete form. Nor is there any convincing teleology on which to argue that this is the shape of things to come.

Consequently, it seems more realistic to suggest we have a mixed system. Nation states remain the dominant players, giving the EU many of the features of a confederation (Forsyth 1982; Warleigh 1998; Chryssochoou 1994). However, they sit alongside the supra- and to some extent postnational institutions of the Commission, Parliament, the European Court of Justice and now the European Central Bank. Meanwhile, the EU has encouraged the growth of political groups of a sub- and a transnational kind. For example, there are now over 3,000 interest groups and 100 regional offices based in Brussels. Many are directly involved in formulating policy via the process of comitology. Correspondingly new levels of decision-making have also emerged that vary according to the policy and groups involved. However, this is not a hierarchical system. There is growing disagreement over core policies, with only ten of the fifteen being members of the EU's putative defence arm, the Western European Union, twelve signing up to the Schengen accords on free movement of peoples and eleven joining the single currency. Even at the centre there is a complicated mix between intergovernmental decision-making, as in the Council of Ministers; potentially transnational, as in the European Parliament; supranational, as in the Commission; and postnational, as with the ECJ. Moreover, all these institutions have to compete and incorporate the various levels of subnational – regional, local, workplace and community – decision-making. Yet there exists no clear lines of demarcated jurisdiction or overarching authority to decide disputes between them.

Even with nation states, it would be wrong to assume that the legitimacy of the polity guarantees the legitimacy of its governing structure or regime. In a mixed polity, however, the legitimation offered by the regime plays an especially important role in determining the legitimacy of the polity itself. In the modern world, democracy has come to be seen as the only legitimate form of state. The resulting democratic imperative holds that the institutional organisation of government (but not necessarily social governance) must reflect the main underlying principles of democracy. Denunciations of the European democratic deficit come into their own here. There is little doubt that the structure of European governance does not fully conform to any meaningful interpretation of the many standard definitions of democracy. There is no political equality in the present system of European representation. Small countries, for instance, are over-represented in both the Council, the Parliament and the Commission. The institutions of direct representation, namely the European Parliament, have no great power; the little they have is mainly as a break upon other institutions, which are in full control of both the political agenda and legislative promotion. No clear majoritarian rule operates in European decision-making; or, when it does, it involves a majority of the member states rather than their citizens. Finally, none of the main European institutions fully satisfies what are usually considered as the important democratic principles of popular responsiveness and accountability; nor is much of the business of government subject to the normative publicity associated with transparent decision-making and freedom of information.

If the European political regime must reflect the democratic imperative to pass the test of direct consensual legitimacy, there are a great many democratic deficits to be overcome. Yet why and how should the democratic imperative apply, given the new conditions in which the European polity and its component nation states now operate? The very principles of democracy may need revision to meet postnational and global conditions, much as they did in taking on their modern representative form during this century as a result of democracy's extension to the masses and its application at a national scale. Addressing the European democratic deficit is not as simple as it appears. It involves both an understanding of what democracy means today and what it can actually do for the legitimation of government.

2. THE DEMOCRATIC IMPERATIVE REVISITED

Democracy has three main meanings that appeal to the democratic imperative frequently conflate. First and most obviously, democracy is a form of government characterised by institutions, rights and practices designed to give people a say in how their community's political affairs are run. Second and more loosely, democracy refers to the underlying values, notably freedom and equality, that define it as a fair scheme of cooperation between formally equal people. Finally, democracy denotes a decision-making process, often identified with majority rule, that applies to groups irrespective of their scope and aims, and so extends beyond the political sphere narrowly conceived. The three meanings are intimately related, so their conflation comes as no surprise. Nonetheless, their analytical distinction reveals the need to disentangle the question of what makes arrangements democratic (and hence what is meant by a deficit of democracy) from what makes democracy a good thing.[5]

Democracy is often unquestioningly regarded as a self-evident and self-justifying good. The force of the democratic imperative clearly draws on this assumption. But if democracy just means a collection of political institutions of a certain sort, it is hard to see what is self-justifying about them. The worth of democracy must refer to other widely approved goods and values, therefore, that are supposedly given political currency by democratic institutions. A standard list consists of liberty, equality, independence and fairness, though different democratic theories combine them in various ways that often reflect divergent ontological assumptions (Held 1987; MacCormick 1997). Following the main contemporary democratic theorists (Habermas 1996; Rawls 1993), we shall assume that modern democracy's main virtue lies in its tendency to underpin and promote value pluralism, at least in ideal conditions. This occurs through the formal incorporation and substantive balancing of different values within its very principles and procedures; through the promotion of consensual decision-making; and through the settlement of disputes arising from either the incommensurability of values or the non-compossibility of rights and liberties, in ways that are recognised as fair and legitimate by the parties involved.

To unpack the value pluralism of democracy, we shall start with its inherent qualities. When considered as values intrinsic to democracy, then liberty, equality, independence and fairness help establish both the principle of democratic authorisation and democracy's procedural character. Liberty entails the presumption that an agent should be free to choose a course of action and to shape the social context in which he or she operates in ways that maximise the conditions for autonomy. As a collective decision-making mechanism, democracy inevitably places limits on the liberty of individuals. But where collective decision-making is both inevitable, because of the social constraints within which agents operate, and necessary, because of the desirability of coordinated action in addressing common problems (Weale 1998), democracy offers a way of preserving the independence of individual members by allowing them to participate in shaping the rules that either limit or enable action.[6] Thus the equal right to liberty and self-determination[7] underlies the authoritative nature of democratic government and establishes the presumption of its legitimacy over other forms of collective decision-making. However, for authorisation to be fully legitimate, some form of consent is needed, and so, inevitably, is some conception of autonomy. These two conditions ground the capacity of community members to make free and responsible choices, providing a formal legitimacy test for democratic authority and substantive criteria for the design of democratic institutions.[8]

Equality and fairness enter here to frame the procedures of democratic authorisation itself. Such values are appealed to when arguing that we owe all individuals equal respect (Cohen and Sabel 1997), that they have equal claims over communal goods, and that their demands should be given equal consideration by the community itself (Dahl 1986, chap. 8). The arguments for equal respect, claims and consideration are the basis for political equality, which is the guiding principle for establishing democracy's procedures in the aggregation of members' opinions and choices and the fair deliberation of reasons (Jones 1983; Sunstein 1991). These arguments also ground the assumptions about the superior legitimacy of democratic methods and arrangements over other forms of collective decision-making.

Both democratic authorisation and its procedural framework rest on values that are considered paramount in modern, post-traditional societies. Herein lies much of the democratic imperative's plausibility. However, that liberty, equality, independence and fairness are intrinsically related to the idea of democracy does not, in itself, guarantee that the effects of democratic government will be consistent with those same values. Nor is there any a-prioristic reason supporting the belief that democracy is conducive to social justice, however this is defined (Van Parijs 1996, 1998). Strictly speaking, the asymmetry between intrinsic values and their promotion is neither a problem of the practical application of ideal requirements nor a question of the compossibility of the demands arising from different values or their various interpretations. The asymmetry is the direct product of the absence of any logical connection between the conditions of choice and its results given the indeterminacy associated with *free* choice (besides various other problems usually associated with collective choice and unintended consequences). From this perspective, the relationship between democracy and either its own or other fundamental values becomes largely instrumental. At best, a virtuous circle may exist between democracy's intrinsic values and their reinforcement through the educative effect of democratic participation (Cohen and Sabel 1997).

Democracy's legitimacy cannot in any case rest on its intrinsic goodness alone, since this needs to be compared to and balanced against the substantial promotion of other values when taken independently (Shapiro 1996, chap. 1). This task involves looking at the beneficial effects of making decisions democratically, so far as these can be reasonably ascertained. Just as the value of democratic principles has been supposed to guarantee its intrinsic goodness, so the virtues of democratic governance are frequently considered self-evident. The literature often fails to indicate whether the benefits of democracy follow logically from its operations or are the empirically ascertainable results of them. To clarify this confusion, let's distinguish between three groups of benefits. A first group concerns the general effects of democratic governance. They consist in the goods of responsive govern-ment, adaptive governance and non-domination. The structure of democratic governance is meant to guarantee a two-way information flow that ensures government is controlled by the ruled and that the rulers are well informed about the needs and views of citizens. This process facilitates adaptive gov-ernance, by developing feedback mechanisms, the pooling of information for collective problem solving, and collective-learning mechanisms both in space and time (Cohen and Sabel 1997). Democracy's ability to adapt to the tasks in hand also means that, as a system of governance, it is apt to take differ-ent institutional forms according to the composition of its membership and its historical and cultural location. Democratic governance is also propitious terrain for securing liberty as non-domination (Pettit 1997). This condition consists not of an absence of interference either by the state or other private actors, but of guaranteeing an environment in which citizens can lead secure lives, plan ahead and feel generally in control, without a sense of their life choices being dictated by more powerful interests.

A second group of benefits concerns the quality of democratic decisions. These are harder to establish without precise empirical evidence. However, by checking arbitrary and self-interested uses of power, while encouraging the formulation of general laws that reflect the common good, democracy is generally conducive to the definition and protection of individual rights and liberties. Moreover, democratic mechanisms foster a degree of social equality by subsuming social and income differences under a commonality of con-cerns that calls for some redistribution of resources. Finally, democracy pro-motes domestic and international peace by establishing a framework within which people are expected to engage in discussion, exchange arguments and find reasonable agreements and compromises, rather than making use of their relative contractual position or physical force.

The third group of benefits follows more clearly from the manner in which democratic decisions are reached (Jones 1983). Democrats contend political participation educates citizens about each other's needs and ideals, thereby fostering toleration if not an equal regard, a concern for the common interest, and an awareness of the importance of cooperation to secure public goods. Some of these effects have already been mentioned in relation to the poten-tial virtuous circle associated with the intrinsic values of democracy (Cohen and Sabel 1997), but they are probably better looked at from a more con-sequentialist perspective. Democracy encourages mutually beneficial types of bargain and forms of reciprocity in the construction of the general will; it formally requires frankness, mutual respect and taking the perspective of others when arguing for one's opinions. These processes facilitate interest and opinion filtering and transformation, so turning private individuals into citizens of the commonwealth (Offe and Preuss 1991; Mansbridge 1992).

Involvement in public affairs may also foster solidarity and trust, contributing to the social capital needed to ease cooperation between different groups and particularly between long-standing majorities and minorities in both politics and society at large.

The catalogue of democracy's beneficial effects is certainly impressive. Prima facie, it reinforces the case for the democratic imperative in modern societies, particularly in view of their increasing pluralism and what Rawls (1993) calls the 'burdens of judgement' in ethical arguments (cf. also Habermas 1996). However, like our earlier consequential refinement of arguments from democracy's inherent goodness, focusing on the good consequences of practising democracy also renders the endorsement of democratic arrangements more discriminating. In both cases, it turns democracy into a partly instrumental good. On the one hand, we value it for *realising* its intrinsic values, not just because they are inherent to democracy per se. On the other hand, our approval of democratic institutions is equally conditional to some degree on their delivering the beneficial effects associated with democratic decision-making. As we have seen, some of these effects are supported by empirical evidence, while others rest on the presumption that, given the right conditions and the appropriate institutional machinery, they are more likely to arise than not. The relatively instrumental and contingent nature of democracy, however, makes its legitimacy no longer self-standing, rendering the democratic imperative less compelling.

Of course, liberals and socialists have always qualified their approval of democracy in ways that appear superficially analogous to those proposed here. Whereas they make their support for democracy conditional on its fostering liberal or socialist values, however, our qualifications rest on the possibility that democratic institutions may either not further democratic principles or fail to produce the benefits that ideally follow from the democratic process. In each case, we evaluate democracy in terms of its instrumental ability to deliver democratic goods rather than those of some other kind. This is not to suggest that all good things are necessarily democratic. Many are only contingently so, and others may be undermined by democracy. As we saw, such reasoning led past European élites to conclude that we could do without democracy much of the time. Libertarians still hold this view, believing as much as possible should be left to the market (Hayek 1982; Buchanan 1975). Advocates of a rights-based Constitution for Europe often take an analogous stance, seeing democracy as limited to and by its contribution to securing rights that might often be better promoted by other mechanisms (Mancini 1989). Much discussion of the democratic deficit involves such a purely instrumental view of democracy. However, these approaches cannot offer the EU the distinctively political legitimacy we have seen it now needs, given that the social and legal legitimacy it currently possesses has proven insufficient. To address this issue one has to consider the intrinsic merits of democracy. Although there are external limits to democracy in terms of economic performance and rights protection which a comprehensive evaluation would have to consider, our concern has been with its own distinct contribution. Moreover, we have shown that many economic benefits and rights are intrinsic to democracy itself and only likely to be realised through it. By judging democracy by its own light, many of the limits that critics believe have to be imposed on democracy can be shown to be internal to it (Bellamy and Castiglione 1997c).

So even in the qualified form we have argued for, democratic values play a vital role in the direct and normative legitimation of regimes. European political integration is no exception. Nonetheless, opinions differ about why and how Europe fails the democratic legitimacy test. Having clarified what is good about democracy in general, we are now in a better position to answer these questions. We shall do so by briefly examining how Europe scores on the three kinds of goods provided by democracy: legitimate authorisation, fair cooperation and the beneficial effects that stem from responsive governance.

The political authorisation of European governance does not come directly from the people(s) of Europe. Direct and consensual authorisation, through the election of the European Parliament, is still largely ineffective. Admittedly, the powers of the EP have recently been increased (see the Amsterdam Treaty), and the Parliament has become more of a partner in European decision-making through having certain powers of control or ratification. On the whole, however, the EP remains a secondary player in the business of European government.[9] Authorisation of the main players, on the other hand, is only partial and indirect. The Commission is selected in ways that correspond more to bureaucratic and diplomatic criteria than to anything resembling democratic mechanisms. Similar notions inform the way it perceives itself and acts politically. The only effective branch of European government that can claim some form of democratic authorisation is the Council. But such authorisation is only indirect. Moreover, it is rare for national governments to be elected on a clear European agenda. Thus, referenda, like those on Maastricht, seem to be the only meaningful form of direct authorisation so far used at the European level. Yet the electorate's message is far from clear on such occasions, given that the vote is often made with national issues in mind; a fact that also applies to elections for the European Parliament. In sum, the little democratic authorisation that European governance can claim is partial, indirect, ineffective and unclear.

If we move to the question of political equality and fair cooperation, however, the bleak picture we have just painted of democratic authorisation appears in a different and less gloomy light. There is no denying the failures on the authorisation front, but the legitimacy that comes with authorisation rests in turn on the legitimacy of the subject that transfers authority. Until some agreement is reached on who is the legitimate 'subject' of the European Constitution: a European demos of European citizens, the citizens of the member states voting nationally, the governments of the member states, or even, in a more cosmopolitan perspective, the values underlying the European Constitution; the terms of both political equality and fair cooperation are uncertain. This problem is largely a question of political identity, to which we shall return in the next section when discussing democratic procedures in more detail. But it also partly depends on the issues raised in section 1 concerning the legitimacy of the polity. As we pointed out, such matters cannot be solved democratically, since democracy itself rests on them. Political equality and fair cooperation presuppose we know who is equal with whom and who can be expected to cooperate or not. In Europe, these questions still remain unanswered.

A similar conundrum applies to the beneficial effects associated with democracy. Until European political institutions are explicitly designed according to democratic principles, arguments about the good consequences of European democracy can only be counterfactual, as can their supposed legitimating force. Supporters of the Community method often maintained that democratic methods and popular participation would bring about neither economic nor political integration. Whether this was true or not, the argument assumed that the benefits of democracy were outweighed by the goods associated with the integration process, mainly peace and prosperity. But now that a fair degree of economic and political integration has been achieved, a degree that most Europeans seem both to take for granted and approve of, the question has become how to sustain it – whether by deepening, widening or halting the process.[10] Hence the shift to a more intentionalist paradigm, which, for some of the reasons already outlined in this section, gives greater value to democracy.

The problem now confronting us is what kind of democratic institutions and what degree of popular participation are necessary to provide the democratic goods without jeopardising the current level of integration. In this respect, critics of the democratic deficit take a sanguine view of the application of the democratic imperative to the European Union. They think political equality must surely apply to the citizens of Europe and that demands for the democratisation of European institutions follow directly from the legitimacy of democratic authorisation. They ask for a more thorough application of majoritarianism throughout the institutions of the Union, and propose we give more power to those involving direct representation. But is this a way out of the democratic deficit? We shall review the logic of these demands in the next two sections by discussing the other two meanings of democracy – as a decision-making procedure and as a form of government.

3. POLITICAL UNITY AND DEMOCRATIC RULES

Most democratic theories hold that majoritarianism – often defined as a majority 'principle' rather than a 'rule' – lies at the heart of democracy. This conviction is both trivial and unfounded. It is trivial because no one disputes that majoritarianism offers *an* application of the principle of political equality, which ensures the vote of each and every member of the community has equal weight. But it is unfounded as the guiding procedural principle of democracy.

The mistake arises from confusing people and majority. This error can best be illustrated by an example. If procedural democracy consisted in following the simple will of the majority of the members of a community, there would be nothing undemocratic in a society where a minority were excluded from the political process (but not necessarily from civil and social rights), as long as all decisions were taken by a majority of the whole community. Thus, for any single decision, the majority of those having political rights (call them A) would need to be larger than the political minority (call them B) and the excluded minority (call them C) put together: A>B+C. On the face of it, this example seems consistent with majoritarianism, but is it consistent with democracy? In the past, many democracies sanctioned the permanent exclusion of minorities (and occasionally, majorities): women, slaves, unpropertied workers, blacks, indigenous populations. But with the universalisation of fundamental human rights, this position is as untenable in practice as it is in theory. Moreover, none of these democracies were founded on the proviso we have specified in our hypothetical example. In the example itself, the minority is not excluded from the community (from the people, that is), but only silenced politically. Indeed, the proviso gives them a certain weight in the political process by allocating them a 'silent' veto power whenever the political and excluded minorities jointly represent the majority of the whole population. The political exclusion of a minority, therefore, does not contradict the majoritarian rule when this is applied to the entire community.[11] But such exclusion is evidently inconsistent with political equality. Indeed, it is the latter that should be regarded as the fundamental procedural principle of democracy, to which all decision-making rules ought ultimately to be subordinated.

To see how the principle of political equality renders democratic decision-making more complex, we shall briefly review some of the shortcomings of majority rule and contrast this procedure with the alternatives of super-majoritarianism, proportionality and deliberation. We will concentrate on three of the main features of majority decision: positive responsiveness, anonymity and issue neutrality (cf. Weale 1997). Each of them possesses certain virtues as part of a procedure that tends to respect the pluralism of preferences and opinions, if not necessarily of strongly held beliefs and values, in the community to which majority decision is applied.

Positive responsiveness implies that, ceteris paribus, changes in an individual's preferences should affect the function of social choice. Majority decision is extremely sensitive to such alterations, as is clearly illustrated in cases when a single vote alters the outcome. By contrast, supermajorities normally need preference shifts in more than a single voter to affect the collective choice. This lack of elasticity seems to give minorities a veto power, as is even more clearly illustrated by the unanimity rule (Saward 1998), so contradicting the principle of political equality. However, this conclusion may be too hasty if it involves the aforementioned confusion between the people and a majority. If, on a whole range of fundamental issues, a society were permanently divided along the same lines, persistent minorities might eventually lose interest in participating in the political process. In their view, such a system would fail to recognise their fundamental interests and contradict the principle of political equality. As Kelsen suggested some time ago (1929), in democracies it is more appropriate to speak of a majority-minority principle, since the one implies the other. The effectiveness of collective decision-making depends on keeping communities together, so that minorities can accept the legitimacy of majority decisions. Majoritarianism must be seen, therefore, as part of a wider process of democratic decision-making that tries to keep a balance between decisiveness in social choice (through competitive mechanisms, based on the equalising function of democracy) and social integration (through cooperative mechanisms, based on the recognition function of democracy). From this perspective, the search for a wider consensus through consociational mechanisms such as the use of super- or concurrent majorities, or occasionally the unanimity rule, is not necessarily undemocratic. In certain circumstances, it may be considered as a way of adapting the principle of political equality to complex polities, where separate political identities coexist that reflect distinct and well-entrenched practices of cooperation and deep differences of interests (Weale 1998; Lijphart 1984; Schmitter 1996b).

Sensitivity to political identity is also central to a discussion of the anonymity feature of majority decision. This stipulates that only the number and not the identity or the status of the members determines the social choice function. As with positive responsiveness, the problem arises when there are persistent minorities. Political equality can be looked at either prospectively, by considering the equality of citizens to influence the making of collective decisions; or retrospectively, by considering whether the interests of citizens have been equally respected in the decision itself (Jones 1983; Saward 1998; Hyland 1995). Because of the anonymity feature, which precludes weighting an individual's voting power according to his or her interest in the matter, majority decision is insensitive to retrospective equality. So, a majority may take decisions on matters that mainly affect a minority, without due regard for the way the minority itself see things. Or there may be cases in which a majority consistently outvotes a minority on related issues, so producing a winner-takes-all situation that reflects unfairly on the real divisions of interests and opinions within the society (Jones 1983). In all such instances, decision mechanisms that result in proportionate satisfaction would better reflect the principle of political equality.

The application of the proportionality rule is not always simple. The most obvious case involves systems of representation. Here majority rule is only undermined indirectly as a result of the consensus and coalition-building politics proportional representation seems to encourage. Moreover, the anonymity feature applies to PR. Things change when we move from second- to first-order decision-making: that is, from the selection of representatives to the making of decisions themselves. Here the only way of weighing the relative interest of the members of the electorate is to do away with anonymity. This can be done in various ways – such as giving stronger representation to certain groups, or by considering both horizontal (across society, through interest-based groups and associations) and vertical (across the territory, through federal and power devolving structures) decentralisation of the decision process, depending on the issues at stake. Majority rule may still be applied in these decentralised structures, but the larger community de facto recognises that there are some (but clearly not all) collective issues for which a recognition of separate political identities may apply.

Finally, we turn to the neutrality of majority decisions. This feature implies the social choice function is determined solely by the number of votes favouring one or other option, rather than by the substantive merits of what is debated. Issue neutrality would raise no particular problem, besides those standardly treated in the public choice literature, if democratic politics just weighed individual subjective preferences. It is only when matters of intrinsic importance have to be discussed that difficulties arise. The application of a seemingly behaviouristic approach to politics (Weale 1992) fails to recognise the essential role played in a democracy by fair discussion and the appeal to arguments that are meant either to convince or to raise doubts in the minds of other voters. The idea of deliberative democracy emphasises the importance of processes and institutions that foster the filtering and transformation of individual preferences by encouraging the educative engagement with others and reflective political judgements (Sunstein 1991). These practices change politics from a market of votes into a forum of principle. Majority decision is not overruled by such institutions, since in pluralist and complex societies there is still plenty of scope for reasonable disagreement and the clash of interests, but its place is hedged in by the forum institutions of politics and, more generally, by the critical function played by the modern public sphere (Habermas 1992b). Counting votes is normally the last stage of a process during which the issues have been discussed on their merits. The dialogic aspect of democracy is as important as the aggregation of views and preferences, and often more so. In simple majority decision, issues may not matter, but in democracy pushpin is not the same as poetry.

If democracy is not just simple majoritarianism, then democratic legitimacy depends on a thick network of institutions more than on thin procedural rules. This analysis also undermines calls for majority rule as the effective cure for Europe's democratic deficit (cf. also, Van Parijs 1998). If, as we have argued, majoritarianism is not the essence of democratic decision-making in the relatively homogenous conditions of the nation state, there is even less reason to believe it can be placed at the core of a future European democracy. Indeed, a European democracy will probably have to wrestle with far more intractable problems of divided political identities than existing nation states, since its component parts have a long history of common engagement, shared culture and feelings of mutual interest that cannot be brushed aside lightly. This sense of commonalty (meant dispositionally, rather than in a strong communitarian sense: cf. Barry 1989; Weale 1997) is further reinforced by the national contexts in which civil networks, civic cultures, political structures and welfare insurance mechanisms mostly operate. The replacement of the sense of civic identity and of national institutions of cooperation, with equivalent structures of trust and reciprocity at a European level cannot be achieved overnight (Offe 1998). Furthermore, the burden of proof must rest with those who attempt to either change or undo institutions that are reasonably efficient and socially legitimate, so to show that the alternatives will do dramatically better.[12]

These are not arguments for the status quo. They suggest merely that calls for the diffusion of democratic procedures at a European level should give greater consideration to issues of political identity than has often been the case. For these are relevant to the fairness of the procedures themselves. More positively, the democratic recognition of different political identities can be incorporated within a Madisonian system of checking and balancing competing interests and powers. The retreat of the nation state need not necessarily lead towards more centralisation. Within the emerging system of European multilevel governance (Marks, Hooghe, et al. 1996), there is scope for more decentralised and contextualised problem solving, for associative democratic governance and other schemes of dispersed and mixed sovereignty that offer an alternative to both top-down statism and deregulated markets (Cohen and Sabel 1997; Schmitter in Marks, Scharpf, et al. 1996; Hirst 1994; Bellamy and Castiglione 1997a, 1997b, 1998). There are also opportunities for a less communitarian-based deliberative framework in which to embed democratic practices. These include the development of a pluralistic and interactive overlapping of national and European legal systems (MacCormick 1993, 1995); the innovative use of European committees, where political interests are disciplined and made more deliberative by the contribution of expert knowledge (cf. Joerges's contribution to this volume); and the creation of a more strongly normative public sphere, applying the test of communicative rationality to the business of politics and administration (cf. Ferry 1992; and Eriksen's contribution to this volume).

Yet, however positive the chances for multi-governance, deliberation and self-reflection may appear, as Habermas reminds us in his contribution to this volume, there still remains an important demand for popular sovereignty and collective self-determination, with the community wanting to exercise 'political influence upon itself'. This is the role traditionally assigned to legislative power in democratic societies, and takes us back to the other reforms standardly invoked to address the democratic deficit in the European Union: more direct representation, more democratic control, more accountability. But can the traditional institutions of modern democracy be transferred to the Union?

4. DEMOCRACY, REGIMES AND POLITIES

As the main thrust of our argument implies, simple demands for more democratic European institutions make too easy a transition from the generic presumption in favour of the democratic imperative to its application to political regimes. There are a-prioristic reasons for using democracy as the main strategy for direct regime legitimation, but these are not enough. Partly instrumental reasons need to be taken into consideration, but they, in turn, depend on the presence of mechanisms designed to bring about the various intrinsic goods and beneficial effects of democracy. As we have also seen, such mechanisms cannot be reduced to strictly procedural rules capable of universal application – the 'rules of the game', in Bobbio's phrase (1987) – but need more substantive specification to perform their tasks. So, what are the concrete institutions of a democratic society?

Talking, as we often do, of democratic societies is only shorthand for saying that some of their fundamental political institutions are run democratically. Neither markets nor families, which determine so much of our social life, are organised according to democratic criteria. Citizens spend most of their time in organisations (schools, firms, corporations) where democracy operates only at the margins, if at all. Even in the public sphere narrowly conceived neither the ordinary administration of justice, policing or the machinery of government are run democratically. There is a sense, of course, in which the passage from status to contract (Maine 1917 [1861]) has democratised social life through making it less hierarchical – a change in which modern political democracy is firmly rooted. But this is more a matter of social equality and independence than strict democracy. In ordinary language, we say that a society is democratic only by use of a synecdoche that treats a part as the whole. There are theories of democracy that argue for a diffusion of democratic practices beyond the confines of politics, maintaining that political democracy itself needs to be propped up by industrial, associational and other decentralised forms of democracy. But even these theorists rarely demand that most decision-making in society should be done democratically; for democratic criteria may not always be appropriate to either the scope or the locus of the kind of decisions to be taken. Furthermore, democracy may sometimes be too cumbersome and time-consuming to be put into operation, or in certain circumstances prove technically unworkable.

All this is fairly uncontroversial. But when we look at strict political democracy, we find precise limits imposed on its operations. These are embodied in some of the 'guardian' institutions of constitutional democracy (separations of powers, role and autonomy of the judiciary, super-partes roles, etc.), whose nature and function is open to interpretation, and whose justification as limits that democracy imposes on itself is questionable (Bellamy and Castiglione 1997c). So, in the relative sense already described, what is democratic about democratic regimes? The question can be answered from three different perspectives, reflecting issues already raised in discussing democracy's values, but which will now be treated at a more descriptive and institutional level. They are political authorisation, the systemic properties of the political regime, and the aims it pursues.

First, a democratic regime is one where the authorisation of collectively binding political decisions is undertaken by the people. This is a very general precondition, whose fulfilment may require different institutions and rights, depending on how one understands the nature and extent of authorisation. For instance, there are significant differences between direct authorisation and authorisation through representatives; there may be disputes over the criteria that are relevant to the assigning of participatory rights and so on. But in essence, a regime can be defined democratic if the people, as a collectivity, have the formal power, and a number of sufficiently effective means, through which to authorise the basic process of legislation.

Second, a regime is democratic if a number of its systemic features allow citizens, acting as free and equal members of the community, to participate in governance. So (partly following Schmitter 1996b), the regime must be organised in such a way that the forms and channels of access to governmental positions are in principle open to all and their holders significantly influenced by the people; the public realm where collective decision-making applies extends to all those issues that are relevant to ensuring the satisfaction of the members' common interests; and the rules followed in making publicly binding decisions ensure a balance between the competitive (voting, elections, individual interests, etc.) and cooperative (bounded nature of the democratic community, common interests, etc.) aspects of democracy.

Third, and from a more consequentialist perspective, a democratic regime is one that ensures that, on the one hand, ordinary citizens exercise both real influence (through selection and authorisation) and control (through transparency and accountability) over their rulers and, on the other, the political leaders gain sufficient information (through the electoral process and the public sphere) to be responsive in their decisions to the ideals and interests of the ruled.

In sum, democratic regimes are characterised by popular forms of authorisation, governance and influence. However, institutional translation of these properties now clearly appears to be a matter of degree. Democratic regimes are not discrete entities. There are no institutions, rights and practices that in themselves can be regarded as sufficient for the establishment of democracy. Some institutional arrangements, such as universal suffrage, territorial representation, representative legislative assemblies, practices of parliamentary accountability, majority decision and so on, are well rooted in democratic theory and practice, but they have emerged historically, and often contingently, in order to fix ways in which to operationalise democratic authorisation and governance. As a regime, democracy is underdefined, therefore: there is no necessary list of democratic institutions and procedures that are required for people to consent to, influence and control the decisions of their rulers. Nor has democracy even been fully realised in any given regime.

Herein lies the difficulty with talk of a democratic deficit. As Neil MaCormick (1997) and Philippe van Parjis (1998) have recently commented, the issue of the legitimacy of political regimes is not whether there is enough (or a maximum) of democracy but whether there is an adequate (or an optimum) amount. The implications for Europe are that an injection of democratic institutions is not sufficient to give political legitimacy to its system of governance; and, conversely, that addressing the question of the legitimacy of the European regime does necessarily require more democracy. So, what is to be done?

The first task is to make a realistic assessment of how the European system of governance currently works. Of course, there is a vast empirical literature, but from a normative perspective the crucial fact to recognise is that most regimes are of a mixed nature. This point has recently and convincingly been made by Neil MacCormick (1997) with particular reference to Europe. The three main branches of European governance form, in his view, a mix of bureaucratic-oligarchic elements, mainly embodied in the Commission (but one could also add the ECJ), with forms of direct (Parliament) and indirect

(Council) democratic control. This clearly makes for a mixed Constitution, but, as he says, one not 'wholly lacking in democratic elements or democratic spirit' (344). From this perspective, reform of the European mixed regime[13] with regard both to its efficacy (in sustaining integration) and an increase in direct forms of legitimation (which are required by the new intentionalist paradigm) is more a matter of prudence, in designing and adapting institutions, than of acting on democratic imperatives (cf. also Schmitter 1996b; Craig 1997). As we have argued elsewhere, the Constitution of Europe should be seen as reflexive bricolage rather than grand architecture (Bellamy and Castiglione 1997b, 1998a; cf. also MacCormick 1997; Curtin 1997).

The second task is to take seriously the new demands that globalisation and multiculturalism pose to democracy in the twenty-first century. As we have argued, a European democracy needs to confront the issue of political identity by finding institutional means through which to parcel out democratic power in ways that are consistent with the principle of subsidiarity (cf. MacCormick 1997). This is a particularly complex task, not only because of the confusion that still surrounds this principle but also because regime legitimacy meshes with the legitimacy of the polity at this point. As we saw, the mixing and overlapping of sovereignties (multiple Demoi and multilevel governance) make Europe a 'mixed polity'. Yet it is also a 'mixed regime' (or commonwealth), in that there is a mixing of different elements of the rule (in the classical sense of the three forms of government). As things stand, these cannot be considered transient features of the European Union. For its political legitimacy depends on the mixture of elements making up the EU being given democratic recognition and expression through a careful and sensitive allocation of powers and the design of inclusive institutions. A mixed polity requires a mixed regime.

CONCLUSION

The underlying values of democracy favour its status as the only legitimate political regime for modern non-hierarchical societies. On the one hand, it ensures that people (both individually and collectively) are in charge of their own affairs. On the other, its general procedures possess a certain fairness appropriate to egalitarian societies. But though the effects of democratic government are generally positive, they cannot be assumed to be so a priori. Democracy only works if it's embodied in a mix of institutions and decision-making procedures that suit the society to which they apply. The democratic deficit can only be addressed in ways that will resolve the EU's current crisis of political legitimacy, therefore, if the proposed democratic regime matches the mixed character of the European polity.

NOTES

1. Research for this chapter was supported by an ESRC Research Grant on 'Sovereignty and Citizenship in a Mixed Polity' (R000222446). For helpful comments, we thank the editors of this volume and participants in the Bergen Conference on 'Democracy in Europe – Integration and Deliberation', February 1998.

2. Weiler (1999, chap. 7) has made use of the same metaphor, but in a reverse form, so to question the cogency of the ideals of Europe after Maastricht.

3. On the process of integration so far and on its ethics, cf. Bellamy and Warleigh (1998).

4. The list of works taking such a turn is growing rapidly. These are some of them, in no particular order: de Burca (1996), Mancini (1989), Curtin (1997), Weiler (1995, 1996, 1999), MacCormick (1993, 1995, 1997), Habermas (1992b), Joerges (1997), Lehning and Weale (1997), Weale (1994), Weale and Nentwich (1998), Shaw (1996, chap. 6), Preuss (1996), Føllesdal and Koslowski (1998) Bellamy and Castiglione (1995, 1997a, 1998).

5. Notice that all three meanings cut across the descriptive/evaluative distinction. We can describe the institutional arrangements of a democratic regime, but we can also prescribe the minimum (or maximum) level of popular involvement required for a regime to be considered a democracy. Similarly, we can not only identify the values that are supported by actual democratic arrangements but also reverse the perspective and argue that political arrangements are only truly democratic if they support certain values. Finally, the identification of democratic procedures is not just an empirical question, as it will be shown in the next section of this chapter.

6. Cf. Kelsen (1929), who expounds on arguments advanced by classical authors such as Rousseau, Kant and Mill.

7. The democratic ideals of liberty and self-determination can be interpreted from either an individualistic or a holistic perspective. For different views, cf. Weale (1997, 1998), Føllesdal (1998a) and Offe (1998).

8. The criteria of consent can take various forms: explicit, tacit or hypothetical; original, recurrent, or sustained. Different theories of democracy may require some or all of these forms. Autonomy can also be given different contents in its specification. From the particular interpretations given to consent and autonomy depend the kind of tests to which democratic institutions can be put in order to satisfy the criteria of democratic authorisation. For instance, with regard to consent, the form of representation and consultation needed in different moments of democratic politics; or, with regard to autonomy, the extension of the franchise and the extent of participation.

9. For an extended discussion of the normative role of the EP, cf. McCormick (Mimeo).

10. We are assuming that, from a very general perspective, supporters of the various strategies are in favour of the kind and level of integration so far achieved (let us call it the acquis communautaire in a non-technical sense), and that their different suggestions are aimed at sustaining it. We are therefore excluding those who may simply wish to undo the Union, who we take to be a very small minority at this stage. As things move on, of course, supporters of the 'halting' strategy may become less

satisfied with the integration process. For some of these, who genuinely proclaim to be in favour of Europe, monetary union may represent a critical threshold.

11. This is true at least for all those instances where a 'positive' decision is taken; the political exclusion of a minority may instead make a difference for all those cases in which the status quo is upheld.

12. Cf. Føllesdal (1998b) and Weale (1998). Pogge (1998, 184) suggests that, because there is no 'pressing emergency' in Europe, this favours the democratic reshaping of European institutions. This is only partly true, for the reason we have just stated in the main text. The lack of emergency may favour a more considered change, but poses a greater normative burden on the arguments for change.

13. MacCormick calls it a 'mixed commonwealth'. We also used 'mixed commonwealth' in Bellamy and Castiglione (1997a), partly borrowing from MacCormick; but, in fact, we there meant what we now call 'mixed polity' as opposed to 'mixed regime'.

Chapter 13

Still in Deficit

Rights, Regulation and Democracy in the EU[1]

Richard Bellamy

INTRODUCTION

Criticism of the EU's democratic deficit has standardly centred on the absence of a European demos and the shortcomings of its institutional arrangements. Though related, these two arguments also work against each other to some degree. Those who emphasise the first critique focus on the low levels of popular identification with the EU, a factor associated with apathy and even antagonism towards EU politics. According to this argument, the lack of a European 'demos', along with the complexity and distance of European decision-making, necessarily weakens the potential for EU-wide democracy. Advocates of the second critique tend to respond that political identification would be strengthened by enhancing the role of democratic institutions within the EU, particularly the European Parliament. However, supporters of the no-demos thesis counter that such measures would deepen rather than alleviate the EU's democratic deficit. Without a demos, EU-wide democratic decision-making risks producing the majority tyranny of one or more demoi over others. On this view, there are limits to what the EU should attempt to achieve if democratic accountability and legitimacy are to be retained.

Recently, this debate has been reinvigorated by two approaches to the problem that challenge the respective presuppositions of these conventional positions. In rather different ways, these scholars relate the EU's legitimacy problems and democratic deficit to parallel difficulties and changes within the democracies of most advanced industrial societies, many of which stem from the impact on nation states of the very global economic and social processes that have given rise to the EU. As a result, the member states are said to have been similarly afflicted by a weakening of affective national bonds and a loss of confidence in the competence of politicians.[2] They argue that the virtual absence of a demos-based, majoritarian parliamentary model of democracy at the EU level merely reflects its attenuation and partial replacement by new forms of democratic legitimation at the member state level.

What I shall call the 'rights-orientated' strand of this argument suggests EU-wide democracy can work, but it needs to be established on a new basis to some form of European identity.[3] This strand stresses how citizens now tend to justify their claims in terms of rights and regard them as constraints on the behaviour of their compatriots and politicians. A commitment to justice is said to be a more powerful political bond within a pluralist society than ethnicity, history or shared cultural values. Most important, it offers the prospect of a postnational form of democracy suited to the EU. After all, the EU has created a transnational legal system guided by international norms of rights and the rule of law. Though EU law originated to secure the basis for a common market, it has reached beyond the narrowly economic sphere. It now disseminates standards of equality and fairness in a whole range of areas: from consumer protection to the recognition of gay relationships. The Charter of Rights and Constitutional Treaty are seen as the culmination of this process and said to offer an alternative, civic basis for a pan-European constitutional democracy to a shared European identity of an ethnic or cultural kind similar to the nationalisms of the member states. As they note, the potential for rights protection at the EU level already provides a focus for many transnational civil society groups.

By contrast, what I shall call the 'public interest–orientated' strand, while not indifferent to these concerns, argues that democratic accountability plays a diminished role in the operation of most states (the prime examples of this strand are, for example, Majone 1998; Moravscik 2002, 603). It proves not just unnecessary but potentially pernicious. EU governance simply reflects this situation. According to this strand, what matters most to citizens are the securing of certain goods – such as high employment, economic growth and environmental protection. Citizens no longer look to states to provide these directly but indirectly, through regulation. Moreover, policies in these areas are often highly technical and susceptible to being distorted to favour particular powerful private interests. What people want in such fields are expertise, efficiency and equity. They look for Pareto-efficient improvements that correct for market failure. Proponents of this strand argue that the democratic output of policies that reflect such public interests do not require – indeed they may even be subverted by – too much democratic input. There should be consultation with affected parties, but this exercise is for information gathering not to promote democratic accountability or responsiveness. Even at the domestic level, technical regulatory issues tend to be delegated to unelected expert bodies. To the extent the EU merely oversees those regulatory problems best tackled at an international level, and of a kind that democratic politicians in any case handle badly, then the relative absence of direct democratic control poses no problem. In fact, intergovernmental democratic bargaining would inevitably raise transaction costs and might well produce distorted and suboptimal outcomes as politicians sought to protect a variety of national-level interests. The indirect control and checks provided by elected politicians within the Council of Ministers and the European Parliament are sufficient.

These two views appear to be at variance with each other: the one advocating the expansion of democracy on a new basis, the other defending the attenuation of older forms. Indeed, some advocates of 'the rights-orientated view' have criticised what they regard as the utilitarian and instrumental emphasis of 'the public interest–orientated view' (Eriksen and Fossum 2004, 439–41). Yet that criticism is not entirely fair. For the 'public interest' view sees the technocratic setting and upholding of regulatory standards as a parallel to, and constrained by, the judicial maintenance of rights standards (Majone 1996, 286; Moravcsik 2004a, 344–46). In that respect, the rights-based view also seeks to limit democracy. Moreover, to a surprising degree, the two views share certain common normative assumptions: namely, that impartial procedures, fostering deliberation and openness among well-informed and appropriately motivated persons, and consulting with affected civil society groups, will generate a consensus on rights or the public interest in their respective areas.

The following examination of these two accounts concentrates primarily on a normative assessment of their common core. In contrasting ways, both views claim they are more 'realistic' than the standard critiques of the EU's democratic deficit. The 'rights-orientated' theory takes issue with the 'no-demos' thesis and contends the emphasis on nationality as a source of political identity harks back to an outmoded, and often malign, ideal of cultural and ethnic homogeneity (Habermas 1992a, 13–8; Eriksen and Fossum 2004, 443–45). The 'public-interest' view criticises those seeking more democratic decision-making within the EU for applying highly idealised standards of an 'ancient, Westminster-style' democracy (Majone 1996, 285; Moravcsik 2002, 605, 2004a, 337). However, I shall argue that both views involve idealised assumptions of their own that are only credible in the context of the very positions they criticise.

The basic problems can be summarised as follows: (1) Both rights and the public interest are subject to reasonable disagreement. As a result, democratic legitimacy cannot be secured by arriving at an 'objective' view of rights or the public interest that all European peoples could be assumed to espouse, regardless of whether they are actually involved in reaching that view or not.

(2) When independent bodies, such as courts or regulators, set such standards they are often controversial. Within established democracies public pressure can be brought to bear on these bodies in ways that render them broadly responsive to sustained majority opinion. Such pressures are often indirect and inadequate, yet when ignored, in whole or in large part, they give rise to concerns about a national democratic deficit. (3) To the extent a consensus exists on rights or the public interest it is because it reflects the majority view of a demos. Therefore, the possibility of such consensuses cannot be used as substitutes for collective democratic decision-making among a people who accept its legitimacy because they feel a sense of commonality and acknowledge the authority of the state to decide issues of public concern within its territorial sphere. If at least part of the reason the EU suffers from a democratic deficit lies in the absence of a demos, then that deficit may be intensified rather than diminished by the development of EU-level rights or regulatory standards possessing minimal democratic endorsement or control by a yet to be created European people.

I shall start by outlining the nature of such disagreements and the role democracy can play in deciding them. I shall also briefly explore whether democracy at the EU level possesses the same normative qualities to perform this role as at the member state level. I then look in more detail at the merits of the postnational rights–orientated view of EU democracy and a public interest-based delegatory democracy. Both are found wanting, with the democratic deficit a continuing problem.

DEMOCRACY AND DISAGREEMENT

The vast majority of citizens within democracies believe in the importance of rights and regard certain state activities to be in the public interest. However, they also disagree about the character and substance of both, and often divide over the policies most conducive to securing them. No doubt self-interest, prejudice and ignorance lie behind many of these differences. However, they also stem from nothing more sinister than the limitations of the human condition. Not only can various worthwhile goals and values prove either contingently or logically incompatible, and so cannot be contained within one social world, but also our evaluations of which mix should be preferred are subject to conflicting appraisals. Such conflicts need not reflect bias or bad faith but simply what Rawls's calls 'the burdens of judgement' (Rawls 1993, 55–7). These burdens range from the difficulty of weighing empirical evidence to the conscientious employment of differing normative standards. All these elements can produce divergent opinions among even reasonable, well-motivated people. Indeed, they lie at the heart of most political debates and divisions. Debates between right and left over the best mix of public and private in running the economy or the legitimacy of social rights are both legitimate and enduring precisely because they do not admit of any definitive, knock-down solution – even if academics and politicians on each side of these and other issues attempt to offer their alternative answers.

The existence of reasonable disagreement in these areas makes the assumption of an underlying European (or national) consensus on rights or the public interest debatable. It also poses a difficulty for the 'objective' setting of standards by supposedly impartial bodies, such as courts and regulators. Either they will disagree as much as the rest of the population or their agreement will reflect a somewhat false professional consensus that fails to take into account many factors that legitimately matter for ordinary people.

Within democracies such as those existing in all the member states, the problem of reasonable disagreement is largely overcome through appeals to rights and the public interest being nested within a national public sphere and democratic system. Indeed, Albert Weale and Jeremy Waldron see reasonable disagreement on matters that nonetheless require a mutually acceptable collective decision as framing the 'circumstances of democratic politics' in much the same way Hume and Rawls regarded moderate scarcity and limited altruism as forming the 'circumstances of justice' (Waldron 1999, 107–18; Weale 1999, 8–13). Four factors lead citizens to accept the authority of democracy to resolve their differences in these cases. The first three factors serve to establish a political community, the fourth concerns the character of democratic decision-making. First, they must share certain common interests and acknowledge that various collective decisions have to be made if their lives are to go well and social cooperation is to be possible. For example, in the case of certain coordination problems, having an agreed collective decision, even one you do not like, can be better than the uncertainty resulting from having no agreed decision at all. Second, the institution towards which the democratic decision is directed must have de facto and de jure authority over the issue – it can actually deliver and is widely regarded as being entitled to do so. Third, there has to be a degree of trust and solidarity among citizens. They need to believe their fellows will honour their mutual obligations and stand by decisions that go against them, and be prepared to make sacrifices to promote certain public goods and common purposes. Finally, they regard democracy as a fair procedure for selecting a collectively binding decision. Two common misconceptions about democracy need to be avoided in this regard. The language of preferences can suggest collective decision-making to be about satisfying conflicting wants. This characterisation misdescribes the nature of political choice. Rather than straightforwardly expressing their own wants, voters are offering judgements on the nature of their common interests and the best ways to promote them. However, democracy is not about producing the 'right' answer on these matters either. Those on the losing side of a democratic vote rarely concede they were wrong – at most they admit to having misjudged the public mood and may even endeavour to win people round next time. People typically accede to a democratic vote to resolve, rather than to dissolve, their continuing disagreements. Indeed, democracy's attractiveness lies in its not requiring their substantive agreement in order to arrive at an agreed decision. It simply offers a fair way of overcoming differences of opinion that is not intrinsically biased towards any given decision. This fairness consists in treating different views on an equal basis and responding to the majority opinion. It also allows mistakes to be corrected and the losers to try again by permitting the periodic revision of decisions and the removal of those responsible for them (on both these caveats, see Waldron 1999, chap. 5; Weale 1999, chap. 7).

A number of features of actually existing democratic decision-making are worth noting for what follows. First, even local democracy usually involves a large degree of delegation to elected representatives. Switzerland apart, citizens rarely vote on individual policies. Rather, they elect politicians to enact political programmes. Basically, elections screen for politicians possessing certain qualities of political leadership and build coalitions between different groups of people, often by log-rolling and arranging trade-offs between their various policy objectives. By allowing those politicians who disappoint to be deselected, elections provide an incentive for them to pursue policies that are in the interests of stable majorities. This system does not rely on voters offering expert opinions on how the economy works, the causes of crime and the best means of reducing it or any other complex policy issue. They merely choose between the different policy prescriptions of the parties in contention and judge on results. As Max Weber noted in a famous analogy (1978, 1456), elections in this respect resemble consumption in the market – most voters no more know how to run the country than they know how to make shoes, but they know when the shoe pinches and likewise when governments fail.

Second, within all democratic states, certain policies are delegated to bodies that are either formally outside the control of democratically elected politicians, or only very indirectly subject to them – such as central banks, courts and other independent regulatory agencies. However, these bodies are not thereby isolated from any political pressure. Both politicians and public opinion more generally will express views on their performance. Usually, these bodies respond to sustained criticism. Moreover, supplementary political action is often required to give real effect to their decisions – giving politicians an indirect source of control.

Finally, the first three of the four factors noted above are, on most accounts, considerably weaker at the EU level than in the member states. Eurobarometer polls reveal that on average a (bare) majority of Europeans believe they benefit from the EU and view EU institutions reasonably favourably, indicating that by and large the first factor applies – if only for just over 50 per cent of EU citizens. So, by implication, does the second factor – at least for the limited policy sphere in which the EU operates. That said, support is lukewarm even among pro-Europeans. Strong enthusiasm for the EU, like hard-line Euroscepticism, is a minority pursuit.[4] However, identification with the EU and fellow Europeans is far lower, suggesting that the third factor of trust and solidarity is very weak. By and large, around 3 per cent of citizens generally view themselves as 'Europeans' pure and simple, with barely 7 per cent saying a European identity is more important than their national one. By contrast, approximately 40 per cent describe themselves as national only and 47 per cent place nationality first and Europeanness second. Indeed, though 89 per cent of these citizens usually declare themselves attached to their country and 87 per cent to their locality, only 58 per cent feel attached to the EU.[5]

As we shall see, 'public interest' defenders of the EU's democratic deficit often argue that criticisms of the EU's political arrangements apply unrealistic democratic standards. However, it does not seem wildly utopian to expect a degree of democratic accountability and control concerning the overall direction of EU policy, the performance of individual decision-makers and the impact of particular decisions – particularly if, as I shall argue below, the deliberations of delegated bodies prove more contentious than is claimed. The issue then becomes how far such democratic control is achieved, possible or acceptable within the EU. Those who cite the absence of a 'demos' as a limiting factor on EU democracy normally focus on the weakness of the first, second and third factors. The 'rights-orientated' strand comes in here, arguing that a common commitment to justice rather than a shared national identity and public culture provide the best basis for trust and solidarity. The difficulty with this argument is that the ties of justice apply to all human beings – not just one's fellow citizens. Moreover, they are themselves deeply contested. As such, they are too thin and controversial to bind citizens to a specific state as the locus where disagreements about their collective interests and rights might be appropriately negotiated and decided.[6] In addition, a shared culture often provides a common language that facilitates public discussion. Though there are many multilingual states and most are multinational, they have tended towards ever greater autonomy of subnational and sublinguistic units. The key issue concerns how far a set of common entitlements and concerns can allow the EU to buck this trend.

RIGHTS-ORIENTATED POSTNATIONAL DEMOCRACY

The rights-orientated, postnationalist strategy conceives the EU 'as building on … principles and rights that are uniquely European and normatively uncontroversial, since every Member State subscribes to them and since these moral norms are increasingly spread worldwide' (Eriksen and Fossum 2004, 447). Their 'presumption is that public support will reside in a *constitutional patriotism*, which emanates from a set of legally entrenched fundamental rights' (Eriksen and Fossum 2004, 446). These rights provide the basis 'both for protecting the integrity of the individual (private freedom) and for making possible participation in the opinion-formation and decision-making processes (i.e. political rights that establish public freedom)' (Eriksen and Fossum 2004, 445). Indeed, these rights are supposedly both the foundations for and the product of a 'European public sphere'.

I think all these claims are flawed. As I have already noted, there is a problem with viewing rights as sources of a European political identity given their allegedly universal status. That ambivalence is present in the contradictory statement, cited above, to the effect that these principles are 'uniquely European' and yet 'increasingly spread worldwide'. They can be hardly be both. If these rights ought to be (and to a large degree are) upheld by all liberal democracies, including those outside Europe – such as the United States, India, Australia or Japan, then they do not provide grounds in and of themselves for any sort of 'uniquely European' allegiance.

Meanwhile, the belief that rights are 'normatively uncontroversial', in part 'since every Member State subscribes to them' is too simple. All member states do 'take rights seriously'. All adhere to the European Convention on Human Rights and have domestic Bills of Rights of various kinds and some form of rights-based judicial review. But though they share roughly the same liberal democratic values, their valuations of them frequently diverge (Nic Shuibhne 2005, chap. 8). For example, though all acknowledge a 'right to participate', 'freedom of speech' and the other 'political rights that establish public freedom', they have very different political and electoral systems. Consequently, they interpret citizenship rights in correspondingly diverse ways. They also employ different constructions of the fundamental rights 'protecting the integrity of the individual', or 'private freedom', such as the right to life. Thus, Belgium and the Netherlands are the only member states that currently allow certain forms of euthanasia, and even they define and regulate it differently.

These different valuations not only differ from each other but also may conflict. For example, Germany understands privacy and its relationship to freedom of speech somewhat differently to Britain. As a result, Chancellor Schroeder was able to prevent *Die Bild* reporting certain details about his personal life that *The Sun* was allowed to publish. Moreover, not only do member state valuations often conflict with each other, but they may also clash with the valuations offered by the ECJ at the EU level, as cases such as *Grogan* notoriously revealed.

These differences render the notion of rights providing a 'normatively uncontroversial' basis for EU democracy somewhat problematic. The aspiration was to see these rights as somehow transcending national differences, but they now seem to be shaped by them. Of course, it might be objected that all these countries already subject themselves to certain common international rights regimes and accept the rulings of international courts, such as the European Court of Human Rights. Arguably, these regimes do pose problems for a democrat. After all, one of the reasons Britain had for incorporating the ECHR was to 'domesticate' the European Convention by 'bringing rights home', as the White Paper introducing the Human Rights Act put it. However, even placing these difficulties to one side, there is a qualitative difference between the role of an international rights regime, such as the ECHR, and the aspirations postnationalists have for an EU rights–based order. The former operates at the margins. Its function is to ensure that all signatories provide political arrangements and policies that can be regarded as plausible readings of the European Convention and to protect those, such as asylum seekers or foreign nationals, who have no voice in the country's democratic system. Consequently, the ECHR employs abstract formulations compatible with widely differing valuations of rights and grants a 'margin of appreciation' to states in many cases. The latter aims to bring into being a European public sphere based on a shared understanding of rights and so motivate agreement on a federal structure for Europe that in various ways goes beyond national allegiances and political cultures (Eriksen and Fossum 2004, 446/7).

As we have seen, at present no such shared understanding exists – indeed, it has been the attempt of the ECJ to give a 'Community' reading of certain rights that departs from their national meaning that has often been a cause of constitutional friction between it and the constitutional courts of the member states (see Weiler 1999, chap. 3, especially the discussion of Case 44/79, *Liselotte Hauer v. Länd Rheinland-Pfalz* [1979] ECR 3,727 at 108–16). That does not mean that member states cannot participate within a common political system. However, they do so in ways that reflect rather than transcend national traditions. For example, though elections to the European Parliament occur under common rules, member states interpret their European political rights in slightly different ways – using different variants of PR, voting on days that fit with local practices and, most importantly, mainly campaigning on domestic issues and debates about Europe under the guise of the same parties that contest national elections. European parties are largely a post-hoc creation within the European Parliament, with a European public sphere – to the extent it exists – being found only among Euro-elites. The absence of a common language, media, political culture and the growing size of the EU all make a genuine EU public sphere unlikely.

European law and rights have been correspondingly 'international' in character – an ongoing dialogue between different national jurisprudential traditions, negotiated between the ECJ and the courts of the member states, notwithstanding the former's insistence on Supremacy, Direct Effect and its own competence-competence (see Weiler 2003). After all, the ECJ's development of a rights jurisprudence came in large part as a result of rights-based challenges from national constitutional courts. The postnationalists believe these practical compromises detract from a potential European normative consensus, risking incoherence and potentially injustice in the process. Yet, given the diversity of European views on rights, such a consensual view would be a false imposition.

Postnationalists make two responses to this sort of critique. The first rests on the role and supposed democratic credentials of constitutional courts as mechanisms for determining the view of the political community. After all, disagreements about rights exist within the member states as well as between them. In many countries, a court resolves these disputes rather than a democratic process. However, some commentators contend this solution need not be seen as anti-democratic but rather as a way of giving effect to the underlying principles of democracy, notably the showing of equal concern and respect to all citizens, in ways that democratic procedures may not through majorities be influenced by prejudice, ignorance or vested interests. Surely, the ECJ would be acting no differently in being the authoritative interpreter of the European Charter of Fundamental Rights. It would be compensating for the inadequacy of European democratic procedures by expressing the substance of a pan-European democratic consensus.

As with the earlier comparison with other international courts, there is a difference of degree. National Courts are not nearly so insulated from democratic influences as the ECJ. They belong to the domestic political system and come under a great deal of direct and indirect democratic pressure. The US Supreme Court is often portrayed as a model of how rights-based judicial review can forge unity and reinforce democratic values within a federal system. Yet, analysts of the Court have observed how throughout its history it has faced periodic democratic challenges, often shying away from federal adjudication for long periods as a result (e.g. see Devins and Fisher 2004, chap. 3). Few successful Court decisions can fly in the face of sustained national majorities – not least because without legislation and government action to promote and enforce them, they are likely to fall into neglect. Moreover, the main successful anti-majoritarian decisions of the US Supreme Court do not provide a particularly edifying example of the democracy-promoting role of courts or their defence of weak minorities. Made during the Lochner era, these struck down some 150 pieces of labour legislation improving working hours and conditions. Only the overwhelming democratic endorsement of Roosevelt's New Deal could right these injustices. Anti-majoritarian checks can not only protect individual rights but also favour entrenched privileges and vested interests. Litigation tends to be an expensive business, with legal avenues in the EU – as elsewhere – being disproportionately exploited by corporate bodies (Harding 1992, 105). Used excessively, litigation can also stunt the evolution of democratic, collective problem solving, and divert attention to ultimately self-defeating forms of individual redress, particularly in the area of compensation and liability (Harlow 1996, 199). Within the EU, where the absence of a European people or public sphere makes it hard to talk of a European majority or, were it to exist, for it to exert much pressure, the dangers of a Court reinforcing rather than diminishing the EU's democratic deficit are particularly strong.

The postnationalists' second response enters here. They argue that the Charter and the Constitutional Treaty, which incorporates it and makes the ECJ the authoritative interpreter of both, can also claim a degree of procedural democratic legitimacy through being produced by a process of democratic deliberation and subjected to subsequent democratic endorsement by either a referendum or parliamentary vote in each of member states.[7] Many postnationalists have set great store by the 'convention method' (Eriksen and Fossum 2004, 453). Though unelected, the conventions used to draft the Charter and Constitution were comparatively representative bodies. Unlike IGCs, they contained a majority of national and European parliamentarians alongside government and commission representatives, and consulted widely with civil society groups. As a result, the main national, supranational and transnational positions were included, along with the central ideological divisions found within each – even if some groups, notably women and ethnic minorities, were conspicuous by their relative absence. Most importantly from their advocates' point of view, decisions within the conventions were taken not by majority vote but by seeking a consensus. Deliberative democrats contend that, on matters of constitutional principle at least, this requirement should lead to participants relinquishing self-serving and partial views and converging only on those reasons and conclusions that would be acceptable to free and equal individuals. In this way, an ideal European democratic process was to give rise to the foundations for a real European democracy.

It is one thing to regard consensus as the logical goal of democratic deliberation, another to believe it a likely or the only rational outcome. Obviously, postnationalists were all too aware of the limitations of any actual deliberative process. However, they tend to regard all differences stemming from national interests or ideological divisions as illegitimate, the product of partiality or prejudice (Eriksen and Fossum 2004, 454). Yet, their source may well be an alternative understanding of rights, freedom and equality. As we saw, the 'burdens of judgement' make reasonable disagreement on such matters possible. Given that innumerable seminars have not produced a consensus among philosophers on these issues, it is perhaps no surprise that the conventions failed to do so. Instead, they generated numerous compromises, with many disagreements being resolved by framing the right or clause so abstractly as to be compatible with almost any reading. In essence, the Charter – and even more the Constitution – represents not a normative consensus, but the most acceptable pragmatic solution to the practical problems currently facing EU decision-making that those involved could agree to (Bellamy and Schönlau 2004, 412; Magnette and Nicolaïdis 2004, 381).

Their status as a time-bound compromise rather than a timeless consensus substantially weakens the claims that can be made for these documents. They reflect the best deal that elites representing different national and European interests could negotiate in present circumstances, not a move towards pan-European democracy. The subsequent referendums and parliamentary debates appear to confirm this scenario. Rather than exercises in pan-European idealism, the key issue has been whether they will ensure that on balance the country concerned benefits rather than loses from EU membership. At best, the Constitution represents a reasonable modus vivendi for regulating the interactions of the various demoi within the EU. As we have seen, quite a few European citizens doubted even that.

There is a vicious circularity to the postnationalist argument. It posits an ideal democratic European consensus as both the underpinning and the potential result of a (properly constructed) real European democratic process. In other words, it makes an assumed European demos the pretext for attempting to bring it into existence. Any failure for this putative demos to emerge gets attributed to shortcomings in the current ground rules. Yet, this thesis builds its conclusions into its premises, and in practice puts the cart before the horse. Though both the normative and empirical bases for the postnational argument are questionable, the plausibility of each rests on the truth of the other. Absent any consensus, then, as I noted, disagreement standardly gets overcome through majoritarian decision-making – but that assumes a demos of the kind postnationalists seek to do without. Indeed, given that the EU has to cope with diversity as well as disagreement, the current rules with their more consociational and Madisonian features are arguably more legitimate than majoritarian ones would be. However, whether they can claim, or need, democratic legitimacy remains at issue.

PUBLIC INTEREST–ORIENTATED DELEGATORY DEMOCRACY

This position more or less forms the starting point for theorists of the public interest model of delegated democracy. They criticise many democratic theorists for applying ideal, utopian criteria to the complicated reality of the EU, noting that proposals for improving democracy must be not only philosophically coherent but pragmatically viable (Moravcsik 2004a, 337). They contend it is the very absence of a European demos that legitimises the use by the EU of 'non-majoritarian' institutions (Majone 1996, 285). Indeed, in many areas – particularly those that most concern the EU – they note that a subset of such non-majoritarian mechanisms, namely expert, regulatory bodies, have become standard even in otherwise majoritarian democratic systems. Yet, curiously, a similar putative European consensus, this time of a technocratic kind, underlies their arguments.

Delegation, the focus here, has a different rationale to many other non-majoritarian schemes. As Majone rightly notes (1996, 285–87), in complex, plural societies, where the dangers of factionalism and minority oppression are said to be greater, it is common to adopt mechanisms aimed at sharing, dispersing and limiting power. Given the EU is split by a number of deep cleavages, from the distinction between small and large states, to differences of language, religion and political culture, the use of such non-majoritarian mechanisms seems appropriate. As we saw, the basic rationale for majoritarian decision-making is that it is a fair procedure among people who share common interests for deciding among their different judgements as to how these might be best pursued. Many of these non-majoritarian schemes share that same logic. They simply note that for some purposes certain groups' interests may not be common, or may be viewed so differently as to make common rules for determining how they should be pursued unsuitable. Thus, the standard form of dispersing power is to devolve it to a particular locality or region. The aim here is to select the functionally or culturally appropriate majority for the issues in question. The prime strictly non-majoritarian strategies arise where there are territorially dispersed consistent minorities, making the federal/devolved option unavailable. These seek to secure either a threshold voice for a given group or a degree of proportionality in decision-making in order to protect the special interests of those concerned. By contrast, delegation – at least in the area of regulation – assumes that all concerned have common interests, but that, for one reason or another, the judgements of ordinary people or those of their chosen representatives are suspect.[8]

Underlying the 'public-interest' account is a crucial distinction between redistribution and regulation (Majone 1996, 294–96). Redistribution is a zero-sum game. As such, it requires democratic endorsement to legitimise the transfer of resources from one group to another. However, regulation aims at improving efficiency and should be a positive-sum game where everyone gains. Such measures dominate the EU agenda and include the removal of trade barriers to improve the functioning of the market, the promotion of food and safety standards that render us all healthier, and the correction of market failures by tackling such negative externalities as pollution. Yet, though intended to make us all better off, they prove more contentious than the advocates of delegation maintain.

As they at least partially acknowledge, the distinction between redistribution and regulation is not clear cut. Regulation aspires to secure diffuse, long-term benefits, but invariably imposes short-term costs on assignable groups and individuals, often in very specific geographical locations. Thus, many EU regulations have significant redistributional effects with identifiable winners and losers. For example, they tend to favour transnational corporations over smaller enterprises producing for the domestic market. Delegation theorists address this problem by arguing that within the EU a condition of 'no wealth effects' holds (Majone 1996, 295). That is, the temporary, adverse effects of a regulatory outcome can be overcome by compensatory measures through the Social Fund, the European Investment Bank and other similar mechanisms. However, these 'political', redistributive decisions can and should be separated from the technocratic, a-political policy decision about the best means to promote aggregate welfare through enhancing efficiency.

Putting to one side the degree to which the 'no wealth effects' condition truly holds in the EU, the argument still remains problematic. 'Efficiency' can be a contested value – both in itself and more especially as a synonym for sound, mutually beneficial policies that promote the public interest. Like rights, it is subject to the 'burdens of judgement'. Different normative considerations and conflicting empirical assessments, including over what evidence is relevant or not, can all lead to as many disagreements among experts as there are likely to be among ordinary citizens. For example, small, family-run farms may produce fewer crops and at greater expense than larger farms, but they may also be more eco-friendly and preserve rural communities, minimising certain social problems in the process. The efficiency of one over the other is a normative judgement, while calculating the costs and benefits of each to come up with a 'no wealth effects' solution is highly problematic. Thus, not everyone will regard rural communities as worth preserving, the costs of not doing so may turn on a number of contingent factors, there will almost certainly be various unanticipated knock-on effects, while the whole chain of cause and effect may be hard to disentangle. Different social and moral theories are likely to highlight different aspects of the problem. Consequently, it is hard to think of a technical or economic decision with no discretionary elements.

Advocates of delegation have tended to respond to these concerns by contending that democracy remains inappropriate nonetheless, while the process of expert decision-making can claim certain democratic credentials. These two claims largely parallel those defending the democracy-promoting properties of judicial review and constitutional rights examined in the last section:

indeed, courts have come to play an increasing role as the people's tribunes in regulatory governance (Majone 1998, 21/22). They also prove similarly flawed. Like the equivalent rights-based arguments, they tend to overstate the parallels with the apparently analogous domestic arrangements and mischaracterise the purpose and nature of democracy. Let's take each in turn.

Democratic accountability is deemed inappropriate because potentially it has huge transaction costs in such areas and introduces biases favouring well-organised and influential sectoral interests. Delegation at the EU level has the particular advantage of overcoming the under-representation or blocking at the national level of the interests of diffuse transnational minorities or even majorities. Moreover, the issues are claimed to be not that electorally salient for most citizens anyway. They tend to be highly technical and often arcane matters that even elected politicians are happy to delegate to experts. Politicians may also want to delegate so they can make long-term commitments in contentious areas that will not be subject to the vagaries of the electoral cycle while being able to shift the blame on to others should these policies prove unpopular (Majone 1998, 13, 16–8; Moravcsik 2004a, 343–48).

Though plausible enough in theory, many of these arguments prove normatively suspect and practically unfounded. For a start, shifting the possibility of being blamed for contentious policies may not only be a means of insulating long-term interests against short-term popular myopia or prejudice but also a way of evading political responsibility for poor decisions. Complaints of an EU democratic deficit stem in part from the tendency of national politicians to attribute certain economic or other failings to decisions by an anonymous 'Brussels', without acknowledging their own part in them. Second, most political decisions involve abstruse technicalities. However, politicians generally specialise in particular areas and get used to consulting, and evaluating, the advice of a range of expert advisors. Moreover, like ordinary citizens, they tend to be especially and legitimately sensitive to the good or bad consequences of policies. Third, Moravcsik and Majone arguably overplay the domestic analogy, underestimating the ways elected politicians control non-majoritarian regulatory bodies in the member states. The autonomy of domestic regulatory bodies is generally limited by various screening and sanctioning mechanisms that allow the political principals to control their technocratic agents. Though many formal instruments appear too costly and arduous to employ with any regularity, potentially impugning the neutrality of the agency and thereby undermining its chief asset, or risking associating the political principals with any failure, a range of less overt and informal measures arguably prove more effective. By selecting friendly yet independent experts, with no direct party or other link to government, and managing the effectiveness of the body through their hold on information or role in implementing its recommendations, politicians can shape the institutional incentives in such ways that regulators propose congenial policies (Thatcher 2005, 347). At the EU level, the plurality of principals and the ability of the Commission to develop a complex network of overlapping agencies, all reduce this influence while introducing the dangers of conflicting forms of accountability. Meanwhile, the possibilities for regulatory capture are increased by the closeness of EU regulation to various 'stakeholders' – notably business and unions (Coen and Thatcher 2005, 341/42). Finally, domestic regulators come under diffuse public pressure from the media and other organs of the national public sphere – a pressure that is far harder to exert at the EU level given the virtual absence of a pan-EU public sphere.

For example, the paradigm case of delegated regulatory power is often taken to be the fixing of interest rates by a central bank. Typically viewed with approval (Majone 2000, 288/89), there is always the danger these regulators will serve the interests of the financial community rather than those of producers and consumers. For far from being pure technical exercises, such decisions have an obvious political dimension involving as they do judgements over the best balance between the risks of inflation and those of higher levels of unemployment (McNamara 2002). As we saw, appeals to efficiency do not get us very far because the factors that might lead one to characterise one position as more 'efficient' than another may be partly 'ideological'. Different economic theories tend to involve value and other judgements that favour and draw on different political perspectives. As a result, the separation of 'policy' from 'politics' is far from clear cut.

These are also decisions that ordinary citizens have a strong interest in, even if most would not claim to have a very sound knowledge of how the economy works or much of an interest in fiscal policy per se. Defenders of delegation sometimes write as if those worried by the EU's democratic deficit are advocating a return to ancient Greece and judging its arrangements by 'an ideal form of perfectly participatory, egalitarian, deliberative politics' (Moravcsik 2004a, 343). Thus, Moravscik proclaims that 'We do not expect complex medical, legal or technical decisions to be made by direct popular vote' (2004, 344). Quite – but whoever suggested we did?[9] By and large, we leave such decisions to professional politicians, who, operating in committees and government departments – invariably with the advice of experts – reveal themselves able to formulate very sophisticated policies in such sensitive and technical areas as taxation. As I remarked above, democratic accountability usually gets exercised post-hoc, when the 'shoe' fails to 'fit'. Citizens may be poor economists but they know when the economy lets them down. Democracy is all about giving politicians an incentive to respond to the needs of the public rather than powerful sectoral interests or fashionable economic theories.

Within the member states, regulatory bodies tend to be embedded within a national democratic culture. Even if banks control interest rates, they can come under public scrutiny via the press and considerable indirect political pressure.[10] Indeed, in the UK (as in New Zealand) the inflation target is set politically, and the Governor can be held accountable if the Bank fails to meet it. The same is true of other regulatory bodies, especially those in the service sector where popular sensitivity to their actions is high. Here, too, policy, as opposed to its implementation, remains firmly under political control. By contrast, such scrutiny is often limited at the EU level. The ECB is particularly insulated, being able to make legally binding regulations without involving the national or European parliaments or other EU institutions.[11] For the reasons explored earlier regarding the absence of an EU-wide public sphere, informal pressures are also much harder to achieve for EU bodies.

Defenders of delegation attempt to rebut some of these criticisms by invoking the democratic qualities instilled by the regulatory bodies themselves. Though delegation aims to isolate the policy-making process from politics, it is said to possess many of the formal, procedural attributes of democratic decision-making. Great play has been made in recent accounts of their 'deliberative' and 'professional' qualities, whereby experts – who are normally national appointees, and so supposedly representative of various local interests – come to adopt more 'cosmopolitan' and impartial outlooks (Majone 1996, 291–94, 2000, 295–98, and see deliberative accounts of the comitology process in Joerges and Vos 1999). However, we have seen there are no reasons for believing deliberation will any more produce a consensus on 'efficiency' than on 'rights'. If any argument involves a naïve, utopian idealisation of the democratic processes, it is surely this claim. Should a consensus emerge, then it probably bears witness simply to the current dominance of a particular view among the profession (Shapiro 2004/5, 9/10). As such, this apparent consensus will reflect more the common identity of the body's members as 'experts' than a convergence of national interests. Nor should we regard the isolation of the decision from such concerns as a good thing. Experts have an unfortunate tendency to overlook issues that are legitimate worries for ordinary folk. People's everyday contact with doctors, lawyers and other professionals means they are well aware that experts can make mistakes or overlook the dilemmas facing those they are supposed to serve. Their use by politicians to bolster unpopular decisions has also resulted in their being scarcely distinguishable from their political masters. Certainly, episodes such as BSE and the French Blood scandal have somewhat tarnished technocracy in the eyes of European citizens. Of course, politicians can introduce compensatory measures post-hoc when certain groups are adversely affected. But it seems naïve to expect the national politicians likely to be held responsible for such costs to wait until the damage is done before seeking to rectify it – especially if they have to gain the consent of possibly unaffected European partners in order to do so.

It's partly to address these problems that there have been moves to make regulatory bodies more transparent and consultative. Majone, in particular, appeals to the American experience in this regard (2000, 293–95). However, the United States proves an ambiguous model, with the differences as instructive as the parallels (Shapiro 2004/5, 5/6). The US bodies originated as creatures of the highly democratically legitimate Roosevelt Presidency as a way of overcoming some of the counter-majoritarian checks on the federal administration. Their opening up was championed largely by a Supreme Court suspicious of technocracy and presidential power. The aim was not to depoliticise these bodies but to ensure a greater degree of political balance within them. Unfortunately, these measures have had mixed results. The guarantees of openness and participation have been mainly used by those interest and other groups best able to organise and fund a team of counter-experts to those favoured by the regulators. Their efforts have often produced regulatory capture or expert stalemate, with specialist courts ending up making the decisions. Majone echoes certain US scholars in justifying this judicial control of the regulatory process as the most functionally appropriate means for protecting individual rights through its being 'insulated from political responsibility and unbeholden to self-absorbed and excited majoritarianism' (Choper 1980, 68, cited in Majone 1998, 22). Thus, a measure that began as a majoritarian initiative for overcoming entrenched counter-majoritarian privileges and interests blocking federal schemes has now been turned into yet another counter-majoritarian strategy, albeit one that claims to articulate a consensus on the public interest and rights. We have come full circle, with the regulatory case for delegation dovetailing with the rights-based argument. Yet, as we saw, both the threats posed by majoritarianism and the democracy and rights promoting credentials of courts are at best contentious. Indeed, there has been something of a democratic backlash against the US agencies amid calls for more effective presidential coordination of economic and other policies (Shapiro 2004/5, 13).

Similar moves within the EU are likely to encounter parallel problems. The White Paper on Governance has been seen as an attempt to open up the technocratic process and boost its democratic credentials by insisting on not only greater openness but also consultation and participation (European Commission 2001, 11–9). However, despite the rhetoric about involving the 'general public', the main proposals for consultation refer to 'civil society organisations', 'interested parties', 'partners' and 'stakeholders' (European Commission 2001, 11, 14, 15, 17, 21). There is a single, ritually pious reference to the importance of European political parties and none at all to their rather more substantial national counterparts. Although the White Paper recognises the dangers of consulting what are often self-selecting and unaccountable bodies, the proposals it offers for overcoming the resulting biases are largely superficial. Therefore, this policy still risks favouring well-funded groups whose interests may well be at variance with that of the public at large. None of these groups need be particularly democratic themselves and involve the citizens they allegedly speak for in their decisions. This weakness is even truer of most consumer and public interest organisations than of certain producer groups. After all, unions at least have a degree of internal democracy. Worse, the ability of many NGOs to criticise regulatory proposals is often constrained by their reliance on EU funds, itself a sign of their low levels of membership (Warleigh 2001, 619). The Commission claims to be able to exercise a general supervisory role, yet unlike elected national executives this too is a technocratic body. The ECJ has also been invoked as being able to ensure due process, yet this will either be purely formal or lead the Court into seeking to second guess the substantive conclusions of democracy. In fact, Americanisation has gone less far than delegatory theorists imagined, with the European Parliament playing an increasing part in overseeing comitology. However, if delegatory theorists are right in believing that the cleavage structure of the Union makes an EU demos unworkable, then the EP's involvement will likewise involve a democratic deficit. In whichever case, the aspiration to substitute technocracy for democracy seems empirically and normatively questionable.

CONCLUSION

Both the rights-based and the public interest arguments attempt to overcome the weaknesses of democratic legitimacy within the EU by positing an EU consensus that can be arrived at by a 'non-political' democratic procedure. At the same time, they tend to mischaracterise the nature and effects of the forms of majoritarian democratic accountability found in most of the member states. Since neither their alternatives nor their criticisms appear that convincing, the standard versions of the EU's democratic deficit retain their force. If an EU demos can be said to exist, then a move should be made towards enhancing the role played by directly elected majoritarian decision-making bodies within the EU. If, as seems more likely, an EU demos and public sphere remain absent with little immediate prospect of being established, then means need to be found for enhancing the democratic accountability of EU decision-makers within the established democracies of the member states.[12] Either way, the current limitations of EU democracy place democratic limits on what the EU should do – even in the name of rights or the public interest.

NOTES

1. An earlier version of this chapter was given at a Conference on Shifting the Boundaries of Sovereignty: Governance and Legitimacy in the EU and Australasia, organised by the National Europe Centre, ANU, and is based on research undertaken while a Visiting Fellow at the Centre as part of the 'Democracy Task Force' of the EU-funded 6th Framework Integrated Project on New Modes of Governance (Contract No CIT1-CT-2004-506392). Later versions have been delivered to the NoSoPhi seminar at the Université Paris 1, the Second Annual Conference of the Consortium on Democratic Constitutionalism at the University of Victoria on 'Supranational Political Community: Substance? Conditions? Pitfalls?' and the Graduate School of Politics and International Studies, Hull University. I'm grateful to the other participants at these events for their comments and to Neil Walker, Jo Shaw, Chris Hilson, David Coen, Andrew Moravscik and Albert Weale for written remarks.

2. It's noticeable, for example, that the White Paper on European Governance explicitly treats the EU's legitimacy problems as symptomatic of various common difficulties confronting advanced democracies more generally (European Commission 2001, 3).

3. The most prominent exponent of this view is Jurgen Habermas (see 1992a, 2001a). Among the many others promoting this strand, see Eriksen, Fossum, and Menéndez (2002, 1–11).

4. For example, when the image of the EU is broken down into 'very positive' and 'fairly positive', then around 7–10 per cent opt for the former category and 35–40 per cent for the latter. A similar division can be found in most assessments of the EU, with the overall positive view fluctuating around 50 per cent with a small but steady decline in support among long-term members, albeit with large differences between member states. See Blondel, Sinnott, and Svensson (1998, 56–62).

5. These figures come from Eurobarometer 60 (2004), and the results of earlier studies reported there. I have used results based on the old fifteen rather than the new twenty-five because these can be placed in the context of a general trend. Figures from Eurobarometer 62 (2004) reveal the new members to be on average a little more positive about the benefits coming from the EU. As a result, the slow decline in approval of the EU from the high point reached in the early 1990s appears, temporarily at least, to have been slightly reversed. In fact, new members almost always boost average support for the EU, after which it declines slightly. The figures relating to identity have been remarkably stable over the past decade or so (see Blondel, Sinnott, and Svensson 1998, 62–5).

6. Arguably Rawls himself partly acknowledges this fact when he explicitly assumes cultural attachments as undergirding agreement on the principles of justice in Rawls (1993, 277).

7. With the French 'Non' and the Dutch 'Nee', the second aspect of this claim has obviously proved false. Yet, the reactions of many academics and EU figures suggest this outcome was largely unexpected and certainly unprepared for.

8. Moravcsik (2004a, 344–46, 355–56) draws a parallel between regulation and judicial review in the area of rights. Some accounts do suggest the rationale for the

judicial protection of rights is to guard against the prejudices or carelessness of voters. As I have implicitly noted in the last section, such arguments are weak. A better case follows the logic of most other non-majoritarian institutions – namely, that we need some way of protecting those who do not share sufficient common interests with the collectivity, or have special interests requiring protection, or who have no say in democratic decision-making. Examples of such groups include children or asylum seekers.

9. The relevant article is rather short on references, but Dahl and pluralists more generally – to name but one name/group of thinkers who are mentioned, seem unlikely candidates for this sort of characterisation. Dahl does criticise 'guardianship' somewhat trenchantly, but not in the name of some utopian ideal democracy but against real, Schumpeter style, competitive party democracy of the kind most actually existing democracies aspire to for most political decision-making (Dahl 1989, chap. 4).

10. See, for example, the following article from the very day I drafted this paragraph – Larry Elliott, 'Manufacturing Woe Raises Rate Pressure', *The Guardian*, 2 June 2005, p. 25.

11. Moravscik (2002, 621) does acknowledge this isolation in the ECB case as a problem, even if Majone regards it as an asset (1996, 288/89).

12. I have explored this issue in Bellamy (2006b).

Chapter 14

Democracy without Democracy?

Can the EU's Democratic 'Outputs' Be Separated from the Democratic 'Inputs' Provided by Competitive Parties and Majority Rule?[1]

Richard Bellamy

Notwithstanding Schattschneider's famous remark that 'modern democracy is unthinkable save in terms of political parties' (Schattschneider 1942, 1), political theorists and political scientists have come increasingly to think the unthinkable. Normative theorists have long been tempted to distinguish the ideal of democracy from the modern reality, favouring the various ideas Joseph Schumpeter lumped together as the 'classic theory' of democracy over his 'other model' of 'that institutional arrangement for arriving at political decisions by means of a competitive struggle for the people's vote' (Schumpeter 1976, 269). While these scholars view this alternative as an accurate account of actual democratic practice, they regard it as normatively limited (e.g. Duncan and Lukes 1963). Meanwhile, declining party membership and voter turnout has begun to challenge the descriptive value of this model, prompting a number of political scientists also to return to the 'classic theory' as a source of democratic ideals that might be better realised by somewhat different democratic practices to those found in most working democracies (e.g. Dalton 2004).

The EU has offered particularly fertile ground for such thinking (Cohen and Sabel 1997; Majone 1998, 2001; Moravscik 2002; Sabel and Zeitlin 2007). With the traditional forms of competitive party democracy and majority rule proving harder to establish and more attenuated at the EU level than in any of the member states, it has become a veritable laboratory of new modes of democratic governance. The basic normative claim of these schemes has been to see democracy in terms of 'outputs' rather than 'inputs'. 'Input' considerations relate to the democratic character of the decision procedure, and in particular the right of all citizens to participate on an equal basis in political decision-making. By contrast, 'output' considerations relate to the degree to which the substance of the decision can be said to promote collective interests in a manner compatible with the democratic goals of equal concern and respect (Scharpf 1999a, 2, 6–13). Their proponents argue that the 'actual existing' model of majoritarian, party democracy may have reasonable, if weakening, credentials on 'input' grounds, but what counts are democratic 'outputs'. These might be achieved better by more idealised forms of democratic decision-making that possess limited conventional democratic 'input'. Indeed, such limitations may be necessary to obtain democratic 'outputs' due to distortions in the standard 'input' process.

What follows explores the merits of 'input' and 'output' democracy in relation to the EU. I start by outlining the basic arguments for democratic 'input', noting how they are broadly met by a system comprising majority rule and competing parties. I then examine two versions of the 'output' argument found in both the literature, and the EU's structures and policies. Neither can justify curtailing democratic inputs. The conclusion briefly proposes how 'input' and 'output' considerations might be met within the EU given the persistent difficulties experienced in establishing the former.

'INPUT' DEMOCRACY

Some commentators suggest 'input' arguments carry no independent weight apart from their contribution to a certain kind of 'output'. Thus, Fritz Scharpf in his influential use of this distinction within EU studies argues that 'modern input-orientated theorists rarely derive legitimacy primarily from the belief "that the people can do no wrong". Instead, they insist that policy inputs should arise from public debates that have the qualities of truth-orientated deliberations and discourses' (Scharpf 1999b, 269). He suggests 'input' assumes not just 'participation' but also convergence on a 'consensus' that reflects the general will – itself only likely among a demos sharing a strong cultural identity, so that 'the justification of majority rule must be considered as the crucial problem of input-orientated theories of democratic legitimization' (1999a, 7). However, this argument misrepresents much mainstream work in democratic theory (e.g. Dahl 1989; Weale 2007), while overlooking why we might value 'input' in itself. Liberal societies regard people as entitled to go their own way, even at the expense of making mistakes. True, part of the reason is so they may learn from their errors. But more significant is the importance of treating individuals as responsible agents, the empirical difficulties as well as the problematic moral justifiability of others defining what is right for someone else, the dangers posed by even an enlightened despotism given human fallibility and so on. None of these issues imply individuals can do no wrong, merely that it is more legitimate for them to take decisions – even wrong ones – than for others to take them on their behalf, especially given these others may err about what is good for them too. Such factors motivate the 'input' account of democracy as much as considerations about good 'outcomes'.

Three related arguments play a key role in justifying democracy: considerations of political equality; the reasonableness of political disagreement and the proneness to the fallibility of most human decision-making; and the need to ensure politicians are accountable and responsive to the public interest (Weale 2007, chap. 3). All three reinforce the importance of 'input' considerations as vital to, and to some degree having a quite independent force from, 'output' considerations.

Many accounts prioritise autonomy rather than equality (e.g. Lakoff 1996, 163; Held 2006, chap. 10). However, viewing democracy as a system of self-government proves hard to sustain (Christiano 1996, chap. 1; Weale 2007, 106–15). All but the most civic minded will experience some tension between their pursuit of personal autonomy in the private sphere and participation in public decision-making. Private autonomy may depend on a public system of rules, giving us an instrumental incentive to play a part in shaping them – a point central to the third argument for democracy. Yet, seeing these collective arrangements as expressions of individual autonomy requires fairly stringent demands be met that amount to a form of anarchism unlikely to be realisable (Wolff 1970). Not only is it improbable that all public decisions could reflect a consensus on what each citizen regards as necessary for their private autonomy but also designing a decision-making procedure in which such a result could theoretically be achieved is practically impossible, given that it would have to include the opportunity to vote on all conceivable options for any potential collective decision. Some accounts that adopt this model seek to overcome these difficulties by employing perfectionist reasoning about the goods and rights needed for individuals to be 'truly' autonomous. These theories tend to shade into 'outcome' versions of democracy – stipulating so many preconditions for citizens to exercise their private and public autonomy that little remains to be decided by the democratic process (e.g. Held 2006, 282). Indeed, their democratic credentials seem circular, stipulating what kinds of 'output' would be democratic and making these preconditions of the democratic process. By contrast, an 'input' perspective distinguishes a process that accords each person equal standing as an autonomous reasoner about our collective life from one that produces decisions that might correspond to and not inhibit the autonomous decisions of each and every citizen. Whereas the latter may be impossible to achieve, the former follows from any process that accords us an equal weight in making and contesting decisions.

The second argument enters here, noting how democratic procedures reflect the need to make collective decisions in the 'circumstances of politics', where those concerned have valid differences about the justification or advisability of different policies based on potentially incommensurable and incompatible normative and empirical judgements (Weale 2007, 12–8; Waldron 1999, 107–13). As Rawls noted, not all political disagreements arise out of, malign, selfish or myopic thinking. Most result from ideological divisions that reflect reasonable disagreements stemming from the 'the burdens of judgement': namely, 'the many hazards involved in the correct (and conscientious) exercise of our powers of reason and judgement in the ordinary course of political life' (Rawls 1993, 55/6). They involve both the empirical difficulties within complex and open societies of weighing up evidence, identifying causal processes, and estimating the consequences of different decisions and policies, and the normative difficulties of assessing which factors are morally relevant or how moral factors of different kinds might be combined or prioritised, overcoming the vagueness of our concepts, especially when it comes to hard cases, and reconciling the divergent moral and political views that people's different life experiences may lead them to adopt (Rawls 1993, 56/7). Accordingly, a consensus is unlikely on what course of action best promotes the public interest on any given issue. Rather, people will hold numerous alternative and potentially equally valid points of view. Consequently, democracy cannot be defined by 'outputs' that supposedly enshrine the democratic values of equal concern and respect. Instead, we need equitable 'input' processes for reaching and contesting decisions – including decisions about these very processes – that ensure all views obtain an equal hearing and policies can be reviewed in the light of evolving views and experience.

Finally, political equality and the 'circumstances of politics' require rulers to be accountable and responsive to the ruled. If political equality demands all citizens be treated equally in their capacity as autonomous reasoners and sources of information about their collective life, while the circumstances of politics suggest they will often disagree, make mistakes and change their minds, then we need mechanisms to encourage rulers regularly to consult the ruled and accord them equal concern and respect. These incentives come from institutionalising ways of screening politicians to select those inclined to respond to public views in an even-handed and effective way, and sanctioning them when they do not, are incompetent or their policies prove flawed.

Taken together, these three arguments give citizens an interest in processes that respond to their concerns in ways that are fair and impartial. Meanwhile, they need not regard the results as 'right', merely as legitimate. What it counts is being included in the process, having their views treated on a par with everyone else, and not feeling permanently excluded from consideration. If a core function of democracy is to allow necessary binding collective decisions to be made despite valid disagreements and uncertainty about their potential effects, these qualities seem vital. In addition, they promote mutual respect and reciprocity among citizens. For the losers in any vote are not being told they are mad or bad, merely that they have been outvoted. Moreover, they can hope to win in future – a possibility that invariably gives them some influence even when they lose.

The case for the Schumpeterian model of democracy that characterises the twenty or so 'working democracies' worldwide lies in its capacity to meet these three 'input' criteria to an adequate degree (Bellamy 2007, chap. 6). Indeed, those that perform best on Freedom House measures tend to be the democracies with the least deviations from this model towards 'output' democracy of the sorts examined below (Dahl 2002, 164/5). The Schumpeter model has two basic elements: majority rule and party competition. Together they promote political equality, respect the circumstances of politics, and ensure decisions are both responsive and accountable.

Majority rule offers a fair and impartial equal weighing of votes that is anonymous, neutral and positively responsive as well as decisive (May 1952). Moreover, the Condorcet jury theory suggests that if there is a better than even chance people are more right than wrong, then the probability is that the majority view will indeed be right too – with that probability increasing dramatically the higher the majority (Condorcet 1976). What about the problems Condorcet revealed of cyclical majorities, and the related Arrovian issues of instability, incoherence or manipulation? Mackie (2003) has shown, though logically possible, these phenomena are rare – not least because party competition socialises voters so their preferences resemble each other sufficiently for cycles to be unusual and eliminable by relatively simple decision rules. Competition in a two-dimensional space also promotes convergence on the median voter, which is generally the Condorcet winner (Ordeshook 1986, 245–57). In these respects, elections do work as a process of 'truth-orientated deliberation' that precedes the simple aggregative phase. Moreover, the fact that most majorities within pluralist societies are shifting coalitions of minorities, means that the proneness of any ruling coalition to cycling gives it an incentive to reach out beyond its immediate membership to excluded groups to retain power (McGann 2004, 56, 71).

These standard features of a Schumpeterian 'actually existing democracy' promote political equality because they instantiate the status of voters as political equals – none has a lower status than anyone else and all are potentially involved in decisions. It meets the 'circumstances of politics' because majority voting on the basis of one person, one vote offers an impartial mechanism for resolving disagreements that neither is biased towards any view nor assumes the superiority of any one of them. However, the dynamics of party competition also encourage equality of concern as well as respect through instituting a 'balance of power' between both different sections of the electorate and rulers and ruled. The need to construct majorities from shifting coalitions of minorities while converging on the median voter means that voters are effectively forced to compromise with each other. Party programmes involve trade-offs between millions of voters that involve either bargains that seek to split the difference between different sets of preferences or identifying agreed second bests. Because an alternative government always waits in the wings, governments must engage in an almost daily referendum, whereby policies are updated in anticipation of a future election. As a result, they are responsive to and accountable for changing attitudes and conditions and policy failure (Bellamy 2007, chap. 6).

None of the above means majoritarian, competitive party democracy works perfectly or even, given voter decline, is in good health. Merely that when it functions reasonably well – with either a plurality or some proportional electoral system – it has the capacity to reflect a coherent set of 'input' criteria. Moreover, these 'input' qualities invariably have positive benefits for the quality of 'outputs'. It is against this background that the adoption of pure 'outcome' approaches needs to be assessed.

'OUTPUT' DEMOCRACY

Scharpf defines 'output' democratic legitimacy as 'collectively binding decisions that "serve the common interests of the constituency"' (Scharpf 1999b, 268; 1999a, 11). Differentiating such decisions from those that result from standard democratic 'inputs' turns on one of two claims (Scharpf 1999a, 12/13, 16; Majone 1998, 2001). On the one hand, 'non-majoritarian' arguments suggest an appropriate process exists for determining substantive democratic outcomes, at least in certain well-defined domains. These render 'input' arguments unnecessary and possibly even subversive of democratic ends. On the other hand, counter-majoritarian arguments seek to correct supposed distortions of the 'input' process so that these favour more equitable outcomes – something especially necessary in culturally diverse societies that do not share a national political identity. Both mechanisms are rampant within the EU. The ECJ, ECB and a host of standard-setting bodies are allegedly 'non-majoritarian'. Co-decision procedures and consensual or qualified majority voting in the Council of Ministers are counter-majoritarian in requiring supermajorities on the grounds that only in this way will the common interests of all concerned be addressed in an equitable manner.

These two arguments share the view that standard democratic 'inputs' distort decision-making by registering false 'positives' or false 'negatives' (Pettit 2004, 60). Non-majoritarian mechanisms aim at avoiding false 'positives'. Their proponents fear electoral incentives could lead politicians to attend too much to unrepresentative groups, such as voters in marginal seats, actual or potential donors to their campaigns, or others able to exercise pressure disproportionate to their electoral strength through their place within the economy, media or other potential sources of social influence on voters' behaviour. Or they may sacrifice long-term goals to short-term electoral advantages – for example, by promising tax cuts that undermine the capacity of future governments to pay for infrastructural improvements. Politicians may also be in a position to skew elections in their own favour, thereby avoiding electoral accountability – say, by manipulating constituency boundaries. In such cases, if the criteria of a fairer and more efficient 'output' are widely agreed, and the means for achieving it technical matters where what counts is expertise rather than political support, then 'depoliticising' strategies that remove such decisions from the influence of democratic 'inputs' may be in the public interest. Counter-majoritarian mechanisms aim at false 'negatives'. This danger arises with consistent minorities. Even in systems of proportional representation (PR), the logical possibility exists for a majority to exclude minority views from the agenda. Counter-majoritarianism seeks to give them a hearing.

Unfortunately, neither of these mechanisms proves better at tackling the respective problem each address than standard 'input' mechanisms, while risking creating the difficulty they neglect – false negatives in the first case, and false positives in the second. Their failings derive from both possessing parallel vices to the virtues of 'input' democracy – namely, not respecting political equality, overlooking the 'circumstances of politics', and being unresponsive and lacking accountability (Bellamy 2009).

Non-majoritarian

There are two forms of non-majoritarian, non-party democracy. The first appeals to deliberation among experts, the second to direct deliberative democracy among the people as a whole or some selected subset. Each claims to be more 'truth orientated', because better designed to weigh impartially all aspects of a problem, than majoritarian democracy. Neither effectively grounds that claim.

Democratic expertise has supplied the main argument for the non-majoritarian account of 'output' democracy (Majone 1996, 1998, 2001; Scharpf 1999a, 15/16; Moravscik 2002). This case turns on a distinction between 'redistributive' and 'regulatory' policies and argues that majoritarian or

counter-majoritarian measures may be appropriate for the former but are
unnecessary or even pernicious for the latter (Majone 1996, 294–96). In the
regulatory arena, citizens look for Pareto-efficient improvements that correct
for market failure. Such measures are the bread and butter of the EU but,
being win-win and highly technical, are uncontentious and consequently
have low electoral salience. These policies require expertise, equity and
efficiency – qualities best provided by experts representing national interests,
yet isolated from short-term electoral considerations or powerful pressure
groups, which tend to produce suboptimal solutions and raise transaction
costs as various influential interests get bought off.

There is a weak version and a strong version of this non-majoritarian
argument. The strong version resembles what Dahl calls guardianship (Dahl
1989, chap. 4). It assumes the availability in certain areas of something like a
science of the public good, and that only specialists will possess such knowledge. The weak argument suggests merely that experts are more likely (or,
in an even weaker version, are as likely) to make conscientious and informed
decisions about certain policies because they are freer from some of the
potentially malign incentives that exist in a system of majority rule.

Given their distinction between redistributive and regulative measures,
Majone and Schapf apparently grant that we have no epistemological grounding for our moral ontological claims to compare with a mathematical proof
or the experimental method in natural science. The difficulty is that most
'purely' technical decisions raise normative issues and are often less clear
cut empirically than is claimed (Bellamy 2006, 734–42). Even policy decisions that rest on reasonably well-attested natural scientific arguments cannot
be decided by scientific experts alone. Thus, scientific arguments for global
warming still leave open a wide range of moral and political choices about
how it might best be tackled, with experts disputing the equity, efficiency or
effectiveness of particular measures. Social science invariably yields even
less clear-cut policy advice. Social scientists may be experts on particular
policy areas, but can never fully account for – and lack expertise in – knock-
on effects in other areas, many of which are unpredictable innovations,
behavioural changes, acts of God and the like. Expert judgements inevitably
rest on assumptions about the way of the world, how things work or people
behave that are at best gross if necessary simplifications, at worst not very
rigorous guesses. Consequently, it is hard to think of a technical decision
without discretionary elements. We know, for example, that differing economic theories or divergent best guesses about how the world economy is
going lead economic advisors to central banks often to disagree about interest
rate increases or decreases (McNamara 2002).

It is sometimes claimed that their disagreements can nonetheless be
resolved more consensually as result of their engaging in a more deliberative

and 'truth orientated' discursive process than, say, legislatures. Whereas the latter involve self-interested bargaining and block votes, the former employ a more public model of reason giving that reflects clear norms of argumentation deriving from shared criteria about a 'good' argument (Pettit 2004; Sunstein 1993, 24/5). Joerges and Neyer (1997) defend comitology on these grounds as deliberative fora where a problem-solving approach overcomes national bargaining to produce agreements that favour the supranational public interest. However, not only are electoral campaigns and debates in legislatures and committees not devoid of deliberation, but the argument also overestimates the epistemic qualities of deliberation itself and the degree to which it takes place (Pollack 2003). Experts can be particularly susceptible to 'group-think', which may be reinforced rather than challenged by such processes. Insider, expert norms can be self-serving products of an entrenched paradigm within a given professional community that may have become immunised from critical scrutiny and/or the legitimate concerns of citizens. Even if deliberation is full, open and critical, valid disagreements may remain – as participants in any seminar know. When a collective decision is needed, these disputes are generally resolved by the much-derided majority vote. We have no reason to believe that the votes of expert bodies are less prone to cycles. Indeed, given the small numbers involved, so that whoever chairs is more likely to know the preference orderings of his or her colleagues, they may be much more liable to arbitrary manipulation arising from agenda setting and voting schedules (Bellamy 2009; Janis 1982; Gambetta 1998).

The weaker version enters here, claiming these expert bodies are nonetheless better informed than the average citizen on such matters. As Moravsick remarks, 'We do not expect complex, legal or technical decisions to be made by direct popular vote' (Moravsick 2002, 344). True – but the 'input' argument never suggested they should be, merely that voters be able to choose between various packages laid out before them in terms they can understand and hold to account those who fail to deliver. For voters can register 'policy spillovers' a given expert body lacks the competence or feedback to tackle or appreciate. Politicians regularly seek expert advice and have proven able to formulate sophisticated policies in such areas as taxation. Yet they must also respond to citizens who, though not economic experts or criminologists, feel the broad effects of a poorly performing economy or rising levels of crime. Most domestic non-majoritarian regulators are embedded within majoritarian systems. It is not just that elected politicians can influence domestic regulatory bodies through various formal or informal screening and sanctioning mechanisms; such bodies are also subject to public opinion through the media. Courts, banks, medical bodies all find it hard to buck sustained national majorities. Such pressures are much less evident in the EU because its public sphere is vestigial and political control and responsiveness more

muted.[2] Worse, the possibilities of regulatory capture may be increased by
the closeness of EU regulation to various 'stakeholders', notably business
and unions (Cohen and Thatcher 2005, 341/42), while the relative obscurity
of their decision-making processes allows national politicians to engage in
blame shifting to an anonymous 'Brussels'.

Direct deliberative democracy through referenda or special consultative
forums with civil society groups has been offered as a corrective both to the
presumed self-interested bargaining of party democracy and self-serving or
selective technical expertise. Many advocated them as mechanisms for legitimising the failed Constitutional Treaty – the convention was a small deliberative forum, the ratification process – usually advocated as a pan-European
affair – was to have been an act of popular deliberation. Yet, as has been
noted with lobbying by civil society groups more generally (Warleigh 2001;
Kroger 2008), the Convention involved considerable political bargaining and
lobbying by unaccountable and unrepresentative groups. No incentive structure existed to consider the public interest as articulated by the public themselves, merely the interests of those with access. Civil society groups could
focus on a single issue without having to balance their concerns against those
of others as part of a public programme. Instead, they could simply push an
arbitrary agenda. Meanwhile, that agenda set the terms of the referenda. The
broader electorate had no mechanism for ensuring the Treaty responded to the
broad range and balance of public concerns except by rejecting it altogether
(Castiglione et al. 2007).

Thus, non-majoritarian devices cannot really substitute for an 'input'
majoritarian process. They fail to overcome the basic case for such mechanisms given by the three arguments explored above. Mechanisms relying
on expertise regard 'political equality', accountability and responsiveness
as inappropriate because they contend the 'circumstances of politics' do not
apply to certain types of technical decision, thereby ignoring the obstacles
posed by reasonable normative and empirical disagreements and fallibility to
attempts to objectively define the common good even in these areas. In the
process, they create false negatives that a democratic 'input' process would
be more apt to correct for and register as many – if not more – false positives.
By restricting access, they increase the likelihood of decision-makers serving partial concerns. They may be denied vital information by foreclosing
feedback from public opinion regarding the impact of their decisions, exhibit
professional bias, be unduly subservient to the politicians or others that select
them, and be more open to regulatory capture. For example, devolving the
setting of interest rates to central banks can insulate from public scrutiny the
neo-monetarist content of orthodox monetary policy choices by presenting
them as the product of 'sound' economic management. Yet, such choices
may serve financial institutions better than the economy at large and be overly

skewed to serve their interests – a prime instance of the sort of 'false positive' problem this mechanism was supposed to guard against (Hay 2007, 113–18). Selective consultation with 'stakeholders' creates a parallel dilemma, with the agenda potentially getting set by the very groups whose interests regulation should be seeking to harmonise with the public interest. Finally, there is nothing particularly deliberative about referenda – its simplistic alternatives between 'yes' and 'no' on a question set by elites on the basis at best of partial consultation lies in stark contrast with the deliberative process of electoral politics, where a constant dialogue gets institutionalised between the multifarious views of different sections of the electorate in the effort of rival parties to build a winning coalition of support. None of the above denies that such mechanisms might occasionally supplement standard forms of 'input democracy', as is the case in many member states. However, they are directly or indirectly controllable by formal or informal political channels that respond to majoritarian politics and public opinion. Thus, central banks have to deal with widespread discussion of their decisions in the media and the governors are often accountable to and removable by politicians. By contrast, no pan-European public sphere exists capable of generating an equivalent pressure in the EU, while political control of the ECB is substantially weaker.

Counter-majoritarian

'Counter-majoritarian' mechanisms tackle the basic 'input' case more directly by seeking to highlight voices liable to go unheard within a majoritarian democracy (Majone 1996, 285–87; Sunstein 1993, chap. 1). These too come in strong and weak forms. Strong forms offer democratic mechanisms for defining the common interest by forcing consensual decision-making. Weak forms merely constrain majoritarianism to correct 'input' bias or protect particular 'outputs'. However, giving extra weighting to potentially excluded voices or 'false negatives' risks their becoming over-represented 'false positives' that exclude equally important voices in their turn.

Some common political devices are sometimes mischaracterised as counter-majoritarian. So PR has been contrasted to majoritarian electoral systems. But the contrast is with plurality systems, PR being merely a more accurate way of calculating the majority. Likewise, federalism and other mechanisms for devolving power simply designate the appropriate community for majority decision-making. They only become counter-majoritarian when particular groups or different federal units are given special weighting, so that collective decisions between different communities have to be made consensually or by supermajorities. Most EU decision-making – both in the Council and the Parliament – requires consensus or supermajorities, with co-decision procedures exacerbating these effects to make it among the most systematically counter-majoritarian political systems in the world, second only to the United States (Fabbrini 2004).

Strong versions of counter-majoritarianism claim a unanimity condition offers a perfect democratic procedure for defining the common interest, ensuring no collective measure gets adopted that does not outweigh the costs, however they are distributed (Buchanan and Tullock 1965, 12, 14). However, this multiplying of veto points is biased towards the status quo, and unless the baseline conditions are entirely equitable, may entrench great injustices (Rae 1969, 1975). Indeed, it is largely advocated by libertarians keen to protect property rights. Within the EU, unanimity voting within the Council offers the prime instance of strong counter-majoritarianism. At one level, it can be justified as ensuring the EU only operates in spheres genuinely mutually advantageous for all member states. Of course, that could mean policies that would benefit the majority of European citizens fail to get adopted. It depends on whether it is more legitimate to view citizens primarily as members of states or members of the EU. Even in the former case, a state might manage to block a reform beneficial to the other states. Moreover, if decisions by state representatives are insulated from domestic majoritarian pressures, they may only respond to sectional interests lobbying on a given issue. CAP offers the prime example, remaining the largest area of EU expenditure despite a decline in the importance of the agricultural sector and external pressures for reform. Each of those with a primary say in the decision – the 'iron triangle' of agricultural ministers, agriculture officials in the commission, and European farming interests – has a vested interest in supporting the other, while the costs of mobilising consumers against CAP is greater than the average cost to each taxpayer (Keeler 1996; Nedergaard 1995).

Weaker versions are designed to protect what US constitutional discourse terms 'discrete, insular minorities', with little or no chance of allying with others to secure political influence. How far this is likely within the EU is debatable, and the degree to which the appropriate minorities are sets of member states rather than dispersed subnational minorities within them even more so. Again, such arrangements risk making it harder for unprivileged minorities to overcome the entrenched position of privileged minorities, as the regressive effects of the United States' system of multiple veto points starkly demonstrate (McGann 2004). Moreover, they favour concentrated overdispersed minorities. If minorities are not discrete and isolated, they have more to gain from being pivotal actors in alliance building than in seeking special protections that may work against them. Consociational arrangements can also give elites incentives to maximise rather than reduce their differences and to solidify group differences rather than allowing them to evolve or reduce (Barry 1975). Indeed, where the legitimacy of the state and the role of given groups within it takes precedence over all other issues, responsiveness and accountability on the quality of government gets severely reduced.

A number of weak counter-majoritarian arrangements exist within the EU, including Qualified Majority Voting in the Council, the need for final resolutions of EU legislation in the European Parliament to obtain a majority of all MEPs, and co-decision. These mechanisms favour a dominant coalition that is ideologically centrist and mildly pro-integration, though the dynamics differ depending on whether the issue has Left-Right or pro-anti integration as the main cleavage. Either way, super-majoritarianism gives power to the dominant partners – the EPP-PS grand coalition in the Parliament and the Franco-German alliance in the Council – and a small number of potential voting partners, depending on the issue, with certain groups permanently excluded (Hosli 1995, 1996, 1997). Once again, the logic of 'input' majoritarianism within the EU systems seems more justified than attempts to structure the system in ways that might produce more favourable outputs or that seek to privilege certain minority positions.

I have left to one side the role of the ECJ. Courts can be characterised as both non-majoritarian and counter-majoritarian. Their operation has been viewed as non-majoritarian, with multi-member courts like the ECJ, seen as models of deliberation, while their effect has been deemed counter-majoritarian. These have been seen as desirable qualities for constitutional courts in particular (e.g. Dworkin 1996, 'Introduction'). However, their effects are often perverse (Bellamy 2007; Waldron 2006). Once again, the non-majoritarian aspect may register false negatives, and the counter-majoritarian aspect produce false positives. The only issues that can be legitimately discussed within a court are those affecting parties with legal standing who have a case as defined by law. These restrictions uphold the 'rule of law' by ensuring the equitable application of settled law to all, but become disadvantages in situations – common to constitutional courts – where court decisions effectively make public policy. For the case under consideration may be untypical and decisions have knock-on effects for important interests and persons whose concerns the court cannot consider. Moreover, those with access to the court and possessing the resources to raise the case may be highly unrepresentative groups.

The ECJ often operates as a de facto Constitutional Court, and suffers from these drawbacks. Partly because the EU's governance structures are so fragmented and its administrative capacity weak, while the move from national to pan-European networks means the parties involved are often unknown to each other, there have been incentives for actors to seek rule-governed, legalistic approaches to regulation at the EU level (Kelemen and Sibbitt 2002). However, the strong judicial enforcement of formal public rules increases judicial discretion and many of the disadvantages of non-majoritarian decision-making. The court has a natural predisposition to reinforce the 'negative' integrationist, market-building agenda enshrined in the four freedoms of capital, labour, services and goods that lie at the heart of the European project. This tendency has produced the effective constitution-alisation of competition law, with the ECJ monopolising judgements on when 'public interest' restrictions apply and challenging the majoritarian decisions of national legislatures and governments – including the exemption of public sector jobs and services (Scharpf 1999a, 54–8). Such changes can be in the interests of consumers and workers alike. But they respond less to such public 'interests' as the 'private' interests of those individuals and bodies possessing access to press for a ruling. Consequently, they risk registering false posi-tives in the manner typical of counter-majoritarian arrangements. That need not always be the case, as in some kinds of public interest litigation (Harlow 1999, 49–52). However, legal avenues tend to be exploited disproportion-ately by corporate bodies (Harding 1992). Used excessively, litigation can also stunt the evolution of democratic, collective problem solving, and divert attention to ultimately self-defeating forms of individual redress, particularly in the area of compensation and liability (Harlow 1996). Unfortunately, the EU has actively encouraged such moves to make up for the democratic defi-cit, often under the banner of citizenship rights. In so doing, the EU is fuelling a more Americanised and adversarial legal culture, which favours those with deep pockets over the resource-poor, compensatory over redistributive jus-tice, and individual over collective benefits. In the process, ECJ decisions can undermine the interpretation of rights that people have made as democratic citizens of the member states. For example, a decision like *Watts*, making health services subject to 'free movement' and allowing individuals to escape waiting lists and other domestic forms of rationing by shopping for treatments elsewhere, undercuts the capacity of states to plan and favours mobile and articulate individuals at the expense of the poor. It also places courts in the quandary of making substantive decisions about an individual's health needs without any obligation to consider their knock-on effects for health and other policies (Newdick 2006).

CONCLUSION

This chapter has defended the virtues of 'input' majoritarian democracy and pointed to various vices of 'output'-orientated non-majoritarian and counter-majoritarian democracy. I have not looked at whether majoritarian democracy is plausible for the EU. Many commentators doubt that it is, at least for the foreseeable future. Size, lack of a common language and media, the absence of shared identities and affective bonds, and the presence of very diverse and well institutionalised national political cultures within the member states, all present powerful obstacles, though over the very long term not necessarily insuperable ones (Scharpf 1999a, 9/10; Bellamy, Castiglione, and Shaw 2006a; Weale 2005). However, the current trend, found in all the member states, is for democracy to be devolved downwards, towards smaller and more culturally homogenous units, rather than upwards, to larger and more diverse political entities (Kymlicka 1999).

Therefore, let us assume that satisfactory majoritarian mechanisms are not available to the EU and unlikely to be so.[3] In these circumstances, are imperfect non-majoritarian and counter-majoritarian mechanisms the best we can get? I noted how some commentators contend that the EU mainly deals with issues that are neither best handled by democratic politics nor electorally salient (Scharpf 1999a, 11–3; Majone 1996; Moravscik 2002). Though I demurred from this analysis, it contains a kernel of truth. If we conceive of the EU as primarily an organisation for cooperation between democratic states rather than as a mechanism for transcending them, then different standards may legitimately apply. One could argue that such situations require arrangements to be mutually advantageous but not that they reflect more stringent criteria of justice that might call for redistribution (Miller 2008, 394–96). The reasoning here is that each of these states has its own internal systems of social justice for which its citizens are co-responsible thorough their equal participation within majoritarian systems of democracy. To the extent the wealth and survival of these states depends on cooperation with other states, it seems appropriate to share the costs and benefits of these arrangements equitably. To provide such agreements with democratic legitimacy, it will be sufficient that the citizens of each member state are satisfied that this is an area where interaction and cooperation are desirable or necessary – for example, in order to set fish quotas so fishing will be sustainable or to promote trade. Moreover, the surpluses generated by such accords need only be Pareto improvements, with each party gaining to an equal degree from the resulting benefits subject to compensatory measures for temporary losers so that a 'no wealth effects' condition holds. For this latter purpose, a mix of non-majoritarian and counter-majoritarian mechanisms between state representatives will be justified since nothing in such a system suggests any change is required with the status quo so far as the relative standing of the parties involved is concerned – quite the reverse. From this perspective, the democratic deficit within the EU brought about by the absence of effective majoritarian democratic mechanisms is twofold. On the one hand, national electorates and parliaments, where these systems function well, ought to have a more decisive voice in deciding the scope and extent of the EU and the spheres it enters (Mair 2007). On the other hand, attempts to move towards majoritarian democracy within the EU become illegitimate, because they suggest an inappropriate role for an EU 'people' in judging its own competences and seeking a more egalitarian distribution among them that transcends national borders (Bellamy 2008; Weale 2005). In sum, the non-majoritarian and counter-majoritarian mechanisms of the EU can be legitimised so long as their scope and operation are controlled by the majoritarian systems of the member states – with them taking over this role from the ECJ. However, when removed from such control, they cannot offer pan-European decision-making with anything but spurious and ineffective democratic credentials.

NOTES

1. Versions of this chapter were presented at the Connex Workshops and conferences at Reading and Manchester. I am grateful to participants for helpful observations, and to David Coen, Christine Reh, Fritz Scharpf and the journal's editors and referees for written comments.

2. Hix (2000) suggests the EP might act as a 'fire alarm', but its 'input' credentials are weak.

3. For the alternative scenario of establishing majoritarian democracy in the EU, see Hix (2008).

Chapter 15

Beyond a Constraining Dissensus

The Role of National Parliaments in Domesticating and Normalising the Politicisation of European Integration[1]

Sandra Kröger and Richard Bellamy

1. INTRODUCTION: THE POLITICAL IDENTITY GHOST IN THE EUROPEAN INTEGRATION MACHINE

The Euro crisis has reinforced the doubts of certain prominent analysts of the EU about whether the course of integration can be addressed adequately in either neo-functionalist or liberal intergovernmental terms (Hooghe and Marks 2009; Scharpf 2015; Vilpisauskas 2013). Both these approaches tend to ignore a development that scholars have dubbed 'politicisation' – the increasing awareness, salience, polarisation of and mobilisation around EU affairs in domestic politics, and the expansion of domestic actors, such as Eurosceptic parties and National Parliaments (NPs), in the EU's decision-making processes (Hutter and Kerscher 2014). This politicisation has gone together with the end of the 'permissive consensus' that characterised the pre-Maastricht phase of European integration and a shift towards what Liesbet Hooghe and Gary Marks (2009, 5) have called a 'constraining dissensus', typified by multiple forms of Euroscepticism. We shall argue that the explanatory weaknesses of neo-functionalism and intergovernmentalism associated with the increased politicisation of EU affairs call for a fresh look at the role that National Parliaments (NPs) should and could play in the context of EU multilevel governance.

As numerous commentators have noted, the Euro crisis has brought to the fore a tension within the integration process that has been present since Maastricht. Following Hooghe and Marks (2009), the fault line of this tension can be located between the functional and economic factors that promote

European integration, on the one hand, and the normative, cultural and social psychological factors associated with political identity and the desire for national self-determination, on the other (Hooghe and Marks 2009, 2). Neo-functionalists hoped that the benefits of economic coordination at the European level would ultimately 'spillover' into an increasing acceptance of the legitimacy as well as the effectiveness of gradually shifting collective decision-making to supranational institutions (Haas 1958; Risse 2006). By contrast, liberal intergovernmentalists contended that so long as the integration process remained under the control of the executives of the member states, then the demands for national democratic legitimacy were satisfied (Moravcsik 2008). If neo-functionalists looked forward to a point where the EU might itself gain both the institutional capacity and the affective allegiance required to resolve the democratic deficit of EU-level decision-making, liberal inter-governmentalists denied the existence of any such problem in the first place.

These analyses have proved too optimistic. Since the debates around the Maastricht Treaty in the early 1990s, what had previously been described as the 'permissive consensus' has come to an end. 'Permissive consensus' referred to the assumed consent of European electorates with the project of integration, which was driven by elites who operated mainly in camera. As the difficult passage of the Maastricht Treaty, the failure of the Constitutional Treaty and the increasing electoral success of Eurosceptic and right-extreme political parties have made abundantly clear, that elite-driven passive consensus no longer suffices. Indeed, the associated shift of legitimate decision-making 'on a range of vital issues … from an insulated elite to mass politics' (Hooghe and Marks 2009, 13) has sparked a legitimacy crisis. For this change has meant the EU has gone public, yet not all of the public likes what it sees. This trend has become yet more pronounced as the Euro crisis has ensured that EU affairs have not only had a prominent place in national debates (Closa and Maatsch 2014; Miklin 2014; Wendler 2014; de Wilde and Zürn 2012) but also become more contested than had hitherto been the case (Hutter and Grande 2014). Crisis-related decisions, such as those to provide financial support to Greece or on measures like the European Stability Mechanism (ESM) or the Fiscal Compact, have prompted wide debate and media attention, and provoked public protest in many member states.[2]

This politicisation of EU affairs has gone hand in hand with declining levels of trust in the EU – especially in those countries worst hit by the crisis (Matthijs 2014). As Eurobarometer polls had long revealed, and the crisis has made ever more marked, identity has not followed function. The EU may have acquired more competences (De Wilde and Zürn 2012), yet citizens have remained attached not just culturally but also politically to their member states. As a result, the growing politicisation of the EU has served not to mobilise greater citizen participation at the EU level, where electoral turnout in European Parliament (EP) elections has steadily declined since 1979, dipping below 50 per cent in 1999 to fall to an all-time low of 42.61 per cent in 2014. Rather, the politicisation of the EU has manifested itself at the national level, most particularly in electoral defeats for governments deemed to have been too submissive towards contested EU-level policies or in the increase of votes for Eurosceptic and anti-system parties. This problem cannot be attributed to a democratic deficit at the EU level alone. The gradual extension of the EP's powers has neither stemmed the process of electoral decline in European elections nor reduced the rise of Eurosceptic parties at both the domestic and the EU level. Instead, the politicisation of the EU within the member states testifies to a democratic 'disconnect' between domestic democratic processes (Lindseth 2010, 234), within which most citizens remain primarily engaged, and EU decision-making by national executives and political and legal actors at the EU level.

In what follows, we shall argue that NPs can play an important role in overcoming this growing tension between European integration and communal self-rule by reconnecting the one to the other. They can do so by providing a means for what we shall call the *domestication* and *normalisation* of EU policy making. The possibility for their so operating arises because the politicisation of EU affairs need not be equated with Euroscepticism and the rise of populist movements. Instead, politicisation should be regarded and deployed as a positive and necessary feature of democratic politics. A number of reasons motivate this argument. First, without politicisation in EU affairs there is a reduction of policy choice. A key feature missing from most domestic EU debates has been the left-right polarisation of EU affairs among the non-Eurosceptic parties and the government and the opposition (Puntscher Riekmann and Wydra 2013). As a consequence, substantial policy choice gets reduced. However, when parties fail to offer citizens such choices they deprive them of political efficacy during elections because they cannot select between alternative government programs. Second, and relatedly, this lack of policy choices means that those who disagree with the governmental position go unrepresented. Given governments tend to adopt pro-integration positions regardless; a representation deficit gets built into the very system of EU decision-making, prompting the Eurosceptical challenge (Bellamy and Kröger 2013). Third, politicisation reduces the scope for blame shifting by politicians as a result of their exploiting the lack of clear lines of responsibility in the EU's multilevel decision-making structure. The more EU affairs get publicly discussed the less it will be possible for governments to participate in EU decision-making, on the one hand, while blaming others for the results of that same decision-making, on the other hand. Finally, the more politicised and public the EU becomes, the more stable it is likely to be as practices of domesticated and normalised opposition overtake populist Euroscepticism as the mainstream form of disagreement and protest. In all these respects, politicisation proves desirable not so much for its potential contribution to supranational demos-creation, as for its beneficial effects for the democratic reconnection of the executives involved in EU policy making with their domestic constituencies. As a result, the growing politicisation of EU affairs within the member states could be moved beyond a mere constraining dissensus on integration into a means for obtaining the active consensus of the various European peoples in the shaping as well as the control of that process. Our contention, though, is that this result can only be achieved by reinforcing rather than supplanting or constraining communal self-rule and established political identities.

We shall argue that the basis for this approach lies in the multilevel and *demoi*-cratic normative ordering of the EU itself (Cheneval and Schimmelfennig 2013; Nicolaïdis 2013). On this account, the legitimacy of EU-level decisions rests on their satisfying the normative logic of a two-level game (Bellamy and Weale 2015; Putnam 1988; Savage and Weale 2009), whereby they must be acceptable not just to the contracting national executives but also to the respective *demoi* they claim to represent. From this perspective, negotiators must treat each other with mutual respect as representatives of their citizens, appreciating that the legitimacy of their decisions depends on their retaining the ongoing, democratic support of all their different peoples. Such an approach rejects the elitism of not only neo-functionalism but also liberal intergovernmentalism. If the failure of a sufficient transfer of affective political allegiances from the national to the EU-level forces the former to continue the *dirigisme* associated with the Monnet method, the latter has too often reflected the capacity of those business and other groups able to profit from integration to promote their interests with governments without addressing the concerns of those for whom the economic, social and cultural advantages often prove less clear cut. By contrast, we characterise our approach as 'republican intergovernmentalism' (Bellamy 2013), seeing the role of NPs as a way of ensuring that the decisions of governments at the EU level operate under the equal influence and control of their peoples, while recognising the obligation of all other member states to operate similarly. The *demoi*-cratic logic of this two-level game entails that European integration needs to show equal concern and respect for the capacity for communal self-rule of its constituent parts (Bellamy and Weale 2015), supporting and sustaining and where necessary supplementing that capacity rather than substituting for it. Yet, these requirements need not be regarded as constraining any further European integration or even as rolling it back – rather, they enable its shaping by the citizens of the European states, a point we underline through a proposal for a positive measure: the Parliamentary Legislative Initiative.

The chapter unfolds as follows. Section 2 outlines the normative basis for the involvement of NPs in EU decision-making within the EU's *demoi*-cratic constitutional order, outlining 'republican intergovernmentalism'. Section 3 explores how far NPs currently live up to this role as mechanisms for the domestication and normalisation of EU policy making, noting the picture to be mixed. Although many of the institutional structures for the domesticating of EU policy making exist, politicians and parties lack the incentives to employ them in a normalising way. Section 4 suggests their performance in this regard might be improved if NPs possessed not only scrutiny powers but the possibility to put forward parliamentary legislative initiatives (PLIs).

2. DEMOCRATIC LEGITIMACY IN A MULTILEVEL EUROPE – TOWARDS A REPUBLICAN INTERGOVERNMENTALISM

Hooghe and Marks have argued that tensions are inherent to the integration process because 'the functional need for human co-operation rarely coincides with the territorial scope of community', so that the demand of communities 'for self rule is almost always inconsistent with the functional demand for regional authority' (Hooghe and Marks 2009, 2; Rodrik 2011). Yet, neo-functionalists could retort that in the long run the change in the locus of communal identification they hypothesise may come about. Of course, as Keynes famously remarked, 'in the long run, we are all dead' (Keynes 1923, 80), rendering the long run 'a 'misleading guide to our current affairs' and its invocation 'too easy, too useless a task' when it comes to meeting the challenges of the present (Keynes 1923, 83). Nonetheless, Hooghe and Marks's thesis might be regarded as resting on a historically contingent set of circumstances. Not only could the conditions that have given rise to this tension pass but also advocates of a federal Europe could argue they should do so, given that such sentiments are most ardently expressed by traditionalists and authoritarians who exploit the temporary plight of the current losers from the integration process. By contrast, we shall suggest that the continued demand for communal self-rule at the national level has both a more justified normative basis and one that is reconcilable with recognising the functional and other demands for greater coordination at the European level. Moreover, NPs play a key role in this reconciliation.

The normative basis for this approach lies in what has been termed the *demoi*-cratic character of the EU: the contention that the EU involves an ever closer union of peoples rather than the evolving formation of a European people or demos, and exists to serve their joint and several interests (Cheneval and Schimmelfennig 2013; Nicolaïdis 2013). On the version of this thesis adopted here (Bellamy 2013), the political and constitutional systems of the member states should be viewed as offering the democratic means whereby their citizens have been able to agree collectively on their mutual rights and obligations as equal participants within a shared political space. This argument goes back to the defence of the moral standing of states elaborated by Kant (Flikschuk 2010; Stilz 2009). According to this thesis, the integrity of the legal and political structures of each of the member states deserves respect as having elaborated over time their own distinctive civic cultures and instantiated various special obligations and an associated political identity among their respective peoples. However, political communities do not exist in isolation. They interact and develop relations of interdependence. Military threats and outright aggression provide the most obvious negative ways one political community may interfere with or dominate another. But there are also numerous other and subtler forms of mutual influence. For example, international trade may be of very unequal benefit if the superior bargaining power of one or more of the trading partners puts them in a position to impose terms on the others. They can also be harmed by, or benefit from, the negative and positive externalities of each other's domestic policies. When one community has laxer environmental regulations than those of its neighbours, say, its neighbours may suffer from the resulting pollution and the competition of cheaper goods, while it may benefit from the clean air and the less competitively priced goods produced by their superior measures. Political communities may also need or wish to cooperate to control a range of activities that operate across their respective borders, from international finance and the operations of multinational corporations, to transnational terrorism. Such activities include the development of mutually beneficial trade relationships, such as the creation of a single market. The EU offers a response to these various developments and their growing importance in an increasingly globalised and interconnected world. On the *demoi*-cratic account, though, its purpose is not to supplant the already-existing political systems of the member states. Rather, the EU's rationale lies in supporting their right to self-government by ensuring these political communities show each other equal concern and respect, and can cooperate effectively and equitably to tackle shared problems. It achieves this result through regulating their mutual interactions and organising their cooperation in ways that avoid domination – not least through forms of supranational governance that treat all contracting member states on equal terms, regardless of population size, military power or wealth, and that remain under their joint and equal control (Pettit 2010).

By contrast to both the neo-functionalist and the liberal intergovernmental approaches, the *demoi*-cratic approach links the functional argument for European integration to communal self-rule. Unlike neo-functionalists, *demoi*-crats do not regard the functional case for supranational institutions and regulations as invoking a quasi-federal teleology involving the formation of a European *demos* and an associated EU-level democratic system on the model of the domestic political systems of the member states. Instead, the *demoi*-cratic approach regards supranational institutions as delegated authorities that are best conceived as agents of the member states (Lindseth 2010, 227). Yet, the normative conditions motivating this view are not satisfied by liberal intergovernmentalism either. A *demoi*-cratic approach requires that governments act with the active rather than the passive consent of their respective peoples, responding to the commonly avowed interests of all their citizens rather than the particular interests of certain well-organised groups. On this account, agreements between member states at the EU level must follow the normative logic of a two-level game (Putnam 1988; Bellamy and Weale 2015): they must both be equally acceptable to the governments that negotiate them and to the citizens that each of these governments represents. The legitimacy of EU-level decisions, therefore, depends on them meeting a dual standard. These decisions must reflect the consent of each of the *demoi* to whom they apply and they must not undermine the capacity for those *demoi* to give or withdraw that consent. As such, this approach operates as a form of 'republican intergovernmentalism' (Bellamy 2013), since it requires the ongoing democratic authorisation and accountability of governments by and to their citizens, albeit indirectly via their elected representatives, in EU decision-making. Our claim is that the growing 'constraining dissensus' results from the integration process having increasingly failed to meet these criteria, as the so-called executive federalism (Habermas 2012) that has characterised the management of the Euro crisis illustrates. Yet, there are also encouraging moves to alter the institutional structures of EU decision-making so as to better satisfy these conditions and so meet the challenge of growing domestic dissent, not least through the new powers allotted to NPs.

The most consistent and prominent articulation of such *demoi*-cratic normative reasoning has come from the German Federal Constitutional Court. In a series of judgements going back to 1974, the Court has insisted that while there are important functional reasons for European integration the resulting arrangements and policies cannot be such as would be incompatible with or undermine the right to communal self-government embodied in the Basic Law of the German Constitution. Increasingly, such arguments have been voiced more widely with the result that they found expression post-Lisbon in Article 4.2 of the Treaty on European Union (TEU), which specifies that 'The Union shall respect the equality of Member States before the Treaties as well as their national identities, inherent in their fundamental structures, political and constitutional, inclusive of regional and local self-government'. In a similar vein, the revised Article 5.2 TEU now insists on 'the principle of conferral', emphasising that 'the Union shall act *only* within the limits of the competences conferred upon it by the Member States in the Treaties to attain the objectives set out therein'. As the German Federal Constitutional Court noted in its Lisbon judgement (2009), this principle upholds the member states as 'the primary political area of their respective polities', with the EU only having 'secondary responsibility for the tasks conferred on it'.

It is no coincidence, therefore, that Lisbon also witnessed a new emphasis on the role of NPs, with Articles 10 and 12 of the TEU recognising them for the first time in the main body of the Treaty as forming an integral part of the EU decision-making process. As Peter Lindseth (2010, 24, 234/35) has noted, from the *demoi*-cratic perspective, as outlined above, the democratic legitimacy of the EU suffers less from a democratic *deficit* within the EU's supranational institutions and more from a democratic *disconnect* between EU-level policy-making and the democratic processes of authorisation and accountability at the member state level. The past sidelining of NPs by executives and EU institutions, to the extent that they were designated as the 'losers' of the integration process (Maurer and Wessels 2001), has played an important part in this disconnect. Consequently, their revitalisation within EU affairs offers a means of democratic reconnection. Once again, the German Federal Constitutional Court has pursued this line of reasoning assiduously by noting how the self-determination of the German *demos* was intimately linked to its Parliament, in this case the *Bundestag*, retaining meaningful influence over German involvement in EU policies, including economic policy post-EMU (Federal Constitutional Court 2014a). As the Court noted in its decision on the ratification of the Treaty Establishing the European Stability Mechanism, the *Bundestag* cannot abrogate its responsibility to decide its own budget nor can the German government undertake an open-ended liability for another state's debts (Federal Constitutional Court 2014b). According to the Court, NPs provide the main mechanism through which people are represented and can influence policy making, albeit indirectly through national elections. They serve as the arena within which people can collectively shape its 'economic, cultural and social living conditions' according to their civic traditions and values. In the Court's view, NPs cannot abrogate that function – indeed, they have a duty to defend it (Federal Constitutional Court 2009).

Two roles emerge for NPs from this analysis. On the one hand, as acknowledged in part in their function as guardians of subsidiarity, NPs have a duty to ensure the EU only undertakes measures that lie within the competences member states have conferred upon it and that could not be achieved as effectively by action at the member state level. On the other hand, they need to ensure that the EU policies agreed and promoted by national governments and carried forward by various supranational actors respond to the democratic will of the various *demoi* and are capable of retaining their ongoing support.

In developing these two roles, NPs can close the democratic disconnect by *domesticating* and *normalising* EU policy making. They domesticate it by taming it and bringing it home. It can be tamed by NPs not only using their subsidiarity checking powers, such as the Early Warning Mechanism (EWM), but also exercising more control over government ministers via EU Affairs and other Committees to ensure EU policies do not unduly encroach on or subvert what the German Constitution Court designates 'essential areas' of domestic 'democratic formative action', such as 'citizenship, the civil and the military monopoly on the use of force, revenue and expenditure including external financing and all elements of encroachment that are decisive for the realisation of fundamental rights' (Federal Constitutional Court 2009). In making use of these instruments, they can also bring EU policy making home and thereby normalise it so that debates about more or less integration get related to the normal domestic debates concerning the character and quality of particular policies in terms of the broader ideological commitments of citizens, particularly their position on the left-right spectrum.

On this account, European integration need neither come at the cost of a loss of communal self-rule nor be regarded as in 'inevitable' tension with it, so that the assertion of one always comes at the expense of the other. Rather, when viewed from a republican intergovernmentalist perspective as a derived fundamental order, the EU can be conceived as needing to be democratically connected to, and dependent for its legitimacy upon, the legal and political systems of the member states. Within this framework, the politicisation of EU affairs can be shifted away from Euroscepticism, undeniable though this phenomenon has been hitherto. Through being domesticated and normalised by the structures and processes of party competition within NPs, politicisation can serve to reconnect the different levels of governance in the EU both to each other and to the citizens of the various *demoi*, thereby improving the quality of representation in the mid and long term. By stemming from, rather than operating against, communal self-rule, politicisation can go beyond the constraining dissensus. For by being channelled within, rather than having to go outside, normal domestic channels, such politicisation can allow a form of European integration to emerge that is capable of obtaining the ongoing assent of the citizens of Europe's various *demoi*.

3. THE ROLE OF NPS IN DOMESTICATING AND NORMALISING EU POLICY MAKING

This section assesses the degree to which the domestication and normalisation of EU policy making, as defined in the previous section, have occurred in NPs, with the subsequent section drawing on this assessment to present a constructive proposal for improvement. The analysis differentiates between the institutional structures NPs have developed to domesticate the EU, on the one hand, and the usage of those structures by individual members of parliament (MPs) and political parties in ways that normalise debates on the EU, on the other. Given parliamentary politics is ultimately party politics, particular attention needs to be given to evaluating how far these domestic institutional structures provide adequate incentives for the main political parties to debate EU policies in ways their reflect their normal ideological commitments and divisions. As we shall see, at present the incentives provided to parties by existing structures are mixed, with the result that NPs currently operate as imperfect channels of domestication and normalisation.

Domestication

NPs were long considered the 'losers of integration' (Maurer and Wessels 2001). Their role was not formally recognised within the EU Treaties, while the integration process allowed executives to circumvent their oversight in a growing number of policy areas. Proposals for improving the democratic credentials of the EU focused on the steady enhancement of the powers of the EP (Rittberger 2005), thereby marginalising NPs yet further. Despite these difficulties, NPs have gradually learnt to 'fight back' and parliamentary attention to EU affairs has clearly increased over the past two decades. NPs have implemented institutional reforms in reaction to the increased importance of the EU (Karlas 2012; Winzen 2012), and the EU has given them more competences in turn. As a result, NPs have developed the institutional capacity to domesticate EU policy making, at least to some extent.

The potential to tame and bring the EU home has been aided by NPs setting up European Affairs Committees (EACs), though important national differences remain as to how powerful these are (Karlas 2012; Winzen 2013). Institutional reforms have been particularly pronounced in member states where both parliamentary authority and Euroscepticism are strong (Raunio 2005; Winzen et al. 2014). Particularly following the Lisbon Treaty all NPs have benefited from improved information and new powers that allow them to scrutinise their own executives more effectively, enter into dialogue with the European Commission, exercise a subsidiarity check and cooperate with other NPs and with the EP to inform and control EU-level decision-making.

According to the new 'Protocol on the Role of National Parliaments', NPs now receive a wide range of documents, including Commission consultation documents and draft legislative acts, directly rather than via their governments, as under the Treaty of Amsterdam.

They also have acquired enhanced scrutiny powers with regard to executive action in the EU, with many NPs adopting either the documentary or especially the mandating models of oversight developed by the UK and Danish Parliaments, respectively, from the 1970s onwards (Lindseth 2010, 200–25). Parliaments differ over whether they scrutinise EU documents or the government's position for negotiations in the Council or both, and whether they offer a written statement or transmit their position to governments orally, in committee. The documentary model involves a 'scrutiny reserve', whereby the government cannot undertake action at the supranational level until parliamentary scrutiny of the relevant proposal is complete. The reserve can only be overridden by Ministers offering 'special reasons' for doing so, this reason giving requirement being further reinforced by the need under the UK model for governments to provide an explanatory memorandum on every European document. The Danish mandating model has been seen as even more demanding, with the government being required to consult on all decisions of major importance and present their negotiating position for approval by the parliamentary committee. Both models potentially improve the ability of legislators to understand EU proposals, on the one hand, while making the positions of national executives more transparent, on the other.

EACs and parliamentary scrutiny more generally not only support the domestic communication and debate of EU policy making but also foster a capacity to tame it by promoting respect for communal self-rule. That occurs both by insisting on the need for domestic democratic authorisation for EU measures and by ensuring the process of European integration respects the primacy of the domestic democratic sphere through being limited to those measures that can be most effectively and efficiently achieved at the supranational level. This latter element lies behind the growing assertion of the subsidiarity principle from the Treaty of Maastricht onwards, culminating in the introduction of the EWM in the Lisbon Treaty, which permits NPs to police subsidiarity and proportionality by way of the so-called yellow and orange cards (Protocol on the Application of the Principles of Subsidiarity and Proportionality, Article 7). The issuing of 'reasoned opinions' by NPs also allows them to enter into political dialogue with the Commission. Following the so-called Barroso Initiative, the Commission undertook to reply to all contributions sent to it by NPs, even those that did not relate to subsidiarity (Jančić 2012). Additionally, NPs can challenge legislative acts on grounds of their infringing subsidiarity by bringing an action before the Court of Justice. Moreover, they are now involved in the evaluation of measures taken within the area of freedom, security and justice (Articles 70, 85, 88), while an individual NP may block Treaty changes under the simplified revision procedures by vetoing the so-called passerelle clause (Article 48). They must also be informed of new applications to join the EU (Article 49).

Finally, NPs engage in inter-parliamentary cooperation. Because the EWM requires coordination among the twenty-eight NPs, it promotes inter-parliamentary networking and the exchange of information (Cooper 2013; Sprungk 2013). COSAC (the French acronym for the 'Conference of Community and European Affairs Committees of Parliaments of the European Union') is the most developed form of inter-parliamentary cooperation. It is officially authorised 'to submit any contribution' that it deems appropriate to the EP, the Council and the Commission. Inter-parliamentary bodies have also developed in those areas where EU institutions and actors operate at the borders of their sphere of competences and possess a degree of executive discretion: namely, Financial and Monetary Policy and Common Security and Defence Policy (see the contribution by Cooper in this issue). Such bodies provide mechanisms for NPs to retain their power to scrutinise executive action in areas where national governments have delegated their authority to EU officials.

In sum, we can see that although the competences of NPs – and governments – have been reduced in the context of European integration, they have begun to acquire the institutional capacities and legal capabilities to control not only their conferral to the EU level but also to monitor and influence their use. As a result, the structures exist for domesticating EU policies along the lines of the republican intergovernmental model outlined in the last section. However, these mechanisms will only operate as a means for democratically reconnecting the EU to the demoi of the member states to the extent they are employed by national political parties and form part of the normal processes of political contestation. Otherwise, the politicisation of EU affairs at the domestic level will remain the terrain of Eurosceptical parties protesting against an ongoing democratic disconnect.

Normalisation

As we noted, politicisation involves the greater salience, polarisation of and mobilisation around EU affairs. By the normalisation of this phenomenon we mean the debate of alternative EU policies by the non-Eurosceptic political parties, according to their characteristic ideological commitments. Such normalised ideological debates would turn less on the legitimacy of the EU or its actions per se, matters that preoccupy the Eurosceptic parties, and more on reasonable disagreements concerning the particular policies that the EU puts forward or implements. In this way, party competition over EU policy could become attuned to the core domestic policy concerns and divisions of voters.

Hitherto the EU institutional space has done anything but encourage the active engagement of domestic political parties in EU affairs. The legal and political structures of the EU have progressively decreased the domestic political alternatives available to national parties in a number of ways (Bellamy and Kröger 2014). They have been restricted a) by way of the transfer of competences to the EU, which limits the available 'policy space' in which parties can intervene (Mair 2007); and b) by the prioritising of the completion and realisation of the internal market over other political aims, which reduces the 'policy repertoire' available to parties and thereby the opportunities for them to disagree and propose alternatives (Mair 2007). These restrictions impact on the degree of political contestation and debate between parties by constraining in their turn the area of reasonable disagreement between them: a) by way of the supremacy and direct effect of EU law as interpreted and upheld by the Court of Justice and its claims to 'competence-competence' in deciding whether it may legitimately override national constitutional objections or not; and b) by way of the party political composition of the main EU institutions (an institutionalised 'grand coalition') and the consensus-oriented nature of the EU's institutional setting more generally, which produces legislative proposals that reflect a somewhat centrist compromise that tries ex ante to anticipate and integrate the interests and concerns of both centre-left and centre-right parties, rendering political conflict about the proposals difficult once they come before NPs. As a result, parliamentary attempts to contest or debate the integration process risk becoming unreasonable. NPs have had no choice but to adapt to and implement EU law. The net effect of these factors is a reduction in political alternatives that national governments – and thereby parliaments and parties – can offer to voters, which in turn decreases electoral competition, rendering elections less decisive (see also Nanou 2013). In turn, parties attempt to avoid the politicisation of EU policies, given that under these conditions it is hardly an attractive electoral issue.

The new parliamentary procedures described above can potentially help overcome these constraints by providing domestic democratic channels through which EU policies can be pursued. The crux is whether parties have adequate incentives to employ them. For parties to politicise an issue in the manner described above, four conditions must usually be met (Miklin 2014). First, the issue must be sufficiently *salient* to affect the choices of the party's voters. Second, the party's position on the issue needs to be *congruent* with that of its voters. Third, its position needs to be sufficiently internally *cohesive* to avoid internal conflicts. Finally, the party's competitors need to hold different positions that allow for *polarisation*. Hitherto, these conditions have only applied to Eurosceptic parties with regard to EU affairs. However, the Euro crisis has undoubtedly raised the awareness of national electorates about the impact of EU policies on their lives. As such, it offers a good test case of the degree to which adequate incentives exist for other political parties to use the new domestic institutional structures to normalise the politicisation of the EU. Although the published empirical evidence is still sketchy, it nonetheless allows us to offer a preliminary assessment with regard to each of the four conditions.

First, the salience of EU affairs in domestic debates and elections, and even in EP elections, has traditionally been low (Reif and Schmitt 1980). However, crisis-related decisions, such as those to provide financial support to Greece or measures like the European stability mechanism or the Fiscal Compact, have generated parliamentary debate (Wendler 2014; Puntscher Riekmann and Wydra 2013; Closa and Maatsch 2014, and the contribution by Wonka and Göbel in this issue) and media attention throughout the Eurozone, and resulted in public protest in many member states. Also, more governments than ever before in the history of the EU have been voted out of office, many clearly as a result of the austerity measures they had felt obliged to implement because of their undertakings as members of the Eurozone. Therefore, the salience criterion has been met.

Second, many non-Eurosceptic parties, particularly the major parties, have traditionally held more positive views towards the EU than their voters (Hooghe and Marks 2008). This lack of congruence has disinclined them from politicising EU affairs. This gap appears to have widened with the crisis, both in debtor and in lender states, with national electorates objecting to the financial cuts or spending, respectively, to which their governments have agreed. By contrast, smaller parties at the extremes of the political spectrum, particularly those on the extreme right, tend to enjoy a greater congruence with their voters on EU affairs and have been able to exploit the crisis to promote their Eurosceptical views (Green-Petersen 2012; Mattila and Raunio 2012).

Third, many parties lack cohesion through being internally divided over the EU. While broadly sympathetic to the idea of European integration, social democrats can worry about the implications of the internal market and of neoliberal policies stemming from the EU. They often see the domestic welfare state as endangered. By contrast, conservative parties often divide along traditionalist lines, as in the UK, with some members seeing the EU as a source of excessively liberal policies in areas such as free movement or anti-discrimination regulations (see Auel and Raunio 2014). We are aware of no literature as yet on whether the internal coherence of mainstream parties on EU policies has increased or decreased since the outbreak of the crisis.

Finally, the fourth condition of polarisation is the most important for democratic reconnection by parties. For the reasons explored above, mainstream parties have hitherto agreed more than they have disagreed about EU policies, particularly in such European integration-friendly member states as Germany (see Auel and Raunio 2014; and Wonka and Göbel in this issue). As a result, public disagreement has focused on the constitutional question of whether there should be more or less Europe rather than on what kind of policies the EU should pursue. Given their own internal divisions and their lack of congruence with their voters, in this context, the main parties could hardly hope to gain votes by highlighting EU issues.

Has this absence of domestic party competition around the EU changed with the Euro crisis? To some degree, it seems so. NPs have debated the Euro crisis, and ideological conflicts between the left and the right have come to the fore (Baglioni and Hurrelmann 2014; Closa and Maatsch 2014; Hutter and Kerscher 2014; Maatsch 2014; Puntscher Riekmann and Wydra 2013; Wendler 2012; and Raunio, and Wonka and Göbel in this issue). Indeed, Frank Wendler contends that the plenary debates in the British, French and German parliaments on the Euro crisis generally adjust to the established logic of party politics at the domestic level (Wendler 2014a). However, it also seems that these ideological divides have often been sidelined by the main parties feeling obliged to act 'responsibly' and simply approve rescue measures (Mair 2011; Puntscher Riekmann and Wydra 2013).

Adapting Wendler's (2014b, 5/6) categorisation of the framing arguments used in parliamentary discourse on the crisis, we can distinguish disagreements of an ideological kind regarding the character and advisability of a given policy, such as we have associated with a normalised politicisation of the EU, from disputes of a pragmatic kind concerning the technical efficacy of EU action, and anti-systemic objections questioning the very legitimacy and justice of the EU, typical of Eurosceptic parties. The evidence Wendler presents suggests that the main parties favoured a pragmatic discussion of austerity measures over a debate that reflected their normal ideological divisions. As a result, more radical parties of left and right have been able to mount anti-systemic challenges to these measures on grounds of their democratic legitimacy and justice. Similarly, Carlos Closa and Aleksandra Maatsch (2014) note this pattern in their study of parliamentary debates of the European Financial Stability Facility (EFSF) in eleven Euro states. They show party positions were mainly polarised between mainstream parties, be they in government or opposition, that adopted pragmatic arguments favouring rescue measures on functional economic grounds, on the one hand, and more extreme right- and left-wing parties that employed arguments of an anti-systemic nature, on the other, with right-wing Eurosceptic parties appealing to national values and interests, and the left-wing parties criticising austerity measures for a lack of solidarity and social justice typical of what they view as the neoliberal structures of the EU (Closa and Maatsch 2014, 13/14). A similar assessment emerges from Puntscher Riekmann and Wydra's (2013) study of parliamentary discussion of legislation relating to the Euro crisis between 2010 and 2012 in Italy, Germany and Austria. The empirical evidence presented shows that legislation relating to the handling of the Euro crisis was passed in NPs by majorities that time and again comprised both government and opposition parties. They also show how the main parties have sought to marginalise criticism of the proposed measures as unrealistic and irresponsible. This suggests opposed positions that might represent the interests of those citizens who could be damaged by particular policies get damned as somehow against the national interest. In consequence, contestation has been left to the largely Eurosceptic parties at the extremes.

Overall, the tendency of major parties to play down the EU varies between member states as mediating factors intervene, such as the national narrative about the EU and media receptiveness to EU issues (De Wilde and Zürn 2012). In fact, EU issues have been most debated in NPs where consensus is greatest rather than where it is weakest (Auel and Tapio 2014). Germany in particular fits this pattern (see the contribution by Wonka and Goebel in this issue). Not only are Eurosceptic parties not represented in Parliament but also the responsibility to take a 'European' decision was in the German case not a matter of passively accepting a decision made by others but, thanks both to its role as the main 'lender' state and to the Federal Constitutional Court's judgement, a decision the Bundestag could potentially shape via its influence on the German government. As a result, its debates were perhaps the most ideologically contested of all (Wendler 2014b). Nevertheless, the evidence suggests that even though the powers of NPs have increased with the Lisbon Treaty, the incentives for most parties to deploy them in ways that normalise the politicisation of the EU remain weak.

At this stage, not much can be said about normalisation via the inter-parliamentary mechanisms that COSAC, the EWM and other bodies provide, given their recent introduction. However, the prospect for normalisation in these contexts seems bleak for several reasons. First, many of their activities are carried out by parliamentary bureaucrats (Högenauer and Neuhold 2014), making them an unlikely candidate for the normalisation of EU affairs through political parties. Second, the fusion of the executive and the legislative in most NPs, which implies that it is the government that provides opinions on EU affairs, will not incentivise all parties and MPs to get engaged with these inter-parliamentary mechanisms and bodies. Third, the policing of subsidiarity under EWM involves both a high threshold and is framed in legalistic terms which will hardly inspire mass public debates. It is also concerned more with the constraining of European integration on 'technical' grounds than shaping the kind of policies the EU should have on the basis of particular ideological views. Finally, the EWM does not allow NPs or parties to criticise inaction by the EU or to promote new areas of integration but is limited to subsidiarity and proportionality checks of legislative proposals.

In sum, the four conditions supporting the normalising of the domestic debate of EU affairs by non-Eurosceptic parties have only arisen under fairly favourable circumstances and, even then, remain weak. In addition to the first condition of the salience of the EU with the electorate, which is now generally present, two further factors appear particularly important. They relate to the second and fourth conditions of congruence with supporters and the possibility of party polarisation. First, parties must not fear giving electoral advantage to smaller Eurosceptic parties on either their left or right. Second, they must feel capable of influencing policy in ways that reflect their distinctive ideological convictions, rather than simply accepting its pragmatic utility or questioning its legitimacy. To a degree, the two are mutually supporting. Only if the EU policies advocated by the main parties can be aligned with their core ideological positions will their policies on the EU be likely to be congruent with those of their supporters and so be capable of being the subject of normal party competition around polarised policy programmes. The next section offers a proposal aimed at promoting the required congruence and polarisation by addressing these two factors.

4. A PARLIAMENTARY LEGISLATIVE INITIATIVE

As we have seen, the Euro crisis provides a propitious context for politicisation to occur. Indeed, it has prompted debates that have involved a discursive coupling of the EU and the domestic levels, even though the management of the crisis was clearly dominated by the European Council (Dinan 2011, 119). However, it is quite possible that once the Euro crisis is settled political parties and NPs will go back to 'business as usual', preferring not to debate EU affairs. To avoid that happening, and to ensure NPs live up to their role in republican intergovernmentalism of reconnecting the integration process to domestic democratic politics, we believe they need to move out of the shadow of the legacies of both the 'permissive consensus' and the 'constraining dissensus'. We propose that one way to achieve the more permanent coupling of the EU and domestic levels through NPs is through a Parliamentary Legislative Initiative (PLI), as a means of fostering the normalised politicisation of the EU by non-Eurosceptic parties, which we shall outline below.

Eric Miklin has argued that polarised legislative proposals can help 'to overcome parliaments' reluctance publicly to discuss and compete on EU issues because such proposals change the incentive structure of those large centrist parties that are able to enforce parliamentary debates' (Miklin 2014, 88). However, Miklin discusses the possibility of 'top-down politicization through polarising Commission proposals' (ibid.). We consider that such polarised proposals are unlikely to come from the Commission, given the grand-coalition-character of politics at the EU level. But more fundamentally, we argue in favour of bottom-up politicisation through greater involvement of

NPs, which is more likely to satisfy requirements of communal self-rule and identification with policies.

By a PLI we mean the possibility for NPs to put forward legislative proposals in regard to issues that are of shared concern with the citizens of the *demoi* of other member states. Such legislative proposals could be either for the EU to initiate legislation in a new policy area, or they could propose the EU modifying or withdrawing from a given policy area. A similar mechanism, the so-called green card, has been suggested recently by both the European Committee of the British House of Lords and the Dutch Parliament, and is now the subject of a consultation exercise by COSAC.[3]

Similar to the rules of the EWM, we propose that the PLI involve cooperation between NPs. A PLI would be triggered by at least one-third of the MPs in a minimum of one-fourth of all the NPs in the EU. The total number of NPs would be calculated by counting each chamber in bicameral systems as 1 and weighting the NPs of unicameral systems as 2. In the case of the threshold being reached, the Commission would be obliged to put forward a legislative proposal to be considered by the normal legislative procedure. As we note below, we set this threshold deliberately below requiring a majority of MPs in 50 per cent of all NPs in order to stimulate debate in part by empowering opposition parties as much as those in government. The *demoi*-cratic legitimacy of any measure would still be guaranteed by the normal legislative process requiring a super majority in the Council and the EP for any proposal to be enacted.

How would a PLI work in favour of the four conditions of salience, congruence between parties and voters, internal cohesion and polarisation so as to provide a positive incentive structure for political parties to normalise the domestic political contestation of EU affairs? We consider that it will be very unlikely that EU policies will return to the shadow of the permissive consensus (De Wilde and Zürn 2012), given that the Euro crisis measures mean they now impact directly on areas that are electorally salient for most citizens and given the high degree of politicisation these policies have already attracted. We also consider that it is next to impossible for parties to not be internally divided – to a greater or lesser degree – over any given policy, and particularly over EU policy. We do not address these two conditions, therefore. Rather, as we noted above, we focus on the impact of the PLI in favouring the two key factors we identified as favouring the crucial conditions of congruence and polarisation, which as we saw are linked.

We contend that the PLI should support the two factors lying behind both these conditions. These factors involved i) mainstream parties considering that the politicisation of the EU does not advantage Eurosceptic parties, and ii) allows them to adopt positions that reflected their core ideological commitments. Being entitled to influence EU affairs positively rather than merely in a reactive way, through subsidiarity checks, favours both factors.

Parties need not be reduced to debating mere technical and pragmatic considerations of a 'responsible' rather than a 'responsive' character, or be forced into opposing the demands for less integration on the anti-systemic grounds deployed by the Eurosceptic parties. Instead, they may seize the initiative to promote a policy measure which accords with their general ideology. Parties in government can push their executives towards adopting proposals that go beyond the compromises they may feel obliged to make as members of an EU-level 'grand coalition'. Such moves could aid their bargaining power by revealing a groundswell of domestic support for particular measures. More importantly, the comparatively low threshold of one-third of MPs is designed to allow opposition parties also to promote such initiatives and thereby to put forward alternative EU policies to the government. That not only empowers the opposition to develop EU policies of their own but provides an additional incentive for government parties to also defend their position on ideological grounds. Meanwhile, the need to cooperate with other NPs under the PLI will work against parties acting purely opportunistically or operating in the manner of Eurosceptic parties to protect a narrowly conceived national self-interest.

We observed in the last section how the ability of parties to promote policies that align closer to their ideological identities supports both congruence with their supporters and polarisation between parties. To the extent the PLI fosters these developments by non-Eurosceptic parties, therefore, it will allow them to reconnect their input into EU policy making with the domestic democratic process. In line with republican intergovernmentalism, they will not be tied to merely passively supporting commitments made by their executives at the EU level. Instead, they may shape those commitments and engage directly in dialogue with other NPs as well as EU-level institutions. In so doing, they can also move the politicisation of EU policy making away from a constraining dissensus monopolised by Eurosceptic parties that challenge the legitimacy of the EU and towards a more active consensus on the kind of integration the citizens of the different peoples of the EU wish to see. By virtue of these proposals coming from different NPs, the likelihood is that they will support rather than subvert communal self-rule. In other words, they will either be in areas that add value to what member states could manage on their own, or be in areas that strengthen the capacity for self-rule by reducing the potential for decisions in one state to create negative externalities that undermine the effectiveness of decisions by others.

CONCLUSION

We have disputed the thesis that the politicisation of EU affairs needs to be linked to an inexorable tension between European integration and communal self-rule. Instead, reconnecting the integration process to the domestic processes of normal party competition can bridge that tension. We have argued that this approach has a normative basis in a *demoi*-cratic understanding of the EU that we have called republican intergovernmentalism. In this approach, NPs play a crucial function as mechanisms for what we termed the domestication and normalisation of EU affairs. EU policies can be domesticated by being brought home and discussed in domestic forums and tamed so that they do not undermine the domestic democratic processes. However, the incentive structure for non-Eurosceptic parties to use these mechanisms in ways that lead to the normalisation of the politicisation of EU affairs along the normal ideological divisions that structure most domestic politics is currently largely lacking. In particular, the main government or opposition parties tend to acquiesce to almost all EU measures on pragmatic grounds, or raise mainly technical objections, thereby lending credence to the attempts by Eurosceptic parties to dispute their legitimacy. To counter this tendency, we propose the creation of a Parliamentary Legislative Initiative (PLI) as a way of fostering such normalised debates of EU affairs. We believe it promotes the two factors we identified as likely to support both polarisation between mainstream parties and convergence with their electorate by stimulating them to compete on rival EU policies that reflect their core ideological commitments. It does so by encouraging the non-Eurosceptic parties, especially those in opposition, to promote a distinctive package of EU policies without fearing they would merely advantage Eurosceptic parties and that reflect their core ideological perspectives and so are more congruent with their voters and liable to promote normal party polarisation through being distinct from those of the government. As a result, EU integration could be reconnected in a positive way to domestic democratic processes.

NOTES

1. We are grateful to the Hanse-Wissenschaftskolleg in Delmenhorst for supporting the research for this chapter. Richard Bellamy also acknowledges the support of the Leverhulme Trust for a Research Fellowship RF-2012-368. We would like to thank the anonymous reviewer, Ben Crum and Cristina Fasone for providing very supportive and helpful written comments, as well as the participants of seminars in Delmenhorst, Ottawa, Zürich, Cardiff and Rome for their constructive discussions of earlier versions of this chapter.

2. Although Schimmelfennig (2014) suggests that neo-functionalists could claim that there has been some supranational institution building in response to the crisis, such as the Fiscal Compact, it is noticeable that such initiatives have had to largely operate outside the established democratic framework of the EU and only been

possible when supported by governments that have been more pro-EU than their populations, and as in Ireland, Italy and Greece, thereby risked rejection by voters once an election occurred. Nevertheless, dissent from the handling of the crisis has not meant that most citizens want to leave the Euro let alone the EU, merely that their support has become more critical (Hobolt and Wratil 2015; Braun and Tausendpfund 2014).

3. HoL EU Committee, 9th Report Session 2013–2014, The Role of National Parliaments in the EU, 24 March 2014, 19–20; Questionnaire for the 23rd Bi-annual Report of COSAC, 23 February 2015, section 2.

Part VI

REPRESENTING EUROPEANS

Chapter 16

Democracy by Delegation?

Who Represents Whom and How in European Governance[1]

Richard Bellamy and Dario Castiglione

Since at least Maastricht, the EU has been in search of novel mechanisms and arguments to ground its democratic legitimacy. An increasingly influential view, which came to prominence with the debate following the Commission's 'White Paper on Governance' (2001), holds that the European Union has evolved new modes of governance (NMG) that either compensate for its lack of democratic legitimacy or offer more participatory and deliberative styles of democratic politics than the traditional electoral and representative forms of democracy associated with the nation state. This view involves two distinct but interrelated arguments. On the one hand, the policy problems dealt with at the European level are said to be mainly regulatory, rather than redistributive, and so can be more appropriately handled by the 'delegation' of powers to specialised, and largely expert (or at least, non-majoritarian) institutions (Majone 1999, 1–24, 2005). On the other hand, the associated NMG involve innovative, less hierarchical and soft-law based decision-making processes that purportedly widen democratic involvement at various levels (Scott and Trubeck 2002, 1–18). Some commentators even argue they form part of an emergent and experimental architecture of governance, whose principles, though mainly instantiated through informal channels and practices, reflect those underpinning democracy more generally (Sabel and Zeitlin 2008, 271–327).

Both these arguments are usually presented in terms of their ability to secure democratic 'outputs' notwithstanding – and possibly because of – their lack of conventional democratic 'input' (Scharpf 1999, 2, 6–13). Nevertheless, these 'output' arguments invoke implicit claims to satisfy certain 'input' criteria for democratic legitimacy, albeit in unconventional ways. These claims rest on delegated bodies and NMG supposedly providing the means to 'represent' social actors, general interests or even an overarching 'European interest' that the conventional democratic channels of political parties, electoral majorities and parliamentary representatives fail to register. As we shall show, their alleged superiority in achieving better democratic 'outputs' largely assume these representative 'inputs'.

We start by outlining the nature of European governance and the role that delegation and NMG play in it. We then assess the representative claims that are made for each of these mechanisms. We argue that lack of effective formal channels for authorising representatives and holding them to account undermines the substantive representative claims of these agents and agencies to 'stand' or 'act' for the European public.

EUROPEAN GOVERNANCE AND NMG

Despite disagreement regarding the scope and nature of European governance, most analysts agree that at its heart lies the so-called Community Method (CM). Majone has characterised this approach in normative terms as involving three constitutional principles – independence, sanctioning and the offering of guarantees – to regulate the interaction between the main Union institutions. 'Independence' underlies the Commission's exclusive prerogative to initiate proposals, execute policies, act as guardian of the Treaties and represent the Community internationally. The Councils of Ministers and the European Parliament (EP) possess the power to 'sanction' the proposals made by the Commission. Finally, the European Court of Justice (ECJ) 'guarantees' a balance between the institutions, while upholding the integrity of the European legal system (Majone 2005, 44).[2] More descriptive accounts of the CM point to how various institutions have assumed particular responsibilities in relation to different areas of policy making. For instance, they distinguish between a stricter application of the CM with regard to areas such as agricultural and fishery policies, and slightly modified sets of rules of engagement and institutional responsibility in areas such as competition policy, regulation and distributional issues (Wallace and Wallace 2007, 339–58). These descriptive accounts imply a greater role for social, sectoral and regional actors, and in some cases for the mechanisms and logic of the market.

From an institutional perspective, the Commission provides the most innovative aspect of this structure of governance. Neither its bureaucratic nor its executive function operate on traditional lines, while its de facto veto power, deriving from its agenda-setting prerogative and role as the guardian of the Treaties, lend it important legislative and quasi-judicial functions. Majone suggests that the 'organizing principle of the Community is not the separation of powers but the representation of (national and international) interests' (Majone 2005, 47). The interlocking of competences and the procedures followed in the decision-making process make the Commission a bearer of political interests, which are balanced with those represented by the other institutions comprising the CM. In Majone's view, the CM offers a form of 'mixed government'. However, as he also notes, this arrangement is characterised by the extensive delegation of powers from the member states (MS) to the Commission, which exercises the role of a supranational non-majoritarian regulator (Majone 2005, 46–51; Tallberg 2003, 23–46; Coen and Thatcher 2005, 330/31). In this capacity, the Commission acts as the 'agent' for the MS. As we shall see, the centrality of this principal-agent relationship in the CM has important consequences for the conceptualisation of the Commission's representative function.

Although the structure of EU governance is fairly innovative compared to decision-making processes within the MS, the CM retains certain traditional elements of governance: notably, a hierarchical division of competences, binding decisions and the more or less uniform and strict implementation of rules through the use of sanctions for non-compliers. However, alongside the CM, there have emerged other modes of governance aimed at policy coordination between different institutional and national actors, and forms of selective transgovernmental cooperation. As Scott and Trubeck note, these depart from both the CM and traditional governance in two important respects (Scott and Trubeck 2002).

The first departure consists in a series of specific variations in how the CM operates, such as the introduction of more flexible and non-binding legislation and the substitution of procedural prescriptiveness for substantive uniformity. Other similar departures comprise the introduction in the policy-making process of new institutional actors, in the form of comitology for instance, to partly direct and control the Commission (Hix 2005, 52/3); and the more frequent recourse to consultation with civil society organisations (CSOs) through ad hoc initiatives or more institutionalised fora and procedures (Scott and Trubeck 2002, 2/3). This kind of departure corrects and transforms the institutional equilibrium and competences of the CM, while giving greater leverage to national and subnational actors in the implementation of policies and in the application of directives and other legislation, without changing the basic principles of traditional governance. Scott and Trubeck call this 'new, old governance' (Scott and Trubeck 2002, 2).

The second kind of departure from the CM is presented as more radical, amounting to a wholesale alternative to traditional models of governance. As argued by Citi and Rhodes, the Open Method of Coordination (OMC) provides the most innovative of these new and alternative instruments (Citi and

Rhodes 2007, 463–82), while Scott and Trubeck list a series of characteristics that in their view set NMG apart. These include:

- the valorisation of forms of participatory governance involving CSOs;
- the full acknowledgement of the multilevel nature of EU governance;
- the recognition that legislation needs to adapt to diversity and subsidiarity;
- the centrality of deliberation in policy making, both as an instrument for problem solving and as a form of legitimation;
- the adoption of soft-law measures, and flexibility in implementation;
- policy-making processes and mechanisms favouring experimentation and knowledge creation (Scott and Trubeck 2002, 3–6).

However, none of these characteristics is entirely new either. In one form or another, they have been integrated into traditional governance, be it as part of the process of policy formulation, or as second-best options, or as a growing trend in international policy coordination (Wallace and Wallace 2007, 349). From this perspective, what distinguishes 'new modes' from 'new, old governance' is their more systematic application, with some claiming that they are embedded in a new architecture or ecology of European governance (Sabel and Zeitlin 2008; Sbragia 2008).

Whether we see NMG as supplementing or substituting for the older forms, with differences a matter of degree or kind, three core elements stand out. First, NMG is heterarchic. Second, it opts for soft-law and flexible instruments, embracing a weak conception of authority and uniformity in organisation and policy making. Finally, it privileges deliberative, consensus-based and reciprocal learning forms of policy making and problem solving. It remains to be seen whether either the old governance of the CM, or these NMG can sustain forms of representation that go beyond those traditionally associated with standard democratic processes.

REPRESENTATIVE CLAIMS IN DELEGATION AND NMG

To represent is either 'to act for' or 'to stand in place of' someone (or something) else. Representation involves a paradox: to make present what is absent (Pitkin 2004, 335; see also Runciman 2007, 93–114). This paradox suggests that representing is a mental construction of a complex relationship in which both the means of representation and the nature of what is represented are continuously negotiated. This negotiation is particularly true of political representation, and especially of democratic politics, where representatives and represented tend to influence and reflexively redefine their respective roles, perceptions and behaviour (see Saward 2006, 297–318).

Political representation often gets equated with modern democracy and the ways the institutions of representative democracy translate the will (or preferences, depending on the approach) of the people into political decisions and action. However, as was evident from the tensions between elites and masses when representative democracies, first developed in the eighteenth and nineteenth centuries (Manin 1997), democratic representation does not exhaust political representation, or representation more broadly. With the spread of universal suffrage and the emergence of political parties, this tension has become less marked. Democracy and representation now appear as complementary and almost synonymous, rather than as alternative forms of government (Plotke 1997). Yet, that they need not coincide has become increasingly evident with the growth of informal and non-electoral forms of political representation.

Analyses of representation in Europe usually focus on the more traditional forms of democratic and electoral representation, and concentrate on either the EP as the representative of the European citizens, or the Council as the indirect representative of the European peoples through their governments (Farrell and Scully 2007). However, these traditional forms of democratic legitimacy are supplemented by informal and semiformal nontraditional forms of representation provided by the Commission and NMG. Moreover, it is these bodies that exercise the main executive and legislative functions of determining European policy. It is to the description and assessment of the degree to which these alternative types of representation can also lay claim to democratic legitimacy that we now turn.

(a) Representation and Delegation in the CM

Although the CM employs the hierarchical and authoritative structures of decision-making typical of 'old' modes of governance, it lacks the classical features of representative and democratic government found in national and federal states. As many commentators have observed, neither the construct of 'people' nor that of 'government', both central to the idea of representative government, applies easily in the EU context. The existence and feasibility of a European demos are famously contested (see Bellamy, Castiglione, and Shaw 2006a for an overview of this and related issues), while what Hix calls the 'double executive' arrangement of the CM can hardly be described as a government in the traditional sense (2005, 27–71). We noted above how the EP and Council can claim to be, respectively, the direct and indirect representatives of European citizens and peoples and to have a responsibility towards their electorates and, in a loose sense, be held accountable for what they do. But, as we have also seen, the CM does not formally rest, as representative and democratic governments do, on its capacity to fulfil the mandate that comes through the formal channels of political representation. Though the Council and the EP can 'sanction' decisions taken at a European level, they have no monopoly over legislative and executive matters. Rather, it is the Commission – a non-elected and non-majoritarian institution – that plays the crucial role of initiating policy. Yet it lays claim to be representative in a different way in virtue of its 'independent' status.

As already remarked, Majone has characterised the resulting institutional structure of EP, Council and Commission as a modern version of 'mixed government'. The key aspect of this arrangement is that each of the three main institutions is 'bearer of a particular interest that it strives to protect and promote' (Majone 2005, 47). Unlike the separation of powers, within 'mixed government' the separate institutions are politically and not merely functionally distinct: they are separate 'political centres', and not separate 'organs' of the state (Majone 2005, 48). They do not operate in distinct spheres of competence but rather cooperate in the decision-making process, bringing to the table different interests whose valence and relative force depends on the nature of the issues at stake.

At the core of the CM's 'mixed government' is a basic 'dualism' of power between 'the MS represented in the Council and the other European institutions'. The Commission and the EP act as the 'bearers' of supranational interests; but whereas the EP is elected by European citizens, and can claim to represent them and their 'interests' (at least formally) at the EU level, the Commission is not, nor is it accountable to the citizens directly – only very indirectly via the EP, which approves its members. If anything, the Commission is an 'expression' of the Council, and its composition reflects the composite nature of the EU as an organisation of separate MS (Majone 2005). Is there, therefore, another way in which the Commission can be said to 'represent' European supranational interests? We contend the Commission's representative claim results from three separate processes, which can be categorised as 'functional', 'societal' and 'delegative' forms of representation, whose combination sets it aside from other European institutions.

Part of the Commission's claim to represent European interests, and thereby justify its role as the formal agenda-setting institution, is its functional responsibility to act as the 'guardian of the Treaties'. This responsibility produces a norm-orientation to act 'on behalf of the abstract "European interest" as defined in the Treaties' (Kohler-Koch 2010). Although the Commission is neither specifically nor personally accountable for the way in which it interprets this task, its position as a kind of 'representative' of the European interest is formally sanctioned by the EU Treaties, and the allocation of powers and responsibilities within the CM. The point is made explicitly in the *White Paper on Governance*, which describes the CM as providing two filters through which the policy-making process arbitrates between different interests. One filter is provided by '*democratic* representation' via the Council and EP; the other is that of 'the *general* interest at the level of the Commission' (European Commission 2001, 8). In this regard, the Commission's role as a functional representative is not dissimilar to that attributed to national constitutional courts with respect to their constitutions, with the important difference that the Commission operates more directly as a political and policy-making actor, so there is no pretence of its operating as a purely judicial power.

From another perspective, the functional representation claimed by the Commission approximates what Dryzek and Niemeyer have recently called 'discursive representation'. They argue that given no definite ontological ground exists to identify the precise entities deserving political representation, 'discourses' – as well as individuals, particular aspects of a person, or groups – can be legitimately represented politically. Indeed, they contend that discursive representation is particularly 'feasible when the representation of persons is not so feasible (especially in transnational settings lacking a well-defined demos)' (Dryzek and Niemeyer 2008, 481). From this perspective, the Commission qua guarantor of the EU Treaties represents the *discourse* of European interests. Theoretically, this approach limits the degree the Commission can act as the bearer of the European interests to the way these are defined by the Treaties. In practice, though, that leaves ample latitude for the Commission to interpret Europe's interests as it sees fit. The Commission de facto constitutes as well as represents the discourse of Europe's interests by virtue of its power to promote policies at the European level. This blank claim to representation gives the Commission a privileged position, at least in principle, even if historically the political conditions in which the Commission operates drastically limit its ability to shape the European agenda and its capacity for autonomous action (Hix 2007, 145–49).

However, such functional representation is rather abstract, and provides the Commission with a weak and ill-defined basis for its claim to represent the general European interest. Moreover, the claim can appear self-serving, while its validity rests more on an 'output' rather than an 'input' perspective. As a result, the Commission has placed increasing emphasis on a second type of representative claim typically couched in the language of democratic 'participation'. This second claim, perhaps best characterised as 'societal representation', consists in the development of procedures and institutional settings for the consultation of CSOs and social partners as a more integral part of European governance. Such initiatives have long existed, going as far back, for example, as the network-building with social NGOs that the Commission promoted with the first anti-poverty programme of 1974. But they were fore-grounded in the 'official' discourse of the Commission and became more for-malised with the *White Paper on Governance* and its commitment to create a 'culture of consultation and dialogue' (European Commission 2001, 16/17).

Rather than establishing legal rules and procedures, which risked slowing down considerably the process of policy-initiation and decision-making, the *White Paper* suggested tightening-up standards for consultation, making it an essential part of the policy process with less ad hoc criteria and procedures for selecting and involving the relevant civil and social organisations. Additionally, the *White Paper* suggested these organisations be required to 'tighten up their internal structures, furnish guarantees of openness and representativity, and prove their capacity to relay information or lead debates in the MS' (European Commission 2001, 17). This opening up was especially necessary for those key policy areas where there were already established histories and channels of consultation, for which the *White Paper* envisaged a structured dialogue through 'partnership arrangements' (European Commission 2001).

This new emphasis on civil society participation and consultation has been described as heralding a new 'regime' in European governance that intro-duces a 'participatory model' alongside the established expert-based and part-nership-based models (Kohler-Koch and Finke 2007, 205–21; Kohler-Koch 2008, 275). The attempt to increase civil society's involvement in European governance also seeks to enhance the *representativeness* of the CSOs and the European institutions that consult them – above all, the Commission. In the words of the *White Paper*, a more participatory and consultative regime will make the Commission 'better placed to act in the general European interest' (European Commission 2001, 34) – not least because it can claim to have listened to a representative sample of relevant European opinion on the issues it tackles, thereby enhancing its standing vis-á-vis those EU institutions with an electoral mandate.

The Commission has no common systematic consultation regime, with practices differing across policies and Directorates, although these differ-ences can be justified as reflecting the nature of the policy good concerned and the type of group that needs to be consulted. While decision-making remains technocratic, formal arrangements for involving social partners, such as the tripartite Advisory Council of representatives from govern-ments, employers and unions used for occupational health and safety policy and consultations European Economic and Social Committee, have worked reasonably well (Smismans 2008, 880–84). However, the evidence is more mixed with regard to the broader consultation with civil society. The selec-tion of CSOs remains biased towards Brussels-based 'umbrella' organ-isations, remote from the constituencies they purport to represent, while lobbying of the Commission favours business and professional organisations over public interest groups by the order of 76 per cent to 20 per cent, and the older and larger over the newer and smaller MS (Coen 2007, 335). Moreover, CSOs are often financed by the EU and have typically been employed by the Commission in the preparatory phases of policy making to legitimise the extension of its influence into areas with a weak or non-existent Treaty base (Kröger 2008). As recent studies have emphasised, the Commission manages lobbying by both firms and societal interest groups to create its own 'insider' organisations that foster trust between elite groups and Brussels officials and improve the flow of information from relevant parties to the Commission and the making of credible regulatory commitments but also allow collusion with and capture by groups with the best organisational and resource advantages (Coen 2007, 335/6). Participation tends to be limited to the early stages of the policy process, continues to be through informal and semiformal rather than formal channels, offers little scope for feedback (Broscheid and Coen 2003) and excludes critical voices unwilling to exchange the possibility of initial consultation for subsequent passive compliance (Hunold 2005).

Finally, the third sense in which the Commission aims to represent European-wide interests derives from its character as a non-majoritarian, supranational regulatory agency to which extensive powers have been delegated. Although, conceptually, delegated and functional forms of representation are not neatly distinguishable, the way the Commission acts as a delegate is specific enough to be considered as separate category. Its role as a regulatory agent follows from the introduction of the Single European Act and the growth of its competences in the area of competition policy so as to facilitate the working of the single market (Coen and Thatcher 2005, 331). Using Franchino's categories, one can locate the Commission at the receiving end of two processes of delegation: one, which Franchino calls 'Treaty delegation', that has the EU MS as the direct principals; the other, 'executive delegation', that has the EU legislators, mainly the Council, but occasionally the EP, in the role of principal (Franchino 2006).

Looked at in a stylised form, regulatory agencies can be considered as the 'representatives' for the principals who select them, give them their regulatory powers, and may dismiss them. Indeed, the formal structure of representation, as identified by Pitkin, can be applied easily to delegation:

A. Representation (delegation) involves a representative (agent) X being authorised by constituency (principal) Y to act with regard to good Z;

B. Representation (delegation) involves a representative (agent) X being held accountable to constituency (principal) Y with regard to good Z (Pitkin 1967; and Castiglione and Mark Warren 2006).[3]

From the perspective of principal-agent theory, democratic representation and regulatory delegation look rather similar, since they can both be nested in an overall chain of 'delegation of powers' from citizens to non-majoritarian institutions, passing through legislative and executive bodies, and occasionally public bureaucracies (Braun and Gilardi 2006, 4–11; Strøm, Muller, and Bergman 2006, 32/33). However, as the literature on regulatory delegation shows, at a more substantive level some of the operations, as well as the mechanisms of role-formation and agent's motivation, are distinctive, following dynamics of their own, which are not entirely reducible to political, or even bureaucratic forms of representation.

Majone characterises the reasons for delegation as being primarily of two kinds: the reduction of decision-making costs, and the enhancement of commitment and long-term credibility. These two reasons align the principal's and agent's preferences in different ways to produce two divergent accounts of delegation (Majone 2005, 64–7). Delegating to reduce decision-making costs assumes that principal and agent share similar preferences. Indeed, the main problem for this kind of delegation is to ensure there are no 'agency losses'. As a result, principals need to design selection procedures and post-delegation mechanisms that avoid dangers such as 'shirking' (when agents follow their own preferences irrespective of their principals'), 'slippage' (perverse institutional mechanisms that make agents' preferences diverge from their principals') and 'capture' (when agents collude with the actors whose behaviour they are meant to regulate) (Coen and Thatcher 2005, 233 and 236). This form of delegatory representation parallels that of mandated political representatives, for whom electoral mechanisms serve to guard against these risks. However, it is unclear that appointed, non-majoritarian bodies have anything as effective as electoral accountability to keep them on their toes. Indeed, their main representative claim rests on the second reason, which, by contrast, requires that delegates be insulated against the need for undue responsiveness to their principals' preferences.

The rationale for delegation to guarantee market credibility and maintain commitments assumes principals suffer from akrasia and act for short-term personal advantages at the expense of long-term collective benefits, even if they ultimately stand to gain from them. Principals can avoid this dilemma by adopting a pre-commitment strategy and selecting agents whose incentive structure coincides with the long-term commitments required by markets rather than the short-term popularity politicians typically need to court. One consequence of this dealignment of preferences between principal and agent is to increase agents' discretion and relax considerably, if not completely, the accountability and control conditions to which they are subjected. Agents no longer 'represent' their principals own short-term understanding of their interests and preferences, but rather respond to their principals' supposed second-order preference. This involves their agents acting according to their own 'independent' judgement as to where their principals' first-order interests and preferences lie *in the long term* so as to produce the commitment and credibility required by the market. Thus, when the Commission acts as a non-majoritarian regulatory agent of the European market, it does not directly represent the MS (as in Treaty delegation) or the EU legislative bodies (as in executive delegation), but rather 'represents' the long-term interests of the European Union and its MS, even if its reading of these interests and preferences diverges from how the other institutional actors perceive them.

The implicit view of the Commission's representative role within this conceptualisation of delegation reinforces other characteristics of how non-majoritarian regulators operate. These features proceed from the way these institutions have emerged as distinct and semiautonomous actors from governments. Many have developed what Coen and Thatcher call 'relational distance', with their own modus operandi and internal and self-referential organisation (Coen and Thatcher 2005). Thus, the European Commission 'has created its own network of national competition regulators', thereby moving delegation further along the line, and making the decisions of these regulators even more distant from their principals. Moreover, the delegation of power to non-majoritarian regulators works as a kind of incomplete contract (Héritier 2005; Thatcher and Stone Sweet 2002, 5–7; and Coen and Thatcher 2005, 334). For the kind of actions and intervention they may need to undertake cannot be fully predicted when power gets delegated, creating a considerable area for them to exercise their discretion in potentially arbitrary ways.

The account of representation implied by the Commission's activity as a delegated regulator in this second sense is that of 'trusteeship'. As Majone observes, it acts as a 'fiduciary' (2005). This fiduciary role is further reinforced by the functional and societal modalities of representation discussed above. Acting in each of these modalities, the Commission claims autonomously to interpret and express the European public interest. It does so in accordance with the various tasks it performs within the CM: as the guarantor of the Treaties, as the mediator with CSOs of European society's interests, and as an expert-based, non-majoritarian regulatory institution. However, as we shall see in the next section, it remains unclear on what basis the Commission can claim to be actually *representing* Europe and European-wide interests, and whether the mechanisms through which the Commission interprets the public interest are effective and have democratic legitimacy. For, though Burke famously championed trusteeship as the prime responsibility of political representatives, it has generally come to be seen as at odds with their democratic status as elected servants of the popular mandate (Burke 1774).

(b) Representation in the NMG

Most of the representative claims made in support of NMG parallel those invoked for the Commission. Indeed, the three modalities of representation – functional, societal and delegative – apply here too. We shall start by briefly examining delegative representation since it operates on the same principles, and through very similar mechanisms to those described for the Commission. We shall then explore the more distinctive forms societal and functional representation takes in this case.

Once again, the delegative modality of representation follows from the delegation of regulatory tasks to independent and non-majoritarian agencies, whose main task is creating markets or correcting their behaviour. Much of the discussion of the fiduciary role played by the Commission can therefore be transposed to NMG more broadly. However, in this case, the principal is often the Commission, which, as we have seen, acts in its turn as the agent for other principals. Consequently, with NMG the chain of delegation gets extended even further, increasing the scope for private organisations and self-regulation and widening the 'relational distance' identified by Coen and Thatcher as one of the ways in which regulatory agents acquire more autonomy and discretion in the decision-making process (Coen and Thatcher 2005). Most importantly, regulation is seen from a sectoral perspective, and so is more dispersed and self-referential.

A similar process of diffusion and segmentation applies to the societal modality of representation. Societal representation by CSOs has two rationales within European governance. The first is to provide one of the preconditions for political representativeness by constructing a 'social constituency' for the European polity in formation (Fossum and Trenz 2006; see also Kohler-Koch 2009, 47–57). It offers a social point of reference for a political system whose links with European citizens are tenuous at best. Kohler-Koch calls this process an exercise in 'imaginary representation' and considers it a 'category that is supposed to help understand the formation of a "political system" and not to assess the democratic functioning of the EU' (Kohler-Koch 2010). The second rationale for societal representation is linked to a conception of participatory governance, whereby policies are said to be more responsive and more likely to be regarded as legitimate through involving those affected in making them.

Both these rationales risks subsuming the European public as a whole into the plethora of civil and social-interest-based organisations that EU institutions choose to consult. Nevertheless, we saw how within the CM, the Commission plays a mediatory and filtering role that – however imperfectly and self-serving in nature – at least attempts to give some unity to the variety of concerns expressed by different autonomous forms of social organisation. It seeks to reconcile different interests and in various ways synthesise them so as to express an overarching European interest. By contrast, within NMG the representation of social interests and particular concerns is often even more haphazard. Different bodies and countries offer different degrees of access, participation tends to be informal and, as is invariably true within the CM, restricted to preliminary consultations. At the EU level, only those groups who can afford to be in Brussels are involved, political parties are excluded, and, as in the CM, experts and technocrats are favoured – especially in comitology, with only MS representatives and the Commission having formal participation rights on the relevant policy-making bodies (Kröger 2007). Indeed, in some cases NMG arrangements for involving social partners and stakeholders have merely detracted from more inclusive mechanisms established within CM (Smismans 2008, 884–90). As a result, NMG threatens to be still more partial and arbitrary in their representativeness of civil society as a whole.

In fact, the participation of stakeholders and organisations of affected parties in NMG is usually justified less on the grounds that they give access to more groups and hence are more representative per se, and more because they are thought to produce better decision-making in a specific sector or activity. However, such partial involvement, and the fact that it is largely consultative, means that at best it gives these decisions a spurious legitimacy, and at worst it fails to assess the impact of policies in a given sector on social interests not directly relevant to its operations or their relative importance compared to measures in other sectors. In this respect, societal representation merges into the functional modality of representation. As we noted, the main features of NMG are said to lie in their offering a heterarchical structure of authority, greater flexibility, and enhanced problem-solving capacity. These qualities supposedly produce a more deliberative decision-making process aimed at achieving consensus on the best policy rather than bargaining to reconcile competing interests, while nevertheless remaining attuned to the diversity and multilevel nature of the EU. By bringing together state and non-state actors, experts and social representatives in a forum orientated towards the sharing of knowledge, mechanisms such as the OMC and network governance are held to foster 'a reasoned discourse between expert and lay people' (Kohler-Koch 2010) that overcomes a '*deficit of mutual awareness* between civil society and public authorities' (Lebessis and Paterson 2000, 27). Strategies such as benchmarking and peer review supposedly encourage those involved to adopt the better rather than merely convenient or self-serving practices, while respecting relevant and legitimate differences stemming from the autonomy and distinctiveness of the MS (Citi and Rhodes 2007, 468–72).

However, one can just as easily imagine these structural constraints having precisely the opposite effect – of producing only mutually advantageous,

Pareto optimal improvements that benefit those already privileged within the status quo by leaving existing inequities and inefficiencies intact. Fair and equitable policies will only emerge from this process if the representation is itself fair and equitable between the main concerns that need to be aired, or if the representatives see themselves as serving public rather than sectional interests. Yet, few (if any) criteria exist to ensure that representation fulfils the requisite standards of either fairness or publicness. It might be argued that when dealing with the largely technical questions that form the bulk of the EU's business both can be met through appointing national experts. However, not only can experts often disagree on technicalities, but most technical questions also have broader social and economic effects. Again, such policy spillovers may go unaddressed without fair representation of non-technical parties from both within and, as we noted above, outside the sector. Health and safety standards for food produce, for example, will have implications for a whole range of actors and policy areas – affecting the viability of different kinds of farming practice, consumer choice, regional development, environmental policies and so on. Quite how all these might be appropriately factored into the deliberative process to ensure all receive their due weighting within the discussion remains obscure. Indeed, the evidence thus far suggests little deliberation occurs within the NMG, be it due to time constraints, the absence of a plurality of actors, or a lack of commitment on the part of those involved (Kröger 2007, 2008).

As with the CM, the claim that NMG represent the European public interest appears more rhetorical than real. Moreover, with NMG this problem gets exacerbated by the fragmented and partial way social interests are represented. But the main issue concerning both modes of governance is whether, conceptually and normatively, clear mechanisms could be said to exist for ensuring that political representation occurs.

CONCEPTUAL AND NORMATIVE ASSESSMENTS

Following Pitkin (1967), one can distinguish formal from substantive concepts of representation. Formal understandings contain two key elements, though different theories may focus more on one or the other: namely, *authorisation* and *accountability*. These provide the formal processes through which representation takes place. We referred to these formal structures above in noting how representation consists in X authorising Y (with regard to Z), and, at the same time, X being accountable to Y (with regard to Z). By contrast, substantive understandings concern the way in which the representative relationship works. Pitkin suggests that, broadly speaking, substantive concepts view representation as a way of either 'standing for' or 'acting for' someone or something else.

'Standing for' suggests a somewhat passive way of taking someone's place and 'acting for' a more independent way of doing so. However, such a sharp distinction would be overdrawn. Representatives who 'stand for' others may be obliged to act in a way that reflects their principals' preferences or spirit but they rarely have a precise imperative mandate from them detailing how they should act on all occasions. Thus, 'standing for', which can take descriptive or symbolic forms, allows representatives some leeway for interpreting their role and a degree of independence in how they perform it. However, overall, the idea of 'standing for' sees representation as involving either a correspondence of interests and views between the representative and those he or she represents, or a mirroring or reflection of those being represented in those that represent them – for example, in their sharing a given quality such as gender or colour.

By contrast, 'acting for' focuses on the substance of the activity performed by the representative. As Pitkin says, 'we are now interested in the nature of the activity itself, what goes on during representing, the substance or content of acting for others, as distinct from its external and formal trappings' (Pitkin 1967, 114). Nevertheless, there is a range of ways of 'acting for' another person: be it as a *substitute,* a *trustee,* a *deputed agent,* a *fiduciary,* or an *expert.* As we shall see below, each of these ways of 'acting for' involves a different view of the relationship between the representative and the represented. Whereas some ways come close to the 'standing for' model, whereby an agent acts as their principals could be expected to, had they the ability or standing to do so; other ways involve agents acting for the benefit of their principals, even if their view of what would most benefit them conflicts with their principals own reading of their best interests. However, all these cases differ from the 'standing for' model in involving some weaker or stronger sense in which representatives exercise their own judgement as to what is necessary to secure the best outcome for the represented, be that a view or knowledge of the most appropriate means, or in the strongest case, of what the better outcome would be.

Analysing the representative claims of the Commission and NMG through Pitkin's grid, it is clear that they emphasise the substantive over the formal aspects of representation. At most, particularly in the case of the Commission, their claims resemble those made by traditional structures of bureaucratic representation, whose representativeness in terms of authorisation and accountability is nested within a more general structure of political and democratic representation involving some appeal to the electorate and public opinion more broadly. However, in the European case these appeals are extremely tenuous, because the chain between the general public and those who make decisions is such a long one. For example, the Commission may be appointed by the MS and subject to approval by the EP, but once in office they operate with a high degree of independence. Likewise, the delegated representatives in regulatory and other non-majoritarian bodies tend to be 'authorised' by governments or the Commission whose own formal authorisation by, and accountability to, a European public is rather thin. Moreover, they then enjoy considerable discretion in view of their role as either *experts* or *credible* agents. Indeed, their credibility is often held to depend on criteria not only external to but deliberately insulated from any need to reflect or be accountable to the declared preferences of those they represent.

The representative claims of European governance are therefore mainly based on the substantive understandings of representation. What we termed the 'societal' modality of representation gestures towards the 'standing for' conception. As we saw, civil society organisations are treated as reflecting the diversity of European society at large. But in the absence of systematic formal mechanisms of authorisation and accountability, such claims are more symbolic than descriptive. Whereas elections give all voters the opportunity to express their views on a range of policies on an equal basis, with majority voting in the context of a system of competing parties offering a fair means for aggregating their different preference schedules in a way that packages them so as to roughly reflect the preference schedule of the electorate (Weale 2005), no equivalent mechanisms exist to ensure that consultations with civil society fairly describe the balance of social views overall. Instead, there is a real danger that this system will overly respond to those with the organisational resources and commitment to gain access. In practice, civil society representatives no less than functional and delegated representatives end up making their representative claims on the grounds that they 'act for' a European society that has yet to develop the capacity to represent itself.

As Pitkin observed, the 'acting for' conception poses two main problems (Pitkin 1967, 112–43). The first is the conceptual problem of whether we can have representation without formal authorisation and accountability – how can we know that such a person is truly acting as a representative? The second is the normative problem of whether any independent purely substantive criteria exist that can enable us to ascertain what it means to act for the good of someone else (or, in our case, in the public interest)

The conceptual problem arises because 'substantive acting for others', as Pitkin puts it, takes many different forms, not all of which can be categorised clearly as a form of representation. Pitkin distinguishes five major forms (Pitkin 1967, 121), which we list here in descending order, from the weakest, which require a stricter adherence to the instructions of the represented, to the strongest, which give considerable autonomy to the person who acts.

(1) Those forms that refer to 'acting for' as the act of someone who is sent or delegated to do something specific (an ambassador, for instance);

(2) those forms that refer to 'acting for' as a kind of 'substitution' (an attorney or someone acting in a vicarious way);

(3) those forms that refer to 'acting for' as the action of an agent, who can, however, be considered as a 'mere' agent, or as a 'free' agent (this ambiguity is typical of the role played by elected representatives, even though Pitkin emphasises that an important distinction remains between an 'agent' and a 'representative', a point to which we return);

(4) those forms that refer to 'acting for' in the sense of taking care, or 'acting in the interests' of someone (a trustee and a guardian are the most common examples); and

(5) and those forms associated with the idea that experts and professionals are acting in the interest of others (a physician, for instance).

These five forms cover a semantic field according to which we can interpret 'acting for' in the two polar senses of either acting 'instead of' mainly forms (1) and (2), or acting 'to the benefit of' forms (4) and (5), with form (3) nicely poised in the middle, since it can be interpreted in either sense. For Pitkin, this ambiguity applies more generally to the very activity of representation (Pitkin 1967, 126). But looking at these different forms within the context of our discussion of European governance, we can confidently assert that both the Commission and the various instruments of NMG are closest to the strongest forms (3) to (5). The implication is that their role as 'representatives' is mainly a function of their actions and decisions being *beneficial* to the European public, rather than *expressing* the public.

As Pitkin notes, it is unclear in what sense these latter claims are representative claims at all. What these strong senses of 'acting for' lack is the idea, central in political representation, that the represented is *present* (hence also responsible) in the action of their representatives. Pitkin distinguishes between a 'representative' and an 'agent' (Pitkin 1967, 125). The latter 'does the actual work' for someone else, so is a kind of tool or instrument; while the former is not a simple instrument, because he or she acts as if they were that person. The 'presence' of the represented in the action of the representative can only be understood if we take the substantive aspect of the idea of representation ('acting for' or 'standing for') *in conjunction with* the formal aspects of authorisation and accountability. But, as we have seen, these formal aspects are lacking in NMG, and this weakens the sense in which we can say that they *represent* the European public. The suspicion arises that they merely represent their own view of what a European public would want. Yet such a public may not exist – it could be entirely 'imagined'.

The normative problem enters here. For their own view need not reflect their own self-interest. It may represent a correct view of the interests of those they 'act for'. The difficulty is how can we know whether this is the case or not? Again, formal mechanisms of authorisation and accountability seem necessary. These exist for physicians and lawyers, say. There are professional standards that they have to meet, and bodies that authorise that they have met them and to whom they are accountable for continuing to do so. As a result, one can at least say they are agents qualified to act for others in pursuance of a given task. It is unclear anything similar exists for political representatives other than a democratic process. As we saw, it was claimed that NMG offer a process of public reasoning, yet we observed how the structural constraints in themselves were unlikely to produce such a result unless there was a fair representation of the public involved. No metric for ensuring reasons do reflect the public interest exists beyond their exposure to public challenge. Likewise, the qualities needed to represent the public lie in large part in the ability to take the public with you. The selection and sanctioning processes of elections serve both these purposes. Of course, the stronger senses of 'acting for' suggest that their principals lack the ability to see their own interests for themselves. By analogy, these cases suggest we should view the European public as too immature, irrational, or ignorant to perceive where their own interests lie – a somewhat paradoxical basis for democratic legitimacy.

CONCLUSION

We have argued that EU governance makes representative claims of a functional, delegative and societal nature.[4] However, these claims are of a substantive kind to 'stand' or 'act' for a European public. The formal mechanisms that might allow this putative public to 'authorise' these claims and hold those who make them to 'account' are residual and imperfect at best. Yet without such formal mechanisms it is unclear whether these claims can be regarded as representative in any meaningful sense. No European public is 'present' within the activities of their putative agents. We have only hinted at the likely consequences of such attempts to separate 'substantive' from 'formal' representation. However, a potential danger exists that those interests that are represented are so partial – being either expert or bureaucratic delegates easily captured by the governmental or commercial interests they are supposed to control, or CSOs that are the creatures of those who not only consult with, but largely finance them – that this system risks magnifying the disadvantages of pork barrel, pressure group politics often associated with conventional democracy, without the benefits of its compensating advantages of promoting political equality and responsiveness.[5]

NOTES

1. A first draft of this chapter was delivered to a Panel on 'Political Representation in Times of Governance' at the ECPR Conference in Potsdam. We are grateful to other participants, especially Chris Lord, as well as Sandra Kröger, David Coen, Christine Reh, Jonas Talberg and Sofia Näsström, and the other participants to a seminar at the Department of Politics of the University of Stockholm and this journal's referees for helpful comments on that version. Research for this chapter was undertaken as part of the 'Democracy Task Force' of the EU-funded 6th Framework Integrated Project on New Modes of Governance (Contract No CIT1-CT-2004-506392).

2. Majone, *Dilemmas*, p. 44.

3. Cf. Hanna F. Pitkin, *The Concept of Representation* (Berkeley: University of California Press, 1967); and also Dario Castiglione and Mark Warren, 'Rethinking Democratic Representation: Eight Theoretical Issues', Paper delivered at the Conference on *Rethinking Democratic Representation*, Centre for the Study of Democratic Institutions, University of British Columbia, 2006.

4. For a discussion of the issues of representation and governance in a more national context, see David Judge, *Representation: Theory and Practice in Britain* (London: Routledge, 1999), ch. 6.

5. For the general issue of the benefits of the democratic process, and the consequences of their absence in those mechanisms that seek to provide democratic 'output' without an appropriate democratic 'input', see R. Bellamy, 'Democracy without Democracy? Can the EU's Democratic 'Outputs' Be Separated from the Democratic 'Inputs' Provided by Competitive Parties and Majority Rule?', *Journal of European Public Policy* (chapter 14 in this volume).

Chapter 17

Three Models of Democracy, Political Community and Representation in the EU

Richard Bellamy and Dario Castiglione

1. INTRODUCTION

Title II Article 10 of the Post-Lisbon Consolidated Treaty of the European Union (TEU) states that the Union is founded on the principles of representative democracy. It identifies three channels whereby European citizens are represented in the EU's political system: directly via elections to the European Parliament (EP), indirectly via their heads of state or government in the European Council or in the Council by their government, and in domestic elections which hold these last democratically accountable to National Parliaments (NPs) or to citizens. One potential difficulty with this arrangement involves a possible tension between the representation of citizens, on the one hand, and of States, on the other, given no clear distinction exists between when and for what purposes citizens are represented as Europeans and as members of States, or of the connections between the two (Kröger and Friedrich 2012, Bolleyer and Reh 2012). Consequently, European-level decisions can be at odds with Member State (MS)-level decisions and vice versa. This chapter explores a related but distinct aspect of this problem. We argue that not only do these three channels represent different subjects – citizens in the first case, States in the second, with the third largely unrelated to European issues, and hence providing no link between the other two but also that each channel involves a different type of representation and form of democracy that reflect divergent conceptions of political community.

Such differences can be productive. For example, bicameral systems often employ different electoral systems and constituencies for each of the chambers, the idea being to bring different voices into the democratic dialogue with short-term and long-term, national and regional, majority and minority interests balanced against each other. Though systems of compound representation can be criticised for multiplying veto points and creating inefficiencies, they have been motivated by an underlying logic of preventing the capture of government policy by sectional interests and promoting among them a concern with the public interest. Our argument is that at present no such logic can be attributed to the EU political system because these three channels are not related to each other in a systematic and coherent manner. Instead, they offer incompatible images of the relations between individuals and States in Europe. Individuals are represented in the first channel as members of a European people, in the second by MS and in the third as members of their various domestic peoples. Each channel not only constructs the interest of a different public but also conceives the public interest in different and ultimately incompatible ways – in terms of a common good, as mutual self-interest and as a shared interest – leading to contradictory policy proposals.

We shall argue that the first two conceptions of the European public interest are at odds with the EU's declared aim 'of creating an ever closer union among the peoples of Europe'. They misrepresent the 'public' of Europe both in their conception of that public – as a European people or simply a collection of States – and in the type of representation they employ and the form of politics it leads to. The resulting problems seem epitomised by current attempts to resolve the Euro crisis, where the proposed measures have failed either to promote a European interest sufficient to allow credit transfers between the MS or to satisfy national interests as these are perceived by domestic electorates. The upshot has been policies widely criticised as suboptimal. We contend the solution lies in the European peoples being represented in a way that allows for greater interaction between them in the collective decision-making of the EU. In line with the TEU's meta-democratic principle of 'equality', a form of representation is required that pays 'equal attention' to citizens as citizens of a Union of peoples rather than as either members of a putative European people or nationals of an MS. In sum, we need to promote a workable form of European 'demoi-cracy' (Nicolaïdis 2003) rather than either a European 'democracy' or a system of democratic States where some tend to dominate others.

The argument proceeds as follows. We start by distinguishing three forms of representative democracy and three related conceptions of political community. If the first form of democracy is 'thick', concerned with the intrinsic promotion of a supposed common good, and the second is 'thin', orientated towards an instrumental protection of individual rights and interests, the third seeks to combine these two in ways that have become characteristic of most working liberal democracies. These three forms of democracy reflect three different political ontologies – what, following Philip Pettit (2005), we term solidarism, singularism and civicity – which conceive the relations between the members of a political community and the appropriate modes of representing them in contrasting ways. We contend that the capacity to promote public policies that give mutual recognition to the rights of individuals can only be found in the interactional form of representation characteristic of a civicity. Turning to the EU, we argue that the supranational, international and national channels of representation within the EU correspond, respectively, to the three forms of representative democracy and political community delineated above. We maintain that the social conditions are lacking for the solidarist account invoked by the EP and the Commission to represent the collective interests of a European people, while the singularist account that legitimises bargaining between the MS prevents their governments moving beyond policies that can be portrayed as Pareto optimal. We propose that if European issues could be introduced into the national channel of representation that might in its turn modify the other two channels sufficiently to move them closer to the form of representative democracy typical of a civicity. The result would be a European demoi-cracy in which political representatives at all three levels would be socially and politically authorised and accountable for policies that show equal concern and respect to the different peoples of Europe. Such policies involve less than the common good of a European people but more than the mutual self-interest of the MS.

2. THREE MODELS OF REPRESENTATIVE DEMOCRACY

In formal terms, representation involves someone taking the place of someone else through a process involving both the authorisation of the representative *by* the represented, and the accountability of the representative *to* the represented (Pitkin 1967). Authorisation concerns the procedures and extent by and to which people transfer their power to either act or decide to other political and/or legal 'persons' or institutions. Accountability deals with the ways and degree by and to which the represented can control what their representatives do in their name. These two moments reflect the initial and the final stage of the representative relationship respectively and are central to the legitimacy of democratic representation.

How political agents enact this formal relationship substantively also matters. A representative may 'stand for' or 'act for' those they represent (Pitkin 1967, 61, 113). The first involves descriptive or symbolic representation, as in a portrait or logo, and hence a degree of identification between representative and represented. The second can be as a delegate or a trustee. Historically substantive disputes about *how* representatives represent have centred on the delegate-trustee dichotomy, though a whole spectrum of possible relationships exists between the two (Pitkin 1967, 115–39). However, despite its limitations (Saward 2010), this dichotomy captures an important dilemma confronting democratic representation. As Pitkin noted, representation involves a paradox whereby it makes 'present' those who are 'absent'. As such, it involves a relationship of relative independence between the representative and the represented (Pitkin 1967, 209). If the legitimacy of representatives tends to rest on their having a mandate of some kind, and so being in certain respects delegates, the activity of representation tends to involve their being able to act to in some ways independently, as trustees.

Our contention is that the manner in which representatives 'act for' their principals depends to a large degree on how they 'stand for' them, and that the extent and nature of the identification between the one and the other conditions how far and in what ways they can bridge the gap between delegation and trusteeship. For the different processes employed to select representatives to 'act for' citizens reflect a particular social relationship between representative and the represented and the way the one 'stands for' the other. How and why citizens are represented determines in its turn the view of the public interest that representatives will seek to construct and the political and social legitimacy they have to do so.

In this section we shall introduce three conceptions of democracy – what we shall call 'thick', 'thin' and 'thick-thin'. We shall argue each involves a different understanding of how representatives may 'act for' citizens which corresponds to a different 'political ontology' or view 'of the relationships and structure in virtue of which individuals in a polity constitute a people, a nation, and a state' (Pettit 2005, 157) which constrains how they 'stand for' them. Following Pettit (2005), we term these three ontologies 'political solidarism', 'political singularity' and 'civicity', respectively. We maintain that both the 'thick' and the 'thin' models of democracy lead representatives to pursue a limited understanding of the public interest that in the one case subsumes the individual into the collective interest and in the other the collective into the individual interest. By contrast, the interactional form of representation typical of the thick-thin model balances the two.

Democratic politics encompasses two main tasks: the positive task of facilitating the equal participation of citizens in the construction of the public interest, and the negative task of protecting the interests of the ruled from being dominated and manipulated by their rulers via their control of the state apparatus. Both the participatory and the protective tasks figure in most theories of democracy. However, different conceptions of the democratic process tend to read either the second through first or vice versa (Macpherson 1977).

Thicker conceptions of democracy emphasise deliberation. Democracy serves an intrinsic purpose whereby the political community can discover and sustain the common good. It aims at generating a general will, which has moral priority over the particular wills of individuals. As a result, the second, protective, task of democratic politics is conceived in terms of the first, participatory, task. The public interest is construed in positive terms, as the product of citizens identifying with each other and the polity.

'Thick' democracy presupposes an organic unity among the demos, and a natural conception of the common good. This unity of interests can be represented in the descriptive and symbolic ways Pitkin describes as 'standing for'. Representatives 'act as' the represented by virtue of certain personal characteristics that allow them either symbolically or descriptively to express the commonality of interests of those they represent. The governing body, be it an elected parliament or an unelected council, gains its authority by reproducing internally the same kind of unity (of the nation, for instance) that allegedly characterises the political body at large. Democratic representation reflects a unity of interests that already exists before the political process is in place and which deliberation among representatives merely seeks to clarify and express.

This understanding of democracy presupposes an ontology of 'political solidarism'. Citizens are conceived as part of a corporate body, whose standing, interests and judgements is both separate and independent from them: they are 'incorporated' into the body politic, which can then act in their collective name. A conception of political relations mainly found today in legal notions of corporate personality, it characterises theories of democracy, such as Rousseau's, that seek to identify the common good with the popular will. This view assumes citizens and their representatives possess a sympathetic identification with each other and an underlying agreement on ethical principles. They regard themselves as forming a stable collective unit with common goals.

By contrast, thinner conceptions of democracy emphasise the protection of private rights to liberty and the aggregation of separate individual interests. Democracy serves an instrumental purpose. The ruled seek to maximise the exercise of their private rights – either by protecting them or combining with fellow citizens who have similar or convergent interests – and to minimise the capacity of others – especially the rulers and the state – to interfere with them. Thus, the positive, participatory, task of democratic politics is conceived largely in terms of the negative, protective, task. The public interest is construed as the product of a system that maximises the possibility of each affected agent to block those interferences with their individual rights they deem unnecessary.

The thin conception's understanding of representation oscillates between privileging either a substantive sense of accountability or the formal processes of authorisation. On the one side, it focuses on the capacity of representatives to deliver certain policies or objectives, while denying that authorisation implies a real transfer of power. On the other side, it stresses the constraints imposed by the authorisation of representatives, but has a limited view of the process of accountability. Adapting Pitkin (1967, 139), the one interprets the role of representatives as 'acting for' in the generic sense of acting 'in the interest of', while the other conceives representatives as 'substitutes' who act 'under instructions'.

Elitist versions of this thin conception, such as Schumpeter's (1947), deny that the democratic selection process is properly representative. Leaders recruit their electors through charisma or the policy package they offer rather than being authorised by them as their representatives. Schumpeter refuses any possibility of a transfer of authority. In Adam Przeworski's words, 'Our institutions are representative. Citizens do not govern' (2010, 15). The representative's responsibilities and responsiveness to the represented are no more than a technical mechanism through which the electors express satisfaction or dissatisfaction with the way in which they have been governed or expect to be governed. Yet, the process of accountability gives liberal elites an incentive 'to act in the interest of' a broad section of the electorate. By contrast, on the substitution and mandate views, the rulers are authorised to represent the interests of the ruled. When acting as substitutes, representatives employ their own judgements as to how the interests of those they represent might best be pursued. Their role is to maximise a return to their diverse supporters. Authorisation gives them the right to do so until it is withdrawn. When mandated, representatives are authorised to act 'under instructions' from the represented, who are conceived as forming a discreet interest group with a shared view on how it should be promoted. However, whether the stress is on accountability or authorisation, the conception of the public interest that issues from these thin views consists of Pareto optimal improvements or the lowest-common denominator. On the elite view, this arises from competing elites striving to win a majority through aggregating individual interests and appealing to as broad a constituency as possible. On the substitution view, it results from substitutes seeking a return for the diverse interests of their backers. On the mandate view, it stems from the delegates of different interests seeking to block any collective decision that might not advantage their principals.

The ontology underlying this account of representation is 'political singularism'. Formal processes of accountability and authorisation are vital because people are assumed to be so distinct that no representative can 'stand for' another. Originating in the natural rights tradition, claims against governments and others are grounded in rights that inhere in individuals by virtue of their humanity rather than their social status. Political society is simply an aggregate of separate individuals with no politically significant relationship to each other apart from their various mutual contractual agreements. They enter these agreements solely to protect their rights and further their interests.

Democracy consists of selecting politicians able to pursue these tasks and removing those who fail through incompetence or corruption.

Each of these two conceptions of democracy has advantages and related disadvantages. The thick conception supports public goods but at the expense of potentially overlooking the pluralism of modern societies. Consequently, social and cultural diversity may be undervalued, with certain private rights overridden and cultural and other minorities marginalised. By contrast, the thin conception emphasises individual rights, but at the expense of so multiplying veto points that it proves hard to move beyond the status quo. Given that power and resources are unequally distributed in society, this arrangement may entrench and potentially enhance existing privileges and inequities. It also risks failing to provide adequately for the public goods on which many rights depend – from the police and legal system to welfare, health and education. Most working democracies seek to balance the two models by making democracy thick enough to promote the public good, but sufficiently thin to allow for the protection of individual and group rights.

This thick-thin model of democracy is sustained by a rather different, relational, view of representation. Neither the thick nor the thin views consider democratic representation as a dynamic and interactive *relationship* between the represented and their representatives. In the thick view, representatives act 'as' the represented by virtue of certain supposed intrinsic similarities. In the thin view, representatives act 'for' the represented either like the executive of a public company charged with maximising the returns to shareholders or by virtue of a mandate. In all these cases, representatives depend on the revealed preferences of their principals. However, a relational view interprets the relationship between representatives and the represented in more dynamic terms. As we noted, representatives are both dependent on the represented, who authorise them and hold them to account, and independent actors in their own right. Such independence results not only from them having to make decisions to meet unanticipated circumstances between elections but also from their being able to persuade voters and recruit a following during them. In Iris Young's words, the moments of authorisation and accountability involve 'a cycle of anticipation and recollection between constituents and representative' (2000, 129), in which both sides of the representation relationship are engaged in mutually constructing what and who is represented, how and by whom.

A thick-thin conception of democracy has this relational dynamic at its core. The process of representation forces citizens to dialogue with each other and obliges them to portray their various rights claims and individual interests in public terms in ways that can relate to those of others. Representatives neither appeal to the passive assent of the unreflective, naked preferences of citizens nor merely reproduce their particular sectional interests, or the alleged pre-political interests of a collective body. Rather, the incentives are such that they need to employ public reasons that can be avowed and shared by a broad cross section of the citizenry. Such public reasoning leads citizens to reflect upon their interests in ways that help construct shared interests (Sunstein 1991). As Bernard Manin (1997, 196) has noticed, contrary to Schumpeter's view the competitive party system has tended to play just this role in facilitating the emergence of a popular general will within elections by making politicians construct programmes of government with broad enough appeal to attract the median voter.

The relational reading of the representative process conceives the public interest as constructed via an ongoing dialogue between the particular interests of citizens. This dialogue occurs both vertically, between the represented and their representatives, and horizontally, among representatives themselves or various sections of the public. In this way, it combines both the intrinsic democratic qualities of 'thick' democracy, with its focus on the common good, and the instrumental qualities of 'thin' democracy, with its emphasis on protecting individual rights and furthering particular interests, so as to construct shared interests that balance both considerations.

This form of democratic representation assumes a political ontology akin to what Pettit calls a 'civicity' (2005, 167). This ontology involves aspects of the other two views. Like political solidarism, citizens within a 'civicity' regard themselves as forming a people with certain common interests and values. However, like political singularism, they also have distinct interests, make divergent rights claims and so differ over many public policies. Citizens combine both perspectives by seeking to resolve their disagreements and differences in public terms that can be seen as plausibly, if for some contentiously, as treating them with equal concern and respect. For example, if a government within a civicity offers a given group a tax break, be it the very poor or the very rich, they will be expected to show how this measure both is equitable and contributes to the welfare of the rest of society. They cannot simply insist that this group is entitled to this money as a privilege and regardless of its effects on others. The measure must treat others in society with equal concern and respect by giving equal weight to their rights and interests, and their views regarding them. Of course, how far the proposal does meet these criteria will be disputed by many, but the fact of free and fair elections forces the government to dialogue with citizens and justify its position to them.

To work, a civicity must possess many of the social conditions identified by pluralist theorists as necessary to the form of democracy they term polyarchy (Dahl 1998, 90). First, while the members of such a society possess diverse interests and values, these must be to some degree cross-cutting. As a result, the danger of a permanent majority or minority is reduced and all are roughly equally affected by collective decisions. Citizens have incentives to seek fair outcomes that show people's different interests equal concern and respect. This condition fosters reciprocity and compromise and facilitates convergence on shared interests and values. Second, it requires a shared public sphere, sufficient to make a genuine public debate possible (Miller 2009, 212). This condition enables different sections of the political community to communicate with each other, and enhances the transparency and responsiveness of government to public rather than sectional concerns. It will be easier to have a discussion among the public as a whole if there are shared cultural instruments, such as a common media – newspapers, blogs, television and radio programmes – that address and are accessible by all, not least because they are in a common language all can understand. Such instruments help the various groups within a society to inform and respond to each other and make it harder for governments to play them off against one another and pander to one group at the expense of another.

The presence of both conditions creates a demos in which citizens regard the democratic system offering a public and fair mechanism for the equal consideration and promotion of their values and interests (Christiano 2010). The weaker these conditions are, the more socially and culturally segmented a society, the greater the likelihood the political community will move from a civicity to singularism and democratic politics will take an individualist and protective turn. It is this problem that currently confronts the EU (Dahl 1998, 114–17).

3. REPRESENTATION IN THE EU: ONE PEOPLE, MANY STATES, OR SEVERAL PEOPLES?

This section relates the supranational, intergovernmental and domestic channels of representation outlined in the TEU to the three conceptions of representative democracy we associated above with solidarism, singularism and civicity, respectively. We shall argue that the second channel possesses a stronger social basis and greater political legitimacy than the first but suffers from the generic risk of 'thin' democracy of potentially producing inequitable and suboptimal solutions to collective problems. To overcome this dilemma, we explore whether the EU can develop the qualities of a civicity. We doubt it can at the supranational level and critique postnational models of democracy that assume it could. Instead, we suggest enhancing the influence of the third, domestic, channel as a way of so modifying the other two channels that the EU's political system operates as a thick-thin model of European *demoi-cracy*, capable of formulating shared European policies that treat the peoples of Europe with equal concern and respect.

We start with the supranational channel of representation. The EP, as a common channel for representing the European citizenry, potentially offers a European-wide perspective. Yet, European elections continue to be second-order and dominated by domestic issues (Hix and Marsh 2011), while the activities of civil society organisations remain similarly tied to the national context, even among the few interest groups possessing the incentives and resources to become more Europeanised (Berry and Kerremans 2007). MEPs represent national parties and constituencies and are largely unauthorised and unaccountable as promoters of pan-European concerns. To so act, they are forced to appeal to an ontology of solidarism and claim that, as a collective body, the EP 'stands for' and can 'act as' a putative European people. For example, though analysts of the EP generally acknowledge the weakness of the formal legitimacy provided by the electoral process, many counter that it nonetheless reflects the broad distribution of ideological positions found across the EU (Hix 2008). As such, it can reflect the common concerns of Europeans despite having no clear mandate to 'act for' them or even the capacity to mobilise European public opinion and provide the catalyst for forming a European public interest on either specific or general issues.

As we shall detail below, no European *demos* with the requisite solidarist qualities of strong mutual identification, agreement on principles and shared collective interests exists. However, these qualities do characterise the majority of political actors within EU institutions (Shore 2000). Indeed, this underlying concurrence of views and backgrounds facilitates the highly consensual decision-making typical of the EU policy process. EU policy makers generally justify articulating such apparently unfounded solidarist assumptions on two related grounds. First, they maintain that the EU tackles largely technical and organisational matters that are issues of 'good' governance (Shore 2011, 291–93). EU polices are deemed to provide public goods most rational actors would regard as beneficial to any view of life, such as the resolution of coordination problems, better and cheaper utilities, or a clean environment. Such policies can be assumed to reflect the collective interest of European citizens, while their efficient and effective delivery is largely a matter of expertise (European Commission 2001, 3–8). Second, as a consequence, the means chosen for providing these goods requires a technocratic rather than popular consensus, such as can be achieved through mechanisms such as the Open Method of Coordination (OMC) which become exemplars of 'thick' deliberative democracy (European Commission 2007). The role of the EP within this system, even under co-decision, is to legitimate rather than legislate, since policy proposals are drafted by the Commission (Burns et al. 2000). Opposition to the EU is regarded as resulting from ignorance and misinformation. Measures purporting to promote democracy and participation invariably turn out to be what is euphemistically called 'public diplomacy' and 'information actions' aimed at forging a European demos among 'opinion multipliers' and 'young Europeans' (Shore 2004).

The Euro crisis has shattered this vision of solidarist 'organic' democratic governance. Moreover, the main actors in responding to the crisis have been the MS governments, with the EP in particular largely sidelined. Within the intergovernmental channel the forms of representation and decision-making conform to the 'thin' democratic model appropriate to the political ontology of singularism. National governments and their ministers operate largely as authorised substitutes and very occasionally as mandated delegates of domestic interests, though with limited electoral accountability for what they do at the EU level given the low salience of Europe in domestic elections. The assumption is that their judgements can be relied on to maximise the interests of their citizens. True, those judgements can only be challenged by defeat in either a parliamentary vote or a referendum, so that only a significant miscalculation of public opinion is likely to be successfully contested. Yet, as primarily domestic politicians, their main incentives lie in promoting national rather than European interests. To a large extent, the national governments 'act for' their principals in the manner of the executive of a joint stock company relative to its shareholders – acting on their own judgement to maximise the several interests of those they serve without assuming a collective interest other than as private investors in a common enterprise.

The political singularism of the intergovernmental channel severely constrains the political solidarism projected by the supranational channel, making it difficult for European institutions to escape national controls (Moravcsik 2008, 334). EU legislation requires a far higher degree of consensus than in any national political system. It must secure consensual support from national leaders within the European Council to be placed on the agenda, a proposal from the majority of the Commission, a formal two-thirds majority – but in practice a consensus – of weighted MS votes in the Council of Ministers, a series of absolute majorities within the EP and the assent and active support of the twenty-seven national administrations, legal systems and parliaments responsible for its implementation. Treaty changes require unanimity between the national governments and ratification by NPs and in an increasing number of cases national referenda as well.

These constraints mean that EU governance mainly provides a mechanism for a singularist type of representation – that is, for democratic rule between and for different states, rather than of and for a people. Yet it also suffers from the limitations and drawbacks typical of such arrangements. First, because agreement is so difficult, it has a status quo bias. It proves hard to reform or drop policies that have outlived their usefulness or failed, or to respond to crises or fast-changing situations. The high consensus requirements not only make European solutions to common policies difficult to agree on but also can inhibit experimentation and innovation at both the national and the European level to improve or adapt those policies once they are agreed. Second, such inflexibility applies even more to the independent institutions – to a degree the Commission and especially the European Central Bank (ECB) and the Court of Justice of the European Union (CJEU) – that monitor particular policies outside of the political process. These bodies risk either applying uniform rules dogmatically to very different situations, or attempting to address such variations and cope with novel circumstances by exercising discretion in ways that may depart from what was intended by the contracting parties. Either way, if their power and competencies have a basis in the Treaties, as is the case with the ECB's remit to maintain price stability at all costs, say, or the CJEU's power to interpret EU law, then it will be near impossible to reverse or effectively challenge their decisions.

The assumption has been that the EU provides solutions to Prisoner's Dilemmas, where a collective agreement is in everybody's interest but there are temptations to free ride or disagreements over the most appropriate solution (Scharpf 2009, 183/4). In both cases, Pareto improvements can be expected. Thus, in areas such as environmental protection or deregulation, that only prove generally beneficial if all adopt them, but that powerful interests at the national level can effectively lobby to block, the EU has operated as an effective self-binding mechanism for tying the MS into mutually beneficial policies. However, the more the EU extends into policy areas where no such win-win solutions exist because of variations between the MS, the more contentious action by the EU will be.

The central dilemma of the EU emerges at this point. European elites embraced a neo-functionalist logic, whereby integration was viewed both as producing endogenous 'spillovers' into ever more sectors and bringing in its wake greater political unity and solidarity (Haas 1958). Mobilising pan-European democratic support for integrationist measures was thought unnecessary. A permissive consensus legitimated elites 'standing for' European citizens until such time as the benefits of integration had forged an active consensus among a European people. However, an ever closer economic and legal union has proceeded against a background of ever greater political and social diversity, not least because of enlargement. Consequently, greater integration has tended to reinforce rather than undermine the EU's political and social ontology of singularism. As we saw, those EU bodies, such as the EP, the Commission, the CJEU or the ECB, which have a role as promoters of common European interests that in principle might balance the singularist ontology with a solidarist one, have a limited capacity to do so. Structural funds apart, the EU bodies do not have the competence to make significant direct transfers between different MS or groups of people. Their policies are regulatory, and biased towards enhancing a single market from which all private actors – be they states or individuals – are presumed to benefit.

Thus, the ECB cannot engage in an effective rescue of the debtor states without violating the no-bail-out clause, Article 125(1), of the Lisbon Treaty. To act in this and other ways would require a Treaty change that would likely attract a German veto, given that Germany would be called upon to underwrite such measures. Since the German government represents its citizens in EU affairs according to the ontology of singularity, their loan must be guaranteed in the simplest manner through decreased spending by the recipient states. Likewise, the CJEU has the remit of promoting the four freedoms. Many have regarded the introduction of Union citizenship and the new European Charter of Fundamental Rights as marking a move away from the market bias of the EU (e.g. Kostakopoulou 2008). Integration through law would no longer simply be integration into a single free market. But the CJEU has little ability to act otherwise. For example, though it has declared that 'a certain degree of financial solidarity' now exists between the MS,[1] the limits to that solidarity have been all too evident in the initial responses to the Euro crisis. The Court can only liberalise and deregulate; it cannot create new European-wide social and economic policy regimes. As decisions such as *Laval*[2] and *Luxembourg,*[3] on the one hand, and *Schwarz*[4] and *Watts,*[5] on the other, indicate, the rights of citizens at the Union level are the rights of private individuals to produce, trade or consume but with no correlative duty to contribute to public goods or provide for social welfare. These are MS' responsibilities. Yet, by conceiving the EU as a whole as simply a collection of rights-bearing individuals along the lines of the ontology of singularity, the CJEU effectively undermines their ability to meet these obligations. The social solidarity of the requisite kind proves entirely alien to this perspective (Scharpf 2009, 190–98).

Is it possible to overcome this impasse? Is it either desirable or feasible to shift the EU towards an ontology of civicity capable of sustaining a more relational form of representation? Those who contest the desirability of enhancing EU democracy have hitherto done so by arguing that the current system of 'thin' democracy suffices for the functions the EU performs (Moravcsik 2008; Majone 2001). A judgement already contestable following the Single European Act (Føllesdal and Hix 2006), even its proponents grant that the debt crisis of the Eurozone has revealed the limits of the current system of governance (Majone 2012). The effects of decisions by the ECB or politicians and bureaucrats in Brussels are apparent not just to experts or special interest groups but to all citizens through their impact on savings, mortgages and public services.

The problem is whether a sufficient basis for an ontology of civicity exists for this proposal to be feasible. Prima facie, this possibility seems doubtful. As we saw, a civicity depends on cross-cutting values and interests and a shared public sphere. However, the EU encompasses too much social, economic and cultural diversity and lacks the necessary common public culture for a viable European *demos*. Moreover, these cultural and social divisions are largely of a segmental kind and correspond broadly to national cleavages between the twenty-seven MS. For example, if one takes views on abortion as an indicator of social values more generally, then the difference between Ireland, which only permits abortion if the life of the mother is in danger, and Sweden, which allows abortion on demand, is immense. Social divisions between the MS are as great. Per capita income in Denmark is getting on for five times that of Lithuania – almost three times the difference between Delaware and Mississippi, respectively, the richest and poorest states of the United States.[6] Meanwhile, despite the spread of English as the lingua franca of the educated classes, news and other media remain firmly national and regional in focus and only Europeanised to a limited extent that mainly benefits government elites (Koopmans 2007). Empirical evidence suggests a European identity to be marginal and fragmentary (White 2011).

Advocates of a fully fledged postnational EU parliamentary democracy contend these difficulties can be overcome. First, they counter that Europeans share basic constitutional values (Habermas 2001a). After all, every MS is a signatory of the European Convention of Human Rights, with the EU itself likely to accede soon. Yet, these rights have been configured differently in each country to reflect domestic democratic preferences regarding welfare, privacy, religion and so on, often in incompatible ways (Bolleyer and Reh 2012, 476–78). Second, they argue that a transnational civil society is emerging, which currently lack representation within national systems. Yet, the evidence for this development is meagre. Only 12 million EU citizens reside in another MS to that of their nationality – 2 per cent of the EU population, mainly from professional backgrounds – and even this group is only modestly de-nationalised in outlook and identity (Favell 2008). Likewise, membership of pan-European civil society organisations is very low – most depend for their funding on EU grants and offer at best 'proxy' representation of assumed interests (Warleigh 2006), while European parties have failed to emerge in electoral as opposed to parliamentary terms.

Of course, segmental divisions exist in the MS too, most of which contain minority national and other groups. However, the main pressures across Europe to resolve this problem are not to shift power upwards, to the European level, but for ever greater devolution of political, legal and economic powers downwards to linguistic, ethnic and religious minorities. Consequently, Europe is becoming more rather than less segmented. Contrary to postnationalist arguments, an abstract commitment to similar liberal democratic values has not of itself generated a willingness or capacity to deliberate on them in common.

So long as the *demoi* of the EU remain predominately national or even subnational, the danger of seeking to create an EU demos is that it will result in consistent minorities and majorities split along national lines. The result will be that the most realistic models of supranational democracy continue either to invoke an elite based ontology of solidarism, or to involve a complex system of multilevel compound representation that remains rooted in the ontology of singularity. Thus, James Bohman concedes that his proposed shift from national to transnational democracy involves a change in forms that 'may sometimes seem like *less* democracy' (Bohman 2007, 21). Indeed, when he refers to the deliberative aspects of this new form it is invariably to agents that have neither formal authorisation from nor accountability to any given *demoi*, such as those allegedly promoted by the Open Method of Coordination (85/86). However, such instruments lack the relative independence and reciprocal influence which we argued are essential to representative democracy within a civicity. Likewise, suggestions for a supranational system involving multiple *demoi* (e.g. Lavdas and Chryssochoou 2011; Fabrini 2010) end up multiplying veto points with all the drawbacks of gridlock, entrenching inequalities, and under providing public goods that we explored earlier (Miller 2008).

We believe a better strategy is to treat the national *demoi* of the MS as the basic building blocks and deliberative contexts of a European democratic association (Christiano 2010). Such an association takes the democratic peoples of Europe as its starting point, and seeks to promote an ever closer Union between them based on principles of political equality and mutual respect. Two criteria govern such a Union (Pettit 2010). First, it seeks to establish and preserve the conditions provided by the ontology of civicity under which the citizens of each MS can be part of a representative democracy based on a shared conception of the public interest. Second, such an association must be under the equal control of the component democratic polities. These criteria seek to prevent any MS dominating another, promote collaboration to tackle common problems and allow citizens to move and trade freely between the MS on equal terms without undermining their separate political systems. They justify MS-level representations in the EU on thicker grounds than those provided by a singularist ontology. They also support the positive and negative roles now accorded NPs within EU decision-making (Article 12 TEU).

The positive role arises from NPs receiving EU legislative proposals and having European Committees to scrutinise them and the decisions made by ministers. They may also send reasoned opinions to the Commission and engage in an informal political dialogue. National politicians currently lack the same legitimacy to act flexibly and to construct the public interest at the European level that they possess at the domestic level. The domestic politics of the MS is only very indirectly linked to the EU system of governance. No dynamic relationship exists between representatives and those they represent when it comes to European issues. Worse, their decisions regarding Europe are increasingly perceived as undermining the established democratic practices within the MS (Mair 2011). Enhancing the influence of parliaments in the European sphere may help foster an interactive relationship between the national *demoi* and their respective governments over EU policy making, thickening the thin democracy of the intergovernmental channel. It may thereby enhance the capacity for ministers and governments to 'act as' the agents of the national *demos*, empowering them to operate more proactively than hitherto, without losing the trust of their citizens.

The negative role relates to the powers NPs possess to police subsidiarity. Though this remains weak due to the high threshold requirement, it does legitimise criticism of the EU for overreaching its competencies. For example, it offers a democratic grounding for Scharpf's proposal (2009, 199/200) that the European Council be able to challenge CJEU interpretations of primary and secondary European law that overstep the intent of the Treaties, as has arguably been the case in a number of decisions relating to Union citizenship. It offers a 'thin' civic check on the 'thick' solidarist aspirations of EU institutions, forcing them to give equal respect and concern to the democratic preferences of the peoples of Europe.

These measures provide a more relational foundation for political representation at the EU level. They enhance the democratic legitimacy of decisions that are not Pareto optimal, but have the wider European interest in view, while enhancing the scrutiny of national governments and subjecting them to greater accountability when they engage in the definition of what the European interest entails. Both roles have also engendered greater cooperation between NPs and with the EP through COSAC. They create the basis for a European civicity, whereby national demoi may construct shared interests in ways characterised by equal respect and concern.

CONCLUSION

We have argued that the EU is caught between a weak form of 'thick' representative democracy at the supranational level, based on an ontology of solidarity, and a strong form of 'thin' representative democracy among the MS, based on an ontology of singularity. Strengthening the former is implausible, but leaves the EU unable to articulate a European interest that goes beyond the mutual interests of the MS. We proposed overcoming this impasse by making MS representatives more authorised and accountable on EU affairs via an improved dialogue with their NPs. In this way, the EU political system might develop the resources of an ontology of civicity within and between its component *demoi*.

NOTES

1. *Grzelczyk v. Centre Public d'Aide Sociale d'Ottignies-Louvain-la-Neuve* [2001] ECR I-6193, para 31.
2. *Laval v. Svenska Byggnadsarbetareförbundet* [2008] IRLR 160.
3. *Commission v. Luxembourg* [2008] ECR I-4323.
4. *Schwarz and Gootjes-Schwarz v. Finanzamt Bergisch Gladbach* [2007] ECR I-6849.
5. *Watts v. Bedford Primary Care Trust* [2006] ECR I–4325.
6. Data refer to 2010 from http://databank.worldbank.org/ddp/home.do?Step=12& id=4&CNO=2.

Chapter 18

An Ever Closer Union among the Peoples of Europe

Republican Intergovernmentalism and Demoicratic Representation within the EU[1]

Richard Bellamy

INTRODUCTION

The aspiration to create 'an ever closer union among the peoples of Europe' has formed the ostensible aim of the European integration process since the Treaty of Rome of 1957. However, this goal has tended to be conceived as the ever greater integration of the various peoples of Europe into a single European people, rather than as increasing and deeper forms of cooperation between them. This chapter defends the latter view on grounds of democratic legitimacy. It develops a thesis of 'republican' as opposed to 'liberal' intergovernmentalism. Whereas a liberal account views democracy as instrumental to upholding individual rights and interests, and therefore as being justifiably constrained should so doing serve to increase these 'outputs' (Keohane, Macedo, and Moravcsik 2009), a republican account regards democratic 'inputs' as of intrinsic worth, and the only legitimate means for pursuing and preserving our rights and interests (Scharpf 2012, 3–13). The terms liberal and republican as employed here denote normative rather than explanatory theories. Nonetheless, they have implications for how we should assess the actual integration process, with the republican account evaluating the EU according to how far it has come about via, and continues to uphold, a legitimate democratic process.

Republicans contend the democratic legitimacy of states rests on their being representative of a people (Pettit 2010b, 144–50). A democratically representative system aims to ensure politicians and their policies are authorised and accountable to citizens in ways that are publicly committed to treating them with equal concern and respect. Such arrangements create a condition of civic freedom in which citizens neither are dominated nor dominate. However, republican democracy at the domestic level can be undermined if states are dominated in their turn by other states or by organisations and individuals operating across states, such as corporations or financial institutions (Pettit 2010a, 77–9). The potential for domination by these various external actors increases as states become more interconnected, posing the problem of how to regulate the movement of goods, capital and persons between peoples in democratically legitimate ways. The solution proposed here is that of an international association of democratic states. This chapter maintains the EU's political system can be interpreted in certain key respects as meeting the requirements of such an association.

The next section explores the normative case for the focus on peoples. It elaborates criteria for a *demos* which can then be deployed to determine the characteristics the people of a given polity require to sustain a democratic regime. This analysis supports the no-*demos* thesis with regard to the EU. However, if the EU is unlikely to achieve democratic legitimacy as the representative of a European people, it might be able to do so as a Union of democratic peoples on the basis of a form of republican intergovernmentalism. The third section elaborates the rationale and criteria for such a Union, while the fourth section argues that the system of representation within the EU can be viewed as conforming to this model. As a result, the EU can be classified as a *demoi*cracy more than a democracy (Nicolaidis 2003, 2013; Chevenal and Schimmelfennig 2013). The fifth section insists that in the EU context the former arrangement possesses greater democratic legitimacy than the latter, a point that the sixth and concluding section illustrates with reference to the Euro crisis.

THE NORMATIVE CRITERIA FOR A 'PEOPLE': DEMOCRATIC LEGITIMACY AND REPRESENTATIVE STATES

The term 'people' may refer to an ethnic, a cultural, a professional or an interest group, or even a haphazard agglomeration of individuals. Here, though, it is employed in a specifically political sense to refer to a group of persons who regard themselves as forming a political community that is capable of self-government. This definition of a people is normative rather than empirical. It involves specifying the criteria for a political order to be legitimate and the qualities a people must possess for such an arrangement to be possible, and only then exploring the social and other conditions under which such qualities are likely to obtain.

Legitimacy can be distinguished from justice and indicates the criteria that determine whether the exercise of coercive power by political institutions over citizens is justified (Pettit 2010b, 142/3). Legitimacy is more permissive than justice in that institutions may be deemed legitimate without being fully just – indeed, it allows for there to be disagreements about justice. While justice may offer *pro tanto* grounds for complying with the laws of a given political institution on the part of those who regard them as just, legitimacy provides *pro tanto* grounds for accepting these laws even if one regards them as unjust, and seeking to alter them through the approved political procedures. Legitimacy may presuppose certain elements of political and even redistributive justice, such as rights to free speech and education. However, even these rights only become legitimate through being established and enforced in ways citizens can endorse as appropriate.

This way of conceiving legitimacy and its relationship to justice follows Rawls (1999) and Philip Pettit (2010a, 2010b) in stressing the normative significance of collective self-government (Macedo 2004, 103). On this account, the use of coercive power by a government can only be legitimate when it is exercised via processes and within constraints that are accepted by those subject to it, and for purposes that correspond to their needs and values. Therefore, a legitimate government must be representative of the views and interests of the governed. These criteria might be met in part within a non-democratic regime, such as those designated by Rawls as 'decent hierarchical peoples' (Rawls 1999, 62–70), in which benign and expert rulers govern according to a moral code subscribed to by the ruled. However, modern societies tend to be pluralist and complex, undermining the possibility of a generally agreed comprehensive conception of the good and rendering the perspective of even well-intentioned and informed rulers partial and limited. Consequently, the representativeness of such regimes can be doubted. Democracies seek to overcome these difficulties by putting in place procedures of authorisation and accountability designed to ensure governments represent the diverse views and interests of all citizens with equal respect and concern (Christiano 2010, 121/2).

Nevertheless, democratic procedures will not operate legitimately unless they likewise function according to norms and serve ends that can be commonly avowed by those involved (Pettit 2010b, 145–49).[2] It will not be sufficient that they involve the public, they must do so on a basis that can be publicly acknowledged by those to whom they apply as fair and appropriate, not least in demonstrably giving equal consideration to their views and interests in framing collective policies (Buchanan 2002). No matter how far such procedures may conform to abstract democratic principles in theory, their legitimacy will be impugned to the extent that their operation is perceived in practice to reflect unduly the values of a subsection of the political community, such as the ruling elite, and of responding disproportionately to their sectional interests (Christiano 2008). As a result, democratic legitimacy will depend to some degree on whether those to whom democratic decisions apply relate to each other in ways that render such a public and equal process possible and appropriate (Rawls 1999, 23–5).

The character of these social, economic and cultural relations, and their suitability for sustaining the public conditions that underpin the legitimacy of common political institutions, serve to define a people or *demos*. First, to justify giving them an equal say, the persons and groups concerned will need to have important issues in common that require a collective decision. Moreover, they must also have a roughly equal stake in the entire set, if not each and every, of these issues and decisions (Christiano 2010, 130/31). These conditions assume not only a high degree of interdependence between the members of a political community but also that their most important interests are more or less equally tied up in that community, and will be so over a long period of time – sufficient for them to care about the impact of present decisions on future generations – at least so far as the whole range of collective decisions is concerned. As a result, it becomes possible to ascribe to them an equal interest in ensuring that the basic structures of social cooperation are fair and equitable, including those employed for deliberating on the public good.

Second, there will need to be what J. S. Mill referred to as 'common sympathies' among members of a political community (Mill 1861, chap. 16; Rawls 1999, 23/24). We can to some extent detach the logic underpinning this idea from Mill's historical and sociological speculations as to its origins in a shared history and political culture of a kind associated with a common nationality. The argument is that to ensure the government pursues the public rather than sectional interests; citizens must both conceive of themselves as a public and be able to act as such and in a public manner (Miller 2009, 212/13). For example, a religious or ethnic group will be more inclined to seek rules that oppose discrimination against all groups, rather than to employ government power to suppress groups different to theirs, where solidarity exists between groups, so that they see themselves as part of the same political community. They must also be capable of sharing certain public principles that extend beyond the convictions of their own particular group, such as a commitment to a given understanding of toleration. Finally, it helps if there is sufficient public communication between groups for politicians to have to address the public as a whole, rendering it harder for them to play different groups off against each other.

Third, as a corollary of the two aforementioned points, democratic legitimacy will be harder the more divided a society is into discrete and insular publics, with distinct interests and views on key issues (Dahl 1989, 258/59). In these circumstances, politics is much more likely to be factionalised, increasing the probability of persistent minorities, with compromises on a common position harder to negotiate. Meanwhile, moves away from the status quo are likely to involve pork barrelling and derogations that increase transaction and policy costs.

The norms and processes that structure decision-making, on the one hand, and their acceptability to and suitability for a given people, on the other, comprise the *regime* and *polity* aspects of legitimacy, respectively (Bellamy and Castiglione 2003). To the extent the one is congruent with the other, it becomes possible for a state to be so organised that its government is representative of its people. Such legitimate representative states provide citizens with civic freedom of the kind republicans associate with freedom as non-domination (Pettit 2010b, 144/45). For the regimes of such polities provide the means for their citizens to secure and advance their interests on an equal basis to each other as defined by public terms and procedures that they can share and control as a people. Citizens can ascertain that the administration and legislation conform to public norms and pursue public purposes, informing and controlling the definition of these norms and purposes as part of an ongoing process of public deliberation among and between the people and their representatives. As a result, governments are constrained from governing arbitrarily – according to their own or some subgroup's views or interests. They can only employ the coercive power of the state insofar as they have been authorised and are accountable to do so on grounds that conform to the commonly avowed views and interests of the people they serve.

Thus, states have legitimacy to the extent they are able to represent peoples in ways that are public and equal and, in so doing, create mechanisms that provide for civic freedom among citizens. Of course, these criteria are not met in full by any actually existing democratic states. No regime represents its polity entirely equally and publicly – not least because peoples are rarely sufficiently homogenous for that to be possible. However, even among quite diverse peoples, the regime can be so tailored to the composition of the polity as to promote equity and publicity among different groups to some degree, as the experience of various multinational and multicultural states indicates. Yet, as these states also illustrate, the more economic, historical and cultural divisions become aligned with territorially concentrated groups and/or the various social cleavages found within pluralist societies cease to be cross-cutting and become segmented in ways that create separate political communities, the less acceptable collective decision-making among them tends to become. Over time, one or more groups begin to question not just the regime but also the polity legitimacy of the state, demanding ever more devolution of power (Kymlicka 2001, 212/13).

This issue poses a potential problem for those who wish the EU to become a polity (e.g. Duff 2011; Habermas 2012), a point to which I return below.

Most commentators acknowledge that while the EU possesses a regime of a supranational as well as an intergovernmental nature, its transnational polity-like features are at present limited (Weiler, Haltern, and Meyer 1995). This situation reflects the nature of the integration process as a series of intergovernmental agreements. Therefore, the issue to be addressed here is whether such a process can be consistent with the account of democratic legitimacy given above, especially if successive agreements give rise to and further empower supranational institutions. In particular, what circumstances might justify such a development and which criteria must the resulting arrangements meet to retain democratic legitimacy?

REPUBLICAN INTERGOVERNMENTALISM AND A 'UNION OF PEOPLES': THE CRITERIA FOR AN ASSOCIATION OF DEMOCRATIC STATES

As was noted above, a legitimate state offers its citizens the conditions whereby they can enjoy civic freedom. These domestic conditions will be insufficient, though, if the ability of the state to represent its people is undermined by bodies external to it, not just other states but also private organisations, such as corporations or financial institutions, that are located in other states or operate to some extent multi- or transnationally (Pettit 2010a, 77–9). External interference by other states – be it intended, as in the case of conquest or the threat of armed conflict, or an unintended product of various negative externalities resulting from domestic decisions – limit the capacity of governments to represent their peoples in fairly obvious ways. A government that must act to palliate or defend against the potential aggression of a hostile state is dominated by that other state. It is inhibited in its actions and to that extent is unfree to respond to and represent the views and interests of its citizens, curtailing their freedom in the process. Likewise, if the domestic policy choices of one state effectively undermine those of another, say by one state polluting upstream from another state that has tried to reduce pollution, then the behaviour of the one reduces the presumptive options of the other in ways that involve illegitimate coercion of one people by another.

Powerful states can also dominate weaker states in numerous ways that fall short of explicit interference (Pettit 2010a, 73–7). For example, they may impose inequitable and disadvantageous terms of international trade on them by exploiting various forms of economic pressure that arise from their control of important markets, their ability to manage various financial instruments, or their access to key resources and so on. Powerful corporations can exert similar forms of pressure and influence, as when they threaten to withdraw from states with taxation or employment policies they regard as unduly reducing their profits. In such situations, governments become to a greater or lesser degree controlled by these alien powers. They feel obliged to act 'responsibly' and satisfy these various external demands lest the domestic economy suffer and be less able to supply the basic needs of the population. Yet such responsible action can lead to a failure to adequately represent the concerns of their own citizens. For example, they might overturn domestic employment laws or cut public spending in ways citizens not only did not desire but also would not have needed to do had it not been for such external demands (Mair 2011).

These examples are not intended to highlight problems of global *distributive* justice per se, although such issues are connected, but rather problems of global *political* justice that result when one state's capacity to be democratically legitimate gets undermined by the dominating actions of another state or of some other organisation based within another state or states (Macdonald and Ronzoni 2012). Even if the aforementioned actions of states and corporations were deemed entirely just in distributive terms, as some libertarians might argue if the pressures involved no direct interference and respected formal rights to freedom of contract and property, they would still infringe the moral interest a people has in collective self-government. At a minimum, therefore, states seeking to have their own democratic legitimacy respected have reason to acknowledge a set of international norms whereby they respect the democratic legitimacy of others by observing a duty of non-intervention (Rawls 1999, 34/35). Yet, in an increasingly interconnected world, states are likely to interact so intensely and frequently that there will be ample scope for some to exert various forms of domination over others. Such domination may stop short of direct intervention but inhibit and intimidate states in ways that undercut their representative character. Interconnectedness also generates problems that can only be effectively tackled through collective action between states, where again powerful states may skew common agreements in their favour without deploying outright coercion. Finally, globalisation has brought with it not simply greater interaction between states but also directly between their peoples and citizens. Not only are peoples involved in global processes of production and exchange but also migration is altering their character, rendering them increasingly multicultural and creating a growing problem of stateless persons and denizens, who belong to dispersed and oppressed peoples and lack citizenship.

As a result of these developments, peoples and persons have a growing interest not only in the legitimacy of democratic decision-making *within* states but also *between* them (Pettit 2010b, 151/52). On the one hand, they will wish their governments to be representative of them when negotiating with those of other states, and for the negotiations to give equal weight to each state so that the ensuing accords tackle matters of common concern in mutually beneficial ways. In other words, they will wish similar criteria of publicity and equality to operate in the international sphere as they do at the domestic. On the other hand, peoples will want their direct interactions with other peoples to involve mutual respect on both sides, with each respecting the domestic rules and regulations of others so long as no peoples discriminate against other peoples when it comes to trading or travelling in a different state to their own. In other words, every state should treat all peoples as equals under domestic law, with a similar rule of non-discrimination operating for those seeking access to citizenship and prepared to undertake the same duties as already-existing citizens.

It might be argued that the easiest way to meet these various desiderata would be to establish an international regime on the model of a domestic state with authority over member states (Held 1995). Yet such an international regime would itself only be capable of democratic legitimacy to the extent it could become suitably congruent with an international polity. However, even advanced processes of globalisation have not generated anything like the same degree of interdependence between states as exists within them, with multinational production estimated at barely 10 per cent of output in the world's most integrated economies (Christiano 2006, 86). As a result, the degree to which citizens of a global democracy would share common issues and have an equal stake in collective decisions is likely to be rather limited at best. Similarly, the common sympathies needed for public reasoning also face the challenge of linguistic and cultural diversity between and within different existing peoples. On both counts, the likelihood of persistent and intense minorities and majority tyranny seems highly probable (Christiano 2010, 132–34).

At the regional level these problems are arguably less severe. Regional economies are far more integrated, especially the EU where intra-EU trade is higher than extra-EU trade in each EU Member State, with the exception of the United Kingdom (Eurostat 2011). However, as the Euro crisis has revealed, integration has not produced economic and social convergence between states. Nor have a European people, sharing a common political identity and public sphere, come into existence. Fewer than 15 per cent of EU citizens consistently identify themselves as Europeans compared to around 40 per cent who consider their identity to be exclusively national, with the 15 per cent being disproportionally composed of the well-educated and highly mobile (Fligstein 2008, 141/2, 156). Likewise, no pan-European media of any significance have come into existence, with European discourse again restricted to elites. At best, there is evidence of some modest Europeanisation of the various national media and the simultaneous and parallel discussion of EU issues (Risse 2010). As a result, pan-European political mobilisation has proven decidedly weak. Parties remain embedded in national systems, with EP elections largely second-order national elections (Hix and Marsh 2011). Much the same can be said of civil society organisations. Again, there is evidence of some Europeanisation of national organisations, yet these remain mainly focused on influencing domestic policy (Beyers and Kerremans 2007). Therefore, the infrastructure needed to connect individual European citizens to legislative power at the EU level in a public and equal way is lacking. Indeed, the politicisation of European integration has mainly fuelled right-wing Eurosceptic populist parties within the MS rather than promoting trans-European federalist political movements (Bartolini 2005).

The rest of this chapter lays out an alternative model for achieving democratic legitimacy within the EU to a European polity – that of an international association of democratic states. Such an international association seeks to promote and be compatible with the possibility for all individuals to live in representative states that possess democratic systems where collective decisions are made in ways that show them equal respect and concern through being under their public, equal control. Four criteria guide this arrangement. First, this argument presupposes a commitment to the values of representative democracy, and their equal enjoyment by all peoples. Second, if the legitimacy of democratic states stems from them offering reasonably effective, public mechanisms for the identification and equal advancement of the interests of their citizens, then the legitimacy of international systems stems from them doing likewise through being in their turn under the shared and equal control of the signatory states acting as the representatives of their respective peoples. Third, citizens of different peoples ought not to be discriminated against in their interactions. The mutual concern and respect that operates among states ought to apply to the citizens of those states in moving and trading between them. Finally, membership of such international systems should be voluntary. Not all states will have an equal stake in collective arrangements on a given issue, and many will not have equal bargaining power. Voluntary arrangements allow states to tailor their international commitments to the interests of their populations and ideally to negotiate the terms of their adherence accordingly.

The next section applies this model to the system of representation within the EU. The analysis shall show how in many respects it proves compatible with these criteria, even if its current practice often falls short of fulfilling them. The resulting republican intergovernmentalist account provides a picture of the EU in which democratic states negotiate an ever closer union of mutual benefit to their peoples while preserving the civic freedom of their citizens.

DEMOI-CRACY AND THE SYSTEM OF
REPRESENTATION WITHIN THE EU

In formal terms, the Post-Lisbon Consolidated Treaty of the European Union (TEU) can be aligned with all four of the criteria outlined above – even if this interpretation is contentious and may fall short in practice. I shall take them in turn.

(1) A Commitment to the Values of Representative Democracy

The first criterion is evident in the preamble, which confirms the Union's 'attachment to the principles of liberty, democracy and respect for human rights', and in Article 2, which notes how these values are 'common to the MS'. The contracting parties also affirm that the deepening of 'the solidarity between their peoples' has to be balanced by 'respecting their history, their culture and their traditions', while the process of 'an ever closer union among the peoples of Europe' has to be one 'in which decisions are taken as closely as possible to the citizen in accordance with the principle of subsidiarity'. Indeed, Article 4 explicitly requires the Union to 'respect the equality of MS before the Treaties as well as their national identities, inherent in their fundamental structures, political and constitutional, inclusive of regional and local self-government' and portrays the Union as based in a principle of 'sincere cooperation' and 'mutual respect'. Thus, the commitment to democratic values goes hand in hand with respect for the ways these may have been configured differently by the various peoples and that as far as possible decisions ought to be taken by each people.

(2) Shared and Equal Control of the International Association by the Signatory States Acting as the Representatives of Their Respective Peoples

The second criterion, whereby an international association should be under the shared and equal control of the signatory states in order to ensure the public and equal advancement of the interests of their respective peoples, emerges from the account of Union's political system in Title II. This commits the Union to being itself organised in accordance with democratic principles and the equality of citizens, with Article 10 explicitly grounding its functioning in representative democracy. This Article identifies three channels whereby European citizens are represented in the EU's political system: directly via elections to the European Parliament (EP), indirectly via their Heads of State or Government in the European Council (EC) or in the Council by their Government, and in domestic elections which hold these last democratically accountable to National Parliaments (NPs) or to citizens.

Of the three, the second channel – whereby citizens are represented in the EC by heads of state or government and in the Council by members of their governments – prima facie corresponds most obviously to the republican intergovernmentalist model. Although the EC has no legislative functions, it 'defines the general political directions and priorities' of the Union (TEU 15.1), not least because any major change would require a revision of the Treaties in which national executives naturally take the lead. Decision-making is also invariably taken by consensus, which nominally at least respects the norm articulated above of giving equal weighting to each MS. The situation in the various configurations of the Council is more complicated, but similar reasoning prevails. Even though qualified majority voting (QMV) is formally the default for decision-making, in practice it operates through consensus wherever possible. Moreover, the proposed double-majority rule for QMV from 1 November 2014, involving 55 per cent of MS representing at least 65 per cent of the population, is designed to ensure that decisions must balance the interests of large and small states by preventing the former imposing a decision on the latter and vice versa.

Although NPs are mentioned in the main text of the Treaty for the first time, the negative and positive roles assigned them in Article 12 TEU play an important role in ensuring that the MS act as representatives of their peoples as the second criteria demands. Executives traditionally exercise wider discretion in foreign compared to domestic policy, and this remains true of the EU despite its significant domestic impact. Hitherto European issues have rarely been salient in domestic elections, and so the election of governments cannot per se ensure they represent citizens with regard to the EU. NPs perform a potentially crucial function in this regard. On the one hand, they have a right to be informed by Union institutions and to see draft legislative acts and have formed European Committees to scrutinise them and the decisions made by ministers. They may also send reasoned opinions to the Commission and engage in an informal political dialogue. Empowering parliaments in these ways can be justified as ensuring Ministers continue to represent their peoples when negotiating within the Council. On the other hand, the Treaty introduces an 'Early Warning Mechanism' (EWM) that assigns national legislatures the right to scrutinize proposed EU decisions and initiatives for compliance with the principles of subsidiarity and proportionality. Furthermore, NPs can have a collective legislative influence in that a majority of them may force, by way of a so-called orange card, an early vote on an EU legislative proposal in the Council and the EP. They are also now involved in the evaluation of measures taken within the area of freedom, security and justice (Articles 70, 85, 88 TEU), may block Treaty changes under the simplified revision procedures (Article 48 TEU) and must be informed of new applications to join the EU (Article 49 TEU). These powers serve the republican intergovernmentalist purpose of providing a means for the component demoi of the EU to ensure the integration process only extends to those areas that clearly require international collaboration, and does not undermine democracy at the national level. Indeed, the enhanced cooperation between NPs within COSAC offers among the clearest expressions of a republican demoi-cracy in facilitating the direct interaction between the representatives of the different peoples of Europe (Cooper 2012).

On the surface, the EP offers a less obvious fit with the model. The wording of Article 10 suggests the existence of a European demos in stating that European citizens are represented directly in the EP. However, Union citizenship derives from being a national of a MS and is 'additional to national citizenship and shall not replace it' (Article 9 TEU). The derivative and additional character of this status is reflected in the way seats are allocated within the EP by MS rather than simply by population, employing the principle of 'degressive proportionality', with a minimum threshold of six seats for the smallest MS and a maximum of ninety-six for the largest (Article 14.2 TEU). The official rationality behind this arrangement has been to ensure that the range of political opinion found in even the less populous MS gets represented. Indeed, European parties do not mobilise a pan-European electorate, but are rather groupings of national parties within the Parliament. As the German Federal Constitutional Court noted in its Lisbon judgement (2BvE 2/08: para. 286), the EP's allocation formula is testimony to the absence of a European demos and the need adequately to represent each of the European demoi. Therefore, the EP can also be conceived as an institutional embodiment of European demoi-cracy.

(3) Mutual Respect and Non-discrimination between the Citizens of the States within the Association

Like the very status of Union citizenship, the representation of citizens even in the EP as members of national constituencies, can also be linked to the third criterion of non-discrimination and equality between citizens of different peoples. This is a key element of Union citizenship (Articles 18–25 Treaty on the Functioning of the European Union (TFEU)). Union citizenship does not does not provide citizens with goods or services through EU funds or agencies. It offers access on a par with national citizens to engage in economic activity with, and enjoy the services and benefits provided by, another MS, and – certain judgements of the Court of Justice of the EU (CJEU) notwithstanding – need not be seen as creating a unified European citizenry. It is only activated through a MS citizen moving to, or trading with, another

MS. Moreover, certain 'limitations and conditions' justified on grounds of public policy, public security or public health protect various non-market liberties associated with national citizenship. Thus, the 1990 Residence Directives, later repealed and incorporated into Article 7 (1) b and c of Directive 2004/38, together with certain provisos of Article 45 TFEU, restrict the right of residence to those engaging in economic activity or possessing adequate funds not to become a burden on the national system of social assurance and covered by sickness insurance. The definition of national citizenship remains a preserve of the MS, and EU citizens resident in another MS can vote in local and European elections but not in national ones.

(4) A Voluntary Association, As Not All States Have an Equal Stake in Every Decision

Finally, the fourth criterion, whereby such an international association should be voluntary and in the long-term equal interest of the peoples concerned, could be regarded as guiding the need for all treaty changes to be negotiated and unanimously approved not just by MS governments but also by their peoples – either directly via referenda or indirectly by a majority of their parliamentary representatives. MS have also negotiated numerous opt-outs from particular EU policies. Such variable geometry reflects a situation in which membership of such an association that is not imposed or compulsory in all respects, but can be tailored to the needs of each contracting people.

THE LIMITS OF DEMOI-CRACY

The resulting political system involves more counter-majoritarian checks and balances than are found in any national democracy. EU legislation must secure consensual support from national leaders within the European Council to be placed on the agenda, a proposal from the majority of the Commission, a formal two-thirds majority – but in practice a consensus – of weighted MS votes in the Council of Ministers, a series of absolute majorities within the EP – which as we saw can itself be viewed as involving a series of coalitions between national parties – and the assent and active support of the twenty-seven national administrations, legal systems and parliaments responsible for its implementation (Moravcsik 2008, 334). In a domestic context, such high consensus requirements ought not to be necessary and would be hard to justify. Among a demos, there should be sufficient solidarity for majoritarian decision-making to be acceptable as providing the fairest and most public means for treating all citizens equally. By contrast, between *demoi* it is not necessary to meet as stringent standards of political and social justice.

As we saw, republican intergovernmentalism aims at ensuring the interactions between representative states are mutually advantageous while protecting their equal rights to collective self-determination (Miller 2008, 394–96). Each of these states has its own internal systems of social and political justice for which its citizens are co-responsible thorough their equal participation within majoritarian systems of democracy. To the extent the non-dominated status, wealth and survival of these states depends on cooperation with other states, it seems appropriate to share the costs and benefits of these arrangements equitably. To provide such agreements with democratic legitimacy, it will be sufficient that the citizens of each MS are satisfied that this is an area where interaction and cooperation is necessary or desirable – for example, in order to set fish quotas so fishing will be sustainable or to promote trade. Moreover, the surpluses generated by such accords need only be Pareto-improvements, with each party gaining to an equal degree from the resulting benefits subject to compensatory measures for temporary losers so that a 'no wealth effects' condition holds. For this purpose, a mix of consensual and super-majoritarian mechanisms between representatives of states and their peoples will be justified since nothing in such a system suggests any change is required with the status quo so far as the relative standing of the parties involved is concerned. Central institutions, such as the CJEU, can be justified as solutions to prisoner's dilemmas and free riding, in order to ensure all states maintain their mutually beneficial commitments in a credible manner. However, to meet the four criteria, they need to be ultimately under the control of the contracting states and peoples.

The difficulties arise when such a political system is forced to operate as if it was representing a pan-European citizenry because its decisions have either undercut the capacity of the MS to respond to the demands of their citizens, or entered policy areas where no such win-win solutions exist. For example, the teleological reasoning of the CJEU in regard to Union citizenship has drawn criticism from some commentators for judgements such as *Schwarz*[3] and *Watts*[4] that give citizens rights to access public services across the Union with no correlative duty to contribute to their provision (Scharpf 2012, 20). Advocate General Stix-Hackl claimed in *Schwarz* that 'shortfalls in tax revenue are [not] to be taken into consideration as matters of overriding general interest' when MS seek to overrule free movement and residence rights. Yet, such matters go to the heart of the capacity for MS to respond to their citizens priorities when setting their budgets (Nic Shuibhne 2008). Not to take them seriously, risks disturbing the reciprocal ties between citizens that make public spending sustainable. Moreover, no mechanism exists to address the problem by transfers between MS, because the EU has neither the competence nor the democratic legitimacy to promote social welfare or public goods at the pan-European level.

Such decisions not only override the *demoi-cratic* decision-making structure of the EU but also undercut democracy at the MS level without creating it at the EU level. This problem has been even more apparent in the series of judgements where the CJEU has prioritised EU-level economic freedoms over MS-level social rights (*Viking*,[5] *Laval*,[6] *Rueffert*[7] and *Luxembourg*[8]). In these cases, the Court has attempted to impose a uniform, minimum standard of wage legislation that overrides local collective bargaining agreements, thereby hindering the exercise of union rights. Neither these decisions nor those regarding access to public services have contributed to the creation of a European *demos* because they dissociate social and economic rights, respectively, from membership of a political community in which all citizens must participate as equals. In the case of access to public services, the Court overlooks the mutual obligations citizens have to contribute to maintaining public goods at a sustainable level for all. In the case of economic freedoms, the Court undermines the politically negotiated balance between labour and capital, designed to achieve a degree of equity between the two. In both cases, the CJEU has misconstrued Union citizenship as if it consisted of a set of human rights to participation in a spontaneously arising and self-sustaining free market, rather than being grounded in the mutual recognition of the rights of citizens within an association of democratic states. This failure to respect the democratic systems of the MS proves self-defeating. For it is these systems that provide the basis for Union citizenship not only formally, in that citizenship of an MS is a precondition for Union citizenship, but substantively, in that it is collective solidarity among citizens of each of the MS that generates the legal, economic and social infrastructure on which the enjoyment of their economic and other rights as Union as well as national citizens depend.

The EU requires the cooperation of the associated MS to implement policy – apart from them its existence is exiguous at best. To flout or circumvent the EU's demoi-cratic structures, therefore, can only undercut both the legitimacy and the efficacy of its decision-making, risking in the process the very forms of interstate domination the avoidance of which provides its most compelling rationale. Yet, these structures limit not just how the EU can act but what it can do. By their very nature they are ill suited to policies that imply or require a demos to be legitimately and effectively pursued.

CONCLUSION: THE
EUROCRISIS – BEYOND DEMOI-CRACY?

This chapter has explored the normative case for conceiving the EU as an 'ever closer Union of peoples' rather than as the formation of a European people. That case rests on considerations of democratic legitimacy and the role a people plays within a system of public and equal political representation capable of securing conditions of civic freedom. A people of the requisite kind are unlikely to exist at the global or European level. However, this case is consistent with representative states forming an international association to secure mutual concern and respect between their peoples given their increased interaction. The EU in many respects resembles such an association, and can be characterised as the product of a process of republican integration.

A demoi-cracy should not be understood as an alternative form of democracy – it has a different scope. It exists to regulate the interactions between states rather than their internal processes. That poses limits to the sorts of policies the EU should attempt to pursue. The Eurocrisis reveals the problems of going beyond these limits all too dramatically. The single currency was supposed to produce a convergence of the MS economies. Instead, it reinforced their divergent dynamics. As a result, the international financial crisis has had a far greater impact on the former soft-currency countries of Greece, Ireland, Portugal, Spain and Italy than on Germany and most northern economies. However, the type of rescue package the EU can offer has been constrained by the capacity of its political system to redistribute between MS. As a result, it has been limited to addressing state-credit crises rather than the underlying economic problems of the debtor economies, and involved strict conditionalities designed to protect the investment of the taxpayers of creditor states. Yet, this approach compounds the original democratic legitimacy problem. For in removing core budgetary decisions from domestic politicians, the discipline imposed by the Fiscal Pact and the EU's Six-Pack Regulations effectively institutionalise a system of domination of the creditor over the debtor states – precisely the sort of situation the EU exists to prevent (Scharpf 2012, 23/24). In George Soros's words, the crisis 'has transformed the EU from a voluntary association of equal states into a creditor-debtor relationship from which there is no easy escape' (Soros 2013, 27). Indeed, these measures have been largely designed outside the Union's demoi-cratic decision-making processes, sidelining not only the supranational institutions of the EP and Commission but also the intergovernmental mechanisms of the Council. As Joseph Weiler has remarked, 'the resort to an extra-Union Treaty, as a centrepiece of the reconstruction, is but the poignant legal manifestation of this political reality' (Weiler 2012, 831).

This problem has led to calls for greater political integration so as to institutionalise republican democracy at the EU level (Habermas 2012). The analysis presented here suggests there are normative as well as empirical problems with this proposal. The experience of existing multinational states suggests that the presence of multiple *demoi* within the EU would give it weak polity legitimacy at most and require a highly complex regime that would be unlikely to be able to provide citizens with public and equal control over governments. Some authors contend that segmental cleavages among national *demoi* might be counterbalanced by transnational cross-cutting cleavages between pan-European interest groups and parties (Bohman 2007, 313). However, such associations are largely artefacts of the EU, operating as umbrella organisations of national associations that are themselves largely not Europeanised. Even the 2 per cent of Union citizens who live in another MS to their own seem only moderately Europeanised (Favell 2008). Habermas's suggestion that a postnational commitment to civil and political rights might overcome the no-*demos* problem obscures the fact that it is precisely such a commitment that underpins *demoi*-cracy at the EU level: for it goes hand in hand with acknowledging the right of each people to institutionalise these rights in their own way.

Therefore, the normative challenge posed by the crisis is to justify transfers between the MS without undermining the right of each people to be publicly and equally represented in national and international decision-making. Paradoxically, though monetary union itself may have overstepped what a republican intergovernmentalism could legitimate, the crisis might justify quite generous if temporary transfers between MS in order to sustain their equal capacity to remain self-governing (Laborde 2010). However, exploring this avenue falls outside the scope of this chapter. What can be affirmed is that, absent a European *demos*, political union would compound rather than assuage the lack of democratic legitimacy of the current rescue package. The EU would prove to be not only a sub optimal currency area but also a suboptimal democracy area, composed of extremely heterogeneous demoi. The challenge, therefore, is to find a solution consistent with the *demoi*cratic character of the EU. Though a survey of the potential solutions lies outside the scope of this chapter, what does follow from the above is that the only policies likely to prove legitimate and lasting in the long run are those that can be made and sustained through the existing demoi-cratic structures.

NOTES

1. Research for this chapter was supported by a Leverhulme Trust Research Fellowship RF-2012-368. Earlier versions were presented at the Universities of Montreal, St. Gallen, Oxford, the Institute for Advanced Studies in Vienna, the Centro Einaudi in Turin and as part of a debate on democracy and the Eurocrisis organised by the European Institute at UCL with funds from the London office of the European Commission. I am grateful to the participants at these events for their helpful comments, in particular Francis Chevenal, David Miller, Glyn Morgan, Kalypso Nicolaidis, Philippe van Parijs and Andrew Walton. I have also benefited from the written comments of Dario Castiglione, Sandra Kröger, Albert Weale and the journal's referee.

2. The criterion of 'commonly avowed' should not be understood as entailing universal consent, which most regard as impossible to meet (Simmons 1976), but rather the weaker notion of equal respect for the views of the governed by virtue of the existence of a plausibly democratic system that gives citizens equal participation in decision-making (see Buchanan 2002).

3. *Schwarz and Gootjes-Schwarz v. Finanzamt Bergisch Gladbach* [2007] ECR I-6849.

4. *Watts v. Bedford Primary Care Trust* [2006] ECR I–4325.

5. Case C-438/05 *International Transport Workers' Federation and Finnish Seamen's Union v. Viking Line* [2008] IRLR 143.

6. Case C-341/05 *Laval v. Svenska Byggnadsarbetareförbundet* [2008] IRLR 160.

7. C-446/06 *Dirk Rüffert v. Land Niedersachsen* [2008] IRLR 467.

8. Case C-319/06 *Commission v. Luxembourg* [2008] ECR I-4323.

Part VII

CONCLUSIONS

CONFRONTING THE EUROCRISIS AND BREXIT

Chapter 19

Political Legitimacy and European Monetary Union

Contracts, Constitutionalism and the Normative Logic of Two-level Games[1]

Richard Bellamy and Albert Weale

1. THE MAKING OF THE LEGITIMACY CRISIS

The crisis of the Eurozone has severely tested the political authority of the EU. Since 2010 the EU and its MS have been forced to improvise policies and processes to deal with the crisis, including the European Semester, a strengthened Stability and Growth Pact, the Treaty on Stability, Coordination and Governance, the European Financial Stabilisation Mechanism (EFSM) and its successors in the European Financial Stability Facility and the European Stability Mechanism (Begg 2013). The European Central Bank (ECB) has embarked upon two rounds of long-term refinancing operations to improve bank liquidity, in effect buying sovereign debt, as well as announcing its willingness to engage in outright monetary transactions (OMT), a policy allegedly leading Jens Weidmann, President of the Bundesbank, to say that this is tantamount 'to financing governments by printing banknotes' (Steen 2012). And still the prospect of deflation looms over European economies (House of Lords 2014c, 13 and *passim*).

The same conditions that gave rise to these policy imperatives have required the EU to find ways of supporting the governments of Greece, Ireland, Portugal, Spain and Cyprus in defiance of the no-bailout clause of the original monetary union (now Article 125 of the TFEU). They have resulted in the Troika imposing restrictions on the national budgets of debtor governments, policies that have been resisted by NPs and opposition movements. They have strengthened anti-EU parties, with a record number of Eurosceptic Members of the European Parliament (MEPs) elected in the European elections of May 2014. They have provoked legal actions in national constitutional courts in both creditor countries like Germany (Federal Constitutional Court 2014a, 2014b) and debtor countries like Portugal (Portuguese Constitutional Court 2014), resulting in judgements that question the legitimacy of the programmes. They have stimulated continued, and sometimes violent, demonstrations against public expenditure austerity packages. They have entailed the installation of technocratic governments in Greece and Italy in 2012, as a way of dealing with the inadequacies of their respective political institutions, as well as the electoral defeat of incumbent governments in Spain and France. In short, they have brought about a crisis of political legitimacy for the EU.

The Lisbon Treaty was widely regarded as having settled the institutional architecture of the EU after nearly two decades of constitutional debate. The Eurozone crisis has reignited those issues. The new policies and processes that have been inaugurated have changed the balance of power within the EU and opened up questions about what 'deep and genuine' economic and monetary union requires by way of institutional change (European Commission 2012; House of Lords 2014a). In these debates, issues of normative political legitimacy inevitably arise, because the EU is a normative order. That is to say, the agreements that it embodies contain principles and values defining norms of behaviour for MS and EU institutions. The Treaty on European Union (TEU) and the Stability and Growth Pact (SGP), strengthened through Title VIII of the Treaty on the Functioning of the European Union (TFEU), together with the Six-Pack and the Two-Pack, have required MS to make progressively stronger commitments to one another in respect of economic and fiscal policy. Those commitments have been reinforced by the Fiscal Compact contained in the Treaty on Stability, Coordination and Governance in the Economic and Monetary Union (TSCG), by which MS have undertaken to ensure that national budgets are in balance or in surplus 'through provisions of binding force and permanent character, preferably constitutional, or otherwise guaranteed to be fully respected and adhered to throughout the national budgetary processes' (TSCG, Article 3.2). Such measures provide a set of rules and principles by reference to which policies and institutional change are justified. Resting on agreed norms and principles, they form a political contract among MS.

Questions of normative legitimacy are raised by the crisis not simply as a result of the EU's being a normative order but also because the construction of EMU rested upon a set of constitutional principles that contained strong – and contestable – normative assumptions. In particular, economic and monetary union was constructed according to the principles of legal constitutionalism (Issing 2008; James 2012). Legal constitutionalism is a political doctrine to the effect that a legitimate political regime must rest on a set of legal rules that constrain the actions of politically responsive decision-makers. In some versions (e.g. Dworkin 1996) such restrictions take a 'left liberal' form; in others (e.g. Hayek 1979), they take a neoliberal form (see Bellamy 2007). Our contention in this chapter is that the developing political contract underlying EMU has produced restrictions on MS with respect to their public budgets that amount to more than simply a treaty agreement; they have given rise to a treaty agreement underwritten by the principles of legal constitutionalism of a neoliberal kind – indeed, of a specific kind within neoliberalism.

The tradition of political analysis that fed into the construction of the single currency and its management is to be found in the work of thinkers associated with the Hayekian version of constitutional liberalism (see James 2012, 6/7). According to this tradition, democratic governments have a tendency to fiscal irresponsibility due to politicians having incentives to buy votes through excessive public expenditure. In seeking re-election, political representatives are motivated to respond to the wishes of special interest groups in the short term rather than framing legislation for the public interest in the long term. Particular manifestations of these tendencies might include the provision of price support schemes for agriculture, the protection of domestic industry from foreign competition, interference in controlling the terms of employment contracts that can be agreed, and expenditure on public works that benefit only localised constituencies. Hayek (1979) held that, to avoid these pitfalls, states need to be constrained by constitutional rules and mechanisms from engaging in excessive expenditure and unduly interfering in the operations of the free market. Behind the construction of the specific set of rules for EMU, therefore, lay a more general set of premises concerning the character of a democratic political order.

The problem with this construction, we argue, is that, when applied to EMU, it neglects the normative logic of two-level games. According to this logic, when governments make commitments to one another about their future behaviour, they *simultaneously* need to be responsible and accountable to their domestic populations in order to retain their political legitimacy. The logic of two-level games was originally developed by Putnam (1988) to account for the outcome of the Bonn economic summit of 1978, and it has been subsequently applied to empirical cases ranging from security issues to economic diplomacy and North-South relations (Evans et al. 1993). As Pollack (2010, 225) has pointed out, it also lies behind liberal intergovernmentalist accounts of EU integration such as that of Moravcsik (1998). However, this framework of analysis neither implies fixed preferences (Crespy and Schmidt 2014) nor has only an empirical use. Beyond its empirical applications, the logic of two-level games also has a normative interpretation (Savage and Weale 2009) providing a model by which we can evaluate the justifiability of constitutional arrangements.

The neglect of the normative logic of two-level games in the construction of EMU is compounded by a second problem within legal constitutionalism, namely its disregard of the existence of reasonable differences in political judgement over the principles that should govern a monetary union made up of different sovereign states, each with their own traditions of economic and monetary policy. Indeed, even within the broadly neoliberal tradition of thinking about economic constitutions, there are important differences of substance as well as emphasis. When the conditions for continuing contestation over policy measures and organisation exists, the putative political legitimacy of EU legal constitutionalist arrangements, such as those underlying EMU, the SGP and the TSCG, reinforce the practical contradiction of the two-level game implicit in the economic constitution. By contrast with this attempt to entrench legal constitutionalism, we suggest that the design of an economic constitution ought to respect the principles of political constitutionalism, with its requirement that governments be responsive to the public reasoning of their citizens within the continuing democratic conversation that makes up a political society (Bellamy 2007).

In pursuing this argument, the chapter proceeds as follows. In section 2 we lay out the normative logic of the two-level game embodied in the construction of EMU. According to this logic, those participating in international agreements have a dual duty: to deal fairly with one another, on the one hand, and to be responsive and accountable to the democratic reasoning of the people whom they represent, on the other. In acknowledging this dual duty, they should also acknowledge that their fellow negotiators have a similar duty in respect of their own peoples. Section 3 indicates why, given reasonable disagreement about the principles that should govern an economic constitution, the legitimacy of EMU cannot be simply secured by framing the related fiscal rules in legal constitutionalist terms. The long-term legitimacy of EMU is compatible only with political constitutionalism. Section 4 concludes that so long as the EU remains subject to the logic of delegation implicit in the normative logic of two-level games, EMU must remain subject to the equal control and influence of the different MS *demoi* – a position we characterise as 'republican intergovernmentalism'. We suggest this result can be achieved through the empowerment of NPs in EU policy making.

2. THE NORMATIVE LEGITIMACY
OF TWO-LEVEL CONTRACTS

At the centre of the issue of political legitimacy is the question of the credibility, and consequently the justifiability, of the reasoning underlying the norms and principles on which the construction of EMU is based. Yet, how might one evaluate such credibility? We approach this question through contractarian political theory. According to contractarian theory, political authority is to be understood as arising from a contract to mutual advantage implicitly or explicitly agreed among the members of a political association. The need for political organisation can be modelled as the solution to dilemmas of collective action (Buchanan and Tullock 1960; Gauthier 1986; Ostrom 1990; Weale 2013). These dilemmas occur when uncoordinated action by separate agents gives rise to potential gains from cooperation, as in an agreement on weights and measures or the rules of the road, or where uncoordinated individual action leads to harmful side effects from otherwise legitimate human activity, of which pollution and resource depletion are the obvious examples. If we think of political associations as having a contractarian logic in this sense, then we can address the issue of credibility by asking what conditions have to be satisfied for actors to find a contract that they can rationally support (Gauthier 1986).

The general logic of contractarian analysis can be applied not only to the study of natural persons but also to relations between states. States can impose harmful externalities on other states and their populations through cross-boundary pollution, trade restrictions or population movements. They can also fail to secure common advantages through a lack of political coordination. The EU has often been portrayed as a mechanism for overcoming these problems in the international arena (Moravcsik 1993). The assumption is that the policies that fall within the competence of the EU are in the long-term common interest of the MS, offering Pareto improvements over a prevailing status quo for all concerned. However, many such issues are subject to the logic of the prisoner's dilemma. Each MS may be better off with an agreed policy that all other MS comply with but it does not, than it would be when it complied as well, even if all would be worse off without any agreement. Yet, if this logic is clear to all, none would rationally comply and so the policy will either never be agreed or will unravel over time. Thus, the fundamental problem to be solved in any political contract between states is that of inducing credibility in others of one's commitment to the policy to be agreed to avoid defection from a mutually beneficial agreement. To overcome this free rider problem requires states to be able to make credible commitments to one another about their willingness to fulfil their obligations even on those occasions when fulfilling those obligations proves onerous.

The logic of the N-person prisoner's dilemma was reflected in the construction of EMU. As Issing (2008, 234–36) has clearly explained, it was thought that, because democratic competition works to create deficit financing, thereby undermining the long-term stability of the currency and public finances, the Euro was designed to represent depoliticised and hence stable money. On this analysis, the political benefits of deficit spending in the form of votes gained by governing parties are enjoyed by national players, while the potential negative effects, notably higher interest rates, are felt by all states. So, it is rational for prudent states to seek to ensure that they do not incur the spillover effects of others' deficit spending and they can attempt to do this by institutionalising a no-bailout rule. The alternative to such a rule is to leave discipline to the markets. However, within a currency union there is no exchange rate risk to a national government from deficit financing, and so borrowing premiums remain low over a period of time and credit risk builds up (Issing 2008, 193/4). Aware of this possibility, no rational state would prudently enter into a currency union without a no-bailout rule. Hence, in order for any such agreement to take place, states must commit to funding their own borrowing. Each state has to be able to make a credible commitment to other states about the maximum deficits that they are willing to tolerate in their public spending plans. This, in short, was the rationale of the no-bailout clause of the Maastricht Treaty. The SGP arose from the recognition that the Maastricht rules of no bailout and no exit were insufficient to prevent MS continuing to run excessive deficits. The idea was that the scope for fiscal adjustments among participating states had to be defined once and for all. Political representatives at the MS level could still coordinate fiscal and monetary policy, but only on condition that the monetary component was fixed exogenously by an independent European central bank, the ECB, which had been deliberately isolated from political interference (see Issing 2008, 193–95).

When Germany in 2002 and then France and Germany in 2003 breached the provisions of the SGP, MS within the contract of monetary union had an incentive to strengthen monitoring and compliance even more. With the coming of the financial crisis, the next stage of the contractarian logic was to embed the SGP in the European Semester, together with the Six-Pack and the Two-Pack, the effects of which were not only to increase the intensity of the monitoring of budgetary plans but also to ensure coordination among MS *before* those plans were put to NPs. The Fiscal Compact, the aim of which is to alter the institutional structure of domestic political arrangements to prevent excessive deficits from arising or rectify them as quickly as possible if they do exist, reinforces these provisions. As contractarian theory predicts, these devices emerge where previous commitment has been shown wanting and there is no alternative to continuing collective association. In other words, when commitments turned out not to be credible, the contractarian logic leads actors to a search for greater compliance by increased monitoring, penalties and institutional restructuring (Weale 2015).

Does this contractarian rationale provide a justification of the political legitimacy of EMU as it has been constructed? It could only do so provided that the states in question could be regarded as unitary actors. Yet, treating states as unitary actors is merely a simplifying assumption, useful for the purposes of some types of analysis but distorting if taken as an accurate representation of an empirical situation. States are collective entities made up of constellations of many actors. In political associations modelled according to the norms of two-level games, the political representatives of each state simultaneously owe obligations to the political representatives of other states and to their own populations (Savage and Weale 2009), with implications for their ability to comply with their contractual commitments.

The credible commitment that each state has to be able to make to every other concerns such matters as the maximum budget deficits that they will allow in their public spending plans, the rate at which deficits will be rectified and the balance between the growth of GDP and the growth of public expenditure. However, the commitment of states in regard to these policy strategies can only be made credible provided that each state enjoys the confidence of its citizens. Only with the confidence of their citizens will these states possess the capacity to implement the policies implied by the international agreement. In the modern world, this confidence and the resulting capacity to implement policy rest upon democratic political legitimation. Monetary union implies, then, that each state can have the confidence that all other states can secure sufficient ongoing domestic support to meet their consequent obligations. Hence, only if states enjoy democratic legitimacy will other states have reason to believe that their commitments are credible.

A similar interlocking logic arises in the relationship of states to their citizens. For international agreements to be credible, the governments responsible for implementing them must be able to give domestic populations good reasons for compliance, showing how an agreement will serve the collective interest. At the same time, each state must recognise that all other states that are parties to the agreement are similarly acting as representatives of their citizens. The state parties are thus engaged in a two-level game, in which the terms of the agreement have to be simultaneously acceptable to other negotiating parties *and* to their domestic constituents. Simultaneity in this context does not mean 'occurring at the same time', but indicates that any international agreement must fulfil two sets of conditions. First, an international agreement requires 'fair dealing' among states in their relations with one another as the representatives of their peoples. Second, states must ensure the general acceptability of the agreement to their respective peoples and be able to justify their international commitments, including any provisions for side payments, as being a reasonable way of advancing their joint and several common interests. Unless this second condition is met, so that a state can guarantee the backing of the people it represents, no other state party to the putative contract can be confident that a commitment made to it is credible.

In short, the logic of collective commitment in a monetary union presupposes the logic of political democracy at the national level. Unless all the state parties to an agreement possess a credible democracy at the national level, it is a practical contradiction at the international level for them to enter into commitments with each other, since, in those circumstances, no state could rationally trust the commitments of the other states or be trustworthy itself. Consequently, *pace* certain analysts of the EU (Majone 2001; Scharpf 1999) input legitimacy at the domestic level cannot be substituted by output legitimacy at the international level – particularly if the beneficial effects of those outputs vary over time and between the different parties to the agreement in ways that might be regarded as unfair (Bellamy 2010; a point acknowledged by the post-crisis analyses of Majone 2012; Scharpf 2011). Therefore, the search for 'an ever closer union of the peoples of Europe' is in effect a search for credible commitment devices among the contracting MS in respect of the peoples whom they represent (Bellamy 2013).

The need for domestic political legitimacy is not simply a political fact; it is also a reason within a normative order. An international agreement involves each state recognising that all other states are embedded within a normative order that governs their internal and external relations. Consequently, each state requires democratic legitimation for its commitments. The most elaborately worked out example of the logic of such a normative order is that provided by the German Federal Constitutional Court in its jurisprudence on EMU starting with *Brunner* (Federal Constitutional Court 1993). That jurisprudence recognises that the German state needs to be able to enter into long-term international commitments in order to be able to secure benefits that are only available through internationally coordinated action. At the same time, the jurisprudence of the Court insists that any international commitment must be consistent with those principles of the Basic Law that bind the German state in perpetuity to the principle of democratic authority stemming from the people. In particular, the voting rights of German citizens should not be compromised by the German parliament losing meaningful control over the direction of economic policy. Therefore, the Court has seen its task as being to make it legally and constitutionally possible for the German state to enter into and honour international agreements that are in its interests and in the interests of other states who are party to the agreement, while at the same time retaining the principle of the democratic self-determination of the German people that is a fundamental element of the Basic Law. In a series of judgements, the Court has reasoned that these different demands can be reconciled through the doctrine of delegation. So long as the international agreement could be said to rest on the delegated authority of the MS and the *Bundestag* retained the power of revoking Germany's participation in the international agreement, then the principle of democratic self-determination was respected.

As Gustavsson (1998) noted, the Court's reasoning in *Brunner* rested upon three assumptions about EMU: its revocability by the *Bundestag*, its marginality in terms of the scope of obligations it implied, and its predictability. The subsequent jurisprudence of the Court has had to deal with the failure of one or more of these assumptions to obtain in practice. Thus, in a recent judgement on the constitutionality of the policy of OMTs by the ECB (Federal Constitutional Court 2014a), a majority of the judges ruled that OMTs were unconstitutional, because they involved an open-ended commitment by the German government. In other words, the scope of the obligations implied by OMT was neither limited nor predictable. Although the Court referred the matter to the Court of Justice of the European Union, it offered its own (sceptical) interpretation of the compatibility of the ECB's planned action with treaty and constitutional requirements. However, the kernel of its judgement turned on the force of Article 38(1) of the German Basic Law. In line with its own previous jurisprudence, the Court interpreted this Article as requiring that state authority not be transferred to the extent to which it makes democratic control nugatory. The right to vote is in effect defined as the right to vote in an election where the result will lead to meaningful parliamentary control over the conditions of collective life, thereby expressing the self-determination of the people. Democratic self-determination means that the scope of the *Bundestag's* authority cannot be rendered nugatory, and, if the German government failed to contest the policy of OMTs, then its actions can be revoked (for this logic, see also Lindseth 2010, 24).

On many matters of international agreement domestic acceptability can be presumed by national decision-makers because the issues involved are technical, have low political salience or can be negotiated with the agreement of specific interest groups who share a consensus on which polices best serve their mutual advantage. In other words, they satisfy something like a marginality requirement. Prior to EMU, the EU's competences largely concerned such low salient issues and hence aroused comparatively little democratic contestation (Moravcsik 2002). However, the logic of monetary union does not fall into any of these categories. Although it is technical, its ramifications are wide. Few items are as politically salient as the reliability of a nation's currency. And interest groups typically take different and incompatible positions on the desirability of different monetary policies. In these circumstances, the assumption that states are acting as authorised representatives of their populations will break down, unless there are good reasons for thinking that the authorisation is open-ended (hence the shift in the post-crisis analyses of Scharpf 2011 and Majone 2012, which, unlike Moravscik 2012, have moved close to the argument made here). However, as the jurisprudence of the German Federal Constitutional Court shows, after 1993 no other state had reason to think that the authorisation was open-ended in the case of Germany.

It was predictable that at some stage the limits of monetary integration would be met. This line of argument can be generalised. For just as other states had no reason for thinking that Germany would have an irrevocable commitment to all the implications of EMU, so no one in Germany could reasonably think that all other states could retain a democratic mandate for abiding by the rules of EMU when those terms became unpredictably onerous.

The practical contradiction at the heart of EMU is that MS could only find the terms of the contract credible on condition that they could assume that the commitments entered into by all other MS went beyond the scope of democratic legitimation within those states. That the contradiction revealed itself in the instability of the political contract on which EMU rested arose in part from the predictable unpredictability of monetary union. That feature in turn stemmed from the fallibility of political judgement within the circumstances of politics, an element of the normative logic that we discuss in the next section.

3. LIBERALISM VERSUS LEGAL CONSTITUTIONALISM

Legal constitutionalism of the sort that underlies the constitution of EMU represents one tradition within of liberal inheritance, one that is notably counter-majoritarian in its implications. According to that tradition, if modern democracies have the characteristics attributed to them by neoliberal legal constitutionalists, these commitments could not be credible, since the governments of the same states that entered into the contract would be prone to myopic and short-term sectional pressures such that they would take any opportunities that might arise to free ride on the cooperation of others. If the temptation to free ride is built into democratic governments in this way, then there is no credible basis for commitment on the part of any potential party to the contract. The only basis for a credible agreement on monetary union would be through the general establishment of legal economic constitutions at the national level, underpinned by powerful counter-majoritarian institutions, so as to break the link between public expenditure and responsiveness to the preferences of the population. Of course, this proposal is an implication of the neoliberal legal constitutionalist analysis, and the first steps along such a path are embodied in the requirements of the TSCG.

However, counter-majoritarian legal constitutionalism in the economic realm is only one way of reading the liberal inheritance. Indeed, that tradition is at odds with another liberal idea, namely the claim that any constitutional political contract should recognise the 'burdens of judgement' in its construction (Rawls 1996, 54–8). The burdens of judgement arise from such general features of human judgement as the complexity of empirical evidence, the different weight that different persons will put on different types of evidence, the vagueness of relevant concepts and the problems of assessing evidence. Given the burdens of judgement, a constitution should refrain from imposing requirements on those subject to it that will be matters of reasonable disagreement, matters in other words in which no knockdown arguments are possible. Rawls used this argument to exclude the constitutional entrenchment of religious doctrines because they rested on controversial philosophical premises, an issue that also arose in the convention on the putative EU constitution (Olsen 2004). However, Rawls (1996, 225) also gives the example of disputed 'elaborate economic theories of general equilibrium' as involving inherently controversial views that should not be given constitutional status. If one takes this view of disputed economic theories, the fair value of political liberties cannot be maintained if some views are given a privileged constitutional position vis-à-vis other views.

Does the entrenchment of a particular form of Hayekian theory in the constitution of EMU fall foul of this condition? There are a number of reasons to suppose that it does. First, Hayek himself opposed EMU in part because he recognised economic policy, even of a libertarian kind, was not a matter that could be legally entrenched. Instead, he advocated free competition between rival currencies provided by private rather than public banks (Hayek 1978). Although this is a position that Issing (2000) attempted to contest on neo-Hayekian grounds, Hayek's scepticism about EMU was a logical consequence of his belief that viable economic orders were the evolutionary product of human action but not of human design (Hayek 1979). In other words, the attempt to construct an international monetary order by political fiat would replicate the fallacies of central planning on which the road to serfdom was based.

Secondly, even within neoliberalism, there are other traditions of theory that take a non-evolutionary view of the economic order. Although sometimes identified with a Hayekian perspective, even by Hayek (1967, 252/3) himself on some occasions, German ordo-liberal economists like Eucken and Röpke took the view that a functioning economy presupposes a moment of constitutional founding in which the rules of its operation are determined (Eucken 1951a, 1951b; compare Goldschmidt 2000; Nicholls 1994; Peukert 2000). As commentators (e.g. Sally 1998; Streit and Wohlgemuth 2000) have noted, this ordo-liberal tradition contrasts with the Hayekian position in being rationalist and constructivist. It presupposes that the institutional form of the economy is determined within an already established legal order and political community. Economic integration is not an instrument to create a political community, but an expression of the political choices of that community.

Thirdly, this ordo-liberal view is consistent with the worries many economists and policy makers had expressed about the sequencing of European political union and monetary union and the design flaws built into EMU before the Euro crisis had revealed these problems. For example, in a paper summarising a wide range of work, Bordo and Jonung (2003, 43/4) pointed out that EMU lacked both a lender of last resort, by contrast with other modern monetary systems where central banks were able to ensure liquidity, and a central authority to supervise financial systems, including the commercial banks. They went on to point out that the absence of any central coordination of fiscal policies within EMU combined with 'unduly strict criteria for debt and deficits ... implies that EMU will not be able to respond to asymmetric shocks and disturbances in a satisfactory way'. Finally, and as many other economists also noted, they pointed out that Europe is too large and diverse an area to form a well-functioning currency union, with the efficiency gains from increased trade not large enough to outweigh the costs of surrendering control over national monetary policies.

Fourthly, it is well established that different national traditions of economic policy making fed into the creation of EMU. For reasons of history and intellectual tradition, German policy making gave pride of place to the goal of price stability underpinned by the independence of the central bank. By contrast, French thinking gave priority to *gouvernement économique*, a view of the relationship between government and the economy in which executive action played a large role in securing the day-to-day steering and coordination of the economy as well as providing capital for investment in major projects (Dyson and Featherstone 1999; Jabko 2006, 168–72). Historically and institutionally rooted traditions do not disappear in a new policy framework, but manifest themselves in different ways. In particular, when it comes to questions of how countries recover from large economic shocks, there will be differences in what is seen as justifiable requirements, for example how quickly and by what methods to re-establish internationally credible debt levels within the framework of the Excessive Deficit Procedure. Similar differences of judgement will affect how countries think about the institutionalisation of debt brakes and other constitutional devices under the TSCG.

The implication of these points is that legal constitutionalism presupposes that there can be agreement on the basis of the constitutional essentials of a European monetary order, although the epistemic conditions do not exist to establish that agreement. Indeed, even the German *Bundesbank*, so often presented as a model a-political central bank, had its independence from the German government tested both by Adenauer and Schmidt (Kennedy 1991, 37–42). If within a single country, with powerful political and intellectual traditions justifying a strong independent central bank, the issue can be contested, it is not surprising that a rigid pan-European economic constitution based on the idea of automatic rules will be contested even more.

4. POLITICAL CONSTITUTIONALISM AND
EUROPEAN ECONOMIC GOVERNANCE

The argument so far may be summarised as follows. Credible commitment by governments at the international level presupposes political legitimacy at the domestic level, but the domestic legitimacy of democratic governments in turn presupposes that commitments may be modified or altered through political processes. Moreover, the epistemic conditions arising from the burdens of judgement reinforce the need for open discussion and democratic deliberation. Legal constitutionalism at the international level, therefore, risks undermining rather than reinforcing the credibility of state commitments if the measures legally entrenched are matters that should be subject to ongoing political debate by domestic electorates.

Political constitutionalism offers an alternative to legal constitutionalism (Bellamy 2007). By contrast to legal constitutionalism, political constitutionalism contends the terms of the political contract must be subject to ongoing debate among citizens with regard to both the procedures of decision-making and the substance of decisions. Judgements about either cannot be legitimately entrenched or handled by judicial or technical bodies that are isolated from democratic processes because such isolation fails to recognise the equal legal and political status of citizens. Political constitutionalists argue that the functional complexity, ethical diversity and openness of liberal societies make individual judgements about the public good inevitably partial and fallible. Because we are inescapably limited in our knowledge and experience, even the most conscientious persons will tend to reason from their own values and interests and be prone to error with regard to the present and future interests of others. If the collective decisions needed to regulate social life are to be not only impartial but also well informed with regard to the views and circumstances of those to whom they apply, so that they treat citizens with equal respect and concern, then citizens must have equal influence and control over the direction of public policy. *Pace* neoliberal thinkers, such as Hayek, such equal influence and control cannot be provided by markets but only by a democratic process, albeit indirectly through the election of decision-makers (Bellamy 1994).

Legal constitutionalism in its purest form tries to place the legal and political system itself and even many public policies beyond political contestation, defining in substantive and concrete terms how both might be best configured so as to realise equal concern and respect. By contrast, political constitutionalism in its purest form regards legitimacy as dependent upon the ability to employ existing political procedures to contest the procedural and substantive adequacy of the democratic system and its policies through the constant struggle of citizens to exercise equal influence and control over both. Most liberal democracies combine different degrees of each of them, some nearer to the political constitutionalist end of the spectrum and others more at the legal constitutionalist end. The various MS manifest considerable diversity in this respect, making all but the most abstract and procedural forms of legal constitutionalism difficult to agree. Hence the need for political constitutionalism between even those MS that have legal constitutionalist regimes (compare Glencross 2013).

From the perspective of the normative logic of two-level games, the legitimacy of the integration process depends on its taking the form of what might be termed 'republican intergovernmentalism' (Bellamy 2013). That is, the governments and their agents can only enter into credible commitments with each other to the extent that they possess ongoing democratic authorisation to represent their respective peoples, and acknowledge the equal right and obligation of all the other governments to represent their peoples (Pettit 2010). This logic stands behind the largely consensual character of much EU decision-making, not least the unanimity rule for any treaty change and the need for such changes to obtain domestic ratification within all twenty-eight MS. Such features have led a number of commentators to remark on how the EU is best characterised not as a democracy, with EU citizens forming a pan-European demos, but as a *demoi*cracy between the different peoples of the MS (Chevenal and Schimmelfennig 2013; Nicolaidis 2013).

We have argued that the legal constitutionalist mechanisms embodied in the TSCG cannot provide EMU with political legitimacy of a normative kind. It is not possible to model the choices of the actors according to the normative logic of the two-level contract in such a way that their practical reasoning is credible. If such reasoning cannot be modelled in a contractarian way, it will not be credible in practice. Instead, EMU must remain part of the political constitution provided by the ongoing democratic influence and control of those subject to it. Within the EU as presently constituted, this political constitution must reflect the normative logic of two-level games. As such, political legitimacy comes not from a single EU demos but from an agreement among the different *demoi* of the Eurozone, as negotiated by their elected representatives. For EMU to be legitimate, therefore, it must be under the *demoi*cratic control of European states. The logic here is that of the delegation of authority, with the problem of democratic legitimacy in the EU not that of the democratic deficit but that of the democratic disconnect – the failure to ensure policy making remains under the equal influence and control of the constituted peoples of the Union via their domestic democratic processes (Lindseth 2010, 234).

Can such *demoi*cratic control be achieved in the case of a currency union? A detailed response lies outside the scope of this chapter. Here we wish merely to indicate the institutional structures needed to place EMU under a political rather than a legal constitution, and to note how these structures exist within the EU to a sufficient degree for this proposal to be plausible. The main lines of such an approach can be found in the German Constitutional Court's judgements from 1993 onwards referred to earlier. According to the Court, the NP, the *Bundestag*, as the representative body of the German people, plays an integral role in realising the 'right to democracy' guaranteed by the German Constitution. Moreover, its budgetary responsibilities form an intrinsic aspect of that role, given that decisions on revenue and expenditure constrain the choice of public policies that shape the collective life of citizens. Adopting reasoning that encapsulates both political constitutionalism and the *demoi*cratic approach, the Court has argued that 'sufficient space' has to exist for the citizens of the MS to be able to interpret the fundamental rights that underlie their 'economic, cultural and social living conditions'. Given reasonable disagreements about the relative importance and nature of these rights and how they might be best interpreted and realised – disagreements that have been resolved in different ways over time within each of the MS, as their different political and constitutional traditions attest – European unification could not be conducted in such a way as to leave no space for the *demoi* of the contracting parties to determine their collective life according to their differing 'cultural, historical and linguistic perceptions' through 'public discourse in the party, political and parliamentary spheres of public politics' (Federal Constitutional Court 2009). As a result, the Court has insisted on the *Bundestag's* right of participation in ESM, particularly in authorising extensions of the guarantees for the fund (Federal Constitutional Court 2014b).

Drawing on this reasoning, two roles for NPs emerge within EMU. The first, domestic, role is to ensure that in negotiating budgetary rules at the EU level, the elected executives of each of the contracting MS act on the authority of their NPs, and that the subsequent undertakings remain subject to their control and scrutiny. There are signs that other NPs are following the German lead. For example, Spain has set up a parliamentary budget office – the *Oficina Prespuestaria de las Cortes Generales* – that checks and assesses the execution of the budget and provides information to the legislature. The French and Italian Parliaments have likewise requested higher standards of information and transparency on issues of European economic governance. The second, inter-parliamentary, role involves NPs working together to ensure that EU measures treat each of the MS with equal concern and respect as self-governing polities. That role was developed formally with Lisbon and the measures relating to their mutual guardianship of subsidiarity, such as the Early Warning Mechanism. Such measures have increased the Commission's obligation to inform and give reasons to parliaments for their policies, while encouraging parliaments to develop the requisite scrutiny and control procedures. Most importantly, the role of NPs was explicitly acknowledged in Article 13 of the TSCG, which provided the basis for the creation of the Interparliamentary Conference on Economic and Financial Governance of the European Union. Although both these roles remain as yet rudimentary and untested, they are the subject of considerable policy interest at present (see for example House of Lords 2014b) and provide the beginnings of the sort of *demoi*cratic political constitution we have advocated for EMU.

CONCLUSION

We have argued that the normative order of the EU requires that contracts between MS be seen as a two-level game, in which executives can only sign credible agreements as the duly authorised agents of their domestic peoples. We termed this *demoi*cratic structure republican intergovernmentalism. We argued that the attempt to view the neoliberal budgetary constraints of the Fiscal Compact as a supranational legal constitution not only conflicted with this normative order but also was unjustifiable in denying the reasonable disagreements among both citizens and MS about economic policy. Instead, such measures have to be subject to a political constitution of a *demoi*cratic kind. The continuing role for NPs insisted on by the German Constitutional Court in its Lisbon Judgement and elsewhere (Federal Constitutional Court 2009) provide the basis for such a political constitutional framework for EMU.

NOTE

1. We are grateful to the special issue editors, two anonymous referees, Peter Lindseth and Christine Reh for their comments. Richard Bellamy acknowledges the support of a Leverhulme Trust Research Fellowship RF-2012-368 and a Fellowship at the Hanse Wissenschaft Kolleg.

Chapter 20

It's the Politics, Stupid!

The EU after Brexit and Its Demoi-cratic Disconnect

Richard Bellamy and Dario Castiglione

We live, perhaps unfortunately, in interesting times. Thirty years ago, when the curtains of the *short* twentieth century (Hobsbawm 1994) came graphically down with the Berlin Wall, the world of international and European politics changed out of recognition. It was not the 'end of History', as it was rather prematurely claimed (Fukuyama 1992), but there was a palpable shift in the scope, languages and sites of politics, requiring also a reassessment of some of the central categories used to interpret it. The change was dramatic, but the end of the Cold War era brought a reassuring sense of optimism with it. For a short while at least, the international scene seemed less conflictual; democracy and rule-of-law systems were in the ascendancy; digital technology and globalisation were creating a more interconnected world, amenable in principle to listening to, if not satisfying, new demands for justice, recognition and environmental sustainability. Although economic equality was everywhere in retreat, and social insurance programmes under pressure and increasingly privatised, the combined effects of the new technological revolution, the emergence of new economic powers and markets on the international scene, and a generally positive (though financially inflated and deregulated) economic conjuncture, all contributed to a diffuse sense of prosperity.

In the narratives of this refashioned world order, the newly named European Union emerging from the Maastricht Treaty played a significant role. Both its 'panglossian' supporters and its 'sceptical' detractors obviously thought so. But even from a more dispassionate perspective, the Union could be seen as an original experiment in multilevel governance across traditional territorial and functional divides, partly responding to the challenges that increasingly porous and interconnected national societies faced from globalisation. The European Union also functioned as the catalyst for the rapid process of democratisation and economic and legal transformation of a significant number of countries that for forty years had operated within the Soviet Union's sphere of influence and dominion. In short, in spite of a number of acknowledged limitations – its top-down formation, the haphazard way in which the Union and its predecessor organisations had developed their legal acquis and the deeply contested *finalité* of the Union itself – by the start of the twenty-first century, the European Union could be regarded as both an effective (albeit opaque) 'model' of regional governance and a promising (though still inchoate) 'project' for a trans- or international form of democracy.

Much has happened in the ensuing thirty years, which have yet again transformed both the international scene and domestic politics across Europe: 9/11 and the economic crisis of 2008 come immediately to mind. There are also other local and global factors that have contributed to such changes. However, in stark contrast to thirty years ago, the resulting transformation comes without any feeling of reassurance and optimism. This is particularly true for the European Union. Brexit – the fact that for the first time the Union is shrinking rather than expanding – poses an existential problem for the European Union. Its mere institutional survival may not be in question, at least for now, but there are no less important strategic doubts as to its ongoing legitimation and long-term viability in its present form. Is the European Union still the right 'model' for regional governance? Can the Union's structure, perhaps suitably reformed, be credibly regarded as the ground on which to base a democratic 'project' in an interconnected world? In the concluding chapter of this collection, we shall assess the state of the Union with reference to the last question in particular.

THE CRISES OF EUROPEAN POLITICS

Brexit is neither the cause of the widespread feelings of dissatisfaction with the European Union nor arguably the gravest of its crises. In the two years since the referendum, the sense of foreboding felt soon after the vote has all but vanished, at least outside the UK. In spite of the many divisions within Europe, and in contrast with the shambolic way in which the UK government has dealt with the exit process, more recent events and economic developments have confirmed to many – perhaps to the point of complacency – that there is some inner resilience in the integration process. True, Euroscepticism is now firmly entrenched across most, if not all, member states, but even where either opposition or government parties successfully mobilise national publics against the Union and some of its key policies, there seems to be little appetite for following the United Kingdom on the exit path.

From a European perspective, Brexit may be seen less as the outright rejection of a broadly defined political integration project, and more as a contingent, though nonetheless grave, result of a series of other crises, which have accumulated since Maastricht and gathered pace, first with the international economic recession, and later with the waves of desperate refugees crossing the Mediterranean Sea. Even though the refugee crisis raised distinctive humanitarian problems related more to international law than the integration process; it ended up getting confused with and heightening a broader cluster of issues: notably, internal mobility of EU and third-country nationals, the impact of more permanent migratory fluxes, and multicultural coexistence in the increasingly securitised post–9/11 world. The political salience of all these issues has swelled in recent years, and for either good or not so good reasons, they have tended to be associated in the minds of national populations across Europe with the European integration process itself. Indeed, the issue of 'immigration', under which most of these particular questions are often lumped together in the media and public debate, is said to have been the single largest factor in determining the Brexit referendum's result, besides fuelling a move towards nationalist, xenophobic and right-wing parties in national elections in the rest of Europe.

At the time of writing, it is not yet clear how Brexit will unfold and what will be the nature of the new relations between the EU and the UK. Such a new partnership (since presumably, though not by any means certainly, some form of partnership will eventually be agreed) may also affect the EU's other external relations, challenging the teleological view of European integration as an inevitable process of enlargement. Brexit, of course, has its own causes and contested rationale when seen from a British perspective. We shall have more to say about its implications for the UK towards the end of this chapter, but our main concern is with the effect of Brexit and the other related crises on the European Union, particularly its democratic credentials.

When discussing the EU's democratic deficit and its simmering legitimation crisis, there is a tendency to examine them as being exclusively related to the Union's institutions and arrangements. From a democratic perspective, however, Brexit and the other European crises should be seen as part of a larger picture involving the transformation of democratic politics at both the national and the international levels. Current discussions of the general crisis of democracy point to the perils of technocracy and populism undermining the established models of constitutional and representative democracy that have prevailed in the majority of advanced capitalist societies since the middle of the twentieth century. Technocratic tendencies are seen as emanating from the very logic of a global-oriented liberal order, while populism is said to threaten such an order through a return to a more atavistic, nationalist and occasionally autarkic kind of politics. For many, the EU is, or should be, the embodiment of some of the ideals of a liberal, cosmopolitan order, and of constitutional democracy on a supranational scale. In this respect, it is threatened in equal measure by each of these twin perils. However, this may be too neat a characterisation of the Union's current predicament, one that tends to locate the perils as lying outside the very process of integration and of the political and social dynamics of European societies. From its beginnings, the EU has been a controversial and contested project, which has partly determined, as well-being shaped by, larger international developments and the internal politics of Europe and of its member states. In this respect, the EU is as much the cause as the effect of its current predicament. Technocracy and populist politics (however vague and often unhelpful the latter's definition may be) should be considered as being in certain respects intrinsically connected to the history of European integration and the fabric of European politics both at the European and the member-states levels. These are not 'external' threats from which European democracy must defend itself, not least because democracy in the EU has so far been more a 'project' than a reality. Technocracy and populism should instead be considered as particular manifestations – or, from a more critical perspective, 'disfigurations' (Urbinati 2014) – of the democratic politics of twenty-first-century advanced capitalist societies operating within a broadly neoliberal international economic system. The EU's legitimation crisis and the retreat of the European democratic 'project' are part of this overall picture, to which the EU itself has contributed through the unresolved problems created by its various phases of integration-without-politics, and by the unthinking repatriation of politics that have characterised the strategic action of national political elites during the last decade or so.

It has belatedly become a commonplace to acknowledge that the post-1989 political acceleration, with both the widening and deepening of European integration, required what Giandomenico Majone (2017) has described as a 'dynamic' rather than 'static' form of adaptation, where the former is characterised by the active presence of institutional and political leadership. It is somewhat dubious that the failure of 'dynamic' adaptation in the EU case mainly lies, as suggested by Majone himself (15–17), in the inability of the Union's leadership to define a clear goal (*finalité*) for the integration process, apart from relying on the vague, procedural formula of an 'ever closer union' (16). There is something more pertinent in the suggestion that the principle of member states equality (backed up by veto power) poses a powerful structural constraint on the formation of a European leadership capable of political action. However, one should not forget that the completion of the Single Market, the adoption of the single currency with the relevant budgetary conditions, the decision to go ahead with enlargement, and even the failed attempt at drafting a Constitution, were all acts of political leadership involving ambitious strategic aims. More than mere absence of leadership, it could be suggested that there has been a failure in the way in which leadership has been exercised. Citing Plamenatz, Majone suggests that strict political leadership (in contrast to managerial and government leadership) consists in the capacity of 'speaking for people', of 'giving expression to aims, beliefs and feelings that people are willing to endorse', and therefore 'defining goals, principles and attitudes that are, or are supposed to be, shared' (2017, 14). This definition approximates what Mike Saward (2010) has more recently identified as the process of representative claim making, insisting on how this very process, and its successful uptake by the relevant audiences, need to be considered an essential part of political and democratic representation. National and European leaders have failed to speak for the peoples of Europe in this precise sense. In their claim making as 'political' representatives – meant here in a broad sense – they have not articulated a narrative of integration that speaks to the citizens, or at least to large majorities within each of the national populations. Only such a narrative could make it possible for those very same peoples to willingly choose to endorse both the underlying principles and the required attitudes necessary for the dynamic process of adaptation that the deepening and widening of integration may call for, and enable them to share in the new policy objectives that seem appropriate for stricter forms of Europe-wide cooperation. The causes for such a failure of leadership can be found in three main areas: the more structural and institutional difficulties besetting the organisation of postnational democratic politics; the subjective shortcomings of the political, economic and intellectual elites, who have misjudged the kind of issues where political leadership was required; and the political leaders' recalcitrance, both at the European and national levels, in adopting policies aimed at redistributing the gains and losses of increasing economic Europeanisation.

These various aspects of the failure of leadership would probably benefit from closer analysis, which is generally lacking in the current literature on the EU, but one key point of our analysis, one that is germane to our republican and demoi-cratic approach as developed in earlier writings, is that the exercise of such leadership requires tackling the problem of the (complex) forms of democratic representation needed in a polity like the European Union. The exercise of power in such a polity rests not only on the democratic legitimacy of the member states, but also on their willingness, and that of their own citizenry, to engage in enhanced forms of transnational cooperation. The maintenance of such sustained (not just one-off) forms of cooperation requires the sharing of institutional processes of decision-making and of burdens and responsibilities. To be legitimate, the required infrastructure of enhanced cooperation must also involve the meaningful internalisation, *through their own* autonomous democratic processes, of the externalities of each member state's actions and decisions (Lord 2019). The realisation of such a complex system of transnational and interstate cooperation is not, as it has been all too often assumed by the national and European elites, one that can be achieved functionally, solely through administrative, legal, or economic integration and coordination. Nor is it a matter of achieving a community of ideals, culture and identity transcending national boundaries. Short of being the result of dramatic events and circumstances, it is difficult to see how such a new identity could be manufactured artificially. Moreover, this would require – as it did in the extended process of the formation of most modern nation states – long and arguably oppressive processes of disciplining and sociocultural homogenisation, which are unthinkable in contemporary European societies, working under the 'banal' constraints of ongoing democratic decision-making and the application of the rule of law. Transnational and interstate cooperation, as envisaged in the European Union, is at bottom a 'political' problem, requiring political mobilisation and political solutions, within already established patterns of social trust and political interactions, which are more firmly rooted at the national than the European level. The failure to perceive the implications of this fact is at the root of the present legitimation crisis of the European Union. To adapt a rather hackneyed phrase: 'it's the politics, stupid'.

POLITICS ENTRAPPED

In the European Union, integration-without-politics takes a variety of forms, but they all suffer from two connected misconceptions. The first can be called the 'autopoiesis misconception', which envisions that a particular kind of integration – administrative, legal, economic, or even sociocultural – can functionally give rise to and sustain a polity. The second is the 'a-political misconception', which assumes that decisions at each of these levels can be taken according to exclusively functional or rational-instrumental criteria, extraneous to the logic of democratic politics, which, on the contrary, is based on procedural and dialogical forms of reconciliation of conflicts, and on the construction of forms of collective unity and responsibility in decision-making. Underlying this second misconception there is usually an understanding of politics as a mere fight for power and sectorial advantage through factional divisions and low forms of compromise. Yet, on those occasions when a broader, more constitutive and transformative view of politics is acknowledged, this misconception tends to identify this kind of politics with an unrealistic and idealised form of high-minded rational deliberation. By contrast, we think of politics as always being a mixture of high and low politics. This mixture applies both to the way the European Union's 'regime' works, and to its development into a polity of sorts. It is this way of conceiving and practicing politics that has been either concealed or underestimated in the European integration process, relying in its stead on other normative grounds to justify the legitimacy of the process of integration and close cooperation.

Three main legitimating rationales are normally offered as alternatives to politics. These three rationales rest, respectively, on appeals to values and ideals, on legal and constitutional arrangements, or on the need for shared regulatory policies in a more globalised economy. We shall examine each in turn to see why they ultimately fail to be fully convincing, and, by contrast, what kind of politics is needed to try to address the current European legitimation crisis.

One argument often advanced to explain the motivating force of the origins of the European project is that integration, even in its limited form of economic cooperation, but even more so when extended through common legal and political structures, has prevented war in Europe, taming the disruptive drive of twentieth-century nationalisms and of competition over trade and power between European states. The same argument is used either in support of federal blueprints for the completion of political integration, or as a cautionary tale against those who wish the disintegration of the European Union altogether. There is no doubt that maintaining peace worked as a strong motivating ideal at the start of the European integration project, particularly for a generation that had witnessed the horrors of World War II and learnt some of the lessons of the interwar period. Strategically, also in the context of the Cold War, it made sense to lock West Germany in an economic alliance that kept peaceful relations between an increasing circle of European nations, with the promise of common prosperity through trade and other forms of cooperation. It is more questionable whether peace as a motivating value can maintain the same hold on the imagination of the current generations of Europeans, who have become accustomed to living in peaceful conditions, thus taking peace in Europe for granted (Grimm 2017, 1–3; Offe 2015, 66). As a motivation for sustaining or even increasing integration, the ideal of peace may therefore count for too little. Indeed, as a kind of moral justification, it may count for too much. For, if the search for peace is considered a strong ground on which to keep the countries of the European Union together, why stop at its borders? The effectiveness of the value of peace as one of the motivating forces at the start of the integration process is not merely due to the abstract nature of peace as a moral value, but to the way in which it worked in the post-war conditions of European politics and societies. Because of such conditions, it was possible to harness it to the project of European integration in a way that, at least for a period, successfully inspired and motivated both national elites and large parts of the different European peoples. Changes in the geopolitical conditions and in the life experiences of Europeans therefore explain the waning power of such an appeal.

Arguably, as spelt out by Claus Offe (2015), a more thorough case for a value- and ideal-inspiring European project, of which peace is only a part, can be made. He identifies seven *finalitées* that are often given as grounds for 'Europe as a "project" intrinsically worth pursuing' (61–80). Since the last one he mentions is of a pragmatic nature, more to do with policies than values, at this stage we shall survey the first six only. In the order in which Offe discusses them, the six *finalitées* comprise the following: (1) peace; (2) economic prosperity and social inclusion; (3) democratic and accountable government; (4) 'soft power' within the international system; (5) diversity of cultures and traditions; and (6) what Offe calls the EU's *mission civilisatrice interne* (63). Offe himself is sceptical that any of these ideal reasons, or even all of them together, can mobilise strong and sustained popular support for the European 'project' beyond the natural appeal they have for a highly mobile European elite, segments of which may, from different perspectives, share a more cosmopolitan outlook.

Leaving aside peace, which we have already discussed, Offe's scepticism is based on a mixture of arguments, partly challenging the empirical connection between the EU's action and the relevant values, and partly questioning the capacity of such values and ideals as embodied by the EU to generate sustained popular support. This mixture of arguments applies in particular to the *finalitées* from (2) to (5). The financial crisis of 2008, and the subsequent debt and monetary crises, together with the adoption of EU-wide austerity policies, have not only put in doubt the link between prosperity and European integration but also magnified the way in which integration, as well as globalisation, spreads prosperity unevenly across states, regions and social classes. The role of the EU in the promotion of democratic government is no less questionable. Apart from the much-debated issue of the EU's democratic deficit, the general trend in all member states has been towards forms of post-democratic governance (Crouch 2004), with increasing powers to delegated and technocratic institutions, and a steady move towards exit- rather than voice-based mechanisms in the running of public services and utilities. Democratic innovations of a more participatory or deliberative kind have on the whole been very marginal, while tendencies towards the strengthening of executive power over the legislative, the personalisation of politics, and the enervation and bureaucratisation of political parties have proceeded apace.

Although the EU (and its predecessor organisations) has been instrumental in helping democratisation processes in countries that joined in the 1980s and at the start of the millennium, it has not halted what Peter Mair (2013) has called the 'hollowing out' of western democracy, increasing the gap between insulated elites and disaffected citizens. Indeed, many indicators show a decline in the support for democracy and trust in government across most, if not all European countries, and, as Offe suggests, 'being part of the EU and undergoing further integration is hardly experienced by the citizens of member states as a gain in terms of their equal liberty and other qualities of democracy' (69).

When we turn to Europe's alleged exceptionalism as either the promoter of 'soft power' in international relations, or as a model for encouraging the flourishing of various forms of 'diversity', there is scant evidence of either being the case. Even though the EU was awarded the Nobel Peace Prize in 2012, its inability in recent years to play a significant and autonomous role with respect to geopolitical issues and areas that are relevant to its sphere of influence and close to its borders, such as the Iraq war, the Middle East conflicts, the relations with Russia, and the Arab Spring and its aftermath, testifies against the distinctiveness of the European Union as a 'soft power', or at least against the effectiveness of such a self-chosen role. The evidence with regard to the EU embodying 'diversity' as a value is even less compelling. The difficulty in reconciling respect for and recognition of cultural minorities while fostering social integration in societies that have become more multicultural and differentiated, and the disquieting return of xenophobic movements and attitudes across Europe, show that the EU as a political area is hardly a model for cultural diversity. As for the intra-European diversity in traditions, intellectual outlooks and styles of life, the integration process, such as globalisation, may actually risk undermining some aspects of this diversity, rather than either facilitating or promoting it. After all, some of this diversity is the product of Europe's past political, institutional and cultural-linguistic fragmentation.

Offe's sixth *finalité* is more intriguing (2013, 71). He highlights how European integration may be looked at as 'a precautionary safeguard against de-civilizing tendencies' undermining long-established standards of civil and human rights. Contrary to the experience in other parts of the world – as in the re-normalisation of the idea of torture in the United States during the Bush Jr presidency – Offe argues that in Europe such regression and the ensuing violations of rights 'could not go undetected and unsanctioned', an achievement 'that cannot be lightly dismissed'. Nonetheless, Offe thinks that the rather 'negative' character of this 'prevention' function is insufficient as a ground for mobilising popular support for the EU. One could raise other doubts about Europe's self-immunisation capacity against de-civilizing tendencies, by asking, for instance, whether this is truly the case; and, if so, whether the safeguards come more from the public cultures and institutions of the member states than from the Union itself. The recent vote of the EU Parliament to trigger Article 7 of the Lisbon Treaty with respect to Hungary is an interesting case in point. On the one hand, this would seem a good example of the way in which the Union may fulfil the (self) civilizing mission that the members states have delegated to it by agreeing to keep to certain internal standards of rights and democratic organisation as part of their membership of the EU (this is, after all, the rationale of Article 7). On the other hand, the fact that the vote has probably come too late to stop the evolution of the Hungarian regime, and that (at the time of writing) it is very unlikely that the Council will take sanctions against one of the member states, may confirm that the Union's *mission civilisatrice interne* is at best ineffective, while ultimately depending on the robustness of the democratic and civil-rights culture of the member states.

However, if one looks closer at the logic of the EU's civilizing mission, as described by Offe, it may appear that it belongs more to the second non-political rationale that we have identified, stemming from the legitimating force of legal and constitutional arrangements. Indeed, Offe refers to the EU's safeguarding role as 'an *institutional* asset' (2015, 71, our emphasis). From such a perspective, the support and legitimacy of the European 'project' is only indirectly linked to the values that it is meant to protect. Its more direct justification is that the Union works as a checking mechanism over the possible lapses of individual member states, which may undermine the kind of democratic, civil and human rights that they have agreed to share as the basis of their cooperation. As Jürgen Habermas, following Offe, argues, the European Union becomes the instrument for the members states' joint efforts to bind themselves in a 'self-paternalistic project' (Habermas 2015, 549). This is a typical constitutional strategy, in line with the argument that moral values or principles are not enough to establish a stable and just order between either individuals or states, but need some form of juridification and constitutionalisation. Accordingly, it has been argued that the legitimation of the European 'project' resides in the progressive accumulation of a legal acquis that has created a new supranational legal order, which has the force of a European-wide Constitution. Those, like Habermas, who do not believe that a Constitution by stealth is sufficient for the legitimation of the EU, have long argued that Europe needs a proper constitutional moment sanctioning the founding of a 'supranational political community' (Habermas 2012, 11) and that this is even more necessary now, in spite of the failed attempt in the first decade of the millennium (Habermas 2012, 2015).

Let's leave aside the general issue of the relationship between constitution-alism and democracy, and the more particular question of the feasibility of a full-blown European constitutional moment, arguments on which we have written in the past, including in essays collected in Part III of this volume. A more pressing problem for the legal- and constitutional-based 'project' lies in the assessment of the integrative and legitimating force of the European legal order, and whether this order can be regarded as a constitutional framework. The idea that the juridification of the Treaties, also through European case law and the interpretation of the European Court of Justice, has de facto resulted in the constitutionalisation of the EEC, and eventually of the EU, is one that has dominated the scholarly debate since the pioneering work of Joseph Weiler (1991). This is not a view on which there is scholarly agreement, however. Many international public lawyers remain unconvinced, regarding the Union as an example, however sui generis, of an international organisation (Klabbers 2001, 224). More recently, Peter Lindseth (2010) has developed a carefully argued case, from the perspective of administrative law, showing that the power of the European institutions should not be seen as a form of post- or supranational constitutional order, but as the *extension* of a post-war constitu-tional settlement that emerged across West European democratic states. As part of such a settlement, there has been an increase in the process of delegation of decision-making to regulatory powers partly independent from the more direct chain of democratic delegation and accountability. Lindseth maintains that this is the appropriate context for the extension of regulatory powers to European institutions, resulting in a form of delegation of administrative capacities and mediated legitimacy, rather than in a transference of sovereignty, as the con-struction of a separate, and arguably superior, constitutional order would imply.

The dispute between these different interpretations of the nature of the EU legal order involves both descriptive and normative elements. As Lindseth argues: 'To call the European public law "constitutional" is to assume some-thing that is fundamentally in historical and political dispute' (Lindseth et al. 2012, 154). In this case, as in many similar ones, *naming* is also to a large degree *doing*. Both scholarly and political discourses find themselves in a bind, unable to unpick normative implications from descriptive understandings and vice versa. The dispute over the nature of the European legal order, and on whether the categories of international, constitutional or administrative law are the most appropriate for it, cannot be settled by fiat, but to a large extent depend on the way in which the social and political agents' understand the relevant facts, and how their understanding orientates their own interactions. On a more formal level, the abandonment of the explicit constitutional project, following the rejection of the 'Treaties establishing a European Constitution' in the Dutch and French referendums of 2005, would seem to support those that insist that the EU is not a constitutional order. But the argument about the constitutionalisation of Europe can be put in a subtler way, which does not necessarily rest on its formal acceptance – even though this itself raises important legitimacy issues. It can be argued that the Treaties and the acquis communautaire have a quasi-constitutional status in function both of the way in which they have been interpreted by the European Court of Justice – an interpretation increasingly accepted within the national legal systems, though intermittently resisted by some of the national constitutional courts – and of the way in which European law directly translates into the national legal orders, and EU policies and directives materially constrain decisions at the national level, particularly on issues of political economy. In some cases, the constitutionalisation of European Treaties and intergovernmental agreements has been done by the member states themselves, as, for instance, in Italy, where elements of the Fiscal Compact were inserted into the Italian Constitution in 2012. In other words, the Treaties work *as if* they were a Constitution, not necessarily in the normative sense recently suggested by Kaarlo Tuori (2016) and correctly criticised by Lindseth himself (2016), but by producing the kind of framing and constraining effects that constitutions normally have, particularly in their role as a linkage between legal and political systems in modern states. The *as-if* constitutional role of the Treaties inevitably creates an imbalance between the formal and material elements in the exercise of power, blurring the distinction between the right of exercising power (*potestas*) and the capacity for doing so (*potentia*) (on this distinction, see Loughlin 2014, 11–2). It is because of this grey area that the nature of the EU legal order remains a matter of intense historical and political dispute, with important implications for political legitimacy and the location of sovereignty.

Brexit may be a good example to illustrate this point. The fact that the UK has decided, through an entirely autonomous process, to exit from the European Union leaves no room for doubt as to where sovereignty lies or the degree of independence that member states' constitutional orders maintain in relation to the Union. Admittedly, the right of withdrawal is also sanctioned by Article 50 of the Treaty of Lisbon. But its first paragraph explicitly states that this right should be exercised in accordance with the member state's own 'constitutional requirements'. The very introduction of Article 50, originally drafted as part of the aborted Constitutional Treaty, was at the time cited as evidence and recognition of the member states being the ultimate repository of sovereignty and the masters of the Treaties – an interpretation underscored by the five national Constitutional Courts who examined Article 50 either as part of the Constitutional Treaty proposal or in the identical version adopted by the Lisbon Treaty (Dixon 2018, 909–14). Article 50 is more about the exit procedures than the right to exit, which, as we said, remains entirely within the member states' constitutional capacities, a fact that marks a clear difference between withdrawing from the EU and the attempts at subnational secession, as in the Scottish and Catalan cases, where the right to separate is either subject to the acceptance and the procedures agreed by the larger unit or denied altogether.

However, this is only half of the story, as the last two years of Brexit negotiations have made only too clear, particularly to the British public and its political class. Even though Brexit may have confirmed that sovereignty remains with the member states, it also shows that the level of entanglement of legal and constitutional orders, of decision-making and regulatory processes, and of a whole range of social interactions, is such that to unravel such capillary forms of integration and cooperation is an arduous task, with very high transactions costs, which make it difficult, if not impossible, to exercise the very right of withdrawal (van Parijs 2016), particularly for those countries that have joined the Euro, as the Greek crisis illustrated only too well. Whereas the decision to join the EU or in the past the EEC (as for the UK with the 1975 referendum) is indubitably momentous; withdrawing is even more dramatic and consequential. Indeed, it is hard to imagine a more momentous constitutional change than the one British politics and society are undergoing at present, with so many, as yet unclear, long-term consequences for the ordinary lives of its citizens, for the UK's position within the international system, and for the very self-understanding of the national community (considering also the possible repercussions on the Scottish and Irish questions). The point here is not about the actual long-term costs of leaving the European Union, which are almost impossible to predict, but the way in which over the years European integration has penetrated and transformed the constitutional order of its member states, locking them in a relationship that is both practically, and arguably normatively, tricky to unpick. By showing the difficulty of undoing forty years of cooperation, Brexit is perhaps proof that the European Union has contributed to create a new constitutional framework in all but name.

Accepting that the EU has created an interstate legal framework with quasi-constitutional features – a 'functional' Constitution (Isiksel 2016), operating in combination with the member states' own constitutional orders – does not imply that such a framework has the same structure and legitimating force that characterise national constitutions in democratic states, thus questioning whether such a quasi-constitutional order can provide sufficient reason for sustaining a project of 'ever closer union' between the peoples of Europe. The difference is not just one of process – the way in which the constitutional order has been consolidated without a proper public debate and without clear statements of intent – but also of form and content. Treating the Treaties as if they had full constitutional status is extremely problematic for a variety of reasons, such as the nature of their content and the ability to change and adapt them over time to changing conditions. Of course, these are controversial issues in constitutional theory itself (Bellamy 2007). There are disagreements on whether constitutions should mainly frame and regulate the political system, defining legal relations and priorities between rightful authorities, or whether and to what extent they should also contain substantive requirements of justice, fixed in a catalogue of fundamental rights. There are also disputes on how rigid and entrenched the constitutional fundamentals should be, and how the powers of adjudication and amendment should be distributed between institutions. But EU Treaties contain a large amount of substantive policies and specific directives that cannot easily be classified as either framing devices or a substantive catalogue of fundamental laws and rights. Moreover, in the present structure of the EU, changing the Treaties is extremely difficult, being subject to agreement and negotiation between all member states. Nevertheless, such rigidity has not precluded changes and extensions by interpretation, thus giving to the European Court of Justice a privileged, and often unchallenged, role in Constitution making over other institutions such as the Council, whose 'legislative' capacity to change the Treaties is curtailed by what Fritz Scharpf calls the 'joint decision trap' (1988, 1999, 76). Dieter Grimm (2017), who has recently explained in some detail the unintended consequences of what he calls the 'over-constitutionalisation' of the Treaties, makes two important points on the skewed character of the present European constitutional order. First, that this arrangement allows for important political decisions, which in democratic societies largely depend on the more directly accountable legislative power, to be taken instead in non-political ways, thus significantly shifting the balance of power away from the legislative to the executive, the judiciary, and the other non-majoritarian institutions. Second, that the legislative weaknesses of the EU tends to deprive the constitutional order of the non-judicial resources on which its legitimacy also and crucially depends.

The distinctive character of the EU's Treaties-based constitutional order has another important consequence that makes it different from modern national constitutions, but which is also relevant to the third rationale often cited in support of the European integration project, as mainly involving issues of economic regulation with limited distributive consequences, and therefore amenable more to problem-solving policies than conflictual politics. Insofar as the functional constitutionalisation of the EU has mainly been focused on issues of economic competition and harmonisation, it has unduly privileged economic liberty over other forms of liberty, often inappropriately extending the logic of either private or competition law to the domain of public law, which is at the core of the European constitutional tradition. As Dieter Grimm has emphasised, there are democratic costs to the way in which the EU has been constitutionalised, and 'the ECJ pursued the goal of market integration with considerable zeal, subordinating other concerns to this goal' (2017, 93). This has resulted, for instance, in the focus on the 'four freedoms' exclusively in terms of economic rights, to the detriment of the broader view that most democratic constitutions take of private and public liberty, where the protection of economic rights is balanced by a consideration of personal, communication, cultural and social rights, all of which have a more collective and public dimension (96). The economic and privatistic bias of the current constitutional order, and its focus on competition and anti-protectionist policies, has also restricted the capacities of the national public authorities to offer social protection, favouring the general trend towards privatisation, and thereby imposing at both the national as well the European level a particular conception of the proper balance between the private and the public, which is arguably one of the main functions of a democratic Constitution.

The way in which the EU quasi-constitutional structure has developed is therefore anything but neutral in terms of policies and their effects on the social fabric of national societies, and the state's capacities for positive, not just negative, types of intervention. As Philippe van Parijs (2016) has noted, the development of the EU as an interstate federal structure, whose main project is the creation of a common economic market, reflects what he calls 'Hayek's Trap'. This trap consists of two main features. The first is the disabling function that the common market and cross-border movement (of goods, services, capital and labour) have on the market constraining and social protection functions of the state, on the one hand, and of other collective organisations, such as trade unions and civil society organisations, on the other. The second is that the multinational character of such a federation weakens some of the identitarian features of the national community on which modern states have relied in order to develop more solidaristic and redistributive policies. A similar story emerges from Fritz Scharpf's influential analysis (1999, chap. 2) of the asymmetries between negative and positive integration in the way in which the EU has developed. He points out that European economic integration presents a fundamental structural dualism between the strength of *negative* measures, through the removal of tariffs and other barriers to free trade, and the weakness of *positive* intervention, through the reconstruction of a regulatory framework with a socially corrective function at the European level. Admittedly, the European Union has not exclusively developed through these ideological lines. Environmental and consumer protection have been central considerations in European legislation, and there has been a growing concern with social and equality-promoting rights. Moreover, one should be wary of reconstructing European integration as the simple story of the functional move to supranationalism. As the historical work of Alan Milward (1992) has shown, European integration played an important role in what he called the rescue of the nation state, by providing important instruments for protecting and developing its problem-solving capacities in the post-war conditions. As we shall discuss in the next section, this is still an important perspective, particularly when we look at the way in which democracy itself may be rescued from some of its disfigurations. Nonetheless, it is also true that the very capacities of the European national states to provide social protection and a balance between private and public freedom, while operating in a more integrated economic area, have been under particular stress in the last two decades, a period that is subsequent to Millward's perceptive historical reconstruction. During this period the kind of output legitimacy that has often been regarded as sufficient for the justification of the European integration project has lost its effectiveness, both in relation to the deterioration of some of the economic benefits attributed to the process of Europeanisation and to the weakening of some of the very mechanisms of output-oriented legitimation. While in national states such mechanisms are balanced and supported by input- and identity-oriented mechanisms, this is not the case at the European level, which relies heavily on the member states for indirectly providing such sources of democratic legitimacy. But, as we shall argue in the following section, the only way in which these different sources of legitimacy can be reconnected is through a return to democratic politics. This is the only way not only to regain some popular support for the European project, but also to keep alive, through the conflicts and compromises of democratic politics, some of the core values, established institutional structures and shared policy aims that have animated the project since its inception.

REGAINING DEMOCRATIC CONTROL?

If we are right that the crisis of the European project can only be resolved through politics, the question that needs to be asked is whether and how to unbound democratic politics in the European Union. Claus Offe (2015) has argued that this is mainly a question of political 'agency', and that either an 'ever closer union' or at least the consolidation of the integration process cannot be left to the force of 'necessity' and neo-functionalist mechanisms supported by a 'permissive consensus' (56–7). As we have already seen, however, Offe excludes that the search for political agency can be motivated by a value-based adhesion to the *finalitées* of the EU, even if those could be agreed upon. He is also sceptical about various other mobilisation options, such as those based on ideological identification (because the pro-European grouping is too fragmented and relatively weak outside certain elites), or on the hegemonic role played by a country like Germany (because of the very reluctance of its political class and the German public at large to pay the relative costs for such an operation). Offe is also convinced, like us, that the 'thin' kind citizenship of the present EU structure is insufficient on its own to be an effective medium for any mobilising political agency. So, what is left?

Given most (if not all) people regard national autarky as a non-starter, and unregulated free global markets unjust as well as likely to be inefficient and prone to failures, one common and well-rehearsed answer to the political conundrum of the EU lies in the suggestion to turn it into a full democratic supranational state, subsuming national democracy and citizenship within some broader scheme for global democracy. Many federally minded Europeans adopt this line of thinking, regarding the development of supranational democracy at the EU level as the first stage in such a process (Habermas 2015). However, this raises the usual concern with the EU's democratic deficit, with Europhiles joining in an unholy alliance with Eurosceptics to argue that in many core areas decisional authority has passed upwards to Brussels without adequate democratic oversight. By and large, proposals for addressing this alleged deficit have turned on the practicality and justifiability of enhancing the powers of the European Parliament (EP) and electing the Commission, be it directly or indirectly, and invariably get linked to arguments for further political integration. Unsurprisingly, the main counter-arguments have mirrored this reasoning. They come from those opposing the justifiability of the integration process on democratic grounds. These critics regard the shift of political authority from national to European political structures as at best diluting the democratic influence of each individual voter, and at worst indefensibly undermining the self-determination of sovereign peoples. Such arguments suggest that the EU could never be democratically legitimate – indeed, that further empowering the EP or electing the Commission might deepen rather than lessen the democratic deficit.

These concerns are further buttressed by some of the arguments already presented on the way in which the EU has the promotion of economic globalisation largely hard-wired into its constitutional structure (Isiksel 2016). Moreover, the transfer of allegiance to the EU has been shallow, mostly associated to 'output' mechanisms of legitimacy, and largely sustained by a broad degree of 'banal' identification for the security and economic benefits with which it has been credited (McNamara 2015). But, as already argued, all this has been sorely tested by the Euro crisis and the more recent association of the EU in many countries with widespread austerity policies and the reduction of public spending, especially on social welfare. As Brexit indicated, those opposing the EU, who account for as much as a third of the electorate or more in many countries across the EU (Usherwood and Startin 2013), are typically far more vocal and passionate than its supporters tend to be (Kriesi 2016). Many pro-Europeans have seen the obvious response as being the adoption by the EU of more socially integrative policies – such as an EU-wide basic income (Van Parijs 2016) or other redistributive schemes addressing substantive issues of social justice (Offe 2015, 121–30) – that might support a transfer of democratic political authority to the EU level. Yet, such a move begs the question of whether EU citizens desire greater social integration in the first place. To many, such a move would be yet another top-down imposition, with a very real risk of further undermining the incomplete but nevertheless far superior social welfare systems existing at the national level, along with the democratic systems that facilitated their emergence (Streeck 2014).

If the full transference of the mechanisms of democratic politics to the European, supranational, level is neither feasible nor convincing, can democratic politics be re-energised in Europe by a step forward into the past? This is, after all, what the supporters of Brexit have advocated by proposing a return to national sovereignty, unbound by the EU structure and the obligations that come from being part of it. Had the referendum on Britain's membership of the EU been decided on the economic case alone, then in all likelihood the UK would have voted to stay in. However, the debate ended up turning as much on politics as economics, and on that issue in particular the Remain campaign offered much weaker arguments, barely mentioning the political risks and costs of Brexit. In this regard, the Leave campaign's winning slogan was the claim that exiting the European Union would allow the people of Britain to 'take back control' – at least indirectly, via their elected representatives in the government and Parliament. The implication was that executive and legislative power over a range of important economic and social policies – not least those relating to immigration – had passed to EU institutions that were largely uncontrolled or inadequately controlled by British citizens, or indeed the citizens of any of the EU member states. Leaving the EU would involve a repatriation of these competences to democratically accountable British administrators and politicians, re-enfranchising the British electorate in the process. Indeed, many Remainers had lent this argument a certain credibility through having contributed to four decades of criticism of the EU's democratic deficit. Stretching back at least to 1979 and the first elections to the European Parliament, the critiques of the democratic failings of the EU by Europhiles all too often paralleled those of Eurosceptics, and in some cases have been even harsher. The comparative failure of the Remain campaign to mount even a negative political case against leaving, let alone to give positive political (or, for that matter, economic) reasons for European integration, served simply to further legitimise the Leave campaign's democratic argument for Brexit.

Yet, the Leave campaign's political case was as misleading and misinformed as much of their economic case is being steadily revealed to be. From the alleged savings on payments into the EU budget and the assumption that a free trade agreement with the EU could be negotiated both swiftly and on advantageous terms to the City and UK producers, to the failure to take

account of the inflationary repercussions of a fall in the pound and a consequent rise in interest rates, the economic claims of the proponents of Brexit
have steadily unravelled. However, the political costs are, if anything, even
greater than the economic. Far from 'taking back control', leaving the EU
involves the British electorate losing control over the global economic and
social processes that shape so many key government policies. Yet, the EU
fosters such control not by subsuming national democracies within a supranational democratic system, as many Europhiles assume – thereby giving rise
to worries about both an EU and a domestic democratic deficit – but by offering a framework within which national democracies can collectively regulate
such global processes in fair ways that, in spite of some of the limits we have
highlighted, overall show the relevant states and their peoples equal concern
and respect. Outside such arrangements, states will inevitably be dominated
by other states as well as by agents and agencies operating trans- or multina-
tionally, such as financial institutions, companies and terrorist groups (Pettit
2010). None of these can be successfully controlled by any single state operating unilaterally. That has proved impossible even for the USA at the height
of its hegemonic sway, with the benefit of massive military might, a large
domestic market and considerable natural resources. It certainly lies outside
the capacity of a medium-sized economic and military power such as the UK,
which is heavily dependent on international trade.

The basic problem can be formulated in terms of what Dani Rodrik has
called 'the fundamental political trilemma of the world economy' (Rodrik
2011, xviii); namely, the impossibility of simultaneously achieving democracy, national self-determination, and economic globalisation – one of these
has to give (Rodrik 2011, xix, 200–5). As he explains, 'If we want to maintain and deepen democracy, we have to choose between the nation state and
international economic integration. And if we want to keep the nation state
and self-determination, we have to choose between deepening democracy and
deepening globalisation' (Rodrik 2011, xix, 200).

How might we avoid this impasse? As Rodrik (2011) notes, an alternative
response to the global 'trilemma' involves collaboration between democratic
states to collectively regulate globalisation in 'smart' ways, as he believed
Keynes's design of the Bretton Woods system achieved for the post-war
period. From this perspective, the democratic legitimacy of the EU lies in
its strengthening and legitimising the democratic systems of the member
states rather than by offering an alternative to them. However, that cannot
be achieved by treating the national self-determination of one state in isolation from that of other states – either morally or practically. The democratic
decisions of almost all states affect, and are themselves affected by, the
democratic decisions of other states, whether they are formally associated
within a structure such as the EU or not. To the extent that democratically

made decisions of one state undercut those of other states, or reduce the options available to them, while being in their turn partially determined by these other states, all states risk losing democratic legitimacy. Meanwhile, as noted above, domestic democracy is further diminished by its inability to tackle problems that require cooperation between states, either because these problems are by their nature global in character – such as global warming – or involve transnational activities and processes among multinational organisations, be it financial movements, migration flows or terrorism. Therefore, a domestic democratic deficit exists from the very fact of democratic states being part of an interconnected world in which autarky no longer offers a plausible or desirable option (see chapter 18 in this volume).

Meeting this challenge requires some regulation of the interactions between states and a mechanism for fostering cooperation among them. To achieve that purpose while still retaining meaningful forms of self-determination for the peoples of these states, we need to reconceive the purpose of supranational bodies. Instead of being superior and independent sources of democratic authority to their constituent states, we should see them as mechanisms that allow democratic communities to coexist on mutually agreed and equitable terms. As such, these bodies have to remain subordinate to their constituent members as a delegated authority under their joint and equal control. The problem of democratic legitimacy thereby changes from being one of a democratic deficit at the supranational level to that of a democratic disconnect between the peoples of the constituent states and the inter- and multinational decisions their domestic representatives make in their name, including the creation and control of supranational regulatory bodies (see chapter 19 in this volume).

This proposal constitutes a 'demoi-cratic' solution to the democratic legitimacy issue, whereby, in Kalypso Nicolaidis's phrase, the peoples of the EU 'govern together but not as one' (Nicolaïdis 2013, 351). This can be achieved through a kind of republican politics that is also capable of internalising interstate externalities whereby decisions conform to the normative logic of what Robert Putnam termed a 'two-level game' (Putnam 1988; Savage and Weale 2009). According to this argument, governments need both to agree among each other on an equal basis at the international level, while at the same time securing the long-term democratic agreement of their citizens. As such, within their negotiations they must respect each other as the democratically authorised and accountable representatives of their respective peoples (Pettit 2010a). Procedurally, that means ministers in the Council should be responsive to their respective national parliaments. Likewise, parties in the EP should be linked more strongly to their national parties, with national parliaments gaining a more direct and collaborative role in EU policy making, not simply through being the guardians of proportionality and subsidiarity, via the so-called 'yellow' and 'orange' cards, but also by being able to propose EU policies via a potential 'green' card (see chapter 15 in this volume). Substantively, it allows for a more differentiated system of integration – one in which, on democratic grounds, states may collaborate more or less than other states, depending on the greater or lesser stake they have in pursuing collective policies at the EU level; opt-out when collective policies infringe domestic constitutional and cultural norms; and insist common rules treat them as equals by taking into account relevant differences (see Bellamy 2019, ch 6). Of course, all states have a moral obligation to participate in those collective policies necessary to secure such basic rights as are to be found in conventions such as the European Convention on Human Rights (ECHR) (Christiano 2016). Similarly, they have to guard against such clear collective harms as global environmental catastrophe and to assist what John Rawls called 'burdened societies' (Rawls 1999, 90, 106) – that is, societies so burdened by extreme poverty, a lack of natural resources and low human capital that basic rights cannot be secured and they lack the means to order themselves effectively in a democratic manner. Yet, the vast majority of the EU's competences operate beyond the morally obligatory. Here, it is appropriate to seek to protect the variety of capitalisms and related welfare systems of the member states (Hall and Soskice 2001), while allowing cooperation to ensure greater efficiency and equity in their interrelations.

To a large degree, the EU already operates in this way. After all, the EU prides itself on seeking to achieve Unity in Diversity. Indeed, it derives much of its legitimacy from this fact, rendering many of the criticisms of its democratic deficit simply misplaced (Moravscik 2008). Some of the intergovernmental processes of the EU and the forms of differentiated integration it produces can and should be regarded not as pragmatic compromises but as matters of principle, whereby the EU seeks to achieve equality of concern and respect among the peoples of Europe (Bellamy 2019: ch. 6). Moreover, the free movement of persons among these peoples further legitimises the Union by ensuring no individual is dominated by such a system through having been born in one state rather than another (Bellamy and Lacey 2018). It gives all citizens an equal opportunity to choose where to live and work without discrimination on the basis of nationality, while at the same time preserving the possibility for the different states of Europe to pursue and experiment with different social and economic arrangements. These opportunities and protections are denied to UK citizens by exiting the EU.

Against the Eurosceptic proponents of Brexit, we have argued we can only exercise control through bodies such as the EU; against some Europhile proponents of political union, we have suggested we achieve control through collaboration among European democracies, not by creating an EU-level democracy. Both these alternatives involve losing control. By leaving the

EU, the British government and those who voted for this proposal have committed a moral and political wrong against themselves and others. They have
placed themselves in a situation where they will inevitably be controlled
and dominated by other states and organisations and can only respond by
seeking, largely vainly, to control and dominate them in turn. The Leave
campaign's favoured slogan had been 'go global' (Cummings 2017). That
represents a more accurate description of what they have achieved, contrary
to the beliefs of many who supported them. In terms of Rodrik's trilemma,
they have delivered a formal façade of national sovereignty, symbolised by
certain immigration controls against the poor and powerless that disregard
their moral obligations to assist those in dire need, combined with a total
openness to global economic processes over which they will have little or no
democratic control.

CONCLUSION

The EU has never taken politics seriously. The creators of what was then
the European Community (EC) sought to legitimise integration indirectly,
providing it with so-called 'output' legitimacy (Scharpf 1999, 6–13) through
what the architect of this strategy, Jean Monnet, referred to as 'concrete
achievements' in the form of desirable policies – notably, an end to war
and improved economic well-being (Müller 2011, 142). Though they hoped
popular endorsement would follow from the success of European integration in securing peace and prosperity, their strategy was in many respects
deliberately technocratic and non-democratic. On the one hand, it reflected
a reinforced liberal distrust of democracy in the wake of the rise of fascism
prior to World War II (Müller 2011, 128), with the EC seen as a mechanism
for constraining demands for popular and national sovereignty that were
widely blamed for the catastrophes of the first half of the twentieth century.
On the other hand, while potential democratic opposition at the member state
level was to be circumscribed in the short term, in the long term the hope was
that increased economic cooperation would steadily create the conditions for
democracy at the supranational, EC, level. However, although this strategy
aimed at weakening the sovereignty of nation states and their peoples, the
acceptance and success of the supranational promotion of economic liberalism depended to a large degree on the democratically created institutions of
these self-same states continuing to provide a source of identification and
solidarity for their citizens sufficient to offer social protection for the losers
of enhanced interstate market competition (Ruggie 1982).

   The economic downturn and domestic adoption of new right policies in
the late 1970s and 1980s gradually placed the post-war compromise under

strain. Meantime, the Maastricht Treaty and the completion of the Single Market and move to Monetary Union created a step change in the EU's fostering of economic liberalisation during the 1990s that limited the possibility for domestic intervention even further: not least, as we have seen, due to the progressive constitutionalisation of the EU's market regulations by a proactive European Court of Justice (Alter 2001; Grimm 2016, chap. 14, 2017; Isiksel 2016). Labour mobility from the less to the more successful economies became the main instrument of European social policy (Ferrara 2014; Isiksel 2016, 175–79; Scharpf 2010, 238; Streeck 2014, 178). It is against this background, made worse by the Euro crisis, that the problem of the EU's democratic deficit came to the fore. The 'output' legitimacy of economic success backed by the rule of law could no longer substitute for the absence of 'input' legitimacy offered by democratic politics (see chapters 13 and 14 in this volume).

Taking our cue from Claus Offe, we have noted above (and in many of the chapters of this book) how the problem confronting the EU lay in the way the EU structures themselves entrapped the possibility for democratic politics. Meanwhile, the more the EU sought to resolve its legitimacy problems by shifting political authority to the EU level, the greater that entrapment has become, not least by constraining in its turn democratic politics within the member states and provoking among large sections of their electorates a Eurosceptical 'constraining dissensus' (Hooghe and Marks 2009; Kriesi 2016; De Vries 2018). As a result, we have advocated an alternative, demoicratic, approach. By conceiving the EU as a union of self-governing peoples, in which the EU provides a mechanism for the fair negotiation of their mutual relations in non-dominating ways, we hope to square the circle and avoid the Scylla of Maastricht and the Charybdis of Brexit.

References

Ackerman, B. 1991. *We the People: Foundations*. Cambridge, MA: Harvard University Press.

Ackerman, B. 1992. *The Future of the Liberal Revolution*. New Haven and London: Yale University Press.

Alter, K. 2001. *Establishing the Supremacy of European Law*. Oxford: Oxford University Press.

Amato, G. 2003. 'Prefazione'. In *La nuova costituzione europea*, edited by J. Ziller. Bologna: Il Mulino.

Anderson, B. 1999. *Imagined Communities*. London and New York: Verso.

Anderson, S. and T. Burns. 1996. 'The European Union and the Erosion of Parliamentary Democracy: A Study of Post-parliamentary Governance'. In *The European Union – How Democratic is It*, edited by S. Anderson and K. Eliassen, 227–67. London: Sage.

Appiah, K. A. 2005. *The Ethics of Identity*. Princeton: Princeton University Press.

Archibugi, D. 1995. 'Immanuel Kant, Cosmopolitan Law and Peace'. *European Journal of International Relations* 1: 429–56.

Archibugi, D., D. Held, and M. Köhler, eds. 1998. *Re-imagining Political Community. Studies in Cosmopolitan Democracy*. Cambridge: Polity.

Armingeon, K. and C. Baccaro. 2012. 'Political Economy of the Sovereign Debt Crisis: The Limits of Internal Devaluation'. *Industrial Law Journal* 41, no. 3: 254–75.

Armstrong, K. A. 1998. 'Legal Integration: Theorizing the Legal Dimension of European Integration'. *Journal of Common Market Studies* 36: 155–74.

Armstrong, K. A. 2002. 'Rediscovering Civil Society: The European Union and the White Paper on Governance'. *European Law Journal* 8, no. 1: 102–32.

Arnull, Anthony. 2003. 'On the Future of the Convention Method'. *European Law Review* 28: 573–74.

Aron, R. 1974. 'Is Multinational Citizenship Possible?' *Social Research* 41, no. 4: 638–56.

Aron, R. 1991–92. 'Une citoyennet, multinationale est-elle possible?' *Commentaire* 14: 695–704.

Auel, K. and T. Raunio. 2014. 'Debating the State of the Union? Comparing Parliamentary Debates on EU Issues in Finland, France, Germany and the United Kingdom'. *Journal of Legislative Studies* 20, no. 1: 13–28.

Aughey, A. 2007. *The Politics of Englishness*. Manchester and New York: Manchester University Press.

Baldwin, P. 2009. *The Narcissism of Minor Differences: How America and Europe are Alike*. Oxford: Oxford University Press.

Balibar, E. 2004. *We, the People of Europe? Reflections on Transnational Citizenship*. Princeton and Oxford: Princeton University Press.

Banchoff, T. and M. P. Smith, eds. 1999. *Legitimacy and the European Union: The Contested Polity*. London: Routledge.

Bankowski, Z. and A. Scott, eds. 2000. *The European Union and Its Order*. Oxford: Blackwell.

Barbalet, J. M. 1988. *Citizenship: Rights, Struggle and Class Equality*. Milton Keynes: Open University Press.

Barry, B. 1975. 'Political Accommodation and Consociational Democracy'. *British Journal of Political Science* 5: 477–505.

Barry, N. 1994. 'Sovereignty, the Rule of Recognition and Constitutional Stability in Britain'. *Hume Papers on Public Policy* 2, no. 1: 10–27.

Bartolini, S. 2005. *Restructuring Europe. Centre Formation, System Building and Political Structuring between the Nation-State and the European Union*. Oxford: Oxford University Press.

Beaud, O. 1995. 'LA Fédération entre l'état et l'empire'. In *L'État, la finance et le sociale*, edited by B. Théret, 283–304. Paris: La Decouverte.

Beetham, D. and C. Lord. 1998. *Legitimacy and the European Union*. Harlow: Longman.

Begg, I. 2013. 'Are Better Defined Rules Enough? An Assessment of the Post-Crisis Reforms of the Governance of EMU'. *Transfer: European Review of Labour and Research* 19, no. 1: 49–62.

Beitz, C. R. 1994. 'Cosmopolitan Liberalism and the States System'. In *Political Restructuring in Europe. Ethical Perspectives*, edited by Chris Brown, 123–36. London and New York: Routledge.

Bellamy, Richard and Albert Weale. 2015. 'Political Legitimacy and European Monetary Union: Contracts, Constitutionalism and the Normative Logic of Two-Level Games'. *Journal of European Public Policy* 22, no. 2: 257–74.

Bellamy, Richard and Alex Warleigh, eds. 2001. *Citizenship and Governance in the European Union*. London: Continuum.

Bellamy, Richard and Alex Warleigh. 1998. 'From an Ethics of Integration to an Ethics of Participation: Citizenship and the Future of the European Union'. *Millennium: Journal of International Studies* 27: 447–70.

Bellamy, Richard and Dario Castiglione. 1996a. *Constitutionalism in Transformation: European and Theoretical Perspectives*. Oxford: Blackwell.

Bellamy, Richard and Dario Castiglione. 1996b. 'The Communitarian Ghost in the Cosmopolitan Machine: Constitutionalism, Democracy and the Reconfiguration of Politics in the New Europe'. In *Constitutionalism, Democracy and Sovereignty: American and European Perspectives*, edited by Richard Bellamy, 111–29. Aldershot and Brookfield, USA: Avebury.

Bellamy, Richard and Dario Castiglione. 1997a. 'The Normative Challenge of a European Polity: Cosmopolitan and Communitarian Models Compared, Criticised and Combined'. In *Democracy and the European Union*, edited by A. Føllesdal and P. Koslowski, 254–84. Berlin: Springer-Verlag.

Bellamy, Richard and Dario Castiglione. 1997b. 'Building the Union: The Nature of Sovereignty in the Political Architecture of Europe'. *Law and Philosophy* 16: 421–45.

Bellamy, Richard and Dario Castiglione. 1997c. 'Review Article: Constitutionalism and Democracy – Political Theory and the American Constitution'. *British Journal of Political Science* 27: 595–618.

Bellamy, Richard and Dario Castiglione. 1998. 'Between Cosmopolis and Community: Three Models of Rights and Democracy within the European Union'. In *Re-Imagining Political Community: Studies in Cosmopolitan Democracy*, edited by D. Archibugi, D. Held, and M. Köhler, 152–78. Cambridge: Polity Press.

Bellamy, Richard and Dario Castiglione. 2000a. 'The Normative Turn in European Studies: Legitimacy, Identity and Democracy'. RUSEL Working Paper 38/2000. http://www.ex.ac.uk/shipss/politics/research/rusel.htm.

Bellamy, Richard and Dario Castiglione. 2000b. 'Democracy, Sovereignty and the Constitution of the European Union: The Republican Alternative to Liberalism'. In *The European Union and Its Order*, edited by Z. Bankowski and A. Scott, 170–90. Oxford: Blackwell.

Bellamy, Richard and Dario Castiglione. 2000c. 'The Uses of Democracy: Reflection's on the EU's Democratic Deficit'. In *Democracy in the European Union – Integration through Deliberation?* edited by Erik Oddvar Eriksen and John Erik Fossum, 65–84. London: Routledge.

Bellamy, Richard and Dario Castiglione. 2001. 'Tra retorica e simbolismo: la Carta dei diritti fondamentali dell'Unione europea'. In *'La Carta dei diritti fondamentali. Verso una Costituzione europea?'*, a cura di Barbara Henry e Anna Loretoni, *Quaderni Forum* XV, no. 2: 67–74.

Bellamy, Richard and Dario Castiglione. 2002. 'Beyond Community and Rights: European Citizenship and the Virtues of Participation'. *Quaderni Fiorentini* 31, no. 1: 349–80.

Bellamy, Richard and Dario Castiglione. 2003. 'Legitimising the Euro-"Polity" and its "Regime": The Normative Turn in European Studies'. *European Journal of Political Theory* 2, no. 1: 1–34.

Bellamy, Richard and Dario Castiglione. 2004a. 'Normative Theory and the European Union'. In *After National Democracy: Rights, Law and Power in America and the New Europe*, edited by Lars Trägårdh, 9–40. Onati International Series in Law and Society, Oxford: Hart.

Bellamy, Richard and Dario Castiglione. 2004b. 'Lacroix's European Constitutional Patriotism: A Response'. *Political Studies* 52, no. 1: 187–93.

Bellamy, Richard and Dario Castiglione. 2008. 'Beyond Community and Rights: European Citizenship and the Virtues of Participation'. In *Constituting Communities*, edited by P. Mouritsen and K.-E. Jørgensen, 162–86. Basingstoke: Palgrave.

Bellamy, Richard and Joseph Lacey. 2018. 'Balancing the Rights and Duties of Union and National Citizenship: A Demoicratic Approach'. *Journal of European Public Policy* 25, no. 10: 1403–21.

Bellamy, Richard and Justus Schönlau. 2004a. 'The Normality of Constitutional Politics: An Analysis of the Drafting of the EU Charter of Fundamental Rights'. *Constellations* 11, no. 3: 412–33.

Bellamy, Richard and Justus Schönlau. 2004b. 'The Good, the Bad and the Ugly: The Need for Constitutional Compromise and the Drafting of the EU Constitution'. In *Political Theory and the European Constitution*, edited by Lynn Dobson and Andreas Føllesdal, 57–71. London and New York: Routledge.

Bellamy, Richard and M. Hollis. 1999. 'Consensus, Neutrality and Compromise'. In *Pluralism and Liberal Neutrality*, edited by Richard Bellamy and Martin Hollis, 54–78. London: Cass.

Bellamy, Richard and Sandra Kröger. 2014. 'Domesticating the Democratic Deficit? The Role of National Parliaments and Parties in the EU's System of Governance'. *Parliamentary Affairs* 67, no. 2: 437–57.

Bellamy, Richard, Dario Castiglione, and Jo Shaw, eds. 2006a. *Making European Citizens: Civic Inclusion in a Transnational Context*. Houndmills: Palgrave.

Bellamy, Richard, Dario Castiglione, and Jo Shaw. 2006b. 'From National to Transnational Citizenship'. In *Making European Citizens: Strategies for Civic Inclusion*, edited by Richard Bellamy, Dario Castiglione, and Jo Shaw, 1–28. Basingstoke: Palgrave.

Bellamy, Richard, Vittorio Bufacchi, and Dario Castiglione, eds. 1995. *Democracy and Constitutional Culture in the Union of Europe*. London: Lothian Foundation Press.

Bellamy, Richard. 1994. '"Dethroning Politics": Constitutionalism, Liberalism and Democracy in the Political Thought of F. A. Hayek'. *British Journal of Political Science* 24: 419–41.

Bellamy, Richard. 1995. 'The Constitution of Europe: Rights or Democracy?' In *Democracy and Constitutional Culture in the Union of Europe*, edited by Richard Bellamy, Vittorio Bufacchi, and Dario Castiglione, 153–73. London: Lothian Foundation Press.

Bellamy, Richard, ed. 1996a. *Constitutionalism, Democracy and Sovereignty: American and European Perspectives*. Aldershot and Brookfield, USA: Avebury.

Bellamy, Richard. 1996b. 'The Political Form of the Constitution: The Separation of Powers, Rights and Representative Democracy'. In *Constitutionalism in Transformation*, edited by Richard Bellamy and Dario Castiglione, 24–44. Oxford: Blackwell.

Bellamy, Richard. 1997. 'Liberal Politics and the Judiciary: The Supreme Court and American Democracy'. *Res Publica: A Journal of Legal and Social Philosophy* 3, no. 1: 81–96.

Bellamy, Richard. 1999. *Liberalism and Pluralism: Towards a Politics of Compromise*. London: Routledge.

Bellamy, Richard. 2000a. 'Citizenship Beyond the Nation State: The Case of Europe'. In *Political Theory in Transition*, edited by N. O'Sullivan, 91–112. London: Routledge.

Bellamy, Richard. 2000b. 'Dealing with Difference: Four Models of Pluralist Politics'. *Parliamentary Affairs: A Journal of Comparative Politics* 53, no. 1: 215–16.

Bellamy, Richard. 2001a. 'Constitutive Citizenship versus Constitutional Rights: Republican Reflections on the EU Charter and the Human Rights Act'. In *Sceptical Essays on Human Rights*, edited by T. Campbell, K. D. Ewing, and A. Tomkins, 15–39. Oxford: Oxford University Press.

Bellamy, Richard. 2001b. 'The "Right to Have Rights"': Citizenship Practice and the Political Constitution of the EU'. In *Citizenship and Governance in the European Union*, edited by Richard Bellamy and A. Warleigh, 41–70. London: Continuum.

Bellamy, Richard. 2003. 'Sovereignty, Post-Sovereignty and Pre-Sovereignty: Reconceptualising the State, Rights and Democracy in the EU'. In *Sovereignty in Transition*, edited by N. Walker, 167–89. Oxford: Hart.

Bellamy, Richard. 2004. 'Which Constitution for What Kind of Europe? Three Models of European Constitutionalism'. Paper presented at the CIDEL Workshop, 12–13 November. *Constitution making and Democratic Legitimacy in the EU*.

Bellamy, Richard. 2006a. 'Still in Deficit: Rights, Regulation and Democracy in the EU'. *European Law Journal* 12: 725–42.

Bellamy, Richard. 2006b. 'Between Past and Future: The Democratic Limits of EU Citizenship'. In *Making European Citizens: Civic Inclusion in a Transnational Context*, edited by Richard Bellamy, Dario Castiglione, and Jo Shaw, 238–65. Hampshire: Palgrave.

Bellamy, Richard. 2007. *Political Constitutionalism: A Republican Defence of the Constitutionality of Democracy*. Cambridge: Cambridge University Press.

Bellamy, Richard. 2008. 'Evaluating Union Citizenship: Belonging, Rights and Participation within the EU'. *Citizenship Studies* 12: 597–611.

Bellamy, Richard. 2009. 'The Republic of Reasons: Public Reasoning, Depoliticisation and Non-Domination'. In *Legal Republicanism: National and International*, edited by S. Besson and J.-L. Marti, 102–20. Oxford: Oxford University Press.

Bellamy, Richard. 2010. 'Democracy without Democracy? Can the EU's Democratic "Outputs" Be Separated from the Democratic "Inputs" Provided by Competitive Parties and Majority Rule?' *Journal of European Public Policy* 17: 2–19.

Bellamy, Richard. 2013. 'An Ever Closer Union of Peoples: Republican Intergovernmentalism, Demoi-cracy and Representation in the EU'. *Journal of European Integration* 35, no. 5: 499–516.

Bellamy, Richard. 2019. *A Republican Europe of Sovereign States: Cosmopolitan Statism, Republican Intergovernmentalism and the Demoicratic Reconnection of the EU*. Cambridge: Cambridge University Press.

Benhabib, S. 2002. 'Transformations of Citizenship: The Case of Contemporary Europe'. *Government and Opposition* 37, no. 4: 439–65.

Benhabib, Seyla, ed. 1996a. *Democracy and Difference: Contesting the Boundaries of the Political*. Princeton, NJ: Princeton University Press.

Benhabib, Seyla. 1996b. 'Toward a Deliberative Model of Democratic Legitimacy'. In *Democracy and Difference: Contesting the Boundaries of the Political*, edited by Seyla Benhabib, 67–94. Princeton, NJ: Princeton University Press.

Benhabib, Seyla. 2004. *The Rights of Others: Aliens, Residents and Citizens*. Cambridge: Cambridge University Press.

Benhabib, Seyla. 2007. 'Twilight of Sovereignty or the Emergence of Cosmopolitan Norms? Rethinking Citizenship in Volatile Times'. *Citizenship Studies* 11, no. 1: 19–36.

Benhabib, Seyla. 2008. *Another Cosmopolitanism*. Oxford: Oxford University Press.

Benjamin, M. 1990. *Splitting the Difference: Compromise and Integrity in Ethics and Politics*. Lawrence: University Press of Kansas.

Berlin, Isaiah. 1969. *Two Concepts of Liberty*. Oxford: Oxford University Press.

Beyers, J. and B. Kerremans. 2007. 'Critical Resource Dependencies and the Europeanization of Domestic Interest Groups'. *Journal of European Public Policy* 14, no. 3: 460–81.

Blondel, Jean, Richard Sinnott, and Palle Svensson. 1998. *People and Parliament in the European Union: Participation, Democracy and Legitimacy*. Oxford: Clarendon Press.

Bobbio, N. 1987. *The Future of Democracy*. Cambridge: Polity Press.

Bodin, J. 1992. *On Sovereignty*, edited by J. H. Franklin. Cambridge: Cambridge University Press.

Bogdanor, V. and G. Woodcock. 1991. 'The European Community and Sovereignty'. *Parliamentary Affairs* 44, no. 4 (October): 481–92.

Bohman, J. 1998. *Public Deliberation: Pluralism, Complexity and Deliberation*. Cambridge, MA: MIT Press.

Bohman, J. 2004. 'Republican Cosmopolitanism'. *Journal of Political Philosophy* 12, no. 3: 336–52.

Bohman, J. 2005. 'From Demos to Demoi: Democracy Across Borders'. *Ratio Juris* 18, no. 3: 293–314.

Bohman, J. 2007. *Democracy across Borders: From Demos to Demoi*. Cambridge, MA: MIT Press.

Bolleyer, N. and C. Reh. 2012. 'EU Legitimacy Revisited: The Normative Foundations of a Multilevel Polity'. *Journal of European Public Policy* 19, no. 4: 472–90.

Bomberg, E. and J. Peterson. 1998. 'European Union Decision Making: The Role of Sub-National Authorities'. *Political Studies* XLVI: 219–35.

Bordo, M. D. and L. Jonung. 2003. 'The Future of EMU: What Does the History of Monetary Unions Tell Us?' In *Monetary Unions: Theory, History, Public Choice*, edited by F. H. Capie and G. E. Wood, 42–69. London and New York: Routledge.

Bork, R. H. 1990. *The Tempting of America*. New York: Free Press.

Bourantonis, D. and J. Weiner, eds. 1995. *The United Nations in the New World Order: The World Organization at Fifty*. Basingstoke: Macmillan.

Braun, D. and B. Gilardi. 2006. 'Introduction'. In *Delegation in Contemporary Democracies*, edited by D. Braun and B. Gilardi, 1–23. London: Routledge.

Broscheid, A. and D. Coen. 2003. 'Insider and Outsider Lobbying of the European Commission: An Informational Model'. *European Union Politics* 4: 165–89.

Brown, Chris, ed. 1994. *Political Restructuring in Europe. Ethical Perspectives*. London and New York: Routledge.

Bryce, J. 1921. *Modern Democracies*. New York: Macmillan.

Buchanan, A. 2002. 'Political Legitimacy and Democracy'. *Ethics* 112, no. 4: 689–719.

Buchanan, J. M. 1975. *The Limits of Liberty: Between Anarchy and Leviathan.* Chicago: University of Chicago Press.

Buchanan, J. M. and G. Tullock. 1965. *The Calculus of Consent: Logical Foundations of Constitutional Democracy.* Anne Arbor: University of Michegan Press.

Burgess, M. 1989. *Federalism and the European Union.* London: Routledge.

Burke, Edmund. [1774] 1987. 'Speech to the Electors of Bristol'. In *The Political Philosophy of Edmund Burke,* edited by I. Hampshire-Monk, 108–10. Harlow: Longman.

Burns, T., C. Jaeger, A. Liberatore, Y. Meny, and P. Nanz. 2000. *The Future of Parliamentary Democracy: Transition and Challenge in European Governance.* Green Paper prepared for the Conference of the European Union, AS/D.

Byrnes, T. A. and P. J. Katzenstein, eds. 2006. *Religion in an Expanding Europe.* Cambridge: Cambridge University Press.

Caporoso, J. A. and S. Tarrow. 2008. 'Polanyi in Brussels: European Institutions and the Embedding of Markets in Society'. Paper presented at APSA 2008 annual meeting, Boston.

Cappelletti, M. 1989. *The Judicial Process in Comparative Perspective.* Oxford: Clarendon Press.

Carens, J. H. 1987. 'Aliens and Citizens: The Case for Open Borders'. *Review of Politics* 49: 251–73.

Castiglione, Dario and Chris Longman. 2007. *The Language Question in Europe and Diverse Societies: Political, Legal and Social Perspectives.* Oxford: Hart Publishers.

Castiglione, Dario and Justus Schönlau. 2006. 'Constitutional Politics'. In *Handbook of European Union Politics,* edited by K.-E. Jørgensen, M. Pollack, and B. Rosamund, 283–300. London: Sage.

Castiglione, Dario and Mark Warren. 2006. 'Rethinking Democratic Representation: Eight Theoretical Issues'. Paper delivered at the Conference on *Rethinking Democratic Representation,* Centre for the Study of Democratic Institutions, University of British Columbia.

Castiglione, Dario, et al. 2007. *Constitutional Politics in the EU: The Convention Moment and its Aftermath.* Basingstoke: Palgrave.

Castiglione, Dario. 1995. 'Contracts and Constitutions'. In *Democracy and Constitutional Culture in the Union of Europe,* edited by Richard Bellamy, Vittorio Bufacchi, and Dario Castiglione, 59–79. London: Lothian Foundation Press.

Castiglione, Dario. 1996. 'The Political Theory of the Constitution'. In *The Constitution in Transformation,* edited by Richard Bellamy and Dario Castiglione, 417–35. Oxford: Blackwell.

Castiglione, Dario. 2000. 'Public Reason, Private Citizenship'. In *Public and Private: Legal, Political and Philosophical Perspectives,* edited by M. Passerin D'Entreves and U. Vogel, 28–50. London: Routledge.

Castiglione, Dario. 2004. 'Reflections on Europe's Constitutional Future'. *Constellations* 11, no. 3: 393–411.

Checkel, J. 1999. 'Norms, Institutions, and National Identity in Contemporary Europe'. *International Studies Quarterly* 43: 83–114.

466 References

Checkel, J. 2001. 'Constructing European Institutions'. In *The Rules of Integration: Institutionalist Approaches to the Study of Europe*, edited by M. Aspinall and G. Schneider, 19–39. Manchester: Manchester University Press.

Cheneval, F. and F. Schimmelfennig. 2013. 'The Case for Demoicracy in the European Union'. *Journal of Common Market Studies* 51, no. 2: 334–50.

Choper, J. 1980. *Judicial Review in the National Political Process*. University of Chicago Press.

Christiano, T. 1996. *The Rule of the Many: Fundamental Issues in Democratic Theory*. Oxford: Westview.

Christiano, T. 2006. 'A Democratic Theory of Territory and Some Puzzles about Global Democracy'. *Journal of Social Philosophy* 37, no. 1: 81–107.

Christiano, T. 2008. *The Constitution of Equality*. Oxford: Oxford University Press.

Christiano, T. 2010. 'Democratic Legitimacy and International Institutions'. In *The Philosophy of International Law*, edited by S. Besson and J. Tasioulis, 119–37. Oxford: Oxford University Press.

Christiansen, T., K. Jorgensen, and A. Wiener. 1999. 'The Social Construction of Europe'. In *The Social Construction of Europe*, edited by T. Christiansen, K. Jorgensen, and A. Wiener. *Journal of European Public Policy* 6 (special issue): 528–44.

Chryssochoou, Dimitis N. 1994. 'Democracy and Symbiosis in the European Union: Towards a Confederal Consociation?' *West European Politics* 17: 1–14.

Chryssochoou, Dimitis N. 1998. *Democracy in the European Union*. London: I. B. Taurus.

Chryssochoou, Dimitis N. 2000. 'Metatheory and the Study of the European Union: Capturing the Normative Turn'. *European Integration* 22: 123–44.

Chryssochoou, Dimitis N. 2001. *Theorizing European Integration*. London: Sage.

Chryssochoou, Dimitris N. 1996. 'Europe's Could-be Demos: Recasting the Debate'. *West European Politics* 19: 787–801.

Cicero. 1999. *On the Laws*, in *On the Commonwealth and On the Laws*, edited by James E. G. Zetzel. Cambridge: Cambridge University Press.

Citi, Manuele and Martin Rhodes. 2007. 'New Forms of Governance in the European Union'. In *The Handbook of European Union Politics*, edited by Knud Erik Jørgensen, Mark A. Pollack, and Ben Rosamond, 463–82. New York: Sage.

Closa, C. and A. Maatsch. 2014. 'In a Spirit of Solidarity? Justifying the European Financial Stability Facility (EFSF) in National Parliamentary Debates'. *Journal of Common Market Studies* 52, no. 4: 826–42.

Coen, D. 2007. 'Empirical and Theoretical Studies in EU Lobbying'. *Journal of European Public Policy* 14, no. 3: 233–45.

Coen, D. and M. Thatcher. 2005. 'The New Governance of Markets and Non-Majoritarian Regulators'. *Governance* 18: 329–47.

Cohen, J. and C. Sabel. 1997. 'Directly-Deliberative Polyarchy'. *European Law Journal* 3: 313–42.

Cohen, J. 1996. 'Procedure and Substance in Deliberative Democracy'. In *Democracy and Difference: Contesting the Boundaries of the Political*, edited by Seyla Benhabib, 95–119. Princeton, NJ: Princeton University Press.

Cohen, J. and C. Sabel. 2006. 'Extra Rempublicam Nulla Justitia?' *Philosophy and Public Affairs* 34: 147–75.

Colley, L. 1992. *Britons: Forging the Nation 1707–1837.* New Haven: Yale University Press.

Condorcet, Marquis de. 1976. 'Essay on the Application of Mathematics to the Theory of Decision-Making'. In *Condorcet: Selected Writings*, edited by K. M. Baker. Indianapolis: Bobbs Merrill.

Constant, B. [1813] 1988. 'The Spirit of Conquest and Usurpation and their Relation to European Civilization'. In *Political Writings*, edited by B. Fontana, 43–167. Cambridge: Cambridge University Press.

Constant, B. [1815] 1988. 'Principles of Politics Applicable to All Representative Governments'. In *Political Writings*, edited by B. Fontana, 170–305. Cambridge: Cambridge University Press.

Constant, B. [1819] 1988. 'The Liberty of the Ancients Compared with that of the Moderns'. In *Political Writings*, edited by B. Fontana, 307–28. Cambridge: Cambridge University Press.

Constant, B. 1822–1824. *Commentaire sur l'ouvrage de Filangeri.* 2 vols, Paris.

Constant, B. 1988. *Political Writings*, edited by B. Fontana. Cambridge: Cambridge University Press.

Cooper, Ian. 2012. 'A "Virtual Third Chamber" for the European Union? National Parliaments after the Treaty of Lisbon'. *West European Politics* 35, no. 3: 441–65.

Coppell, Jason and Aidan O'Neill. 1992. 'The European Court of Justice: Taking Rights Seriously?' *Common Market Law Review* 29: 669–92.

Coulmas, F. 1997. 'Introduction'. In *The Handbook of Sociologuistics*, edited by F. Coulmas, 1–11. Oxford: Blackwell.

Craig, P. 1997. 'Democracy and Rule-making Within the EC: An Empirical and Normative Assessment'. *European Law Journal* 3, no. 2: 105–30.

Crespy, A. and V. Schmidt. 2014. 'The Clash of Titans: France, Germany and the Discursive Double Game of EMU Reform'. *Journal of European Public Policy* 21, no. 8: 1085–101.

Crouch, C. 2000. 'Introduction: The Political and Institutional Deficits of European Monetary Union'. In *After the Euro: Shaping Institutions for Governance in the Wake of European Monetary Union*, edited by C. Crouch, 1–23. Oxford: Oxford University Press.

Crouch, C. 2004. *Post-Democracy.* Cambridge: Polity.

Cummings, D. 2017. 'On the Referendum #21: Branching Histories of the 2016 Referendum and "the Frogs Before the Storm"'. https://dominiccummings. wordpress.com/2017/01/09/on-the-referendum-21-branching-histories-of-the-2016-referendum-and-the-frogs-before-the-storm-2/.

Curtin, Deirdre. 1993. 'The Constitutional Structure of the Union: A Europe of Bits and Pieces'. *Common Market Law Review* 30: 17–69.

Curtin, Deirdre. 1997. *Postnational Democracy: The European Union in Search of a Political Philosophy.* The Hague: Kluwer Law International.

Dahl, R. A. 1986. *Democracy, Liberty and Equality.* Oslo: Norwegian University Press.

Dahl, R. A. 1989. *Democracy and its Critics*. New Haven: Yale University Press.

Dahl, R. A. 1998. *Democracy*. New Haven: Yale University Press.

Dahl, R. A. 2002. *How Democratic is the American Constitution?* New Haven: Yale University Press.

Dahl, R. A. and E. R. Tufte. 1973. *Size and Democracy*. Stanford: Stanford University Press.

Dalton, R. J. 1999. 'Political Support in Advanced Industrial Democracies'. In *Critical Citizens: Global Support for Democratic Governance*, edited by P. Norris, 75–6. Oxford: Oxford University Press.

Dalton, R. J. 2004. *Democratic Challenges, Democratic Choices: The Erosion of Political Support in Advanced Industrial Democracies*. Oxford: Oxford University Press.

David, Judge. 1999. *Representation: Theory and Practice in Britain*. London: Routledge.

De Búrca, G. 1996. 'The Quest for Legitimacy in the European Union'. *The Modern Law Review* 59: 349–76.

De Búrca, G. 1999. 'The Institutional Development of the EU: A Constitutional Analysis'. In *The Evolution of EU Law*, edited by P. Craig and G. de Búrca, 55–82. Oxford: Oxford University Press.

De Búrca, G. 2001. 'The Drafting of the EU Charter of Fundamental Rights'. *European Law Journal* 26: 126–38.

De Vries, C. 2007. 'Sleeping Giant: Fact or Fairytale? How European Integration Affects National Elections'. *European Union Politics* 8, no. 3: 363–85.

De Vries, C. 2018. *Euroscepticism and the Future of European Integration*. Oxford: Oxford University Press.

De Wilde, P. and M. Zürn. 2012. 'Can the Politicization of European Integration be Reversed?' *Journal of Common Market Studies* 50, no. 1: 139–53.

De Witte, Bruno. 1991. 'Droit communautaire et valeurs constitutionelles nationales'. *Droits* 14: 87–96.

De Witte, Bruno. 1999. 'Direct Effect, Supremacy and the Nature of the Legal Order'. In *The Evolution of EU Law*, edited by P. Craig and G. de Búrca, 177–213. Oxford: Oxford University Press.

De Witte, Bruno. 2002. 'The Closest Thing to a Constitutional Conversation in Europe: The Semi-Permanent Treaty Revision Process'. In *Convergence and Divergence in European Public Law*, edited by P. Beaumont, C. Lyons, and N. Walker, 39–58. Oxford: Hart.

De Witte, Bruno. 2004a. *The National Constitutional Dimension of European Treaty Revision – Evolution and Recent Debates, The Second Walter van Gerven Lecture*. Groningen: Europa Law Publishing.

De Witte, Bruno. 2004b. 'The Process of Ratification of the Constitutional Treaty and the Crisis Option: A Legal Perspective'. *EUI Working Papers*, Law 2004/16.

Deloche-Gaudez, Florence. 2001. 'The Convention on a charter of Fundamental Rights: A Method for the Future'. Notre Europe Policy Paper. http://www.notre-europe.asso.fr/fichiers/Etud15-en.pdf.

Devins, N. and L. Fisher. 2004. *The Democratic Constitution*. Oxford: Oxford University Press.

Diez, T. 1999. 'Riding the AM-Track through Europe; or, The Pitfalls of a Rationalist Journey through European Integration'. *Millennium: Journal of International Studies* 28, no. 2: 355–69.

Dinan, D. 2011. 'Governance and Institutions: Implementing the Lisbon Treaty in the Shadow of the Euro Crisis'. *Journal of Common Market Studies* 49, The JCMS Annual Review of the European Union in 2010: 103–21.

Dryzek, J. and S. Niemeyer. 2008. 'Discursive Representation'. *American Political Science Review* 102: 481–93.

Duff, A. 1994. 'Building a Parliamentary Europe'. *Government and Opposition* 29: 147–65.

Duff, A. 2005. *The Struggle for Europe's Constitution*. London: Federal Trust.

Duff, A. 2011. *Federal Union Now*. London: Federal Trust.

Duncan, G. and S. Lukes. 1963. 'The New Democracy'. *Political Studies* 11, no. 2: 156–77.

Duverger, M. 1995. *L'Europe dans tous ses Etats*. Paris: Presses Universitaires de France.

Dworkin, Richard. 1985. *A Matter of Principle*. Oxford: Clarendon Press.

Dworkin, Richard. 1986. *Law's Empire*. London: Fontana.

Dworkin, Richard. 1995. 'Constitutionalism and Democracy'. *European Journal of Philosophy* 3: 2–11.

Dworkin, Richard. 1996. *Freedom's Law: The Moral Reading of the American Constitution*. Oxford: Oxford University Press.

Dyson, K. and K. Featherstone. 1999. *The Road to Maastricht: Negotiating Economic and Monetary Union*. Oxford: Oxford University Press.

Eco, Umberto. 2003. *Dire quasi la stessa cosa. Esperienze di traduzione*. Milan: Bombiani.

Einem, Caspar. 2004. *Die Quadratur der Sterne- So schrieben wir Europas Verfassung (und was daraus geworden ist)*. Wien: Kremayr & Scheriau Verlag.

Eleftheriadis, P. 1998. 'Begging the Constitutional Question'. *Journal of Common Market Studies* 36: 255–72.

Elgström, E. O. and C. Jönsson. 2000. 'Negotiation in the European Union: Bargaining or Problem-Solving?' *Journal of European Public Policy* 7, no. 5: 684–704.

Elkin, S. L. 2006. *Reconstructing the Commercial Republic*. Chicago: University of Chicago Press.

Elliott, Larry. 2005. 'Manufacturing Woe Raises Rate Pressure'. *The Guardian*, June 2, 2005.

Elster, J. 1996. *Argomentare e negoziare*. Milan: Anabasi.

Eriksen, E. O. 2001. 'Why a Charter of Fundamental Rights?' In *The Chartering of Europe*, edited by E. O. Eriksen, et al. Oslo: Arena Report No. 8/2001.

Eriksen, E. O. and J. E. Fossum, eds. 2000a. *Democracy in the European Union – Integration through Deliberation?* London: Routledge.

Eriksen, E. O. and J. E. Fossum. 2000b. 'Post-National Integration'. In *Democracy in the European Union. Integration through Deliberation*, edited by E. O. Eriksen and J. E. Fossum. London and New York: Routledge.

Eriksen, E. O. and J. E. Fossum. 2002. 'Democracy through Strong Publics in the European Union?' *Journal of Common Market Studies* 40, no. 3: 401–24.

Eriksen, E. O. and J. E. Fossum. 2004. 'Europe in Search of Legitimacy: Strategies of Legitimation Assessed'. *International Political Science Review* 25: 439–41.

Eriksen, E. O., ed. 2005. *Making the European Polity: Reflexive Integration in the EU*. London and New York: Routledge.

Eriksen, E. O., J. E. Fossum, and A. J. Menéndez, eds. 2004. *Developing a Constitution for Europe*. London and New York: Routledge.

Eriksen, E. O., J. E. Fossum, and A. J. Menéndez. 2002. 'The Chartering of a European Constitution'. In *Constitution Making and Democratic Legitimacy*, edited by E. O. Eriksen, J. E. Fossum, and A. J. Menéndez. Oslo: ARENA Report, No 5/2002: 1–11.

Eucken, W. 1951a. *The Foundations of Economics: History and Theory in the Analysis of Economic Reality*, translated by T. W. Hutchinson. London: William Hodge and Company Limited.

Eucken, W. 1951b. *The Unsuccessful Age or The Pains of Economic Progress*, with an introduction by John Jewkes. Edinburgh: William Hodge and Company Limited.

Eurobarometer Report 48, March 1998.

Eurobarometer Report 52, April 2000.

Eurobarometer Report 60, February 2004.

Eurobarometer Report 62, December 2004.

European Commission. 2001. *European Governance. A White Paper*. Brussels: Commission of the European Communities. Brussels 25.7.2001, Com (2001) 428.

European Commission. 2007. 'Open Method of Coordination'. *Europa Glossary*. http://europa.eu/scadplus/glossary/open_method_coordination_en.htm.

European Commission. 2012. *A Blueprint for Deep and Genuine Monetary Union: Launching a European Debate*. Brussels. COM (2012) 777 final.

Evans, P. B., H. K. Jacobson, and R. D. Putnam, eds. 1993. *Double-Edged Diplomacy: International Bargaining and Domestic Politics*. Berkeley, Los Angeles and London: University of California Press.

Everson, M. 1995. 'The Legacy of the Market Citizen'. In *New Legal Dynamics of European Union*, edited by J. Shaw and G. More, 73–89. Oxford: Clarendon.

Fabbrini, S. 2004. 'Transatlantic Constitutionalism: Comparing the United States and the European Union'. *European Journal of Political Research* 43: 547–69.

Fabbrini, S. 2010. *Compound Democracies*. Oxford: Oxford University Press.

Farrell, David M. and Roger Scully. 2007. *Representing Europe's Citizens? Electoral Institutions and the Failure of Parliamentary Representation*. Oxford: Oxford University Press.

Farrell, H. and A. Héritier. 2003. 'Formal and Informal Institutions Under Codecision: Continuous Constitution-Building in Europe'. *Governance* 16, no. 4: 577–600.

Fasone, C. 2012. 'Interparliamentary Cooperation and Democratic Representation in the European Union'. In *The Challenge of Democratic Representation in the*

European Union, edited by S. Kröger and D. Friedrich, 41–58. Basingstoke: Macmillan.

Favell, A. 2008. *Eurostars and Eurocities*. Oxford: Blackwell.

Featherstone, K. 1994. 'Jean Monnet and the "Democratic Deficit" in the European Union'. *Journal of Common Market Studies* 32: 149–70.

Ferrajoli, L. 1994. 'Dai diritti del cittadino ai diritti della persona'. In *La Cittadinanza. Appartenenza, Identita, Diritti*, edited by D. Zolo. Roma and Bari: Laterza.

Ferrajoli, Luigi. 1995. *La Sovranità nel Mondo Moderno. Nascita e Crisi dello Stato Nazionale*. Milano: Anabasi.

Ferrajoli, Luigi. 1996. 'Beyond Sovereignty and Citizenship: A Global Constitutionalism'. In *Constitutionalism, Democracy and Sovereignty: American and European Perspectives*, edited by Richard Bellamy, 151–60. Aldershot and Brookfield, USA: Avebury.

Ferrara, M. 2014. 'Social Europe and its Components in the Midst of the Crisis: A Conclusion'. *West European Policy* 37, no. 4: 825–43.

Ferry, J.-M. 1992. 'Une "philosophie" de la communaute'. In *Discussion sur l'Europe*, edited by J.-M. Ferry and P. Thibaud, 127–212. Paris: Calmann-Levy.

Fioravanti, M. 1992. 'Quale futuro per la "costituzione"?' *Quaderni Fiorentini* 21: 623–37.

Fischer, J. 2000. 'Vom Staatenverbund zur Föderation: Gedanken über die Finalität der Europäischen Integration'. Lecture given at Humboldt University. Berlin.

Fitoussi, J. P. 2002. *La régle et le choix. De la souveraineté économique en Europe*. Paris: Seuil.

Fligstein, N. 2008. *Euroclash: The EU, European identity and the future of Europe*. Oxford: Oxford University Press.

Flikschuh, K. 2010. 'Kant's Sovereignty Dilemma: A Contemporary Analysis'. *Journal of Political Philosophy* 18, no. 4: 469–93.

Føllesdal, A. 1998a. 'Democracy and Federalism in the European Union'. In *Democracy and the European Union*, edited by Føllesdal and Koslowski, 231–53. Berlin: Springer-Verlag Berlin Heidelberg.

Føllesdal, A. 1998b. 'Democracy, Legitimacy and Majority Rule in the European Union'. In *Political Theory and the European Union*, edited by A. Weale and M. Nentwich, 34–48. Routledge.

Føllesdal, A. 2014. 'A Common European Identity for European Citizenship?' *German Law Journal* 15, no. 5: 765–75.

Føllesdal, A. and P. Koslowski, eds. 1997. *Democracy and the European Union*. Berlin: Springer-Verlag.

Føllesdal, A. and S. Hix. 2006. 'Why There Is a Democratic Deficit: A Reply to Majone and Moravcsik'. *Journal of Common Market Studies* 44, no. 3: 533–62.

Fontana, B. 2002. 'The Napoleonic Empire and the Europe of Nation'. In *The Idea of Europe*, edited by A. Pagden, 116–28. Cambridge: Cambridge University Press.

Forsyth, M. 1982. *Union of States – The Theory and Practice of Confederation*. Leicester: Leicester University Press.

Fossum, J. E. and H. J. Trenz. 2006. 'The EU's Fledging Society: From Deafening Silence to Critical Choice in European Constitution-making'. *Journal of Civil Society* 2, no. 1: 55–77.

Foucault, M. 1980. *Power/Knowledge*. New York: Pantheon.

Franchino, Fabio. 2006. 'Delegation in the European Union: Debates and Research Agenda'. In *Delegation in Contemporary Democracies*, edited by D. Braun and B. Gilardi, 216–38. London: Routledge.

Franklin, Julian H. 1991. 'Sovereignty and the Mixed Constitution: Bodin and His Critics'. In *The Cambridge History of Political Thought 1450–1700*, edited by J. H. Burns and Mark Goldie, 298–328. Cambridge: Cambridge University Press.

Freeman, S. 1990. 'Constitutional Democracy and the Legitimacy of Judicial Review'. *Law and Philosophy* 9: 327–70.

Friese, H. and P. Wagner. 2002. 'Survey Article: The Nascent Political Philosophy of the European Polity'. *The Journal of Political Philosophy* 10, no. 3: 342–64.

Fudge, J. 2002. 'The Canadian Charter of Rights: Recognition, Redistribution and the Imperialism of the Courts'. In *Sceptical Essays on Human Rights*, edited by Campbell et al. Oxford: Oxford University Press.

Fukuyama, F. 1992. *The End of History and the Last Man*. Harmondsworth: Penguin.

Galston, W. 1991. *Liberal Purposes: Goods, Virtues and Duties in the Liberal State*. Cambridge: Cambridge University Press.

Gambetta, D. 1998. '"Claro": An Essay on Discursive Machismo'. In *Deliberative Democracy*, edited by J. Elster, 19–43. Cambridge: Cambridge University Press.

Gauthier, D. 1986. *Morals by Agreement*. Oxford: Clarendon Press.

Geddes, A. 1995. 'Immigrant and Ethnic Minorities and the EU's "Democratic Deficit"'. *Journal of Common Market Studies* 33: 197–217.

Gellner, E. 1983. *Nations and Nationalism*. Oxford: Blackwell.

George, S. 1991. *Policy and Politics in the European Community*, second edition. Oxford: Oxford University Press.

Gilpin, R. 1987. *The Political Economy of International Relations*. Princeton, NJ: Princeton University Press.

Glencross, A. 2013. 'The Absence of Political Constitutionalism in the EU: Three Models for Enhancing Constitutional Agency'. *Journal of European Public Policy* 21, no. 8: 1163–80.

Glendon, M. A. 1991. *Rights Talk: The Impoverishment of Political Discourse*. New York: The Free Press.

Goldschmidt, N. 2000. 'Theorie auf Normativer Basis: Anmerkungen zum ordo-liberalen Konzept von Walter Eucken'. In *L'ordoliberalisme allemand: aux sources de l'économie sociale de marché*, edited by P. Commun, 119–31. Cergy-Pontoise: CIRAC.

Goldsmith, Lord Peter. 2000. 'Consolidation of Fundamental Rights at EU-level – the British Perspective'. In *The EU Charter of Fundamental Rights*, edited by K. Feus, 27–38. London: Federal Trust.

Goldsmith, Lord Peter. July 17, 2000. Interview data comes from Justus Schönlau, 'The EU Charter of Fundamental Rights: Legitimation through Deliberation', PhD thesis, University of Reading, Reading 2001.

Green-Pedersen, C. 2012. 'A Giant Fast Asleep? Party Incentives and the Politicisation of European Integration'. *Political Studies* 60: 115–30.

Greenwood, J. 1997. *Representing Interests in the European Union*. London: Macmillan.

Greve, Morton F. and K. E. Jorgensen. 2002. 'Treaty Reform as Constitutional Politics: A Longitudinal View'. *Journal of European Public Policy* 9, no. 1: 54–75.

Grimm, D. 1995. 'Does Europe Need a Constitution?' *European Law Journal* 1: 282–302.

Grimm, D. 1995. *Braucht Europa eine Verfassung?* Berlin: Carl Friedrich von Siemens Stiftung.

Grimm, D. 2016. *Constitutionalism: Past, Present, Future*. Oxford: Oxford University Press.

Grimm, D. 2017. *The Constitution of European Democracy*. Oxford: Oxford University Press.

Gustavsson, S. 1996. 'Squaring the Circle? Provisional Suprastatism and Democratic Accountability in the 1993 Maastricht Verdict of the German Constitutional Court'. Paper presented to ECPR Joint Sessions, Workshop 2 on the Political Theory of Constitutional Choice, Oslo, 29 March–3 April 1996.

Gustavsson, S. 1998. 'Defending the Democratic Deficit'. In *Political Theory and the European Union: Legitimacy, Constitutional Choice and Citizenship*, edited by A. Weale and M. Nentwich, 63–79. London: Routledge/ECPR.

Gutmann, A. and D. Thompson. 1996. *Democracy and Disagreement*. Cambridge, MA: Harvard University Press.

Haas, E. B. 1958. *The Uniting of Europe: Political, Social and Economic Forces 1950–57*. Stanford: Stanford University Press.

Haas, E. B. 1997. *Nationalism, Liberalism, and Progress: The Rise and Decline of Nationalism*. Ithaca: Cornell University Press.

Habermas, J. 2015. 'Democracy in Europe: Why the Development of the EU into a Transnational Democracy Is Necessary and How It Is Possible'. *European Law Journal* 21, no. 4: 546–57.

Habermas, Jürgen. 1992a. 'Citizenship and National Identity: Some Reflections on the Future of Europe'. *Praxis International* 12: 1–19.

Habermas, Jürgen. 1992b. 'Further Reflections on the Public Sphere'. In *Habermas and the Public Sphere*, edited by C. Calhoun, 421–61. Cambridge, MA: The MIT Press.

Habermas, Jürgen. 1996a. *Between Facts and Norms*. Cambridge: Polity.

Habermas, Jürgen. 1996b. 'Three Normative Models of Democracy'. In *Democracy and Difference: Contesting the Boundaries of the Political*, edited by S. Benhabib, 21–30. Princeton, NJ: Princeton University Press.

Habermas, Jürgen. 1997. *Solidarietà tra Stranieri. Interventi su 'Fatti e Norme'*, edited by L. Ceppa. Napoli: Guerini e Associati.

Habermas, Jürgen. 1998. *The Inclusion of the Other: Studies in Political Theory*. Cambridge: Polity.

Habermas, Jürgen. 1999. 'The European Nation-state and the Pressures of Globalisation'. *New Left Review* 235: 46–59.

Habermas, Jürgen. 2001a. 'Why Europe Needs a Constitution'. *New Left Review* 11: 5–26.

Habermas, Jürgen. 2001b. *The Postnational Constellation: Political Essays*. Cambridge: Polity.

Habermas, Jürgen. 2006. *The Divided West*. Cambridge: Polity Press.

Habermas, Jürgen. 2012. *The Crisis of the European Union: A Response*, trans. Ciaran Cronin. Cambridge: Polity Press.

Hall, P. A. and D. W. Soskice, eds. 2001. *Varieties of Capitalism: The Institutional Foundations of Capitalism*. Oxford: Oxford University Press.

Hampshire, S. 1991. 'Justice is Strife'. *Proceedings and Addresses of the American Philosophical Association* 65: 19–27.

Harding, C. 1992. 'Who Goes to Court? An Analysis of Litigation against the European Community'. *European Law Review* 17, no. 1: 105–25.

Harlow, C. 1996. '*Francovich* and the Problem of the Disobedient State'. *European Law Journal* 2, no. 3: 199–225.

Harlow, C. 1999. *Citizen Access to Political Power in the European Union*. Florence: EUI Working Paper RSC No. 99/2.

Harrington, James. 1992. *The Commonwealth of Oceana*, edited by J. G. A. Pocock. Cambridge: Cambridge University Press.

Hart, H. L. A. 1961. *The Concept of Law*. Oxford: Clarendon Press.

Hay, C. 2007. *Why We Hate Politics*. Oxford: Blackwell.

Hayek, F. A. 1948 [1939]. 'The Economic Conditions of Interstate Federalism'. In *Individualism and Economic Order*, edited by F. A. Hayek, 255–72. Chicago, IL: University of Chicago Press.

Hayek, F. A. 1960. *The Constitution of Liberty*. London: Routledge.

Hayek, F. A. 1967. *Studies in Philosophy, Politics and Economics*. London: Routledge & Kegan Paul.

Hayek, F. A. 1978. *Denationalization of Money – The Argument Refined*, second edition. London: The Institute of Economic Affairs.

Hayek, F. A. 1979. *Law, Legislation and Liberty*, three volumes. London: Routledge.

Hayek, F. A. 1982. *Law, Legislation and Liberty*. London: Routledge.

Hegel, G. W. F. 1942 [1821]. *Philosophy of Right*. Oxford: Clarendon Press.

Hegel, G. W. F. 1952. *Philosophy of Right*, edited by T. M. Knox. London: Oxford University Press.

Held, David. 1987. *Models of Democracy*. Cambridge: Polity Press.

Held, David. 1995. *Democracy and the Global Order: From the Modern State to Cosmopolitan Governance*. Cambridge: Polity Press.

Held, David. 2006. *Models of Democracy*, third edition. Cambridge: Polity Press.

Heller, H. 1927. *Die Souveränität. Ein Beitrag zur Theorie des Staats- und Völkerrechts*. Berlin and Leipzing: W. de Gruyter.

Herdegen, M. 1994. 'Maastricht and the German Constitutional Court: Constitutional restraints for "an ever closer union"'. *Common Market Law Review* 31: 235–49.

Héritier, Adrienne. 2005. 'Managing Regulatory Developments in Rail'. In *Redefining Regulatory Regimes: Utilities in Europe*, edited by D. Coen and A. Héritier, 120–44. Cheltenham: Edward Elgar.

Heun, W. 1995. 'The Evolution of Federalism'. In *Studies in German Constitutionalism*, edited by C. Starck. Baden-Baden: Nomos Verlagsgesellschaft.

Hirschman, A. O. 1970. *Exit, Voice, and Loyalty: Responses to Decline in Firms, Organizations, and States*. Cambridge, MA, London: Harvard University Press.

Hirschman, A. O. 1994. 'Social Conflict as Pillars of Democratic Market Society'. *Political Theory* 22: 203–18.

Hirst, Paul and Graham Thompson. 1996. *Globalisation in Question: The International Economy and the Possibilities of Governance*. Cambridge: Polity Press.

Hirst, Paul. 1994. *Associative Democracy*. Cambridge: Polity.

Hix, S. 1995. 'Parties at the European Level and the Legitimacy of EU Socio-Economic Policy'. *Journal of Common Market Studies* 33: 527–54.

Hix, S. 2000. 'Parliamentary Oversight of Executive Power: What Role for the European Parliament in Comitology?' In *Committee Governance in the European Union*, edited by T. Christiansen and E. Kirchner, 62–78. Manchester: Manchester University Press.

Hix, S. 2005. *The Political System of the European Union*. Basingstoke: Palgrave MacMillan.

Hix, S. 2007. 'The European Union as a Polity (I)'. In *The Handbook of European Union Politics*, edited by Knud Erik Jørgensen, Mark A. Pollack, and Ben Rosamond, 141–58. New York: Sage.

Hix, S. 2008. *What's Wrong with the European Union and How to Fix It*. Cambridge: Polity.

Hix, S. and M. Marsh. 2011. 'Second-order Effects Plus Pan-European Political Swings: An Analysis of European Parliament Elections Across Time'. *Electoral Studies* 30: 4–15.

Hobbes, T. 1991. *Leviathan*, edited by R. Tuck. Cambridge: Cambridge University Press.

Hobhouse, L. T. 1964 [1911]. *Liberalism*. Oxford: Oxford University Press.

Hobsbawm, E. 1994. *Age of Extremes. The Short Twentieth Century, 1914–1991*. London: Michael Joseph.

Hoffman, S. 1966. 'Obstinate or Obsolete: The Fate of the Nation State and the Case of Western Europe'. *Daedalus* 95, no. 3: 862–915.

Hoffman, S. 1982. 'Reflections on the Nation-State in Western Europe Today'. *Journal of Common Market Studies* 21: 21–38.

Hollis, M. and S. Smith. 1990. *Explaining and Understanding International Relations*. Oxford: Clarendon Press.

Holmes, S. 1993. *The Anatomy of Antiliberalism*. Cambridge, MA: Harvard University Press.

Holmes, S. 1995. *Passions and Constraint: On the Theory of Liberal Democracy*. Chicago and London: University of Chicago Press.

Holmes, S. 1998. 'Gag Rules or the Politics of Omission'. In *Constitutionalism and Democracy*, edited by J. Elster and R. Slagstad, 19–58. Cambridge: Cambridge University Press.

Hooghe, L. and G. Marks. 2009. 'A Postfunctionalist Theory of European Integration: From Permissive Consensus to Constraining Dissensus'. *British Journal of Political Science* 39, no. 1: 1–23.

Hosli, M. O. 1995. 'The Balance Between Small and Large: Effects of a Double Majority on Voting Power in the European Union'. *International Studies Quarterly* 39: 351–70.

Hosli, M. O. 1996. 'Coalitions and Power: Effects of Qualified Majority Voting in the Council of the European Union'. *Journal of Common Market Studies* 34: 255–73.

Hosli, M. O. 1997. 'Voting Strength in the European Parliament: The Influence of National and Partisan Actors'. *European Journal of Political Research* 31: 351–66.

House of Lords. 2014a. European Union Committee. *'Genuine Economic and Monetary Union' and the Implications for the UK.* London: The Stationery Office Limited, HL Paper 314.

House of Lords. 2014b. European Union Committee. *The Role of NPs in the European Union.* London: The Stationery Office Limited, HL Paper 151.

House of Lords. 2014c. EU Economic and Financial Affairs Sub-Committee. *Euro Area Crisis: An Update.* London: The Stationery Office Limited, HL Paper 163.

Hunold, C. 2005. 'Green Political Theory and the European Union: The Case for a Non-integrated Civil Society'. *Environmental Politics* 14, no. 3: 324–43.

Hurrelmann, A., A. Gora, and A. Wagner. 2013. 'The Politicization of European Integration: More than an Elite Affair?' *Political Studies*. doi: 10.1111/1467-9248.12090.

Hutter, S. and A. Kerscher. 2014. 'Politicizing Europe in Hard Times: Conflicts over Europe in France in a Long-Term Perspective, 1974–2012'. *Journal of European Integration* 36, no. 3: 267–82.

Hutter, S. and E. Grande. 2014. 'Politicizing Europe in the National Electoral Arena: A Comparative Analysis of Five West European Countries, 1970–2010'. *Journal of Common Market Studies* 52, no. 5: 1002–18.

Hyland, J. L. 1995. *Democratic Theory.* Manchester: Manchester University Press.

Imig, D. and S. Tarrow, eds. 2000. *Contentious Europeans: Protest and Politics in an Emerging Polity.* Boulder: Rowman & Littlefield.

Isaac, J. 1988. 'Republicanism vs. Liberalism: A Reconsideration'. *History of Political Thought* 9: 349–77.

Isiksel, T. 2016. *Europe's Functional Constitution: A Theory of Constitutionalism Beyond the State.* Oxford: Oxford University Press.

Issing, O. 2000. 'Hayek, Currency Competition and European Monetary Union'. Occasional Papers 111. London: The Institute of Economic Affairs.

Issing, O. 2008. *The Birth of the Euro.* Cambridge: Cambridge University Press.

Jabko, N. 2006. *Playing the Market: A Political Strategy for Uniting Europe, 1985–2005.* Ithaca and New York: Cornell University Press.

Jachtenfuchs, M., T. Diez, and S. Jung. 1998. 'Which Europe? Conflicting Models of a Legitimate European Political Order'. *European Journal of International Relations* 4, no. 4: 409–45.

Jackson, Robert. 1999. 'Sovereignty in World Politics: A Glance at the Conceptual and Historical Landscape'. *Political Studies* 47 (special issue *Sovereignty at the Millenium*, edited by Robert Jackson).

James, Alan. 1999. 'The Practice of Sovereign Statehood in Contemporary International Society'. *Political Studies* 47 (special issue *Sovereignty at the Millenium*, edited by Robert Jackson).

James, H. 2012. *Making the European Monetary Union: The Role of the Committee of Central Bank Governors and the Origins of the European Central Bank*. Cambridge, MA: The Belknap Press.

Jančić, D. 2012. 'The Barroso Initiative: Window Dressing or Democracy Boost?' *Utrecht Law Review* 8, no. 1: 78–91.

Janis, I. L. 1982. *Groupthink*. Boston: Houghton Mifflin.

Jeffrey, C. 2000. 'Sub-National Mobilization and European Integration'. *Journal of Common Market Studies* 38, no. 1: 1–25.

Jennings, J. 2009. 'Constant's Idea of Modern Liberty'. In *The Cambridge Companion to Constant*, edited by H. Rosenblatt, 69–91. Cambridge: Cambridge University Press.

Joerges, C. 1997. 'The Impact of European Integration on Private Law: Reductionist Perceptions, True Conflicts and a New Constitutional Perspective'. *European Law Journal* 3: 378–406.

Joerges, C. and E. Vos, eds. 1999. *EU Committees: Social Regulation, Law Politics*. Hart.

Joerges, C. and J. Neyer. 1997. 'Transforming Strategic Interaction into Deliberative Problem-Solving: European Comitology in the Foodstuffs Sector'. *Journal of European Public Policy* 4: 609–25.

Joerges, C. and M. Everson. 2004. 'Law, Economics and Politics in the Constitutionalization of Europe'. In *Developing a Constitution for Europe*, edited by E. O. Eriksen, J. E. Fossum, and A. J. Menéndez, 162–79. London and New York: Routledge.

Jones, P. 1983. 'Political Equality and Majority Rule'. In *The Nature of Political Theory*, edited by D. Miller and L. Seidentop, 155–82. Oxford: Clarendon Press.

Jones, R. J. Barry. 1993. 'The Economic Agenda'. In *International Politics in Europe: The New Agenda*, edited by G. Wyn Rees, 87–110. London and New York: Routledge.

Jones, R. J. Barry. 1995a. *Globalisation and Interdependence in the International Political Economy: Rhetoric and Reality*. London and New York: Pinter.

Jones, R. J. Barry. 1995b. 'The United Nations and the International Political System'. In *The United Nations in the New World Order: The World Organization at Fifty*, edited by D. Bourantonis and J. Weiner, 19–40. Basingstoke: Macmillan.

Joppke, C. 2001. 'The Evolution of Alien Rights in the United States, Germany and the European Union'. In *Citizenship Today: Global Perspectives and Practices*, edited by A. Aleinikoff and D. Klusmeyer. Washington, DC: Carnegie Endowment for International Peace.

Kant, I. 1991. 'On the Common Saying: "This May Be True in Theory but Not in Practice"'. In *Kant Political Writings*, edited by H. Reiss and trans. by H. B. Nisbet, 61–92. Cambridge: Cambridge University Press.

Kantner, C. 2006. 'What is a European Identity? The Emergence of a Shared Ethical Self-Understanding in the European Union'. *EUI Working Paper RSCAS*. 2006/28.

Karlas, J. 2012. 'National Parliamentary Control of EU Affairs: Institutional Design after Enlargement'. *West European Politics* 35, no. 5: 1095–113.

Katzenstein, Peter J. 2005. *A World of Regions: Asia and Europe in the American Imperium*. Ithaca: Cornell University Press.

Keeler, J. T. S. 1996. 'Agricultural Power in the European Community: Explaining the Fate of CAP and GATT Negotiations'. *Comparative Politics* 28: 127–49.

Kelemen, R. D. and E. C. Sibbitt. 2002. 'The Globalisation of American Law'. *International Organization* 58: 103–36.

Kelsen, H. 1929. *Vom Wesen der Demokratie*, second edition. Tübingen: J. C. B. Mohr.

Kelsen, Hans. 1920. *Das Problem der Souveränität und die Theorie des Völkerrechts. Beitrag zu einer Reiner Rechtslehre*. Tübingen: Mohr.

Kennedy, E. 1991. *The Bundesbank: Germany's Central Bank in the International Monetary System*. London: Pinter Publishers, The Royal Institute of International Affairs.

Keohane, Robert O. and Stanley Hoffman. 1991. 'Institutional Change in Europe in the 1980s'. In *The New European Community: Decision Making and Institutional Change*, edited by Robert O. Keohane and Stanley Hoffman, 1–39. Boulder, CO and Oxford: Westview Press.

Keohane, Robert O., S. Macedo, and A. Moravscik. 2009. 'Democracy-enhancing Mulitilateralism'. *International Organisation* 63, no. 1: 1–31.

Keynes, J. M. 1923. *A Tract on Monetary Reform*. London: MacMillan.

Kiljunen, Kimmo. 2004. *The European Constitution in the Making*. Brussels: Center for European Policy Studies.

Klabbers, J. 2001. 'The Changing Image of International Organizations'. In *The Legitimacy of International Organizations*, edited by J. M. Coicaud and V. Heiskanen, 221–55. Washington, DC: United Nations University Press.

Kochenov, D. 2011/12. 'A Real European Citizenship: A New Jurisdiction Test: A Novel Chapter in the Development of the Union in Europe'. *Columbia Journal of European Law* 18, no. 1: 55–109.

Kohler-Koch, Beate. 2008. 'Does Participatory Governance Hold its Promises?' In *Efficient and Democratic Governance in Multi-Level Europe*, edited by B. Kohler-Koch and F. Larat, CONNEX Report Series, Volume 9.

Kohler-Koch, Beate. 2009. 'The Three Worlds of European Civil Society – What Role for Civil Society for What Kind of Europe?' *Policy and Society* 28, no. 1: 47–57.

Kohler-Koch, Beate. 2010. 'Civil Society and EU Democracy: "Astroturf" Representation?' *Journal of European Public Policy* 17, no. 1: 100–16.

Kohler-Koch, Beate and B. Finke. 2007. 'The Institutional Shaping of EU–Society Relations: A Contribution to Democracy via Participation?' *Journal of Civil Society* 3, no. 3: 205–21.

Koopmans, R. 2007. 'Who Inhabits the European Public Sphere? Winners and Losers, Supporters and Opponents in Europeanised Political Debates'. *European Journal of Political Research* 46: 183–210.

Koopmans, T. 1992. 'Federalism: The Wrong Debate'. *Common Market Law Review* 29: 1047–52.

Kostakopoulou, D. 2008. 'The Evolution of European Union Citizenship'. *European Political Science* 7, no. 3: 285–95.

Kriesi, H. 2016. 'The Politicization of European Integration'. *Journal of Common Market Studies* 54, no. S1: 32–47.

Kröger, S. 2007. 'The End of Democracy as We Know it? The Legitimacy Deficits of Bureaucratic Social Policy Governance'. *European Integration* 29, no. 5: 565–82.

Kröger, S. 2008. 'Nothing but Consultation: The Place of Organised Civil Society in EU Policy-making Across Policies'. EUROGOV No. C-08-03. http://www.connex-network.org/eurogov/pdf/egp-connex-C-08-03.pdf.

Kröger, S. and D. Friedrich. 2013. 'Democratic Representation in the EU: Two Kinds of Subjectivity'. *Journal of European Public Policy* 20, no. 2: 171–89.

Kukathas, C. 2005. 'Immigration'. In *The Oxford Handbook of Practical Ethics*, edited by H. LaFollette, 567–90. Oxford: Oxford University Press.

Kumm, M. 2005. 'To be a European Citizen: Constitutional Patriotism and the Treaty Establishing a Constitution for Europe'. In *The European Constitution: The Rubicon Crossed?* ARENA report No. 3/05.

Kymlicka, W. 1999. 'Citizenship in an Era of Globalization'. In *Democracy's Edges*, edited by I. Shapiro and C. Hacker-Cordon, 112–26. Cambridge: Cambridge University Press.

Kymlicka, W. 2001. *Politics in the Vernacular: Nationalism, Multiculturalism and Citizenship*. Oxford: Oxford University Press.

Kymlicka, W. 2008. 'Liberal Nationalism and Cosmopolitan Justice'. In *Another Cosmopolitanism*, edited by S. Benhabib, 128–44. Oxford: Oxford University Press.

Laborde, C. 2002. 'From Constitutional to Civic Patriotism'. *British Journal of Political Science* 32: 591–612.

Laborde, C. 2010. 'Republicanism and Global Justice: A Sketch'. *European Journal of Political Theory* 9, no. 1: 48–69.

Lacroix, J. 2002. 'For a European Constitutional Patriotism'. *Political Studies* 50, no. 5: 944–58.

Ladvas, K. and D. Chrissochoou. 2011. *A Republic of Europeans: Civic Potential in a Liberal Milieu*. Cheltenham: Edward Elgar.

Laffan, B. 1996. 'The Politics of Identity and Political Order in Europe'. *Journal of Common Market Studies* 34: 81–102.

Lakoff, S. 1996. *Democracy: History, Theory, Practice*. Boulder: Westview Press.

Laponce, J. A. 2002. 'Language and Politics'. In *Encyclopedia of Government and Politics*, edited by M. Hawkesworth and M. Kogan, vol. 1, 587–602, 2nd edition. London and New York: Routledge.

Le Monde. June 15–16, 2003. 'Un texte de compromis pour un Union á 25'.

Lebessis, L. and J. Paterson. 2000. 'Developing New Modes of Governance'. In *Working Paper of the Forward Studies Unit*. Luxembourg: European Commission. http://ec.europa.eu/comm/cdp/working-paper/nouveaux_modes_gouvernance_en.pdf.

Lee, Steven. 1997. 'A Puzzle of Sovereignty'. *Californian Western International Law Journal* 27, no. 2: 241–63.

Lehning, P. and A. Weale, eds. 1997. *Citizenship, Democracy and Justice in the New Europe*. London: Routledge.

Lijphart, A. 1968. *The Politics of Accommodation: Pluralism and Democracy in the Netherlands*. Berkeley: University of California Press.

Lijphart, A. 1977. *Democracy in Plural Societies. A Comparative Exploration*. New Haven and London: Yale University Press.

Lijphart, A. 1984. *Democracies. Patterns of Majoritarian and Consensus Government in Twenty-One Countries*. New Haven and London: Yale University Press.

Lindseth, P. 2010. *Power and Legitimacy: Reconciling Europe and the Nation State*. Oxford: Oxford University Press.

Lindseth, P. L. 2016. 'The Perils of "As If" European Constitutionalism'. *European Law Journal* 22, no. 5 (September 2016): 696–718.

Lindseth, P. L., et al. 2012. 'Special Book Review Symposium: Power and Legitimacy'. *European Constitutional Law Review* 8: 128–64.

Linklater, Andrew. 1998. *The Transformation of Political Community: Ethical Foundations of the Post-Westphalian Era*. Cambridge: Polity.

Lipset, S. M. and S. Rokkan. 1967. 'Introduction'. In *Party Systems and Voter Alignments*, edited by S. M Lipset and S. Rokkan, 1–64. New York: Free Press.

Locke, J. 1960. *Two Treatises of Government*, edited by P. Laslett. Cambridge: Cambridge University Press.

Lodge, J. 1994. 'Transparency and Democratic Legitimacy'. *Journal of Common Market Studies* 32: 343–68.

Lord, C. 2019. 'Externalities and Representation beyond the State: Lessons from the European Union'. In *Creating Political Presence: The New Politics of Democratic Representation*, edited by D. Castiglione and J. Pollack, 281–59. Chicago, IL: Chicago University Press.

Lord, C. and D. Beetham. 2001. 'Legitimizing the EU: Is there a "Post-parliamentary Basis" for its Legitimation?' *Journal of Common Market Studies* 39: 443–62.

Loughlin, M. 2000. *Sword and Scales: An Examination of the Relationship between Law and Politics*. Oxford: Hart.

Loughlin, M. 2014. 'Constitutional Pluralism: An Oxymoron?' *Global Constitutionalism* 3, no. 1: 9–30.

Luhmann, Niklas. 1981. *The Differentiation of Society*. New York: Columbia University Press.

Luhmann, Niklas. 1996. 'La costituzione come acquisizione evolutiva'. In *Il futuro della costituzione*, edited by G. Zagrebelsky, P. P. Portinaro, and J. Lüther, 129–66. Turin: Einaudi.

Lyons, C. 1996. 'Citizenship in the Constitution of the European Union: Rhetoric or Reality?' In *Constitutionalism, Democracy and Sovereignty: American and European Perspectives*, edited by Richard Bellamy, 96–110. Aldershot and Brookfield, USA: Avebury.

Maatsch, A. 2014. 'Are We All *Austerians* Now? An Analysis of National Parliamentary Parties' Positioning On Anti-crisis Measures in the Eurozone'. *Journal of European Public Policy* 21, no. 1: 96–115.

MacCormick, Neil. 1993. 'Beyond the Sovereign State'. *Modern Law Review* 56: 1–19.

MacCormick, Neil. 1995. 'Sovereignty, Democracy and Subsidiarity'. In *Democracy and Constitutional Culture in the Union of Europe*, edited by R. Bellamy, V. Bufacchi, and D. Castiglione, 95–100. London: Lothian Foundation Press.

MacCormick, Neil. 1995. 'The Maastricht-Urteil: Sovereignty Now'. *European Law Journal* 1: 255–62.

MacCormick, Neil. 1996. 'Liberalism, Nationalism and the Post-Sovereign State'. In *Constitutionalism in Transformation: European and Theoretical Perspectives*, edited by Richard Bellamy and Dario Castiglione, 141–56. Oxford: Blackwell.

MacCormick, Neil. 1997. 'Democracy, Subsidiarity, and Citizenship in the "European Commonwealth"'. *Law and Philosophy* 16: 331–56.

MacCormick, Neil. 1999. *Questioning Sovereignty: Law, State, and Practical Reason*. Oxford: Oxford University Press.

MacCormick, Neil. 2004. *The European Convention: What's in it for Wales?* WiRe: University of Aberystwyth.

Macdonald, T. and M. Ronzoni. 2012. 'Introduction: The Idea of Global Political Justice'. *Critical Review of Social and Political Philosophy* 15, no. 5: 521–33.

Macedo, S. 2004. 'What Self-governing Peoples Owe to One Another: Universalism, Diversity and *The Law of Peoples*'. *Fordham Law Review* 72: 101–17.

MacIlwain, C. H. 1958. *Constitutionalism: Ancient and Modern*. Ithaca, NY: Cornell University Press.

Mackie, G. 2003. *Democracy Defended*. Cambridge: Cambridge University Press.

Macpherson, C. B. 1977. *The Life and Times of Liberal Democracy*. Oxford: Oxford University Press.

Maduro, M. Poiares. 2000. 'Europe and the Constitution'. In *What If This Is as Good as It Gets?* Constitutionalism web papers. http://les1.man.ac.uk/conweb/ConWeb No. 5/2000.

Maduro, M. Poiares. 2003. 'Europe and the Constitution: What If This Is as Good as It Gets?' In *European Constitutionalism beyond the State*, edited by J. H. H. Weiler and Marlene Wind, 74–102. Cambridge: Cambridge University Press.

Magnette, P. 2004a. 'When Does Deliberation Matter? Constitutional Rhetoric in the Convention on the Future of Europe'. In *Deliberative Constitutional Politics in the EU*, edited by C. Closa and J. E. Fossum. Oslo: ARENA report No.5.

Magnette, P. 2004b. 'Deliberation or Bargaining? Coping with Constitutional Conflicts in the Convention on the Future of Europe'. In *Developing a Constitution for Europe*, edited by E. O. Eriksen, J. E. Fossum, and A. J. Menéndez, 207–25. London and New York: Routledge.

Magnette, P. and K. Nicolaïdis. 2004. 'The European Convention: Bargaining in the Shadow of Rhetoric'. *West European Politics* 27.

Maher, I. 1998. 'Community Law in the National Legal Order: A System Analysis'. *Journal of Common Market Studies* 36: 237–54.

Maine, H. 1917 [1861]. *Ancient Laws*. New York: Dutton and Co.

Mair, P. 2007. 'Political Opposition and the European Union'. *Government and Opposition* 42: 1–18.

Mair, P. 2007. 'Political Parties and Party Systems'. In *Europeanization: New Research Agendas*, edited by P. Graziano and M. P. Vink, 154–66. Basingstoke: Palgrave Macmillan.

Mair, P. 2011. 'Smaghi vs. the Parties: Representative Government and Institutional Constraints'. Paper prepared for the Conference on Democracy in Straightjackets: Politics in an Age of Permanent Austerity. Ringberg Castle, Munich.

Mair, P. 2013. *Ruling the Void: The Hollowing of Western Democracy*. London: Verso.

Majone, D. 2005. *Dilemmas of European Integration*. Oxford: Oxford University Press.

Majone, G. 1994. 'The Rise of the Regulatory State in Europe'. *West European Politics* 17: 77–101.

Majone, G. 1995. 'La communauté européenne come état régulateur'. In *L'État, la finance et le sociale*, edited by Bruno Théret. Paris: Editions La Decouverte.

Majone, G. 1996. 'Regulatory Legitimacy'. In *Regulating Europe*, edited by G. Majone, et al., 284–301. London: Routledge.

Majone, G. 1998. 'Europe's "Democratic Deficit": The Question of Standards'. *European Law Journal* 4: 5–28.

Majone, G. 1999. 'The Regulatory State and its Legitimacy Problems'. *West European Politics* 22, no. 1: 1–24.

Majone, G. 2000. 'The Credibility Crisis of Community Regulation'. *Journal of Common Market Studies* 38, no. 2: 273–301.

Majone, G. 2001. 'Nonmajoritarian Institutions and the Limits of Democratic Governance: A Political Transaction Cost Approach'. *Journal of Institutional and Theoretical Economics* 1: 57–78.

Majone, G. 2012. 'Rethinking the European Integration after the Debt Crisis'. European Institute UCL Working Paper No. 3/2012.

Majone, G. 2017. 'The European Union Post-Brexit: Static or Dynamic Adaptation?' *European Law Journal* 23, nos. 1–2: 9–27.

Mancini, F. and J. H. H. Weiler. 1998. 'Europe – The Case for Statehood ... and the Case Against. An Exchange'. Harvard Jean Monnet Chair Working Papers Series, no. 6.

Mancini, G. F. 1989. 'The Making of a Constitution for Europe'. *Common Market Law Review* 26: 595–614.

Mancini, G. F. 2000. *Democracy and Constitutionalism in the European Union*. Oxford: Hart Publishing.

Manin, B. 1997. *The Principles of Representative Government*. Cambridge: Cambridge University Press.

Mann, M. 1987. 'Ruling Strategies and Citizenship'. *Sociology* 21: 339–54.

Mansbridge, J. 1992. 'A Deliberative Theory of Interest Representation'. In *The Politics of Interests. Interest Groups Transformed*, edited by M. P. Petracca, 32–57. Boulder: Westview Press.

Margalit, A. and J. Raz. 1990. 'National Self-determination'. *Journal of Philosophy* 87: 439–61.

Marks, G. 1999. 'Territorial Identities in the European Union'. In *Regional Integration and Democracy: Expanding on the European Experience*, edited by Jeffrey J. Anderson, 69–91. Lanham: Rowman & Littlefield.

Marks, G., F. W. Scharpf, P. Schmitter, and W. Streek. 1996. *Governance in the European Union*. London: Sage.

Marks, G., L. Hooghe, and K. Blank. 1996. 'European Integration from the 1980s: State-Centric v. Multi-level Governance'. *Journal of Common Market Studies* 34: 341–42.

Marshall, T. H. 1950. *Citizenship and Social Class*. Cambridge: Cambridge University Press.

Matthijs, M. 2014. 'Mediterranean Blues: The Crisis in Southern Europe'. *Journal of Democracy* 25, no. 1: 101–15.

Mattila, M. and T. Raunio. 2012. 'Drifting Further Apart: National Parties and Their Electorates on the EU Dimension'. *West European Politics* 35, no. 3: 589–606.

Maurer, A. and W. Wessels, eds. 2001. *National Parliaments on Their Ways to Europe: Losers or Latecomers?* Baden-Baden: Nomos.

May, K. 1952. 'A Set of Independent, Necessary and Sufficient Conditions for Simple Majority Decision'. *Econometrica* 10: 680–84.

McAllister, I. 1999. 'The Economic Performance of Governments'. In *Critical Citizens: Global Support for Democratic Governance*, edited by P. Norris, 201–3. Oxford: Oxford University Press.

McCormick, J. P. 2000. 'Parliament and the Court in the European Union: An Evaluation of their Potential as Supranational Democratic Institutions'. Mimeo version, by kind concession of the author.

McGann, A. J. 2004. 'The Tyranny of the Supermajority: How Majority Rule Protects Minorities'. *Journal of Theoretical Politics* 16: 53–77.

McKeever, Robert J. 1995. *Raw Judicial Power? The Supreme Court and American Society*, 2nd edition. Manchester: Manchester University Press.

McKinnon, C. and D. Castiglione. 2003. 'Reasonable Toleration'. In *The Culture of Toleration in Diverse Societies: Reasonable Tolerance*, edited by C. McKinnon and D. Castiglione, 1–11. Manchester: Manchester University Press.

McNamara, K. 2002. 'Rational Fictions: Central Bank Independence and the Social Logic of Delegation'. *West European Politics* 25: 47–76.

McNamara, K. R. 2015. *The Politics of Everyday Europe: Constructing Authority in the European Union*. Oxford: Oxford University Press.

Merlingen, M. 2001. 'Identity, Politics and Germany's Post-TEU Policy on EMU'. *Journal of Common Market Studies* 39: 463–83.

Miklin, E. 2014. 'EU Politicisation and National Parliaments: Visibility of Choices and Better Aligned Ministers?' *The Journal of Legislative Studies* 20, no. 1: 78–92.

Mill, J. S. 1861 [1972]. *Considerations on Representative Government* in *Utilitarianism, On Liberty and Considerations on Representative Government*, edited by H. B. Acton. London: Dent.

Miller, D. 2008. 'Political Philosophy for Earthlings'. In *Political Theory: Methods and Approaches*, edited by David Leopold and Marc Stears, 29–48. Oxford: Oxford University Press.

Miller, David. 1994. 'The Nation-state: A Modest Defence'. In *Political Restructuring in Europe. Ethical Perspectives*, edited by Chris Brown, 137–62. London and New York: Routledge.

Miller, David. 1995. *On Nationality*. Oxford: Clarendon Press.

Miller, David. 2000. *Citizenship and National Identity*. Cambridge: Polity Press.

Miller, David. 2006. *The Liberty Reader*, second edition. Edinburgh: Edinburgh University Press.

Miller, David. 2007. *National Responsibility and Global Justice*. Oxford: Oxford University Press.

Miller, David. 2008. 'National Responsibility and Global Justice'. *Critical Review of International Social and Political Philosophy* 11: 383–99.

Miller, David. 2008. 'Republicanism, National Identity and Europe'. In *Republicanism and Political Theory*, edited by C. Laborde and J. Maynor, 133–58. Oxford: Blackwell.

Miller, David. 2009. 'Democracy's Domain'. *Philosophy and Public Affairs* 37: 201–28.

Milward, A. 1992. *The European Rescue of the Nation-State*. London and New York: Routledge.

Modood, T. 1993. 'Kymlicka on British Muslims'. *Analyse und Kritik* 15: 87–91.

Moravcsik, A. 1993. 'Preferences and Power in the European Community: A Liberal Intergovernmentalist Approach'. *Journal of Common Market Studies* 31: 473–524.

Moravcsik, A. 1995. 'Liberal Intergovernmentalism and Integration: A Rejoinder'. *Journal of Common Market Studies* 33: 611–28.

Moravcsik, A. 1999. *The Choice for Europe: Social Purpose and State Power From Messina to Maastricht*. London: UCL Press.

Moravcsik, A. 2002a. 'In Defence of the "Democratic Deficit": Reassessing Legitimacy in the European Union'. *Journal of Common Market Studies* 40, no. 4: 603–24.

Moravcsik, A. 2002b. 'Europe Without Illusions'. Paper presented at the Third Spaak Foundation, Harvard University Conference. Brussels.

Moravcsik, A. 2004a. 'Is There a "Democratic Deficit" in World Politics? A Framework for Analysis', *Government and Opposition* 39: 336–363.

Moravcsik, A. 2004b. 'The Unsung Constitution', *Prospect*, March 20: 112.

Moravcsik, A. 2005. 'The European Constitutional Compromise and the Neofunctionalist Legacy'. *Journal of European Public Policy* 12, no. 2: 349–86.

Moravcsik, A. 2008. 'The Myth of Europe's "Democratic Deficit"'. *Intereconomics* 43: 331–40.

Moravcsik, A. and K. Nicolaïdis. 1998. 'Keynote Article: Federal Ideas and Constitutional Realities in the Treaty of Amsterdam'. *Journal of Common Market Studies* 36 (Annual Review): 13–38.

Moravscik, A. 2012. 'Europe after the Crisis: How to Sustain a Common Currency'. *Foreign Affairs* 91, no. 3: 54–68.

Morgan, G. 2005. *The Idea of a European Superstate: Public Justification and European Integration*. Princeton and Oxford: Princeton University Press.

Mulhall, Stephen and Adam Swift. 1996. *Liberals and Communitarians*, second edition. Oxford: Blackwell.

Müller, J. W. 2007. *Constitutional Patriotism*. Princeton and Oxford: Princeton University Press.

Müller, J. W. 2011. *Contesting Democracy: Political Ideas in the Twentieth Century Europe*. New Haven, CT: Yale University Press.

Nanou, K. 2013. 'Different Origins, Same Proposals? The Impact of the EU on the Policy Direction of Party Families'. *West European Politics* 36, no. 1: 248–69.

Nedergaard, P. 1995. 'The Political Economy of CAP Reform'. In *The Political Economy of European Integration*, edited by F. Laursen, 111–44. The Hague: Kluwer.

Nentwich, M. and A. Weale. 1998. *Political Theory and the European Union*. London: Routledge.

Neunreither, K. 1994. 'The "Democratic Deficit" of the European Union: Towards Closer Cooperation between the European Parliament and the National Parliaments'. *Government and Opposition* 29: 299–314.

Newdick, C. 2006. 'Citizenship, Free Movement and Healthcare: Cementing Individual Rights by Corroding Social Solidarity'. *Common Market Law Review* 43: 1645–68.

Nic Shuibhne, N. 2005. 'The Value of Fundamental Rights'. In *Values in the Constitution of Europe*, edited by M. Aziz and S. Millns. Dartmouth.

Nic Shuibhne, N. 2008. 'Case Comment on Schwarz, Commission v Germany, and Morgan & Bucher'. *Common Market Law Review* 48: 771–86.

Nicholls, A. J. 1994. *Freedom with Responsibility: The Social Market Economy in Germany, 1918–1963*. Oxford: Clarendon Press.

Nicolaïdis, K. 2003. 'The New Constitution as European Demoi-cracy?' *Critical Review of Social and Political Philosophy* 7, no. 1: 76–93.

Nicolaidis, K. 2013. 'European Demoicracy and its Crisis'. *Journal of Common Market Studies* 51, no. 2: 351–69.

Norris, P. 1997. 'Representation and the Democratic Deficit'. *European Journal of Political Research* 32: 273–82.

Nuotio, K., ed. 2004. *Europe in Search of 'Meaning and Purpose'*. Helsinki: Forum Iuris, Faculty of Law University of Helsinki.

Nussbaum, M. 1996. 'Patriotism and Cosmopolitanism'. In *For Love of Country: Debating the Limits of Patriotism*, edited by J. Cohen, 3–17. Boston: Beacon Press.

Offe, C. 1998. 'The Democratic Welfare State: A European Regime under the Strain of European Integration'. Mimeo, by kind concession of the Author.

Offe, C. 2000. 'The Democratic Welfare State in an Integrating Europe'. In *Democracy Beyond the State? The European Dilemma and the Emerging Global Order*, edited by M. Greven and L. Pauly, 63–90. Lanham: Rowman & Littlefield.

Offe, C. 2003. 'Is There, or Can There Be, a "European Society"?' In *Demokratien in Europa*, edited by I. Katenhusen and W. Laming, 71–89. Opladen: Leske+Budrich.

Offe, C. 2015. *Europe Entrapped*. Cambridge: Polity Press.

Offe, C. and U. K. Preuß. 1991. 'Democratic Institutions and Moral Resources'. In *Political Theory Today*, edited by D. Held, 143–71. Cambridge: Polity.

Offe, C. and U. K. Preuß. 2016. *Citizens in Europe: Essays on Democracy, Constitutionalism and European Integration.* Colchester: ECPR Press.

Olsen, J. 1997. 'Institutional Design in Democratic Contexts'. *Journal of Political Philosophy* 5, no. 3: 203–29.

Olsen, T. V. 2004. 'Europea: United under God? Or Not?' In *Political Theory and the European Constitution*, edited by L. Dobson and A. Føllesdal, 75–90. London and New York: Routledge.

Olson, M. 1974. *The Logic of Collective Action: Public Goods and the Theory of Groups*, revised edition. Cambridge, MA: Harvard University Press.

Ordeshook, P. C. 1986. *Game Theory and Political Theory.* Cambridge: Cambridge University Press.

Ostrom, E. 1990. *Governing the Commons: The Evolution of Institutions for Collective Action.* Cambridge: Cambridge University Press.

Paine, T. 1989. *Political Writings*, edited by B. Kuklic. Cambridge: Cambridge University Press.

Passerini, L. 2003. *Memoria e Utopia. Il Primato dell'intersoggettività.* Torino: Bollati Boringheri.

Patten, A. and Will Kymlicka. 2003. 'Introduction: Language Rights and Political Theory: Contexts, Issues and Approaches'. In *Political Theory and Language Rights*, edited by Will Kymlicka and Alan Patten, 1–51. Oxford, Oxford University Press.

Pattie, C., P. Seyd, and P. Whiteley. 2004. *Citizenship in Britain: Values, Participation and Democracy.* Cambridge University Press.

Pernice, I. and R. Kanits. 2004. 'Fundamental Rights and Multilevel Constitutionalism in Europe'. *Walter Hallstein-Institut Paper* 7, no. 4.

Peterson, J. 1995. 'Decision-making in the European Union: Towards a Framework for Analysis'. *Journal of European Public Policy* 21, no. 1: 69–93.

Pettit, P. 1997. *Republicanism: A Theory of Freedom and Government.* Oxford: Clarendon Press.

Pettit, P. 1998. 'Reworking Sandel's Republicanism'. *Journal of Philosophy* 95: 73–96.

Pettit, P. 2004. 'Depoliticizing Democracy'. *Ratio* 17: 52–65.

Pettit, P. 2005. 'Rawls's Political Ontology'. *Politics, Philosophy and Economics* 4, no. 2: 157–74.

Pettit, P. 2010a. 'A Republican Law of Peoples'. *European Journal of Political Theory* 9, no. 1: 70–94.

Pettit, P. 2010b. 'Legitimate International Institutions: A Neo-republican Perspective'. In *The Philosophy of International Law*, edited by S. Besson and J. Tasioulis, 139–60. Oxford: Oxford University Press.

Pettit, P. 2012. *On the People's Terms: A Republican Theory and Model of Democracy.* Cambridge: Cambridge University Press.

Peukert, H. 2000. 'Walter Eucken (1891–1950) and the Historical School'. In *The Theory of Capitalism in the German Economic Tradition: Historism, Ordo-Liberalism, Critical Theory, Solidarism*, edited by P. Koslowski, 93–145. Hamburg: Springer-Verlag.

Phillips, A. 1995. *The Politics of Presence*. Oxford: Oxford University Press.

Pierson, P. 1996. 'The Path to European Union: An Historical Institutionalist Account'. *Comparative Political Studies* 29: 123–64.

Pinder, J. 1994. 'Building the Union: Policy, Reform, Constitution'. In *Maastrict and Beyond: Building the European Union*, edited by A. Duff, J. Pinder, and R. Pryce, 269–85. London: Routledge.

Pitkin, Hanna F. 1967. *The Concept of Representation*. Berkeley, Los Angeles, London: University of California Press.

Pitkin, Hanna F. 2004. 'Representation and Democracy: Uneasy Alliance'. *Scandinavian Political Studies* 27, no. 3: 335–42.

Plotke, David. 1997. 'Representation is Democracy'. *Constellations* 4, no. 1: 19–34.

Pocock, J. G. A. 1995. 'Conclusions: Contingency, Identity, Sovereignty'. In *Uniting the Kingdom: The Making of British History*, edited by A. Grant and K. J. Stringer, 292–302. London: Routledge.

Pogge, T. 2008. *World Poverty and Human Rights: Cosmopolitan Responsibilities and Reforms*, second, expanded edition. Cambridge: Polity Press.

Pogge, T. W. 1998. 'How to Create Supra-national Institutions Democratically. Some Reflections on the European Union's "Democratic Deficit"'. In *Democracy and the European Union*, edited by Føllesdal and Koslowski, 160–85. Berlin: Springer-Verlag.

Pogge, Thomas W. 1994. 'Cosmopolitanism and Sovereignty'. In *Political Restructuring in Europe: Ethical Perspectives*, edited by C. Brown, 89–122. London and New York: Routledge.

Polanyi, K. 1944. *The Great Transformation*. New York: Rinehart.

Pollack, M. 2003. 'Control Mechanism or Deliberative Democracy? Two Images of Comitology'. *Comparative Political Studies* 36: 125–55.

Pollack, M. A. 2001. 'International Relations Theory and European Integration'. *Journal of Common Market Studies* 39, no. 2: 221–44.

Preuß, U. K. 1996. 'Prospects of a Constitution for Europe'. *Constellations* 3: 209–24.

Preuß, U. K. 2003. 'The Ambiguous Meaning of Citizenship'. Mimeo.

Preuß, U. K. 2005. 'Europa als politische Gemeinschaft'. In *Europawissenschaft*, edited by G. F. Schuppert, I. Pernice, and U. Haltern, 489–539. Baden-Baden: Nomos.

Prosser, T. 1996. 'Understanding the British Constitution'. In *Constitutionalism in Transformation: European and Theoretical Perspectives*, edited by Richard Bellamy and Dario Castiglione, 61–75. Oxford: Blackwell.

Puntscher Riekmann, S. and D. Wydra. 2013. 'Representation in the European State of Emergency: Parliaments against Governments?' *Journal of European Integration* 35, no. 5: 565–82.

Putnam, R. D. 1988. 'Diplomacy and Domestic Politics: The Logic of Two-Level Games'. *International Organization* 42, no. 3: 427–60.

Rae, D. 1969. 'Decision-Rules and Individual Values in Constitutional Choice'. *American Political Science Review* 63: 40–56.

Rae, D. 1975. 'The Limits of Consensual Decision'. *American Political Science Review* 69: 1270–94.

Raunio, T. 2005. 'Hesitant Voters, Committed Elite: Explaining the Lack of Eurosceptic Parties in Finland'. *Journal of European Integration* 27, no. 4: 381–95.

Rawls, J. 1971. *A Theory of Justice*. Oxford: Clarendon Press.

Rawls, J. 1993. *Political Liberalism*. New York: Columbia University Press.

Rawls, J. 1996. *Political Liberalism: With a New Introduction and 'Reply to Habermas'*. New York: Columbia University Press.

Rawls, J. 1999. *The Law of Peoples*. Cambridge, MA: Harvard University Press.

Raz, J. 1994. *Ethics in the Public Domain: Essays in the Morality of Law and Politics*. Oxford: Clarendon Press.

Reif, K. H. and H. Schmitt. 1980. 'Nine Second-order National Elections – A Conceptual Framework for the Analysis of European Election Results'. *European Journal of Political Research* 8, no. 1: 3–44.

Risse, T. 2000. '"Let's Argue!" Communicative Action in World Politics'. *International Organization* 54, no. 1: 1–39.

Risse, T. 2004. 'European Institutions and Identity Change: What Have We Learned?' In *Transnational Identities. Becoming European in the EU*, edited by R. K. Herrmann, T. Risses, and M. B. Brewer, 247–71. Lanham: Rowman & Littlefield.

Risse, T. 2005. 'Neofunctionalism, European Identity and the Puzzles of European Integration'. *Journal of European Public Policy* 12, no. 2: 291–309.

Risse, T. 2010. *A Community of Europeans? Transnational Identities and Public Spheres*. Ithaca, New York: Cornell University Press.

Rittberger, Berthold. 2005. *Building Europe's Parliament. Democratic Representation Beyond the Nation State*. Oxford: Oxford University Press.

Rodrik, D. 2011. *The Globalization Paradox Democracy and the Future of the World Economy*. New York and London: W.W. Norton & Company.

Rokkan, S. 1974. 'Dimensions of State Formation and Nation Building'. In *The Formation of National States in Western Europe*, edited by C. Tilly. Princeton, NJ: Princeton University Press.

Rubio Llorente, F. 1998. 'Constitutionalism in the "Integrated" States of Europe'. Harvard Jean Monnet Chair Working Papers Series, no. 5.

Ruggie, J. G. 1993. 'Territoriality and Beyond: Problematizing Modernity in International Relations'. *International Organisation* 47, no. 1: 139–74.

Rusconi, G. E. 1996. 'La cittadinanza europea non crea il "popolo europeo"'. *Il Mulino* 45: 831–41.

Sabel, C. and J. Zeitlin. 2008. 'Learning from Difference: The New Architecture of Experimentalist Governance in the EU'. *European Law Journal* 14, no. 3: 271–327.

Sabel, Charles F. and Jonathan Zeitlin. 2007. 'Learning from Difference: The New Architecture of Experimentalist Governance in the European Union'. *European Governance Papers (EUROGOV)*. No. C-07-02. http://www.connex-network.org/eurogov/pdf/egp-connex-C-07-02.pdf.

Sally, R. 1998. *Classical Liberalism and International Economic Order: Studies in Theory and Intellectual History*. London and New York: Routledge.

Sandel, M. 1987. 'The Political Theory of the Procedural Republic'. In *Constitutionalism and Rights*, edited by G. Bryner and N. Reynolds, 141–55. Provo, Utah: Brigham Young University Press.

Sandel, M. 1996. *Democracy's Discontent: America in Search of a Public Philosophy*. Cambridge, MA: Harvard University Press.

Sangiovanni, A. 2007. 'Global Justice, Reciprocity, and the State'. *Philosophy & Public Affairs* 35: 2–39.

Savage, Deborah and Albert Weale. 2009. 'Political Representation and the Normative Logic of Two-Level Games'. *European Political Science Review* 1, no. 1: 63–81.

Saward, M. 1998. *The Terms of Democracy*. Cambridge: Polity Press.

Saward, M. 2010. *The Representative Claim*. Oxford: Oxford University Press.

Sbragia, Alberta M. 2008. 'Distributed Governance: The Changing Ecology of the European Union'. In *Efficient and Democratic Governance in Multi-Level Europe*, edited by B. Kohler-Koch and F. Larat. CONNEX Report Series, Volume. 9.

Scanlon, T. 1999. *What We Owe to Each Other*. Cambridge, MA: Harvard University Press.

Scharpf, F. 1988. 'The Joint Decision Trap'. *Public Administration* 66: 239–78.

Scharpf, F. 1997. *Games Real Actors Play: Actor- Centred Institutionalism in Policy Research*. Boulder: Westview.

Scharpf, F. 1999a. *Governing in Europe: Effective and Democratic?* Oxford: Oxford University Press.

Scharpf, F. 1999b. 'Legitimacy in the Multi-actor European Polity'. In *Organising Political Institutions: Essays for Johan P. Olsen*, edited by M. Egeberg and P. Laegreid, 261–88. Oslo: Scandinavian University Press.

Scharpf, F. 2009. 'Legitimacy in the Multilevel European Polity'. *European Political Science Review* 1, no. 1: 173–204.

Scharpf, F. 2011. 'Monetary Union, Fiscal Crisis and the Preemption of Democracy'. MPIfG Discussion Paper 11/11. Munich: Max Planck Instituten für Gesellschaft.

Scharpf, F. 2012. 'Legitimacy Intermediation in the Multilevel European Polity and its Collapse in the Euro Crisis'. MPIfG Discussion Paper 12/6.

Scharpf, F. 2015. 'After the Crash: A Perspective on Multilevel European Democracy'. *European Law Journal* 21, no. 3: 384–405.

Schattschneider, E. E. 1942. *Party Government*. New York: Holt, Reinhart & Winston.

Schmidt, V. A. 2006. *Democracy in Europe: The EU and National Polities*. Oxford: Oxford University Press.

Schmitter, P. C. 1998. 'Is it Really Possible to Democratize the Euro-polity?' In *Democracy and the European Union*, edited by Føllesdal and Koslowski, 13–36. Berlin: Springer-Verlag Berlin Heidelberg.

Schmitter, Phillipe C. 1996. 'If the Nation State were to Wither Away in Europe, What Might Replace It?' In *The Future of the Nation-State: Essays on Cultural Pluralism and Political Integration*, edited by S. Gustavsson and L. Lewin, 211–44. Stockholm: Nerenius and Santérus.

Schmitter, Phillipe C. 1996. 'Imagining the Future of the Euro-polity with the help of new concepts'. In *Governance in the European Union*, edited by G. Marks, et al. London: Sage.

Schmitter, Phillipe C. 2000. *How to Democratize the European Union ... And Why Bother?* Lanham: Rowman & Littlefield.

Schmitter, Phillipe C. 2001. *What is There to Legitimise in the European Union ... And How Might This be Accomplished?* Florence: EUI mimeo.

Schönlau, Justus. 2004. 'Time was of the Essence: Timing and Framing Debates in the European Convention'. In Carlos Closa and John Erik Fossum, ARENA Report 05/04, Oslo.

Schumpeter, J. A. 1954 [1943]. *Capitalism, Socialism and Democracy*. London: Allen and Unwin.

Schuppert, G. Folke. 1995. 'The Evolution of a European State: Reflections on the Conditions of and the Prospects for a European Constitution'. In *Constitutional Policy and Change in Europe*, edited by J. J. Hesse and N. Johnson, 329–68. Oxford: Oxford University Press.

Scott, J. 1998. 'Law, Legitimacy and the EC Governance: Prospects for "Partnership"'. *Journal of Common Market Studies* 36: 175–93.

Scott, Joanne and David M. Trubeck. 2002. 'Mind the Gap: Law and New Approaches to Governance in the European Union'. *European Law Journal* 8: 1–18.

Shapiro, I. 1996. *Democracy's Place*. Ithaca and London: Cornell University Press.

Shapiro, M. 2004/5. '"Deliberative", "Independent" Technocracy v. Democratic Politics: Will the Globe Echo the EU?' IILJ Working Paper 2004/5. Global Administrative Law Series.

Shaw, J. 1996. *Law of the European Union*, second edition. London: Macmillan.

Shaw, J. 1998. 'The Interpretation of European Union Citizenship'. *The Modern Law Review* 61, no. 3: 293–317.

Shaw, J. 1999. 'Constitutionalism in the European Union'. *Journal of European Public Policy* special issue 6, no. 4: 579–97.

Shaw, J. 2000a. 'The "Governance" Research Agenda and the "Constitutional Question"'. In *Governance and Citizenship in Europe: Some Research Directions*, 22–25. Brussels: European Commission.

Shaw, J. 2000b. 'Process and Constitutional Discourse in the European Union'. *Journal of Law and Society* 27, no. 1: 4–37.

Shaw, J. 2000c. 'Constitutionalism and Flexibility in the EU: Developing a Relational Approach'. In *Constitutional Change in the EU: From Uniformity to Flexibility*, edited by G. De Búrca and J. Scott, 337–58. Oxford: Hart.

Shaw, J. 2003. 'Process, Responsibility and Inclusion in EU Constitutionalism'. *European Law Journal* 9: 57–66.

Shore, C. 2000. *Building Europe*. London: Routledge.

Shore, C. 2004. 'Whither European Citizenship?' *European Journal of Social Theory* 7, no. 1: 27–44.

Shore, C. 2011. 'European Governance or Governmentality? The European Commission and the Future of Democratic Government'. *European Law Journal* 17, no. 3: 287–303.

Siedentop, L. 1979. 'Two Liberal Traditions'. In *The Idea of Freedom*, edited by A. Ryan, 153–74. Oxford: Oxford University Press.

Simmons, A. J. 1976. 'Tacit Consent and Political Obligation'. *Philosophy and Public Affairs* 5, no. 3: 274–91.

Simmons, A. J. 1979. *Moral Principles and Political Obligation*. Princeton, NJ: Princeton University Press.

Skinner, Q. 1996. *Reason and Rhetoric in the Philosophy of Hobbes*. Cambridge: Cambridge University Press.

Skinner, Q. 1998. *Liberty before Liberalism*. Cambridge: Cambridge University Press.

Skutnabb-Kangas, T. and R. Phillipson. 1995. *Linguistic Human Rights: Overcoming Linguistic Discrimination*. Berlin and New York: Mouton de Gruyter.

Slaughter, A. M. 2004. *A New World Order*. Princeton and Oxford: Princeton University Press.

Sørensen, Georg. 1999. 'Sovereignty: Change and Continuity in a Fundamental Institution'. *Political Studies* 47 (special issue *Sovereignty at the Millenium*, edited by Robert Jackson): 590–604.

Steen, M. 2012. 'Weidmann Isolated as ECB Plan Approved'. *The Financial Times*, September 6.

Stein, E. 1981. 'Lawyers, Judges and the Making of a Transnational Constitution'. *American Journal of International Law* 75: 33–50.

Stilz, A. 2009. *Liberal Loyalty: Freedom, Obligation and the State*. Princeton, NJ: Princeton University Press.

Stone Sweet, A. 2000. *Governing with Judges: Constitutional Politics in Europe*. Oxford: Oxford University Press.

Stone Sweet, A. and W. Sandholtz. 1997. 'European Integration and Supranational Governance'. *Journal of European Public Policy* 4, no. 3: 297–317.

Streeck, W. 1996. 'Neo-Voluntarism: A New European Social Policy Regime?' In *Governance in the European Union*, edited by Marks, et al., 64–94. London: Sage.

Streeck, W. 2014. *Buying Time: The Delayed Crisis of Democratic Capitalism*. London: Verso.

Streit, M. E. and H. Wohlgemuth. 2000. 'The Market Economy and the State. Hayekian and Ordoliberal Conceptions'. In *The Theory of Capitalism in the German Economic Tradition: Historism, Ordo-Liberalism, Critical Theory, Solidarism*, edited by P. Koslowski, 224–69. Hamburg: Springer-Verlag.

Strøm, K., W. C. Muller, and T. Bergman. 2006. 'The (Moral) Hazards of Parliamentary Democracy'. In *Delegation in Contemporary Democracies*, edited by D. Braun and B. Gilardi, 27–51. London: Routledge.

Stuart, Gisela. 2003. *The Making of Europe's Constitution*. Fabian Ideas 609. London: Fabian Society.

Sunstein, C. 1991. 'Preferences and Politics'. *Philosophy & Public Affairs* 20: 3–34.

Sunstein, C. 1993. *The Partial Constitution*. Cambridge, MA: Harvard University Press.

Sunstein, C. 1996. *Legal Reasoning and Political Conflict*. New York: Oxford University Press.

Swank, D. 2002. *Global Capital, Political Institutions and Policy Change in Developed Welfare States*. Cambridge: Cambridge University Press.

Tallberg, Jonas. 2003. 'Delegation to Supranational Institutions: Why, How, and with What Consequences?' *West European Politics* 25, no. 1: 23–46.

Tamir, Yuli. 1993. *Liberal Nationalism*. Princeton, NY: Princeton University Press.

Taylor, Charles. 1989. 'Cross-Purposes: The Liberal-Communitarian Debate'. In *Liberalism and the Moral Life*, edited by N. L. Rosemblum, 159–82. Cambridge, MA: Harvard University Press.

Taylor, Charles. 1994. 'Why Do Nations Have to Become States?' In *Reconciling the Solitudes. Essays on Canadian Federalism and Nationalism*, edited by G. Laforest, 40–58. Montreal and Kingston: McGill-Queen's University Press.

Taylor, Charles. 1995. 'Invoking Civil Society'. In *Philosophical Arguments*, 204–224. Cambridge, MA and London: Harvard University Press.

Taylor, C. 1998. 'The Dynamics of Democratic Exclusion'. *Journal of Democracy* 9, no. 4: 143–56.

Telò, M. 1994. 'L'integration sociale en tant que réponse du modèle européen à l'interdépendance globale? Les chances, les obstacles et les scenarios'. In *Quelle Union Sociale Europeenne?*, edited by M. Telò. Bruxelles: Université de Bruxelles.

Thatcher, Mark and Alec Stone Sweet. 2002. 'Theory and Practice of Delegation to Non-majoritarian Institutions'. *West European Politics* 25, no. 1: 1–22.

Thatcher, Mark. 2005. 'The Third Force? Independent Regulatory Agenices and Elected Politicians in Europe'. *Governance* 18: 347–73.

Thibaud, P. 1992. 'L'Europe par les nations (et réciproquement)'. In *Discussion sur l'Europe*, edited by J.-M. Ferry and P. Thibaud, 19–126. Paris: Calmann-Levy.

Thomassen, J. and H. Schmitt. 1997. 'Policy Representation'. *European Journal of Political Research* 32, no. 2: 165–84.

Tönnies, F. 2001. *Community and Civil Society*, edited by Jose Harris; translated by Jose Harris and Margaret Hollis. Cambridge: Cambridge University Press.

Tully, J. 1995. *Strange Multiplicity: Constitutionalism in an Age of Diversity*. Cambridge: Cambridge University Press.

Tully, J. 1999. 'The Agonic Freedom of Citizens'. *Economy and Society* 28, no. 2: 161–182.

Tully, J. 2001a. 'La conception républicaine de la citoyenneté dans les sociétés multiculturelles et multinationals'. *Politique et Sociétés* 21, no. 1: 123–47.

Tully, J. 2001b. 'Introduction'. In *Multinational Democracy*, edited by A.-G. Gagnon and J. Tully, 1–34. Cambridge: Cambridge University Press.

Tully, J. 2002. 'The Unfreedom of the Moderns in Comparison to their Ideals of Constitutional Democracy'. *Modern Law Review* 65: 204–28.

Tuori, K. 2015. *European Constitutionalism*. Cambridge: Cambridge University Press.

Turner, S. 1997. 'Citizenship Studies: A General Theory'. *Citizenship Studies* 1: 15–8.

Tushnet, M. 1999. *Taking the Constitution Away from the Courts*. Princeton: Princeton University Press.

Urbinati, N. 2014. *Democracy Disfigured: Opinion, Truth, and the People*. Cambridge, MA: Harvard University Press.

Usherwood, S. and N. Startin. 2013. 'Euroscepticism as a Persistent Phenomenon'. *Journal of Common Market Studies* 5, no. 1: 1–16.

Valentini, L. 2012. 'Ideal vs. Non-Ideal Theory: A Conceptual Map'. *Philosophy Compass* 7, no. 9: 654–64.

Van Parijs, P. 1996. 'Justice and Democracy: Are They Incompatible?' *The Journal of Political Philosophy* 4: 101–17.

Van Parijs, P. 1998. 'Should the European Union Become More Democratic?' In *Democracy and the European Union*, edited by Føllesdal and Koslowski, 287–301. Berlin: Springer-Verlag Berlin Heidelberg.

Van Parijs, P. 2016. 'Thatcher's Plot and How to Defeat It'. Social Europe. https://www.socialeurope.eu/thatchers-plot-defeat.

Viner, J. 1958. 'Adam Smith and *Laissez-Faire*'. In *The Long View and the Short: Studies in Economic Theory and Policy*, 213–45. Glencoe, IL: Free Press.

Vink, M. P. 2001. 'The Limited Europeanisation of Domestic Citizenship Polity: Evidence from the Netherlands'. *Journal of Common Market Studies* 39: 875–96.

Voggenhuber, Johannes. 2001. 'Die Wahrheit ist bloß eine Behauptung'. In *Die Grundrechtecharta der Europäischen Union,* edited by Sylvia Kaufmann. Bonn: Europa-Union Verlag.

Waever, O. 1995. 'Identity, Integration and Security: Solving the Sovereignty Puzzle in EU Studies'. *Journal of International Affairs* 48, note. 2: 389–431.

Waldron, J. 2006. 'The Core Case against Judicial Review'. *The Yale Law Journal* 115: 1346–406.

Waldron, Jeremy. 1989. 'Rights in Conflict'. *Ethics* 99: 503–19.

Waldron, Jeremy. 1999. *Law and Disagreement.* Oxford: Oxford University Press.

Waldron, Jeremy. 1999. *The Dignity of Legislation.* Cambridge: Cambridge University Press.

Walker, N. 1996. 'European Constitutionalism and European Integration'. *Public Law, Sum*: 266–90.

Walker, N. 2002. 'The Idea of a European Constitution and the Finalité of Integration'. Faculdade de Direito da Universidade Nova de Lisboa, Francisco Lucas Pires Working Papers Series on European Constitutionalism, Working Paper 2002/01.

Walker, N. 2003. 'After the Constitutional Moment'. The Federal Trust Constitutional Online Paper Series No. 32/03. Available at SSRN: https://ssrn.com/abstract=516783 or http://dx.doi.org/10.2139/ssrn.516783.

Walker, N. 2004a. 'The EU as a Constitutional Project'. *Federal Trust Online Constitutional Papers* 19, no. 4.

Walker, N. 2004b. 'The Legacy of Europe's Constitutional Moment'. *Constellations* 11, no. 3: 368–92.

Walker, N. 2005. 'Europe's Constitutional Momentum and the Search for Polity Legitimacy'. *International Journal of Constitutional Law* 4, no. 2: 211–38.

Walker, Neil. 2003. 'After the Constitutional Moment.' The Federal Trust Constitutional Online Paper Series No. 32/03. Available at SSRN: https://ssrn.com/abstract=516783 or http://dx.doi.org/10.2139/ssrn.516783.

Wallace, Helen and William Wallace. 2007. 'Overview: The European Union, Politics and Policy-Making'. In *The Handbook of European Union Politics*, edited by

Knud E. Jørgensen, Mark A. Pollack, and Ben Rosamond, 339–58. New York: Sage.

Wallace, Helen. 1985. 'Negotiations and Coalition Formation in the European Community'. *Government and Opposition* 20: 453–72.

Wallace, Helen. 1990. 'Making Multilateral Negotiations Work'. In *The Dynamics of European Integration*, edited by W. Wallace, 213–28. London: Pinter.

Wallace, Helen. 1996. 'Politics and Policy in the EU: The Challenge of Governance'. In *Policy Making in the European Union*, third edition, edited by H. Wallace and W. Wallace, 39–64. Oxford: Oxford University Press.

Wallace, William. 1999. 'The Sharing of Sovereignty: The European Paradox'. *Political Studies* 47, no. 3: 503–521.

Walzer, M. 1981. 'Philosophy and Democracy'. *Political Theory* 9: 379–99.

Walzer, M. 1983. *Spheres of Justice: A Defence of Pluralism and Equality.* Oxford: Martin Robertson.

Walzer, M. 1994a. 'Notes on the New Tribalism'. In *Political Restructuring in Europe. Ethical Perspectives*, edited by Chris Brown, 187–200. London and New York: Routledge.

Walzer, M. 1994b. *Thick and Thin: Moral Argument at Home and Abroad.* Notre Dame: University of Notre Dame Press.

Walzer, M., ed. 1995. *Toward a Global Civil Society.* Providence, RI: Berhahan Books.

Ward, I. 1999. 'Amsterdam and the Continuing Search for Community'. In *Legal Issues of the Amsterdam Treaty*, edited by David O'Keeffe and Patrick M. Twomey, 41–56. Hart Publishing.

Warleigh, A. 1998. 'Better the Devil You Know? Synthetic and Confederal Understandings of European Unification'. *West European Politics* 21: 1–18.

Warleigh, A. 2001. ''Europeanizing' Civil Society: NGOs as Agents of Political Socialisation'. *Journal of Common Market Studies* 39: 619–39.

Warleigh, A. 2006. 'Making Citizens from the Market? NGOs and the Representation of Interests'. In *Making European Citizens: Civic Inclusion in a Transnational Context*, edited by R. Bellamy, D. Castiglione, and J. Shaw, 118–32. London: Palgrave.

Weale, A. 1992. 'Social Choice'. In *The Theory of Choice. A Critical Guide*, edited by S. Hargreaves Heap, et al., 199–215. Oxford: Blackwell.

Weale, A. 1994. 'Single Market, European Integration and Political Legitimacy'. Paper presented at the 'Evolution of Rules for a Single European Market', ESRC Conference, University of Exeter.

Weale, A. 1995. 'Democratic Legitimacy and the Constitution of Europe'. In *Democracy and Constitutional Culture in the Union of Europe*, edited by Richard Bellamy, Vittorio Bufacchi, and Dario Castiglione, 81–94. London: Lothian Foundation Press.

Weale, A. 1997. 'Majority Rule, Political Identity and European Union'. In *Citizenship, Democracy and Justice in the New Europe*, edited by P. B. Lehning and A. Weale, 125–41. London and New York: Routledge.

Weale, A. 1998. 'Between Representation and Constitutionalism in the European Union'. In *Political Theory and the European Union*, edited by A. Weale and M. Nentwich, 49–62. London and New York: Routledge.

Weale, A. 2005. *Democratic Citizenship and the European Union*. Manchester: Manchester University Press.

Weale, A. 2007. *Democracy*, second edition. Basingstoke: Palgrave.

Weale, A. 2013. *Democratic Justice and the Social Contract*. Oxford: Oxford University Press.

Weale, A. 2015. 'Political Legitimacy, Credible Commitment and Euro Governance'. In Dawson Mark, Henrik Enderlein, and Christian Joerges (eds.), *Beyond the Crisis: The Governance of Europe's Economic, Political and Legal Transformation*, 1–21. Oxford: Oxford University Press. DOI: 10.1093/acprof: oso/9780198752868.001.0001.

Weale, A. and M. Nentwich, eds. 1998. *Political Theory and the European Union. Legitimacy, Constitutional Choice and Citizenship*. London and New York: Routledge.

Weber, Max. 1968. *Economy and Society: An Outline of Interpretive Sociology*, edited by Guenther Roth and Claus Wittich. New York: Bedminster.

Weber, Max. 1978. 'Parliament and Government in a Reconstructed Germany'. In *Economy and Society*, Volume 2. Appendix, pp. 1381–1469. Berkeley: University of California Press.

Weiler, J. 2012. 'In the Face of Crisis: Input Legitimacy, Output Legitimacy and the Political Messianism of European Integration'. *Journal of European Integration* 34, no. 7: 825–41.

Weiler, J. H. H. 1991. 'The Transformation of Europe'. *The Yale Law Journal* 100: 2403–83.

Weiler, J. H. H. 1993. 'Parliamentary Democracy in Europe 1992: Tentative Questions and Answers'. In *Constitutionalism and Democracy: Transitions in the Contemporary World*, edited by D. Greenberg et al., 249–63. Oxford and New York: Oxford University Press.

Weiler, J. H. H. 1994. 'Journey to an Unknown Destination: A Retrospective and Prospective of the European Court of Justice in the Area of Political Integration'. *Journal of Common Market Studies* 31: 1–30.

Weiler, J. H. H. 1995. 'Does Europe Need a Constitution? Reflections on Demos, Telos, and the German Maastricht Decision'. *European Law Journal* 1: 219–58.

Weiler, J. H. H. 1995. 'Idéaux et construction européenne'. In *Démocratie et construction euroéenne*, edited by M. Telò, 99–122. Bruxelles: Université, de Bruxelles.

Weiler, J. H. H. 1996. 'European Neo-Constitutionalism: In Search of Foundations for the European Constitutional Order'. In *Constitutionalism in Transformation: European and Theoretical Perspectives*, edited by Richard Bellamy and Dario Castiglione, 105–21. Oxford: Blackwell.

Weiler, J. H. H. 1999. *The Constitution of Europe: 'Do the New Clothes Have an Emperor?' and Other Essays on European Integration*. Cambridge: Cambridge University Press.

Weiler, J. H. H. 2000. 'Does the European Union Truly Need a Charter of Rights?' *European Law Journal* 6: 95–7.

Weiler, J. H. H. 2000. 'Fisher: The Dark Side'. In *What Kind of Constitution for What Kind of Polity? Responses to Joschka Fischer*, edited by C. Joerges, Y. Mény, and J. H. H. Weiler, 235–47. Florence: Robert Schuman Centre.

Weiler, J. H. H. 2001. 'European Democracy and the Principle of Toleration'. In *A Soul for Europe: Vol 1 A Reader*, edited by F. Cerutti and E. Rudolph. Leuven: Peeters.

Weiler, J. H. H. 2001. 'Federalism with Constitutionalism: Europe's *Sonderweg*'. In *The Federal Vision: Legitimacy and levels of governance in the United States and the European Union*, edited by K. Nicolaïdes and R. Howse, 54–70. Oxford: Oxford University Press.

Weiler, J. H. H. 2002. 'A Constitution for Europe? Some Hard Choices'. *Journal of Common Market Studies* 40, no. 4: 563–80.

Weiler, J. H. H. 2003. 'In Defence of the Status Quo: Europe's Constitutional *Sonderweg*'. In *European Constitutionalism Beyond the State*, edited by J. H. H. Weiler and M. Wind, 7–20. Cambridge: Cambridge University Press.

Weiler, J. H. H. with U. R. Haltern and F. C. Mayer. 1995. 'European Democracy and its Critique'. In *The Crisis of Representation in Europe*, edited by J. Haywood, 4–39. London: Frank Cass.

Wenar, L. B. and B. Milanovic. 2009. 'Are Liberal Peoples Peaceful?' *Journal of Political Philosophy* 17, no. 4: 462–86.

Wendler, F. 2012. 'Debating the European Debt Crisis: Government Leadership, Party Ideology and Supranational Integration as Focal Points of Parliamentary Debates in Austria, Germany and the United Kingdom'. Washington, DC: American Consortium on European Union Studies (ACES), *ACES Cases*, No. 2012.3.

Wendler, F. 2014a. 'Justification and Political Polarization in National Parliamentary Debates on EU Treaty Reform'. *Journal of European Public Policy* 21, no. 4: 549–67.

Wendler, F. 2014b. 'Debating the Eurozone Crisis in National Parliaments: Contesting the Utility, Principles, and Legitimacy of Crisis Management'. Paper prepared for the Research conference: 'Crisis Contained, Democracy Diminished? The Politics of the Eurozone Crisis'. Carleton University, Ottawa.

White, J. 2011. *Political Allegiance after European Integration*. Basingstoke: Palgrave.

White, S. *The Civic Minimum*. Oxford: Oxford University Press.

Wiener, A. 1998. *'European' Citizenship Practice: Building Institutions of a Non-State*. Oxford: Westview.

Wilks, S. 1996. 'Regulatory Compliance and Capitalist Diversity in Europe'. *Journal of European Public Policy* 3: 536–59.

Williams, S. 1990. 'Sovereignty and Accountability in the European Community'. *Political Quarterly* 61, no. 3: 299–317.

Wilterdink, N. 1990. *Where Nations Meet: National Identities in an International Organisation*. Florence: EUI Working Paper.

Wilterdink, N. 1993. 'An Examination of European and National Identity'. *European Journal of Sociology* 34: 119–36.

Winch, D. 1978. *Adam Smith's Politics*. Cambridge: Cambridge University Press.

Winckler, A. 1995. 'L'Empire revient'. *Commentaire* 15: 17–25.

Wincott, D. 1994. 'Is the Treaty of Maastricht an Adequate "Constitution" for the European Union?' *Public Administration* 72: 573–90.

Wincott, D. 1995a. 'Political Theory, Law and European Union'. In *New Legal Dynamics of European Union*, edited by J. Shaw and G. More, 293–311. Oxford: Clarendon Press.

Wincott, D. 1995b. 'Institutional Interaction and European Integration: Towards an Everyday Critique of Liberal Intergovernmentalism'. *Journal of Common Market Studies* 33: 597–609.

Winter, G. 1995. *Reforming the Sources and Categories of EC Legal Acts*. Report for the General Secretariat of the European Consortium.

Winzen, T. 2012. 'National Parliamentary Control of European Union Affairs: A Crossnational and Longitudinal Comparison'. *West European Politics* 35, no. 3: 657–72.

Winzen, T. 2013. 'European Integration and National Parliamentary Oversight Institution'. *European Union Politics* 14: 297–323.

Winzen, T., et al. 2014. 'Parliamentary Co-evolution: National Parliamentary Reactions to the Empowerment of the European Parliament'. *Journal of European Public Policy*. doi: 10.1080/13501763.2014.881415.

Wolff, R. P. 1970. *In Defence of Anarchism*. New York: Harper & Row.

Wolkenstein, F. 2018. 'Demoicracy, Transnational Partisanship and the EU'. *Journal of Common Market Studies* 56, no. 2: 284–99.

Young, I. M. 2000. *Inclusion and Democracy*. Oxford: Oxford University Press.

Zolo, D. 1992. *Democracy and Complexity*. Cambridge: Polity.

Zolo, D. 1995. *Cosmopolis: La prospettiva del governo mondiale*. Milan: Feltrinelli.

Cases Cited in the Volume

Deutscher Bundestag, *Die Charta der Grundrechte der Europäischen Union*, Berlin, 2001.

Cologne European Council, 3./4.06.1999, Annex IV.

Tampere Council 15/16.10.1999, Annex, A iv.

Cologne European Council Meeting 3-4.06.1999, Annex IV, establishing the Charter Convention.

The Laeken Mandate, European Council 15.12.2001, Document SN 273/01.

GERMAN FEDERAL COURT: *Ruling, Second Division, Dated 12 October 1993*, 2BvR 2134/92 2BvR 2159/92, English version.

Cowan v. Le Trésor public Case 186/87 [1989] ECR 195, *Konstantinidis v. Stadt Altensteig* Case C-168/91 [1993] ECR I-1191.

'Solange I' Internationale Handelsgesellschaft [1974] 2 CMLR 549.

'Solange II' Wunsche Handelsgesellschaft [1987] 3 CMLR 225.

Solange II, Brunner [1994] 1 CMLR 57.

Cinéthèque v. Fédèrations nationales des cinémas français Cases 60-1/84 [1985] ECR 2605.

ERT v. Dimotiki Etairia Piliroforissis Case C-260/89 [1991] ECR I-2925å.

Watts v Bedford Primary Care Trust C-372/04 [2006] ECR 1185.

Federal Constitutional Court (2009) *Lisbon Judgement* BVerfG, 2 BvE 2/08.

Federal Constitutional Court (2014a), *Outright Monetary Transactions*, available as: 2 BvR 2728/13 vom 14.01.2014, Absatz-Nr (1-105), https://www.bundesve rfassungsgericht.de/entscheidungen/rs20140114_2bvr272813.html. (Accessed 15 August 2014).

Federal Constitutional Court (2014b), *European Stability Mechanism*, available as: 2 BvR 1390/12 vom 18.3.2014, Absatz-Nr. (1-245), https://www.bundesve rfassungsgericht.de/entscheidungen/rs20140318_2bvr139012.html. (Accessed 15 August 2014).

Federal Constitutional Court (1993) *Brunner*, available as BVerfG (1994) C.M.L.R. 57.

Federal Constitutional Court (2009) *Lisbon Judgement* BVerfG, 2 BvE 2/08.

Federal Constitutional Court (2014a), *Outright Monetary Transactions*, available as: 2 BvR 2728/13 vom 14.01.2014, Absatz-Nr (1-105), available online at https://www.bundesverfassungsgericht.de/entscheidungen/rs20140114_2bvr272813.html. (Accessed 15 August 2014).

Federal Constitutional Court (2014b), *European Stability Mechanism*, available as: 2 BvR 1390/12 vom 18.3.2014, Absatz-Nr. (1-245), available online at https://www.bundesverfassungsgericht.de/entscheidungen/rs20140318_2bvr139012.html. (Accessed 15 August 2014).

Portuguese Constitutional Court Decisions 187/2013, 474/2013, 602/2013.

Costa v. ENEL, case 6/64.

Internationale Handelsgesellschaft Case 11/70 [1970] ECR 1125 p. 1134.

Internationale Handelsgesellschaft [1974] 2 CMLR 549.

Nold v. Commission [1974] ECR 503.

Frontini v. Ministero dell Nice e Finanze [1974] 2 CMLR 372.

Rutili v. Minister for the Interior Case 36/75 [1975] ECR 1219.

Nicolo [1990] 1 CMLR 173.

Charter of Fundamental Rights Nice, 2000.

Conclusions of the Cologne European Council Meeting.

Convention 17 of 20.03.2000.

Convention 28 of 05.05.2000.

European Convention on Human Rights.

'Consolidated Version of the Treaty establishing a Constitution for Europe', published as document CIG 87/04 on 06.08.2004.

Protocol on the Application of the Principles of Subsidiarity and Proportionality, CONV 850/03.

Case 44/79, *Liselotte Hauer v. Länd Rheinland-Pfalz* [1979] ECR 3,727.

Case C-64-65/96 *Uecker and Jacquet* [1997] ECR I-03171.

Case C-413/99 *Baumbast* [2002] ECR I-07091.

Case C-200/02 *Zhu and Chen* [2004] ECR I-9925.

Case C-85/96 *Martinez Sala* [1998] ECR I-02691.

Case C-456/02 *Trojan*i [2004] ECR I-07573.

Case C-138/02 *Collins* [2004] ECR I-02703.

Case C-405/01 *Colegio de Oficiales de* Marina Mercante Espanola [2003] ECR- I-10391.

Internationale Handelsgesellschaft, [1970] ECR 1125, 1134.

29/69, *Stauder v. Ulm*, [1969] ECR 419.

Case 159/90, 4 October 1991, reported in [1991] 3 CMLR 689.

Case 11/70, *Internationale Handelsgesellschaft*, [1970] ECR 1125 at 1134, [1972] CMLR 255 at 283.

Case C-148/02 *Garcia Avello* [2003] ECR I-11613.

Case C-135/08, *Rottmann* [2010] ECR I-1449.

Case C-34/09, *Ruiz Zambrano* [2011] ECR I-0000.

Case C-434/09, *McCarthy* [2011] ECR I-0000.

Case C-147/03 *Commission v Austria* [2005] ECR I-05969.

Case C-263/86. *Humbel* [1988] ECR 5365.

Case C-76/05 *Schwarz and Gootjes-Schwarz v. Finanzamt Bergisch Gladbach* [2007] ECR I-6849.

Cowan v. Le Trésor public Case 186/87 [1989] ECR 195.

Konstantinidis v. Stadt Altensteig Case C-168/91 [1993] ECR I-1191.

Case C-184/99 *Grzelczyk v. Centre Public d'Aide Sociale d'Ottignies-Louvain-la-Neuve* [2001] ECR I-6193.

Case C-158/96, *Kohll* [1998] ECR I-1935.

Case C-157/99: *Geraets-Smits v Stichting Ziekenfonds VGZ* [2001] ECR I-5473.

Case C-385/99 *V.G. Muller-Faure v. Onderlinge Waarborgmaatschappij O.Z. Zorgverzekeringen U.A* [2003] ECR 1-4509.

Case C–372/04 *Watts v. Bedford Primary Care Trust* [2006] ECR I–4325.

Case C-438/05 *International Transport Workers' Federation and Finnish Seamen's Union v Viking Line* [2008] IRLR 143.

Case C-341/05 *Laval v Svenska Byggnadsarbetareförbundet* [2008] IRLR 160.

C-446/06 *Dirk Rüffert v Land Niedersachsen* [2008] IRLR 467.

Case C-319/06 *Commission v Luxembourg* [2008] ECR I-4323.

Case C-120/78, *Rewe-Zentral AG v Bundesmonopolverwaltung für Branntwein* (1979) ECR 649.

Grzelczyk v Centre Public d'Aide Sociale d'Ottignies-Louvain-la-Neuve [2001] ECR I-6193, para 31.

Laval v Svenska Byggnadsarbetareförbundet [2008] IRLR 160.

Commission v Luxembourg [2008] ECR I-4323.

Schwarz and Gootjes-Schwarz v. Finanzamt Bergisch Gladbach [2007] ECR I-6849.

Watts v. Bedford Primary Care Trust [2006] ECR I–4325.

Schwarz and Gootjes-Schwarz v. Finanzamt Bergisch Gladbach [2007] ECR I-6849.

Watts v. Bedford Primary Care Trust [2006] ECR I–4325.

Case C-438/05 *International Transport Workers' Federation and Finnish Seamen's Union v Viking Line* [2008] IRLR 143.

Case C-341/05 *Laval v Svenska Byggnadsarbetareförbundet* [2008] IRLR 160.

C-446/06 *Dirk Rüffert v Land Niedersachsen* [2008] IRLR 467.

Case C-319/06 *Commission v Luxembourg* [2008] ECR I-4323.

Index

Biographical Notes

Richard Bellamy is Professor of Political Science at University College London (UCL), University of London, and Director of the Max Weber Programme at the EUI. He has taught at Oxford, Cambridge and Edinburgh and held chairs at UEA, Reading and Essex, and visiting fellowships at Nuffield College, Oxford; the EUI, Florence; and CAS, Oslo. He was Academic Director of the ECPR 2002–2005, Director of the School of Public Policy at UCL 2005–2010 and is currently Director of the European Institute there. His *A Republican Europe of States: Cosmopolitanism, Intergovernmentalism and Democracy in the EU* is Published by Cambridge University Press in 2019. His other publications include *Liberalism and Pluralism: Towards a Politics of Compromise* (1999), *Rethinking Liberalism* (2000, 2005) *Political Constitutionalism: A Republican Defence of the Constitutionality of Democracy* (2007) and *Citizenship: A Very Short Introduction* (2008). Among other volumes he has also co-edited *The Cambridge History of Twentieth Century Political Thought* (2003); *Lineages of European Citizenship* (2004) and *Making European Citizens* (2006).

Dario Castiglione teaches Political Theory in the Department of Politics at the University of Exeter and is Director of the Centre for Political Thought. He has held the Gaetano Mosca visiting Chair in 2008 at the University of Turin, and has been visiting fellow at numerous other international institutions in the United States, Germany, Italy and Australia. His main research interests are in the History of European Political Thought, and theories of Democracy, Constitutionalism and Civil Society. Recent publications include two edited volume on representation: *Creating Political Presence* (2019) and *Les Défis de la Représentation* (2018). Other publications include a co-authored book on *Constitutional Politics in the European Union* (2007) and co-edited volumes: *The Handbook of Social Capital* (2008); *The Language Question in Europe and Diverse Societies* (2007); *The Culture of Toleration in Diverse Societies: Reasonable Tolerance* (2003); *The History of Political Thought in National Context* (2001); *The Constitution in Transformation: European and Theoretical Perspectives* (1996).

www.ingramcontent.com/pod-product-compliance
Lightning Source LLC
Chambersburg PA
CBHW022344280326
41935CB00007B/68